HEMINGWAY

By James R. Mellow

Charmed Circle:
Gertrude Stein & Company

Nathaniel Hawthorne
in His Times

Invented Lives:
F. Scott and Zelda Fitzgerald

Hemingway:
A Life Without Consequences

A Life Without Consequences

HEMINGWAY

JAMES R. MELLOW

Houghton Mifflin Company
BOSTON NEW YORK LONDON
1992

Library of Congress Cataloging-in-Publication Data

Mellow, James R.
Hemingway : a life without consequences / James R. Mellow.
p. cm.
Includes bibliographical references and index.
ISBN 0-395-37777-3
1. Hemingway, Ernest, 1899–1961 — Biography. 2. Novelists, American — 20th century — Biography. I. Title.
PS3515.E37Z74176 1992
813'.52 — dc20
[B] 92-9549
CIP

Printed in the United States of America

DOH 10 9 8 7 6 5 4 3 2 1

Book design by Melodie Wertelet

For permission to print or reprint previously unpublished or published materials, the following are gratefully acknowledged:

Charles Scribner's Sons, an imprint of Macmillan Publishing Company, for scattered excerpts from *Ernest Hemingway: Selected Letters, 1917–1961* by Carlos Baker, copyright © 1981 The Ernest Hemingway Foundation; for selected passages from *The Nick Adams Stories,* copyright © 1972 The Ernest Hemingway Foundation.

Charles Scribner's Sons, an imprint of Macmillan Publishing Company, for selections from the following works by Ernest Hemingway: *In Our Time,* copyright 1925, 1930 by Charles Scribner's Sons, renewal copyrights 1953, 1958 by Ernest Hemingway; *Men Without Women,* copyright 1927 by Ernest Hemingway, renewal copyright 1955 by Ernest Hemingway, copyright 1927 by Charles Scribner's Sons, renewal copyright 1955 by Ernest Hemingway; *Winner Take Nothing,* copyright 1932, 1933 by Ernest Hemingway, copyright 1932, 1933 by Charles Scribner's Sons, renewal copyrights © 1960 by Ernest Hemingway, © 1961 by Mary Hemingway; *The Short Stories of Ernest Hemingway,* copyright 1936, 1938 by Ernest Hemingway, renewal copyrights © 1964, 1966 by Mary Hemingway; *The Fifth Column and the First Forty-Nine Stories,* copyright 1938 by Ernest Hemingway, renewal copyright © 1966 by Mary Hemingway; *The Sun Also Rises,* copyright 1926 by Charles Scribner's Sons, renewal copyright 1954 by Ernest Hemingway; *Death in the Afternoon,* copyright 1932 by Charles Scribner's Sons, renewal copyright © 1960 by Ernest Hemingway; *Green Hills of Africa,* copyright 1935 by Charles Scribner's Sons, renewal copyright © 1963 by Mary Hemingway; *For Whom the Bell Tolls,* copyright 1940 by Ernest Hemingway, renewal copyright © 1968 by Mary Hemingway; *Across the River and Into the Trees,* copyright 1950 by Ernest Hemingway, renewal copyright © 1978 by Mary Hemingway; *The Old Man and the Sea,* copyright 1952 by Ernest Hemingway, renewal copyright © 1980 by Mary Hemingway. For scattered excerpts from *Ernest Hemingway: A Life Story* by Carlos Baker, copyright © 1969 by Carlos Baker, copyright © 1969 by Mary Hemingway; *By-Line: Ernest Hemingway,* edited by William White, copyright © 1967 by Mary Hemingway; *Dateline: Toronto,* edited by William White, copyright © 1985 by Mary Hemingway, John Hemingway, Patrick Hemingway, and Gregory Hemingway.

Charles Scribner's Sons, an imprint of Macmillan Publishing Company, for quotations from unpublished letters of Max Perkins to Charles Scribner and Ernest Hemingway and from a report by William Brownell on *The Sun Also Rises* from the Scribner Archive at the Princeton University Library. Copyright © 1992 Charles Scribner's Sons.

Charles Scribner's Sons, an imprint of Macmillan Publishing Company, for quotations from the following works by F. Scott Fitzgerald:

The Letters of F. Scott Fitzgerald, edited by Andrew Turnbull, copyright © 1963 by Frances Scott Fitzgerald Lanahan; renewal copyright © 1991 by Joanne J. Turnbull, Joanne T. Turnbull, Frances L. Turnbull, and Eleanor L. Lanahan, Matthew J. Bruccoli, Samuel J. Lanahan, Sr., Trustees u/a dated July 3, 1975, created by Frances Scott Fitzgerald Smith; *Dear Scott / Dear Max: The Fitzgerald-Perkins Correspondence,* edited by John Kuehl and Jackson R. Bryer, copyright © 1971 by Charles Scribner's Sons.

The Ernest Hemingway Foundation: Permission has been received from the Ernest Hemingway Foundation to quote from the unpublished writings of Ernest Hemingway.

Jack Hemingway: Permission has been received from John H. Hemingway to quote from the unpublished writings of Hadley Richardson Hemingway Mowrer.

New Directions Publishing Corporation: For unpublished letters of Ezra Pound, copyright 1992 by the Trustees of the Ezra Pound Literary Property Trust; used by permission of New Directions Publishing Corporation, agents. For 4 lines from "Hugh Selwyn Mauberley" by Ezra Pound, *Personae,* copyright 1926 by Ezra Pound, reprinted by permission of New Directions Publishing Corporation. For 12 lines from "Canto XIV," "Canto XVI," and "Pisan Cantos" by Ezra Pound, *The Cantos of Ezra Pound,* copyright 1934, © 1962 by Ezra Pound, reprinted by permission of New Directions Publishing Corporation.

Mrs. John Dos Passos: For excerpts from five unpublished letters from John Dos Passos to Ernest Hemingway and excerpts from two letters from Katy Dos Passos to Pauline Hemingway. Copyright © 1992 by Elizabeth H. Dos Passos. All rights reserved. For excerpts from previously published letters by John and Katy Dos Passos in *The Fourteenth Chronicle,* copyright © 1973 by Elizabeth H. Dos Passos and Townsend Ludington. All rights reserved.

Mrs. Elizabeth B. Carter: For excerpts from a February 21, 1951, letter from Carlos Baker to Ernest Hemingway, copyright © the Estate of Carlos Baker, all rights reserved, and for the use of related materials from the Carlos Baker Papers.

The Estate of Walker Evans, John T. Hill, executor: For a passage from Walker Evans's 1933 diary and for the reproduction of a 1933 photograph of a Havana movie house. Copyright © 1992 The Estate of Walker Evans. All rights reserved.

The Estate of Josephine Herbst, Hilton Kramer, executor: For unpublished passages from the manuscript of "The Hour of Counterfeit Bliss," by Josephine Herbst. Copyright © 1992, the Estate of Josephine Herbst. All rights reserved.

The Estate of Gertrude Stein: For passages from unpublished letters of Gertrude Stein to Ernest Hemingway.

Constance Hammett Poster, attorney in fact, for Marion H. Smith: For excerpts from previously unpublished letters of William Smith to Ernest Hemingway and Carlos Baker and an unpublished memoir, "The Hunter's Eye," in the Hemingway Collections at the John F. Kennedy Library; the Princeton University Libraries; the Yale Collection of American Literature; and the Carlos Baker Papers. Copyright © 1992, Marion H. Smith. All rights reserved.

Harcourt Brace Jovanovich: For an excerpt from "Burnt Norton" in *Four Quartets,* copyright 1943 by T. S. Eliot and renewed 1971 by Esme Valerie Eliot, reprinted by permission of Harcourt Brace Jovanovich, Inc. For excerpts from *88 Poems by Ernest Hemingway*, edited by Nicholas Gerogiannis, copyright © 1979 by The Ernest Hemingway Foundation and Nicholas Gerogiannis, reprinted by permission of Harcourt Brace Jovanovich, Inc.

The University of Wisconsin Press: For quotations from *Ernest Hemingway: The Writer in Context*, edited by James Nagel. Copyright © 1984, the Board of Regents of the University of Wisconsin System. All rights reserved.

The Julian Bach Literary Agency, Inc.: For excerpts from the diary and the letters of Agnes von Kurowsky published in *Hemingway in Love and War*, Northeastern University Press, copyright © 1989 by Henry Serrano Villard and James Nagel.

Carol Publishing Group: For passages from *Hemingway in Cuba* by Norberto Fuentes. Copyright © 1984 by Norberto Fuentes. Translation copyright © 1984 Lyle Stuart, Inc. All rights reserved. Published by arrangement with Carol Publishing Group.

W. W. Norton & Company: For quotations from *The Hemingway Women* by Bernice Kert. Copyright © 1983 by Bernice Kert. All rights reserved.

Princeton University Press: For quotations from Reynolds, Michael, *Hemingway's First War*. Copyright © 1976 by Princeton University Press. Reprinted by permission of Princeton University Press.

Blackwell Publishers, Oxford, England: For passages from *The Young Hemingway* by Michael Reynolds. Copyright © 1986 by Michael Reynolds. All rights reserved.

Oxford University Press: For quotations from *Along With Youth* by Peter Griffin. Copyright © 1985 by Oxford University Press. All rights reserved.

Alfred A. Knopf, Inc.: For excerpts from *How It Was* by Mary Welsh Hemingway, copyright 1951, © 1955, 1963, 1966, 1976 by Mary Welsh Hemingway, reprinted by permission of Alfred A. Knopf, Inc. For 6 lines from "Esthétique du Mal," from *Collected Poems* by Wallace Stevens, copyright © 1947 by Wallace Stevens, reprinted by permission of Alfred A. Knopf, Inc.

Yale Collection of American Literature, Beinecke Rare Book and Manuscript Library, Yale University: For quotations from letters from the Pound collection, the Dial collection, and the Charles Fenton file correspondence.

The Princeton University Libraries: For permission to quote from materials in the following collections: F. Scott Fitzgerald Papers, Hemingway Papers, Scribner's Archives, Sylvia Beach Papers. Published with permission of Princeton University Library.

for Augie,
for June

And out of what one sees and hears and out
Of what one feels, who could have thought to make
So many selves, so many sensuous worlds,
As if the air, the mid-day air, was swarming
With the metaphysical changes that occur,
Merely in living as and where we live.

—WALLACE STEVENS

And, in memoriam, for Celia and Jim

And the end of all our exploring
Will be to arrive where we started
And know the place for the first time.

—T. S. ELIOT

Contents

BOOK FOUR

The Gulf Stream

List of Illustrations

President Woodrow Wilson and King Victor Emmanuel during Wilson's January 1919 tour of Italy (courtesy Charles Bakewell Collection, Yale University)

Hadley and Hemingway on their wedding day, with Carol, Ursula, Leicester, and Hemingway's parents (courtesy The Hemingway Society, John F. Kennedy Library)

The groom among his bachelor friends. From the left: Jock Pentecost, Charles Hopkins, an unknown friend, Dutch Pailthorp, Hemingway, Bill Smith, Bill Horne, Carl Edgar, another unknown friend (courtesy The Hemingway Society, John F. Kennedy Library)

Bobsledding at Chamby-sur-Montreux, winter 1922–1923. "If you want a thrill of the sort that starts at the base of your spine in a shiver and ends with you nearly swallowing your heart . . . try bobsledding," Hemingway advised the readers of the *Toronto Daily Star.* (courtesy John F. Kennedy Library)

Gertrude Stein and Alice B. Toklas, minding their godson, Bumby, 1924. Jack Hemingway remembered the pair as "the two giant women gargoyles of my childhood." (courtesy John F. Kennedy Library)

F. Scott Fitzgerald, Zelda, and Scottie in Paris, Christmas 1925 (courtesy Princeton University Library, Department of Rare Books and Special Collections)

Robert McAlmon at Shakespeare and Company, photographed by Sylvia Beach (courtesy Princeton University Library, Department of Rare Books and Special Collections)

Sylvia Beach and James Joyce at Shakespeare and Company (courtesy Princeton University Library, Department of Rare Books and Special Collections)

Following page 466

Mussolini's March on Rome, October 28, 1922. "Mussolini was a great surprise. He is not the monster he has been pictured," Hemingway wrote on his first interview with the Duce. Seven months later he would call him "the biggest bluff in Europe." (courtesy AP/Wide World Photos)

Hitler in Landsberg Prison following his aborted Beer Hall Putsch of November 8–9, 1923. Hemingway later remarked, lecturing Ezra Pound on twentieth-century politics, "The great qualification to

B O O K

O N E

Soldier's Home

1

The Country Is Always True

It must have seemed to Ernest Hemingway, as it had to his hero Harry Walden, the dying writer of "The Snows of Kilimanjaro," that he had come to a time when he was too tired to care much, a time without affect, a time when, facing the prospect of death, he had edged beyond pain: "For years it had obsessed him; but now it meant nothing in itself. It was strange how easy being tired enough made it."

Harry, the victim of a careless accident, lying in his cot in the African bush country, sees death at the edge of the clearing, circling toward him, sniffing, like a predatory but cautious animal. Looking out at the scene, he thinks back on his past — the bitterness and rivalry of a successful literary career, the long history of adventures, accidents, the casual friends, the necessary wives — and is characteristically sardonic.

That is one way of putting it; imagining that Hemingway, facing death, might have felt what Harry Walden had felt facing death. Death and the moment of death figured prominently in Hemingway's fiction. In dire moments the Hemingway hero reflects on his past life, reconsiders his experiences, tries to puzzle them out anew. He takes the hard view. If Harry, in his bitter ruminations, is not precisely an alter ego for Hemingway, he is the different self the author has concocted, though modeled after the personal experiences and private defeats that mirrored Hemingway's own. Astonishingly, Hemingway's story of the dying writer had been written when the author was in his mid-thirties; young, with a prospect of many years ahead. He had, seemingly, foreseen the time when he, too, would pass beyond curiosity, would welcome the tiredness that meant, almost, the end of regrets: "He had seen the world change; not just the events; although he had seen many of them and had watched the people, but he had seen the subtler change and he could remember how the people were at different times. He had been in it and he had watched it and it was his duty to write of it; but now he never would." As much as any writer of his generation, Hemingway had seen the world.

Generations of readers have judged Hemingway's story of the failed writer as one of his principal masterpieces, and rightly so. But only another writer, perhaps, would appreciate how close to the truth Hemingway had come to that sense of failed ambition and the terrible, fixed preoccupation, the irreducible selfishness of the writer's life; how the dogged practice of the craft takes hold — the time spent, the time wasted — with few things, other than war or marriage or a love affair, nearly as real or compelling or of more consequence than what was on the page in front of him. There had been, for Hemingway, after the writing of "The Snows of Kilimanjaro," fallow years of dissipation and failure redeemed somewhat by For Whom the Bell Tolls *and* The Old Man and the Sea, *and the critics, like the hyenas of his story, nosed around and made the inevitable connection between Harry and the later life of his author.*

Or, to put it another way, Hemingway had — unwittingly, perhaps — put more of himself on paper than he had intended, and his enemies had seized on his weaknesses: the too insistent masculinity; the too easy, shallow, romantic views of love and women; the corrupting need to create a self-image that would, inevitably, fail him in the end. "After all . . . there is the career, the career," he told Gertrude Stein, who, meanly, quoted him in her memoir, claiming he was too "yellow" to tell the real story of his life. Yet, after all, it was his sense of craft and career that had been the real measure of his talent. He had put his faith in that — the unique world he had created for generations of readers.

Once, in his youth, he had aspired to create, in prose, landscapes as rigorous and right as those Cézanne had painted. It was his fantasy that he — and the reader — could move into, inhabit, them. But had that lovely dream survived the later years, when he grew sour, self-absorbed, embittered?

Men supplied a steadying influence in his life and work, envious, admiring, affectionate, companionable, ready to confirm the image of masculinity he projected. (Perhaps he despised them a little for being so willing to serve. Certainly he had abrupt quarrels with several male friends who, in his mind, had crossed him.) But women were somehow more problematic, as the four wives and the unsatisfactory affairs along the way suggest. In life, women seldom conformed to the pattern he wanted or imagined that he wanted. In his fiction, they were often half-realized, victims of his wish fulfillment rather than the creatures of his shrewd observational powers. There were exceptions. In "Snows," the rich-bitch wife complains about Harry's surliness, his urge for destruction, and elicits from Harry a meaningful confession. "I don't like to leave anything. . . . I don't like to leave things behind."

If, at the end, there had been too much anger, too much drink, too many quarrels, too much of the backbiting literary life, too much jealousy, too many wives, too much of the company of the rich and idle, the dumb and the fawning, the toadies . . . too much "Papa" . . .

If, at the end, he looked back, over the road he had come by, wondering where it had begun, where the wrong turn had been taken, perhaps he remembered the work and the fragmentary truths left among the false starts in the scattered papers he would leave behind. And, perhaps, he might have recalled a telling bit of his own private testimony. "Of the place where he had been a boy he had written well enough. As well as he could then."

Perhaps he looked back to that fresher scene, to the country that he claimed was always true, and to the early mornings of childhood on a lake in Michigan, his father rowing, the rhythmic scrape of the oarlocks, the brief interruptions of talk . . . a question asked in a murmur, an answer given . . . and then the electric whir of fast-beating wings, the reverberating crack of a rifle shot echoing around the shore . . . a mallard in midflight plunges into the water with an innocuous splash . . . and then the sudden empty silence after the kill, and the obliterating calm of early morning — mist rising, the soft lapping of small waves at the water's edge — as if he were, then, incredibly close to the still point of the world. . . .

II

The details of a writer's childhood may not be as significant as the way in which he later shapes his recollections of it. His actual experiences may be no more than those he shared with other children of his age and time. What he makes — or remakes — of his childhood, twenty or thirty years later, is of more consequence to the writer.

There were, in fact, two childhoods in the life of Ernest Hemingway. The one that he lived and experienced: a calendar of days and events, some of it unrecoverable now, but much of it still available in the five keepsake albums his mother, Grace Hall Hemingway, made for him until he was eighteen — photographs pasted onto album pages and captioned in her neat hand — and in the memory books Grace kept for her other children as well. There are Ernest's awkward childhood letters and the abundant family correspondence — the gossip of daily life and special occasions, salvaged by history because of the fame of one of its members. There are the reminiscences of Hemingway's sisters and his younger brother, Leicester, written years later in an effort to correct or soften or, unintentionally, confirm the public image of the Hemingway family which Ernest had promoted. There are the later, sometimes self-serving, recollections of childhood friends or schoolmates and later literary acquaintances, requisitioned by biographers hoping for explications of genius and talent.

Then there is the more problematic childhood that Hemingway, years after the events, reconstructed in his imaginative fictions — and the equally fictional, misleading recollections he gave out to friends. There are the family stories, true and fabled, which Hemingway told his sons and which they repeated in their memoirs. The distinctions between the two childhoods were not always clear-cut. That remembered childhood — boisterous memories improved by fiction — conformed to an inner need in Hemingway to construct a more heightened, sometimes embittered version of his early years: the need to be a writer, to put a frame on life.

Family photographs preserve the time of that more accessible childhood. On the surface, at least, in Grace Hall Hemingway's keepsake albums, Hemingway had a happy childhood. The boy depicted in the family chronicle is attractive, tough, frank, and immediately responsive, even in babyhood. Grace recorded his infant activities: "He is contented to sleep with Mama and lunches all night." Papa is the first name he pronounced, she reports. When the child reached up to pat his mother's thick, light brown hair, she was Kitty, the affectionate nickname Hemingway later used for some of his wives. He was a loving child who lisped, "Fweetie, fweetie," when he cuddled up to his mother. "He comes and slaps you if you don't suit him," Grace recorded, proud of his little displays of manly assertiveness, "and kisses you when he is sorry." She also reported Ernest's answer when, as a toddler, he was asked what he was afraid of: "'Fraid a nothing!" he said.

Clarence Edmonds Hemingway and Grace Hall did not fit the stereotypical image of late-Victorian parents — if, indeed, there was anything as easily definable as a typical upper-middle-class family in melting-pot America, even in the fashionable and sedate Chicago suburb of Oak Park, where Hemingway was born on July 21, 1899. Hemingway's parents were individualists. They may have shared the religious and social values of the time, but on their own terms. And they were both professionals. Before her marriage, Grace Hall had been a successful music teacher with a well-trained contralto voice, who had had a try at an operatic career in New York but had given it up in favor of marriage. She had traveled abroad, widening her experience, and before and after she married she had given voice lessons, earning, at times, as much as a thousand dollars a month — substantially more than her doctor-husband commanded at the beginning of his career.

Grace was vain about her English heritage. Her father, Ernest Hall, had been born in Sheffield, England, in 1840, the son of a silversmith. He had moved to the United States as a youth, settling with his family on a farm in Dyersville, Iowa. He hated the hardships and boredom of farm life and ran away as a young man, working as a day laborer along the Mississippi, only to return home at the outset of the Civil War. He subsequently enlisted in the First Iowa Volunteer Cavalry, and in April 1862, in Warrensburg, Missouri, was shot in the left thigh. As his military records ambiguously phrased it, the wounding was "not in the regular discharge of his duties, though from an enemy in arms against the authority of the U.S." He was, nonetheless, honorably discharged after five months in the hospital. Back in Dyersville, Ernest Hall married Caroline Hancock, moved to Chicago, and went into the cutlery business with a brother-in-law. Caroline, whose father had been an English sea captain (she had sailed the Horn with him), was artistic, a painter as well as an accomplished pianist. Grace was born in 1872. A buxom girl with a pleasant voice, her musical interests were thoroughly encouraged by her mother. Caroline Hancock Hall was strong-willed, determined that nothing — least of all, domestic chores — would stand in the way of her daughter's eventual career in opera. "You tend to your practicing," Caroline would tell her daughter. "There is no use any woman getting into the kitchen if she can help it." Ernest Hall was equally fond of music and regularly took Grace, the favorite of his three children, to the performances of the Chicago Opera Company. He also taught her to play billiards, their evening games held in the family billiard room.

The Hall house at 439 North Oak Park Avenue, built in the 1880s, was an ample, dark Victorian with a fashionable turret. Across the street, at number 444, was the modest clapboard house of Anson and Adelaide Hemingway. The Hemingway family could trace its roots back to the early New England settlers. A Ralph Hemingway had lived in Roxbury, Massachusetts, in 1633. Later Hemingways moved to East Plymouth, Connecticut, where Anson was born in 1844, and then to Chicago, where Anson's father set up a wholesale clock business for the Seth Thomas Company. Hemingway's grandfather on his father's side had also served in the Civil War, in the Seventy-second Illinois Infantry. Anson Hemingway was particularly proud of his military service and, in later years, marched in full dress uniform and medals in the annual Oak Park Memorial Day parades. Hemingway liked to quote his grandfather, who had fought under General Grant at the battle of Vicksburg, as saying that "anytime you could wake Grant you could get a sound answer from him."

After the war, Anson graduated from Wheaton College in Illinois and married Adelaide Edmonds, a fellow student. A man of strict religious principles, a friend and admirer of the evangelist Dwight Moody, Anson first worked as a secretary for the YMCA. But unable to support a wife and growing family on charitable intentions, in the mid-1870s he established a real estate business in Chicago profitable enough to allow him to send his six children to Oberlin College. (His eldest son, Clarence, born in 1871, continued the family tradition by fathering six children.) Adelaide Hemingway, handsome and as erect in her carriage as her husband, was an avid botanist and an amateur astronomer who taught her children and grandchildren to study nature and the stars. Ernest's older sister, Marcelline, recalled her grandmother pointing to a flower and saying, "But do you *really* see it?" She then gave her four-year-old granddaughter a complete botanical breakdown — calyx, corolla, stamen, and pistil. "Suddenly the flower was a whole new wonderful creation to my childish eyes."

Clarence Hemingway and Grace Hall had known each other as childhood neighbors and then as high school acquaintances, but it was not until 1894, when Caroline Hall became ill with terminal cancer, that the two became more intimately involved. Clarence Hemingway, who had completed his medical training at Rush Medical College in Chicago, was an assistant to the Halls' family physician, Dr. William Lewis, and frequently attended the dying woman.

Clarence had had a robust childhood; camping and hiking, fishing and hunting, with his brothers and friends were among his fondest memories. Interested in Indian culture, he collected Indian artifacts, chiefly dug from the local mounds of the Potawatomi tribe, remnants of which still lived along the nearby Des Plaines River. After his college years at Oberlin, where he had played on the football team, Clarence had made an excursion with a group of male friends on a geological expedition to the Great Smokies in North Carolina, one of the significant events in his life and one that he often described to his children. He had served as the camp cook.

Clarence had more than a conventional interest in Christian service; he was especially devoted to his brother Willoughby, who was a medical missionary in China. (Uncle Willoughby was also one of young Ernest's heroes.) Clarence organized a local Agassiz Club, spoke to boys' groups on the subjects of nature and personal hygiene (a sometime euphemism for sex education, about which he held decided views). He regularly took his children and members of the Agassiz Club on nature walks, pointing out the flora and fauna with an expert eye. Though a crack marksman and hunter, Clarence Hemingway had a horror of physical violence. A family story had it that as a child, he had been chased into his own house by a bully and badly beaten in front of his mother. Adelaide Hemingway, holding strictly to the Christian tenet of turning the other cheek, would not allow him to strike back. As a doctor, Clarence offered his services free to local orphanages and readily took on other charitable cases. It was also part of the family legend that he had designed a new form of laminectomy forceps, an improvement over the crude instruments used at the time. Clarence refused to patent his design, insisting that it was not right to profit from anything that would benefit humanity.

Apparently Clarence Hemingway had developed no serious interest in a woman until he became involved with Grace Hall, whom he courted while treating her mother. During his visits, Grace found him a comfort to be with, regarded him as sensible and manly. They began taking afternoon walks and buggy rides together. When, during the summer of 1895, Clarence made a trip to Scotland, visiting a medical clinic in Edinburgh, he wrote her often. (The Hemingways would be a letter-writing family; when separated from his wife, Clarence would become depressed when he had no word from her.) It was during one of their rides together, when the horse had coincidentally come to a halt in front of a justice of the peace, that Clarence got up the nerve to ask Grace to marry him and she had said yes. Nevertheless, it says something about her independence that after her mother's death on September 5, 1895, she was still determined to follow through on her plans for an operatic career, perhaps out of some need to fulfill her mother's dream.

That fall, she went to New York to study with Madame Louisa Cappianni, a well-known opera coach who had trained Amelita Galli-Curci and who worked with some of the stars of the Metropolitan Opera Company. Madame Cappianni was impressed with Grace's ripe contralto voice. (Clarence would later tell his children that it was Grace's voice that he had first fallen in love with.) According to Marcelline Hemingway Sanford, Grace was offered a contract with the Metropolitan but put off making a commitment, despite Madame Cappianni's urging. During the 1895–1896 season, Grace gave a concert at Madison Square Garden but found that during the performance her eyes were terribly bothered by the bright footlights. This, according to the family legend, was one of the principal reasons she decided to give up a professional career. Grace attributed her sensitivity to bright light to the aftereffects of an attack of scarlet fever when she was seven, which left her temporarily blind. Since there is little medical history of blindness attributable to scarlet fever, and since Grace's affliction disappeared as mysteriously as it had appeared, it's likely that the cause was psychosomatic. She had had, it appears, a dramatic restoration of her sight while she was sitting alone at the piano and her parents were at church. But, thereafter, she suffered from poor eyesight and severe migraine headaches that were so painful she had to lie down in her room with the shades drawn. In the family circle, she maintained that if she had continued her career instead of marrying, she would probably have occupied the spot on the Metropolitan's bill then taken by the great Austrian-American contralto Ernestine Schumann-Heink. The realization must have been all the more acute when Schumann-

Heink made her American debut in Chicago, playing Gertrude in *Lohengrin* in 1898, the year in which Marcelline was born. "But I have you children," Grace would say.

Grace's retreat from her promising professional career took the form of an extended trip to Europe in the company of her widowed father, after which she returned to Oak Park and married Clarence Hemingway on October 1, 1896, in the First Congregational Church. The wedding was small out of respect for the recent death of her mother, but Grace had a taste for the sumptuous in dress. According to Marcelline, the wedding gown, with its elaborate puffed sleeves and double train, required some ninety yards of white organdy.

The newly married couple moved in with Ernest Hall at North Oak Park Avenue. Grace's father had a great affection for his son-in-law, called him "dear boy," and spoke of him to others as "the blessed doctor." Clarence's office was off the landing between the first and second floors. His medical and nature specimens, however, were kept on high shelves in the circular attic room of the turret. (In Hemingway's short story "Now I Lay Me," Nick Adams remembers the jars of snakes and other specimens bleaching white in the depleted alcohol, and, in a bitter metaphor of marriage, his parents' wedding cake, a petrified souvenir hanging suspended from a rafter in a tin box.) Four of the Hemingway children were born in the Hall house: Marcelline on January 15, 1898, and Ernest a year and a half later. He was a healthy infant, weighing nine and a half pounds. His birth, as Grace reported in her album, was orchestrated to the chirping of robins. Two more girls were born in the sturdy brass bedstead on the second floor: Ursula in 1902 and Madelaine (nicknamed Sunny because she resembled the smiling Sunny Jim on a cereal package) in 1904. The later children, Carol and Leicester, were born elsewhere: Carol in the Hemingway cottage at Walloon Lake in Michigan in 1911 and Leicester Clarence in Grace's new, modern "dream house" on Kenilworth Avenue in 1915.

It was understandable that the Hemingway children found their parents imposing. Clarence Hemingway was powerfully built, standing six feet tall, strong-featured with a firm brow, deep-set dark eyes, and a black mustache and beard that his son Ernest maintained hid some elemental weakness. Hemingway, in a fictional but still vivid autobiographical account, gives Nick Adams's impressions of his doctor father:

> When he first thought about him it was always the eyes. The big frame, the quick movements, the wide shoulders, the hooked, hawk nose, the beard that covered the weak chin, you never thought about — it was always the eyes. . . . They saw much further and

> much quicker than the human eye sees and they were the great gift his father had. His father saw as a bighorn ram or as an eagle sees, literally.

Outside the family, Clarence Hemingway was considered a charmer. But with the children he could turn suddenly gruff or stern when they misbehaved or neglected to perform some chore. In serious cases, he took a razor strop to them. After punishment, they were told to kneel down and ask God for forgiveness. As they grew older they realized that their father made decisions only reluctantly and that if they asked permission to do something or go somewhere, his first answer was apt to be no. They soon learned that it was better to ask their mother first.

Grace Hemingway, five feet eight, was plump and fair-skinned, with bright blue eyes. Her complexion was described as "English." Her cheeks, deeply dimpled, were so rosy she considered them something of an embarrassment and toned them down with a liquid powder. Her daughter Marcelline remembered the lily of the valley scent that clung to her, the perfume specially imported from Paris.

Grace had an unexplained penchant for wanting to pass off her two eldest children, Marcelline and Ernest, as twins, dressing them alike, sometimes in dresses and floppy organdy hats, or, in the summer, in boys' overalls (or "overhauls," as she spelled it). She kept up the illusion (or delusion) of twinhood through kindergarten age and beyond. (Marcelline was held back a year in kindergarten so that she and Ernest could enter the first grade together in the fall of 1905.) Marcelline recalled that she and her brother "played with small china tea sets just alike; we had dolls alike; and when Ernest was given a little air rifle, I had one too." At preschool age, they both had Dutch boy haircuts, which embarrassed Marcelline. In 1902, at the age of three, at Christmastime, Ernest was concerned that Santa Claus might not recognize that he was a boy. But as a child, Hemingway seems not to have suffered any dire psychological effect from the early cross-dressing. Every evidence suggests that he had a boisterous, rough-and-ready boyhood and adolescence. There may have been the later embarrassment of a self-conscious boy looking at his childhood pictures in an album. Perhaps it sharpened his sense of masculine competitiveness in boyhood sports and at hunting and fishing. Still, some aspect of the sexual transference of brother into sister, and vice versa, kept its fascination for a lifetime, served him as a theme in later stories and quite probably inspired the ambiguous combinations of sexual play between heroes and heroines in his novels, particularly the posthumously published *The Garden of Eden*.

Early on in childhood, Hemingway developed a predilection for names for himself; at first he was Nurnie. But then he moved on to other identities — Bobbie the squirrel, or Carlo (his toy dog), or Prince, the family horse, or Pawnee Bill. Called by any other name, he refused to answer. He had a vivid imagination even from his earliest years. Once, at about the age of five, he claimed to have stopped a runaway horse single-handedly. Grandfather Hall, whom Ernest called Abba Bear, remarked to Grace, "Chumpy dear, this boy is going to be heard from some day. If he uses his imagination for good purposes, he'll be famous, but if he starts the wrong way, with all his energy, he'll end in jail, and it's up to you which way he goes."

A routine piety prevailed in the Hall-Hemingway household. Every morning, in the first-floor parlor, Grandfather Hall officiated at the family's prayer sessions, which consisted of readings from a gilt-edged volume titled *Daily Strength for Daily Needs.* He also said grace at the evening meal, a duty Clarence Hemingway gladly relinquished. In his retirement, "Abba" Hall was affable and gentle, though a bit sinister-looking with his bushy black eyebrows and fluffy white muttonchop whiskers. Immaculately dressed, top-hatted, erect, Grandfather Hall took his daily walk downtown to see after his stock investments. Every Saturday, in the basement, he gave his Yorkshire terrier, Tassel, a weekly bath. According to Marcelline, Tassel looked like nothing so much as "the frayed end of a rope." Grandfather Hall appreciated routine. After his meals, he retired to his library, the sliding doors drawn shut, to smoke a cigar with his companionable brother-in-law, Benjamin Tyley Hancock, a traveling salesman, or "drummer," for Miller, Hall and Sons, manufacturers of brass bedsteads. Uncle Tyley had a room awaiting him at North Oak Park Avenue whenever he returned from his Midwest tours.

Clarence Hemingway was stricter in the faith than his father-in-law. He disapproved of drinking, dancing, smoking, and cardplaying. When the Hemingway girls reached the proper age, Grace and Adelaide Hemingway had to intercede for them for permission to attend school dances. His birthday messages to Ernest invariably stressed the Christian virtues and manliness. When Ernest turned eight his father wrote him, "Your Daddy loves you and prays that you may be spared many years to praise God and help your parents and sisters and others about you, to have a good time and do something always to help some one else." When Ernest turned sixteen: "I am so pleased and proud you have grown to be such a fine big manly fellow and will trust your development will continue symmetrical and in harmony with our highest Christian Ideals."

Boundlessly active, Clarence Hemingway taught his children,

girls and boys alike, to hunt and fish. Well in advance of talk about vitamins, he had theories about food and nutrition. Even before the babies were weaned, he insisted on feeding them on diets of fresh vegetables and meat broths. Grace once complained that he had brought Marcelline to her to nurse "with onion on her breath." He hated fussiness at the dinner table; what wasn't eaten on the plate would be served cold at breakfast. He was not keen on literature, though his attitude changed when his son became a promising, even famous, writer. The family library included the requisite sets of Shakespeare, Scott, and Dickens, but Clarence preferred that the children be out of doors playing or helping with the chores, rather than lounging and reading in the living room. (Hemingway, in his youth, loved nature stories and adventure tales, the works of G. A. Henty and Captain Frederick Marryat.) Clarence regularly took the children on excursions to the Field Museum of Natural History in Chicago and the Lincoln Park Zoo. When a dinosaur bone was dug up in Forest Park, he took them to see it as well. Confronting the evidence of evolution, he considered it necessary to explain to them that — as the Bible stated — God had, indeed, created the world in seven days but that no one had ever explained how long the days were. New knowledge, he told them, only added to the truths they had learned in Sunday school.

III

One by one, when small, the children were taken to the Hemingway summer retreat, Windemere, the family cottage on Bear Lake in the Traverse Bay area of northern Michigan. It would become the pattern of their days: the freedom of summers at the lake, the fall and winter regimen of school in Oak Park. Grace had named the cottage after the famous Lake Windermere in the English Lake District, but family usage had eroded the spelling somewhat. Marcelline was brought there at the age of seven months in 1898, the year in which Grace and Clarence bought the property and before the camp was built on the near acre of ground between Henry Bacon's farm and Murphy's Point. Ernest was a mere six weeks old, in 1899, when the family made the summer trek once again in order to oversee the building of the cottage. That year, they stayed only a few weeks into September. The spot was rustic, with a wide beach, the land wooded with white birch and hemlock. Clarence considered the spring-fed lake ideal for fishing, abundant in pike and perch and largemouth bass. Nearby there was a camp of Ojibway Indians who peeled bark for tanning. On the Boyne City side of the lake, there was an old sawmill that remained in operation for a few more years. When the wind blew in the right direction, one could hear the "screaming" of the saws.

Virtually every summer, from Hemingway's first to his eighteenth year, the growing family would set out from Oak Park to Chicago, where they would embark on a Lake Michigan steamer — generally the *State of Ohio* and sometimes the *Manitou* — which took them across the lake to Harbor Springs in northern Michigan. There, they took the rail line to Petoskey, where they once more transferred the luggage, this time to the dummy train for Walloon Village. The final phase of the journey was on one of the two-decker wood-burning steamers — the *Tourist* or the smaller *Outing* — which made the regular circuit of the lake.

Petoskey, the still-rustic summer resort, and Bear Lake (later renamed Walloon Lake), as well as the region around Lake Charlevoix (where Uncle George Hemingway had a cottage), would become important country for Hemingway. In his early fiction, writing about his childhood and adolescence, he staked out the territory as his own; the region, the place-names, became an indivisible part of his career and reputation and, more important, one that he claimed for American literature. Equally important was the journey; leaving behind the hampering proprieties of Oak Park, it became a ritual passage. As a young man, when writing to his male friends, suggesting fishing and hunting trips to Walloon Lake and upper Michigan, Hemingway spelled out the proposed itineraries, gave detailed lists of the necessary supplies, as conscientiously as if he were dealing in categorical imperatives: the needed ammunition, the best flies for trout fishing, where to buy the cheapest liquor. Such details would also figure prominently in Hemingway's many fictional accounts of hunting and fishing expeditions. For Hemingway, ever after, journeys became ritual affairs.

They were the same careful preparations that his father had established for the family summers. A few days after their arrival at Windemere, the family would receive notice that their order of foodstuffs from Montgomery Ward had arrived in Petoskey. Clarence and one or more of the children would make the journey to check the bill of lading, verifying the order — the barrels of flour, the hams and slabs of bacon, the supplies of gingersnaps and the marshmallows for roasting over nighttime fires on the beach — before the shipment was delivered by horsedrawn dray. Annually, Clarence bought a flock of ducklings that were allowed to range along the lakefront property, though they were sometimes decimated by foxes or neighboring dogs. Occasionally, he bought one or two piglets that were fattened up for the summer before being sent off to market in the fall, much to the dismay of the children. Milk and fresh eggs were brought from the nearby Bacon farm. (It was on one of the daily runs to the farm that Ernest had one of the first of many accidents that would plague him all his life. Running downhill with a stick in his mouth, he tripped and fell, gouging his throat and tonsils. Fortunately his father was on hand to cauterize the wound.)

Each summer (Hemingway would only vaguely remember his earliest summers) Grandfather Hall would pay a visit to Windemere, out of a sense of familial duty. It was seldom a pleasure to the fastidious old gentleman, who did not care for the helter-skelter meals and the informal life of a rural cottage. Abba Hall much preferred his lunches at home or his dinners at Henrici's in downtown Chicago, where the napkins and tablecloths were white damask and the waiters were attentive. At Windemere, he regularly wore his starched collar and tie and a suit coat. Great-uncle Tyley Hancock, a lifetime bachelor, however, seemed to blossom amid the informality, the lunches on the porch, the outings on the lake, and the fishing expeditions on which he could wear his baggy trousers, his jacket pockets stuffed with his pipe and tobacco pouches and his incidental fishing gear. He regularly took part in the summer festivities, the sing-alongs in the evenings, the Fourth of July celebrations. He could easily be persuaded to dance the hornpipe or do a little buck and wing when Grace played the parlor organ. Uncle Tyley, however, had a problem with drink and sometimes had to be rescued from Forest Park saloons by Dr. Hemingway. On these occasions, Clarence told the children that Uncle Tyley was sick and couldn't be disturbed for a day or two. At Walloon Lake, however, he was always sober. Hemingway admired Uncle Tyley. It was from one of Tyley's stories, about a voyage around the Horn with his captain father, that Ernest got the inspiration for an early composition for his sixth grade English class at the Holmes Grammar School. "My First Sea Vouge" was written as a first-person narrative, with faith in the sovereignty of detail. It is a brief but rambling tale of how Ernest H. had been born in a little white house on Martha's Vineyard and how his mother had died when he was four (as Tyley's mother had) and how on the voyage aboard the schooner *Elizabeth,* sailors, using a biscuit for bait, hooked an albatross but let it go ("for they are very superstitious about these big birds") and how the sailors had also harpooned a porpoise ("or sea pig as they called them") and cut the liver out and fried it for supper and how it "tasted like pork only it was greesier."

Grandfather Hall's visits to Walloon Lake ended in 1905. That spring, after his customary annual visit to his son Leicester in California, Abba Hall returned to Oak Park seriously ill. Dr. Lewis's diagnosis was Bright's disease (a then fatal form of nephritis, or kidney failure), and the old man died slowly and painfully in his front bedroom in the house on North Oak Park Avenue in May. One of Hemingway's family stories had it that his Grandfather Hall had kept a revolver under his pillow, planning to commit suicide when the pain became too unbearable, and that Clarence Hemingway, who disapproved, had removed the bullets. Abba Hall had tried to shoot himself with the empty pistol.

Later in life, Hemingway would recall his grandfather's funeral in a disguised form. In one of the false starts in the manuscript version for *The Sun Also Rises,* Jake Barnes recalls attending the funeral of a favorite namesake-uncle as a young boy. (The uncle is alternately named Raphael and Ernest, and in the last revision, Jacob.) Though deleted from the final version of the novel, the scene has its odd relevance to the life. Jake notes that his parents, when he was quite young, "were going through a period of great religious fervor" and his mother had made it plain there were several things she would "rather see me in my grave than do." Jake's ironic commentary on these transgressions — smoking, gambling, and drinking — is that they were not very plausible at his age, the latter two especially, being "quite unthought of and far off sins." Nevertheless they were much on his mother's mind because gambling and drinking were vices said to run in her family and to have caused "the disgrace or extinction of various uncles who contributed much to the Romance of boyhood." This was particularly the case with his Uncle Jacob, who, in fact, was thought to have succumbed to other vices "too terrible even to be warned against." Jake, however, remembers his uncle very fondly "because of his notable gifts at Christmas time and because he was the first man in town to own an automobile and one of the notable patrons of the horse show . . . and in other ways a source of great pride to me and not a little income."

In the claustral atmosphere of the funeral service, abounding with black-garbed mourners dabbing their eyes with handkerchiefs, and floral tributes banked beside the altar, young Jake makes a careful study of the straining vocal chords of the female soloist, until his eye casually notices the "high, gallant, hooked purple nose" of his Uncle Jacob, rising above the bouquets. In a comic confession, Jake recalls that afterward, when his mother told him of the things she would rather see him in his grave than do, he irresistibly thought of himself in his uncle's position, nose up in flowers. "It seemed strange that any thing I could do would make her wish to see me in that condition and it prejudiced me against all her views and moral values."

It was, of course, grandfather Ernest Hall's funeral that Hemingway had attended at that early age. (Uncle Tyley did not die until he was in his nineties.) In one of those useful or psychological subversions of real life which writers consciously or unconsciously indulge in when writing fiction, Hemingway perversely merged his pious grandfather and his alcoholic great-uncle to create a travesty version of Grace's revered father, Hemingway's real namesake, who would become the tiresome model Grace held up to him in his unruly adolescence.

ϒϒϒ

Grace Hemingway eased her grief over her father's death with plans for building a new house. She was determined to sell the dark, turreted house at 439 and with her inheritance build a new and spacious home on North Kenilworth Avenue and the corner of Iowa Street. All that summer, at Windemere, she planned and dreamed of the house that would satisfy her ambitions and the family's needs. That summer, too, against the advice of her husband, who was wary of extravagance, she bought a forty-acre farm across the lake from Windemere. It was being sold for back taxes. (It was another of Grace's dreams that someday she would build a little cottage on a hill there to serve as an occasional retreat for herself and her husband, away from the increasingly cramped quarters of Windemere.) Clarence insisted the farm be leased to a tenant farmer on a sharecropping basis, providing for the upkeep of the property and outbuildings and the planting of crops and hay, and the cutting of winter ice to be stored in the icehouse for the next summer. Grace objected at first but then agreed. Clarence eventually replenished the run-down orchard, putting in new peach, plum, cherry, and apple trees on one of the slopes of what the family dubbed Red Top Mountain. Grace named the new purchase Longfield Farm. Over the next several years, there were barrels of apples and potatoes to be shipped to Oak Park in September. It was Clarence's stock joke, when asked what he raised on Longfield Farm, to answer, "The best thing we raise is the flag."

Summers, then, at Walloon Lake became the happy succession of events recorded in the family albums. In a 1904 photograph, Grace stands stiff and corseted in a skirt and starched shirtwaist, holding a seven-and-a-half-pound pike she has caught while her son and daughters look on, bashfully. Ernest, still in his Dutch bob, is wearing an Indian outfit with fringes on the sleeves and leggings. It would be another two years before he was allowed a boy's haircut, much to his mother's regret, an event commemorated by clippings of his hair. "My precious boy, a 'real boy,'" Grace reported.

Birthdays at the lake were special occasions, days set aside for picnics and feasts and duck dinners. Birthday trees were cut or planted, then decorated as if it were Christmas. Ernest's birthdays were regularly celebrated. "All Four Children on Ernest's Birthday, July 21, 1905," Grace captioned one of the group photographs of his sixth birthday at the lake. He is sitting on his Uncle Tyley's lap, smiling the wide, sun-drenched, midday smile of old, overexposed photographs that are innocent of any historic intent. He holds his birthday gift, an air rifle, aslant, the barrel pointed upward. Next to him, in the row of stiff kitchen chairs set out on the unkempt grass, are his younger sister Ursula, then Marcelline, and next, baby Madelaine, an infant of eight months, sitting on Grace's lap. Grace had been having difficulty breast-feeding the baby because her milk was scarce. That homely detail, too, is set down in the family record. Time in sepia.

⸺

It was a sign of Grace's assertiveness that the house she was having built on Kenilworth Avenue would incorporate every modern convenience that came to her mind. With the help of a local architect, who drew up the plans, construction began in the fall of 1905. By the following August, the family was ready to move into the large three-story oblong house with gray stucco walls and white trim. Grace had insisted upon a cement cellar with ample storage facilities for the vegetables, pickles, and jams that Clarence put up each year. The kitchen had plenty of built-in cupboards and hard maple countertops for uninterrupted working space, as well as a vent for removing smoke and cooking odors. The dining room, with five large windows, looked out over the back yard. A frieze of Caroline Hall's landscape paintings was built into three of the dining room walls. Having read up on the science of acoustics, Grace designed her own separate but connected music room, thirty feet square, with the ceiling height one half that measure, and one wall broken by a balcony. The bronze-painted radiators were equipped with containers of water to keep her new Steinway in tune. The children used the practice piano in the dining room for their lessons, but the music room became the social center of the house, the setting for concerts and family parties and the recitals of Grace's music students. There were occasions when it held as many as a hundred guests. It was in the music room that Christmas and Boxing Day (Grace kept up the English tradition) were celebrated with a huge

Christmas tree. It was a house clearly designed not only for family use but for entertainment and company.

Clarence had an office on the premises, and a small library was his waiting room. The bookshelves were stocked with the wholesome classics Grace brought with her from her father's house. The library also housed Clarence's collection of stuffed owls, a chipmunk, and raccoon. Marcelline would remember with fascination, in the back room of her father's office, the specimens of a preserved appendix and a tiny human fetus, kept in glass jars. A skeleton, which Clarence had dubbed Suzy Bone-a-part and which the children were allowed to take to class on occasion, hung in a closet.

Although nothing in Hemingway's known childhood experiences seems traumatic enough to justify his later prolonged vendetta against his mother, he would use the move to the North Kenilworth Avenue house when he was six years old to situate one of the fictional bits of evidence in his indictment. In the short story "Now I Lay Me," Nick Adams recalls that after his grandfather's death, in preparation for the move to the new house his mother had designed and built, his father's snakes and other specimens were tossed out and burned, "and I remember those jars from the attic being thrown in the fire, and how they popped in the heat and the fire flamed up from the alcohol. I remember the snakes burning in the fire in the back-yard." Critics and some biographers refer to Grace as the culprit in this destruction of her husband's boyhood trophies. But in this instance, Hemingway was more clever than he is sometimes given credit for. Nick admits that he could not remember who had thrown out the specimens on that first occasion. But in a second instance, he more than implies that the guilty party was the doctor's wife. In the new house, Mrs. Adams, given to sudden attacks of housecleaning, burns her husband's treasured Indian artifacts — arrowheads, stone skinning knives, and pottery shards. Her timing seems deliberate. She has done this while he was off on a hunting trip. Not, in fact, when he went off, but strategically just before his expected return. He arrives home to find the bonfire in progress. Hemingway's timing suggests a calculated act of retaliation. The terseness of his style gives the episode a mean authority. "I've been cleaning out the basement, dear," Mrs. Adams greets her husband from the porch, smiling. When the doctor starts to pick through the rubble, searching out the charred and blackened artifacts — "The best arrow-heads went all to pieces," he tells his watching son — his wife has conveniently disappeared into the house.

How closely this fictional episode relates to some actual circumstance is hard to determine. Marcelline's recollections make it clear that at least some of Dr. Hemingway's medical specimens survived the move to the new house. She also indicates that among the treasured Indian artifacts were prized beaded mocassins, decorated deerskin articles, and baskets of quillwork and sweet grass — and these do not figure in the story. Nor does it appear that Grace Hemingway was as given to rampages of housecleaning as Mrs. Adams. At least one of Hemingway's biographers, Jeffrey Meyers, believes that the fictional episode was invented and that Clarence Hemingway retained his collection of Indian artifacts until the day he died. But whether it was actual or imagined, the episode would become — consciously or unconsciously — another item in the bill of particulars against the fictional Mrs. Adams that Grace's son compiled over the years. The truth is that the real-life incidents of Hemingway's childhood — when they can be determined factually — were never as devastating as the fictional treatments he derived from them. Even if one grants that Hemingway, the writer, became something of a master at analyzing the cruelties that lie beneath the surface banalities of family life, there is little in his early life, freed from the fictional overlays, that warrants the vengefulness he would feel toward his mother in time.

Grace Hemingway, despite her nagging piety, her presumed selfishness, was hardly the villain Hemingway would depict in his fiction and in his letters to friends. Her greatest crime, perhaps, was that she made no apologies for her unwillingness to become an ordinary housewife and helpmate. As a girl, she had been something of a tomboy, donning her brother Leicester's trousers in order to ride his bicycle out on the street when it was not considered the ladylike thing to do. As a wife, she took up her husband's hobbies of fishing and target shooting; at Windemere, she had her own .22 smokeless Winchester and took part in the trapshooting there. She was particularly generous and sympathetic to the young girls she hired to do the housework and made a practice of giving them voice lessons if they had talent or inclination. One of them, Ruth Arnold, came to live with the family at the age of thirteen, studying voice while working as a baby sitter and part-time cook. She developed a lifetime devotion to Grace, whom she referred to, in letters, as "Dearest Muv."

Grace felt it her duty to further her husband's career. In 1908, she funded a four-month postgraduate course in obstetrics for her husband at New York's Lying-In Hospital that made it possible for him to become, first, a specialist and, later, the chief of obstetrics in the Oak Park Hospital. Clarence returned from his course in obstetrics by way of New Orleans, taking what appeared to be a well-earned vacation there. (Marcelline recalled that her mother had provided the money for it as well, from the inheritance left her by Abba Hall.) But, judging from Grace's letters to her husband, there may have been some family secret involved, such as one of Clarence's periodic spells of depression. "Do you want me to let the local press know about this vacation?" she wrote Clarence on October 17. "Don't you think it perhaps wiser to let them keep the 1st idea in their minds that you are taking 'post grad' work in N.Y." The following day, she advised him not to read the Oak Park newspapers and get himself "into the old train of thought."

IV

In September 1913, Ernest and Marcelline were enrolled together in their freshman year at the Oak Park and River Forest Township High School. Hemingway was not an indifferent student; during his four years of high school, his grades were above average and in his English courses he consistently ranged between 85 and 95. He had equally good grades in ancient and American history. With years of summer camping and woodsmanship — at Walloon Lake, he had learned woodcrafting from Billy Gilbert, one of the local Ojibway — it was not surprising that he got a grade of 90 in manual training. His lowest grades, in the 70s to mid-70s, were in his three years of Latin, which he elected out of deference to his father, who, from the time that Hemingway was eleven, had tried to interest him in a career in medicine. On a visit to the Mayo Brothers Clinic in Rochester, Minnesota, Clarence sent his son a postcard: "Your Dad is having an excellent trip, it will be only a few years before you and Papa will be visiting clinics together." Marcelline recalled that Hemingway, as a young boy, once signed the guest book for one of the family dinners as *Ernest Hemingway, M.D.* She also recalled that her brother had been allowed to help Dr. Hemingway in his office and was on hand while he treated the Indians at Walloon Lake: "Once I remember it was a gunshot wound that Ernie watched being cleaned out."

In high school, Hemingway was not as interested in team sports like baseball and football — though he did make the junior varsity football team in his sophomore and junior years, and the major team in his final year. He served as manager for the track team in his senior year and played cello in the school orchestra. He was popular with a close-knit group of schoolmates, his young "bachelor friends," as Grace referred to George Madill (inevitably nicknamed "Pickles"), Lewis Clarahan, and Harold Sampson, who, in the summers, were sometimes invited to pal with him at Windemere. There was also Morris Musselman, called Mussie, one of the liveliest and most popular of his classmates. (Hemingway would encounter him years later in Hollywood, when Musselman was a successful screenwriter.) Hemingway had a teasing streak in his character exhibited in the nicknames he thought up for himself and for others. For Marcelline's benefit, he invented the nickname for himself "the Old Brute" and called her "Ivory." But throughout high school he adopted the name Hemingstein and, sometimes, just plain Stein. (Grace, accordingly, was called Mrs. Stein.) Occasionally, he referred to his father as "the Great Physician" — irreverently, since that was how Clarence spoke of God.

Judging from Marcelline's memoir, *At the Hemingways,* the house at North Kenilworth Avenue was a gathering place for friends after school and for Saturday parties or Sunday suppers, in contrast to the homes of the more pious members of the community who strictly observed the Sabbath. It was a time for socializing. Even Clarence's objections to dancing did not hold up against Grace's demands that both Marcelline and Ernest be allowed to take lessons so they could attend the dances at the nearby Unitarian Church House. Clarence begrudgingly drove the two young people to Miss Marybelle Ingram's Saturday classes at the Colonial Club in his new Model T Ford. "Leads to hell and damnation . . . it's all your mother's idea," Clarence grumbled along the way.

At the beginning of his sophomore year, Hemingway was less interested in dancing than Marcelline. According to Grace's memory album, he now stood at five feet ten and a half inches and weighed 140 pounds. Handsome, dark-haired, he was attractive to the girls, though some found him "no particular prize" because he was too unkempt, not quite "sharp." Supposedly, Hemingway had little interest either in girls or dancing and glumly escorted Marcelline to the proms, uncomfortable in his high starched collar and conspicuously polished shoes, standing by the door, chatting with other boys, and waiting for his sister to finish so he could take her home. But at the beginning of the school year in 1914 Hemingway took an interest in an attractive dark-haired freshman, Dorothy Davies, and in January had his first "date," taking Dorothy to a basketball game. "All his bachelor friends," Grace reported, "were nearly in a state of apoplexy over it" — a first mention of the intense air of mutual possessiveness that marked Hemingway's early male friendships. Dorothy was subsequently replaced by Frances Coates, whom Hemingway first noticed when she sang in the high school production of *Martha.* (Like his father apparently, he was first attracted to the voice.) Too shy to invite her to the junior prom — he escorted Marcelline, though she had other invitations, according to Grace — he nevertheless took Frances on a canoe trip and picnic up the Des Plaines River, accompanied by Marcelline and Harold Sampson.

⁂

In his earlier years, Hemingway's reading habits tended to be indiscriminate and voracious. As a child, he was much taken with the stories of Ralph Henry Barbour in *St. Nicholas* magazine, waiting eagerly for each issue. Before leaving for Walloon Lake each summer, both Ernest and Marcelline would load up on books from the Oak Park Library, enough to carry them through the better part of the vacation. "There was one summer," Marcelline recalled, "when Ernest couldn't get enough of Horatio Alger." One spring, both she and Hemingway came down with the mumps and the two were home from school together. They plowed through the classics from the waiting-room library, including Shakespeare's tragedies, Dickens, and Thackeray's *Vanity Fair,* the last "from cover to cover." Robert Louis Stevenson was a favorite, particularly *Treasure Island* and the less well known *The Suicide Club.*

In high school, the curriculum stressed the traditional English masters: Chaucer, Spenser, Milton, and Pope. Rudyard Kipling was to be one of the more potent influences on Hemingway's early poetry, but Wordsworth, Keats, Browning, and Matthew Arnold were also required reading.

The American works on the school's list were few. Franklin's *Autobiography* was required reading in freshman English, but there seems to have been no course description for a class on American literature. The school library, also deficient in American literature, had several copies of Owen Wister's *The Virginian,* and during Hemingway's years it acquired works by Bret Harte, Hamlin Garland, and Jack London. (Hemingway's parents considered London too coarse and violent for the home library.) Hemingway would later champion Twain's *Adventures of Huckleberry Finn,* perhaps read in high school, as the great American novel. His admiration for Ring Lardner, whom he imitated in articles for *Trapeze,* the high school weekly, was probably acquired from reading Lardner's "In the Wake of the News" columns in the *Chicago Tribune.*

Hemingway would later confess his lack of interest in "Emerson, Hawthorne, Whittier and Company"; they were, apparently, too gentlemanly for his midwestern tastes. "They had minds, yes," he conceded. "Nice, dry, clean minds." Considering his lifelong interest in nature, he was surprisingly critical of Thoreau's writings, finding them too "literary." It was only later, after he escaped Oak Park, that he looked at the American realists Theodore Dreiser and Frank Norris.

Fortunately for Hemingway the future writer, there were high school teachers who exercised an important early influence on his career. The first, probably, was his freshman English teacher, Frank J. Platt, the chairman of the department, a "dignified, rather quiet, unexpressive man," who held his classes in the English Club room — leather armchairs, oak paneling, beamed ceiling. Platt praised both Hemingway and Marcelline for their creative approach to English composition. Marcelline appreciated his interest, but Hemingway, in later years, would characterize Platt as merely an amiable fool.

His favorite teachers, the ones he remembered long after, were Margaret Dixon, brusque and mannish, his English teacher in his junior year, and Fannie Biggs, who taught English V and VI, the latter a course in journalism. A classmate of Ernest's and later an English professor himself, Edward Wagenknecht recalled that Dixon "was a very frank, straightforward, honest, down-to-earth person." Her liberal sympathies, which she expressed in the classroom, did not always sit well with the overwhelmingly Republican Oak Park community. She adored Woodrow Wilson and loathed Theodore Roosevelt but kept her opinions within the bounds of decorum. She was full of praise for her favorite students, like Hemingway, and a severe critic when they did not measure up to her standards. Wagenknecht remembered her as being "more interested in movies than most high school teachers admitted they were in those days."

Fannie Biggs, who taught the senior elective courses, had less panache but was a more substantial figure in Hemingway's development. Thin and wiry, with a birdlike face and sharp nose, her hair piled atop her head in an unkempt bun, she was the perfect caricature of the old-fashioned schoolmarm. In character, she was abrupt, bristling with energy and curiosity. In class, she appreciated and encouraged unusual approaches to a subject. At one of Grace's musicales, she once startled Hemingway. Nodding toward a young girl in a wheelchair, she remarked to him, "She has ripe eyes." Though taken aback, Hemingway agreed. Miss Biggs could be impish and daring on occasion. She felt considerable disdain for the high school principal, Marion R. McDaniel, and resented his authoritarian manner, though he was, it seems, an able enough administrator. McDaniel had a disconcerting tendency to meddle, even pry into matters which earned him the name Gumshoe. Once, in the school lunchroom, Miss Biggs, deftly and without the principal's notice, dropped a piece of ice down his neck as she was leaving. For

Marcelline and Ernest, neither of whom liked McDaniel, she became an instant heroine.

Fannie Biggs, who developed a more personal relationship with Hemingway than his other teachers and was invited to the house at North Kenilworth Avenue, was a sometimes caustic observer. Late in life, she would remember the Hemingway family, with a bit of condescension, as being on the fringe of Oak Park society: "I never saw any of the family at the Country Club, Tennis Club, etc., which, locally, were much used for entertaining (and where teachers were frequently invited) nor at the clubs in town (Chicago) where well-to-do Oak Park and River Forest people went for lunch or dinner instead of to restaurants." She noticed, too, that Hemingway seemed to bear a grudge against his parents. When other boys got into scrapes at school, their parents would come to their defense. "Neither of *my* parents would come to school for *me* no matter *how right* I was," Hemingway once blurted out. "I'd just have to take it." She also remembered Hemingway's confiding to her, "When I go to get married, I hope I find a girl that doesn't have to be cuddled up to get her over a peeve. I hope we can just plain talk it over together."

Her visits with the Hemingways gave her a peculiar vantage point on Hemingway's relationship with his mother. Miss Biggs was critical, as others were, of Grace's methods as a voice teacher, especially with her training on the high notes because Grace "liked a dramatic 'edge' on the tone, which seemed disagreeable to many listeners." Ernest, she noted, was aware of this. "I know," he told her, "people don't like my mother's singing. But I remember her singing to me when I was little." Fannie Biggs was struck by the remark and would remember it later: "Thinking of his mother's exuberant vitality, the rich curves of her every move, the warmth of her personality, I have wondered if Ern would find a wife with the lush motherhood he knew."

In his junior year, pressured by the faculty adviser for *Trapeze,* Arthur Bobbitt, Hemingway began contributing regular bylined articles on football games and extracurricular activities like the meetings of the Hanna Club, the school's debating society. By the end of the year, Bobbitt remembered, Hemingway "was recognized as the best writer on the staff." In 1917, both he and Marcelline became members of the editorial board, taking turns, along with other students, as editors of the weekly. And although, at first, Hemingway gave the impression of being diffident about contributing to the high school literary magazine, *Tabula,* he allowed his teachers — Platt or Dixon — to bring his stories to the attention of the *Tabula* editors. Having broken the ice, he contributed more stories and poems.

The three Hemingway stories published in the *Tabula* were competent high school exercises, more interesting for what they reveal of Hemingway's early preoccupations than for any precocious narrative skills. The first, "Judgment of Manitou," published in the February 1916 issue, establishes the fact that Hemingway, well before any traumatic experience in his life, had already begun to work toward the grammar of violence and death that marked his later work. It is a fast-paced story of murder and suicide. Two trappers in a remote Canadian territory, Dick Haywood and his partner, Pierre, who is half French and half Cree, are friends. But Pierre unjustly suspects Haywood of having stolen his wallet. He has set a snare for him out along the trap lines. Haywood, inspecting the lines, senses that he is being followed. (A band of timber wolves has been trailing him.) Meanwhile, Pierre, lying in his cot in their backwoods cabin, discovers that it was a red squirrel that had taken his wallet. In the freezing cold, he starts out to save his friend. "After a gasping, breathless, choking run he came upon the spruce grove. Two ravens left off picking at the shapeless something that had once been Dick Haywood, and flapped lazily into a neighboring spruce. All over the bloody snow were the tracks of My-in-gau, the timber wolf." Pierre then becomes the victim of his own tactic: he steps into the open bear trap that Haywood had come to tend. "It is the judgment of Manitou," Pierre tells himself as he lies, crippled, in the snow. "I will save My-in-gau, the wolf, the trouble." He reaches for his rifle. For Hemingway, wild beasts and carrion birds had already become associated with death, well before they would announce the imminence of death in the bullrings and the African plains of his later stories.

The two other *Tabula* stories also dealt with physical violence in heavy-handed fashion. "A Matter of Colour," which appeared in the April 1916 issue, is a boxing yarn. (At sixteen, with his father's approval, Hemingway had begun boxing lessons in a Chicago gym.) Hemingway's big "Swede," though not a boxer, has been hired to fix a bout. Standing behind a stage curtain, he knocks out one of the fighters with a baseball bat. Unfortunately, he hits the wrong man, and Joe Gans, a "pusson of color," wins the fight. Written as a sustained bit of dialogue, the story ends with a stale joke for a punch line. Confronted with his mistake, the Swede explains, "I bane color blind!"

"Sepi Jingan," too, is a story in dialogue. (The title is the name of the dog belonging to the Ojibway protagonist, Billy Tabeshaw.) A fugitive Indian, Paul Black Bird, has murdered the game warden,

John Brandar, Billy Tabeshaw's cousin. Black Bird's fate, reputedly, is that having gotten drunk on the Fourth of July, he fell asleep on the Pere Marquette tracks, near Walloon Lake, and was killed by a train. But the true story, as Tabeshaw relates it to the young narrator of the tale, is that Tabeshaw had trailed Black Bird through Canada for two years without success. When Black Bird doubled back through Mackinaw to the Petoskey region, Tabeshaw caught up with him, but only to be bushwhacked as he trailed him along the tracks. If it hadn't been for his dog, Sepi Jingan, who crept up on Black Bird and instinctively sprang for the jugular, Tabeshaw would have been killed himself. "It was really a very neat job, considering," Tabeshaw tells the narrator as the pair are sitting out on a grassy hill in the glare of a full moon. "The Pere Marquette Resort Limited removed all the traces."

2
The Two Good-byes

In photographs now — it is his senior year in high school — Hemingway stands nearly as tall as his father, though it is difficult to tell because he slouches, giving his father the advantage. He looks uncomfortable in his dark suit and vest. The father and son shake hands awkwardly, standing in front of the budding trees in the back yard of the Kenilworth Avenue house. Clarence Hemingway takes his preferred pose (it occurs in snapshot after snapshot), his body in near profile, his head inclined to one side. He looks directly at his son. Ernest, smiling, thrusts his hand far out to clutch his father's, which is held close to the body. It is an image of their wary relationship: admiration, but distance on Clarence's part.

It was not surprising that Indian life and Indian lore should figure prominently in Hemingway's early fiction. His father's association with the neighboring Indians at Walloon Lake, treating them when they were ill, was a matter of pride with the Hemingway children. Clarence was an expert marksman who had been given the name Ne-teck-ta-la, "Eagle Eye," by Indian friends. "He was a beautiful shot, one of the fastest I have ever seen," Hemingway would admit, though not without a disclaimer, "but he was too nervous to be a great money shot." Clarence's gaze, however, could be unsettling. Sunny recalled the disturbing effect of her father's penetrating stare: "Dad had keen, piercing eyes that looked right through you when he was serious."

Hemingway's father took pride in his Indian name and liked to boast about his prowess. One summer, when he was obliged to stay behind in Oak Park while the family was at Windemere, he confided in a letter to Ernest, "Don't tell, but I saw a great grey cat in our chicken coop the other evening while Uncle Tyley had the chickens out in the yard." Clarence related how he had gotten out Grace's .22 Winchester and took aim just as the cat, nervily staring him in the eyes, came out into the yard: "in an instant a Squibb like report and Mr. Tom Cat turned a summer-sault in the air — and will never steal eggs . . . again — So you see your Daddy is still a good 'Eagle-Eye' with the trigger when there is game or tin cans." Although there was no truth to it, Hemingway liked to claim that his father had Indian blood from the Edmonds side of the family. And true or not, he also enjoyed telling the story that when he was a youngster, an old Indian on the Wind River Reservation asked him if he were an Indian boy. "Sure," Hemingway told him. The Indian asked, "Cheyenne?" to which Hemingway answered, "Sure," again. The old Indian's comment on the Cheyenne was blunt: "Long time ago good. Now no good."

⁂

In his adolescence, Hemingway seems to have made a careful study of the local Ojibway who worked for the nearby mill as sawyers or peeled hemlock bark for tanning. On Sunday mornings, the Indian women from the camp would come to the back doors of the lakeside cottages to sell baskets made from sweet grass and artifacts decorated with porcupine quills. Once a year, a tribe of Indians would come down from the Garden River area of Ontario, to give performances of "Hiawatha" at Round Lake, north of Petoskey. Hemingway and his sisters were eager to attend the dramatization in the outdoor setting. Albert Wabanosa, a member of the visiting tribe, was a friend of Clarence Hemingway's. Wabanosa claimed that his grandfather had been Longfellow's guide.

Hemingway often accompanied his father, the only doctor on the lake at the time, on emergency calls to the camp about a mile distant from Windemere. The treatments were largely a matter of broken bones, infections, occasionally a stabbing. On his own, Hemingway played with some of the Indian children. Perhaps from a strange adversarial viewpoint, developed early in his life, he refused to accept the popular stereotypes of the Indian. In "Sepi Jingan," he made it plain that Billy Tabeshaw "is not the redskin of the popular magazine. He never says 'ugh.' I have yet to hear him grunt or speak of the Great White Father at Washington." Nor did he depict the Indian as the noble savage of early Westerns, fierce in battle. He did look at them with the expectable prejudices of white Oak Park society, depicting Indians, more often than not, as shiftless, sly, hard-drinking, and ingratiatingly amoral. Billy Tabeshaw; Nick Boulton and his children, Prudence and Richard; Billy Gilbert; and Simon Green were the Indians he knew best at Walloon Lake. They would figure in the later Nick Adams stories with their real names intact or only slightly changed — an indication, perhaps, of callousness on Hemingway's part. He thought little about hurt feelings or possible reprisals for describing them in not very complimentary fashion. But it was also true that early in his career, Hemingway, in the first drafts of stories or novels, often primed his imagination with the names of actual people, whether palefaces or red men. And it is probably true that in his later rebellion against his family and its Oak Park values, he found the Indians convenient surrogates for types of behavior he approved of or wanted to give the impression of endorsing. The Indian was a man of the outdoors, a renegade spirit, absolved from the pieties and frustrating inhibitions of the white man, or so it seemed to the young Hemingway.

One of the more flagrant of his early attempts to flaunt censorship is a queer, incomplete, adolescent play titled "No Worst Than a Bad Cold." It seems doubtful that his parents were allowed to read it; it was perhaps his first and only effort at closet drama. Two Indians, a sixteen-year-old named Richard Boulton, and an older man, Albert, nicknamed Paw Paw Keewis, discuss an "Indian Passion Play" they plan to perform in a natural setting. Juvenile jokes and racial slurs constitute most of the dialogue. But in its graphic attempts at masculine sexual discussion, it probably reflects the urgencies of Hemingway's adolescent sexual drives. Richard Boulton — at first, at least — proves to be as inhibited as any member of the Plymouth League, the young people's church group to which Hemingway and Marcelline belonged. When Paw Paw Keewis brings up the subject of Richard's girlfriend, an offstage presence in the play, Richard is shy about discussing the relationship. Paw Paw advises him to make out with the girl, but Richard says no. "She's a good kid," he claims; he doesn't want to "get mixed up with her." Paw Paw answers, "Ain't any mixed up with Indians. Fuck'um say goodbye, you never seen 'em again." Paw Paw even suggests that if Richard isn't interested, he might "take her" himself.

The character of the offstage girl in this early drama may well have been inspired by Prudence Boulton, the Ojibway girl, two or three years younger, whom Hemingway knew. Sunny Hemingway, a year or so younger than Prudy, remembered how Prudy tagged along (as she herself did) when Ernest and the real Richard Boulton went on hunting expeditions in the woods. But Prudence, Sunny maintained, was not good-looking, only a good sport. "I never saw any evidence of Ernie's liking her or even wanting her along on our exploring trips or squirrel-hunting jaunts. Stories! Stories!" she claimed. Sunny gives the impression that it was she, more often than Prudence, who was so eager to go off with Ernest and his friend Rich Boulton, wanting to be companionable when they talked about hunting or fishing or the proper way to skin animals. She didn't mind when Ernest told her to "lay back, we want to talk private," which usually meant they wanted to talk about girls or some other taboo subject. Perhaps Hemingway showed no visible interest in Prudence in the presence of his younger sister. But Prudence nonetheless would become, both in Hemingway's early and later fictions, an enduring symbol of indulgent and gratifying female sexuality. In that respect she was more the creation of a young man's lust and amoral sexual fantasies than a factual reality.

What is actually known about Prudence Boulton and her relationship with Hemingway is scant and speculative. Yet she haunted Hemingway's fiction through nearly every decade of his adult life. Some twenty-eight years later, Hemingway would tell his fourth wife, Mary Welsh, that Prudence Boulton was the first girl he had "pleasured" (the "pleasured" was probably Mary's euphemism), but the story could well have been one of Hemingway's highly credible inventions. Whether he had had sex with Prudence in his budding adolescence matters little in terms of the persuasive power of her image in his fiction. The truth is that for Hemingway's generation, a young man's randy feelings may not have found such easy sexual gratification. But the objects of one's youthful lust can command indelible loyalty; Prudence Boulton may have provided only the necessary image of a boy's desire that endured — undisturbed — for years.

Her life in Hemingway's Nick Adams stories has a curious history. She appears first as Prudence Mitchell in "Ten Indians," where, as the cliché has it, she broke Nick's heart. Nick, having spent the Fourth of July celebrating with the neighboring Garner family in Petoskey, returns to have supper with his father. He has taken a bit of railing from the two Garner boys, especially Carl, for having an Indian girlfriend. ("Nick . . . felt hollow and happy inside himself to be teased about Prudence Mitchell. 'She ain't my girl,' he said.") Carl, obviously jealous, makes snide comments about the smell of Indians, which he meanly compares to the odor of skunk. But Carl is put down by Mrs. Garner, who, allying herself with Nick, reminds her son that he has no girlfriend, "not even a squaw." In the episode with the Garners, Hemingway creates a real sense of family warmth and conviviality, and of the open, accepting, sly sexuality between Joe Garner and his wife which neither attempts to hide from the children or Nick.

The supper at the Adamses' cottage has a distinctly different feeling. Nick eats in the kitchen while his father watches, pouring him a glass of milk, cutting a piece of huckleberry pie for him. Hemingway's description of the lamp on the oilcloth-covered table, the cold pitcher of milk, the hard light casting the father's shadow large on the kitchen wall, the constrained talk between father and son, fix the scene with the clarity of an Edward Hopper painting, giving it a nighttime sense of loneliness, isolation. (Nick's mother, for unexplained reasons, does not appear in the story; Dr. Adams is either widowed or perhaps separated from his wife.) When Nick asks what his father did that afternoon, Dr. Adams mentions that while walking in the woods behind the Indian camp, he had come across Prudie and Frank Washburn having "quite a time" together. When Nick insists on knowing what they were doing, his father hedges by saying that he didn't hang around but then makes it unmistakably clear, adding, "I just heard them threshing around." Nick, crestfallen, stares at his plate.

In his bedroom, trying to sleep, Nick buries his face in the pillow. "My heart's broken," he thinks. "If I feel this way my heart must be broken." He finally falls asleep, awakening briefly in the middle of the night, hearing the sound of a brisk wind in the hemlocks and the waves breaking on the shore of the lake. Hemingway ends the story with one of the simple unalterable lines that characterize his major work: "In the morning there was a big wind blowing and the waves were running high up on the beach and he was awake a long time before he remembered that his heart was broken."

But every story has its quixotic history, and Hemingway did not arrive at that perfect ending as inevitably as it might seem. He had begun "Ten Indians" in the fall of 1925 in Chartres. In 1926, in Spain, he made two revisions of it (one of which was titled "A Broken Heart"). It was not until May 1927, at Grau-du-Roi, where he was honeymooning with his second wife, Pauline, that he finally resolved the ending. The title was taken from the popular rhyme about the ten little "Injuns" who disappear, one by one, until the last:

> One little Injun livin' all alone.
> He got married and then there were none.

In the Hemingway version, the first nine Indians get drunk during a Fourth of July celebration and are lying along the road. The tenth, ostensibly Prudie Mitchell, does not exactly suggest the fate of the concluding couplet — unless one takes it as a pun on the fact that she and Frank Washburn were playing at "marriage" in the woods. Nor did Prudence Mitchell's betrayal figure in the first version of the tale at all. That came only with the two Madrid versions. Ironically, Hemingway introduced the theme of Prudie's infidelity when he was himself feeling guilty and remorseful over his infidelity to his first wife, Hadley.

It is also one of the personal peculiarities of Hemingway's Indian stories that they are almost invariably associated with his father in the fictional portraits of Dr. Adams. The doctor figures importantly in "Indian Camp," "Ten Indians," "The Doctor and the Doctor's Wife," and "Fathers and Sons." In the Madrid versions of "Ten Indians," Hemingway dwells sympathetically and pointedly on the relationship of father and son and on the loneliness of Dr. Adams.

In one of the scrapped episodes, before going to sleep Dr. Adams, full of remorse for having disillusioned his son, kneels and prays, "Dear God, for Christ's sake keep me from ever telling things to a kid. . . . For Christ's sake keep me from telling a kid how things are." Getting into the big double bed, he lies crossways, "to take up as much room as he could. He was a very lonely man." It is instructive to learn that when Hemingway was writing those passages in Madrid, he was separated from both his wife, Hadley, and from Pauline and was afflicted with "a certain vague loneliness."

The more full-blown account of Nick Adams's loss of sexual innocence occurs in a steamy flashback in the later story "Fathers and Sons," in which Nick remembers his first sexual experience with an Indian girl now called Trudy Gilby. Written when Hemingway was in his early thirties, it is regarded by most critics and biographers as the mature man's elegy to a young man's initiation into the sexual act. In the story, Nick Adams is himself a father, driving with his son, who is not quite twelve, through a southern town. When his son asks what it was like to hunt with the Indians as a boy, Nick, who has been thinking of his father and of their hunting and fishing trips together and of his early sexual exploits, is startled. The story is, on one level, a story about the inevitable contest between fathers and sons. Nick has been thinking about his father's suicide (another of those inescapable autobiographical elements that infuse much of Hemingway's fiction) and trying to come to terms with the fact of it. Nick's recollections of their hunting and fishing trips are among the most poignant and sensitive tributes to another man Hemingway would ever write: "His father came back to him in the fall of the year, or in the early spring when there had been jacksnipe on the prairie, or when he saw shocks of corn, or when he saw a lake, or if he ever saw a horse and buggy, or when he saw, or heard, wild geese." His depiction of the traditional sexual advice of father to son, however, is a comic put-down: "His father had summed up the whole matter by stating that masturbation produced blindness, insanity, and death, while a man who went with prostitutes would contract hideous venereal diseases and that the thing to do was to keep your hands off of people." One can only wonder if it accurately reflected the views of a doctor, particularly one who had specialized in obstetrics. Nick Adams, too, wonders what his father knew, aside from the nonsense he told him. The father is an enigma in one of the story's stranger passages (a fragment not used). Nick vividly recalls a scene that hints at some mystery of male sexuality:

> I've seen him when we used to row in the boat in the evening, trolling the lake quiet, the sun down behind the hills, widening

> circles where the bass rose, ask me to take the oars because it was too uncomfortable.
>
> "It's the hot weather," he said. "And the exercise." I would row, not knowing what it was about, watching him sitting in the stern, the [big] bulk of him, the blackness of him, he was very big and his hair and beard were black, his skin was dark and he had an indian nose and those wonderful eyes, and I didn't know what it was that made him so uncomfortable. I had not started to be uncomfortable that way yet.

As if in contrast to Dr. Adams's old-fashioned notions on sex, Nick remembers his own healthier attitude on a day when he was out hunting in the woods with Trudy and her brother Billy. Trudy is depicted as a child of nature, uninhibited in her appetites. She and Nick have sex twice, the first time in front of her brother. ("I no mind Billy. He my brother.") Afterward, Nick feels "hollow and happy," the same feeling he experienced when he was teased about Prudence Mitchell in "Ten Indians." She manages to arouse Nick again by feeling for his penis through his pocket, and the two have sex again. Billy, disgusted ("Son a bitch. . . . What we come? Hunt or what?"), goes off to hunt for black squirrel. Trudy wonders, without too much concern, if they have made a baby. ("Make plenty baby what the hell," she says.) Nick realizes he cannot explain — not to his son, certainly, and probably not to another adult — what he obviously views as the lyrical force of the occasion. He asks himself,

> Could you say she did first what no one has ever done better and mention plump brown legs, flat belly, hard little breasts, well-holding arms, quick searching tongue, the flat eyes, the good taste of mouth, then uncomfortably, tightly, sweetly, moistly, lovely, tightly, achingly, fully, finally, unendingly, never-endingly, never-to-endingly, suddenly ended, the great bird flown like an owl in the twilight.

It is not absolutely certain that Hemingway ever knew what became of the Indian girl who had prompted his early lust. In February 1918, Prudence Boulton and her lover, Richard Castle, committed suicide together by taking strychnine in his father's house at Charlevoix and became an item in the local papers, including the *Petoskey Evening News.* Prudence, sixteen at the time, was pregnant. It is possible that Hemingway heard about it when he was in Michigan in the late spring that year, just before he went overseas as an enlistee in the Red Cross Ambulance Corps. One might wonder at the circumstances that led Prudence and her lover to take their lives; yet the sadder realization is that their deaths would have remained an item of local history if Prudence Boulton had not caught the eye and stirred the fantasies of a young writer in Michigan.

II

In another snapshot, taken on Graduation Day, June 13, 1917, Hemingway and Marcelline stand in the bright sunshine on the front lawn at 600 North Kenilworth Avenue. He is slightly taller than she, having gained an inch or two in height; his new haircut is noticeable. There are other photographs from the day: the six children on the lawn, bright and self-conscious, smiling their broad, dimpled family smiles. There is another with the whole family, including Dr. Hemingway, again in profile; Grace in a long dress with a dowdy lace collar; the girls in light-colored dresses. Sunny has a huge bow in her hair, and Leicester, two years old, is still in a knee-length dress for the occasion.

At the graduation ceremonies that day, Hemingway read the class prophecy, which he had written; Edward Wagenknecht gave the valedictory address. Among the several commencement speeches, Marcelline's was on "The New Girlhood." The class oration, given by LeRoy Edward Huxham, addressed the time-honored theme for young men and women about to conquer the world, "Dreamers as World Builders." Senior class president Robert Mason Cole delivered probably the most topical speech, "Doing Our Bit"; in April, the United States Congress, at the request of President Woodrow Wilson, had declared war on Germany.

Clarence Hemingway refused to allow his son to volunteer, as some of Ernest's classmates had done. He wanted Ernest to go to Oberlin, where Marcelline was already enrolled. But Hemingway objected. For a time there was a prospect that Uncle Leicester Hall might find him a job in California. Failing that, Clarence was agreeable to Ernest's going to Kansas City, where his brother Alfred Tyler Hemingway, who knew Henry Haskell, chief editorial writer for the *Kansas City Star,* offered to help his nephew get a job as a cub reporter. Hemingway eventually learned that there would not be an opening until the fall. He had thought of applying for a job on the *Chicago Tribune* and could not make up his mind whether to enroll at the University of Illinois. It was an unsettling time. It was probably a relief to have an excuse for spending the summer at Walloon Lake.

Clarence, that year, decided to make the summer journey overland in his Ford. Marcelline and the girls were to make the usual lake crossing on the SS *Manitou*. Grace, with little Leicester riding on her lap much of the way, and Ernest, who would be needed to help with setting up camp along the way, accompanied Clarence. They packed a tent and the necessary camping equipment; they also brought a saw for cutting branches, which would provide traction getting up the sandy roads and hills of upper Michigan. According to Clarence's diary, the journey of some 480 miles, including detours along the way, took more than five days. He was rather proud of the venture. They arrived at his brother George's camp at Ironton late on the fifth day, too tired and dusty to make the additional drive to Walloon Lake. A photograph taken at Uncle George's camp shows the family (together with George's wife, Anna, and their children) looking the worse for wear but smiling still. Clarence, stiff and formidable in his vest and dark hat, which covered his brow, stares full-face out of the picture. Grace, bespectacled, wisps of hair straggling out from under her automobile cap, is wearing an ankle-length duster. Ernest, looking lean and rangy, smirks in the summer glare and lounges against the Ford in his Oak Park High School team sweater and baggy pants. Leicester, a knee-high waif in a forest of adult legs, wears a sun hat and long, dark overcoat. A family fixed in a moment of vanished time.

⁊ ⁊ ⁊

It was a summer of hard work. Marcelline recalled that, with the help of a local farmer, Warren Sumner, and his team of mules, Ernest and Clarence moved the Longfield farmhouse off the property and built a new icehouse by the apple orchard. But Clarence had had a hernia operation in May and was not likely to have engaged in such strenuous work. That, more than likely, was the reason Hemingway did sweat labor for much of the summer. He helped Sumner cut the acres of hay on the hilly land at Longfield and also tended the extensive vegetable gardens through a dry summer that by August threatened the potato harvest. Hemingway tented at Longfield, taking his meals at Pinehurst Cottage, the restaurant run by Liz Dilworth (Aunty Beth to the children) at Horton Bay, two miles from the farm. Liz's husband, Jim, was the town blacksmith. Sometimes Ernest stayed over at Pinehurst.

It was not all work, however. The summer before, he had become reacquainted with Bill Smith and his sister, Katy, who, for years, had been summering with their Aunty Charles — "the Madam," as Hemingway called her — just outside Horton Bay and about four miles from Longfield Farm. Her husband, Dr. Joseph Charles ("Unk"), an optometrist in St. Joseph, Missouri, was seldom at their farm, and the children had a good deal of freedom. Sandy-haired, tall, and lithe, Bill Smith was not quite twenty-one and a student at the University of Missouri when he had met Hemingway again in 1916. Katy was twenty-two, pert, with hard, green eyes, not beautiful, but attractive enough that Hemingway would picture her, in his fiction, as resembling the figure of Anna Held which he had seen on cigar boxes. An avid reader, with literary aspirations, Katy was a source of good books for Bill and for Ernest, whom she treated affectionately, but as a younger brother. Lively, educated, with a casual wit, Katy also had a sharp tongue. The Smiths' older, married brother, Yeremya Kenley, known in the family simply as Y.K., worked in the advertising business in Chicago.

The Smiths — whose mother had died of tuberculosis when the children were small — acquired their literary and intellectual interests from their father. William B. Smith was a somewhat eccentric professor of Greek, mathematics, and philosophy at the University of Missouri and, later, at Tulane. A man with an analytical bent, a scholar of religion, he published two or three controversial books on the historicity of Christ. His treatise, *The Birth of the Gospel,* on which he worked for years, was published posthumously by his children. When he visited Horton Bay, he was not welcome at his sister-in-law's summer house; Aunty Charles thought his neglect of his family had contributed to her sister's death. On his visits to his children at Lake Charlevoix, he put up at the Dilworths'. A family story had it that, once, when Y.K. and his friends were out sailing on the lake and a severe storm came up, Aunty Charles, frantic about the children, ran to Professor Smith's study to rouse him. The professor walked down to the lakeshore and shouted out over the waters, "Oh, Lord, give up Thy dead," then turned and went back to his work.

Bill Smith recalled that when he and Hemingway first met as youngsters, they hadn't particularly liked one another. They would greet each other occasionally at the general store in Harbor Bay with little more than a hello. "Ernest was a husky, sharp-eyed kid in short trousers — usually with a pack on his back." Their families had unwittingly set them against one another by extolling the other's willingness to work at chores: "Young Ernest Hemingway works like a grown man on *his* father's farm," Bill's Aunty Charles would tell him. For a number of summers, the two were indifferent to each other. "It took an old pal of mine, Carl Edgar," Smith recalled, "and most of a long summer to put Ernest and me on really good terms. Carl was wild about fishing and he took to Ernest instantly." That would have been in the summer of 1916 or 1917. Edgar, a Princeton graduate, nearing thirty, worked in Kansas City. His family had a cottage at Pine Lake, and he was assiduously courting Katy Smith at the time. In less than a few weeks, the three were out at the Point, fishing from the dock, day and night. Smith, in short order, acquired a full quota of the nicknames that Hemingway invented for friends — Bird, Boid, Jazzer — while Hemingway, for inexplicable reasons, preferred to be called Wemedge.

In the summer of 1917, Smith and Hemingway instituted a "change-work" program that cemented the friendship even further: Bill helped dig potatoes and pull beans at Longfield, and Hemingway reciprocated by picking apples and chopping wood at Aunty Charles's farm. During the long summers of 1916 and 1917, he and Bill swam together and went fishing often, usually out on the Point, the pine woods behind them, the bay in full view. Bill Smith remembered that Hemingway often came by night, taking the trail from Longfield barefoot "to keep the feel of it," cutting through scrubby pines, skirting the swampy land, crossing the narrow log bridge across Horton's Creek, his voice coming out of the darkness, "Hi, Boid! They ought to be in there tonight — I heard a big one jump."

The friendship between Smith and Hemingway established the pattern for many of Hemingway's male friendships in the years that followed. That they involved men older than he by some four or five years, whom he would dominate, despite his younger age, was characteristic of his closer male relationships. Hemingway instinctively assumed the role of expert and organizer; that, too, was part of the habit. With Bill Smith, in those first years of the friendship, the fishing expeditions were clearly high-spirited; the two shared a kind of feisty humor, enjoyed punning — their letters to each other were full of banter. When they fished Horton's Creek, which emptied into Lake Charlevoix, they had no hip-length waders, simply worked their way up through the deep, achingly cold water. They referred to the ordeal as "penal servitude."

It was in those early summers, too, that Hemingway seems to have studied Katy Smith with some care. He may even have developed a crush on her. Certainly, he observed her relationship with Carl Edgar, whom Hemingway swiftly christened Odgar, in life and in his short stories. Katy, called Butstein, usually took Edgar for granted or was annoyed by his mooning after her — a situation not without interest to Hemingway, who regarded the older man condescendingly. At some point Hemingway began to fantasize that Katy — though she was nearly five years older than he and considered him a youth who didn't scrub under his nails well enough — would have preferred his attentions. Like Prudence Boulton, Katy would have the doubtful honor of appearing in a highly erotic episode in one of Hemingway's later stories.

⁊⁊⁊

It was in the summer of 1917 that Hemingway began to exhibit the early signs of rebellion against his parents and their conventional values. He was unsettled about the future, uncertain about taking the Kansas City job. By August 6, after twelve-hour days of haying and sweltering farm work, he was ready to take it easy. So he informed his grandfather Anson in a belated thank-you note for his birthday present: "I may stay up here thru October working for [Jim] Dilworth and I am not going to the U. of Illinois this fall." His uncle Tyler and uncle George and family were coming to the cottage for a visit on the following day. He was still toying with the idea of going to California or perhaps getting a job on the *Chicago Tribune.* If so, in a year's time he would be "fixed" to go to college.

Things were not going smoothly at Windemere. Clarence, writing to his wife, who had taken one of her summer escapes from the family, reported that Ernest

> is just as headstrong and abusive and threatening as ever. I am sure if he can *work & board* at [Dilworth's] & pay his board it would be *good* for him. I am about to my limit with the *Six* alone. I try to make them happy and the more I do for them, the more they take advantage of me. No word whatever from Uncle Leicester. Ernest had not written him up to yesterday. He is so pessimistic, says it wouldn't do any good.

Clarence's solution to family unrest was apparently culinary. In a self-congratulatory style and with his usual exactitude, he told Grace, "I made all very happy making three extra fine *blue berry pies* between 10:30 a.m. and 11:15 a.m."

Yet, as with many of the eruptions within the Hemingway family, incidents taken out of context sometimes give the impression of more dramatic confrontations between Hemingway and his parents than actually occurred. After his return to Oak Park, Clarence seemed pleased to learn that Ernest was doing well at the Dilworths': "very glad to hear you are happy in your work." Ernest, in return, wrote him a chatty account of his labors at Longfield. Because of the continuing dry spell, the ground was so powdery he doubted the late beans would ever ripen. He was sending a barrel of apples down by the lake steamer *Missouri* and a "sack of spuds." He had had to dig the potatoes himself because Warren Sumner was "all crippled up. In his joints." He advised his father that it would be best to ship all sixty bushels of marketable potatoes home since Wesley Dilworth, Aunty Beth's son, was paying only 85 cents a bushel. "I wanted to hire the Polacks to pick up," he told his father, "but they wanted 5 cents a bush[el] so I told them nothing doing." He planned to leave for Oak Park by the first of October. He gave every evidence of being a capable and dutiful son.

Among the minor skirmishes and tactical feints and truces of family life, it is difficult to sift out the real truths of the family chronicle. In Hemingway's case, it is particularly difficult to extrapolate the early life from the public versions he created in his fiction. Bill Smith, for instance, remembered — though he may have been wrong about the date — that on his way home to St. Louis in October 1917, he had stopped at Oak Park to visit Hemingway. While there, Ernest had mentioned the toolshed at Windemere and said that that was where, in a moment of anger after his father had punished him, he had sat with his shotgun cocked, drawing a bead on his father's head as Clarence puttered around in the tomato patch.

Hemingway described a more complex fictional version of such an incident in "Fathers and Sons," giving it an odd psychological twist. The episode, described in the most economical terms, is painfully intimate and humiliating. As a boy, Nick Adams hated the smell of his father. When he had had to wear a suit of underwear that had gotten too small for his father, it made him feel sick. He had taken it off and put it under two stones in the creek.

> He had told his father how it was when his father had made him put it on but his father said it was freshly washed. It had been, too. When Nick had asked him to smell of it his father sniffed at it indignantly and said that it was clean and fresh. When Nick came home from fishing without it and said he lost it he was whipped for lying.

Afterward, Nick sits in the woodshed with the door open, the shotgun his father had given him, loaded and ready. Looking across to his father reading in the screened-in porch, Nick thinks to himself, "I can blow him to hell. I can kill him." Certainly, Hemingway's ambivalence toward his father was enduring, both in his life and in his work; bitter characterizations were sometimes overturned by moments of pity and forgiving remembrance. It remains one of the most problematic aspects of Hemingway's art, however much critics and biographers try to explain it. When dealing with Hemingway's departure from Oak Park — for Hemingway at eighteen did decide to take the Kansas City job — biographers ever since Carlos Baker have made use of the episode, have invoked the scene in *For Whom the Bell Tolls* when Robert Jordan recalls leaving home for the first time. It is a justly famous scene that has become something of an icon among Hemingway's male biographers. Jordan's father accompanies him to the station and kisses him good-bye. "May the Lord watch between thee and me while we are absent the one from the other," he tells his son. It is a touching and awkward moment.

> His father had been a very religious man and he had said it simply and sincerely. But his moustache had been moist and his eyes were damp with emotion and Robert Jordan had been so embarrassed by all of it, the damp religious sound of the prayer, and by his father kissing him good-by, that he had felt suddenly so much older than his father and sorry for him that he could hardly bear it.

It is possible, maybe even probable, that such a scene had actually taken place when Hemingway left home; the pressure to say something important or meaningful on such an occasion, the sense of finality, the rush of emotion, might have moved even a man as guarded as Clarence Hemingway. It is also possible that Hemingway might only have wished it had happened in just that way.

III

When Hemingway's train pulled into Kansas City's Union Station on the afternoon of October 15, it was met by Uncle Tyler, who took his nephew home to his new house on fashionable Walnut Street. But Hemingway's Kansas City relatives did not expect him to board with them for any undue length of time. Or, perhaps, Hemingway, eager to escape family surveillance, announced at the beginning that he would be looking for his own place shortly. In one of his first letters home, he mentioned that Aunt Arabella wanted him to stay at least until the end of the week. He also wrote that he and Carl Edgar — who was working for a fuel oil company and whom he had seen on his first evening — were planning to get rooms together since they were both alone. What he didn't tell his family was that he found Uncle Tyler insufferably vain and pompous. It was understandable, then, that within a very short time, Hemingway made interim arrangements, moving to Miss Haines's boardinghouse on Warwick Avenue.

Hemingway kept his family regularly informed about his work. Uncle Tyler had accompanied him to the offices of the *Star* for his interview with Henry Haskell, Tyler's Oberlin classmate. Haskell turned Hemingway over to George Longan, who informed him that he would be put on a thirty-day trial period at a salary of $15 a week. Hemingway's immediate superior was C. G. "Pete" Wellington, a "stern disciplinarian, very just and very harsh." Wellington told the cub reporter that he was expected to know the *Star* style sheet, a long galley of 110 dos and don'ts: "Use short sentences. Use short first paragraphs. Use vigorous English. Be positive, not negative." Hemingway would later praise the style sheet as "the best rules I ever learned for the business of writing. I've never forgotten them." Writing to his parents after the first day on the job, he boasted that he had three stories in that day's issue. His hours, he informed them, were from eight A.M. to five P.M., with Sundays off.

His assignments took him on what was called the "shortstop run": the number 4 police station on Fifteenth Street, the General Hospital, and Union Station, the settings for some of the shabbier aspects of Kansas City life. "He liked action," Wellington said, remembering Hemingway's bad habit of taking off in the hospital ambulances without letting the city desk know he was leaving. "He always wanted to be on the scene himself." At the Fifteenth Street station, Hemingway recalled, "you covered crime, usually small, but you never knew when you might hit something larger." Still, it was preferable to the Kansas City that lay just across the river and the state line. The composer Virgil Thomson, born three years before Hemingway, who grew up in Kansas City, Missouri, boasted that "the Union Depot, hotel life, banking, theaters, shopping — all the urbanities — were in Missouri." People who lived in Kansas City, Missouri, during the early decades of the twentieth century seldom spoke about its Kansas counterpart, with its packinghouses and stockyards, and never went there except on business, Thomson maintained. It was "Yankee territory, windy and dry, with blue laws on its books; and the women from there wore unbecoming clothes and funny hats."

The stories that Hemingway covered, the people he interviewed and wrote about, furnished local color items of no more than a few brief paragraphs. Still, on occasion, he managed to make something memorable out of them. One night ambulance attendants brought in the victim of a street brawl, identified only by the name George Anderson on a receipt for a down payment on a house in a little Nebraska town:

> The surgeon opened the swollen eyelids. The eyes were turned to the left. "A fracture on the left side of the skull," he said to the attendants who stood about the table. "Well, George, you're not going to finish paying for that home of yours."

A black man was badly cut up by a razor:

> "It was just a friend of mine, boss," the negro replied weakly to questioning. The sergeant threatened and cajoled, but the negro would not tell who cut him. "Well, just stay there and die, then," the officer turned away exasperated.

> But the negro did not die. He was out in a few weeks, and the police finally learned who his assailant was. He was found dead — his vitals opened by a razor.

At least one of the incidents from the underside of life in Kansas City concerning a cigar store robbery in which two Italians were shot (it is not clear whether Hemingway wrote up the incident at the time) would later be honed to perfection by the more practiced writer. It served as one of the vignettes for *in our time.* Hemingway made the robbers Hungarians in order to effect the ironic ending when the Irish cop who shot the two men maintains their deaths would cause no difficulty since they were Italians. Asked how he knew they were Italians, he brags: "Wops . . . I can tell wops a mile off." Hemingway would use a Kansas City setting for two later, lesser short stories: "A Pursuit Race," about an advance man spaced out on dope in a Kansas City hotel, and "God Rest You Merry, Gentlemen," a grim tale, heavy with Christian symbolism, about a sixteen-year-old boy, so troubled by "awful lust" that he begs a doctor at the city hospital to castrate him. The doctor tries to convince him that what he is feeling is a natural thing, but without success. "It is wrong," the boy answers. "It's a sin against purity. It's a sin against our Lord and Saviour." In the end, the boy mutilates himself on Christmas morning. The tale is Hemingway's parable about the evil effects of unnatural virtue.

In Kansas City, Hemingway also learned how to get on in the world. He sought out the more experienced reporters on the *Star* and the *Times,* the paper's morning edition, and asked them how they developed their stories. He clearly wanted to learn the ropes. "He was a big, good-natured boy with a ready smile," Pete Wellington remembered, "and he developed a friendship with all those on the staff with whom he came in contact." That may have been the generous judgment of a later time when Hemingway had become famous; but Hemingway, as he always would, made the most of any opportunity. His appreciation of Wellington, who, despite his stern appearance, had a habit of putting his arm around a reporter and talking to him as a friend rather than a boss, was equally complimentary: "Working under Pete was like serving under a good officer."

More than likely, working at the *Star* fueled Hemingway's literary ambitions, sharpened his competitive edge as a writer. Russel Crouse, an older, more experienced reporter on the sports desk, claimed, "Every newspaper man I knew was secretly working on a novel." One of the more colorful figures Hemingway encountered at the paper, Lionel C. Moise, had turned up there only the year before Hemingway arrived. Ten years older than Hemingway, he had a reputation as a heavy drinker, a barroom battler, and a cop slugger. He had acquired a badly bent nose, the result of one of his brawls — a fact that did not seem to damage his reputation as a ladies' man. Moise was considered a no-nonsense reporter who admired Saint-Simon, Mark Twain, Kipling, and Conrad. His journalistic credo was forthright: "No stream of consciousness nonsense; no playing dumb observer one paragraph and God Almighty the next. . . . In short, no tricks." But the truth is, his credo and the better part of his reputation as a two-fisted reporter of the *Front Page* variety came later, not in 1917. Within two years of meeting Hemingway, in fact, Moise was back to his roustabout life, working for a time as an orderly in the King's County Hospital in New York, paying off his hospital expenses after another of his brawls, this time with a bunch of "Mexican sailors." It was there that he met Dorothy Day, a radical young newspaper woman who would later become a Catholic convert and founder of the *Catholic Daily Worker,* with whom he had a brief, unhappy affair. (Moise was bad news for women; Day attempted suicide, then had an abortion in an East Side flat. Moise failed to come for her after the abortion. Instead he left her a farewell note and a little money from a bum check he had managed to cash.)

In the scattered trail of drafts, sketches, and fragments of stories that Hemingway left behind him in his career as a writer, there is a brief sketch of Moise, paying tribute to his skills as a reporter who could carry four stories in his head and go to the telephone and take a fifth and then write all five at full speed to catch an edition. Moise was, Hemingway recalled, "the fastest man on a typewriter I ever knew." But Hemingway's instinct for violence also brought to mind a particularly brutal episode:

> [Moise] drove a motor car and it was understood in the office that a woman had given it to him. One night she stabbed him in it out on the Lincoln Highway halfway to Jefferson City. He took the knife away from her and threw it out of the car. Then he did something awful to her [broke her jaw]. She was lying in the back of the car when they found them. Moise drove the car all the way into Kansas City with her fixed that way.

In later years it became a verity that one or another member of the *Star* staff must have influenced Hemingway's journalistic style, and Moise, because of his colorful career, seemed an obvious candidate. Hemingway denied it: "I never, to my knowledge, heard him discuss writing seriously. His style of journalism as I recall it at that time was flamboyant and rhetorical and what amazed me was the facility with which he turned it out. I saw very little of him because we worked in different parts of town." And Moise himself objected: "Like all real writers, he owes his well-deserved eminence not to any 'influence' but to his ability to select from a host of influences — part of that little thing called genius."

✓✓✓

The two men with whom Hemingway did develop important relationships at the *Star* were to become close personal friends. Charles Hopkins, when Hemingway met him, was assignment editor for the morning *Times,* a lively, often amusing man with a good deal of vitality, whom Hemingway nicknamed Hop and Hophead when they were on more familiar terms. Hopkins was always hard up for reporters and Hemingway eagerly covered extra assignments for him. He was decidedly impressed with Hemingway's abilities and no doubt earned his gratitude when he assured Hemingway — as Hemingway reported to his high school teacher Fannie Biggs — "Don't let anyone ever say that you were 'taught' writing. It was born in you."

Some weeks on the job, Hemingway acquired another new friend, twenty-two-year-old Theodore Brumback, the son of a prominent Jackson County circuit judge, who afforded him the opportunity of playing the seasoned reporter to a new recruit. At Cornell University, Brumback had suffered an accident on the golf course which had resulted in the loss of one eye. Even with that disability, he had managed to join the American Field Service as an ambulance driver in France for four months in 1917. After his return to the States, with a little pull from his influential father, he had gotten a job on the *Star.* On his first day at the newspaper, Brumback was impressed by Hemingway's furious pounding on a typewriter. The keys kept jamming. Handing his story to a copyboy, Hemingway looked up and explained, "When I get a little excited this damn type mill goes haywire on me." He shoved out a hand. "My name's Hemingway — Ernest Hemingway," he said. "You're a new man, aren't you?" Brumback's impression was that Hemingway could turn out more copy than any two reporters.

Perhaps because of Brumback's example, and probably because of his eagerness for real adventure, Hemingway was still dreaming of getting into the war. His chances for the army were not good because of defective vision in his left eye. "We all have that bad eye like Mother's," he wrote Marcelline. "But I'll make it to Europe some way in spite of this optic. I can't let a show like this go on without getting in on it." Not long after his arrival in Kansas City, not wanting to be considered a slacker, Hemingway joined the Home

Guard, organized when the Kansas City National Guard had left for France in August. By mid-November he was already involved in practice drills and maneuvers. By December 6, after he had moved into an apartment with Carl Edgar on Agnes Street, he had received his woolen olive drab uniform and overcoat. "They are the regular army stuff, we have the Black and Gold hat cord of Missouri State," he wrote his parents.

It was a busy and active time, and Hemingway enjoyed every moment of it. Aside from his newspaper work, which included occasional late-night hours working for the Sunday edition, and his Home Guard activities, he was keeping late hours, frequenting the Kansas City dives with *Star* companions. On one occasion, he came to the rescue of a fellow reporter who was being taunted by a teamster in a cafeteria one night. Hemingway knocked the teamster out with a haymaker and became the office hero. There was a good deal of heavy drinking and heavy talk, so Carl Edgar remembered, though no serious involvements with young women. Occasionally Hemingway accompanied Edgar on his regular weekend visits to his parents in St. Joseph. Edgar sensed that the emancipated Kansas City life was having an effect on the rather diffident boy he had first met in Michigan. Hemingway had become "very aggressive and opinionated and moreover an apostle of the violent." But that, it is well to remember, was a judgment Edgar arrived at many years later.

It was perhaps on one of the Saturday nights that Hemingway had remained in town that he invited Ted Brumback, after work, to stay over at the Agnes Street apartment. After the long streetcar ride to the dismal, tiny attic room (Hemingway and "Odgar" slept, well bundled up, on a frigid sleeping porch), Brumback was ready for bed. Hemingway, however, insisted on reading Robert Browning aloud while drinking from a handy bottle of "dago red." When Brumback woke up, lying on the floor with a pillow under his head, it was four o'clock; Hemingway was still droning on. The next day Hemingway managed to get through his work as if nothing had happened. Brumback concluded; "Sometimes I think that's the outstanding characteristic of genius — boundless energy."

Hemingway's move to Agnes Street, his unsupervised companionship with men older than he, and, evidently, a recent visit from his St. Louis friend Bill Smith, caused worries in Oak Park. Grace wrote him a warning letter about his current friends and his failure to attend church. Hemingway responded, "Now dry those tears Mother and cheer up. You will have to find something better than that to worry about. Don't worry or cry or fret about my not being a good Christian. I am just as much as ever and pray every night and believe just as hard so cheer up!" The reason he didn't go to church on Sunday was because he had to work till one A.M. — and sometimes to three and four A.M. — getting out the Sunday *Star.*

But he had something more on his mind. "Now Mother," he went on, "I got awfully angry when I read what you wrote about Carl and Bill. I wanted to write immediately and say everything I thot. But I waited until I got all cooled off. But never having met Carl and knowing Bill only superficially you *were* mighty unjust." Carl, he assured her, was a prince and the most sincere and real Christian he knew and was a better influence than anyone he had ever ever known. "I have never asked Bill what church he goes to because that doesn't matter. We both believe in God and Jesus Christ and have hopes for a hereafter and creeds don't matter." He ended with a rebuke: "Please don't unjustly criticize my best friends again. Now cheer up because you see I am not drifting like you thought."

The war on the home front did not last too long. By early March, Hemingway was writing "Dear Mither" to thank her for the box of cake and foodstuffs she had sent. He had opened it in the pressroom, and the cake had been devoured there; the other goodies he took home for himself and Carl. He found an appropriate biblical analogy: the cake had fed "a multitude of starving and broke newspapermen," and the fellows all agreed that "Mother Hemingstein must be some cook." He was still working on his latest assignment, the recent hospital scandal, charges that several politicians and members of the health board were guilty of $27,000 in graft. "I have about five conferences with the Managing Ed. per day and am getting along swell. We sure are making them hunt cover. The reason they are trying to keep me out of the joint is because I have enough on them to send them all to the pen pretty near."

IV

Early in 1918, when a team of Italian Red Cross officials reached Kansas City on a recruitment drive for men to serve as ambulance drivers in Italy, Hemingway and Brumback were ready to sign up. The fact that Brumback had a glass eye and Hemingway's eyesight was poor did not make a difference; the Red Cross could recruit only men not fit for military service in the U.S. draft. Later in life, Hemingway would claim that, worried about his poor eyesight, he had used a ruse to get accepted. Another member of the staff had memorized the eye chart. "He came back and I learned it from him." It may have been one of Hemingway's inventions; if Brumback passed muster with a glass eye, there would have been little need for Hemingway to resort to trickery. Having been accepted, he and Brumback gave their notice to the *Star;* they planned to quit at the end of April. Though it was not likely he could spend a last full summer in Michigan — there was no telling exactly when he would be called up — he still intended to make a farewell trip there and encouraged his friends to join him. Writing to his family about his future plans, Hemingway mentioned that he expected to get back to Oak Park by May 2.

If Clarence was still wary about Hemingway's serving in the army, he seems to have relented when it came to the idea that Hemingway would be providing a useful Christian service as a noncombatant. Grace was enthusiastic and supportive. On April 17, both his parents wrote him. "Your good letter rec'd," Clarence wrote. "I am proud of you and your success." He appreciated "the fact you have in seven months got a profession that you can take anywhere in the world and earn a living — Both Mother and I love you devotedly. . . . We both agree your judgment at this time is *good.*" Grace, addressing her letter to "Dear Old Kid," said she was looking forward to seeing her "Newspaper Man" home again. In a burst of enthusiasm she gave her hearty approval to the planned trip to Michigan: "Gee! But I'm glad you can go there and get fit again. (Don't bother to write Mother.) I can wait till you get rested up north for my next letter . . . God bless you my own precious boy." Neither she nor Clarence was a clutching or possessive parent.

Hemingway's response to this parental approval seemed genuine. "I sure was glad to hear from you both Dad and Mother. Everything is going fine down here. It is raining hard now and has been all day. I put my old mackinaw on and turn the collar up and let it rain." He had been writing a lot of recruiting stories about the army, navy and the British Canadians. He sent clippings in his letter. "Some of them go pretty good," he concluded.

As soon as Hemingway received his final paycheck, he, Edgar, Hopkins, and Bill Smith took the train to Chicago. Ted Brumback, at the last moment, decided to stay with his family in Kansas City, planning to meet Hemingway in New York. In Oak Park, Hemingway's parents entertained the men. Clarence, mindful of the occasion, snapped a photo of Bill Smith, Edgar, and Hopkins standing in the back yard with Sunny, Ursula, and Marcelline. Hemingway, wearing his boyhood cap, has his arm around Grace, gazing at her rather than at the camera. She has the broad beaming smile of a proud mother. The trees are barely budding in the northern spring; a light wind is catching at Sunny's skirt.

The next day, or soon after, the group of friends left for Michigan. The past being at the mercy of the erosions of personal memory, it is not altogether certain which of the friends took part in that last fishing trip. Hemingway was decidedly a member of the party, as was Charles Hopkins. Hemingway, awaiting the results of a recent physical and word about his traveling orders, was concerned about being out of reach. Clarence agreed to send a wire when word came. Bill Smith recalled that he had not joined the party, but he was sure that Ted Brumback was a member of the group. Carl Edgar remembered that Bill Smith had been there, along with Hopkins, Hemingway, and himself, and that they had fished at Horton Bay and the Pine Barrens beyond. Edgar remembered that word came so late that Hemingway had had to leave for New York in his fishing clothes, a nice detail. Marcelline's story was that the men had gone as far north as the Canadian Soo line to a spot where no town existed. Her father had had to wire a telegraph operator at a whistle-stop and an Indian runner had been dispatched to find the little fishing party in the wilderness.

Whatever the story, there is a letter from Clarence to Hemingway dated May 7, sent to Horton Bay, alerting him to the fact that the telegram had arrived, that his physical examination was acceptable, and that he should proceed with his passport application. For further instructions he should consult Red Cross Headquarters. Leicester, only three at the time, remembered that all four men, including Ted Brumback, had rushed to New York to be outfitted in Red Cross uniforms before their assignment to Italy. But the memory of a three-year-old can't be trusted, since Edgar, after twice having failed the physicals for National Guard outfits, was drafted into the army with no problem, and Charlie Hopkins, according to Marcelline, did his training at the Great Lakes Naval Station and was a frequent visitor at Oak Park while Ernest was overseas. At some point in the confusion of Hemingway's return to Oak Park before taking the train to New York, he must have had time to say good-bye to Fannie Biggs. She remembered the request he made: "If it comes to a death notice for me, I want *you* to write it, because you'll tell it the way it was, and no gushing."

On May 12, he wrote his parents from aboard the train that was taking him, along with fifteen other volunteers from New Trier and Evanston, to New York. They were fast approaching Buffalo, he noted, having run along Lake Erie all day. He hoped his parents would see Ted Brumback, who would pass through Chicago, and that they had had "Hop" Hopkins out to dinner. The roadbed, he said, was very rocky, which accounted for the "rotten" handwriting. The food had been very good so far.

✓✓✓

In New York, Hemingway was quartered at the Hotel Earle on Washington Square ("The heart of Greenwich Village," he wrote his parents), close to the Washington Arch. The Red Cross paid his hotel bills and meals. The rumor had it that he would be leaving in about a week. The men in his unit, he wrote, were "dandy fellows." On the morning after his arrival, May 13, he had met Ted Brumback, and the two were now rooming together. Ted, he reported, was very glad that Dad had met him at the station, sorry that he hadn't been able to get out to meet the family in Oak Park. That same morning he had had his smallpox inoculations and his physical. He had passed it with a B, mostly because of his poor eyesight. The doctor had recommended that he see an oculist and get a pair of glasses. But Hemingway did not bother. He had been issued $200 worth of military uniforms and equipment, including an officer's trunk, which, in his eagerness, was already packed.

The next morning, May 14, he had his uniform fitted, and in the afternoon he and Ted and a cluster of new friends (Howell Jenkins, "Harve" Osterholm, Jerry Flaherty — he seems to have acquired them on the spot through some special magnetism) had gone downtown to the Battery and visited the aquarium. They had also been up to the Woolworth Tower. Somewhere in this crowded two-day schedule, Hemingway had also managed to go up and down Riverside Drive and see New York "from the Harlem River on [the] North and Grant's Tomb . . . to the Libber of Goddesty [Goddess of Liberty] in the South." Hemingway then made a casual remark that would cause a storm of consternation in Oak Park. "As soon as I don my officers' uniform I have an engagement with the Mrs. and have already investigated the possibility of the Little Church around the Corner. I've always planned to get married if I could ever get to be an officer, you know."

The unlikelihood that Hemingway, on the second day after his arrival in New York, with a busy schedule of examinations, fittings, and sightseeing trips with his buddies, would have met, courted, and proposed marriage to a woman, escaped the notice of his parents. They were immediately thrown into a fit of worry; letters and cables flew off to New York. Grace was shocked past believing; she must have been a very poor mother, she wrote, if her son showed such a lack of confidence in her. She had asked him about girls and he had never mentioned any. Now there was news of an engagement. "I do trust you will think twice before making such a mistake as to marry at 18, and without any income or visible means of support," she wrote. "I fear you do not realize what a laughing stock you would make of yourself." Her letter continued with a little homily on the matrimonial state:

> Marriage is a beautiful and wonderful thing; but it is sacred in proportion to the prayerfulness with which it is entered into. You may come home disfigured and crippled; would this girl love you then? A marriage ceremony should be followed by constant companionship, a little home nest, a bit of heaven roofed over & walled in, for just two loving souls.

After which she said her prayers. "God help you, dear boy; I cannot; I can only keep on loving you and praying that you will use your best judgment and ask God's guidance."

Clarence was more circumspect; nevertheless, he cabled some cautionary advice: "PLEASE CONSIDER MOST SERIOUSLY ANY ADVENTURE THAT MIGHT TEMPT YOU. MUCH LOVE." In the flurry of correspondence and cables that resulted over the next few days, Clarence tried to instill in Hemingway a sense of his obligations to his parents. On May 18, he sent a cable and a letter in which he wrote, "You could do no greater kindness to your Mother and Father . . . than to write to us often and *confide* in us, as no one will ever love and be willing to sacrifice for you as we do and have." He reminded his son of all the good times, the eighteen wonderful summers on Walloon Lake. "If you did get married — write us all about her? Who and where and how etc. — But please relieve our minds. A girl that marries a fellow of 18 or 19 — seldom is at all satisfied with him when he is 23 or 25 years old. Never be ashamed to say *NO* and to tell the *truth*. God bless you dear boy."

Grace, that same day, wrote in terms that Hemingway, as a skilled writer, would learn to depict as a form of subtle but exacting emotional blackmail. Little Leicester, Grace told Hemingway, had come in that morning with a fistful of dandelions and a wonderful smile for his mother. "It reminded me so of you, Ernest. It was only yesterday that you were Mother's little yellow headed Laddie, and used to hug me tight and call me 'Silkey Sockey.' Don't forget, Darling, that any girl who is worthwhile is worth waiting for and working for; and if she really loves you she will be willing to wait till you are a man, and able to take care of her." Family tyranny was all the more constraining for being so well meant.

On May 19, Hemingway sent a cable and a letter explaining that it had all been a joke: "Cheer up Ye old Pop for nobody gets my insurance save yourself. Also the matrimonial status is negative and will be for some years." He also informed his parents that he was scheduled to sail on the following Wednesday. Clarence wrote him as soon as he had received the telegram. But it was clear that damage had been done. Both his parents were relieved but not altogether convinced. Clarence wrote, "Your wire explaining the 'joke' which has taken five nights sleep from your mother & father received about half-hour ago. So glad to receive it, hope you have written your dear mother, who was broken hearted. *No one* knows what mother & I know and never will. God bless & keep you, dear boy."

The joke apparently had been effective enough that Hemingway decided to embellish the story when he wrote to one of his colleagues at the *Kansas City Star,* Dale Wilson. In the version he produced for Wilson on May 18, his fiancée was none other than Mae Marsh, the twenty-three-year-old film star, whom he had first seen in Griffith's *The Birth of a Nation.* Hemingway stressed that his gossip was not for publication in the *Star,* "but I have been out to see Mae several times and am out there for dinner tomorrow evening . . . Miss Marsh no kidding says she loves me. I suggested the little church around the corner but she opined as how ye war widow appealed not to her." He had, however, sunk 150 dollars in a ring and he was engaged. Once more he cautioned, "But for god's sake don't let it get out amongst the gang and in the sheet."

Boasting a bit, he informed Wilson that the Great Hemsteith, "by virtue of his manly form and perfect complexion," had been appointed the right guard of his squadron and that he had paraded down Fifth Avenue and, at eyes right, had had "a fine look at Woodrow." The president and his wife had reviewed the 75,000 marchers in a parade launching a Red Cross drive. "Woodrow," he said, "resembles nothing so much as his pictures."

During his ten-day stay in New York, Hemingway made the most of his time. The New York socialites, eager to demonstrate their hospitality toward servicemen, especially officers, had invited them to parties and dances, driven them around town in their chauffeured limousines. But it was not the elegance or chic of New York that would figure in Hemingway's memories or fiction. There was an element of coarse sexuality in Hemingway's character, both early and late, that occasionally edged over into the vulgar, encouraged a fascination with the darker corners of passion. And he needed to demonstrate his awareness of the world well beyond Oak Park. It had surfaced in his high school production, the "Indian Passion Play." For some reason, in his later years, it would be associated with his New York visit. Whether Hemingway had actually witnessed such events or merely heard about them in New York, or whether he invented them out of a later, broader acquaintance with the animal strangeness of lust is not clear, but they crop up in a sequence of interrelated, unpublished sketches, titled "Crime and Punishment," written around 1932, when Hemingway was still finishing *Death in the Afternoon.*

Of the two related manuscripts, one is a series of lurid sexual episodes too scurrilous, it might seem, even for Dante's *Inferno;* the other a near-complete short story. They are, plainly, as pornographic as Hemingway's writing would ever become. Those that are associated with New York chiefly deal with sailors and homosexuals. There is a sketch of the homosexual activities around Grant's Tomb, depicted as a gathering place for perverts who let sailors piss in their beards for seventy-five cents. ("They did a good business when the fleet was in. There was another fellow you could take him in a vacant lot and shit on his bare chest for five dollars. I swear to God.") Another is an account of a homosexual theater manager named Big Jack who took on twenty-two sailors one night in Brooklyn, paying them a dollar apiece. But Big Jack could hold his own in a fight and nearly killed a sailor who bragged he would beat the shit out of him. ("I have to do that," he said. "Nobody has to do it with me that doesn't want to. But you come over here just looking for trouble. All right. You got it.") In the story, two men are bumming on the freight cars, one a tough con released after a twenty-year sentence from San Quentin. He wants to get to Brooklyn: "I used to have a lot of fun in Brooklyn. It was the hell of a fine place." He learns that the narrator is from Petoskey — "The hell . . . I come from Traverse City" — and eventually tries to proposition him. In the course of the conversation he reveals, in graphic terminology, that he and a fellow sailor had been put away for sodomizing a younger sailor aboard ship: "He took it all right the first time. I swear to Christ he took it and he liked it. . . . Then when we wanted it the second time, with a wet deck, he wouldn't take it and he squealed."

Not all of the sketches relate to New York; the heterosexual episodes occur elsewhere. (There are mentions of bullfights, of the Escorial near Madrid and of St.-Rémy in Provence.) There is a mordant sketch of a beautiful whore in Panama:

> Thirty seven dollars in one dollar bills in her stocking from that many sailors and she was the most beautiful girl I ever saw. In Panama. With a smooth lovely skin and beautiful dark hair parted in the center and drawn back smooth off her forehead and fine looking eyes and a beautiful mouth. Like a regular madonna. You've got a wonderful chin for a pair of balls, lady [sentence crossed out]. She'd play the flute and swallow the wad all right. That's the only way she'd take it.

The sketches form a montage of sacred and profane variations on a theme. Reworked versions of a Spanish religious procession with banners of the Sacred Heart of Jesus hung from the balconies of houses, the guards with bayonets protecting the Host, the blaring music of a marching band, are juxtaposed with encounters with a Spanish woman, possibly a whore. The sexual episode with the woman ("so hot and brown to scald and then firm saddled to ride, scalding until the great bird flies") bears a distinct resemblance to that with the Indian girl Trudy in "Fathers and Sons," also written in 1932. But the most disturbed and disturbing sequences of this phenomenology of the sexual urge revolve around New York City. From the first, it seems, Hemingway's New York was always to be the special hell of perversion and depravity.

Considering Hemingway's tangled relationship with his parents, is it at all strange to discover that it was not, after all, Clarence Hemingway but Grace who, in a last letter written before her son's departure from New York for the uncertainties of the war in Italy, gave the poignant blessing Hemingway would later attribute to Robert Jordan's father? "Dear Boy," Grace wrote Hemingway on May 20, "no one knows of your 'church around the corner' idea but your Father & I and we shall not let it get out. If you are really engaged, won't you let us know to whom? I want to learn to love the girl who will be as dear to me as my own daughters, but if you are only joking, please tell the truth to your Mother, who loves you so dearly." She ended with, "This is my good-bye letter to you, so again, 'Mizpah' which means — The Lord watch between me & thee while we are absent, one from the other. Your loving Mother Gracie."

3

And Wounds Don't Matter

TWO DAYS of glorious weather, warm and calm, then a storm that cleared the dining room with great regularity. Hemingway wrote his family that the *Chicago* was the rottenest tub in the world. He had been sick only four times, which he considered a record. He, Ted Brumback, and Howell Jenkins (nicknamed Jenks or the Carper) were now pals. They had met two Polish lieutenants bound for Paris — "Count Galinski and Count Horcinanowitz, although it is not spelled that way," Hemingway wrote home. There was, he discovered, "a big difference between polacks and Poles." Fortunately there had been no contact with any German subs; the only ship they had seen was a big American cruiser returning home. It had been a silent passing in the midst of the wide Atlantic; a heliographed message, signal flags sent up snapping in a brisk wind. At night, it was pleasant on deck, where they watched the phosphorescent wake of the ship trailing away in the dark. In four days they expected to land in Bordeaux.

In time — seven years later — Hemingway's Atlantic crossing would become a deepened fictional experience, a young man's rite of passage rather than the straightforward account of his letters home. Hemingway would use real names in the opening draft for an uncompleted novel, *Along with Youth*; Jenkins would figure as the Carper in the novel, and Leon Chocianowicz would become a new confidant for Nick Adams. (Hemingway, with his capacity for attracting male friends like a magnet in the midst of stray nails, learned the correct spelling when Chocianowicz wrote to him, later, in Italy.) Hemingway added a sexual angle (which may or may not have been based on an actual occurrence) in the persona of a female passenger named Gaby, whose father had some connection with the French Line and who was returning to Paris with an aunt. Gaby spends her time making out with men in the lifeboats. Hemingway's description of her is vivid: "She had blonde hair which was always coming down, a loud laugh, a good body, and a bad odor of some sort."

Nick, however, does not bother with Gaby. He spends his nights talking with Chocianowicz, drinking wine in a suspended lifeboat, talking over serious matters. As is frequently the case in Hemingway's fiction, the older or more experienced man pushes the friendship while the young hero exhibits a certain restraint.

> "You'll get better wine than this in France," Leon said.
> "I won't be in France."
> "I forgot. I wish we were going to soldier together."
> "I wouldn't be any good," Nick said.

They talk about fear. Nick wonders if he will flinch under fire. It is obvious to both that the Carper is frightened; he has been drinking for two weeks. Chocianowicz assures Nick, "He's not like us. . . . Listen Nick. You and me, we've got something in us." Nick responds, "I know. I feel that way. Other people can get killed but not me. I feel that absolutely."

And they talk about girlfriends. Nick, who has a girl back home, is engaged. Leon admits that he has never slept with a girl. Nick says that he's been with girls in whorehouses. "That isn't what I mean," Leon says. "I done that. I don't like it. I mean sleep all night with one you love."

What the episode is really about is male intimacy in the face of danger, a kind of male ethic. Gaby is the ambiguous symbol of female promiscuity, sluttishness. Yet, as the story breaks off, Nick adds that his girl would have slept with him if he had wanted. "Sure," Leon says. "If she loved you she'd sleep with you." Nick, still clinging to propriety, answers, "We're going to get married."

⁂

Ted Brumback's recollection was that on the day of their arrival in Paris the city was under the German bombardment of Big Bertha. Spurred by the shell bursts, Hemingway acted as if he were tracking down a headline story, commandeering Brumback and hiring a taxi. After an hour in pursuit of the action, they caught up with a burst near the Madeleine which knocked a stone segment from the facade. Writing home, Hemingway told his parents that Parisians were so used to the shelling they no longer paid attention to it. Hemingway, Brumback, Howie Jenkins, and Bill Horne, a graduate of Princeton and another of the new friends Hemingway had picked up in New York, did a good bit of sightseeing: Napoleon's Tomb at the Hôtel des Invalides, the Arc de Triomphe, the Champs-Élysées, the Tuileries. Paris, Hemingway claimed in a letter to his parents, was a great city but "not as quaint and interesting as Bordeaux. If the war ever ends I intend to bum all through this country." He informed his straitlaced parents that he had gone to the Folies-Bergère that evening, June 5, and that it would be his last night out.

He was scheduled to leave for Milan on the following night. On Thursday evening, he and the hundred or more volunteers boarded a train at the Gare de Lyon. At Modane they transferred to boxcars for transportation through the Mont Cenis tunnel. Arriving in Milan at the end of a tiresome, crowded trip, he and his friends were registered at the Hotel Vittoria.

Hemingway's initiation into the disasters of war came not on the battlefield but on his first day in Milan. On the afternoon of June 7, he heard a terrific explosion; a munitions factory some twelve miles from the city had blown up. Hemingway was one of a group of available volunteers, including Milford Baker from Hemingway's unit, who were rushed to the scene in a Red Cross staff car. Baker, who kept a diary of his Red Cross service in Italy, provides a detailed account of the episode in all its horrendous detail.

> A terrible sight greeted us. . . . In the barbed wire fence enclosing the grounds and 300 yards from the factory were hung pieces of meat, chucks of heads, arms, legs, backs, hair and whole torsos. We grabbed a stretcher and started to pick up the fragments. The first thing we saw was the body of a woman, legs gone, head gone, intestines strung out. Hemmie and I nearly passed out cold but gritted our teeth and laid the thing on the stretcher. . . . One place we found a perfect body of a nude woman with only the head gone.

Hemingway, too, would write about that scene, but not until fourteen years later in a section of *Death in the Afternoon* titled "A Natural History of the Dead." The differences between his version and Baker's are significant. Hemingway, too, recalled the shock of what he termed the "inversion" of the usual sex of the dead in wartime:

> I must admit, frankly, the shock it was to find that these dead were women rather than men . . . and the most disturbing thing, perhaps because it was the most unaccustomed, was the presence and, even more disturbing, the occasional absence of [the] long hair. I remember that after we had searched quite thoroughly for the complete dead we collected fragments. Many of these were detached from a heavy, barbed-wire fence which had surrounded the position of the factory.

In Hemingway's account, the morbid details of the youthful, amazed Baker have been replaced by the more calibrated observations of an older man and professional writer. For Hemingway, the ride back to Milan was the occasion for a philosophical discussion: "I recall one or two of us discussing the occurrence and agreeing that the quality of unreality and the fact that there were no wounded did much to rob the disaster of a horror which might have been much greater." Hemingway's little discourse sounds callous, a bit of artistry where one expected numbness or compassion. But it is instructive to read Baker's artless final comments in his diary: "After the first shock we worked mechanically with no thought of the pieces being parts of human bodies, but only as hunks of meat. We returned to town in the late evening and were at once surrounded by the bunch. We were the envy of the whole bunch. . . . Golly I was lucky. What a fine initiation."

At Milan, Hemingway, Baker, Brumback, Jenkins, and Horne were assigned to Section Four, the Red Cross ambulance unit in Schio, a wool-manufacturing town in the lower foothills of the Dolomites. A few days later they were on their way, traveling by train to Vicenza, arriving late in the afternoon, then transferring to the ambulances that took them to Schio, about four miles from the Austrian lines. The huge second-floor barracks of the officers' quarters, in a former factory, was lined with cots and afforded little privacy. The section had its own mess hall: the chef, reputedly, had worked in London; Italian waiters served the hearty meals and liberal quantities of red wine. There was a local inn, the Albergo Due Spadi (Two Swords), where the officers gathered at night. During the daylight hours, in their cumbersome gray Fiat ambulances, gears wrenching, the drivers made the slow climb up Monte Pasubio to pick up the wounded and sick at the medical receiving stations and transport them to nearby hospitals. The smaller Fords were used for transporting supplies and patients with contagious diseases.

At the "Schio Country Club," their days off were enlivened by ball games and swimming, or visits to and from men in other units. Later in life, Hemingway and John Dos Passos, who had earlier been assigned to the Section One ambulance unit in the Bassano region, would convince themselves that they had met each other during such a visit. It made a colorful story of two writers, later friends, having met and conversed in the midst of the war zone, unaware of their literary interests. Dos Passos's post was more active than the one at Schio: the Austrians intermittently shelled the town, and the shopkeepers had fled so there were no cafés open. Dos Passos busied himself with an active schedule of writing and reading, Boccaccio and Leopardi in Italian, the poems and ballads of Swinburne. Had he and Hemingway actually met then, they might not have agreed on much. Hemingway, full of youthful enthusiasm, idealized the Italians, officers and fighting men alike. Unfortunately, Dos Passos detested the Italian military, found the Italian officers too bootlicking toward their superiors, too arrogant in their dealings with underlings. "God they are a nasty crew!" he wrote a friend. The fact is that he and Hemingway did not meet: on May 30, Dos Passos left the Bassano region for good, "joyful at the idea of going." That was more than a week before Hemingway had even arrived in Italy.

In mid-June the Austrians mounted a new offensive in the mountain passes around Bassano and Schio. On their stepped-up ambulance runs, Hemingway, Baker, and Brumback began picking up "a wonderful lot of souvenirs." At the Schio barracks, Hemingway and his friends were photographed with their captured carbines, bayonets, and pistols, Hemingway grinning under a Boche helmet, shouldering a rifle. When the northern offensive failed and the Austrians began to dig in farther south along the Piave River, Hemingway's unit chief, Lieutenant Charles Griffin, asked for volunteers to man the canteen stations in the southeast sector at Fossalta di Piave and San Pedro Norello. They would be in charge of the relief stations behind the lines, where soldiers could relax, get hot food, write letters home. They would also be responsible for bringing chocolate and cigarettes and postcards to the Italian soldiers at the front. Hemingway, Jenkins, and Horne volunteered. Toward the end of June, they made the trip in ambulances to Mestre, a railhead north of Venice. There they were put under the command of Captain James Gamble, Inspector of Rolling Canteens, a thirty-six-year-old Yale graduate, a Main Line Philadelphian, and an amateur painter. Living in Italy at the outbreak of the war, Gamble had signed up for ambulance duty. He gave the new men a pass for the night to Mestre, as Venice was off limits.

The following morning the volunteers were driven to their stations. Bill Horne and fellow officer Warren Pease chose San Pedro Norello, headquartering in a run-down building in which, on the second floor, there were racks of silkworms industriously feeding on mulberry leaves. Hemingway chose the canteen at Fossalta di Piave, a battered farmhouse in a lonely spot that had seen much damage.

American Red Cross volunteers were allowed to eat at the company messes with the Italian officers. In Hemingway's case, it was the officers' mess of the Brigata Ancona, the Sixty-ninth and Seventieth Infantry units. There, Hemingway struck up an acquaintance with an amiable chaplain from Florence, Don Giuseppe Bianchi, who would later figure in both Hemingway's life and his work in that oblique but important way in which lesser lives, innocently enough, are caught up in the affairs of the famous.

There was little to do at Fossalta; the major supplies had not arrived. When Hemingway bicycled to San Pedro Norello for an overnight visit, he found Bill Horne disgruntled with the inactivity, the swarms of mosquitoes, the uninterrupted feeding of the silkworms, which kept him awake at night. He and Hemingway talked late about their families and their future plans to the sound of the steady chewing. Horne, discouraged with the assignment, would soon ask to be reassigned back to Schio. But the innocuous visit — the setting, the nighttime talk, the blind silkworms feeding as remorselessly as time — would provide Hemingway with the inspiration for one of his finest war stories, "Now I Lay Me."

Close enough to the front and the action, Hemingway felt he was, at last, a part of the war. With characteristic exaggeration, he wrote an Oak Park friend, Ruth Morrison, "You see I'm ranked a soto Tenente or Second Lieut. in the Italian Army and I left the Croce Rosa Americana Ambulance service a while back, temporarily, to get a little action down here." His offhand remarks and exaggerations would be the source of many of the myths about his military service, including the later lies that he had served in various branches of the Italian army. He could not avoid adding an element of danger to his activities. "I crawled out over the top this afternoon and took some darby pictures of the Piave and the Austrian trenches." He was lonesome for the sight of an honest-to-God American girl, he said. He would give all the war souvenirs he had "captured" and his chances for the war cross "for just once dance."

II

Just after midnight, on July 8, Hemingway and three Italian soldiers to whom he was delivering cigarettes and chocolate were crouching in a forward position beyond the front lines. Hemingway heard the *chuh-chuh-chuh-chuh* of a trench mortar being lofted from the Austrian lines. Within moments, he felt an explosion of light which came with the force of a furnace door bursting open. He then experienced what he attempted to describe on at least four different occasions: "I died then . . . I felt my soul or something coming right out of my body, like you'd pull a silk handkerchief out of a pocket by one corner." In the confusion that followed, he heard the *tat-a-tat-tat* of machine guns and the sound of rifle fire. Overhead he saw star shells bursting, then drifting downward. He heard a soldier screaming in pain.

So Hemingway would describe the event in the several fictional and factual accounts of his baptism by fire, most of them contradictory and many of them elaborated on over the years. He once claimed that the depiction of Frederic Henry's wounding in *A Farewell to Arms* came closest to the truth. There, except for the fact that the three wounded soldiers, one of whom was dead, were depicted as four Italian ambulance drivers, Hemingway's account seems to jibe with the official citation for his receiving the Medaglia d'Argento al Valore — though the bureaucracy of heroism may not necessarily be correct in every detail, either. "Gravely wounded by numerous pieces of shrapnel from an enemy shell, with an admirable spirit of brotherhood, before taking care of himself, he rendered generous assistance to the Italian soldiers more seriously wounded by the same explosion and did not allow himself to be carried elsewhere until after they had been evacuated."

Over the years, the episode of Hemingway's wounding would expand to include the heroic rescue of one of the wounded Italian soldiers, whom, with superhuman will, he carried back to the first-aid dugout, despite being subsequently hit by machine-gun fire in both legs. But his citation does not confirm these details. Hemingway, at first, claimed that he had learned what had actually happened only the next day when an Italian officer told him about them. It was the same officer who informed him that he would be nominated for the silver medal. The story would be subject to many variations. In a later version — whether it was indeed the case or one of his self-deprecating ironies that made a story more credible — Hemingway claimed that the soldier he had carried back with such pain was dead when he reached the safety of the dugout. But in *A Farewell to Arms,* where truth may have been of more consequence to the writer, Lieutenant Henry, when questioned, denies the heroism: "I didn't carry anybody. I couldn't move."

At the dressing station in Fornaci, he was given morphine and tetanus shots. It was there, probably, that Italian doctors removed some twenty-eight fragments of shrapnel: "They did a fine job of bandaging and all shook hands with me and would have kissed me but I kidded them along." The regimental chaplain, Don Giuseppe Bianchi, might have included Hemingway in his blessing of the wounded there, though it seems doubtful, as Hemingway later claimed, that the priest had baptized him. The next phase of Hemingway's painful journey was the trip over bumpy roads, swinging in the ambulance sling, to the field hospital in Treviso. There he spent several days recuperating before his transfer to the newly opened American Red Cross Hospital in Milan.

At Treviso, Captain Jim Gamble visited Hemingway regularly. They had met only briefly before but soon became warm friends. Gamble seems to have courted Hemingway, obviously out of concern for a wounded man under his command, but perhaps, also, from a personal sense of loss or bereavement. Three weeks earlier, on June 16, Gamble's close friend and fellow officer Lieutenant Edward McKey, an American portrait painter who had lived and studied in France and Italy and who had been assigned to the Fossalta canteen, had been killed in the line of duty. As the Red Cross officially reported it, McKey was "killed by a shell while conferring as to arrangements with two Italian officers." Supposedly, his last words had been "How splendidly the Italians are fighting!" Hemingway, so soon on the scene, must have heard about McKey's death.

It was more than duty, then, that prompted Gamble to accompany Hemingway on the wearying train trip to Milan. And Gamble, later, would make a point of visiting Hemingway there, another step in their developing friendship. In fact, Gamble may have been in love with Hemingway. Five years later, Hemingway, remembering the kindness of his friend, wrote Gamble with genuine affection, "That trip to Milan from the Piave had all the bad part smoothed out by you. I didn't do a thing except let you make me perfectly comfortable."

⁂

The first news the Hemingways heard of their son's wounding was an early cable. As Hemingway explained later, "Capt. Bates thought it was best that you hear from me first rather than the newspapers. You see I'm the first American wounded in Italy and I suppose the papers say something about it." The papers did. The *Kansas City Star,* reporting from a Red Cross telegram, carried a story of his wounding on July 14. Three days later it published the report that Hemingway had been recommended for the Italian Cross for Valor for having, despite his wounds from a trench mortar explosion, brought "several wounded Italian soldiers" to the dressing station. The Oak Park weekly *Oak Leaves* carried similar stories.

Since Hemingway was still not well enough to write his family more fully, Ted Brumback, who arrived at the hospital as soon as he heard the news, immediately wrote Clarence and Grace, filling them in on the details that would add measurably to the legend:

> The concussion of the explosion knocked him unconscious and buried him in earth. There was an Italian between Ernest and the shell. He was instantly killed, while another, standing a few feet away, had both his legs blown off. A third Italian was badly wounded and this one Ernest, after he had regained consciousness, picked up on his back and carried to the first aid dug-out.

In a modest postscript, Hemingway added, "I'm not near so much of a hell roarer as Brummy makes me out." Clarence wrote his son as soon as he had received the initial cable, "I do hope and pray you will speedily recover . . . Dear Mother gets more proud of you every day and hour." Carried away by the awesomeness of the occasion, Clarence became noticeably formal in his letters. After receiving the official wire, he wrote Ernest, "Please believe that the Great Physician will take care of you and restore you. . . . Do write us often and give us particulars."

When he wrote his parents, Hemingway tried to put their minds at ease. The surgeon, a Dr. Sammarelli, who knew one of the Mayo brothers, was waiting for the bullet in his patient's right knee to become encysted before operating. ("That is wise don't you think Dad?") Hemingway assured them that there would be no permanent effects from the wounds since there were no bones shattered, no fractures in either kneecap. A week later he wrote his mother that his wounds were "coming on in rare shape." But, he joked, "I will never look well in kilts." On August 18, in a lengthy letter, he gave his parents the summary details of his wounding, the two hundred and more flesh wounds, and the developing story of the heroic rescue of the Italian soldier:

> The Italian I had with me had bled all over my coat and my pants looked like somebody had made currant jelly in them and then punched holes to let the pulp out. . . . They thought I was shot thru the chest on account of my bloody coat. But I made them take my coat and shirt off. I wasn't wearing any undershirt, and the old torso was intact. Then they said I'd probably live. That cheered me up any amount.

Under the headline "WOUNDED 227 TIMES," *Oak Leaves* published Hemingway's vivid account. Clarence and Grace, under the onslaught of press coverage and official messages, burgeoned with pride. At a meeting at the First Congregational Church, Clarence, by request, read aloud from his son's letters. Grace was even prouder than her husband: "I thank God for you everyday," she wrote Ernest. "You are like your grandfather Ernest Hall. *Clean clear* thru." She signed it as one of the boys, "Your old Pal & Mother."

One evening, in a Chicago movie theater, Marcelline and a friend were watching a newsreel when Ernest suddenly appeared on the screen. He was sitting in a wheelchair, being pushed by a pretty nurse along the hospital terrace. Dressed in his military overcoat, he waved his crutch and smiled. Marcelline was "hysterical with excitement." She called her parents, and the next evening the whole family trooped to the theater. It had been six months since they had seen him and they all shed tears of joy.

Hemingway, enjoying the acclaim back home, wrote his father; "Anyway, don't worry about me because it has been conclusively proved that I can't be killed. And I will always go where I can do the most good you know and that's what we're here for." In one of his letters, he even turned a bit philosophical. "And wounds don't matter," he told his family; he wouldn't mind being wounded again because he knew what it was like. "There are no heroes in this war," he said. "We all offer our bodies and only a few are chosen." If he had died, he said, it would have been very easy for him. People back home didn't realize, he said, that they'd suffered a thousand times more. "And how much better," he concluded, "to die in all the happy period of undisillusioned youth, to go out in a blaze of light, than to have your body worn out and illusions shattered." Apparently, he wanted to give his parents a demonstration of his newfound maturity: "Does all that sound like the crazy wild kid you sent out to learn about the world a year ago?" he asked. By now, he was experienced enough to know that his testimonial to bravery would find its way into public print — and it did, in the pages of another local paper, the *Oak Parker.*

But it would take years before Hemingway's brush with death, the traumatic experience of being wounded, would leave his mind. At first, he suffered from insomnia, could not go to sleep without a light on for fear he might die in the night. Whether the affliction lasted for several months or several years is another of the clues and false clues with which Hemingway, like an Indian, covered his tracks in life. His boastful letters to his family and the testimony of friends and hospital witnesses suggest that he made a remarkable recovery — even that he was too spunky, too assertive, as the young hero. Nevertheless, there is no doubt that the experience touched him in a profound way. Three years after he was wounded, he would write a curious anniversary poem on the subject of death in battle, curious because of its point of view and gender. A dead soldier is remembered by his wife or lover. The date in the title leaves no ambiguity about the death in question:

Killed Piave — July 8 — 1918

Desire and
All the sweet pulsing aches
And gentle hurtings
That were you,
Are gone into the sullen dark.
Now in the night you come unsmiling
To lie with me
A dull, cold, rigid bayonet
On my hot-swollen, throbbing soul.

The poem is rudimentary — romantic, lacking the exactitude of a major poet. What is striking is not Hemingway's metaphorical merger of sex and death but his assumption of the feminine role, that of the loved one robbed of sexual satisfaction by the death of a lover. It is possible to read into it evidence of Hemingway's sensitivity to the feminine role, but it also suggests his glorification of male potency. The more interesting fact relating to the poem is the extra-curricular, but relevant, knowledge that another, presumably earlier, version of the poem carried the date June 15, 1918. The implication is that the inspiration for the poem had come from Jim Gamble's friend Edward McKey, killed on June 16. Had Hemingway borrowed the death of another man to enhance the impact of a poem written about himself?

The whole subject of Hemingway's wounding has precipitated a long critical and biographical debate about the validity of the evidence, the nature of his wounds, and the psychological effect they had upon his psyche and his career. But whatever the controversy — and the queer mystifications of the self that prompt a writer as concerned about his image as Hemingway proved to be — it does not annul the fact that Hemingway, in Italy, had narrowly escaped death, and had been wounded seriously enough to require extensive surgery and treatment. Common sense argues that the ordeal had an effect on his life. Nor is there any doubt that it influenced his work; the confrontation of death proved to be one of his most vital and obsessive themes.

In a moment of candor and modesty in his later life, Hemingway stated what would stand as one of the negotiable truths in his career as a writer of fiction: "In Italy, when I was at the war there, for one thing that I had seen or that had happened to me I knew many hundreds of things that had happened to other people who had been in the war in all its phases. My own small experiences gave me a touchstone by which I could tell whether stories were true or false and being wounded was a password."

III

In a letter to his mother, Hemingway abruptly announced that he had a girl: "Also Mom, Im in love again. Now don't get the wind up and start worrying about me getting married. For I'm not; as I told you once before. Raise my right hand and promise! So don't get up in the air and cable and write me. I'm not even going to get engaged! Loud cheers. . . . You're a dear old kid and you're still my best girl. Kiss me. Very good."

The girl in question was Agnes von Kurowsky, a twenty-six-year-old American-born Red Cross nurse. Exceptionally attractive, with captivating gray-blue eyes and rich chestnut brown hair, she was a favorite with the patients in the recently opened Ospedale Croce Rossa Americana. A lively conversationalist with a pert wit and an affable, easy manner with men, she was something of a flirt.

Agnes von Kurowsky had trained as a nurse at Bellevue Hospital in New York and on graduation applied for overseas duty in Italy with her classmates, Ruth Brooks and Loretta Cavanaugh, and her former supervisor, Katherine de Long. Her visa, however, had been held up because of her father's German origins. (Of Polish descent, her father had served as an officer in the German army before marrying the daughter of a retired American brigadier general.) Agnes was not able to leave for Italy with her friends. It was not until June 15, 1918, that she made the crossing on the steamer *La Lorraine* with fellow nurse Caroline Sparrow. At the time, she was engaged to an older Bellevue physician, a Dr. S., whom she referred to as "Daddy." Aboard ship, nevertheless, she was highly popular with a contingent of Belgian officers, who, in the fortunes of war, having been stationed in Russia at the time of the revolution, were returning home by way of Siberia and America. A Belgian adjutant, teaching Agnes French in exchange for lessons in English, was particularly attentive. "I'm afraid I'm forgetting Daddy already," Agnes wrote in her diary.

Hemingway's love affair with Agnes von Kurowsky is another of those episodes that have perturbed biographers and critics over the years. Whether it was a passionate sexual affair or only a romantic interlude involving a young wounded ambulance driver and an attractive American nurse seven and a half years older than he, remains an unanswered question after years of critical speculation and debate. Whether Agnes was the real and only model for Catherine Barkley in *A Farewell to Arms* is another of the issues that have been investigated and disputed over the years. Since the evidence brought forward to prove Hemingway and Agnes von Kurowsky had sex together is the same evidence that proves they did not — there is nothing conclusive, either way — the chronology of the relationship is of considerable interest. Agnes's chatty, informative, but hardly intimate diary, covering the period from June 12 to October 20, 1918 — recently published in full — does a good deal to clarify the nature and extent of her "affair" with Hemingway.

It was not until June 27, after a stopover in Paris, that Agnes and Caroline Sparrow arrived in Milan ready to take up their duties — that is, some three weeks before Hemingway entered the American Red Cross Hospital as a patient. Since there were no accommodations ready at the newly opened hospital, Agnes and Caroline were put up at the Hotel Manin. Within a week Agnes was being wooed by Captain Enrico Serena, an impetuous Italian officer. Serena, who spoke English, was blind in one eye and had a limp, but was "simply full of personality, and attractive in spite of his disfigurement." So Agnes reported. Her diary reveals that she was intrigued by the idea of being romanced by an Italian officer, but it also indicates that her notions of love and romance were safe, old-fashioned, and largely literary. She considered herself a cut above less inhibited American nurses like her classmate Ruth Brooks, whose exploits caused Agnes to make clucking remarks. Still, as Agnes confided in her diary, she spent a "wonderful evening" with Brooksie "exchanging romances & experiences. Of course she has much more romance to tell than I have, as she always was inclined to draw romance to her, and I have only lately broken out." Her first weeks in Milan were taken up with a hectic social life: a Fourth of July celebration in honor of the Americans in Milan and a weekend with fellow nurses at Lake Como. There were, too, lunches with a group of American aviators, whom she had met one evening at the Duomo.

On July 8, the night Hemingway was wounded on the Piave, Agnes was assigned her first patient, a Mr. Rochefort, an English lieutenant who had suffered a serious concussion in a train accident. She reported for duty on July 9, not at the Red Cross Hospital, but the Italian Ospedale Maggiore. The first person she saw on the officers' floor was Captain Serena: "Talk about Fate! He presented me with a letter he wrote me last week, the cutest letter in English asking if he might see me again." Captain Serena was nothing if not persistent. He called for her at the hotel, wearing white gloves, a green hat, and carrying a cane. Agnes was slightly embarrassed: "I'm glad my Amer. friends didn't see him. . . . And yet I feel sorry for him. . . . He's nothing but wounds & yet as bright as can be & full to the brim with energy." By July 13, the captain had begun to make minor advances: "It's so funny, he tries to kiss my hand, & I get furious & go into my patient's room, & then my patient kisses my hand. It must be the air of Italy."

It was not until July 16 that Agnes took up residence in the third-floor nurses' quarters at the American Red Cross Hospital at 4 via Cesare Cantú. Her patient, Mr. Rochefort, remained behind at the Ospedale Maggiore, and she continued to tend to him during the day. It was then that Captain Serena made a habit of walking her home at night. On July 20, Agnes made the first mention of Hemingway in her diary: "The Capt. walked home with me again & came in this time. He seemed delighted with our Hospital and took quite a fancy to Mr. Hemingway — who has the honor of being the 1st Amer. wounded in Italy. He has shrapnel in his knees, besides a great many flesh wounds." On the following day, there was a party on the ward: "Sunday, July 21: Mr. Hemingway's birthday, so we all dressed up, & had Gelati on the balcony and played the Victrola. Then Mr. Seely brought him a large bottle of 5 star Cognac & they did make merry. I simply can't get to bed early these nights."

Agnes's first incidental mentions of Hemingway in her diary give no indication that she was particularly impressed with him, other than as the legendary first American wounded in Italy. Her flirtation with Captain Serena, however, waned and waxed: "This tempestuous Italian mode of wooing is certainly terrifying. He tells me how much he loves me, & when I say but I don't love you, it squelches him but a moment & then he begins again." She had her moments of loneliness at night and confided in her friend Nurse Cavanaugh: "Cavie thrills over all the tidbits of romance I tell her & it makes it more interesting to have an audience." And Captain Serena pressed onward: "My Capt. grows even more ardent, & I am beginning to enjoy it, I believe."

On July 29, with much hustle and excitement, her patient Mr. Rochefort — still suffering from moments of going "off track" mentally — was transferred to the American Red Cross Hospital. On July 30, Agnes began a period of several months of night duty. The next day, she reflected on her situation: "Wednesday, July 31: This has been a fascinating month in some respects. I have gone pretty far in the emotional pathway. Somehow, things you read about never seem quite the same when they become one's own experience." With perfect irony, her experiences as a Red Cross nurse in Italy would become something to read about.

⸙⸙⸙

The American Red Cross Hospital in Milan was spacious, clean, "a peach of a hospital," with eighteen American nurses to take care of four patients — so Hemingway informed his family on his nineteenth birthday. The top floor, the hospital ward, had fifteen interconnecting bedrooms, half of which had small balconies. The other half opened onto a broad terrace with awnings and potted oleanders. The rooms had been newly refurbished, the walls calcimined a soft cherry tint, and the furniture had been newly varnished. Though small compared to the Ospedale Maggiore, there was room for a small operating room. On the third-floor nurses' quarters, there was a library and lecture hall, a dining room and reception area. Ten years later (with an appropriately renovated setting for Lieutenant Frederic Henry's love affair with Catherine Barkley) it would serve as the model for the hospital in *A Farewell to Arms*, even down to the smell of the new varnish.

Hemingway, with his youthful looks and liveliness, was popular on the ward. The other patients liked him and did favors for him, especially during the first weeks when he was confined to bed. Many of the nurses liked him, too, especially Elsie MacDonald, an older hand on the ward, a Scot. Temperamental and easily slighted, she nonetheless struck up an immediate bantering friendship with Hemingway, who called her the Spanish Mackerel or Spanish Mac; MacDonald called him her "broken doll." There were nurses who took a dislike to Hemingway. Charlotte Heilman thought him rude and "smarty," uncooperative and spoiled: "He always seemed to have plenty of money which he spent freely for Italian wine and tips to the porter who brought it." The empty bottles of cognac, Cinzano vermouth, and Chianti piled up in the armoire, which served as the closet in his room. In time, Hemingway's heavy drinking would bring on house inspections by the disapproving supervisor of nurses, Katherine de Long, whom Hemingway referred to as Gumshoe.

As usual, Hemingway began to gather a circle of male friends, the most noticeable being Captain Serena, who would serve as the model for Lieutenant Frederic Henry's Italian doctor friend, Rinaldo Rinaldi. Agnes, in her quizzical way, noted the friendship promptly, commenting on it several times in her diary. The captain, along with an artist friend, Lieutenant Brundi, took to visiting the ward at night, "ostensibly to call on Mr. Hemingway," Agnes noted, convinced that it was a ploy to see her, since she was on night duty. The remarkable fact is that, at first, Hemingway championed Captain Serena's cause with Agnes. (Agnes's diary, Sunday, August 4: "Last night I had a lecture from Kid Hemingway on the subject of my 'meanness to the Capitano.' I can't help laughing every time I think of it.") Hemingway, she noted, "is devoted to that man — and they tell each other all their secrets."

In August, Bill Horne turned up as a patient, suffering with enteritis. Elsie MacDonald took to mothering him. Also in August, Hemingway made friends with a new patient in the room adjoining his, Lieutenant Henry Villard, an ambulance driver from Section One. Villard, eight months younger than Hemingway, was slight of build, thinned down even more by malaria and jaundice. He was impressed by Hemingway's stoical acceptance of pain, stretched out in bed with one leg in a cast and the other swathed in bandages: "a good-looking son-of-a-gun . . . lying there fresh-faced and clean-shaven on the white-painted iron bedstead, and good-natured, too, considering that he appeared totally disabled." Hemingway immediately told him, "You'll like it here. . . . They treat you royally."

Only one of Hemingway's newly acquired friends proved to be a problem, a Mr. Englefield, an Englishman in his fifties, a brother to one of the Lords of the Admiralty — so Hemingway informed his mother, who would appreciate such credentials. Mr. Englefield, who had been "younger sonning it in Italy for about twenty years," had adopted him, visited him often, made a practice of bringing him gifts — everything from eau de cologne to the London papers and bottles of Marsala. Later in life, however, Hemingway would remember Mr. Englefield in an acid sketch in a letter to a friend. On his visits to the hospital, Mr. Englefield, it seems, "got wet about wanting to see my wounds dressed. At that time I didn't know well-brought-up people were like that. I thought it was only tramps. I explained to him that I was not that way and that he couldn't come to the hospital anymore and that I couldn't take his Marsala." By then, Hemingway claimed, "it was getting comic and awfully like Proust when you know Albertine is the chauffeur." Agnes had her views about Hemingway's charismatic attractiveness to other men. She would tell Hemingway's fourth wife, Mary Welsh, assuming it was as apparent to Mary as it had been to her, "You know how he was. Men loved him. You know what I mean."

⁂

It was because Hemingway nagged ("Oh, go out to dinner with the Captain, Ag"), Agnes claimed, that she finally agreed to have dinner alone with Captain Serena. As she later described it in a 1971 interview, Serena had made reservations at the Lorenzo and Lucia in a private room in which a couch was prominently featured. It was an expensive restaurant and a famous one. Throughout the meal, a fine one, Agnes had been very apprehensive: "I thought this is some sort of place for seduction." When the meal was over, she promptly excused herself and returned to the hospital. She was aware that Serena didn't have much money and must have "spent a ton" on the occasion. But she thought that it served him right for "thinking Americans are easy." It was the evening of the day on which Hemingway was operated on to remove the bullets and shrapnel fragments from his right leg. "He was the one that kept telling me to go," Agnes remembered, "and then he was mad when I was out during the evening that he was post-operative." Hemingway had blasted her, "You weren't here!"

If there were such a thing as an etiology of love, then a biographer might have diagnosed Ernest's case on Agnes von Kurowsky as having begun on August 10, 1918, with that apparent burst of jealousy. It was, understandably, a serious operation and Hemingway would have been concerned about how well he would walk afterward. Agnes remembered that he *was* worried about the outcome. The operation on his right knee and foot required twenty-eight stitches. Nonetheless, Dr. Sammarelli, according to Hemingway's later report to his family (and using one of his favorite metaphors at the time), did a "peach of a job." Before surgery, Hemingway had joked with the doctor, saying that if he did not survive, his back pay, his insurance, and his bloody boot from the front were to go to Elsie MacDonald. So Elsie MacDonald remembered. Tears had come to her eyes. On the following morning, she couldn't get to the Red Cross office fast enough to cable Hemingway's father about the successful operation. Certainly, Hemingway's irritation with Agnes that night would have been understandable.

Yet Agnes's diary gives a quite different account of her date with the captain, and of Hemingway's postoperative mood, than the one she told late in her life:

> Saturday, August 10: This A.M. Mr. Hemingway was operated on bright & early — our first op. here. Everything went off beautifully. The Ital. doctor flashed smiles all around & learned a few Eng. words such as "needle — strong — enough." Then I had my 1/2 night off & the Capt. came for me at 6 P.M. We went to the Parco & saw the monument of Mt. Grappa. Then to a restaurant — Sempioncius — where at first we seemed to be the only guests. We tried 2 tables on the balcony, & finally it got cold, & he made me go into a little private room, much as I disliked the idea. However, I got home early and he seems to be more decent than I thought at first.

The tricks of memory: the circumstances are different, the restaurant is different, Agnes's feelings toward Captain Serena are different. There is no scolding from Hemingway on that night or the day after or the day after that because, in fact, the first intimations of a bourgeoning romance between Agnes von Kurowsky and Lieutenant Hemingway had not even begun until two weeks later — at least so far as Agnes thought. According to her diary, Hemingway did not make a play for her until more than a month after his admission to the hospital, and two weeks after his operation. The striking fact is that it was not until late in August, after Captain Serena announced that he was leaving Italy, that Hemingway made his move. Something about his relationship with the captain evidently held him back. Agnes, who had been observing their friendship, noted that when Serena was out of town for a few days and didn't return when expected, Hemingway was upset. She had been glad of Serena's absence because she was busy, "but how the Kid worried. He was sure 'we' had been jilted." When Serena did turn up on the night of Saturday, August 24 — with "a whiff of beer about his breath & a stronger whiff of perfume in his hair which was curlier than ever," it was to tell them that he would be leaving Milan for good on Monday, August 26.

Hemingway wasted little time. On Sunday, Agnes made her first diary note of Hemingway's interest in her: "Now, Ernest Hemingway has a case on me, or thinks he has. He is a dear boy & so cute about it. It does beat all how popular I have become in the last 6 mos." The next day, the day of Captain Serena's departure, she expressed relief that her "old affair" with him was over. "Thanks be!" she commented. Rather abruptly, however, she turned her attention to the Kid: "Ernest Hemingway is getting earnest. He was talking last night of what might be if he was 26–28. In some ways — at some times — I wish very much that he was. He is adorable & we are very congenial in every way." Hemingway, for his part, had no doubts. Four days later, he wrote the letter informing his mother that he had a girl, but that she was not to worry about his getting married.

His fellow patients were soon aware of the love affair. Villard, who had also developed a crush on Agnes, now considered himself out of the running. It was evident "that Ernie had been smitten to a far greater extent than the rest of us, and I knew that he had the inside track to her affections when I caught him holding her hand one afternoon in a manner that did not suggest she was taking his pulse." Bill Horne watched the budding intimacy and, despite the difference in their ages, thought Agnes's "romance with Hem was a beautiful thing to watch." After August 27, when the cast came off and he was able to hobble about the ward on crutches, Hemingway began to resent the intrusions of other visitors, including friends like Elsie MacDonald, who, like Hemingway, also suffered from insomnia. "You had a great case on her," Elsie wrote Hemingway years later. "Remember how I could not sleep and would come up to visit her on night duty when out you would come on your crutches and lay me out, call me all manner of Spanish names. . . . That was great fun." On the afternoon of August 30, Agnes reported in her diary, she took Hemingway ("mia ammalato") on his first visit to the outside world in two months, "which we both enjoyed hugely." And on the following evening Hemingway took her to dinner at the Hôtel du Nord.

One has to wonder about Agnes's sudden encouragement of Hemingway. On September 11, their relationship had developed to the point that Agnes gave Hemingway a ring to wear. He was thrilled and she was astonished at "how little an act will give a huge amt. of pleasure to someone." But she was also feeling guilty about her doctor in America ("I feel like a criminal at times"). On August 12, she and Hemingway had a "gay" day, taking in the races at San Siro, along with Mac; another nurse, Ruth Fisher; and Lieutenants Lewis and Pay. ("I didn't win a cent, & lost 30 lire — but enjoyed it nevertheless.")

Still, it would be premature to translate Agnes's idea of an "affair" as serious sex even at this stage of the romance. A week later, when she came on night duty to relieve Nurse Fisher and found her "having a high old time" with Lieutenant Lewis on a chaise longue on the terrace, she was incensed. "It was so common. I couldn't get over them," she wrote in her diary. Hemingway, she reported, was "furious" too. This notation suggests that she and Hemingway had not reached the stage of sexual activity in their lovemaking. Perhaps they were into heavy petting. There was, for instance, the episode involving one of Agnes's hairpins: "Lo'dy, Lo'dy, Goodness me — Mac found one of my yellow hairpins under Hemingway's pillow, & she and Mr. Lewis will never let me forget now. I think both Ernie & I got through it pretty well." But that had occurred on September 7, even before Agnes had been so taken aback by Ruth Fisher's behavior with Lieutenant Lewis. For Hemingway, who had a lifelong erotic fascination with women's hair, the incident would inspire the scene in *A Farewell to Arms* when Frederic Henry loosens Catherine Barkley's hair when she comes to him in his room at night: "I would take out the pins and lay them on the sheet and it would be loose and I would watch her while she kept very still and then take out the last two pins and it would all come down and she would drop her head and we would both be inside of it, and it was the feeling of inside a tent or behind a falls."

Two months later, Hemingway would boast to one of his male friends that it took a trained nurse to make love to a man with one leg in a splint — a boast that, fortified by the fictional account in *A Farewell to Arms,* would give rise to a good deal of speculation about how Hemingway and Agnes, the disabled patient and the on-duty nurse, managed to routinely indulge in sex on a hospital bed in a not too private ward. But the truth is, unless the chronology of Agnes's diary is incorrect, that Hemingway was already out of his cast and ambulatory before he had begun to make a play for Agnes and before she would have begun taking him seriously enough to go to bed with him. Agnes, in later years, irritated by persistent questioning, would deny that she was ever Hemingway's mistress. "I think Hemingway and I were very innocent at that time — very innocent — both of us," she claimed in a late interview. "In those days we were all pretty innocent. As a nurse I didn't know that much." Judging from her diary, at least, which suggests schoolgirl crushes alternating with righteous prudery about nurses who went beyond proper limits, she seems to have been telling the truth.

Again, if, as the diary chronology implies, the love affair became serious only after the departure of Captain Serena in late August and, presumably, after Agnes's September 19 criticism of Nurse Fisher's laxity with Lieutenant Lewis, Agnes and Hemingway had little time together to indulge in the kind of serious sexual affair enjoyed by Nurse Barkley and Lieutenant Henry. On September 24, only five days later, Hemingway and another of the volunteers who had come over on the *Chicago,* John W. Miller, Jr., a Minnesota boy and a Section Two ambulance driver, went off for a week-long convalescent leave at Stresa on Lago Maggiore. Miller, who had been decorated for valor for having rescued a wounded soldier under fire, had been admitted to the hospital on August 30 for pneumonia. While recuperating, he had promptly developed a crush on the flirtatious Ruth Brooks. He and Hemingway supplied the Asti Spumante for the impromptu parties on the nurses' floor. Agnes, however, concerned about Hemingway's drinking, began cautioning him when he went off to the Anglo-American Officers' Club with his friends. Hemingway would promise to drink only anisette. "Maybe I am 'reforming' him after all," Agnes wrote.

On Hemingway's first night away from the hospital on his visit to the lakeside resort, Agnes wrote him — "at midnight as per order" — that his empty room haunted her so that she couldn't stay in it. She also promised to remove the empty bottles he had left behind, putting them in Lieutenant Lewis's room since it was rumored that Miss de Long was going to clean house in Hemingway's quarters while he was away. "Don't forget to come back to me, Boy O.M. [of mine]," she wrote him, "cause I miss you most awfully."

At Stresa, Hemingway spent his time reading, rowed out on the lake with Miller, or sat around under the trees listening to the music. Even with his limp, he managed to take the cog railway up the Mattarone. He was struck by the beauty of the scenery, the mountains rising above the lake. "This beats paradise all to hell!" he told Miller. Even his brief period of rest and recreation at Stresa gave rise to further additions to the Hemingway legend. At the Grand Hotel, he and Miller were adopted by the vacationing Bellia family of Torino, invited for drinks and to dinner. Signor Bellia was an agreeable old scout, "one of the richest men in Italy," Hemingway wrote his family. The meeting would give rise to a posthumous legend that Hemingway had proposed marriage to the youngest of the three Bellia daughters, Bianca, who turned him down — a possibility that casts some doubt upon the absoluteness of his devotion to Agnes. (Agnes would teasingly remind Hemingway of the Bellia connection in later letters.) At Stresa, Hemingway was caught up in the off-season social swirl. A countess, he told his family, had "taken a great fancy to the Old Master" and was now calling him "dear boy." But he was more impressed by his acquaintanceship with an ancient Italian diplomat and nobleman, Count Emanuele Greppi, with whom he played billiards at the hotel. Greppi, who would be one hundred in March, "took charge of me and introduced me to about 150 people. He is perfectly preserved, has never married, goes to bed at midnight and smokes and drinks champagne. . . . He has had love affairs with all the historical women of the last century it seems and yarned at length about all of them." A man with fastidious manners, courtly and alive and interested in the present, Greppi would appear as Count Greffi in *A Farewell to Arms*. Hemingway would credit the count with being his first instructor in the world of European politics — a tall order for such a brief, busy social encounter. More than that, Hemingway claimed that the old count had tried "to bring me up so I would have the beautiful manners a Gentleman should have." Characteristically, he would undercut the patronizing compliment with a feisty aside: "A couple of years later I was bouncing in a whore-house and writing day-times."

Eager to return to Milan, Hemingway cut short his ten-day leave three days early, arriving on the night of September 30, stepping off the elevator, cane in hand, looking for Agnes's greeting. ("My Kid came back tonight," she wrote, "& I feel so different. It seemed wonderful to be together again.") Yet, within a week's time, Agnes was making some critical assessments of their relationship. The Kid had a jealous disposition, she recorded in her diary on October 7: "Every time I try to tease him I'm made sorry for it after, as he goes off at a tangent, without waiting to find out for sure." It irritated her enough that she wrote him about it: "And, Mister Kid, my dear — if you dare to once let that expression of absolute desolation glitter in your beamish eye I'll lay off and — well — there's no telling what I'll do, but it's most likely you'll be unable to appear before the Bellias when they come to town."

For a few days in October, Agnes went on day duty, which meant she had little time for Hemingway on the busy wards and he was deprived of her usual company at night. He was forced to visit with her on the nurses' floor after hours. Agnes, perversely, or perhaps because Ruth Brooks had been called on the carpet by Miss de Long for her frequent dating, made a point of inviting Cavie to sit with her in the evenings. That put Hemingway out of sorts. He sulked for much of the evening: "He says he can't stand seeing me all day like this, & not be able to say what he likes." That was October 13. Only two days later, Hemingway became even more depressed early in the morning when Elsie MacDonald woke him to tell him that Agnes was assigned to Florence and was expected to catch the noon train. Hemingway got up and dressed by nine A.M. ("an unprecedented performance," Agnes commented) to take her to the station. Suspicious that Agnes had volunteered for the assignment, he was so rude to Mac that she was close to tears. Agnes tried to scold him for it, but Hemingway was so obviously broken up that she didn't have the heart to say much. She had a miserable twelve-hour train ride, "an awful trip in the rain."

IV

After her sudden departure at the Milan railroad station, Agnes's love affair with Hemingway was largely epistolary. She would remain in Florence for nearly four weeks on night duty, caring for a seriously ill influenza patient, Lieutenant Hough. Then Elsie Jessup, the American Red Cross nurse who had been tending the patient on days, became ill as well. Agnes did not return to Milan until November 11, Armistice Day. After that, she and Hemingway had little time together before she was sent off again on another assignment. Surprisingly, her letters to Hemingway from Florence (and for the remainder of Hemingway's stay in Italy) were forthright in their expression of love and affection, partly, one presumes, in response to Hemingway's demanding correspondence. (Hemingway's letters to Agnes have not survived.) On that first night of her trip to Florence, possibly on request, Agnes wrote him from the train, saying she felt sorrier for him than for herself; she was going someplace new, he was left behind with nothing to occupy him. She was watching the couple sitting across from her (Hemingway had noticed them at the station), the husband fussing over the wife, who seemed to be suffering with a cold. "Perhaps that's why I like to imagine that you are here, offering me these little attentions, & putting my cape around me, etc." She suspected that if the couple were not there, their places might have been occupied by some interesting Italian officers she had observed on the train. (She was teasing again, but "niente — niente," she added.) The next day, Agnes mentioned the couple again in a letter. Seeing them, she said, she "kept wishing I had you alongside of me, so I could put my head on that nice place — you know — the hollow place for my face — &

go to sleep with your arm around me." Although this was clearly a wish that Hemingway had been beside her on the train with his arm around her, later commentators have too easily read into the remark a hidden confession that in their lovemaking, Agnes had been practicing fellatio. In an updated letter to her "Dear old furnace man," however, Agnes had made a reference to borrowing Hemingway's manly chest in a bit of doggerel:

So tonight when you've gone to rest, my dear
Tonight when you've gone to rest,
While the rain it doth pour
I'll open the door
And ask for the loan of your chest.

But in the letter in which she sent her verse, she also remarked, "This is what comes of refusing, & turning you down. The Woman Pays." At best, her references to Hemingway's chest are highly ambiguous, though teasing.

Separation made Agnes bolder than she was in her diary references to Hemingway. Her letters were filled with endearments, referring to Hemingway as "Why Girls Leave Home" and "The Light of My Existence"; she signed a letter "Your Mrs. Kid." She made a point of reassuring him that her nights were most lonely, that she was not enjoying herself in the vast empty building. "Gosh — if you were only here, I'd dash in & make you up about now, & you'd smile at me & hold out your brawny arms. What's the use of wishing?" She was, perhaps, more caught up in the image of their relationship than in the relationship: "Everything I see or read seems applicable to the Case of You & Me," she wrote him. "I find a parallel in every romance."

It soon became clear that she would have to stay longer in Florence. She tried to put a good face on it. Hemingway had been hoping to pay a visit to Florence along with his "3 old pals," Brumback, Horne, and Jenkins, and that would be encouraging. (Agnes jokingly referred to them as "the 3 original Campfire Girls of Sec. 4.") But something still grated on her mind — one of those irritations that thread their way through a relationship. She reminded him of his complaint when she was on day duty, just before she left Milan: "But anyhow, you said you couldn't stand seeing me around all day as you did for days, so it is probably for the best, anyhow." There were other problems. She was concerned that they were writing each other too often; the frequency of his letters was creating a bit of a stir. "Miss Jessup thinks that you are merely an infatuated youth, whom I allow to write me, & I've let her think so — for reasons of state. You must never think I am ashamed of you." Though she tried to be tactful, this only aggravated Hemingway's suspicions.

Agnes filled him in on the interesting Miss Jessup with whom she had struck up a friendship. She thought Hemingway would like her. Tall, blond, independent in her attitudes, Jessup smoked heavily, had her own pensione for days off. She carried a swagger stick that had belonged to her fiancé. (In her diary, Agnes confided, "I like Miss Jessup, the day nurse, so much. She has only been home once since the war began & has experiences by the bookful.") When she learned that Jessup's fiancé, a British officer, had been missing in action since April and that she wore mourning for him, she became fearful about Hemingway: "Don't let me gain you only to lose you, after I've just found out what I've gained." Agnes thanked him for the relayed message from his mother. "I wish I knew her," she added. (Grace had written, "Give HER my best, I always love all the nice girls.")

Agnes was still in Florence in October when the Italians began the final offensive against the Austrians, which started near Bassano and Monte Grappa and would end with the Vittorio Veneto and the hasty Austrian surrender on November 4. Hemingway, eager to be in on it, returned to Schio to visit Jenkins, Horne, and Brumback but learned that his friends had been transferred to Section One, near Bassano. When he reached there, he indulged in a night of heavy drinking and heavy reminiscing with Bill Horne while under the steady barrage from the Italian bombardment. He also may have helped move some of the wounded. He managed to catch sight of a contingent of Arditi shock troops and was impressed. The encounter would later become part of the myth he spun around himself, claiming he had fought with the Arditi throughout the final offensive. But the truth was that, within a few days, having come down with a severe case of jaundice, he returned to the Milan hospital before the battle ended.

Agnes wrote him as soon as she learned that he was back in the hospital. A letter from Sis Cavie assured her that he was all right, so, she said, she just buried her face in her pillow and laughed for joy. "Last night," she wrote him, "I was wishing I was with you on the big couch on the terzo piano." Her subsequent letters were full of enthusiasm over the spate of Italian victories: the fall of Trieste, then the taking of Trento and the abrupt truce with Austria. Her patients had been playing the Victrola for hours. On November 5 to 6, she wrote that she hoped to be back in Milan soon; Elsie Jessup, just getting over the flu, would be coming back with her on a convalescent leave. Agnes warned Hemingway in advance that the chances were she wouldn't be seeing him that often since she wouldn't be on night duty "& I remember how you burst out before I left." She added, "But my but I'm hungry for a sight of you even if you are Mongolian in cast — cause you are still & more than ever, my love Ernie." Still, her stay was hardly settled ground between them. On November 7, she told him that she would definitely be returning on November 11, but confessed, "Yours of the 4th (I believe) I got yesterday & you scared the life out of me by your wild threats of disappearing before I get back to Milan. . . . My goodness," she asked, "what would be the good of that?"

⸙ ⸙ ⸙

On the night of the Armistice, Hemingway wrote his family, "Well it's all over! And I guess everybody is pretty joyous." His letter was full of plans; after completing his physical therapy, which would take about a month and a half, he wanted to see something of Italy and Austria, since it was not likely he would be back in Europe for several years. By next fall he was going to commence the real war: "The war to make the world safe for Ernie Hemingway." He did not mention Agnes in his plans, only that in several years' time, he expected to bring his children over to view the battlefields. In the meantime, after his treatments, he might spend two weeks of hunting and trout fishing in the province of Abruzzi with an Italian officer friend he had met in Milan. Hemingway must have felt that his family would not object. In an earlier letter home he had broached the subject of remaining abroad after the war, and his parents had been receptive. Clarence had written him, "We trust you will be guided wisely about returning home." He went on to assure his son, "I am always glad to do all I can you know and you are oh so welcome to all we have and with your ability as a Journalist you will easily make good here or there."

Although he had been depressed during Agnes's absence, Hemingway nonetheless managed to take up with two new friends who would be important to his work. One was the Italian captain Nick Nerone, who had fought on the Alpine front and had been wounded several times. He had also served in the battles of Gorizia and the Isonzo and in the final battle of the Vittorio Veneto and had been awarded a war cross. In October 1917, he had been in the mountains during the humiliating defeat at Caporetto in which the Austrian army had poured into Italy through the mountain passes and, taking up a position along the Piave River, threatened Venice. It was Nerone, who was from the Abruzzi region, who had been urging Hemingway to spend two weeks there, hunting and fishing.

Hemingway's other new friend was a British officer, Eric "Chink"

Dorman-Smith, twenty-three, an acting major in the Northumberland Fusiliers. Hemingway was enthralled with Dorman-Smith's stories of his fighting in the battles around Mons and Ypres on the Belgian Front. Like Nick Nerone, he had also been several times wounded and awarded a military cross for exceptional heroism. He had recently been active in fighting on the Asiago Plateau but had come down with dysentery and was just out of hospital. (Hemingway, not to be outdone, gave Dorman-Smith the impression that he had been wounded fighting with the Arditi near Monte Grappa.) Lean and tall, with a brush mustache and a calm manner, Dorman-Smith was nearly a caricature of the typical British officer — brave, tight-lipped, with a dry humor. He and Hemingway hit it off immediately and it would remain one of Hemingway's long-term friendships. The two went out often together, dining at Biffi's, drinking at the Cova, the most popular of the officers' night spots. It was Chink Dorman-Smith whom Hemingway told that it took a trained nurse to make love to a man with his leg in a splint — a fact that did not seem to deter Hemingway from introducing his new friend to Agnes when she returned to Milan. Chink thought her a gay and charming person but must not have spoken with her often since he somehow got the impression that Agnes was South African.

Hemingway's fast-growing relationship with Dorman-Smith must have compensated for the lack of time he was able to spend with Agnes. The hospital was now crowded with patients, many of them down with Spanish influenza. When Hemingway was able to spend a few hours with her in the afternoons, riding in the park or visiting the racetrack, Agnes often had Elsie Jessup in tow.

And then on November 21, ten days after her return to Milan, Agnes, together with Loretta Cavanaugh, was sent to Treviso to operate a busy field hospital that would soon be filled with American doughboys, also the victims of the flu epidemic. It was not the easiest assignment: the wards were in bad shape and there was only one medical corpsman. Soon after arriving there, having brought some order to the chaos and the minimal care, Agnes wrote Hemingway, perhaps too cheerfully, "I am very happy indeed, because I feel I am doing some really worth while work." Hemingway was evidently glum. A few days later, in response to some complaint in his letter, Agnes answered, "Please don't think I'm ashamed of you and don't dare to say it again. I thought I made you eat those words once, but you said them again in your letter, and it hurts me."

With his girl "up at the front," he was very lonely, he wrote his parents. He was attending the opera at La Scala — *Aida, Moses, The Barber of Seville* with Toscanini conducting — and was planning to see D'Annunzio's *La nave,* a gory historical drama set in Venice. It was one of the first indications of Hemingway's lifelong fascination with the Italian poet, playwright, and soldier of fortune, who, months earlier, had flown over Vienna, dropping propaganda leaflets in one of the daredevil, self-promoting acts that marked his gaudy life.

Hemingway had also begun to write. In a brief sketch, written on Red Cross stationery, borrowing Nick Nerone's first name, he sketched out the grim tale of Nick Grainger, a wounded American soldier from Petoskey, Michigan, who lies wretched and depressed in a hospital bed, severely wounded, having lost both legs and an arm. For his heroism, he has been awarded the Silver Medal of Valor and the war cross, little consolation to him, while, outside in the streets, throngs are shouting "Viva la Pace, Viva Wilson!" following the announcement of the Armistice. Listlessly, he studies his medals and the "flowery" Italian citation, which reads a bit more impressively than Hemingway's own: "Wounded twice by the machine guns of the enemy, he continued to advance at the head of his platoon with the greatest coolness and valor until struck in the legs by the shell of a trench mortar." With a crooked smile, Nick folds the paper. Having stolen a bottle of bichloride of mercury, he intends to commit suicide. "I had a rendezvous with Death," he says, "but Death broke the date and now it's all over. God double crossed me."

It's a melodramatic tale, with borrowings from his own experiences and Nick Nerone's more heroic feats. Nerone's exploits at Caporetto would provide much more valuable background material for *A Farewell to Arms* some ten years later. And it would be from Chink Dorman-Smith and his stories of the action around Mons that Hemingway would derive the clipped British dialect and the sangfroid of the narrator in one of the incisive military vignettes in *in our time*: "We were in a garden at Mons. Young Buckley came in with his patrol from across the river. The first German I saw climbed up over the garden wall. We waited till he got one leg over and then potted him." But that would be the work of a far more practiced writer.

V

Not long after the Armistice, Jim Gamble wrote Hemingway, offering to stake him for a year abroad, suggesting that they winter together at Madeira or the Canary Islands, then travel around. Hemingway was tempted; Gamble would pay all his expenses. Ernest broached the subject to Agnes, who was still at Treviso. "Dearie me," she answered, "how nice that trip to Madeira sounds — but I'm afraid you'd never want to go & be somebody worth while. Those places do get in one's blood . . . I'd hate like everything to see you minus ambition, dear lad." She was plainly not happy about the prospect. Perhaps she was suspicious about Gamble's offer. In a late interview with Mary Hemingway, Agnes claimed, "My idea was to get him home to the United States because he was very fascinating to older men. They all found him very interesting . . . I told him he'd never be anything but a bum if he sponged off someone else." She also claimed that even at that time, she had already decided not to marry Hemingway and was waiting only until he was back home before telling him so. But that was all in hindsight. In the letter she wrote him, in fact, she had explicity held out the hope: "I sometimes wish we could marry over here, but since that is so foolish I must try & not think about it," she told him. Agnes's letters, during the last weeks of Hemingway's stay in Italy, reveal that she had encouraged him in every way. There were optimistic discussions of marriage. She told him that she loved him, said she needed him. She teased him about a planned visit to Treviso, saying how often she looked out the window, "and every now & then jump because I think I see a familiar stalwart figure in a good-looking English uniform & overseas cap with a cane."

When Hemingway finally made the trip, he hitched rides on camions, then at Torréglia, at the 105th Siege Battery, visited a British officer, a Lieutenant Hey, whom he had met at the officers' club in Milan. On the following morning, December 9, he managed to ride the colonel's hunter, taking ditches and fences with his bum leg. That afternoon, he rode with the lieutenant to Treviso in a staff car; Hey was anxious to see his girlfriend, Gertrude Smith, a nurse at Treviso. Hemingway arrived in full uniform with wound stripes and medals in full array, probably to fulfill Agnes's expectations. It was a mistake; the wounded and ailing American doughboys, according to Agnes, had laughed at him behind his back. He and Agnes, Lieutenant Hey and Nurse Smith, visited the ruins of the battlefield, saw the former Austrian trenches, and had a midnight breakfast before Hemingway started back on the tiresome journey to Milan.

Despite the briefness of the visit, Agnes appeared even more committed. The day after, she wrote him encouraging words; the Treviso hospital would probably be shut down soon and, perhaps, they might return home together. The Red Cross nurses would have to return home from Italy, which was a bitter disappointment: "I'd hoped to get back to Paris for a few days anyhow. Do you think we'll be able to get over again some day? If so, I shan't worry about seeing everything now." A few days later, she was even more affirmative about their future: "I wrote to my mother that I was planning to marry a man younger than I — & it wasn't the Doctor — so I expect she'll give me up in despair as a hopeless flirt."

For the moment, Hemingway seemed to have agreed, with Agnes's strong urging, to turn down Jim Gamble's offer. He wrote his family: "For a while I was going to go down to Madeira and the Canaries with Capt. Gamble, but I realize that if I blow down there and bum I will never get home. The climate and this country get you and the Lord ordained differently for me and I was made for to be one of those beastly writing chaps y'know." Hemingway also informed Bill Smith about his decision: "So I'm going to hit the States and start working for the Firm. Ag says we can have a wonderful time being poor together." He was scheduled to sail from Genoa on January 4, aboard the *Giuseppe Verdi,* he told Bill. It was clear that he was eager to marry Agnes: "Every minute that I'm away from that Kid is wasted," he said. He expected Bill to be his best man. "Now try to keep your finger off the trigger," he added, "cause you may be in the same fix yourself sometime." He had been planning to spend time in Michigan after his return. But now, after the visit to Treviso, a new seriousness was detectable. He told Bill, "So now all I have to do is hit the minimum living wage for two and lay up enough for six weeks or so up North."

Agnes was surprised at the suddenness of his decision: "Your news was somewhat startling — about going home I mean. And I do hope I'll get to Milan for Xmas or it will be a miserable day." But she hedged; everything at Treviso was undecided. One day she heard she wouldn't be needed after the end of the week; the next day it seemed the hospital would never get the patients removed by Christmastime. "Besides, I think the officers want us to stay to make things a little more cheerful & homelike for them." The casual mentions of officers and men were bound to be unsettling to Hemingway. And toward the end of their relationship, Agnes gave him additional cause for worry. In another letter, she made one of her more acute observations about herself and Hemingway: "It's strange how circumstances can affect one. When I was with Jessup I wanted to do all sorts of wild things — anything but go home — and when you are with Capt. Gamble you felt the same way. But I think maybe we have both changed our minds — & the old Etats Unis are going to look tres tres bien to our world weary eyes." On December 20, Agnes wrote Hemingway the bad news: "Be nice, now, & don't get rash when you hear I'm not coming to Milan — as I'm afraid it looks that way. By this I mean don't lap up all the fluids in the Galleria." Agnes, too, had her worries: "It makes me shiver to think of your going home without me. What if our hearts should change? Both, I mean, & we should lose this beautiful world of us?"

Hemingway had remained in Milan until sometime before Christmas, so Katherine de Long wrote Agnes: "Your steady is here but going away tomorrow for a nice trip." In a surprising change of heart, she added, "Now don't laugh when I say I am going to miss him very much. He is a good boy & has been so kind & thoughtful for me. I am glad though, that he is going to America, for I do not want him to waste his time — he is too fine!" Hemingway's "nice trip" was undoubtedly the trip he made to Taormina in Sicily at the invitation of Jim Gamble, who had rented a villa with a garden from an English artist there. Writing Hemingway, he complained, "Now the only thing lacking is company & I only hope you will take care of that. There is plenty of room in the house, two studios, lots of atmosphere, and I should think plenty about which to write." Hemingway accepted. Perhaps, as a young man, flattered by Gamble's attentions, impressed by Gamble's sophistication and wealth, Hemingway was also casually stringing his friend along, though he clearly was fond of Gamble. Hemingway would remember the Taormina visit with considerable pleasure — the walks through the city, he and Gamble pleasantly drunk, strolling under a Mediterranean moon, Mount Etna smoking in the distance. In Taormina, Gamble introduced him to his friends, a pair of English artists named Woods and Kitson, a British major and his affable wife. He and Gamble joked about Jim's cook, whom they nicknamed Mange Uova, because his specialty was eggs. He also met another of those interesting nonagenarians, this one the duke of Bronte, supposedly a descendant of Admiral Nelson, who wanted — so Hemingway claimed — to bring him up as a gentleman.

Yet, clearly, something about the visit made him feel embarrassed or defensive. When he returned to Milan, he concocted a story for Chink Dorman-Smith's benefit, boasting that he had seen nothing of Sicily "except a bedroom window because his hostess in the first small hotel he stopped in had hidden his clothes and kept him to herself for a week. The food she brought him was excellent and she was affectionate. Hem had no complaints except that he saw very little of the country." Dorman-Smith, who treated many of Hemingway's stories with an unwarranted credulousness, when relating the episode, commented, "I don't know what Hem told Ag!" Little wonder that in a sentimental poem in praise of his friend, Hemingway recalled their heavy drinking sessions and their talk, talk, talk of the Empire, the separate trades of soldiering and writing, the necessity of money, overdrafts, and how to handle tailors. What

Hemingway appreciated in his friend was that "when drunk I boasted and you never minded."

✓✓✓

Biography: even the very well trod ground occasionally yields up new discoveries. The common assumption in all Hemingway biographies has been that Hemingway's last meeting with Agnes was his December 9 visit with her at the field hospital at Treviso. Strange that a man so ardently in love would not have made every effort to see Agnes just before his departure for home. Particularly since he had made just such an effort to visit his friend Jim Gamble in Sicily. But the past, providentially, is never settled ground. A careful reading of a letter to Hemingway which Agnes began on New Year's Eve 1918 and then continued on New Year's Day reveals that she and Hemingway did, in fact, have a final rendezvous in Milan on December 31, just before Hemingway took ship for America. (In fact, Agnes's letter had been written in Milan.)

In her New Year's Eve summing-up, Agnes tried hard not to be the submissive female, though not always successfully. She was realistic when it came to Hemingway's character and made a sharp assessment of his probable reactions to their parting. It was, she said, the hardest letter she had ever written:

> If I'm doleful you'll cause the boat to sink — and if I'm troppo cheerful you'll blow up in your very characteristic style and get the old boat all full of smoke, thereby causing consternation among those of an elderly order. So the only solution I can find, is a happy medium (if you know what that is) and I shall endeavor to dispense cheer & yet give the impression of subdued spirits.

Posing as his "superior officer," Agnes offered Hemingway a few bits of advice, some of them comic, some of them motherly: "Don't chew tobacco in the presence of ladies"; "Don't wear loud neckties in the States just 'cause the Italian ufficiali can't dress decently in mufti. You hadn't orter copy their styles"; and "Don't use no perfume, curling irons, nor tooth-picks. Don't like em — that's all." She made a point of explaining that back home she didn't want him to work too hard or undermine his health, which was now one of his "chief assets." She also encouraged him to take the vacation in Michigan with Bill Smith which he had been talking about: "I'm not the one to put a stop to that and I certainly don't want to be responsible for your going into a decline early." But throughout the letter — addressed to "Dear Boy" — was the very evident manner of an older woman writing to a temperamental young man.

Hemingway had exacted conditions at their parting; he expected her to write him every day. Agnes, however, had balked. ("You know I wouldn't promise because I wasn't sure I'd be able to fulfil my oaths," she reminded him in a later letter.) But on New Year's Day, she had yielded: "I'm beginning the New Year right in one respect. I'm writing to you." She made it plain, however, that she was not keen on returning home. Hemingway would be off in Oak Park or in Michigan, and the likelihood was that he wouldn't be there to meet her when she arrived in New York. Also, she was sure that she would find nursing in the United States "particularly dull and uninteresting" after her experiences in Italy. "But, you made me promise not to stay here on this side of the water so I must needs go."

There had been, too, some trying moments in their good-bye meeting. Hemingway was not in the best frame of mind. Agnes wrote him, "So now when you get blue & can't find your ideas as fast as you'd like & things look particularly low & hellish (scuse me) just remember I'm looking to you for my future life. You've got to make good, and things never stay low for long." Something had plainly gone wrong between them: "You were a dear last night tho', and I shouldn't complain of things in the past which must be forgotten & forgiven — on both sides, of course." Her next remark should have warned him about their future: "Dear Ernie, you are to me a wonderful boy, & when you add on a few years & some dignity & calm, you'll be very much worth while." But she did express her confidence in him: "Now Ernie, I'm looking to you to do big things."

One of the first clues that Agnes's "December 31 — and then some" letter had been written in Milan is her reference to a conversation she had had with Captain Charles Moore, a physician stationed in the Milan hospital, and her friend Ruth Brooks: "Capt. Moore was teasing me today about my fondness for Italian officers. Brooks was praising up the British, but I said, 'Well, we all come back to a perfectly good American just the same.'"

In the plausible scenario of their final meeting in Milan, based on the pieces of the puzzle culled from Agnes's correspondence, she and Hemingway seem to have run into Lieutenant Brundi, the painter friend of Captain Enrico Serena whom they both knew. Also Agnes had taken Hemingway to a tearoom in Milan, and he had not liked the place: "I forgot to tell you I saw Brundi again on Sun. in the St. Margherita tea room, which you turned up your nose at, when I took you there. He hasn't seen nor heard of Capt. Serena." It is certain that when Hemingway left Jim Gamble in Sicily, Gamble had given him money to buy some paints and send them to him in Taormina. But things in Milan had gotten too hectic and the date for his sailing was moved up (at least Hemingway claimed so in a letter to Gamble) and he had turned that errand over to Agnes at the last minute. Unimportant items, perhaps, in the record of a particular life, but it is out of such minor confirmations that a biographer sometimes manages to build a case.

What is more important is that passing references in Agnes's letters written after Hemingway's departure, like shards in an archaeological site, indicate that prior to that last good-bye, Hemingway had met Agnes in Padua and the two had traveled to Milan together. On the twelve-hour train trip they had a significant lovers' quarrel; Agnes felt that Hemingway had acted like "a spoiled child." She had held back from saying so in order not to hurt his feelings. Their quarrel was about her decision to remain behind in Italy after he had left. In the prior biographical literature, there are no indications at all that Hemingway and Agnes had ever spent time together in Padua. But Agnes's letters do indicate that both in Padua and in the final meeting in Milan, she and Hemingway had indulged in bouts of picture-taking. (For Hemingway, as for much of his family, the camera was the recording angel.) In a January 9 letter, Agnes acknowledged receiving some photographs Hemingway had sent her just before he sailed, but stated that she "badly" wanted the films Hemingway had taken in Milan; she wanted to send photographs of herself to her mother and friends. Conceivably, these might have been taken during her brief stay in Milan in mid-November. But writing from Torre di Mosto (a further outpost to which she was later assigned), she also referred to photographs she and Hemingway had taken in Padua. ("This was the first [spring?] day since I came, so I was able to finish up that film we started in Padova.")

The evidence suggests that Agnes stayed in Milan for several days after Hemingway's departure. She appears not to have mailed her New Year's letter to Hemingway, and one or two others written in Milan, right away — first because she had no stamps and secondly because she decided to mail them from Padua "to escape the R.C. censor" in Milan. Her reason for remaining in Milan was the January 5 grand reception for the touring President Woodrow Wilson and his wife. Held in the Palazzo Reale, it was a white-glove affair; liveried flunkies lined the velvet-carpeted stairs. During the long wait, the nurses in full dress uniform sweltered in the overheated salon. ("Hence, we suffered for our country as never before," Agnes wrote.) Elsie MacDonald, having a British passport, barely managed to get a ticket and was peevish. When the great moment came, it was a disappointment. In the general excitement, the crowd surged forward, hoping to shake the president's hand. All Agnes managed to see was "his ear & Mrs. W's hat."

4

The Art of the Short Story

IT WAS Hemingway's luck, or misfortune, never to want for celebrity. His return to the United States on January 21, 1919, was heralded by an eager dockside reporter from the *New York Sun*. In an interview, published the next day under a page 8 headline, "Has 227 Wounds, But Is Looking For Job / Kansas City Boy First To Return From Italian Front," Hemingway enlarged upon the already accumulating and inaccurate legend. In the latest version of his story, he claimed that after serving with the Red Cross in France, he had transferred to the Italian Front. He described his wounding — "the slugs from the shell felt like the stings of wasps" — indicating that the surgeons in Milan had extracted thirty-two fragments from his head and body and advised him he would need further operations over the next year, in addition to the dozen he had already undergone in Italy. He had been bored, he said, with the inactivity after the slugs were removed and had returned to the front and remained there until the Armistice. His former service as a reporter on the *Kansas City Star* proved to be a media advantage. Hemingway made a point of telling the interviewer that he would take on any New York paper "that wants a man that is not afraid of work and wounds." His arrival in New York had also been noted in the *Chicago American* with an even catchier page 3 headline, "Worst Shot-up Man In U.S. On Way Home."

Hemingway spent a few days in New York, visiting with Bill Horne and his girlfriend, and then wired his family that he was taking the train to Chicago. It was a cold, snowy night at the La Salle Street station when Marcelline, who was working at a Congregational church training school in Chicago, stood at the head of the stairs while Dr. Hemingway waited on the platform below. Marcelline, impatient, finally caught a glimpse of Ernest in his khaki uniform and black cape as he came limping forward, leaning on a cane. Hemingway climbed the stairs awkwardly. His father, offering help, said, "Here boy! — Here, lean on me!" But Ernest brushed the aid aside: "Now Dad, I've managed all right by myself all the way from Milano." At the head of the stairs, Marcelline hugged him and burst into tears.

At North Kenilworth Avenue, the Hemingway house was ablaze with lights. Grace and the family and a collection of neighbors gave him a hero's welcome. Cocoa with marshmallows was served. The younger children were allowed to stay up late. Hemingway hoisted four-year-old Leicester up on his shoulders; then Carol wanted to be lifted up as well. Leicester remembered, "It was pretty glorious stuff being kid brother to the guy who had personally helped make the world safe for democracy."

✓✓✓

In the mornings, Hemingway, still recuperating, stayed late in his green-painted iron bed, bundled up in the Red Cross patchwork comforter he had brought home as a souvenir. It kept him from being homesick for Italy, he said. Marcelline, home on weekends, and Sunny and little Leicester were allowed occasional visits to Hemingway's third-floor sanctuary. The walls were lined with maps and pictures of Europe; his war trophies — bayonets, pistols, an Austrian carbine, a gas mask, all shipped home in a trunk — were on display. He kept his medals in a velvet-lined case. In the beginning, Hemingway preferred not to talk about the war with his family. (Leicester, however, remembered that Ernest was eager enough to discuss the subject with his male friends, who hefted the unloaded rifle and sighted it out the windows, snapping the trigger.) The family pampered him; his sisters brought up plates of lobster sandwiches at lunchtime. "Brain food," Hemingway decided. In the afternoons, walking out in uniform and cane (he polished his boots daily), he visited the high school or the library. Marcelline recalled that he read everything in the house, including the *A.M.A. Journal*s in his father's office.

Hemingway did his drinking in his room, the bookshelves camouflaging a variety of liqueurs. Sometimes, he pushed drinks on the girls, encouraging Sunny, then fourteen, to sample one of the potent spirits, then handed her a cigar, telling her, "Smoke that, kid, and we'll be friends again." Perversely, he taught her a few "beautiful" Italian swear words and "a really dirty song" that he and his friends had sung in Italy.

Marcelline recognized that her brother's wounds were still causing him pain, also that he was dissatisfied. Once, discouraged about a personal problem and looking for sympathy, she visited him in his room. He urged her to take a "nipper" of kümmel. "Don't be afraid to taste all the other things in life that aren't here in Oak Park," he told her. "There's a whole big world out there full of people who really feel things. . . . Sometimes I think we only half live over here." During the first weeks of her brother's return, Marcelline noticed that he was on good behavior, trying not to shock the sensitivities of their parents. But it was at some cost: "For Ernest it must have been something like being put in a box with the cover nailed down to come home to conventional, suburban Oak Park living, after his own vivid experiences." Later in life, Hemingway would claim that his sister Ursula, sixteen at the time, had seen him through the bad times after the war. When he was out at night, she waited up for him, would have a light drink with him in his room. He could not sleep without a light on and Ura, he claimed, sometimes even slept with him, "so I would not be lonely in the night."

Nonetheless, he enjoyed his role as local hero. Asked by his old high school teacher Frank Platt to speak to the debating club, Hemingway showed up in his field outfit and medals and gave a lively account of his wounding, then passed around his blood-stained, punctured trousers so the boys could count the shrapnel and bullet holes. "There was some laughter," Platt recalled, "but I think they felt that this man had been through the war and these were the dents of his armor, and it was a very impressive evening."

For months after that, Hemingway was much in demand; for a small fee he spoke at social clubs, church societies, meetings of women's groups. The bullet-riddled trousers and the battle trophies became props while the stories of his wounding and his exploits in Italy were further elaborated. At a high school assembly, reported in *Trapeze,* the students memorized a welcoming song — "Hemingway, we hail you the victor / Hemingway, ever winning the game." Hemingway regaled them with stories about the fierce Arditi troops and a wounded Arditi captain: "He had been shot in the chest but had plugged the holes with cigarettes and gone on fighting." He gave them a vivid account of his own wounding: "When the thing exploded . . . it seemed as if I was moving off somewhere in a sort of red din. I said to myself, 'Gee! Stein, you're dead' and then I began to feel myself pulling back to earth." He related in full detail how he had carried a wounded soldier back to the trenches while a machine-gun bullet struck him in the thigh "like a snowball, so hard and coming with such force" that it had knocked him down. The reporter for *Trapeze,* having related Lieutenant Hemingway's "modest story," went on to explain that Hemingway had been awarded the highest decoration of the Italian government and that one of his medals "was conferred personally by the King of Italy."

Probably as a result of the publicity, early in the year, members of the Italian-American organizations in Chicago approached the

Hemingway family about hosting a party in honor of the war hero to be held at his home. Clarence and Grace were reluctant; the date suggested was a Sunday, and they were uneasy about accepting the committeemen's proposal that the members would supply all the necessaries. Ernest and his sisters were all in favor.

Sunday, February 16, 1919, was to be a gala day on North Kenilworth Avenue. The hosts brought bulging hampers of food; Italian chefs from the better restaurants in Chicago prepared it in the Hemingway kitchen. Pastas and meat dishes, salads and cheeses, were set out in the dining room. Wine was served in what had always been temperance quarters. There was a small Italian band — violins, guitars, and a mandolin — and members of the Chicago Opera Company gave a concert. Ernest in full uniform, his family, the musicians, and members of the Chicago Italian community posed for a commemorative photograph.

A second party was held some weeks later, again on a Sunday. This one, however, lasted too long, starting at noon and finishing past midnight. It was a larger crowd, and good-byes were lengthy and noisy in the quiet neighborhood street. Two of the Oak Park boys Hemingway and his sisters had invited were found sleeping off the effects of too much wine, one behind the davenport in the music room and the other in Ernest's bedroom. Luckily, Hemingway's father never learned about the leftover guests — they were shepherded outside into the cold air. But Clarence, not given to large and noisy entertainments, worried about the neighbors. "You've let this sort of thing go too far," he complained, and the Oak Park Italian festivals came to an end.

⁂

"They've tried to make a hero out of me here," Hemingway wrote Jim Gamble on March 3. "But you know and I know that all the real heroes are dead. If I had been a really game guy I would have gotten myself killed off." His letter to Gamble was embarrassingly sentimental and slurred; quite possibly he had been drinking when he wrote it. He apologized for not having written sooner, then launched into a complaint: "Every minute of every day I kick myself for not being at Taormina with you. It makes me so damned homesick for Italy and whenever I think that I might be there and with you. Chief, honest I can't write about it." He remembered "old Taormina by moonlight and you and me, a little illuminated sometimes, but always just pleasantly so." When that mood was on him, his remedy was a trip to the bookcase to pour himself a tall stiff drink and set it by his typewriter "and think of us sitting in front of the fire after one of mange uova's dinners and I drink to you, Chief. I drink to you."

He was working hard at the typewriter: "I've written some darn good things Jim. That is good for me." He was launching an assault on *The Saturday Evening Post* and had already sent a first story. He planned to send so many and such good ones ("no, I haven't really got the big head") that the magazine would have to buy them in self-defense. It was natural that several of the stories Hemingway wrote after his return should have an Italian connection. But, in one of those unpredictable patterns of association that make the human mind a puzzle, the act of writing had a curious effect on Hemingway's emotional state. Writing to Gamble, he confessed, "Really Chief, I'm so homesick for Italy that when I write about it it has something that you only get in a love letter. A love letter, not a mash note."

Hemingway modeled these earliest attempts at fiction along the lines of the adventure yarns in pulp magazines. "The Woppian Way," retitled "The Passing of Pickles McCarty," involves a prize-fighter, Pickles McCarty, alias Nick Neroni, who disappears from public view in order to join an Arditi battalion. He fights in the battle of Asolo, knives in both hands, with extraordinary tenacity. The principal interest of the story, however, is Hemingway's use of a topical event. The narrator, a forty-two-year-old journalist, encounters Nick en route to Fiume, where, in September 1919, the swash-buckling, real-life D'Annunzio and his band of insurrectionists were bent on taking the city for Italy, although it had been ceded to Yugoslavia under the terms of the Versailles treaty. The narrator, as fascinated with the poet and patriot as Hemingway, ruminates about "the great amourist who had exhausted the love of women and now was wringing the last drops from love of country onto his white hot soul."

The story, not unpredictably, was turned down by *The Saturday Evening Post* and *Red Book,* much to Hemingway's disappointment. In the most improbable of the early stories, "The Ash Heel's Tendon," a smart Irish police detective manages to capture a hired killer named Hand Evans by the novel device of playing a record of Caruso singing "*Vesti la giubba.*" Evans is totally overcome by Leoncavallo's "soul-searing" music. His real name, it turns out, is Guardalabene, and it is his Italian heritage, his love of music, that proves to be his Achilles' heel.

"The Mercenaries" is a story within a story: three soldiers of fortune meet in a Wabash Avenue bar in Chicago. Two of them — a Frenchman named Denis Ricaud and an American, Perry Graves — discuss plans for an upcoming operation in a border battle between

Peru and Chile. The third man, the narrator, is Rinaldi Renaldo. The dialogue is tight-lipped:

> "Wop?" asked Graves, lifting his eyebrows and his adam's apple simultaneously.
>
> "Grandfather was Italian," I replied.

There is much talk about a dashing Italian hero, Il Lupo, the Wolf. (Il Lupo is a parody of D'Annunzio.) Graves summarily deflates the legend with a roundabout story of his own encounter with the great man. On a trip to Sicily, Graves is unexpectedly invited home by an Italian signora who has mistaken him for an American captain she has heard about from mutual friends. Naturally, the signora is beautiful, with "blue-black hair and a face colored like old ivory and eyes like inkwells and full red lips." She and her husband, an aviator off with the "Wop army of preoccupation," do not get along well. The signora is pleased and happy that Graves has come along to cheer her up for a few days. They have a lovely meal that night. The dinner is described in detail, from *antipasto di magro* to roast young turkey and dessert ("funny crumpily things they call *pasticerria*"), ending with black Turkish coffee and "a liqueur called cointreau." After the meal, they sit out in the garden under the orange trees. There are blue-black shadows on the jasmine-covered walls. "Away off you could see the moon on the sea and the snow up on the shoulder of Aetna mountain." Hemingway leaves their night together up to the reader's imagination.

At breakfast, the husband makes a predictable and highly dramatic entrance, wearing a scar on his cheek, a gorgeous blue cape, black boots, and a sword. He dashes in crying "Carissima!" It is, of course, Il Lupo. He immediately challenges Graves to a duel, pistols on the table, four feet apart. The fastest man on the draw will be the inevitable winner. Intentionally or not, the duel is pure ithyphallic farce. Il Lupo's weapon is "one of those little 7.65 mm. pretty ugly, short little gats," while Graves, naturally, has the more powerful piece: "My big forty-five made a big handful." Il Lupo cheats, grabbing for his gun on the count of "Dua," but Graves expertly shoots the weapon out of his hand.

The beautiful signora who offers her hospitality is straight from the tale Hemingway invented for Chink Dorman-Smith; the meal and the moonlight are from his Taormina vacation with Jim Gamble. The garbled Italian is the effort of a young author to prove himself a knowledgeable man of the world. The stories are heavy-handed in their humor, irredeemably bad considering the writer Hemingway was to become. Their only value is that of biographical curiosities.

II

Agnes's letters from Italy tell a brief story. In mid-January she wrote Hemingway from Torre di Mosto. Her patients, for the time being, were orphaned children and severe cases of typhoid. She and Loretta Cavanaugh and two Italian nurses, one of whom she found too bossy, alternated on the night shift and did district nursing during the day. The town, badly damaged during the war, was a ruined mudhole in winter. Walking on the roads, she had to hitch up her skirts but still came back from her visits mud-bespattered. There was a medico, "a little tenente" and an ambulance driver named Bruno, but the Ford ambulances were nearly all in need of repair. Agnes experienced the tragic aftermath of the war: one day four children were brought in by oxcart, bleeding from head to toe. They had been playing with a bomb they had found in their yard and it had exploded. (Two other children were killed outright.) "We all worked like mad over them for about 2½ hrs. Cavie & I — the Ital. dr. & nurse." Fortunately, when they had finished dressing them, Bruno showed up in the one working ambulance and took the children to a larger hospital five kilometers away. Despite the hardships, she wrote, "Sometimes I think I'd rather enjoy living in Italy some day, and, then, I get disgusted again and change my mind." She expected that Hemingway was back in Oak Park by now. "Don't forget your promise to send me your stories," she reminded him.

There was a growing tendency in Agnes's letters to bring up matters she knew would worry Hemingway: the little *tenente* she mentioned "is giving me a desperate rush — now don't get excited." The future had become a puzzle for her; she didn't know whether to go home or apply for more foreign service. "Of course, you understand this is all merely for the near future, as you will help me plan in the next period, I guess." Lately, Cavie had been accusing her of being a flirt, putting her in Brooksie's class: "You know I don't do anything like that, don't you." A contingent of Arditi was camping nearby — "the wildest of them all. You'd certainly adore them." The Arditi captain had come to sleep at the hospital until he could find lodgings: "The ladies all liked him until they heard he beat the prisoners so."

Cavie was to go to Rome and leave Agnes in charge of the hospital at Torre di Mosto. When it became time to turn the facility over to the Italians, she would have the chance to spend a year in Rome, "but, I'm thinking strongly of going to the Balkans — so I'm rather undecided as yet." Her mother had advised her to stay as long as she wanted; work in the States would likely prove very dull after her life abroad. "Maybe you are finding it so now." On March 1, she wrote Hemingway that she had received a whole bushel of his letters but told him not to write so often: "I can't begin to keep up with you, leading this busy life I do." Loretta Cavanaugh, by then, was in Rome, and Agnes had been left in charge of the hospital and the housekeeping duties. The staff was now feeding thirty-five to forty-five people at noon.

Among the newer visitors was an Alpini major, a friend of the Italian nurses. He was thirty years old and very small, had been five years at the front minus forty months spent in hospitals. "One arm is paralyzed, but, he's full of pep." He spoke English, which was an advantage. And Agnes had taken up smoking and had learned a new gambling game at which she won ten lire. "Oh, I'm going to the dogs rapidly, & getting more spoiled every day." Then she added, "I know one thing. I'm not at all the perfect being you think I am. But as I am, I always was, only it's just beginning to creep out." She was, she said, feeling "very *cattiva* [wicked] tonight. So goodnight, Kid, & don't do anything rash, but, have a good time." She signed the letter "Afft, Aggie."

On March 7, Agnes wrote the letter Hemingway had probably been anticipating. Before he left, Agnes said, she had had to convince herself that theirs was a real love affair "because we always seemed to disagree, & then arguments always wore me out so that I finally gave in to keep you from doing something desperate." She was still very fond of him but more as a mother than a sweetheart. "So Kid (still Kid to me & always will be) can you forgive me some day for unwittingly deceiving you? You know I'm not really bad & don't mean to do wrong." It was her fault in the beginning that Hemingway cared for her and she regretted it from the bottom of her heart. "But, I am now & always will be too old, & that's the truth, & I can't get away from the fact that you're just a boy — a kid." Someday, she was sure, she would have reason to be proud of him, "but, dear boy, I can't wait for that day & it is wrong to hurry a career." The final blow came at the end of her letter: "Then — & believe me when I say this is sudden for me, too — I expect to be married soon." She hoped and prayed that after he had had time to think things out, he would forgive her and start a wonderful career and "show what a man you really are."

In the biographical literature, Agnes's new man turns up as a lieutenant, a captain in the Arditi, and as an Alpini major. The two latter identifications have been culled from passing mentions in Agnes's letters, but there is no clear indication that either of them was the man she fell in love with. If he was the little Alpini major, whom she had met only two weeks before her Dear John letter, then her marital plans were, indeed, unexpectedly sudden. Agnes's later interviews provide a name: Domenico Caracciolo, an officer in an unspecified unit, a Neapolitan and an heir to an Italian dukedom. From photographs and from Agnes's account of him, Caracciolo was not a prepossessing figure: short, pear-shaped, with an arrogant smile. Agnes, nevertheless, found him "very gentle, a gentle, nice soul — much more interesting to me than a nineteen year-old Hemingway."

Whatever his earlier suspicions, Hemingway was devastated by Agnes's farewell letter. According to Marcelline, he took to his bed, physically ill, for several days. When she asked what was wrong, he thrust the letter at her, saying, "Read it," then thinking better of it, perhaps feeling too humiliated, he took back the letter and told her that Agnes was not coming home to America, that she was going to be married in Italy. Then he turned to the wall. Yet on the day that he received Agnes's letter, he managed to write Bill Horne with some equanimity, "I'll tell you the sad truth which I have been suspecting for some time, since I've been back. . . . She doesn't love me Bill. She takes it all back. A 'mistake.' One of those little mistakes, you know. Oh, Bill, I can't kid about it, and I can't be bitter because I'm just smashed by it." The devil of it was, he said, that it would never have happened if he hadn't left Italy. "You make love to a girl and then you go away. She needs somebody to make love to her. If the right person turns up, you're out of luck." Agnes was his ideal, he said, "and Bill, I forgot all about religion and everything else because I had Ag to worship." He tried to be forgiving: "The dear Kid. I hope he's the best man in the world. Aw, Bill, I can't write about it."

By the time Jim Gamble wrote him in mid-April, inviting him to spend time at his family place, Eagle's Mere in the Allegheny Mountains, Hemingway was philosophical. He was now a free man, he said. "All entangling alliances ceased about a month ago and I know now that I am most damnably lucky." He wasn't sorry it had happened, "cause Jim I figure it does you good to love anyone. Through good fortune I escaped matrimony so why should I grumble? Not being philosophical though, it was a devil of a jolt, because I'd given up everything for her, most especially Taormina." Gamble was sympathetic: "Poor Hemmy, I bet you had a hard time but am glad to see that you have had more sense than to pity yourself." Like many of Hemingway's male friends, Gamble was ready with comfort and advice: "Don't get caught on the rebound," he warned.

In mid-June, Hemingway learned that Agnes's marriage plans had been canceled. He wrote Howie Jenkins, full of genuine concern: "She has fallen out with her Major. She is in a hell of a way mentally and says I should feel revenged for what she did to me. Poor damned kid. I'm sorry as hell for her." But there was nothing he could do. He had cauterized the memory of her, burned it out "with a course of booze and other women and now it's gone."

It is no credit to Caracciolo — or to Agnes for submitting — if, as has been generally conceded to be the case, he demanded to read Hemingway's love letters and then burned them. (In one interview, Agnes said that Caracciolo threw them away.) It does seem characteristic of Caracciolo that he was persuaded by his mother not to marry Agnes. She strenuously objected, considered Agnes an adventuress. One catches a parting glimpse of Caracciolo — again from the biographical literature — after his breakup with Agnes. On a visit to Naples, Agnes and Cavie were taking a carriage ride with two "very jolly" Englishmen they had picked up on the train. A man in a passing carriage stood up and stared all the way back at them; it was Caracciolo. "He was with his mother I think," Agnes remembered. "I pretended that I didn't see him."

⁂

A love affair is an agreed-upon fiction. Hemingway would treat his affair with Agnes as grounds for fiction on several occasions. It may well have been the subject for a first, lost novel, begun a year or two after his return to the States. He took up the story, once again, in an untitled vignette first published in the limited Paris edition of *in our time* in 1924. It provided the basis for the love affair between Catherine Barkley and Lieutenant Frederic Henry in *A Farewell to Arms*. The first published version of the vignette was a minor masterpiece, a mere seven paragraphs retelling (with variations) the details of the affair. In it, a nurse named Ag and an unnamed soldier patient have a sexual affair. (Characteristically, however, the sex is discreetly implied, rather than spelled out in graphic terms.) The setting, as in life, is the hospital in Milan and it is to Torre di Mosto that Ag is sent after her soldier returns home. Hemingway retained the names for the 1925 edition of *In Our Time,* published by Boni & Liveright, where it appeared as "A Very Short Story," rather than as a vignette. But in 1930, when Scribner's was preparing a new edition, Hemingway, rather late in the game, worried that the story might be considered libelous, changed the nurse's name to Luz and gave the cities as Padua and Pordenone — a thin disguise but a clear indication that he had misgivings.

In the story, Ag is present at the soldier's operation; the soldier and the nurse have a little on-the-ward joke about friend or enema. The two plan to marry. When the soldier returns to the front, he receives a batch of Ag's letters. (In life, of course, the reverse was true.) Hemingway's fictional use of Agnes's letters from Florence, Treviso, and Torre di Mosto is a fairly accurate summary, considering that he may have punitively exaggerated Agnes's professions of love out of a need to indicate how much she had deceived him: "They were all about the hospital, and how much she loved him and how it was impossible to get along without him and how terrible it was missing him at night." In the vignette, Hemingway sketched out the terms of their parting agreement: "he should go home to get a job so they might be married. Luz would not come home until he had a good job and could come to New York to meet her." In life, meeting her was not a condition Agnes had imposed; instead she seems to have welcomed his not being able to meet her in New York as an excuse for staying in Italy a bit longer. "It was understood he would not drink" is a close-to-life version of Agnes's worries about Hemingway's heavy drinking.

The parting is unhappy, its autobiographical significance enhanced by the fact that Hemingway and Agnes had, in fact, taken a similar train trip: "On the train from Padua to Milan they quarrelled about her not being willing to come home at once. When they had to say good-bye, in the station at Milan, they kissed good-bye, but were not finished with the quarrel. He felt sick about saying good-bye like that." But the fragile truce of Hemingway's last meeting with Agnes, recounted in her Dear John letter, has the sharper edge of the actuality: "I tried hard to make you understand a bit of what I was thinking on that trip from Padua to Milan, but you acted like a spoiled child & I couldn't keep on hurting you. Now I only have the courage because I'm far away."

The admission, two months later, that she could tell him only with the distance of the ocean between them reveals more about Agnes's ambivalence and her character than the story perhaps required. The fictional Ag returns to Pordenone to open a new hospital. It is a rainy and lonely spot. She falls in love with a major in a battalion of Arditi quartered there. The major makes love to her; "and she had never known Italians before, and finally wrote to the States that theirs had been only a boy and girl affair. She was sorry, and she knew he would probably not be able to understand, but might some day forgive her, and be grateful to her, and she expected, absolutely unexpectedly, to be married in the spring."

While it was hardly true that Agnes had no experience of Italians (except in the biblical sense, which Hemingway intends in the story), the paraphrase of Agnes's letter is true enough. It makes one wonder if Hemingway hadn't the letter in hand, or the words etched in his memory, when he wrote the vignette. To his instructive tale of love lost, Hemingway added a bitter coda: "The major did not marry her in the spring, or any other time. Luz never got an answer to the letter to Chicago about it. A short time after he contracted gonorrhea from a sales girl in a loop department store while riding in a taxicab through Lincoln Park."

The ironic smartness of the ending is, arguably, a flaw in an otherwise perfectly controlled bit of writing. In the earliest known manuscript version of the vignette, written in first-person narrative, the ending was brutally abrupt: "The major never married her and I got a dose of clap from a girl in Chicago riding in a yellow taxi." Hemingway, nervous about censorship, did some telltale fidgeting with the closure in the typescript, at one time crossing out the vernacular "got a dose of the clap" and toning it down to "had gotten sick." Finally, he settled for the published version. No story inevitably matches the life circumstances of the writer, incident by incident. The details — the alterations of detail — are evidentiary. Hemingway's brief story is, in fact, a remarkable case history of the transaction between real life and fiction, and the personal rationalizations deployed in both. He is the author negotiating a different, perhaps more significant, truth than the one life had presented.

There is no indication that Agnes ever read "A Very Short Story." But she too would construct her fictional versions of the affair: late in life, for instance, she denied using the terms of endearment that appear in her letters. "That's some of his writing," she maintained. She claimed, too, that if she had misled Hemingway it was only to get him home to his family so that he wouldn't bum around Europe with Jim Gamble. "I think I felt — more or less an obligation to look after him a bit. I don't think I was ever crazy mad about him." She also maintained that she had never intended to marry Caracciolo: "I was fascinated by him but never expected to marry him." Testimony to how malleable the personal past can be.

What disturbed Agnes deeply was the implication that she was the Catherine Barkley of *A Farewell to Arms,* the nurse who had slept with Lieutenant Frederic Henry. In the novel, Hemingway, the fully matured writer, would gather up the factual details of his seven months in Italy, his wounding, his love affair, to effect the altered state of fiction. Agnes and Miss Jessup with her swagger stick somehow merged; Captain Serena, the amiable priest who was not from the Abruzzi, the temperamental and jealous Elsie MacDonald, and the inexperienced young man who was Hemingway at that time were fictionally endowed with qualities not so evident in the biographical record. The Agnes of the brief wartime affair in Milan would become the more interesting and more complex Catherine Barkley of the novel — more sensual, slightly perverse, even a bit "crazy," as she admits. She is a more sophisticated woman with an edge of bitterness in her voice and manner — not, after all, the naively romantic, vital nurse of the Agnes diaries and letters, who flirted with and misled the lieutenant from Oak Park. And, in the end, it matters little to the life in the fiction whether the real Agnes and the invalided Hemingway had managed sex, however ingeniously, in a hospital bed in Milan.

But it is clear that the fiction had mortified Agnes. Years later she worked as a librarian in the Key West library. By then, Hemingway was dead and his former home on Whitehead Street had been turned into a local museum. A 1918 photograph of her was hanging on the wall, a ghost of Hemingway's past. It irritated her greatly to learn that tour guides and people in Key West referred to her as the nurse Hemingway had written about in his novel. She had become, unwillingly, a woman touched by fame.

III

It was one of the oddities of "A Very Short Story" that the serious young soldier, returned home, does not pick up with his old friends. He has taken up a solitary life: "he did not want to see his friends or any one in the States." That was another point of difference between Hemingway and the fictional alter ego of the story. The fact is that there would be very few times in Hemingway's life when he did not surround himself with companionable male friends. His correspondence after his return home reveals that he made himself a clearinghouse for news and reports involving his old prewar friends in Michigan and Oak Park and the new friends he had made in Italy: Howie Jenkins was in town "and we foregather pretty often"; so was Art Newburn, he wrote Jim Gamble. He wrote to Larry Barnett, another Schio veteran, enrolled at the University of Wisconsin, asking for the "dope" about the school. His parents wanted him to go to college and were pushing for Wisconsin: "I don't know anything about it except that there is nobody of the male sex from Oak Park that I recall that is worth a damn that goes there." He wasn't keen on going to college but frankly didn't know what else he wanted to do. "Wish I could go to Schio instead of any of them."

Although he was the free man he claimed to be in his letter to Gamble, Hemingway did not accept his friend's invitation to Eagle's Mere. He began writing his response but entered the hospital before he could send it. Clarence had finally persuaded him to have his tonsils removed by a specialist. The results were not all that successful according to Hemingway's brother, Leicester, who claimed that afterward and throughout his adult life, Hemingway "was plagued with more sore throats than an average opera star." When Hemingway took up the letter to Gamble again, he was full of excited plans for a fishing expedition in Michigan with his old friends Bill Smith, Carl Edgar, and Charles Hopkins. He did his best to persuade Gamble to join them. In a lengthy and hyperbolic letter, he described his chums in glowing detail, touted Horton Bay and the Pine Barrens and the Big and Little Sturgeon rivers. ("Fine country. Good color, good northern atmosphere. Absolute freedom, no summer resort stuff, and lots of paintable stuff.") Gamble, however, did not join him that summer.

Nor did his friends Odgar and Hopkins get to Michigan for the fishing. But Howie Jenkins and Larry Barnett managed to join Hemingway in July for a hunting and fishing expedition in the Pine Barrens. Hemingway had planned the trip and listed the needed equipment as if it were a major expedition. Writing Jenks he produced an itemized listing: Barney should go to Von Lengerle and Antoine's and buy himself a ten-foot fly rod and line. As for guns, he had a .22-caliber automatic pistol, a rifle and a .32 automatic, and a 20-gauge shotgun: "You birds better bring some 22 cal. cartridges. These are the kind you want. 22 cal. 'Lesmok' 'Long Rifles.' *Not* smokeless. Lesmok is *semi* smokeless. Better get about 1000 as they are cheap there and we will do a lot of shooting." And he added old blankets or canvas, old clothes, and, since Prohibition was in the offing, "grog."

It was to be a summer of fishing and camping which he would draw from, for years, in his later fiction. In September he and his high school friend Jack Pentecost (also known as Jock, or "Ghee") and another buddy, Al Walker, spent a week in the wilds, fishing the Big and Little Fox rivers near Seney, fifteen miles from the Pictured Rocks on Lake Superior. The Big Fox, he reported to Jenks in one of his letters, was "priceless," with ponds forty feet across; they had caught some two hundred trout in the week they were there. "Fever, I lost one on the Little Fox below an old dam that was the biggest trout I've ever seen. I was up in some old timbers and it was a case of horse out. I got about half of him out of wasser and my hook broke at the shank!"

Out of the country near Seney, with his ritual need for order and the mundane details of bait and gear, the lore of fishing, Hemingway would create the setting and the action for one of his most famous and audacious stories, "Big Two-Hearted River," about a young man, Nick Adams, "coming home beat to the wide from a war." Nick goes off into the woods, sets up camp, and, in solitude, fishes the stream. He has a dire need to leave everything behind him, "the need for thinking, the need to write, other needs. It was all back of him." It was a story in which Hemingway deliberately set out to test his mettle as a writer and one in which he proved a critical theory that the best stories were those in which what the writer omitted was as important as what the writer put in. He was determined to show that in Hemingway country, there would be no need for a message. Hemingway's own explication of "Big Two-Hearted River" in the essay "The Art of the Short Story" remains the best: "So the war, all mention of the war, anything about the war, is omitted. The river was the Fox River, by Seney, Michigan, not the Big Two-Hearted. The change of name was made purposely, not from ignorance nor carelessness but because Big Two-Hearted River is poetry."

But it was an uneasy summer all the same. Since late spring, Grace Hemingway had been caught up in plans to build her long-dreamed-of cottage on Red Top Mountain at Longfield Farm across the lake from Windemere. She wanted a quiet retreat of her own where she could work at her musical compositions away from the children and the business of family life. She had not been feeling well. She wanted, she told Clarence, "a little haven of refuge" where the two of them "could sleep, and be alone, for a while or have just the little children with us." It was her understanding that Clarence had told her to go ahead and see what could be done.

However, when she drew up the plans and got an estimate, Clarence balked, making it seem an unwarranted financial burden. Even when Grace found a second contractor who agreed to build the cottage for less than the original estimate and explained that she would assume the entire expense, Clarence, feeling threatened or put upon, wrote the contractor, Mr. Morford, a queer and demeaning letter denying any responsibility for the actions of his "dear wife Grace Hall-Hemingway": "This [I] want you to know, that she assumes herself without my advice and agrees to pay for herself with her own money. She holds the title to the land. I own no land in my name. All was placed in her name. I am unable to understand the necessity."

Clarence also wrote to Grace, who, against his objections, went ahead with her plans and was at Windemere while the cottage was being built. Clarence, who had been spending less and less time with the family in Michigan, had remained in Oak Park continuing his practice. Obviously hurt, Grace drafted a long, defensive letter to her husband, answering his objections and presenting her case. Windemere, she said, had been very pleasant and adequate for eight or nine years, but after two attacks of typhoid fever which had undermined her health, to say nothing of other causes, "the place became hateful to me, so much so that I had a nervous breakdown summer after summer when ever I was forced to spend a summer there, shut in by the hills & lake, no view, no where to go, acting the part of the family drudge, standing at sink & cook stove."

During the summer of 1919, when Ruth Arnold was helping Grace with the chores and the children, they spent their evenings braiding rugs for the cottage. When the cottage was finished well enough to move in, she went with Ruth and the smaller children, Carol and Leicester. Sometimes she got away by herself. In the nights the children could hear the music of her piano echoing across the black water. When she wanted to return, she hung out a piece of sheet or a bath towel and one of the children — or Clarence, when he was at the lake — would pick her up in the motorboat. But all that summer, Grace Cottage, as she called it, was a subject of contention in the family. Hemingway spent most of his time with Bill and Katy Smith, or put up at the Dilworths', or was off camping with his friends; he was seldom around to do chores. Ernest took his father's side in the argument. He would claim that building the cottage was an act of selfishness, that his mother had used money that would have paid for the younger girls to go to college. Perhaps he believed so at the time, but both Ursula and Sunny would attend college, a fact that did not alter his story in later years. And even though he had no real desire for a college education, he would also claim that Grace had deprived him of the opportunity by spending the money on her cottage.

Grace, in a confidential talk with Marcelline, who sided with her mother, tried to explain her need to be alone: "Some women cling to their husbands and their children. They want to possess them. . . . Others like to share their abilities and their interests, but they need solitude and communion with God — the source. I think I am one of these people. I must have quietness and peace to live."

"Your father," she told Marcelline, "does not always understand this need for me to be alone occasionally. He is kind and willing for me to have this cottage, but he feels he is giving in to a woman's whim. There are times when I feel sure he thinks I *want* to be away from *him,* that my need for quietness is some personal slight to him. That's not true."

There is sufficient evidence that Clarence, that summer, was undergoing some mental crisis. It was one of the principal reasons he had remained behind in Oak Park. But the family debate over Grace Cottage was not the only source of trouble. When Ruth Arnold returned to Oak Park at the beginning of August, Clarence erupted over some now unknown cause and refused to let Ruth in the North Kenilworth Avenue house, where she had been living for years. The situation had not been resolved at the end of August when Marcelline returned to Oak Park along with Ursula and Sunny, who were scheduled to resume their high school classes. Marcelline found it impossible even to invite Ruth to see the children because, as she reported to Grace, her father was acting "so insane on the subject."

In the meantime, Ruth's pleading letters to Grace, to whom she was totally devoted, only made the problem more disturbing. "No distance," Ruth wrote, "can separate my soul from the one I love so dearly." Grace wrote to Clarence, noting that he seemed to be no better for the two months' rest he had had from the family. She had hoped and prayed that with God's help the quiet would have improved his mental attitude. "If your mental attitude is really not a thing within your control, then you can count on me to help you all in my power, as long as I live." But she could not forget the loyal service Ruth had given her and the family so many years. "This is my platform," she wrote. "I shall desert none of you, for fancied wrongs on the part of anyone of the number. You are each one as dear to me as life, and no one in the world can ever take my husband's place unless he abdicates it to play at petty jealousy with his wife's loyal girl friend who has an unhappy and unsympathetic home life." It is not clear from the family correspondence what the problem was; letters that might have explained the situation seem to be missing. Biographers have speculated that there may have been some taint of lesbianism in the relationship between Ruth Arnold and Grace Hemingway. Perhaps, in his troubled state of mind, Clarence might have felt displaced or uncomfortable about the relationship. Whatever Ernest suspected — in a curious revelation he told one of his sons that Grace was "androgynous" — if he was at all deeply concerned at the time, he seems to have kept it to himself.

* * *

That fall, Hemingway remained behind in Michigan, away from family squabbles, boarding with the Dilworths. When Liz Dilworth closed down Pinehurst for the season, he rented a room at Mrs. Eva Potter's white-frame boardinghouse on State Street in Petoskey. The rent was $8 a week, with a month's lease. Hemingway settled into his first exhilarating stint as a free-lance fiction writer, and with a typewriter borrowed from Bill Smith he made good use of his time. Edwin Balmer, a journalist and short story writer who had a summer place in Bay View near Petoskey, and whom Hemingway had first met that summer, had given him some professional advice. Hemingway would remember Balmer with a certain affection as an old pro — albeit a writer of "pot boilers" — who had helped him when he was young. Balmer warned him not to expect easy success or, for that matter, ready failure. "The funny feature of the writing business," he told Hemingway, "is that you simply can not tell what will go. I've seen things in print that I wouldn't believe anyone could possibly buy." He gave Hemingway the names of the more enterprising editors, like George Horace Lorimer of *The Saturday Evening Post* and Charles MacLean of *Popular Magazine* and suggested that Hemingway keep in touch with him.

Hemingway had reason to remember Balmer's cautionary advice. In December he wrote Bill Smith, who was in St. Louis, that Lorimer had turned down "The Passing of Pickles McCarty," but that he had sent "The Mercenaries" to MacLean at *Popular Magazine*: "Hope to God he may buy it. Non hearage from him is a good sign at any rate. A better sign would be a large check." Smith, who was looking for a job without success, commiserated. He suspected, he said, that his own final means of support might be his "organ." In the comic, raunchy style in which Hemingway and his male friends often communicated, Smith related his last night's "ghastly dream." It was awash in Freudian implications that seemed to have passed unnoticed. In a hotel in which danger clearly lurked, a cold-blooded man had grabbed Bill and destroyed his "organ." He felt a dread realization that the man was going to keep him alive for years and use him for "experimental purposes." Bill added, "I don't suppose my description gets it across, but believe me Bird, it was grisly. Never have I felt such abject, crushing fear as when that cursed flash destroyed the organ. Could it be prophetic? Will the organ soon catch a bad cold altho I have done naught to expose it?"

Smith, in one of those coincidental competitions that occur between friends, was also making a stab at writing. An even greater coincidence was that both he and Hemingway should have been struck by a continuing series of stories written by E. W. Howe which made a first appearance in the November 7 issue of *The Saturday Evening Post*. Howe, adopting the strategy of the poet Edgar Lee Masters's *Spoon River Anthology*, had worked up a sequence of brief prose sketches of small-town characters under the title "Anthology of Another Town." Bill wrote Hemingway with generous enthusiasm, claiming that Hemingway's "stuff" had the Howe collection beat. He suggested that they collaborate on sketches "anent the

Bayites." Together, he said, "we could tear them off easy. I don't know about alone." He sent along a sketch he had done in a half hour about a local farmer named Bert. Within a week Hemingway responded with five sketches of his own. Smith pronounced the one about Hemingway's old Indian pal Billy Gilbert "a whang — a pearl of the primal hydrazation." The others he liked less well, they weren't quite human enough and he knew Hemingway could do better. They needed more dialogue, Bill thought. Character, he said, "can be well divulged thru the medium of conversation." It was an astute observation, since Hemingway would become a master at revealing character through dialogue.

Of Hemingway's early writings, the Horton Bay sketches were the most promising. Instead of indulging in tough-guy heroics, he had begun to take the measure of small-town life. The Billy Gilbert sketch, which Bill had praised so highly, was not the most effective of the sketches that Hemingway, under the rubric of "Crossroads: An Anthology," labored at that fall and winter in Petoskey. It had a sense of the topical: Gilbert comes home from the war to discover that his shack at Susan Lake is padlocked and his wife has gone off with another man, taking the children. In his Black Watch kilt and medals, he is a figure of fun among the Bayites. The sketch of Ed Paige, the lumberjack, who has his one moment of glory on the night that he stays the six rounds of a forfeit match with the boxer Stanley Ketchell and takes home the $100 prize, ends with the kind of concision Hemingway would bring to the *in our time* vignettes: "But now most everyone has forgotten all about it, and quite a few say they'll never believe Ed really did it."

A more relevant story is the character sketch of Pauline Snow, in essence a tryout for Hemingway's later short story about a village seduction, "Up in Michigan." Pauline, an attractive young girl with some sensitivity, appears, like the other characters in the sketches, to have been based on an actual person. She is prodded by her guardian into walking out with Art Simmons, "the only regular fellow around the Bay." At first, she is frightened of him, "with his thick blunt fingers, and his manner of always touching her when he talked." When she comments on a vivid sunset, "Don't you think that's awfully pretty, Art," Hemingway closes in for one of his typical fade-outs: "We didn't come down here to talk about sunsets, kiddo!" Art says, and puts his arm around her as they walk alone on a deserted road. Pauline yields, and the relationship becomes a local scandal. Hemingway ends the story with a pair of straightforward sentences that prefigure the style for which he would later become famous: "After a while some of the neighbors made a complaint, and they sent Pauline away to the correction school down at Cold-water. Art was away for awhile, and then came back and married one of the Jenkins girls."

↿↿↿

As usual, Hemingway had at least one close male friend in Petoskey, Dutch Pailthorp, home on sick leave from the University of Michigan. He and Pailthorp hung out in the bar at the old Park Hotel. Hemingway regaled his friend with stories of his overseas adventures, of the gruesome exploits of the Arditi, as well as the tall tale of the Sicilian landlady who trapped him in her pensione and took his clothes away for a week of heroic pleasure. He seems also to have told Dutch about his wartime love affair with Agnes, for when *A Farewell to Arms* was published, Hemingway inscribed a copy for his friend: "For Dutch Pailthorp to whom I told this story in the winter of 1919–1920 in Petoskey, Michigan."

But one of the more ostensible reasons for his move to Petoskey was to be near Marjorie Bump, an attractive, redheaded seventeen-year-old high school girl who had been a waitress at Pinehurst that summer and with whom Hemingway had struck up a more than passing friendship. When he had finished his morning stint at writing, Hemingway waited for Marjorie after school. For a time, he also dated an attractive college girl, Irene Goldstein, on vacation with her aunt and uncle. Hemingway played tennis with her and occasionally was invited to dinner.

Often, too, he went on walks with a fourteen-year-old girl, Grace Quinlan, whom, in brotherly fashion, he nicknamed Sister Luke. He took Grace to one of the local dances but was such a terrible dancer the two sat out the waltzes and talked. Grace remembered that he talked a lot about the stories he was writing. Naturally enough, some of the local citizens disapproved of what they considered a grown man hanging around the streets with high school girls. Nor did they approve of his appearance — dressed in a mackinaw, old pants, and old shoes, with a stubble of beard — or his lack of gainful employment. But with the girls, Hemingway was sociable and proper. Often enough, he and Marjorie, and Marjorie's younger sister, Georgianna, called Pudge, did nothing more than meet with Sister Luke in the Quinlan kitchen, pop corn, and listen to records — and talk. Having been burned in his affair with Agnes, Hemingway must have felt more comfortable with high school girls.

It would become a fact of Hemingway's life that his closer male friends were likely to become involved in his love affairs and marital decisions. At times he seems to have sought their approval of his current girlfriends. And sometimes, they offered advice on their own. When Hemingway mentioned to Bill Smith, early in the fall, that he was going from the bay to Petoskey on a weekend, Bill assumed that he had a date with Marjorie. He reprimanded Hemingway: "Fie on you. I'd as soon it was Connie." (Connie Curtis was another of the waitresses at the Dilworths' that summer.) In his letters, Smith was concerned that Marjorie Bump was too young for Hemingway to be courting. Now, it appeared, the gossips of Petoskey, having acquired "the gift of tongues," had begun spreading rumors about Hemingway's engagement to Marjorie. Smith wrote Hemingway frankly, "But remember that I said Marj would be sure to misinterpret your attentions. . . . I speak with the voice of discretion when I say that unless you are more careful you'll make hash of the poor kid's life." It was nonsense for Hemingway to pretend that he didn't "rate" with Marjorie; as a matter of fact, Marjorie definitely had a crush on him. How would Hemingway look at it, Bill asked, if he, Bill, "were to hopelessly beguile the fancy of let us say Pauline Snow? I am not one to bellow 'I told you so,' but it doth appear that there was much in my opinions. Regardless of how they were disregarded."

However Hemingway chose to regard it, as a case of a friend's meddling in his affairs or an easy excuse for removing himself from a sticky situation, Bill's interference had a fictional consequence. Hemingway commemorated it in a back-to-back pair of later stories, "The End of Something" and "The Three-Day Blow." In the first, Nick Adams, in the course of a night-fishing expedition on the lake, breaks up with his girlfriend, Marjorie, in a shamefully callous way, precipitating a quarrel with her on the feeble grounds that she now knows everything he has taught her about fishing: "You know everything. That's the trouble." Marjorie recognizes that Nick is talking nonsense and asks what really is the matter. Nick tells her that their relationship isn't fun anymore. He is plainly dissatisfied, perhaps going through some emotional crisis: "I feel as though everything was gone to hell inside of me." When Marjorie asks, "Isn't love any fun?" Nick gives her a blunt "No." Marjorie, rebuffed, decides to leave. No sooner is she gone than Nick's friend Bill comes out of the woods, asking "Did she go all right?" making it clear that the breakup had been prearranged. Bill asks if there had been a scene, asks how Nick feels. Irritated, Nick blurts out, "Oh, go away, Bill!" then softens it: "Go away for a while." Bill, picking up a sandwich from the lunch basket, goes off to check the two fishing rods set up at the water's edge.

There is, however, an odd, jarring interruption at the end of the story when Bill emerges from the woods. Hemingway notes, "Bill didn't touch him, either." Presumably it relates to an earlier moment when Nick and Marjorie are sitting on the blanket together "without touching each other," watching the moon rise. The curious feature is that in the first manuscript version of the story, Bill's arrival is described as a peculiar physical circumstance: "He lay there until he felt Bill's arm on his shoulder. He felt Bill coming before he felt his touch." In this story in which a young man sends his girl away, reverting to the companionship of another male, Hemingway may have wanted to avoid any sense of a homosexual connection. He changed the wording to "He felt Bill's hand on his shoulder." Finally, Hemingway dispensed with even that, adding the preliminary mention that Marjorie and Nick had not touched each other and that Bill had not touched him either. The changes, that is, seem to have been dictated more by the author's fearfulness than by the narrative logic of the story. In Hemingway's prose, it is one of the earlier indications that he recognized that his celebrations of male camaraderie might have dangerous implications.

In "The Three-Day Blow," Nick and Bill, during the first of the autumn storms, get progressively drunk on whiskey in Bill's father's cottage. They talk about baseball and books and writers. They are young men as comically high on literature as they are on baseball and booze, discussing the merits of George Meredith and Hugh Walpole as seriously as those of the Giants and the Cardinals. Only toward the end of the drinking session do they get around to discussing what has been the undercurrent of their conversation, Nick's breakup with Marjorie. Bill tries to convince Nick, "Once a man's married he's absolutely bitched. . . . He hasn't got anything more. Nothing." Bill's adamant views about marriage — ostensibly, his fear of it — have had a not altogether unwelcome influence on the ambivalent Nick. "I tell you, Wemedge," Bill says, "I was worried while it was going on. You played it right." If Nick had married Marjorie, he'd have been married to the family and everything that that entailed, the boring Sunday dinners, the mother-in-law telling her daughter what to do and how to act.

But Nick, now, is not so certain; there is the danger that he might start up again with Marge. That thought gives him a certain happiness: "Nothing was finished. Nothing was ever lost." The Marge business no longer seems so tragic. "None of it was important now," Nick thinks to himself at the end of the storm and the end of the story. He and Bill leave the cottage, shotguns in hand, to go hunting. The wind, Hemingway explains, has blown the problem of Marjorie out of Nick's head — but not quite. "Still," he thinks, "he could always go into town Saturday night. It was a good thing to have in reserve."

Hemingway's reliance upon the factual in these early, unromantic stories of young love and sexual exploration — and the distortions he introduced for artistic or personal reasons — underscores the irreconcilable differences in the uneasy marriage of fact and fiction in a writer's works. In "The End of Something," the meticulously described method of bottom fishing for rainbow trout, using skinned perch as bait, is the method Hemingway and Bill Smith had evolved and one that Hemingway lovingly relayed in precise detail in his letter to Jim Gamble, inviting him to Michigan. The real-life Marjorie denied that the fishing episode in the story had ever taken place, which suggests that it is an instance of Hemingway's transference of a masculine episode to a male-female exchange in the story. The books that Nick and Bill have read in the story are those that Hemingway and Bill Smith were reading at the time. ("It was the kind of thing we read in those days, Chesterton, Walpole, Hewlett, Meredith," Bill Smith recalled in an interview.) The rumored engagement between Hemingway and Marjorie talked about in Bill's letters was useful to the story. Nick denies that they were engaged but admits they were planning to get married nonetheless. When Bill asks what the difference is, Nick is nonplussed, but insistent: "I don't know. There's a difference."

In the two stories, Nick has moments of hostility and resentment toward Bill, feeling pressured into actions he is not quite ready to make. And the vital, but probably unanswerable, question is whether Bill Smith's views about marriage are accurately reflected in the story or whether they were those that Hemingway himself felt but fobbed off on the fictional friend. (In an interview, Bill Smith would recall that Marjorie's family owned the local hardware store in Petoskey. Pressed by the interviewer about whether he thought a doctor's son was too good to marry a hardware man's daughter, Smith responded, "No. I don't honestly think it was that. It's just that I thought Wemedge had a lot more potential than that.") In Hemingway's case, where the evidence is available, the telltale connections between life and art are too obvious to deny. That Hemingway, in the practice of his craft, could rely so persistently on actual experience suggests something more than mere convenience, something deeper and more necessary to his sense of the creative process. And it is in the distinctions between the life and the work that one is more likely to find those clues that suggest a writer's motivations, the exercise of the creative mind.

⁊ ⁊ ⁊

It is now part of the Hemingway legend, except for those biographers who believe that Hemingway's affair with Agnes was sexual, that it was with another of the waitresses at Pinehurst — not Marjorie Bump, but an unnamed, older waitress — that Hemingway had his first sexual experience. She appears as Liz Coates in one of Hemingway's first and most famous short stories, "Up in Michigan." (The waitress's name was contrived from Liz Dilworth and probably Frances Coates, the girl from Oak Park whom Hemingway had had a brief crush on in high school.) In the story, Hemingway is more sensitive to the heroine's emotional responses than he was in the Pauline Snow vignette. He gives a vivid accounting of Liz's rising physical interest in Jim Gilmore, the blacksmith who takes his meals at the village restaurant. "Liz liked Jim very much. She liked it the way he walked over from the shop and often went to the kitchen door to watch for him to start down the road." One night, when he is slightly drunk, Jim takes her on the landing dock: "The boards were hard. Jim had her dress up and was trying to do something to her. She was frightened but she wanted it. She had to have it but it frightened her." It is an effective bit of writing. But it is also a queer, convoluted report on sexual arousal in which the author panders to a male's fantasies about his prowess as a lover, including the size of his penis. (Liz cries, "'Oh, it isn't right. Oh, it's so big and it hurts so. You can't. Oh, Jim. Jim. Oh.'")

That Hemingway, early in his career, felt it necessary to describe the sexual act in prose that would be considered objectionable to the polite readership is evident (though it would hardly be considered obscene by present standards). That he had begun the story before his first trip to Paris seems very likely. Bill Smith remembered that he and Hemingway had worked up a little joke about the pornographic implications of the title. Bill suggested that Hemingway's next story should be called "Even Further Up in Michigan." But in Hemingway's career, the most important feature of "Up in Michigan" was that, as a young writer, he had discovered the underground current of sexuality that exists in every life and underlies much that passes as humor or wit or whim; that gives rise to dreams and finds channels into art and music and literature; that affects relationships and enmities in the personal life; and that may be tapped or dammed up with damaging results or run into strange tributaries that linger for years like dry creek beds waiting to rise only at unexpected flood times — but which, in the main, run their steady course from the beginning of a life to its delta ending.

IV

In mid-December, Hemingway gave a lecture in the Petoskey library on his war experiences for the benefit of the Ladies Aid Society. On that occasion, he wore his full-regalia dress uniform and his black cape with the silver clasp. As for previous lectures, he brought along his bullet-and-shrapnel-riddled battle trousers. In his best form, he provided the audience with a dramatic moment when he told them that after being wounded and while waiting to be evacuated from a roofless shelter, it had seemed to him "more reasonable to die than to live."

The women were impressed, none more than Harriet Connable, a friend of Hemingway's mother and the wife of Ralph Connable, head of the F. W. Woolworth chain in Canada. The Connables were planning a winter vacation in Palm Beach, Florida, and wanted a hired companion to stay with their crippled nineteen-year-old son, Ralph Jr., in their well-staffed mansion on Lyndhurst Avenue in Toronto. They offered Hemingway the job. Mr. Connable explained that he wanted Hemingway to give Ralph the right slant on life, particularly regarding sports and pleasures. The boy had been handicapped since birth; his right hand and arm had not fully developed. The father felt that Hemingway's example would be beneficial. Hemingway would receive a salary of $50 a month plus expenses for entertainment for Ralph and himself. A chauffeured car would be at his disposal and he would be free to work at his writing as he chose. For Hemingway, the most attractive feature of the proposal was that Mr. Connable was an influential man in Toronto and had promised he would introduce Hemingway to his friends on the *Toronto Star Weekly.* Yet in one of his later revisions of his personal past, Hemingway would claim that his most pressing need to leave Petoskey was that he was in love with four girls, "engaged, or partly so, to one of them and in trouble with a fifth." Reason enough to feel he "should get the hell out."

Writing to Howell Jenkins about the Toronto job, he claimed it was "the original Peruvian Doughnuts," a catch phrase from his story "The Mercenaries," which had made the circuit of his friends. He planned to be in Chicago, "the city of sin and sometimes gin," for five days before leaving for Canada. He suggested Jenks get tickets to the Ziegfeld Follies. He would send "the kale," but he was nearly broke. When he got home, he said, he would "tap the banco" and repay him. It was to be a busy and bibulous holiday. Jenkins had arranged for a meeting of the clan (fifteen of the "Arditi" from the ambulance service) on the North Side. Hemingway also lunched with Jenkins and Jock Pentecost at the Venice Cafe. Clarence had put aside six mallards for a Sunday supper for Hemingway and his friends. And he was scheduled to hear Titta Ruffo sing *Pagliacci.* "So it doesn't look like there'll be much time spent studying the S.S.

[Sunday School] lesson," he wrote his fourteen-year-old friend, Grace Quinlan.

⁂

Hemingway would remember the dry cold of the Toronto winter and the warmth of his welcome into the Connable household. Mr. and Mrs. Connable and their daughter, Dorothy, had not yet left for Palm Beach. In the evenings, the senior Connable liked to play billiards and, according to Hemingway, nearly always beat him by a slight margin. Hemingway got on well with Dorothy, slightly older than he and a Wellesley graduate who had worked with the YMCA in France and Germany after the war. They had pleasant chats in her room; he thought of her and of himself as "very young old soldiers." They became friends. It somehow crossed Hemingway's mind, then or later, that the Connable household, with its "wonderful worthless servants," was a proper subject for Henry James's delicate touch. Mrs. Connable, "one of the finest, loveliest and most lovely looking" women he had ever known, was a fitting Jamesian heroine. (His job as the paid companion to a lame son would have fitted the classic Jamesian plot, as well.) Hemingway may have enjoyed socializing with the Connables and their friends, but there was little time for fiction writing. Mostly he took Ralph to hockey games and boxing matches, sometimes accompanied by Dutch Pailthorp, who was working in Toronto and living in the local YMCA. Hemingway found Ralph Jr. a bit crafty. He managed to convince himself that Ralph was an "exceptional child," his problems the result of a "high forceps delivery."

Before the Connables left for Florida, Hemingway pushed the issue of writing for the *Toronto Star* and Mr. Connable introduced him to the advertising chief, Arthur Donaldson, who showed him around the plant on King Street West. Donaldson introduced him to the staff members, including Gregory Clark, the features editor of the weekly. At first, Clark was a bit suspicious of the young reporter, although he recognized that having worked on the *Kansas City Star* was a very good recommendation. He let Hemingway cool his heels for a time. Hemingway thereafter hung around the newsroom, hoping for an assignment.

His family, informed of the bright possibilities ahead, particularly the opportunity to write for the *Toronto Star,* encouraged him to make the most of his opportunities. Clarence was sure Ernest's arrangement with Mr. Connable was "a great character builder and will give you a chance to see things with a new responsibility. . . . Get acquainted with as many nice people as you can. They are the every one a real asset in life's bank as the years go on." (In the Hemingway family, banking was a noticeable metaphor in parental discussions of life and morals.) When Hemingway sent his mother a gift of a lily at Easter, both his parents were moved. "I was very pleased you so beautifully remembered your dear Mother on Easter," Clarence wrote. "I assure you it touched her very deeply." Hemingway could have been in little doubt of it. Grace's letter was effusive; her eyes were brimming over with joyous tears, she said. Recalling the baby picture of her son that hung in his room, she reminded Hemingway that he then called himself Cozy Curls. "Oh! I cannot tell you how happy you've made me, tonight, with your thoughtfulness. God bless and keep you pure and noble my Big son."

Greg Clark finally relented — largely, it seems, because Hemingway haunted the office, distracting the other reporters. But Hemingway's youthful persistence paid off; Clark took him in to see J. Herbert Cranston, the editor of the *Star Weekly*. Cranston was sufficiently impressed to give the young reporter a chance, partly on the basis of his ebullient talk. Hemingway gave Cranston the impression that he had done a good deal of bumming around the country. He also made the most of his ambulance service, modestly mentioning his medals. His first article, published on February 14, was about a circulating library of paintings initiated by a group of wealthy socialites who preferred to hang the work of local modern artists who had "introduced anger into art." He followed it up with a snappy piece about the hazards of getting a free shave at the local barber college. Clarence wrote approvingly, "The Free shave etc. story was very good indeed. I am sure you will succeed." One of his more sarcastic sketches was "How to Be Popular in Peace Though a Slacker in War," a put-down of Canadians who had crossed the border to work in American munitions plants to avoid being sent overseas, then returned home, with a good deal of money, to confront the awkward social problem of being asked about their military service. Hemingway advised them to read a good history of the war: "You will be able to talk intelligently on any part of the front." He also suggested they buy themselves secondhand trench coats, a far better advertisement of military service than the military cross.

Cranston approved of Hemingway's ability to write plain Anglo-Saxon; he also welcomed a writer with a sense of humor, though he did not, at the time, expect great things from him. Between February and May, Hemingway wrote some sixteen articles for the *Toronto Star,* all but one of them bylined and published in the weekly edition. They were a mix of comic and sardonic articles about local affairs and out-of-the-way social events, none of them topflight journalism or important news stories. The best were the articles on trout fishing drawn from his expeditions of the summer before in Michigan. Greg Clark was not, at first, as easily impressed by Hemingway's charisma as Cranston. An ex–infantry officer, he was, for one thing, skeptical of Hemingway's war record. It was not, apparently, until after Clarence had sent Hemingway's war cross and citation to Toronto that the features editor became a believer. "As long as I live," Clark recalled, "I shall never forget the cold chill that leaped out, radiating, from my back and over my shoulders and into my cheeks. For on the edge was inscribed: '*Tenente* Ernesto Hemingway.'"

When the Connables returned in March, they invited Hemingway to stay on. He told them he could do nothing for Ralph and preferred to devote his time to his articles for the *Star Weekly*. Mr. Connable, however, insisted that he keep his quarters and continued to pay him, over Ernest's objections. Hemingway claimed it was an amiable ruse, since Connable invariably won back the money in their weekly billiard games. The odd feature of Hemingway's life among the well-to-do was that at Mrs. Connable's request, he slept in the same room with Ralph Jr. "I did this for her because I was truly fond of her." But by the end of spring Hemingway was feeling restless; he began making plans for the yearly vacation in the Michigan woods. Perhaps he was influenced by an enthusiastic report from his father, who had taken a May vacation, fishing at Advance Creek. "Say, I renewed my youth ten years at least," Clarence wrote his son. "I had the best trouting by far since the trip I made across the Plains several years ago." Later that month, Hemingway said his good-byes to his surrogate family and returned to Oak Park to wait for Bill Smith to make the annual migration to Michigan.

On June 1, Hemingway wrote Harriet Connable, apologizing for the delay in thanking her for her hospitality. "You were awfully good to me and I want you to know how much it meant to me to know you all in addition to the priceless time I had." He was looking forward to seeing the Connables in Petoskey, hoped they would pay a visit to Windemere. The family was expecting to make the move to Michigan in a week's time. There was peace at home: "Marcelline, my older sister, and I are the best of pals now, so I've no one at all to row with."

5

A Life Without Consequences

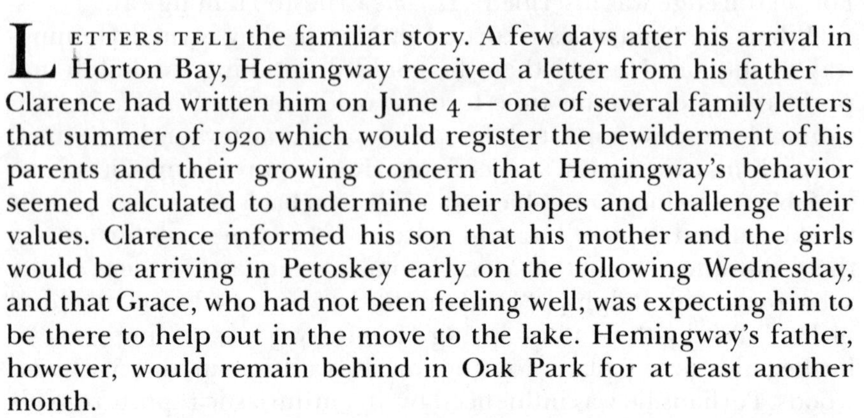

LETTERS TELL the familiar story. A few days after his arrival in Horton Bay, Hemingway received a letter from his father — Clarence had written him on June 4 — one of several family letters that summer of 1920 which would register the bewilderment of his parents and their growing concern that Hemingway's behavior seemed calculated to undermine their hopes and challenge their values. Clarence informed his son that his mother and the girls would be arriving in Petoskey early on the following Wednesday, and that Grace, who had not been feeling well, was expecting him to be there to help out in the move to the lake. Hemingway's father, however, would remain behind in Oak Park for at least another month.

Clarence's letter was an occasion for a sermon indicating that Hemingway was already proving troublesome: "Do hope dear Ernest that you will think more of what others have done for you and try to be charitable and kind and gentle. Do not doubt that I am proud of your ability and independence, but try and soften your temper and never threaten your Father and Mother . . . I want you to represent all that is good and noble and brave and courteous in Manhood, and fear God and respect Woman." There was an uneasiness in Clarence's letter; Hemingway had asked for his "little Wop automatic," and Clarence noted that he was sending it with Grace, wrapped "exactly as you handed it to me." His peculiar insistence suggests that he expected to be accused of some crime or misdemeanor: "I have never touched it since you handed it to me. All the shells I know anything of for it are herewith as you handed them to me. Wish when I went upstairs to bid you good bye you had thought of it."

Hemingway, believing he had drudged enough that winter, expected to relax, fish, congregate with his friends. At first he had stayed at the Dilworths' at Pinehurst, working part-time with Bill Smith on the Charleses' farm. Later he would put in some time working with Warren Sumner at Longfield, but not enough to satisfy his father. That summer, Ernest saw a good deal of Bill and Katy Smith, and of Odgar, who had arrived on the scene still mooning after

Katy. They sailed, swam off Wesley Dilworth's dock, and played tennis. It was a source of irritation to his parents. Things got no better when Ted Brumback arrived to spend time with Hemingway and his friends. (For a time Hemingway and Brumback would put up in the guest cottage at Windemere.) Grace, alone with the younger children, felt put-upon, facing the daily chores she detested. Nor did she have the help of Ruth Arnold, who tactfully put off visiting Windemere until after Clarence had taken his vacation.

Throughout June, Clarence wrote to Grace, expressing concern about Ernest, still at Horton Bay. "Dear Ones at Windemere: Hope Ernest has been over to help you," he wrote on June 11. Two days later: "I will write to Ernest this afternoon. Hope he has been over and helped you." In a letter to Ernest that afternoon, Clarence expressed the same hope again. He also noted that he had a fine front seat at the big Republican Convention held in Chicago that summer — the convention that eventually nominated the dark horse candidate Warren Harding on the tenth ballot: "I heard three nominating speeches and saw the first four ballots cast. . . . It was very exciting and I wished that you had been with me." On June 16, he wrote Grace, "I had a letter from Ernest in this morning's mail. He expected to go over and see you soon. He was expecting Jack Pentecost. Says he and Bill have worked very hard all the time since he arrived." On June 28, he reported on the sweltering heat: "92 Saturday, 94 Sunday and right now at three o'clock it is 96." He was expecting to hear from Dr. Potoff, who he hoped would take over his practice so that he could get up to Walloon Lake. He had had a postal from Ted Brumback, saying "he and Ernest were away over on the Black and would go over to see you all at Walloon when they returned."

It was not until July 1 that Clarence wrote his wife that he was now able to get away on his vacation. During his two weeks at Windemere, he and Grace must have discussed their problems concerning Ernest. It was evident that the situation had worsened and that Ernest was becoming belligerent. But Clarence did not confront his son while there, only gave him some chores to attend to, a letter to be handed to Warren Sumner regarding the haying, and a request that Ernest do some spraying, for which he would pay him $5. Clarence waited until he was back in Oak Park to write his son about a decision that would obviously stir up more hard feelings. On July 18, he reported to Grace that he had written Ernest: "I advised him to go with Ted down Traverse City way and work at good wages and at least cut down his living expenses. I also most sincerely hoped now that he had attained the legal age he would be more considerate of others and use less vitriolistic words." On July 21, Hemingway's birthday, Clarence wrote Grace that although he had not heard from Ernest yet, he "took it for granted he had done the spraying as per your Thursday letter, and so sent him the five dollars and the birthday five." But on the following day he felt "greatly distressed" to learn from Warren Sumner that Ernest had not delivered the letter about the haying, as instructed:

> I think Ernest is trying to irritate us in some way, so as to have a witness in Brummy in hearing us say we would be glad if he was to go away and stay . . . I will write to him and enclose herewith for you to read and hand to him. Keep up your courage, my darling. We are all at work and very soon he will settle down and suffer the loss of his friends the way he is fast using them up. He will have to move into new fields to conquer.

In the meantime, on July 21, Grace prepared a special birthday dinner for Hemingway to which Ted Brumback and Bill Smith were invited. It was to be the source of the legend, perpetuated by Leicester, that after the dinner Grace had handed her son a perfidious letter kicking him and his friend Ted Brumback out of the house. But in actual fact, it was Clarence who had twice written Hemingway that they should leave. The second letter, of course, had not arrived in time for the birthday celebration. On July 25, Clarence wrote to Grace, "In the last mail last night I received your big envelope letter and the letter of Thursday evening, after Ernest's birthday supper. I hope he went back to the Bay with Bill and that you read and have mailed him the letter I wrote to him to stay away from Windemere until he was again invited. You surely gave him and his friends a good time."

In the rush of daily letters, it was clear that Hemingway's parents were involved in a serious campaign to remedy a situation they felt had become intolerable. On July 26, Clarence wrote "My dear Gracie," hoping she had by now read and handed Ernest his letter, "advising him he must move on and get to work and stay away from Windemere until he is again invited to return." He was also distressed that Hemingway still had not delivered the letter to Warren Sumner as he had been asked. "I so wish that Ernest would show some decent loyalty to you and not keep on the sponge game with his friend Ted. I will write him again at the Bay . . . I will also write Ted at the Bay advising him it is altogether too much for you to entertain him longer at Windemere . . . I shall continue to pray for Ernest."

Unknown to Clarence a family crisis had occurred on the night of July 26. What contributed to it may well have been Clarence's second letter telling Hemingway and Brummy to stay away from

Windemere until they were invited. (Grace wrote her husband that she had given it to Hemingway that morning: "Your letter I handed to Ernest on Monday morning. . . . After reading it, he chopped a few pieces of wood, enough for 2 days, about, then he tried to fix the pier, and *did* after a fashion though it is very wobbly.") What precipitated the new crisis was a secret midnight picnic that Ursula and Sunny, along with two of the children of the Hemingways' neighbors the Loomises and a pair of visiting teenage friends, decided to have at Ryan's Point on the lake. The plan was that they would all sneak out at night after the adults were asleep. The Hemingway girls had persuaded Ernest and Brummy to come along as chaperons, and the older men had reluctantly agreed. It was an innocent enough affair, but Hemingway, angry over his father's letter, may have become involved out of malice.

At three o'clock in the morning, as Grace explained in a letter to her husband, Mrs. Loomis and her older daughter pounded on the door, wanting to know where their children were. Grace, certain that hers were in their rooms — though she remembered that they had gone to bed with a good deal of ostentation — discovered that they were gone. In her nightgown she had gone out searching for them with a lantern, without success. When the culprits finally returned in the early hours of the morning, so Sunny recalled, "the air was *blue* with condemnations." On the following day Grace informed Clarence about the incident, embellished by Mrs. Loomis's three o'clock visit in a towering rage and Mrs. Loomis's threat that "she would pack up & take her whole family back to Oak Park unless we could do something to get rid of those grown men loafing around." Grace furnished a detailed account of Ernest's behavior that makes it clear he had few difficulties in standing up to his parents:

> Of course Ernest called me every name he could think of, and said everything vile about me; but I kept my tongue and did not get hysterical. . . . Oh! but he is a cruel son. I got supper for him when he came home at 9 o'clock last night and sat down with him for I had had none, and he insulted me every minute; said "all I read is moron literature," . . . and asked me if I read the *Atlantic Monthly* just so someone would see me doing it. I did not explain to you that the escapade last night was a plan of the Loomis boys and girls to have a midnight eats, and fire, up the lake, not wicked; except in the deceit practiced and the general lawlessness that Ernest instills in all young boys and girls. He is distinctly a menace to youth. I think our girls have had a very good lesson but its most killed their mother.

That next morning, as she informed Clarence, Grace confronted Ernest and his friend: "I called Ernest and [Brumback] into the living room & told them to pack up all their things and leave this morning, that I did not wish to see them again this summer." But Grace, too, that same morning had handed Ernest a lengthy letter, this one the letter of an aggrieved mother, reminding her son of his debt to motherhood and religion, in the same accounting terms that Clarence favored. It read like a moral ultimatum from the nineteenth century to the unruly, ungrateful twentieth:

> Unless you, my son, Ernest, come to yourself, cease your lazy loafing, and pleasure seeking — borrowing with no thought of returning — stop trying to graft a living off anybody and everybody — spending all your earnings lavishly and wastefully on luxuries for yourself — stop trading on your handsome face, to fool little gullible girls, and neglecting your duties to God and Your Savior, Jesus Christ — unless, in other words, you come into your manhood, there is nothing before you but bankruptcy: *You have over drawn.*

In the letter, she advised him, "Do not come back until your tongue has learned not to insult and shame your mother. When you have changed your ideas and aims in life you will find your mother waiting to welcome you, whether it be in this world or the next — loving you, and longing for your love."

By July 28, Clarence had had a letter from Ernest, one which had crossed in the mails apparently, but which was nonetheless a very definite letter of denial of everything that had or might be charged against him. Clarence's account of it in his letter to his wife was the quintessential parental response to the widening gap between the generations:

> He is a very unusual youth that does not realize that his mother and father have done a lot more for him than any of his chums. He is sure to suffer a lot. I will pay no attention to his statements that he has done nothing wrong at Windemere. He says Brummy was there at your particular request and that he had painted the house for you, and dug garbage holes and washed dishes and done all the work of a "hired man." Let it go. . . . He did not tell me a kind thing. . . . He says he does not want to hear from me any more along those lines . . . I shall not let his fiery letter bother me and I will wait a while to write to him again.

Two days later, Clarence wrote Grace of his great relief on learning that Ernest had at last left Windemere:

> the last act of his was his finish, and it will be just so all along the line. Oh, if he alone could do the suffering. . . . If those big boys had gumption at all they would have volunteered all the paint work and had it done long ago . . . Ernest's last letter to me after reading the one I sent you to hand him, does not require an answer. It was

> written in anger and was filled with expressions that were untrue to a gentleman and a son who has had everything done for him. . . . He must get busy and make his own way, and suffering alone will be the means of softening his Iron Heart of selfishness.

Ernest, strangely, turned to fifteen-year-old Grace Quinlan to air his grievances about being kicked out of his home, along with Brumback, without even being allowed to tell his side of the story. "Mother was glad of an excuse to oust me as she has more or less hated me ever since I opposed her throwing two or three thousand seeds away to build a new cottage for herself when the [jack?] should have sent the kids to college. That's another story. Fambly stuff. . . . Am so darned disgusted I don't care to have anything more to do with them for a year at least."

The expulsion, however, had not dampened his enjoyment of a fishing expedition on the Black River with Brumback, Jock Pentecost, Howell Jenkins, and a new friend named Dick Smale. Hemingway's account of the trip is a glowing one of a life apart from the wrangle of family aggravations, the enjoyment of boon companions in the wilderness. At night, Brummy played the mandolin by the fire, and Hemingway read the tales of Lord Dunsany. "Didn't we rate a great moon the first of last week?" he wrote his young friend. "It was great in camp lying all rolled up in the blankets after the fire had died down to coals and the men were asleep and looking at the moon and thinking long long thoughts. In Sicily they say it makes you queer to sleep with the moon on your face. Moon struck. Maybe that's what ails me."

In mid-September, Clarence, trying to smooth things over, wrote to Hemingway asking him to help Grace close up the cottage for the winter. "In as much as there were a few misunderstandings between you and your mother this summer I am sure if you will make this effort, you may right the matters and I will continue to pray that you will love one another as you should."

Clarence's moralizing reveals the custom of a time and place, that youth is apt to be callous, that a midnight picnic was not the major sin that frightened neighbors might suspect — as even Grace Hemingway recognized. It situates the trials of the Hemingway family in the summer of 1920 in Michigan. Clarence and Grace had stuck to their principles, as they had been brought up to do in a world of values that were fading. And Hemingway, unable to forgive his father for being the man he was, reserved his scorn for his mother, whom he blamed for all the trouble. It seems not to have occurred to him that happy families, being all alike, are not the subject of fiction.

⸙ ⸙ ⸙

In "Soldier's Home," a story written in Paris four years later, Hemingway tried to come to terms with his complicated and resentful feelings as a son, a returned veteran of the war, confronting a family life that he no longer felt a part of. But the story was not just a personal statement; it would become a classic in the literature of alienation following World War I, a definition of a generation returned from the war, dissatisfied with the goals and values of American life.

There are differences between Hemingway's hero, Harold Krebs, and Hemingway himself. Krebs, a graduate of a Methodist college in Kansas, was a marine in World War I. He took part in the campaigns at Belleau Wood, Soissons, the Argonne, and returned home late in the summer of 1919 when the parades and the heroes' welcomes were over. But there is much of Hemingway's experience in Harold Krebs's situation. He is disaffected with his family. He sleeps late in the mornings, spends time around town, visits the library regularly. He reads a history of the war and of the campaigns he took part in. Hemingway implies that in reading about the war, Krebs is clutching at the one thing that seems real in his life, something that offsets the boredom and dissatisfaction he feels in his dull Oklahoma hometown.

Krebs is a hero to his two young sisters (as Hemingway was to Sunny and Ursula). One of them in fact wants him to be her "beau." Hemingway refers to Krebs's musical background; for lack of something better to do, Krebs practices on his clarinet in the evenings. He does not, at first, talk about the war with his family. He lies to others about his experiences overseas: "His lies were quite unimportant lies and consisted in attributing to himself things other men had seen, done or heard of, and stating as facts certain apocryphal incidents familiar to all soldiers. Even his lies were not sensational at the pool room." (Hemingway, later, would admit to similar experiences: "In the war that I had known men often lied about the manner of their wounding. Not at first; but later. I'd lied a little myself in my time. Especially late in the evening.") The consequence of Krebs's lying is that he has lost the good feeling he once had: "A distaste for everything that had happened to him in the war set in because of the lies he had told."

The cautious, fussing, pious lifestyle of Grace and Clarence — as Hemingway viewed it, though it was not, altogether, the actual truth — is reflected in his story as well. But Krebs's mother is not Grace Hemingway, for Grace, whatever her faults, was a spirited and independent woman. Nor was Grace unaware of her son's interior struggle. "Ernest is very like me," she once told Marcelline.

"When Ernest gets through this period he's going through of fighting himself and everybody else, and turns his energy toward something positive, he will be a fine man." Mrs. Krebs, on the other hand, is a drab, worn, overly devout woman who frets over her son. (Mr. Krebs, more of an offstage presence in the story, is a man who believes that "all work is honorable" and is concerned about his son's failure to take hold of opportunities.) Yet Grace and the events of the summer of 1920 play an incisive role in "Soldier's Home." Nothing exemplifies Hemingway's genius as a writer so well as the way he reduced the familial complexities of that difficult summer to a simple yet powerful focus. Early in his career Hemingway learned not to dwell on the minutiae of personal experience. He recognized that an author's bitter personal motivations might give the story away, so to speak. His scorn — and a covert sympathy for Mrs. Krebs which was not evident in his treatment of Grace at Walloon Lake in the summer of 1920 — were condensed into a brief exchange between mother and son in "Soldier's Home."

In the climactic moment, Mrs. Krebs blackmails her guilty son into kneeling down and praying with her, an episode aptly calculated to make the reader — particularly the modern reader — cringe. But to bring it off, Hemingway cut out the smugness, the blackmailing demands for affection and affirmation that Grace set down in her expulsion letter. Grace's view of the claims of motherhood were, in truth, such a smothering caricature of motherhood they could hardly serve as credible fiction. In her "bankruptcy" letter, Grace itemized the overdrawn accounts:

> Interest in Mother's ideas and affairs. Little comforts provided for the home; a desire to favor any of Mother's peculiar prejudices, on no account to outrage her ideals. Flowers, fruit, candy or something pretty to wear, brought home to Mother, with a kiss and a squeeze. The unfailing desire to make much of her feeble efforts, to praise her cooking, back up her little schemes; a real interest in hearing her sing, or play the piano, or tell the stories that she loves to tell — A surreptitious paying of bills, just to get them off Mother's mind; Thoughtful remembrances and celebration of her birthday and Mother's day (the sweet letter accompanying the gift of flowers, she treasures most of all). These are merely a few of the deposits which keep the account in good standing.

Taken by itself, Grace's letter would be enough to make anyone believe in the vilifications Hemingway would heap upon his mother in later life. And nowhere in this reckoning, it should be noted, does Grace mention Hemingway's obligations to his father.

In "Soldier's Home," the confrontation scene is etched in acid simplicity:

> "Don't you love your mother, dear boy?
> "No," Krebs said.
> His mother looked at him across the table. Her eyes were shiny. She started crying.
> "I don't love anybody," Krebs said.
> It wasn't any good. He couldn't tell her, he couldn't make her see it. It was silly to have said it. He had only hurt her.

Moments later, full of the mortifying guilt only a mother can induce, Krebs lies. He says he didn't mean it, that he was angry about something else. Having given in, he is then forced to beg his mother to believe that he loves her, that he didn't mean what he had said.

> Krebs kissed her hair. She put her face up to him.
> "I'm your mother," she said, "I held you next to my heart when you were a tiny baby."
> Krebs felt sick and vaguely nauseated.

ııı

But Harold Krebs's excruciating confrontation with his mother is not the only fictional intent of "Soldier's Home." In every major Hemingway story, the human incident points the way to larger issues that are not, at first, so apparent. A river, for instance, runs through many of Hemingway's major stories and his most important novels. Generally, in such Hemingway fictions, the river serves as a cleansing baptism, an absolution for past sins, a healing experience, a rite of escape from the outside world as the Big Two-Hearted is for Nick Adams in the story of that name, as the Irati is for Bill Gorton and Jake Barnes in *The Sun Also Rises,* as the Tagliamento is for Lieutenant Frederic Henry in *A Farewell to Arms.* But in one of the cleverest touches in any Hemingway story, and in a paragraph that perfectly epitomizes the Hemingway style, Hemingway describes Krebs in a souvenir snapshot: "There is a picture which shows him on the Rhine with two German girls and another corporal. Krebs and the corporal look too big for their uniforms. The German girls are not beautiful. The Rhine does not show in the picture." In those few objectively reported statements, as in a banal snapshot, Hemingway has nevertheless summed up a good deal of information and social observation: that Krebs is a corporal who served with the occupying army; that the German girls are most likely whores, or women in a defeated country who have turned to prostitution; that the vast effort of the war, with its national hatreds, its millions dead and wounded, has been reduced to casual exchanges between soldiers and enemy prostitutes. The absence of the Rhine is, perhaps, a signal that there is no redemptive symbol in Krebs's circumstances — or in the story.

Back in the States, Krebs, who was under no illusions about the German and French girls he had known, eyes the young hometown girls. He is reluctant to get involved with any of them: he does not care to live in their "complicated world of already defined alliances and shifting feuds." Krebs feels neither the energy nor the will to engage that world. Yet in a wonderful Proustian aside, Hemingway says of Krebs, "He liked to look at them from the front porch as they walked on the other side of the street. He liked to watch them walking under the shade of the trees." Still, he does not want to become any more involved in the intrigue and the politics of courtship than he wants to become involved in family life and loyalties. He tells himself that he does not need a girl, that needing a girl is another of the lies men tell themselves. Being in the army, in the company of men, had disabused Krebs of that notion. You needed girls only when you thought about them; sooner or later you got one anyway. Krebs is a man opting out of society, tired of himself, tired of the lies he has told. In one of the story's more telling but awkward observations, Hemingway notes, "Krebs acquired the nausea in regard to experience that is the result of untruth or exaggeration." He is, in fact, more comfortable in the company of other returned servicemen, where he can adopt the "easy" pose of the old soldiers among other soldiers, admitting to himself "that he had been badly, sickeningly frightened all the time. In this way he lost everything." Lying is for Krebs a failed attempt at staving off the sudden emptiness that Hemingway heroes suffer at crucial moments in their lives.

After his brush with death, after the affair with Agnes, after the suffocating dissatisfactions of family life, Hemingway had begun to entertain a philosophy — impossible though it might be to maintain — of playing always against the odds. He summed it up by saying of Krebs, "He did not want any consequences. He did not want any consequences ever again. He wanted to live along without consequences."

II

Reports from the life: after that summer of 1920, Hemingway gave up living with his family. Writing to Howell Jenkins, he explained, "Having been barred from my domicile I know not where I will linger in Chicago. Probably ask Vigano [the proprietor of a local speakeasy] to leave me a couple of blankets in the Venice [Cafe]." Like Harold Krebs, he was thinking about a move to Kansas City. "Will be in Chicago a few days and then allez to either Toronto or K.C. Had a letter from K.C. asking me to name my figure!" The Kansas City job was imaginary.

That summer and fall, Hemingway wrote occasional articles for the *Toronto Star Weekly.* A few of them suggest he was grubbing around for subjects. His article on trout fishing in the August 28 issue started out authoritatively: "At present the best rainbow trout fishing in the world is in the rapids of the Canadian Soo," though the article in fact merged his summer fishing expeditions on the Black River with Brumback and Jack Pentecost and his recollections of the trip he had made to the Canadian Soo three years before in 1917. "Canadians Wild/Tame" dealt with Americans' stereotyped views of their neighbors to the north as bewhiskered types who wore mackinaw blanket pants and fur caps and were pursued by the Mounties, or tame specimens who wore spats and small mustaches and looked very intelligent and politely bored. Another suggested trading celebrities in the way baseball teams traded players; thus the United States might acquire Anatole France, Jean-Jacques Rousseau, and Voltaire in return for the potboiling American novelists Harold Bell Wright, Owen Johnson, and Robert W. Chambers — with $800,000 thrown in to sweeten the deal.

It was an indication of Hemingway's charisma that his male friends — at least in the beginning of their relationships — were so willing and able to help him whenever necessary. Bill Horne, working in Grand Rapids with the Eaton Axle Company, was slated to move to Chicago. He came up with a plan to solve Hemingway's problem. They would share an apartment together, preferably in a suburb, where it would be cheaper. Horne offered to grubstake Hemingway until he found a suitable job. "It being now decided that we have to live together until an act of God or some woman shall do us part (she being to our tutored and jaundiced eye most decidedly no act of God) now it behooves us to foregather in solemn conclave and reason where and how much." Horne suggested that Hemingway try the advertising game. "It's bushels of fun, keeps you writing and thinking, teaches you quite a lot about a million things, pays you a little more than enough to live on and gives you plenty of spare time to really write." He was ready to lend Hemingway money if needed. He confessed that he was so excited by the prospect of their sharing an apartment that he found it difficult to write an intelligent letter. "But the big thing Hemmy is just you and me. If you need me as much as I need you, why we had better hurry —

that's all. I haven't changed basically yet, but there's no time to lose in getting out the old antidote — come live with me and be my 'life preserver.'" In his youth Hemingway elicited from his male friends a kind of devotion that was almost sensual in its unabashed warmth and sincerity.

But before moving in with Bill Horne, Hemingway stayed in the apartment of Bill and Katy Smith's older brother, Y. K. Smith, and his wife, Doodles, at 63 East Division Street. Twelve years older than Hemingway, Y.K. worked for McCann Erickson, the advertising agency. Through his business connections, he was a welcome source of theater and opera tickets. Something of an intellectual, Y.K. was well acquainted with writers and painters in Chicago and took a generous and genuine interest in Hemingway's career. Bill Smith recalled that his brother was the first to call Hemingway a genius, even before there was much to base that judgment on other than Hemingway's lively conversations.

Y.K.'s wife, Genevieve — no one referred to her as anything other than Doodles — was short, on the plump side, gray-eyed, brown-haired. (Fussy about her hair, she set great store by it.) She and Y.K. had met at the Trudeau Sanatarium in Saranac, New York, where they were both under treatment for tuberculosis. Their union, as Bill recalled, was strictly a case of "propinquity." Doodles had ambitions of becoming a classical pianist; Y.K. had bought her a Mason and Hamlin grand piano, referred to in the household as the Twins. She was a lazy housewife; Katy Smith took a perverse pleasure in writing "Doodles" in the dust atop the piano. Doodles had one great gift as a pianist, an ability to sight-read that allowed her to play difficult compositions perfectly the first time. Her first renditions of Bach and Mozart were always her best. Unfortunately, as Bill remembered, "practice made *her* imperfect, despite lessons from various teachers." She was an inveterate flirt — an easy accomplishment, since the Smiths had taken in three male roomers: Don Wright, a womanizer who worked in an advertising agency, and a young man named Bobby Rouse, as well as Ernest. Doodles's catchphrase for her husband or almost anything in pants was "a good-looking young man." She was known to have affairs; she and Y.K. were early practitioners of the open marriage.

It was at a party at the Smiths' late in October, soon after he had moved in, that Hemingway met Elizabeth Hadley Richardson. She was tall, sturdy, handsome rather than pretty. Hemingway, who always noticed a woman's hair, found her auburn hair especially attractive. Hadley's friends called her Hash. The moment Hadley entered the room, Hemingway claimed afterward, "an intense feeling came over me. I knew she was the girl I was going to marry."

During the three weeks Hadley was in Chicago, they were together much of the time. She found Hemingway immediately attractive, ruddy-cheeked, with a broad smile — a "hulky, bulky something masculine." Hemingway, who had adopted his father's habit of focusing his attention on one person to the exclusion of others, seemed to be courting her. But Hemingway's age made Hadley doubt that he was being anything but friendly. Of that first meeting, she later confessed, "I tho't he likes me because my hair's red and my skirt's a good length but wait till he hears that I'm a player of classical music and do not care for Harold Bell Wright."

Hadley was twenty-nine. As a child, she had been invalided, having fallen out of a second-story window with resulting back injuries that eventually responded to treatment. Her mother, however, overprotected her throughout her childhood and somehow managed to convince her that she was physically and even, perhaps, psychologically fragile. She did, however, encourage her to take up music as a suitable avocation. Like Grace Hemingway, Florence Richardson was a determined woman with musical interests — a talented pianist, who in her later years developed an interest in the occult, dabbled in theosophy and mental science and automatic writing. Hadley's father, James Richardson, an executive in the family pharmaceutical business in St. Louis, was a gentleman with a tendency to drink. When Hadley was twelve, he committed suicide, putting a revolver to his head, presumably as a result of business losses. Hadley had attended a private girls' school, Mary Institute, graduating in 1910, then went on to Bryn Mawr for a year.

At college Hadley became friendly with her roommate Edna Rapallo and visited her family in Windsor, Vermont. Mrs. Constance Rapallo, Edna's mother, was an artist, had studied with Howard Pyle, and was friendly with Maxfield Parrish, her highly successful neighbor in nearby Cornish, New Hampshire. Parrish was famous for his androgynous and languid nymphs lolling in chill and autumnal settings. It was there that Hadley had a brief spell of emancipation from the strictures of family life in St. Louis. She played strenuous tennis with the local Harvard boys and rode around the hilly countryside in an old surrey with Edna. She was introduced to the local artists like Parrish and Kenyon Cox and their rich patrons and admirers, who had settled in the little colony established by Augustus Saint-Gaudens some years before and were wildly fearful that Cornish "would become a second rate political summer haunt."

Mrs. Rapallo became astonishingly attached to her young guest, taking Hadley under her wing, so much so that Hadley's mother became suspicious that Mrs. Rapallo might be a lesbian. Florence

Richardson discouraged any further relationship between her daughter and the two women, thereby adding to Hadley's sense of insecurity. About Mrs. Rapallo, Hadley later explained to Hemingway, "I sort of appealed to her or something as a helpless little somebody — as I was and in order to help me out, she managed to show me how much pleasanter life was with her and Edna — best friend at college, freshman year — tremendous amount of jealousy. Then this rotten suggestion of being evil — and being very suggestible, I began to imagine I had all this low sex feeling and she for me." The whole experience was so demoralizing that she quit Bryn Mawr after a year. But as she assured Hemingway,

> Well, you needn't fear me on that side, my dear. There was a time when someone liking me that much made me think I liked them that much, but I know now that I don't. I like other kinds better — very few women and a great many kinds of men. Between family's throwing off on the horrible male sect and thinking my relations with women were low if things were demonstrative, I must have been somewhat bound down for company for a while there, eh?

Back in St. Louis, Hadley found herself hemmed in, her life dominated by her mother and her younger sister, Florence, known as Fonnie, who was married and lived with her husband and children in the apartment below. Hadley, by then an accomplished pianist, devoted herself to her music. She saw occasional boyfriends, none of whom were particularly important to her, except for Harrison Williams, her piano teacher. Williams, however, seemed content to carry on an a largely aesthetic friendship. They talked literature and music and art when they were together.

The summer of 1920 was difficult for Hadley because her mother was slowly and painfully dying of Bright's disease and Hadley had taken on the burden of caring for her. When Florence Richardson died at the end of the summer, Hadley was particularly grateful to hear from Katy Smith, her classmate at Mary Institute. Katy, who was working in Chicago and living at the Arts Club, wrote her suggesting that she come to Chicago for a long visit. Hadley could stay with her brother Y.K. and his wife on East Division Street.

Hemingway's claim to love at first sight seems to be borne out in his letters to friends. He promptly let it be known that he was more than casually involved with Hadley. He wrote his teenage confidante, Grace Quinlan, "Hadley Richardson was here for three weeks and we tore around together and had a terrible good time. She's a peach and I've been leading a kinda quiet life since she's gone." Hemingway said that he was trying to cinch an advertising job, one that would pay him "some real Jacksonian." In the meantime, he said, he was also "grinding out stuff every day for the Star."

Within a month he and Bill Horne had found interim quarters on North State Street, and he was writing Bill Smith about a jovial party Horne had given in a private dining room at the Victor House at which Katy, Hash, and he had been present. The dinner had included "two rounds of Bronxes [cocktails], the acids and liqueurs." Then they had gone dancing at the College Inn. "Hash is a good scout of the einst wasser and a splendid hand with the grog," he said. "She can also in the writer's opinion spot Doodles a trio of pianos and still be fighting for her head in the stretch." It was the first time he had seen Katy up against the weather from drinking, the effect, perhaps, of some personal problems, for Hemingway's letter implied that Edgar had made a bumbling attempt at suicide: "What would have caused J. C. Odgar to attempt self mortage and enabled him at the same time to be unable to locate the morter." It had left Katy, he said sarcastically, "in the finest of shape."

In a pre-Christmas letter to his mother, who was visiting her brother in California (Grace had taken young Leicester with her), Hemingway talked familiarly about Hadley, who had made a recent weekend visit to Chicago. "Came one Saturday night and allezed Monday night. We had a most excellent time. She wants me very badly to come to a big New Year's eve dinner and party at the University Club in Sin Louis — but I can't negotiate the grade. Being about as well seeded as the navel orange." A good deal of his letter was bent on creating the impression that he was leading a sober and responsible life. The most important news was that he had gotten a job on a magazine called *The Cooperative Commonwealth,* "the organ, mouth organ, not pipe organ for the Co-operative movement." The circulation was 65,000, and the current issue had eighty pages of reading matter and about twenty pages of ads. "Most of the reading was written by myself. Also write editorials and most anything. Will write anything once."

Hemingway had been going out to Oak Park on Sundays, so he wrote Grace. Y.K. and Doodles were invited out for Christmas dinner with the Hemingways at Oak Park. Doodles would be going to New York to study with a piano teacher after Christmas, and Hemingway would be moving back into the East Division Street apartment while she was away. "It's a very extra comfortable apartment, seven rooms, and the priceless Della to cook for us. There will be five of us there in batchellor quarters." On such occasions, Hemingway could be the joyful opportunist. Writing to Bill Smith, he acknowledged that his new job was not bad except at the end of the month, when he had to "work like hell." He could spend a good deal of time at the apartment, his hours were elastic; he went to the office about nine in the morning and took a two- or three-hour lunch break. "I'm supposed to do a good deal of thinking and planning of editorials at home."

Life at the Men's Club on East Division Street turned out to be very agreeable. Y.K. was gregarious and entertaining; he liked company. Frequently, there were guests for dinner. Writing to his mother, Hemingway informed her that Isaac Don Levine, the *Daily News* correspondent in Russia, had been there for a midday dinner. Levine was an excellent fellow "and gave us the cold dope on Rooshia." Then the group went to a concert by the pianist Benno Moseiwitch at Orchestra Hall. He played Chopin and Debussy and Liszt as well as "some modern stuff . . . I think he has it on Rachmaninoff or Gabrilowitch." He told his mother that he had just gotten a $10 raise and was now earning $50 a week. "I am in good shape. I eat well. I sleep well. I do everything but work well."

***

There is no question that the affair between Hemingway and Hadley Richardson had been sudden; at a restless time in both their lives, they had discovered each other. Both were serious about the relationship, but it was a matter, at first, of assumption rather than declaration. There is also no doubt that Hemingway's affair with Agnes von Kurowsky had been painful, even crippling, in some psychological way. Hemingway was cautious. At first he and Hadley went through a time of testing. When Hemingway wrote her, in one of his rare surviving courtship letters, that he wouldn't be able to get to St. Louis over the New Year's holiday ("I'd be much happier too, Hash Darling — but I can't come — you see I hate and loathe and despise to talk about seeds"), Hadley was disappointed. She had already warned him that she was a very fly-by-night girl sometimes and that she would be going to the New Year's party with a former boyfriend, Dick, who was "a nawful good sport — That must make you very jealous." In another letter she told him, offhandedly, that it was very likely that Dick would get drunk and want to kiss her all night. For Hemingway, it must have been a sensitive time, if he remembered, as he probably did, the uneasy New Year's Eve farewell with Agnes the year before. Hadley's ploy was successful. Hemingway answered, "Suppose when you tell me how nice Dick is and so on I ought to counter with how enjoyable it is to dance with [Marilyn?] and how nice she looks topside of a horse and so on — but when I think of anyone in comparison with you, you are so much dearer and I love you so much . . .'Course I love you. I love you all the time." On New Year's Day, Hadley gave him a detailed report: "I was feeling so blue thru all this and thinking so hard of you — wondering where you were . . . Dick did kiss me goodnight in the quietest way — and I let him — cause I do like Dick and feel sorry for him." Hemingway had told her about the welcoming party when he moved into Y.K.'s new apartment and the "corking little Irene," who had liked him best of all. He hinted that there was further competition, as well. Of Irene, Hadley countered, "Wasn't it good of her to tell you when it got too much for her, and in such a selfish way." She accused Hemingway of "press-agenting." His uncertainty was showing.

Ironically, there was another test over the holiday season, this one from masculine quarters. Hemingway wrote her that he had heard from his old friend Captain Jim Gamble, who had suggested he spend a year in Italy with him, at Gamble's expense. Hemingway added that his father thought it a good opportunity. "Jim Gamble is great," Hemingway told Hadley, "and I love him a lot. But not like I love you." He wondered what Hadley thought.

Hadley was probably no more pleased with the idea than Agnes had been, but she was more subtle. "Rome sounds so wonderful. I would be so envious of you! . . . I would *miss* you pretty frightfully . . . I hope it's not too unfair to say so." Hemingway cabled Gamble, turning down the offer. His typewritten copy read, "Rather go to Rome with you than heaven stop [Not married. crossed out] Too sad for words stop. Writing and selling it stop [Unmarried. crossed out] but don't get rich stop all authors poor first then rich stop. me no exception stop. Wouldn't we have a great time stop Lord how I envy you." The odd feature of Hemingway's telegram is that twice he intended to tell Gamble he was not married — and that twice he thought better of doing so.

Still the dream of Italy died hard. On January 12, he suggested to Hadley that they should make a "bold penniless dash for Wopland" and forget everything. Yet it was clear that he did not want to leave everything behind. He stipulated that they would have to wait until Bill Horne and perhaps Howell Jenkins could join them. Hadley answered rather dryly that she perhaps could take tickets at a Milan movie house. At the same time she was willing to acknowledge that the most important thing was Hemingway's writing. "I want to be your helper — not your hinderer," she wrote him. Throughout their courtship, Hadley made it plain that her interests would be subservient to his, however chancy. "I'm not at all the woman [who] wants her practical future guaranteed," she said.

If anything, Hadley's letters — which ran from twelve to twenty pages each — reveal that she was all too willing to be what Hemingway wanted her to be, to do what Hemingway wanted her to do. From the beginning, it seems, she had recognized that it was the right strategy, that behind Hemingway's gruff pose he was overly sensitive, uncertain, dependent on a woman. She was flattering: she wanted to be "picked up and loved to death — won't hurt you a bit or me either . . . any woman with a gram of sense would adore you." She was not coy or prudish: "to be everything to you is the only thing that can satisfy me physically. . . . Funny, if it had been anyone else but you loving me, I'd have felt it was *very* wrong. I know there's a fine, clean quality in you, it runs clear through, that evaporates nauseating memories." When Hemingway told her about his war service, his affair with Agnes, she was calmly supportive, reminding him,

> Do you remember the morning at Y.K.'s you came in very panting and seething and told me about the girl you loved so much and she gave you so much and then went away? Then a lot of talk we had about that kind of experience and then I remember clear as a bell telling you not to marry for a long time. That was good impersonal wisdom wasn't it? Hmmm.

Unlike Agnes, Hadley was frank about the age question and dismissed it forthrightly: "Ernest, *I* never have taken an attitude of olderness to your youngerness in anything that mattered, have I? God knows I don't feel that way, honey." When he wrote that he was hoping to get to St. Louis in a few weeks, she answered, "It's about time. I'll eat you alive."

Though no formal announcement had been made they had already decided on marriage. When it was clear that Hemingway still wanted to go to Italy, she took the reasonable tack, that the decision ought to be "thought out, not felt out." But she valued his ambition as a writer too much, "So anything you suggest that means putting the work in a secondary place has no backing from me." The trip to Italy, for whatever reasons — perhaps as restitution for what he had been cheated out of by Agnes — had become an obsession with Hemingway. He had been putting money away to buy Italian lire. Hadley sent him money to buy lire for her as well.

It was at the Men's Club that Hemingway, early in the year, met two influential writers, the poet Carl Sandburg and the novelist Sherwood Anderson. Anderson, like many of the Chicago writers, had worked in an advertising agency. By his own legendary account, he had walked out on the job to become a serious writer. He was an inveterate talker (Anderson would talk to a chair if he had no other audience, Margaret Anderson, editor of *The Little Review,* once claimed). His *Winesburg, Ohio* had been published in 1919, establishing his claim as a leading figure in the Chicago Renaissance, which included such figures as Sandburg, Edgar Lee Masters, Ben Hecht, and Harriet Monroe, the editor of *Poetry.* Both Sandburg and Anderson had appreciated Hemingway's spirited reading of *The Rubaiyat of Omar Khayyam* in Y.K.'s parlor the first time they met. And Anderson, generous to young midwestern writers, had invited Hemingway out to his house at Palos Park. He and his wife, Tennessee, were on the verge of a trip to Europe, funded by the critic Paul Rosenfeld. Anderson was definitely encouraging, and Hemingway was impressed by the successful writer. Hadley was impressed, too. She thought it was wonderful that "those two 'old fellows' think so much of your work." She remained his greatest supporter and was particularly infuriated when she learned that Aunty Charles and even Bill Smith had told her sister Fonnie that Hemingway had exaggerated ambitions as a writer. In April, Hemingway sent word that he had begun work on a novel and had three chapters done. Hadley was ecstatic "bout the novel busting loose in your brain":

> Juvenilia! Pooh. Thank the Lord, some young one's gonna write something young & beautiful. Some one with the clean, muscular freshness of young things right on him at the moment of writing. You go ahead. I'm wild over the idea Ernest and the *start.* Thas the way for a novel to start with real people talking and saying what they really think! . . . I'm *all for it* and so violently for *you* as a person and a writer and a Lover I can't put it down on this paper.

"My feeling for you, best beloved person," Hadley told him, "is like yours for your writing — *no one can take it away.*" She asked him if he had a typewriter, if he would like a Corona for his birthday. Two days later, she joked, "I will give you a Corona and you will consequently marry me."

Though he was living frugally, Hemingway was also keeping up an active social life. He had met an intelligent young man named Krebs Friend, a staff member at *The Cooperative Commonwealth.* (Hadley, who had met Friend on a visit to Chicago, thought it was a shame that he had a fine mind but a crummy body. She liked his "sheer gaiety," however.) Hemingway had taken up boxing with Y.K. and with Nick Nerone, who was now working at the Italian consulate in Chicago. ("Kate says Nick is *mad* over you," Hadley wrote Ernest. "Wish I *had* met him.") Hemingway was also seeing a good deal of Katy during that spring and summer, dating her frequently, taking her to the theater and the local night spots. He was seeing other women, among them a Ruth Lobdell, apparently with Hadley's blessing. Late in April, she counseled him, "Don['t] get too awfully lonesome ever. Get someone. Someone charming. Miss Lobdell or

Katie or someone knows ye." She even conceded that when Hemingway had taken Katy to a tough joint, it must have been fun. "And Butstein would pep up anyone." But a little more than a week later she was peevish about scarves that Katy had borrowed from her and never returned and the fact that Katy had lit into Ernest when he had asked for one of them back. "How many scarves of mine does she want, anyway. Got two now — shall I send another?" she fumed. Applying some heavy strokes to the pen, "Getting Mad," it was her own fault, she said, "for believing for a minute she had any sense of obligation."

When Hemingway and Katy participated in a dance contest in one of the local night spots, Hemingway sent Hadley a poem about the incident, titled "Lines to a Young Lady on Her Having Very Nearly Won a Vogel."

> Through the hot, pounding rhythm of the waltz
> You swung and whirled with eager, pagan grace
> Two sleepy birds
> Preen in their wicker cages
> And I
> Am dancing with a woman of the town.

Throughout the spring and summer of their courtship, Hemingway seemed to be taunting Hadley with Katy or Ruth Lobdell or with a woman named Frances or "the svelte jewess" Irene Goldstein. Hadley bore up under it with determination. When Hemingway finally gave her some explanation of his relationship with Katy, Hadley professed her understanding: "Very, very sorry and frightfully admiring of Butstein, for the way she's been. . . . Course you love her — love her like mad. At the same time I'm 'always to remember you don't love anyone but me'? . . . *Think* I know, honey, how you feel about Katie — hope I understand it right, hope it's all right." The subject of Hemingway's feelings for Katy brought out in Hadley a kind of passive understanding that was not quite so innocent as it seemed:

> It's amazing you happened by some chemical accident not to fall for her, hard. Worth about three of me, anyhow, and probably be a better lover and worker for you, and everything. My but its queer the way things happen, and if you didn't want me pretty hard, as I think you do, I'd make you throw me over and do yourself justice.

Hemingway had been feeling discouraged and anxious. Like his mother, it seems, under stress he suffered severe headaches. For months he had been hoping to pin down a job with the *Toronto Star*, preferably as a correspondent for the paper in Italy. But John Bone, the managing editor of the *Toronto Daily Star,* had delayed and delayed, and Greg Clark, now Hemingway's friend, kept him alerted but had no firm offer to report. More than that, Hemingway's friends were not exactly encouraging about his marital plans. Y. K. Smith, in the course of a train trip back from a Sunday dinner at Oak Park, had advised him that marriage would be a drag on his promising career. Howell Jenkins had given him the same advice. When Bill Smith told Ernest that he thought Hadley's age was a problem, Hemingway's response was "At least she'll have lived." It did not help that Hemingway reported their conversations to Hadley, who had to console him frequently, bolster his spirit, and combat the negative advice.

In late April, Hemingway wrote Bill a long complicated letter, baring his anxieties in the course of writing what was an elegy to the outdoor life. For the past two weeks, he told Bill, he had been having killer headaches; he'd been taking Veronal, but it didn't seem to have "the wallop" he needed. It bothered him that he was not likely to get up to Michigan that summer:

> Sometimes get thinking about the Sturgeon and the Black during the nocturnal and damn near go cuckoo. . . . Dats the way tings are. Guy loves a couple or three streams all his life and loves 'em better than anything in the world — falls in love with a girl and goddam streams can dry up for all he cares. Only the hell of it is that all that country has had as bad a hold on me as ever — there's as much of a pull this spring as there ever was — and you know how it's always been — just don't think about it at all daytimes, but at night it comes and ruins me.

Nor had things been going well at the Men's Club, which had transferred its occupancy to a fourth-floor apartment at 100 East Chicago Avenue. Doodles was back with her gardenia perfume and easy habits. "She plays worse than ever," Hemingway wrote Bill Smith. Hemingway, unfortunately, had put himself, in a meddling way, in the middle of Doodles's carrying on with her off-time boyfriend "Dirty Don" Wright. Hemingway, intending to do a service for Y.K., had had words with Wright and now Wright would no longer show up at the apartment when Hemingway was there. Instead he and Doodles met outside. Doodles complained to her husband, and Y.K. complained to Hemingway. Hemingway told Bill, who had no love for Doodles, either, "Yen's words to me are 'You can never understand what Don means to Doodles.' Yen is right. I can't . . . Jo Eezus. This Wright rates the rope." It had all been better, Hemingway felt, when Doodles was in New York; then they had had "a high grade time." Now he had taken to sleeping on the roof. He had made up his mind that after he and Hadley were married, they would not be moving in with the Smiths even though Y.K. had made the offer: "The enditer would sooner take his promised bride to the back room of the second floor of a brothel in Seney Michigan." Hadley had had second thoughts about the unsavory living conditions with the Y.K. Smiths back at the East Division Street apartment, what with the drunks running in and out and Howell Jenkins turning up with a bunch of "chorines." Bill Horne, Hadley wrote Ernest, "was the only person who seemed to know how squalid the whole situation was." When Ernest complained that Doodles had propositioned him one night, Hadley answered that she was not surprised. She had once interrupted one of Doodles's tête-à-têtes with Wright, while Y.K. was sleeping in his room. Wright had rushed out of the room "stuttering with terror and laughing hysterically." Doodles, however, was unperturbed.

It was during Hemingway's Memorial Day visit to St. Louis (Bill Horne had accompanied him) that he and Hadley made some decisions about their wedding. Throughout June they discussed the details and arrangements. They planned to have the wedding in September in the white-frame Methodist church in Petoskey. Hadley was happy to have an excuse for taking the arrangements out of her sister Fonnie's hands. She and Hemingway both wanted a simple ceremony. Grace and Clarence had offered them Windemere for their honeymoon. Hemingway had asked Bill Smith to be the best man. Katy Smith would not give a ready answer when they asked her to be a bridesmaid, then said she would but made a point of saying that she would decide what she would wear. The formal announcement was made at a party in St. Louis given by Hadley's close friend Helen Breaker. (Her husband was the lawyer who handled Hadley's trust funds.) Hemingway was not there, but Hadley sent a report to her future mother-in-law and thanked her: "Ernest has written me from time to time of your sweetness and generosity in planning for our happiness in September. I can't think of any better way to spend our honeymoon than North and in the woods." It was a polite and gracious letter. But Hadley had formed her opinion of Grace months earlier, in March, when Hemingway had taken her out to meet his parents in Oak Park. Of Grace, Hadley said frankly, "We were not made to be friends, but she worked at it."

Hemingway, unaccountably still clinging to his teenage confidante, wrote Grace Quinlan, inviting her to the wedding. "Suppose you want to hear all about Hadley," he said. "Well her nickname is Hash — she's a wonderful tennis player, best pianist I ever heard and a sort of terribly fine article." A month later, he commissioned young Grace, in a joking vein, to find them a suitable preacher. "In your wide and diverse acquaintance can you recommend a capable minister to perform this ceremony? Hash says she doesn't care particularly what breed of priest it is, but prefers one that doesn't wear a celluloid collar or chaw tobacco." He sent news to Marjorie Bump as well. Marjorie, writing him from a summer camp in Wisconsin, offered her congratulations. "I think it is grand," she said. "We have had a rather queer friendship, but it is going to be the strongest ever now isn't it? I do love you lots, Stein, as the best old pal in the world." Even on the eve of his marriage, Hemingway was oddly reluctant to give up his teenage girlfriends. Perhaps he was still clinging to his boyhood, to the life without consequences in rural Michigan.

The impending wedding must have brought with it some doubts. In early July, he was suffering through a spell of depression, even considering "mortage." Hemingway's letter was serious enough to worry Hadley, who took a sympathetic and mothering but firm line. "Old dear — what's this?" she wrote him promptly on July 7. "*Not* truly so low as to crave mortage are you? The meanest thing I can say to you on that point is remember it would kill me to all intents and purposes. . . . Don't ever get confused when such a moment comes — don't ever forget That responsibility to me. You *gotta* live first for you and then for my happiness." The crisis seemed to be solved by a hasty weekend trip to Chicago to be with him. By July 13, back in St. Louis, she had received the "dearest letter" from him. Her emotions were in such a whirl she had immediately sat down at the piano and played and played, the malagueña and a Chopin étude and a Brahms ballad, "all played unto you — dedicated — on the spot." Though the trip home had been "ghastly" and the state of domestic affairs at the "Domicile" was aggravating, she had had a wonderful time, she said. Hemingway had introduced her to some of his colleagues at *The Cooperative Commonwealth,* the whistling "Il Larietto" and Hans with the "so easily forthcoming" smile. "And Kate dancing," she made a point of mentioning, "that's the most graceful thing!" Best of all was finding Ernest's warming and softening glances at her across the table at the bar they had visited on an evening out together. "And I love white wine," she noted. In his letter, Hemingway had sent two "warm weather pomes" that she appreciated so much she read them aloud to her friend Ruth Bradfield. One of them, quite likely, was "Flat Roofs":

It is cool at night on the roofs of the city
The city sweats

Dripping and stark.
Maggots of life
Crawl in the hot loneliness of the city.
Love curdles in the city
Love sours in the hot whispering from the pavements.
Love grows old
Old with the oldness of sidewalks.
It is cool at night on the roofs of the city.

For Hadley, the poems must have recalled the roof at Y.K.'s Domicile, where she and Ernest retreated to be together. "I'm awfully grateful that you have the Roof to compensate for some of the lack there, Old deah!" she wrote him. "But it *isn't* enough." For Hemingway, however, the images in the poem must also have recalled the evenings with Agnes and the roof of the American Red Cross Hospital in Milan. In Hemingway, women seemed to merge, one with the other, in some dream of fulfillment. Another of the possible "warm weather" poems written at the time was, perhaps, too suggestive to be read to Ruth Bradfield:

At night I lay with you
And watched
The city whirl and spin about

Katy Smith: the references to Kate — how she had borrowed Hadley's scarves, how she fussed about what she was to wear at the wedding and what the other bridesmaids would be wearing; how Ernest felt or said he felt about her — cropped up continually in the courtship correspondence between St. Louis and Chicago. A typescript, clearly intended for Hadley (was it ever sent?), gives a curious impression about Hemingway's state of mind prior to the wedding. He and Horney and Stut (Katy) had spent an evening stretched out on the big bed in the front room of the Cile "and talked and jibed about this wedding. Stut says as how she thinks you oughta allow her to wear half mourning. Something bout the shade of the typer ribbon." They had talked about what the men should wear — probably flannel trousers, which seemed to be the popular thing at summer weddings. Katy talked about decorating the church at Petoskey, but mostly she teased:

> Said that she'd try and act as though there wasn't anything between us much in order to keep people from talking. Said she'd try and remember it was your wedding and try and make you feel so. . . . Said she suddenly woke up the other night and decided that my loving you this way couldn't last and that she ought to call me up on the phone and tell me so — Says she gives us a year at the longest —

says you'll be off of me inside of a year and that then she'll come over and live with us to hold the home together.

When Hemingway showed Katy some recent pictures of himself and Hadley, she pretended not to know who the "sweet boy" was and when told, claimed that that was what Hadley had done to him. "Said she'd always known me as large, solid, rough, rabelasian, cosmic force and here first pictures she sees of you and I together I look like slim young Flemish poet." He kept up the joke, noting that he and Katy had had "a good time throwing off on each other — I always greet her for past couple of weeks with how terrible she is looking and she says Wemedge I've never seen you look worse." If Hemingway had, in fact, sent such a letter to Hadley, it was one of the odder epistles a bridegroom ever sent his intended.

The wedding was held, as planned, in the white clapboard Methodist church in Petoskey on Saturday afternoon, September 3. Hadley had come down from Wisconsin, where she had been vacationing with friends until the wedding. Hemingway, still clinging to old habits, had managed a three-day fishing expedition on the Sturgeon with Howell Jenkins and Charlie Hopkins prior to the wedding. A suitable preacher had been found; the church was decorated with swamp lilies and bittersweet and boughs of balsam. Helen Breaker was Hadley's maid of honor. Ursula and Katy Smith and Ruth Bradfield were the bridesmaids. Sunny, much to her regret, was away at a girls' camp in Wisconsin, and Marcelline was ill with what her mother described as a bad case of "nerves" and was recuperating in New Hampshire. Neither of them attended the wedding. (Marcelline's was not the only case of family nerves at the time; Clarence had somehow gotten the notion that his son did not want him at the wedding and wrote to Ernest, saying that if that were the case, he would return to Oak Park. Hemingway had to reassure him.) Hemingway's male friends showed up en masse, dressed, as the groom was, in white trousers and dark jackets. Young Leicester would remember Ernest's legs trembling beneath his trousers.

Hadley, coming down the aisle on the arm of Helen's husband, George, was radiant in her bridal gown and veil, her hair still damp from an afternoon swim. She carried a bouquet of baby's breath. She remembered that in the confusion of leaving the church, surrounded by friends and well-wishers, Hemingway had stepped on her white satin slippers; she thought it a bad omen at the time. After the ceremony there was a picture-taking session and a reception and dinner at the Dilworths' Pinehurst Cottage. When it was dark, the couple left for Walloon Lake. Ernest rowed his bride across the lake to Windemere.

Clarence wrote up the report on the wedding for the newspapers. The names of the principal guests at the reception were listed for posterity. There was, strangely, little mention of the bride or her family background. Clarence continued the myth of Ernest's having been a first lieutenant in the Italian army. The notice ended with a tribute to his son's war record: "Many telegrams were received from people of high social and state positions in Italy where Lieutenant Hemingway received such signal honors and decorations at the close of the war." A press agent couldn't have done better.

It was not the ideal honeymoon. Both Hadley and Hemingway came down with colds and were ill for several days. After a decent interval of isolation, Hemingway insisted on taking Hadley to meet his abandoned young girlfriends in Petoskey. She remembered the ordeal of standing in the kitchen of a dark-haired and attractive young girl, probably Grace Quinlan, who stood by the kitchen table all the while they were there. The poor girl had looked so embarrassed and ill at ease, Hadley thought that she must really have had a terrible crush on Ernest.

The future settled their uncertainties about where to live. Florence Richardson's estate was settled in October; trust funds from that, as well as those from Hadley's banker grandfather, allowed her a monthly income of slightly less than $300. Hemingway was given a post as the *Toronto Daily Star*'s foreign correspondent, covering political events and sports in Europe. He made arrangements to sail on the French liner *Leopoldina* from New York, on December 8. Sherwood Anderson, back from France, convinced them that Paris was the place an aspiring young writer should live. He gave Hemingway letters of introduction to people he should meet: Gertrude Stein, with whom Anderson had struck up an immediate friendship; Ezra Pound; and Lewis Galantière, an American translator and writer who worked for the International Chamber of Commerce.

In Chicago, Hemingway had found a seedy interim apartment on North Dearborn Street. He and Hadley did not stay with the Y. K. Smiths. Doodles, spurned, had made slurring remarks about Hadley, saying she had flirted with Don Wright. (Wright, spitefully, had told Doodles this.) Hemingway, assured by Hadley that no such thing had taken place, threatened to beat up on Wright, but Hadley had persuaded him not to. So, at least, one version of the break has it. The friendship with Y.K. definitely ended when Hemingway wrote to tell him that he and Doodles would not be welcome at his parents' twenty-fifth wedding anniversary party on October 1 even though the Hemingways had sent them an invitation. Ernest said he would pick up the remainder of his belongings at the flat, including his "probably well-thumbed correspondence." Y.K. answered that Hemingway's belongings were in the storeroom. The janitress had the key: "You can readily understand that your having written me as you have makes your presence in my house quite impossible, at any time, under any circumstances."

The break with Y.K. was one more manifestation of Hemingway's break with his past. But despite the frailty and perverseness of human relationships, the people of his past had been preserved, recorded in the wedding photographs that Clarence and others had taken. They stand there, figures in the glancing light of a September afternoon: the bride in her lacy wedding dress, her veil crowned with flowers; the groom in white trousers and dark jacket; Mother Grace, dimpled and beaming in a sprigged tunic; Clarence in his rumpled linen suit and wing collar, posed in profile. Leicester, pouting, stares at the camera. They are figures in a rural wedding, frozen in a moment, or moments, of time in the late summer of 1921. The male friends of the groom are posed, arms linked, in a chorus line of bright smiles and white flannel trousers. Bill Smith and Charlie Hopkins, Carl Edgar and Howell Jenkins and Bill Horne: the representatives of Hemingway's gregarious past. They had shared Hemingway's experiences: the fishing expeditions on the Black and the Sturgeon, the stint on the *Kansas City Star,* the ambulance service in Italy. They had borne witness to the unhappy affair with Agnes. And now they had come together to witness the first marriage in their crowd. The photographs commemorate the end of the little society of friends that had centered around Ernest Hemingway.

Time would darken the friendships, bleach the photographs. But the past would have an indelible life in Hemingway's prose.

BOOK

TWO

A Lost Generation

6

The Mecca of Bluffers and Fakers

A cold ocean lay between him and the past. In Paris, where they arrived in late December, the winter weather was wet, bone-chilling. They put up in the Hôtel Jacob on the Left Bank, which Sherwood Anderson had recommended. It was clean and cheap. They discovered the local cafés: the Rotonde, which was in the process of being redecorated, and the Dôme, where they could warm themselves, drinking hot rum punches, sitting close to the charcoal braziers. (The drinks, Hemingway claimed, entered you like the Holy Spirit.) They found an inexpensive restaurant, Le Pré aux Clercs, at the corner of the rue Bonaparte and the rue Jacob, serving decent wines and a meal for two costing about 12 francs — about a dollar. "Paris is cold and damp but crowded, jolly and beautiful," Hemingway wrote Howell Jenkins. He and Hadley took long walks through the city. At night, walking home, he thought how, centuries before, wolves would slink into Paris after dark. And he thought about François Villon, the streetwise poet of the Middle Ages, and of the gallows at Montfaucon. "What a town," he told Anderson.

Sherwood's friend Lewis Galantière contacted the Hemingways right away. Twenty-six, a former Chicagoan, Galantière was bright, witty, and, for an American, very well informed about French culture (he was translating some of Anderson's stories for French publication). In short, Galantière was a good person to know. He promptly invited the Hemingways to have dinner with him and his girlfriend, Dorothy Butler, at Michaud's, where James Joyce regularly dined. The report in Paris, so Hemingway wrote Anderson, was that Joyce and all his family were starving, "but you can find the whole celtic crew of them every night in Michaud's." He and Hadley could barely afford to dine there once a week, he complained.

At dinner, Hemingway, taking the offensive in a new male relationship, talked up boxing, then insisted that Galantière come back to the hotel for a round or two of sparring. After a spate of vigorous shadowboxing, when Galantière's guard was down, Hemingway suddenly lunged forward, delivering a punch to the face that broke Galantière's glasses. Fortunately, Galantière escaped any cuts, but it made for an awkward end to the evening.

Both Hemingway and Hadley were homesick. Hemingway, keeping up his contacts with male friends, wrote several letters to Bill Smith and worried when he received no replies. He wrote Smith about their brief stopover at Vigo on the coast of Spain, described the landlocked harbor — "about as long as little Traverse Bay" — and the fleet of tuna-fishing boats and the big brown mountains behind. "That's the place for a male," he said. At Vigo, the water was green and the beaches were sandy. He planned to go back there someday. He wrote Anderson about the rattling train ride to Paris through Normandy, past long fields and smoking manure piles and bare pleached trees. He wrote Howell Jenkins that he had bought himself a new tailored suit of Irish homespun, with slacks and knickers, for 700 francs. He and Hadley were having a priceless time and he was working like hell. "Written a chunk of my novel and several articles."

Galantière, an accommodating friend, found them an inexpensive apartment at 74 rue du Cardinal-Lemoine. It was in a run-down working-class district, on the Left Bank, near the place de la Contrescarpe. In ancient times it had been the haunt of Villon and Rabelais. Hemingway told Jenks, with considerable exaggeration, that the apartment was "a high grade place." (Thirty years later, he would describe the neighborhood in grubby detail, thereby embellishing the legend of the poor but loving honeymoon couple starting out in Paris.)

Before they settled into housekeeping in their cramped apartment, they decided, despite the cost, to take a real honeymoon. They wanted to get away from the rain and dampness, the closed shop doors and wet-black streets of Paris. Even though the exchange rates were better in France and in the Austrian Tyrol, they went to Switzerland. The Swiss towns that were so popular before the war, Hemingway claimed in an article for the Toronto Daily Star, now looked like "the deserted boomtowns of Nevada." Early in his career, Hemingway realized that in journalism it was possible to suggest a greater degree of knowledgeability than one actually possessed; he had never seen the deserted mining towns of Nevada.

The chalet where they stayed in Chamby-sur-Montreux was comfortable and neat. Hemingway remembered the snow falling soundlessly through the spiky pines and, in the cold silence of the night, the sound of the snow crunching beneath their boots as they trudged home. They had books for reading and, warm in bed, they looked out through the opened windows at skies full of bright stars. He and Hadley had been much in love, then, in the mountains. So, at least, he would remember it.

When they returned to Paris, he rented a room in a hotel where he could work in peace. Hemingway gave out the romantic story that it was the hotel in which Verlaine had died, though this was not the case. (Whether it was a local legend he chose to believe or sheer invention on his part is not clear.) His room was on the top floor, up steep flights of stairs. It had a small fireplace and a view that looked out over the rooftops of Paris. It was, he claimed, in this hotel room, or in a warm café when it was too cold in his room, that he began his real vocation, writing in his cheap blue copybooks poems, stories about Michigan and Bill Smith and fishing and the people of Horton Bay. The weather of Paris, he said, settled into the stories. If he was *writing about himself and Bill up in Michigan, and the weather outside the café was wild, cold, blowing, that was how it would be in his story. When he finished his writing stint for the day, he walked slowly back up to his flat and Hadley. The gray rain of Paris then was no longer the rain of his stories. It had become "only local weather and not something that changed your life."*

Nothing in Ernest Hemingway's life, before or after, would match the importance of the years that were centered in Paris. It would not be too much to say that Paris changed Hemingway's life as a writer — for better and worse, and significantly in both cases. A writer's truths may be provisional truths, more exhilarating than the actuality. It was in Paris, as a young man, that Hemingway became the master of that conjunction of the real and the fictive that marked his work. Years later, writing as an "old newsman," he would make a clever distinction between truth and mere fact. "All good books are alike," he said, "in that they are truer than if they had really happened." When you finished reading a good book, he said, you felt that it had all happened to you: "the good and the bad, the ecstasy, the remorse and sorrow, the people and the places and how the weather was." Many a good writer would see through that useful deception and pass on; but no great writer could survive without wanting to believe it.

II

Early in February, the Hemingways sent out Sherwood Anderson's letter of introduction to Gertrude Stein and received a prompt invitation to pay a visit to the studio at 27 rue de Fleurus, where Stein lived with her companion, Alice B. Toklas. "Will you and Mr. Hemingway come to tea with us Wednesday, the eighth," Stein wrote. "I do like Anderson so much and I would like to meet his friends." Hadley readily accepted: she and Hemingway were delighted and would come on the following day. "Sherwood has told us so many nice things that we are glad to come right away to see you." The Wednesday teatime visit, on February 8 — earlier than the March date that biographers have previously supposed — was the beginning of a complex relationship between Hemingway and the forty-eight-year-old expatriate. Her Left Bank salon had witnessed two distinct phases of the twentieth-century avant-garde revolution. First it was a virtual private museum of modern art, harboring the works of the Postimpressionist painters Cézanne, Renoir, Bonnard, and ending with the Fauvist and Cubist painters Matisse, Picasso, and Juan Gris. And second, it had become a station stop for visiting American writers, editors, and composers — Anderson, Carl Van Vechten, Robert McAlmon, William Carlos Williams, Djuna Barnes, Virgil Thomson, Paul Bowles — the famous, the passing famous, the later neglected figures of the age.

Hemingway's account of his visits to the rue de Fleurus in *A Moveable Feast,* written with the residual bitterness of the quarrels of thirty years past, nevertheless conveys the charm of the atmosphere — the high-ceilinged studio with its brusque Picasso nudes and Cubist landscapes, the idyllic Cézanne bathers. "It was like one of the best rooms in the finest museum except there was a big fireplace and it was warm and comfortable and they gave you good things to eat and tea and natural distilled liqueurs made from purple plums, yellow plums or wild raspberries." He remembered, mostly, the great pictures and the conversation.

The paintings were more than a collection, they were a history of modern art. A magisterial portrait of Madame Cézanne provided a balance with Picasso's celebrated portrait of Stein herself. Painted within two decades of each other, the two pictures marked the division between the old master of the preceding age and the new master of the Cubist style, bridging the years between. The Picasso portrait, with its earthy colors, its masklike face and solemn features (after many sittings, Picasso, dissatisfied with the likeness, painted it over without the sitter), became an icon of the modernist school.

On that first visit to the studio, Hemingway was struck with Stein's appearance — short, sturdy, and big-breasted. (He estimated, so he told Hadley, that Stein's breasts must have weighed ten pounds apiece.) Stein had "beautiful eyes and a strong German-Jewish face." She reminded him, he said, of some northern Italian peasant woman because of her "clothes, her mobile face and her lovely, thick, alive immigrant hair." In conversation, Stein talked and talked, mostly about people and places.

While Stein and Hemingway talked by the fire, Hadley tried, unsuccessfully, to listen from the corner, where she sat with Alice Toklas; she admitted, however, that she was "petrified" by Gertrude's presence. It was the practice at the Stein salon that wives were delegated to Alice Toklas, tiny, with a pleasant voice, and, on her upper lip, the trace of a mustache that would grow more noticeable with age. With company, Alice sat at her appointed place near the front of the studio, unobtrusive but controlling, working her needlepoint, attending to the tea, conversing with the wives and women guests about domestic matters or current affairs. But her presence carried weight; she was the iron armature that structured every occasion at the rue de Fleurus. Hemingway thought there was something frightening about her — or, at least, claimed that he had felt it from the beginning. From long practice, Alice "made one conversation and listened to two and often interrupted the one she was not making." Hemingway, for months — and Hadley, for years — would address Alice as Miss Tocraz when they wrote to her.

Sherwood Anderson's enthusiastic introductory letter — "Mr. Hemingway is an American writer instinctively in touch with everything worthwhile going on here" — was an example of his generosity, since Hemingway, except for his journalism, was a largely unpublished American writer. But it had broken the ground for a headlong friendship between Gertrude Stein and the youthful writer. On March 9, a month after their first meeting, Hemingway wrote Anderson, "Gertrude Stein and me are just like brothers and we see a lot of her." There had been, in their early discussions, some talk about Stein's vanguard rival, James Joyce, and his alleged poverty. Stein claimed that Joyce reminded her of an old woman she had known in San Francisco, whose son had struck it rich in the Klondike but who went around wringing her hands, crying, "Oh! my poor Joey! My poor Joey! He's got so much money!" Hemingway relayed the story to Anderson, commenting, "The damned Irish, they have to moan about something or other, but you never heard of an Irishman starving." Nevertheless, he told Anderson that Joyce's *Ulysses*, just published in Paris, was "a most god-damn wonderful book!" He added that he had, himself, been writing some pretty good poems in rhyme lately. He ended the letter with "We love Gertrude Stein." Stein, writing to Anderson, was equally taken with the Hemingways: "They are charming. He is a delightful fellow and I like his talk." As a practical economy, she was teaching Hemingway to cut his wife's hair. "We have had a good time with them and hope to see more of them."

⁂

Gertrude Stein was old enough to be Hemingway's mother, just a year and four months younger than Grace Hemingway. The relationship that developed between the two in those early years of friendship might have passed for that of a son and a proud and approving mother. But it was more than that. Stein found Hemingway an extraordinarily handsome man, "rather foreign looking, with passionately interested, rather than interesting eyes." Where Grace Hemingway was suspicious and disapproving of her son for taking advantage of his looks, Stein found him all the more attractive. She was flattered by Hemingway's attentiveness and encouraged their relationship. Whether by accident or design, when Hemingway finished his writing stint for the day, he often met Stein in the Luxembourg Gardens, one of her favorite afternoon walks. He was invited to the studio to continue their talks and soon was told to call at the rue de Fleurus whenever he was in the neighborhood. But more than that, their relationship was based on a mutual interest in the writer's craft, the French sense of *métier,* a dedication to the practice of one's trade. It was a concept Stein had adopted and one that Hemingway took up, as well.

It is clear that Stein had discussed her indebtedness to Cézanne with Hemingway. It had been under the *Portrait of Madame Cézanne,* Stein claimed, and directly under the influence of Cézanne's method, with its infinitely patient repetition of one stroke laid next to another, that she had written her early prose masterpiece *Three Lives,* a sequence of portraits of commonplace women — two German immigrants and a young black girl, Melanctha Herbert — rendered in a bluntly realistic, declarative style, one sentence upon another, in controlled repetitions. Stein had her theories: "A sentence is not emotional a paragraph is," she declared. What she had discovered in Cézanne's method, early in her career, was the sense of overall composition in which each part, each sentence, was as significant as any other part, a composition in which nothing seemed to happen, but one which, through reiterative phrases and shifting emphases, moved forward to the culminating paragraph. It was out of this patient bricklaying method that she evoked the portraits of the women in *Three Lives,* just as, she felt, Cézanne had evoked the stolid figure of his wife from the carefully repeated strokes of his brush. Published in 1909 at Stein's expense, *Three Lives* was to have, for years, an underground reputation among serious writers.

In the rue de Fleurus studio, Hemingway had carefully studied the portrait of Madame Cézanne and the little Cézanne bathers as well. The painter and his method would become a familiar topic in Hemingway's writing. He would claim Cézanne as one of his tutelary heroes, an inspiration for his own literary style. "He wanted to write like Cézanne painted," Hemingway's Nick Adams ruminates in a deleted segment of "Big Two-Hearted River," one in which Hemingway acknowledged the influence of Stein's Cézannes: "Cézanne started with all the tricks. Then he broke the whole thing down and built the real thing. It was hell to do. . . . He, Nick, wanted to write about country so it would be there like Cézanne had done it in painting. . . . He felt almost holy about it."

In Paris, Hemingway's quest was for a simple and direct style, a search for what he called the "one true sentence." More than a year after meeting Stein, he would write the critic Edmund Wilson, extolling Stein's method as "invaluable for analysing anything or making notes on a person or a place. She has a wonderful head." He told Wilson that he would like to review one of Stein's old books, probably meaning *Three Lives.*

Stein was a mother figure whom Hemingway could approve. Well acquainted with the expatriate literary life of Paris, she championed the sense of freedom the city provided. It was not what Paris gave you, she once claimed, but what it did not take away. She was not bogged down in the social pieties that ruled Oak Park. Like any serious writer, like Hemingway, she was fond of gossip and intrigue. Then, too, she was an old soldier of sorts. From 1917 until the Armistice, Stein and Toklas, an unlikely pair of ministering angels in their gotten-up uniforms, had worked for the American Fund for the French Wounded, rumbling along the roads of France in a converted Ford van, distributing hospital supplies. In their travels, they adopted the dozens of French and American doughboys they met as their military godsons. "Soldiers like a fuss," Stein wrote in one of her wartime poems. "Give them their way."

The line was from "Work Again," one of the poems shortly to be published in her volume *Geography and Plays*. Sherwood Anderson wrote a preface for the book, which, coincidentally, had arrived at about the time of Hemingway's first meeting with Stein. Anderson applauded Stein's style as a brave attempt at refreshing the language. With his usual hyperbole, he saw Stein's work as "a rebuilding, an entire new recasting of life in the city of words." Hemingway, having read the preface, wrote Anderson that he had liked it very much, adding, "It made a big hit with Gertrude." It may have been more than gratuitous praise. Hemingway would later endorse Stein's doctrine of the rehabilitation of the language as one of his own aims as a writer. In *Death in the Afternoon,* he tells the old lady who serves as the straight man for his monologues, "Madame, all our words from loose using have lost their edge."

Stein encouraged Hemingway's interest in contemporary painters: Picasso, obviously, and Juan Gris, for whom she felt a special affection — artists whom Hemingway later acknowledged as the great painters of his Paris years. She even suggested that he become an art collector himself. Hemingway said he would never have money enough to buy a Picasso, and Stein agreed. But she advised him to concentrate on the serious artists of his own age. At the time, she was interested in a young Frenchman, André Masson, then painting in a late variation of the Cubist style. Stein was impressed with Masson's mastery of white, a difficult color, and with what she termed the "wandering line" of his compositions. When, however, Masson later fell under the sway of the Surrealists, Stein's interest faded. She considered the Surrealists "vulgarizers" who mistook "the manner for the matter." Hemingway would also develop an antipathy to the Surrealists in an even more virulent form. But, during that first year and a half in Paris, he struck up a friendship with Masson and, in time, acquired one or more of his paintings and drawings. Hadley claimed that in those early years, Hemingway had been "profoundly occupied" with the theories of Stein and Ezra Pound, and that Masson's paintings had been important for him. "Everything was grist to a superfine powerful mill," she acknowledged, but added that Hemingway was "much too strong in his own right" to be "permanently influenced" by anyone.

///

One evening, Stein and Toklas paid a visit to the Hemingway apartment on the rue du Cardinal-Lemoine. Hemingway, as Stein recalled it, brought out all the writing he had done thus far. She liked the short poems he had been writing for some time, finding them "direct, Kiplingesque." She was less interested in the "inevitable" novel that he had begun. There was too much description in it, she told him: "Begin over again and concentrate." In Hemingway's account of the session, Stein balked when she read "Up in Michigan," with its graphic seduction scene. Stein admitted it was a good story but said it was "*inaccrochable,*" meaning its sexual explicitness would make it impossible to publish. She told him there was no point in doing it: "It's wrong and it's silly." Hemingway had definitely rewritten the story in Paris, and it is possible that the version with his rue du Cardinal-Lemoine address is the one that he showed Stein. If so, the apparently earlier versions of the typescript might indicate that Hemingway had, on his own, arrived at the use of repetition ("She liked it about his mustache. She liked it about how white his teeth were when he smiled") that critics have attributed to Stein's influence. But certainly her method confirmed and gave authority to what had been a tendency in his style.

Even late in life, Hemingway acknowledged the impact of Stein's method: "She had . . . discovered many truths about rhythms and the uses of words in repetition that were valid and valuable and she talked well about them." And certainly, in the early years of their friendship, he was as convinced an advocate as Gertrude Stein might wish for. In his boyish enthusiasm, he could write Bill Smith, "She's the best head I know. Never wrong. Geest she can pick them — painters, etc., when nobody can see it. Never picked a loser. . . . She's sure given me straight dope. . . . She's trying to get at the mechanics of language. Take it apart and see what makes it go. . . . But she aint no fool."

In that first rush of friendship, Hemingway and Stein had, as he wrote Anderson, gotten on like brothers. Stein, perhaps wanting to repeat one of her excursions with her military godsons, found a perfect occasion. In late March, when the countryside was pushing into leaf and the orchards were just budding, the "Steins," as Hemingway referred to Gertrude and Alice, and the Hemingways traveled out to Meaux in Gertrude's Ford runabout, nicknamed Godiva. The plan was to pay a visit to Stein's old friend Mildred Aldrich, an American writer and critic in her late sixties. Aldrich had lived through the early battles of World War I and had given a stirring account of her experiences in her books *A Hilltop on the Marne* and *On the Edge of the War Zone.* Her home, La Creste, near the village of Huiry, commanded a fine view of the countryside. In the first September of the war, Aldrich had stood her ground and, from her garden, witnessed the German bombardments of the farming villages to the north. Stout, white-haired, and doughty, she was one of the feckless older women for whom Hemingway had a ready affection.

Writing to Howell Jenkins, Hemingway described Aldrich as "a fine old femme." He reported with genuine enthusiasm, "We saw the woods where the Uhlans were in 1914 and bridges the English blew up and the whole thing. . . . Aldrich was there during the battle and she told us all about it." It was an occasion for some heady drinking. At lunch on the way to Huiry, he had "morted a fiasco of wine," he confessed to Jenkins, and he had had a good cup of three-star Hennessey before making the return trip. Aldrich, writing to Stein after the visit, commented on the brisk weather. "I am hoping that you didn't quite freeze before you got to your 'ain fireside.'" Tactfully, she added, "I hope Mr. Hemingway didn't fall off."

III

It was not long after their return to Paris that the Hemingways were invited to tea at Ezra Pound's apartment at 70 bis Notre-Dame-des-Champs. The studio room was cold, with a disorderly clutter of books, manuscripts, Japanese prints, modern sculptures, and the paintings of Wyndham Lewis and Pound's wife, Dorothy Shakespear, arranged haphazardly along room-length shelves. Pound, a rabid conversationalist, lounged in one of his homemade boxwood chairs, consuming endless cups of tea. Hadley thought him cantankerous and not too lovable. She preferred Dorothy Pound and her refined English manners. What surprised Hadley on that first meeting was the unlikeliness of Hemingway's seeming so deferential, sitting rapt at Pound's feet and listening as if he were in the presence of an oracle.

Lewis Galantière, however, recalled that Hemingway had been decidedly put off by Pound's bohemian appearance and his pontificating style. In fact, he claimed that Hemingway had shown him a bitter satirical portrait of the poet, which he planned to give to Margaret Anderson and Jane Heap, the editors of *The Little Review,* with whom Hemingway had just been talking. Since Pound was one of the stalwarts of the magazine at the time, it was unlikely that the editors would have published it. Galantière convinced Hemingway that it was the wrong thing to do and, according to him, Hemingway tore it up. The fact that Margaret Anderson and Jane Heap did not settle in Paris until the following year casts some doubt on an otherwise lively story.

⁂

"One has to keep going east to keep one's mind alive." That was Ezra Pound's explanation for his troubadour existence. In 1908, at the age of twenty-two, Pound had quit America, dissatisfied with what he called, in his cranky phonetic style, the "enfeebled or adolescent Amurkn mind." For twelve years, with occasional trips home, he lived in England. There, he was befriended by Ford Madox Hueffer (before he changed his last name to Ford), the editor of *The English Review;* served as secretary for the Irish poet William Butler Yeats; and had some essential but random encounters with the most eminent of the old guard American exiles, Henry James. He and James, so Pound wrote his parents, had "glared at one another across the same carpet." In one of Pound's early poems, "Moeurs contemporaines," James would serve as the admired relic of an age of civility: "They will come no more, / The old men with beautiful manners."

Among his contemporaries, Pound developed a long-term but testy friendship with the sharp-tongued Wyndham Lewis, writer, artist, editor of the short-lived magazine *Blast.* Pound could be as abrasive as Lewis and as opinionated as any of the displaced American writers abroad. ("Mistrust any poet using the word *cosmic.*") But he was generous to a fault in promoting the work of his compatriots. He did what he could to further the careers of T. S. Eliot and the "Vurry Amur'k'n" Robert Frost, who were trying to make reputations for themselves in London. Pound was the bohemian poet par excellence. Of medium height, with a mane of sandy reddish hair and a sharply pointed Mephistophelian beard, he was a familiar figure at the Vienna Cafe near the British Museum and the Eiffel Tower restaurant on Percy Street. He dressed his part, slightly unkempt, wearing a wide collar and flowing necktie, a single earring, corduroy jacket, and green trousers. In London, he had published several volumes of poetry in the early years of exile (*A lume spento, Personae, Canzoni, Ripostes*). It was one more of his grievances against his native land that he had made his reputation in London before receiving recognition in New York. An indefatigable literary modernist, he was a founding father of the Imagist school of poets. (According to one legend, Pound, addicted to the English custom of afternoon tea, invented Imagism in a Kensington bun shop.) He and Amy Lowell — "the only hippopoetess in our zoo" — were the leading exponents of the school until they quarreled over questions of orthodoxy and rank. He had little patience with female writers; nonetheless he made a distinct impression on wealthy, unmarried women eager to serve as patronesses of the arts. He was a literary scout for and contributor to Harriet Monroe's *Poetry* and Harriet Weaver's *The Egoist.* (Miss Monroe, he said, had "the swirl of the prairie wind in her underwear." Harriet Weaver was Joyce's secret patron during the writing of *Ulysses.*)

By December 1920, Pound had decided it was useless to try to drive "any new idea into the great passive vulva of London." Pound believed in the primordial notion that the creative and procreative functions were intimately linked and were largely the prerogative of the male. The brain, he surmised, was a "sort of great clot of genital fluid held in suspense or reserve." (He may well have engendered a similar notion in Hemingway.) Accordingly, he next settled in Paris, where he continued his charitable efforts, editing and promoting Eliot's seminal poem *The Waste Land* and sponsoring a fund for getting the poet out of his time-consuming post in Lloyd's Bank. For a brief period, Pound served as the Paris correspondent for *The Dial,* writing book reviews, prose and poetry, monthly chronicles. He was not overly impressed with the French capital. ("The literary life of Paris is insular. They know even less of the outer world than do the elder generation of English, though not less perhaps than the Georgians.") In Paris he wrote, sculpted, and worked at an opera based on François Villon's *The Testament,* with needed counsel from a young American pianist and composer, George Antheil, whom he immediately began publicizing. In his energetic way, he readily established himself as one of the movers and shakers of the avant-garde in the American colony of expatriates.

In Paris, Pound clearly represented a challenge to Gertrude Stein's authority on the scene, which probably accounted for the mutual lack of enthusiasm they felt for each other. For her part, Stein was put off by Pound's pedagogical manner. She considered him a "village explainer." Consequently, she and Pound saw little of each other. Scofield Thayer, the acerbic coeditor of *The Dial,* had witnessed the two together when he arrived in Paris in midsummer

1921, on his way to a course of treatment under Dr. Freud. Pound and he paid a visit to the rue de Fleurus. Thayer immediately sensed the rivalry between the two American vanguardists. Stein, whom Thayer described as having "the homely finish of a brown buckram bean-bag," had decided to outshine Pound in an argument. Thayer observed, "In conversation, she put it all over Ezra, who got back by saying all sorts of things on the way home." The legendary explanation of their rift, however, was that Pound, in the course of his argument, sat down too emphatically in one of Stein's favorite armchairs and tipped over backward, breaking it. It was not an unusual occurrence, since Pound had an ironclad reputation for clumsiness, forever dropping his cane or treading on toes, both literally and literarily. Thayer acknowledged the poet's special talent for disruption. Pound, he said, was "so awkward as unintentionally to knock over a waiter and then so self-conscious as to be unable to say he is sorry."

Fisticuffs and fiction writing did not necessarily go hand in glove with Hemingway, but when he spotted real competition, whether physical or literary, he was ready to get in the ring and prove himself the better man. Probably at Pound's request, Hemingway was soon giving the poet boxing lessons. Wyndham Lewis happened into one of the practice sessions in Pound's studio and caught sight of Pound flailing away in his attempts to land a punch at "a splendidly built young man, stripped to the waist," who was effortlessly parrying every one of Pound's hectic blows. After a final swing, the exhausted Pound fell back on his settee. Hemingway, however, would later claim that Lewis had deliberately encouraged Pound to keep fighting in the mean hope of seeing Ezra flattened. Pound was no boxer, Hemingway informed Sherwood Anderson; he led with his chin and had the general grace of a crayfish. But it was "pretty sporting of him to risk his dignity and his critical reputation" at something he knew nothing about. Hemingway concluded, "He's really a good guy, Pound, with a fine bitter tongue onto him."

⁂

Ezra Pound was thirty-six when he met Ernest Hemingway — too young, obviously, to be Hemingway's surrogate father but old enough to register the younger man among his many protégés. Despite her own reservations, Hadley was convinced, then and later, that Pound's talk had had a distinct effect on Hemingway. "I believe some of the ideas lasted all his life," she said. She was also astonished and pleased when Pound demonstrated his interest by promoting Hemingway's writing with his editor friends. As she reported to her mother-in-law, "Ezra Pound sent a number of Ernest's poems to Thayer of the 'Dial' and has taken a little prose thing of his for the 'Little Review' also asked him to write a series of articles for the 'Dial' on American magazines. . . . It is all surely most flattering." Like many an older man, Pound was struck by Hemingway's youthful charisma. His first impressions are given in his letter to Scofield Thayer, submitting Hemingway's poems:

> the chap seems to have his head screwed on straight; he arrived here with introd from Sherwood Anderson; has read serious works, and is allowing himself five years for his first novel. I think, as you know, that the Dial shd occasionally take in a little new blood, and H. seems to me as sound a chance as is likely to offer. He is discontented with the softness of some of the local stars.

Thayer turned down the poems; he was of the opinion that *The Dial* had "enough young blood already to make it decidedly rough reading." (He was, as well, dissatisfied with Pound and his "silly cantos" and was planning to sack him as the Paris correspondent.)

It had long been Pound's intention to write an epic poem, a "poem including history." By the time Hemingway met him, he had begun his lifetime work, the *Cantos,* an extraordinary, mind-cluttered epic that in its progress through the years became a swollen river, pulling down from its banks and into its mainstream every evidence of Pound's reading and ruminative thought — Greek myths, the songs of the Provençal troubadours, the analects of Confucius (Dorothy Pound calligraphed the Chinese ideograms); episodes from his peripatetic life — bits of remembered conversation, descriptions from his travels, vivid snapshots from his personal memories; a hortatory flood of prejudices, political animadversions, and crank economics based on the theories of Major C. H. Douglas, founder of the Social Credit Movement, which attributed the world's ills to the hoarding of capital by the few (the principal villains being the banks and "international Jewry"), providing Pound with a long-term metaphor: usury. Time was the modus operandi for this lifelong poem. The *Cantos* flowed on, muddied by erudition, foreign phrases, sweet lyrical passages followed by anti-Semitic diatribes, an open-ended journey through time and one man's mind, moving always toward unforeseeable conclusions. It was also a poetic diary, an often perverse intellectual chronicle of the life and crimes of the twentieth century and a testimony to Pound's belief in Machiavelli's observation, "Mankind lives in the few."

There is no doubt that Hemingway was impressed with Pound's credentials as a poet, and he would speak highly of them throughout much of his life. Early on in their relationship, he paid Pound the tribute of "borrowing" — or, in his competitive vein, improving upon — a stanza from Pound's "Hugh Selwyn Mauberley":

> The "age demanded" chiefly a mould in plaster,
> Made with no loss of time,
> A prose kinema, not, not assuredly, alabaster
> Or the "sculpture" of rhyme.

In double-edged fashion, Hemingway honored and updated Pound's Edwardian example in his "The Age Demanded," a 1922 poem later published in the German magazine *Der Querschnitt* (*The Cross Section*). He challenged Pound's stilted phrases with gutsier language:

> The age demanded that we sing
> and cut away our tongue.
> The age demanded that we flow
> and hammered in the bung.
> The age demanded that we dance
> and jammed us into iron pants.
> And in the end the age was handed
> the sort of shit that it demanded.

Hemingway was at a critical and impressionable stage in his career, and Pound was a valuable fund of information and literary lore. Pound's outspoken views on the American university system, "which aims at filling the student's head full of facts to paralyze him with data instead of developing his perspicacity," probably appealed to Hemingway, who had skipped college and whose suspicions of academics ripened with age. Pound's feelings that women and wives represented a threat to the writing male would be sympathetically echoed in Hemingway's views. Moreover, in his personal letters, Pound was masculine, bawdy, and blunt. (Writing to his old friend and confidant William Carlos Williams, for instance, Pound suggested that he and Williams were the "two halves of what might have made a fairly decent poet," except that they were separated by the "——— buttocks of the arse-wide Atlantic Ocean.") Both he and Hemingway were to have reputations for daring publishers with four-letter words and obscenities.

Politics and economics were the subjects on which Hemingway and Pound parted company. Pound, when Hemingway met him, was in the habit of writing scolding letters of advice on political and economic matters to the leaders of the world, including presidents, prime ministers, and politicians of every persuasion. In his letters to

Hemingway he attempted to proselytize by way of his diatribes on "sodomitical usurers" and the "buggaring money" the banks were garnering at the expense of mankind. (Sexual perversion and usury were analogous tropes in the *Cantos.*) In his letters, Hemingway rather promptly began pandering to Pound's anti-Semitism, referring, for instance, to an acquaintance as a "Celto-Kike," or a young woman as a "19 year old Bloomsbury kike intellectual," but he was never, for a moment, swayed by Pound's politics or his economic theories. Pound considered it a flaw of Hemingway's fiction that he never dealt seriously with the economic factor.

Hemingway could be ambivalent, both generous and yet wary of crediting too much to Pound's influence on his writing. It depended on the impression he wanted to make with a particular correspondent. In a letter to the critic and biographer Charles Fenton, Hemingway asserted that Pound had seen only a half dozen things that he had written, a plausible disclaimer. The initial phase of his friendship with Pound in Paris must have been brief: Pound left for Italy on March 27, 1922, and for much of the year Hemingway was away from Paris on newspaper assignments or on trips with Hadley and friends. He and Pound were both in Paris during part of June and July and later in the fall, when Hemingway returned from an assignment in Constantinople. For a brief time in 1923, the Hemingways and the Pounds were together in Rapallo. And in 1924, Pound was again in Paris before leaving permanently for Italy.

For much of their lives, in fact, the relationship was kept alive by way of their feisty correspondence. In public print and in private letters, Hemingway several times acknowledged that Pound had taught him a great deal about prose writing, had taught him, for instance, to "distrust adjectives," or flatteringly told Pound that he had "learned more about how to write and how not to write from you than from any son of a bitch alive and have always said so." Hemingway's admiration for Pound the writer was largely based on the cantos, and chiefly those that had not been warped by Pound's economic propaganda. He had serious reservations: "There is also several stale jokes and quite a lot of crap in the Cantos," he said, "but there is some Christwonderful poetry that no one can better." What Hemingway balked at, particularly as he developed his own declarative, uncluttered style, was Pound's display of pedantry. "Erudition shouldn't show" was Hemingway's doctrine; the writer should know everything he needed to know, but he shouldn't use it. "Ezra," he said, "can't leave any erudition true or false out of a poem."

As for Pound, he promoted Hemingway with editors and publishers, praised his work in early letters, but oddly, he said little of it in print in the form of reviews. As Hemingway became more successful, Pound's commentaries became more critical. He later claimed that Hemingway had "sold himself to the god dollar." The most damaging charge was Pound's observation that Hemingway, as a man and, presumably, as a writer, "never knew one human being from another . . . and never much cared."

IV

Despite the fact that he had written Bill Smith several letters and received no reply, Hemingway was shocked when, late in February, he received a letter from Smith breaking off their friendship. Smith gave Hemingway's quarrel with his brother Y.K. as the root cause. Blood was thicker than water, he told Hemingway, adding that there had been profound and very unwelcome changes in Hemingway: "The 1922 Edition of E.M.H. is so radically different from earlier Editions . . . that I can only hope time will show equal changes in a reverse direction." He sent regards to Hash, nevertheless.

Hemingway vented his sorrow and anger — both genuine — in a letter to Howell Jenkins. The trouble, Hemingway claimed, was "the Madam," Aunty Charles, who had been "poisoning" Bill against him. He was tempted, he said, to tell Bill "to take his whole damned family and jam them as far as they will go up some elephant's fanny — but I'm still fond of him, so I'm making no answer." He was clearly grieved by Bill's letter. "Isn't that a goddam hell of a letter from a guy whose been like Smith and I have been?" He pictured himself as the injured party: "It's hell when a male knifes you — especially when you still love him."

Hemingway may or may not have answered Smith. Hadley tried to persuade him not to, but Hemingway's vendettas, once aroused, did not subside readily. Early in their relationship, Hadley noticed that Hemingway seldom gave up on his grudges: "Once he took a dislike to someone you could absolutely never get him back [to the person]." Hemingway did, however, write a bitter poem about the loss of his friendship:

> "Blood is thicker than water,"
> The young man said
> As he knifed his friend
> For a drooling old bitch
> And a house full of lies.

His anger at the Smiths one and all, however, was tempered by the fact that Katy Smith, to whom Hemingway had also written several times and who had not replied, was holding "about eight hundred dollars worth of wop drafts." It was the money he and Hadley had put aside for their Italian trip. Hemingway had asked Katy to forward them when he had a proper address in Paris. Now, he told Jenkins, he would be needing some of the money for a trip. (He had been assigned by the *Star* to cover the Genoa Economic Conference.) He feared that Katy might be "off" him as well, and he didn't want to risk writing her again. He asked Jenkins to look her up. He was "fonder of Stut than of Bill," he said, "but a man gets a little bit backed about pushing his mush in the dust after a certain length of time." He asked Jenkins to tell Katy, "I still feel the same as ever."

The loss of Bill Smith's friendship rankled and preoccupied Hemingway for several years. It was a loss that he felt more deeply than his estrangement from his family. It would cast a shadow over his work, especially the stories he wrote during his early years in Paris when he tried to recapture the special quality of his life in Michigan. In "The End of Something," "The Three-Day Blow," and "Big Two-Hearted River," for instance, Hemingway not only explored his relationship with Smith — sometimes affectionately, sometimes ambivalently — but he used it as counterpoint: the human adventure in contrast to the vast consoling indifference of nature. In those early stories, Hemingway recreated the life he had shared with Smith and Edgar, Hopkins and the "Ghee," on their fishing expeditions in the north. Ironically, it was in the midst of the expatriate colony of Paris that he created for himself a half-remembered, half-invented life of male companionship in the wild, a life free of the pieties, taboos, and inhibitions of Oak Park.

Y. K. Smith, remembering the "prehistoric" Hemingway of the Chicago period, would claim that in the early days, Hemingway had created a society of his own. It was a private club to which Hemingway admitted only a few members, while casting out those who failed to meet his standards. The true insider of the group, of course, was Hemingway himself; his attitude toward the subordinate members, Smith maintained, was one of "irony and ambivalence." Someone like Sherwood Anderson might be admitted out of Hemingway's need but was marked for eventual slaughter: Anderson's sin "was that of being larger than the founder of the club." Smith felt that eventually Hemingway came to despise several members of his crowd because they refused to live by the "gospel of hard work and worldly achievement" that he subscribed to. The more likely and more serious cause was that Hemingway felt a certain condescension toward those members of the happy few who had so readily allowed him to dominate them. The hero was also a hero worshiper: he seldom looked up to a man he could look down on.

For Bill Smith the break was a wrenching experience as well, one that he had delayed making. His relationship with Hemingway reached back to their adolescence and youth. Writing about Hemingway in an unpublished memoir, Smith remembered an expedition when he and Hemingway fished the Little Pigeon River while Edgar and Hopkins were working the Big Pigeon some distance away. The fishing was poor; the trout were not taking the bait or the flies. Hemingway, with a fisherman's instinct for seasons and causes, attributed it to the heavy rains the night before, which had roiled up the smaller streams and made them muddy. He persuaded the others, all older than he, to make the trek to the Indian River. It meant cutting across the rough terrain of the Pine Barrens, with the dark coming on and no one familiar with the trails. Bill objected, but Hemingway insisted that if they kept the wind on their right they would inevitably connect up with a road going north. It was heavy going, over twisting miles with heavy clouds and some rain, but they had made their way. Smith, trekking through the dark, was convinced that it was sheer guesswork on Hemingway's part. But when they made their destination, he had to admit he had been wrong. Hemingway's sense of direction, he said, was "almost instinctive." Hemingway, Bill claimed, was alert to every clue from nature. Like an Indian, he had a "hunter's eye."

Hemingway, too, had vivid memories of those gone days. Whatever his disappointment or resentment, he did not give them up easily. A vision of an Eden without an Eve haunted his early fiction. "All the love went into fishing and the summer," he would write in an elegiac segment of his story "Big Two-Hearted River," begun two years after his break with Bill. In a long, Steinian, autobiographical passage (deleted before the story was published), he remembered the summers with Bill Smith:

> He had loved it more than anything. He had loved digging potatoes with Bill in the fall, the long trips in the car, fishing in the bay, reading in the hammock on hot days, swimming off the dock, playing baseball at Charlevoix and Petoskey, living at the Bay, the Madame's cooking, the way she had with servants, eating in the dining room looking out the window across the long fields and the point to the lake, talking with her, drinking with Bill's old man, the fishing trips away from the farm, just lying around. He loved the long summer.

It seemed to be the nature of Hemingway's male relationships that they were with men for whom he had a charismatic presence. Despite his youth, he was — or appeared to be — more assured, bolder, than they. Often enough, his chosen friends were men who had some weakness in their character or felt some lack of self-worth or identity. There is ample evidence in Hemingway's correspondence with Bill Smith that Hemingway played the role of the more experienced and emotionally mature friend, a position that Smith, in his easygoing diffidence, accepted. Smith, it appears, had periods of self-doubt and depression in his early years. In their correspondence, Hemingway was always ready to give advice about work and about writing. He invariably counseled Smith on sexual matters. (As he grew older, Hemingway cast himself in the role of a master mechanic of sex.) J. C. Edgar — the Odgar — recalled that during the period of Hemingway's courtship and marriage or soon after, Smith had had a manic-depressive episode. The emotional disturbance quite probably had its bearing on Smith's break with Hemingway.

In Paris, isolated from his old friends, Hemingway began to question the failure of his old relationships, especially the loss of his friendship with Smith. Time and distance, perhaps, were also the causes that darkened the scattered keepsakes, like the photographs of the two of them, dressed in overalls and country caps, all smiles, standing on a rickety pier, holding up their catches, or Hemingway, all but nude in a jockstrap and comic hat, his leg bandaged from his war wounds, prancing on a lonely stretch of beach on a lake.

Hemingway, strangely, took credit for what had been important in their friendship. He said that Bill had never fished before they had met — an unlikely claim — implying that he had initiated Smith into the art. It was after that, Hemingway maintained, that the two had discovered all the rivers, the Black and the Sturgeon and the Upper Minnie. What is, perhaps, the most telling aspect of Hemingway's relationship with Bill Smith was that in his remembered idyll in "Big Two-Hearted River," he, consciously or unconsciously, cast Bill in an ambiguously feminine role: "Bill forgave him the fishing he had done before they met. He forgave him all the rivers. He was really proud of them. It was like a girl about other girls. If they were before they did not matter. But after was different."

He had lost them all, Hemingway ruminated fictionally: Bill Smith, Odgar, the Ghee — "all the old gang." In the persona of Nick Adams, Hemingway convinced himself that his marriage had made the difference. Marrying Hadley (Helen in the story) had been an admission that there was something more important than the camaraderie of the hunting and fishing trips with his old gang. It had cost him his friends. "Was it because they were virgins," Nick/Hemingway asks himself. "Helen thought it was because they didn't like her." Hadley, in a sarcastic moment, referred to Hemingway's meddlesome friends as a "heart-busted bunch."

V

"The scum of Greenwich Village, New York, has been skimmed off and deposited in large ladles on that section of Paris adjacent to the Café Rotonde," Hemingway claimed in one of his early articles for the *Toronto Star.* Where bohemianism was concerned, Hemingway was an Oak Park Savonarola — at least in public print. He pictured the Rotonde as a raucous birdhouse in a zoo, the chattering patrons in exotic plumage, the waiters rapidly working the tables "like so many black and white magpies." Hemingway assured his Canadian readers, "You can find anything you are looking for at the Rotonde — except serious artists." And he wrote in another of his derisive articles, "Paris is the Mecca of the bluffers and fakers in every line of endeavor from music to prizefighting."

The targets were easy. Hemingway had little difficulty in catering to philistine tastes, concentrating on the never-before-heard-of American dancers, the phony artists, the previously unknown prizefighters, whose reputations in Paris bloomed overnight and then faded away. He considered them the perfect illustration of the gullibility of the provincial Parisians. In his newspaper pieces, so he explained to Gertrude Stein, he was obliged to express what he called "the canadian viewpoint."

True enough: postwar Paris was crowded with expatriates who, by day, loafed in the cafés, and by night frequented such tourist traps as the Folies-Bergère, Maxim's, and the So-Different, confident that they were seeing the real Paris. Dissatisfied at home, escaping Prohibition, attracted by the exchange rates, young and restless Americans, after brief apprenticeships in Greenwich Village, joined the migration to the City of Light. Many were tourists looking for "a super-Sodom and a grander Gomorrah," as Hemingway claimed. Others hoped to write new scenarios for their lives, escaping the sexual taboos and the presumed cultural poverty of America, in order to accomplish something important — at least until the money ran out.

Hemingway's news stories were self-serving as well as entertaining. He established a voice for himself, avoiding the usual impersonality of the reporter. In the early phases of his professional career, he created a contrived journalistic identity, the man-of-the-world who knew the ropes and was privy to the stories behind the story. Even as a novice of a bare three weeks in Paris, he was advising his readers, "It is from tourists who stop at the large hotels that the reports come that living in Paris is very high. The big hotelkeepers charge all they think the traffic can bear." In his later career as a journalist, when he was "Papa," the international celebrity, he had a different persona, confidential, a man who felt no qualms about admitting to his fears and failures or naming his debts to older writers and editors, of whom he spoke gratefully. But that later persona, touching and intimate as it was, was a bit false, too.

Hemingway's Parisian reports had a clever malice that underscored his efforts to distance himself from the crowd of expatriates and tourists flocking to the gay life of the French capital. The man who dressed in sober Irish homespun ("Cook and Co . . . a famous London house. You know em of course") was not to be mistaken for the gaudily dressed patrons of the Rotonde. But Hemingway was doing something more than merely separating himself from his compatriots. His ambition, his need to coax a satisfactory identity out of his work, took root in his journalistic pieces. What he wanted to promote was the convincing image of the serious and hardworking author.

His diatribe against Greenwich Village types carried with it some of the residual fascination and distaste he felt for Greenwich Village and New York City during his brief stays in 1918 and 1919. In his early years abroad — and, in fact, for much of his life — Hemingway prided himself on "never having lived in New York any longer than was necessary to catch a boat." But the view of Paris — and its Greenwich Village exiles — which he tossed off for the readers of the *Toronto Star* was for public consumption. His more crafted observations were set down in a series of six one-sentence vignettes, titled "Paris, 1922." They had the visual impact of a few frames from a newsreel and were drawn from such recent experiences as his visits with Hadley to the racetracks at Auteuil and Enghien, a glimpse of an American entertainer in a popular and expensive night spot, and a scene from the May Day riots which he seems not to have actually witnessed but had read about in the Paris papers:

> I have seen the favourite crash into the Bulfinch and come down in a heap kicking while the rest of the field swooped over the jump . . . I have seen Peggy Joyce at 2 A.M. in a Dancing in the Rue Caumartin quarreling with a shellac haired young Chilean who had manicured fingernails, blew a puff of cigarette smoke into her face, wrote

> something in a notebook, and shot himself at 3:30 the same morning . . . I have watched the police charge the crowd with swords as they milled back into Paris through the Porte Maillot on the first of May and seen the frightened proud look on the white beaten-up face of the sixteen year old kid who looked like a prep school quarterback and had just shot two policemen.

The prose might have gained something from Stein's use of repetition; the concise imagery might have been prompted by Pound's Imagist practice, but the rapid-fire one-sentence accounts represented the true beginnings of the Hemingway style.

⁂

Examples of sobriety in expatriate Paris were admittedly few. Gertrude Stein and Alice Toklas avoided Parisian nightlife completely, having no taste for it. Another worthy example was Sylvia Beach, proprietor of Shakespeare and Company, the bookshop at 12 rue de l'Odéon, which Hemingway had ventured into not long after his arrival. Beach, a Presbyterian minister's daughter, lived quietly with a French companion, Adrienne Monnier, in Monnier's apartment, not far from the bookshop. The two women were dedicated to literature and to each other: "my sister born beyond the sea," Monnier wrote in a poem to Sylvia. "Behold my star has found your own." Except for physical appearance, their lives and careers were mirror images of one another. Monnier, plump, round-faced, outfitted in full cape and ankle-length dresses that gave her the appearance of a peasant *and* a nun, owned the Maison des Amis des Livres, across the street at 7 rue de l'Odéon. A writer and publisher as well as a bookseller, she spoke of her shop as "half convent and half farm." Since its beginnings in 1915, it had been the lively meeting place of such French writers as Apollinaire (then in uniform and recuperating from his war wound, complaining that there was no copy of *Alcools* on the shelves), Valéry, the Monsieur Teste of poetry, protesting that it was only by fluke that he was a poet, and André Gide, defending himself against Monnier's charge that *The Counterfeiters* revealed a coldness and fundamental unkindness in his nature. Erik Satie once gave a rare performance of his *Socrate* there, introduced by Jean Cocteau. Monnier admired Cocteau, but his prissy authority gave her migraines. She had the French gift for incisive observation; in the battle for modernism, she observed, Cocteau was never the first to mount the breach, "but it is always he that plants the flag."

Sylvia Beach, small, thin, self-effacing, usually garbed in a velvet smoking jacket and flowing tie, stocked her shelves with the works of English and American authors, both contemporaries and the famous dead, while their photographs punctuated the sackcloth-covered walls above. (The expatriate Americans Man Ray and his assistant, Berenice Abbott, were the official photographers for Shakespeare and Company.) When she first opened her shop at another location in 1917, Beach trafficked in Hardy, James, Yeats, and Conrad, promoted Emerson and Whitman. In the twenties, she backed the contemporary writers — Joyce, Eliot, Pound, and Anderson. (Anderson, on his first visit to Paris, was thrilled to see a copy of *Winesburg, Ohio* in the bookstore window.) The shop, with its lending library, its racks of English and American periodicals — *Poetry, The Dial, The Egoist, The Little Review* — became the club for visiting Americans and expatriate writers and a haven for Sorbonne students. Pound was often there, lounging full-length in a small, straight-backed chair, or Joyce, staring out implacably from behind thick lenses, clasping his ashplant cane in his long fingers.

When Hemingway first met Beach, she was in the throes of publishing the first edition of Joyce's *Ulysses,* garnering subscriptions for the publication, and Hemingway, like many of the regulars, pitched in and did his share. But he could hardly match the dedication of Robert McAlmon, the publisher of the Contact Editions of contemporary writers, who used the bookstore as a postal drop and warehouse for his stock of unsold books. McAlmon, freshly married to an English heiress, Winifred Ellerman, daughter of the millionaire shipping magnate John Ellerman, had been set up in business by the generosity of his father-in-law. McAlmon preferred the excitements of Paris; his understanding wife, who wrote under the pen name Bryher, preferred the company of Ezra Pound's former sweetheart, Hilda Doolittle (the poet H.D.), who was ensconced in Territet, Switzerland. McAlmon, equally understanding, made no objections. In Paris, with true noblesse oblige, he pushed the subscription sales of *Ulysses* in his nightly rounds of the bars.

Hemingway was charmed by Sylvia Beach. "Brown eyes that were as alive as a small animal's and as gay as a young girl's, and wavy brown hair that was brushed back from her fine forehead" — that was his remembered first impression. He was equally impressed with Shakespeare and Company: the cozy warmth of the big stove, the thoughtful photographs along the walls. "Even the dead writers looked as though they had really been alive," he said. He became one of the best customers of the lending library, taking out volumes of Turgenev, Lawrence, Dostoevsky, Tolstoy's *War and Peace.* He and Hadley were soon invited to dinner (Monnier was a notably good cook). Hemingway took the two women to the six-day bicycle races (one of his new enthusiasms) and to boxing matches, sporting events they had never witnessed before. Sylvia Beach's relationship with

Hemingway was never disturbed by quarrels; she remained a steadfast friend and admirer throughout his career. "No one that I ever knew," Hemingway said of her, "was nicer to me."

Hemingway's welcome in the Beach-Monnier ménage was a further example — as were his frequent invitations to the Stein-Toklas household — of his tolerance for women who were observably lesbian in their tendencies or otherwise intimately involved with one another. Although Hemingway despised male homosexuals throughout his life, he had a peculiar fascination with lesbian relationships; they crop up often in his stories and novels. But his toleration of lesbianism casts an odd light on one of the deliberately comic and demeaning episodes in his later memoir, *A Moveable Feast*. There Gertrude Stein elects to instruct Hemingway on the psychology of abnormal sexual practices. Stein, so Hemingway's version goes, informed him that the act male homosexuals committed was "ugly and repugnant," and afterward the men were disgusted with themselves, took to drugs, and made frequent changes of sexual partners. Therefore, they were never happy with themselves. In lesbian relationships, the opposite was true. The women "do nothing that they are disgusted by and nothing that is repulsive and afterwards they are happy and they can lead happy lives together."

Stein, who, after all, had had some medical training at Johns Hopkins and presumably some objectivity about sexual matters, seldom discussed sexual topics with acquaintances, referred to them in guarded terms in her published writings, and hardly ever mentioned them in intimate letters with close friends. This, despite the fact that, during much of her life, she surrounded herself with an entourage of male homosexuals whom she and Alice treated in motherly fashion and who would have more than welcomed her confidences. Her relationship with Alice, though obvious on the surface, was a closeted one so far as her circle of acquaintances, male and female, was concerned. (Even Virgil Thomson, as privy to the Stein household as any of her friends, admitted that Gertrude had never acknowledged the nature of her relationship with Alice. "You have to find someone who had gotten upstairs at the rue de Fleurus and knew what the sleeping arrangements were," he said.) It is possible that Stein may have made an exception in Hemingway's case and decided to be frank and open on the subject and expressed the views he attributed to her. But it is equally possible — perhaps even probable — that, given his sympathetic interest in lesbians as against male homosexuals, Hemingway may have adulterated his report of Stein's fatuous comments with a few illuminating prejudices of his own.

VI

"Paris," Gertrude Stein once claimed, "was where the twentieth century was." It was in Paris, under the city's heady influences, that Hemingway launched his career as a modern writer. It was in Paris that he staked out the theme — the old Jamesian theme of the American abroad — that would characterize the work of his early fame and success as a writer. His major novels — *The Sun Also Rises, A Farewell to Arms, For Whom the Bell Tolls* — were continental novels, an odd circumstance for a writer considered, perhaps wrongly, as the quintessential twentieth-century American writer. And if it was only in his stories that he explored his American background, many of those stories, among the earliest and best, were written in Paris.

Odd, that Hemingway should have been so bent on exposing the seamy side of Parisian life, but explainable; as a journalist, he meant to be controversial. Expatriate life in Paris in the twenties was as disorderly and wasteful as he had pictured it, but life there was also more exciting, more complex, and more intricately corrupting and rewarding than Hemingway had acknowledged in his provocative stories for the *Toronto Star.* Its street life had sustained a long tradition of poets from Villon to Apollinaire, who had captured the place, the pulse, the time. Even in Hemingway's time it could inspire the aged photographer Eugène Atget, who still trudged the streets in his shabby clothes, carrying his cumbersome old-fashioned equipment, faithfully recording the unadulterated look of the city, its avenues and misted quais, its vendors, ragpickers, and fat *poules,* its shops, its rain-wet streets. (When Atget died in 1927, it was a fortunate chance that his lifework was rescued from oblivion by the photographer Berenice Abbott, who preserved his fragile glass negatives. How much of documentary history depends on such chance encounters?)

Expatriate life in Paris in the twenties was a convergence of egos, libidos, intellects, rivalries, and profound ambitions. Like Stein, the painter Joan Miró found Paris the vital center of his life and work. "I don't know why it is," he once remarked, "but those who lose contact with the world's brain fall asleep and turn into mummies." In Paris, freewheeling sexual relationships, regular and irregular, were the norm. The tourist life existed, but at the fringes of creativity. Yet serious artists, as Hemingway soon learned (if he hadn't already known it at the time he wrote his blistering articles) were just as much in evidence in the bistros and cafés as the loungers and wasters. The influential figures of the period, the writers and artists whom Hemingway respected and then later disowned, those who aided and abetted his career because of his youthful charisma or out of belief in his talent (and those who did not), could be found daily or nightly at the Dôme and the Rotonde, the Sélect, the Coupole, the Deux Magots. Hemingway, himself, favored the Dingo, on the rue Delambre, where Jimmie Charters, the gossipy cockney bartender "Jimmie the Barman," presided. At the Nègre de Toulouse, Hemingway and Hadley dined regularly enough to have their red-and-white-checked napkins saved in the napkin rack. In the mornings, Hemingway sat on the terrace of the Closerie des Lilas, writing in his blue copybooks, undisturbed — all of which he would later lovingly describe in *A Moveable Feast,* an old man's romantic idyll and a vengeful summing-up.

It was at the Dôme, usually, that the stragglers from the night before gathered for their morning coffee and croissants. Josephine Herbst the novelist met her husband-to-be, John Herrmann, also a novelist, at the Dôme. Both were midwesterners (Herrmann was from Michigan and knew Hemingway's summer territory well); both were to become friends and admirers of Hemingway's, and then, in the way of things in the literary life of the twenties and thirties — and in Hemingway's special case — less than friends. At the Dôme, Sinclair Lewis, triumphant after *Main Street* and *Babbitt* but ignored by the snobbish Paris crowd, stood up and drunkenly made mention of himself and Flaubert in the same breath, and someone shouted, "Sit down. You're just a best seller." Lewis got his revenge by writing about the shiftless bohemians of Paris in an article for *American Mercury* at home.

At the Rotonde across the street, the Soviet poet and journalist Ilya Ehrenburg, who had known the café both before and after the war, regarding it as "a seismographic station where men recorded impulses not perceptible to others," sat for hours over his empty coffee cup, surveying the scene. It was at the Rotonde that the Russian poet Mayakovsky mused about the violet evenings of Paris, drinking his coffee through a straw, morbidly afraid of catching a disease. (Life, perhaps, was the fatal disease.) In Paris, Mayakovsky wrote in his cramped bedroom at the Hôtel Istria, ordered White Horse whiskey at the Coupole, and read his poems to admiring audiences of surrealists in Montparnasse bistros. Hemingway, in the *Toronto Star,* was more aware — even mildly tolerant — of the White Russian émigrés who sold their jewels on the rue de la Paix and spent their afternoons in the cafés, recalling the good times under the czar and waiting for the revolution that would bring them back to power. "Like all the rest of the world," Hemingway concluded, "the Russians of Paris may have to go to work. It seems a pity, they are such a charming lot."

At the Rotonde one evening, Malcolm Cowley, historian (*aller et retour*) of the American exiles, accompanied by Peggy Guggenheim, heiress and modern art collector, and her husband, Laurence Vail (painter, poet, and current acquisition), the Surrealist poet Louis Aragon, and Tristan Tzara, precipitated a war of insults with the surly *patron*. Cowley finally took a sock at him. Roughed up by insulting *flics*, Cowley would have been sentenced to a month in jail if a delegation of respectable-looking French and American friends hadn't impressed the magistrate. (Cowley "ran with the idiot fringe," hung out with the "cafe characters," Hemingway claimed late in life, unmindful of Cowley's championship of his work and reputation.)

Djuna Barnes, on her first visit to Paris, decided the Rotonde was like the Brevoort back in Greenwich Village. She found it difficult to settle down to work: "Everyone just sits around and says, 'Gosh isn't it great to be here!'" But once settled in at the Hôtel Jacob, she wrote in bed in the mornings, her breakfast brought by the chambermaid. At the Stryx, the Swedish restaurant popular with the women expatriates, Barnes dined with her lover, the American sculptor Thelma Wood, the model for Robin in *Nightwood*. At the Stryx, too, one might discover the beautiful Mina Loy, poet and shopkeeper, dining with the visiting Harriet Monroe — beaming, bespectacled, lace-collared, a schoolmarm on sabbatical. "A faintly sensitized, dried up old bitch who runs a long dead magazine," Hemingway said of her, even after she had been kind enough to publish six of his early poems in *Poetry*:

For we have thought the longer thoughts
  And gone the shorter way.
And we have danced to devils' tunes,
  Shivering home to pray:
To serve one master in the night,
  Another in the day.

And E. E. Cummings, a more accomplished poet, living in Paris in an awkward time in his life, tried to make up his mind whether to marry Elaine Thayer, the ex-wife of his very close friend Scofield Thayer. (Cummings had written the couple's epithalamion — "her eager body's unimmortal flower knew in the darkness a more burning rain" — and received a $1000 check from the groom. Three years later, before the divorce, Cummings was the father of Elaine's child.) Cummings toured the Parisian bistros with Louis Aragon, Matthew Josephson (chronicler of the Surrealist insurrection), and John Peale Bishop, poet, critic, and friend of Scott Fitzgerald and Edmund Wilson. (Bishop, praising Cummings's high-wire skills, assured Wilson, "He, I may add, keeps himself completely removed from both the French Dadaists — of course the better ones now repudiate the title — and their American hangers-on, Josephson, Cowley, etc.") Hemingway, who admired and probably envied Cummings's wartime memoir, *The Enormous Room,* reported to Ezra Pound on the long-delayed nuptials in suitable Poundese: "E. E. Cummings married to Scofield Buggaring Thayer's first wife."

At the popular Bricktop's in Montmartre, where the city's black musicians gathered nightly, one could find Man Ray and his mistress, the famed Latin Quarter model Kiki, or Florence "Flossie" Martin, the former Ziegfeld showgirl, loudmouthed, orange-haired, Rubenesque, and generous-hearted, especially where sailors were concerned. (In the banner year 1924, the crews of the USS *Detroit, Memphis,* and *Pittsburgh* were in town. Flossie and her drinking companion, the English painter Nina Hamnett, according to Jimmie the Barman, vigorously entertained the American fleet.) At the Café Cyrano, Nancy Cunard, heiress of the Cunard Line fortune, socialite, publisher (The Hours Press), and minor poet (Pound wrote her by way of criticism, "Damn it all, midnight is midnight, it is not 'this midnight hour'"), her thin arms laden with African bracelets, was the centerpiece of the Surrealist congregation: André Breton, René Crevel, Philippe Soupault, and Louis Aragon, Nancy's lover pro tem.

Ezra Pound, though not a heavy drinker, was among the notables photographed at the inauguration of Le Boeuf sur le Toit, the nightclub promoted by Jean Cocteau and the meeting place for Satie and the members of Les Six: Milhaud, Honnegger, Poulenc, et al. (Cocteau appeared there regularly, keeping an eye on his sixteen-year-old lover, Raymond Radiguet, who asserted his independence by dancing with the *poules.*) Pound also fraternized with the peripatetic editors of *Broom,* drinking with Harold Loeb at the Dôme, or dining well at the Deux Magots at the expense of Alfred Kreymborg. ("What Broom and the Skyscraper primitives will die of is what Dada is dead of; impotence," Hemingway claimed.)

Harold Stearns's outpost was the Sélect; there, glued to the bar, he argued with the argumentative *patronne.* In 1921 Stearns had barely completed his preface for *Civilization in the United States,* a symposium by thirty intellectuals on the cultural, social, and intellectual barrenness of American life, when he embarked for Europe, escaping prohibition and "the unlovely aftermath of the great Wilson crusade." In Paris, he lived a down-and-out existence relieved by periods of gainful employment as a newspaperman. (For several years, he was the racetrack handicapper Peter Pickem for the Paris edition of the *Chicago Tribune.*) Part of the time he lived on the support of generous women and scorned the "self-conscious and self-assured brotherhood of Montparnasse" — though, often enough, he was obliged to cadge drinks or a room for the night from that same brotherhood. Hemingway befriended him, gave him cash or paid his bills, got his typewriter out of hock, and was rewarded by kind words in Stearns's autobiography, *The Street I Know:* "He has never let me down." Forced to return to the United States in 1932 because of illness and eye troubles and the Depression, Stearns looked back on his Paris years with equanimity: "It was a useless silly life — and I have missed it every day since."

Harry Crosby, playboy nephew of J. P. Morgan and publisher of the Black Sun Press, and his wife, Caresse, preferred the Right Bank establishments like Fouquets and did their drinking at the Ritz Bar. Crosby, having escaped to Paris from "the City of Dreadful Night — Boston," gave lavish and scandalous parties in his rue de Lille town house, parties that sometimes turned into orgies of twining flesh alongside a huge sunken marble tub. Despite their fabled dissipations, the Crosbys' productive publishing career resulted in an extensive list that included an unwarranted percentage of Crosby's romanticized cult-of-the-sun-and-death poems and an eclectic assortment of volumes by Poe, Oscar Wilde, D. H. Lawrence, Lewis Carroll, James Joyce, Hemingway (the Paris reprint of *The Torrents of Spring*), and Hart Crane.

Crosby had met Crane at the Deux Magots and, having a penchant for rebellious and violent types, wined and dined the poet and gave him room and board in his Paris house and at his country mill so that he could complete his masterpiece *The Bridge.* But Crane, given to nasty drunks, barroom brawls, and homosexual extravagances (he seduced a visiting count and a chimney sweep who left sooty footprints on the white walls, and laid siege to the Crosbys' chauffeur), had little time to finish his series of poems. He ended up in La Santé Prison after a furniture-busting fight at the Sélect, and Crosby provided the poet with a ticket to America on the White Star Line. In an exuberant postcard to a friend, Crane summed up his Paris sojourn from beginning to end: "Dinners, soirees, poets, erratic millionaires, painters, translations, absinthe, music, promenades, sherry, aspirin, pictures, Sapphic heiresses, editors, books, sailors. *And How!*"

VII

Out of pride or caution, Hemingway made it clear that he was not a member of the "strange-acting and strange-looking breed" that crowded the tables of the Café Rotonde. He preferred a different

Paris, the Paris of the local *bals musettes,* where the sailors and apaches hung out with their girls. He preferred to be among people who "enjoy life, without respecting it." It was to one of the local *bals* near his apartment that he usually took Hadley dancing to the music of a wheezing accordian with, on weekends, the steady tattoo of a drum. Hadley was amused and a little frightened by the toughs who spun her around the floor. But Hemingway, she noted, danced "with anything he could get his hands on."

All the same, he was a young man on the make, eager to get on with his career. Hemingway made it his business to know everyone worth knowing in the Paris of the expatriates, whether they frequented the Rotonde or not. It may never have seemed a calculated effort to many of the people he won over with his "sudden marvelous smile," his brusque camaraderie, his eagerness to learn — and to teach. It was, nevertheless, one of the facts of his life that there were few friendships that Hemingway made during his first four or five years in Paris that did not, in some way, benefit him or his career.

///

As early as his March 9 letter to Anderson, Hemingway began complaining about his work assignments. "This goddam newspaper stuff is gradually ruining me," he said. He was going to cut loose from it and do his own writing for three months. Despite the complaints, he frequented the weekly Wednesday meetings of the Anglo-American Press Club, listening to gossip and behind-the-scenes stories from the regulars. He struck up useful relationships with older, more experienced newsmen like Frank Mason of Hearst's International News Service and Guy Hickok of the *Brooklyn Daily Eagle,* with whom he frequently lunched. Mason would later hire him to double up on special assignments, covering stories for the INS. Hickok became a warm friend and supplied Hemingway with press tickets to boxing matches and sporting events. The two would later take a trip in Hickok's old Ford through Mussolini's Italy, an excursion that Hemingway first wrote up as a sardonic news sketch for *The New Republic.* Hickok, who took pride in Hemingway's later success and admired Hemingway's ambition, furthered Hemingway's legend by writing articles about him and his wartime exploits for the *Eagle.* He treasured a photograph he had taken of the youthful Hemingway; on the back, Hickok had written, "'I did it,' said Cock Robin.")

Among the rivalries and backbiting of the profession, few writers had their careers launched with such good will as Hemingway. In 1922, he was at the threshold of becoming a recognized author. In its May issue, *The Double-Dealer,* a lively New Orleans magazine that published Sherwood Anderson, Djuna Barnes, and Edmund Wilson, among others, printed "A Divine Gesture," Hemingway's burlesque fable of a harried Lord God and his yes-man, the angel Gabriel, in the Garden of Eden. (He had written it in Chicago.) Then, in its June issue it printed Hemingway's sardonic quatrain "Ultimately":

> He tried to spit out the truth;
> Dry mouthed at first,
> He drooled and slobbered in the end;
> Truth dribbling his chin.

It appeared on the same page as "Portrait," a poem by the young William Faulkner. (Hemingway, who harassed the editor of *The Double-Dealer* for payment, could not remember, in later life, whether Sherwood Anderson, who was in New Orleans that spring, had arranged his publication there.)

Although Ezra Pound had not been successful in getting Scofield Thayer to publish Hemingway's poems in *The Dial,* six of them ("Mitrailliatrice," "Oily Weather," "Roosevelt," "Riparto d'assalto," "Champs d'Honneur," and "Chapter Heading") would appear under the title "Wanderings" in the January 1923 issue of Harriet Monroe's *Poetry.* If *The Little Review* did not publish the first Hemingway sketch that Pound sent, Margaret Anderson and Jane Heap did lead off their Spring 1923 "Exiles" issue with six of the prose vignettes that would later appear in Hemingway's *in our time.* In the same issue, the editors also printed Hemingway's "They All Made Peace — What Is Peace?" a satirical poem in the Stein manner, based on his coverage of the Genoa Economic Conference.

Gertrude Stein wrote the first review of Hemingway's first book *Three Stories and Ten Poems,* published by Robert McAlmon's Contact Editions. It appeared in the November 27, 1923, issue of the Paris *Tribune.* She followed it up with one of her odd "word portraits," "He and They, Hemingway," in the December 1923 issue of *Ex Libris,* published by her friend W. Dawson Johnston, director of the American Library in Paris. Adrienne Monnier would publish the first French translation of a Hemingway story, "L'Invincible" ("The Undefeated") in her magazine, *Le Navire d'argent.*

There would be a long string of such favors in Hemingway's climb to success. The honors were sometimes in dispute. The perenially young American composer George Antheil, not always a reliable source, claimed he had been responsible, through his friend Count Hans von Wedderkop, editor of *Der Querschnitt,* for Hemingway's initial publication in the vanguard German art and literary magazine. Between 1924 and 1925, the magazine published a number of Hemingway's bawdy but innocuous poems, among them a satire on the "Lady Poets," including such slow-moving targets as Edna St. Vincent Millay, Sara Teasdale, and Amy Lowell, as well as "The Earnest Liberal's Lament":

> I know monks masturbate at night,
> That pet cats screw,
> That some girls bite,
> And yet
> What can I do
> To set things right?

Without offering any alternative explanations, Hemingway denied that Antheil had any connection with his appearances in the magazine.

Hemingway flattered but never fawned over his mentors and promoters; he seems to have recognized that independence was a more attractive and effective quality than obsequiousness. He did what he could to promote those who were promoting him. Their names appeared in the gossipy news notes he forwarded to *Poetry* or, later, wrote for the *Transatlantic Review.* In the January 1923 issue of *Poetry,* Harriet Monroe informed her readers, "A letter from Ernest Hemingway gives us all kinds of news, in brief: that Gertrude Stein is doing a new book while living in St.-Rémy in Provence this winter . . . that James Joyce is ill and having a difficult time with his eyes; and that Padraic Colum is likewise in Paris." Hemingway, in those early years, carefully linked his name with the names he was publicizing. His compliments and put-downs were double-edged. As he remarked, in print, on his uneasy friendship with Antheil, "If George Antheil asks you to write a Jazz Opera with him say, 'Yes George,' and let it go at that. He asks all his friends. It is his way of paying a delicate compliment."

Ezra Pound's generosity was the shining example for Hemingway. And there would be ample evidence in Hemingway's career of his assistance to writers who were down and out financially. When he believed in their talents, he proposed their names to editors who were looking for contributors. But friends with sharper eyes, like Scott Fitzgerald, another writer dazzled by Hemingway, took a harder look at Hemingway's generosity. Fitzgerald noted that Hemingway's helpfulness was often strategically placed: "Ernest would always give a helping hand to a man on a ledge a little higher up."

7

Chasing Yesterdays

LATE IN MARCH 1922, Hemingway had his initiation into the world of international politics. John Bone of the *Toronto Star* had assigned him to cover the International Economic Conference at Genoa, Italy. It was the first major summit meeting following the Versailles Peace Conference. Convened by the Allies to take up the issues of the economic reconstruction of Europe, it was the first international meeting to which a defeated Germany had been invited as a full participant. (The French, however, were determined that the conference should not become a platform for German protests against the staggering war reparations assessed against the enemy nation.) And it was the first major conference in which the new Soviet government, eager for diplomatic recognition and seeking economic aid and commercial relations with the West, took part.

For a twenty-two-year-old reporter, it was an important assignment, a greater challenge than the dispatches on the new fad for sparrow-bedecked hats and the efforts of the French Anti-Alcohol League he had been sending from Paris. Hemingway made the most of the opportunity. He wrote or cabled some twenty-three pieces, which appeared in the *Daily Star* between April 10 and May 13. Some were brief dispatches of a few sentences; others, full-length stories written in a brisk anecdotal style that, here and there, revealed some grasp of the underlying issues involved. Hemingway noted the ominous public context of the conference, the squads of highly visible carabinieri, whose function was to prevent clashes between the local Italian Communists and the aggressive young Fascisti who were gaining power in the industrial towns of northern Italy. Hemingway's sympathies were clearly not with the Italian Communists, whom he depicted, condescendingly, as good fathers and good workingmen who drank in the cafés and talked interminable politics on Sunday and chalked up slogans on the walls on their way home. With doubtful authority, he reported on "the casual and childish nature of ninety-seven out of every hundred Red demonstrations in Italy," although he had been in Genoa only a week or more. He recognized that the Fascists represented "almost as great a danger to the peace of Italy" as the Reds ever were, but he was more admiring of them in print, describing them as "young, tough, ardent, intensely patriotic, generally good-looking," with "the valor and intolerance of youth."

His articles were gossipy and youthful: he reported on the German delegation largely in terms of personalities, trying hard — perhaps too hard — to give a vivid impression of Germany's statesmen. Chancellor Joseph Wirth looked, he said, like a tuba player in a German band; his speech at the opening session was "a masterpiece of tact and kindliness — but it did not say anything." He described Walter Rathenau, the German foreign minister and pro-Western industrialist, as "coldly intellectual," with a "polished billiard-ball head." Hemingway aptly noted that the hard line taken by the French even before the conference had begun meant that Germany, reluctant to attend the meeting in the first place, "had nothing to gain and everything to lose." He duly reported on the shock created by the surprise treaty that Germany and Russia, both frustrated by the intransigence of the Allies, had signed in Rapallo on Easter Sunday, but he did not assess its significance. A hurried affair, the Rapallo treaty gave diplomatic recognition to Russia and afforded the Germans some leverage in dealing with the Allied powers on questions of reparation. France and Italy threatened to walk out unless the treaty were abrogated. Except for the old-fashioned diplomacy of David Lloyd George, "the greatest compromiser politics has ever seen," Hemingway claimed, the conference might have broken up entirely. Reporting on the press meeting that the British prime minister had called to discuss the consequences of the Russian-German treaty, Hemingway gave cameo portraits of the dignitaries: Lloyd George — "His charm, his fresh coloring — almost girlish — the complexion of a boy subaltern just out of Sandhurst." And of Jean-Louis Barthou, the head of the French delegation, he repeated what was a favored description, "like the left hand one of the Smith Brothers of cough-drop fame." He described the shabbiness of the hardworking English press corps and the closed motorcars lined up in the hot sun in the courtyard of the Palazzo San Giorgio, waiting to bear the diplomats away, housed in glass.

Later historians, like George Kennan, have acknowledged that the unyielding policies of the French had undercut Rathenau's position at the conference and provided the perfect excuse for the "Easterners" of the German delegation, like Chancellor Wirth, to make an accommodation with the Soviets. The Soviets, in turn, were convinced of the effectiveness of their strategy of driving a wedge between the capitalist nations. The Genoa Conference had been a major victory for Soviet diplomacy and a forewarning of the new politics of Europe in the wake of Versailles. Hemingway, a novice in the field, had begun to master the color and excitement of the scene, but he had not yet grasped all the complexities of the political event.

He was certainly alert to every professional opportunity the conference offered. He made it clear to his readers each time that he had personally interviewed any of the major celebrities, reporting on the Soviet foreign minister, "Chicherin said to me . . . 'The rights of foreign capital will be perfectly secured but Russia will resist all attempts by consortiums to make Russia a colony.'" And he implied that Chicherin had responded to another of his questions about the opposition socialists then on trial in Russia. Chicherin insisted that they were not being "persecuted" but were being prosecuted for real offenses like blowing up banks and ammunition dumps, or shooting at Lenin. "We are changing our penitentiary system to educate and reform criminals," Chicherin added. Hemingway took a safe stance toward Russia. He explained to his Canadian readers that he was not pro-Bolshevik; one might hate the things the Soviets did and the system of government they represented, but he admired the fact that they were the hardest-working delegation at the conference.

The most significant of the lessons Hemingway learned at Genoa was the unpredictable nature of political power. Four years earlier, Hemingway noted, Chicherin had been confined in an English jail as a political agitator; now he was a leading representative of the Russian government at the conference. Four years earlier, Maxim Litvinov, with whom Hemingway also had a private interview at the heavily guarded Soviet delegation in Santa Margherita, had been expelled as the Soviet ambassador to Britain; now he was sitting at the conference table with the venerable Lloyd George. Whatever the political intricacies and intrigues, Hemingway, with a novelist's eye, had recognized that he and the other reporters at the conference had been chronicling "the dawn of a new era."

⁄ ⁄ ⁄

Hemingway's coverage of the conference was a remarkable performance. "I worked very hard at Genoa and wrote some very good stuff," he boasted to his father. "Met L. George, Chicherin, Litvinov and many others." Despite his grumblings that newspaper work was ruining him, he had worked industriously. His articles tended to be at one and the same time precocious in their knowledgeability and naive in their descriptive characterizations. In his earlier reports from Paris or in his letters home, there had been no inkling of any detailed awareness of political events in Italy. Yet within days of his arrival at Genoa, he was sending back full-blown accounts of the political rise of Fascism and what read like eyewitness reports on the brutal power struggle that had been taking place between the Communists and Fascists during the past two years. More surprising, he seemed to have developed a flair for firsthand accounts of people and events that he could only have learned about secondhand from other sources. On April 28, the *Daily Star* printed his insider's views on the German industrialist Hugo Stinnes, Rathenau's enemy, whom Hemingway described knowingly as "the industrial dictator of Germany today," a man whose hold on German newspapers, he said, was as firm as Lord Northcliffe's grip on the British press. Stinnes, however, was not at the conference, and there is no evidence that Hemingway had ever seen him, except, perhaps, in a newsreel or photograph. Still he gave a full-fledged description of the man with his "black derby hat and his ready-tied neckties, his celluloid collar and the meanest face in Europe." Stinnes, Hemingway wrote, was casting a shadow over the conference that gave one "the same sensation as seeing the black eagle on the flag that hangs over the German consulate at Genoa."

In a month's time, it seems unlikely that he would have found the necessary documentary sources or the foreign periodicals (many in languages he did not read) in order to cover the wide range of subjects he wrote about at Genoa, besides covering the meetings and press briefings. The probability is that Hemingway, a remarkably quick study, had been picking up an amazing education in the politics and economics of postwar Europe from the more experienced reporters on the scene. He had ample opportunities. On the train to Italy, he had made the aquaintance of George Slocombe, only five years older than Hemingway but a seasoned reporter for the British Communist paper the *London Daily Herald.* (Covering an earlier conference at Spa, in Belgium, Slocombe had overheard Stinnes forcefully haranguing the German delegation into settling with the Allies on the question of coal deliveries from the Ruhr mines.) Hemingway also met the American journalist William Bird, head of the Consolidated Press in Paris, with whom he struck up a warm and useful friendship. In Genoa, Hemingway met George Seldes, head of the *Chicago Tribune*'s Central European Bureau in Berlin, who knew Hugo Stinnes as a secretive fellow resident at the Adlon Hotel, who took his meals in his rooms. It is one of the Hemingway legends that the young reporter, having just learned "cablese," had excitedly taken his first efforts to the fifty-six-year-old muckraking journalist Lincoln Steffens, claiming, "This is a *new* language." But Steffens, covering the conference for the Hearst papers, did not arrive on the scene until May, after Hemingway had returned to Paris. With the others, however, Hemingway spent a good many evenings drinking in the local trattorias and discussing the day's events.

At the opening session of the conference, Hemingway met Max Eastman, the American journalist and editor, who was sitting directly behind him, engaged in awkward conversation with Marcel Cachin, head of the French Communist party and editor of *L'Humanité*. ("[Cachin] has a very rich wife and can afford to be a Communist," Hemingway quipped.) Eastman, en route to Russia, was covering the conference for the *New York World*. Thirty-nine, tall, lean, handsome, prematurely white-haired, he looked, to Hemingway, like "a big, jolly, middle-western college professor." Either Hemingway or the *Star* editors mistakenly described Eastman as the editor of the *Masses*, although that radical publication had been effectively shut down in 1917 by the Wilson administration, with a much-publicized trial under the Espionage Acts. He had subsequently started up a new Socialist monthly, the *Liberator*. Eastman, who had a marked distaste for the bohemianism of Greenwich Village and Paris, was much taken with Hemingway's personable appearance, enthusiasm, and proper attire. Hemingway, he noted, was "gentle and unassuming, dressed in easy-fitting but conventional suits of clothes and distinguished mainly by a winning laugh, a handsome face and the most beautiful row of teeth I ever saw in man, woman or child." He and Hemingway saw each other frequently during their stint in Genoa, and Eastman remembered Hemingway's modestly telling him "all about how scared he had been in the war."

Either in Genoa, or possibly later, when the two men were together in Paris, Hemingway pressed his opportunity and asked Eastman to read some "descriptions of scenes and incidents" he had been experimenting with. "They weren't stories," Eastman recalled. "They were just a paragraph or two long." Hemingway asked if they might be suitable for the *Liberator*, and Eastman, having just resigned his editorship of the paper before coming to Europe, offered to send the sketches to his successors, Mike Gold and Claude McKay. Nevertheless, he felt Hemingway's efforts were not really satisfactory; his later opinion was that Hemingway's journalistic training had had a detrimental effect on his literary style. The sketches never appeared in the *Liberator*.

One warm spring day, Hemingway joined Eastman and George Slocombe on the long, dusty, eighteen-mile drive to Rapallo to pay a visit to Max Beerbohm, the author of *Zuleika Dobson* and the celebrated caricaturist of the Edwardian era. The rumpled trio of reporters (Slocombe was wearing his customary bohemian anarchist's vast black felt hat) sat with their fastidiously dressed host on the terrace of his villa, looking out over the blue sea, sipping Marsala wine. They discussed journalism versus art, a subject much on Eastman's mind. Hemingway fretted over his journalistic bondage. Eastman noticed that Hemingway was attentive but unusually quiet and thoughtful. Driving back to Genoa, Eastman made a point of jotting down a few of Beerbohm's remarks. Hemingway gave him a brief laugh and, tapping his forehead, said: "I have every word of it in here." Eastman was sure it was true. That may well have been the case, but the Rapallo excursion did not turn up in Hemingway's published dispatches to the *Star*.

II

Reunited in Paris, Hemingway and Hadley took a forty-mile hike through the forests of Chantilly and Compiègne. Spring had arrived, but unfortunately, Hemingway came down with his old complaint, a sore throat that put him to bed for several days — so he wrote his father. Perhaps by way of recuperation, or as reparation for his weeks away from Hadley, the two made plans for another excursion to Chamby-sur-Montreux, this time to meet with Hemingway's army friend Chink Dorman-Smith. They intended to do some fishing and mountain climbing. Then Hemingway and Hadley would take that long-ago planned sentimental journey to Italy to revisit the sites of his Red Cross service. But their plans were stalled for a brief time by a proposal from the *Star* of a news-gathering trip to Russia.

The Russian assignment, never carried through, was an ambiguous affair. Whether Hemingway, having learned about Eastman's forthcoming Russian tour, had entertained the idea seriously and then, for some personal reason, defaulted, is not clear. In Genoa, during his interview with Maxim Litvinov, he had brought up the possibility of the Russian visit, and Litvinov had assured him he would have no trouble. For the next few months, Hemingway played up the proposed Russian trip in his letters. From Paris on May 2, he wrote his father that the Russian trip would soon take place, and again, from Chamby on May 24, he told his father that the *Star* had sent his credentials for the Russian trip. As late as July, when he wrote Harriet Monroe from Paris with the necessary biographical information for *Poetry*'s contributor's column, he listed himself as the *Star*'s correspondent in Russia but explained that his passport was in fact three weeks overdue. He was hopeful, however; Max Eastman's visa had just come through. In the end, the Russian trip never took place. One of the *Star*'s in-house reports claimed that Hemingway refused to go because Russian hotel accommodations were notoriously poor and uncomfortable. Perhaps Hadley, relieved to have him back, had balked at the idea of another lengthy separation.

Clearly he and Hadley were eager to get away on their vacation. In mid-May, from Chamby, Hadley wrote to Stein and Toklas, "Wasn't that an awful way to rush off from a nice city like Paris! Hope you found out we'd gone before you came over as you'd promised. We have your picture with us and it's a great comfort." They had found a fishing stream and a tennis court, Hadley said, and they were both "*very* happy."

In the Swiss mountains, the lower valleys were blooming with narcissus; along the country roads, the chestnuts were in full bloom. With the snowmelt, the streams were running swiftly, roiled by fast currents. Nevertheless, Hemingway found an ideal fishing spot, a little stream on the Rhône canal, some distance from Aigle, where he caught several fine trout. Always eager to communicate nature notes to his father, Hemingway wrote Clarence, "It is all fly fishing and as the trout have been fished for over two thousand years or so they are fairly shy. I haven't been skunked on them yet though." He and Hadley and Chink, climbing the Dent du Jaman, had caught sight of two martens, just below the snow line. Hadley, he reported, was healthy "and as red and brown as an Indian. She never looked better." He had gained back all the weight he had lost in the past few weeks and was feeling fine again.

The hike to Italy through the Great St. Bernard pass, which was not yet officially opened, proved arduous, however. Hadley had not brought the proper hiking shoes for the still deep snow. "I believe I wanted Chink to admire my trim legs," she said later. Before they had reached Aosta, walking twenty minutes and resting ten, her feet swelled so badly that her stylish American oxfords had to be cut open. They rested up for two days at Aosta before taking the train to Milan.

In Milan (where Chink left them to return to his outfit in Cologne), Hemingway wrote Stein that he and Hadley had been regularly playing the races at San Siro and that Hadley, with "alcoholic clairvoyance," was picking winners "as easy as cracking peanut shucks." Their plan was to visit the old wartime sites, traveling to

Schio and the Piave and Venice before returning to Paris in mid-June.

It was in Milan that Hemingway had his first interview with Benito Mussolini. Hemingway was aware of the politics of terrorism as practiced by Mussolini's Fascist squads; the political opponents murdered in the streets, or forced to drink castor oil; the foreigners roughed up because they failed to take their hats off or show respect when the Fascist anthem, "Giovinezza," was played. A week or so before the interview, Mussolini's black-shirted Fascist youths, many of them recruits from Hemingway's admired Arditi, had "taken" Bologna, burned the postal and telegraph offices, beat up protestors, and then withdrawn. The Italian political scene, Hemingway noted prophetically, "has the quiet and peaceful look of a three-year-old child playing with a live Mills bomb."

He was, however, very favorably impressed with the man he interviewed in the offices of *Il Popolo d'Italia.* "Mussolini was a great surprise," Hemingway wrote. "He is not the monster he has been pictured." His portrait of the Fascist leader was that of a big, brown-faced man with a slow smile, a somewhat "intellectual" look, sitting at his desk, fondling the ears of a wolfhound puppy.

There were some random characteristics of the Italian leader that Hemingway might, perhaps, have identified with. Mussolini was a writer (though of pulp romances), an editor, and a successful journalist. (At one point, the Hearst syndicate would pay Mussolini as much as $1500 a week for articles that had in fact been ghostwritten for him by his brother Arnaldo and others.) He was forceful; his bullying tactics, his shrewd manipulation of warring political factions — and the indulgence of a series of weak and ineffectual Italian governments — had brought him to the Chamber of Deputies, where he could wield even greater power. His political philosophy was blunt. "The crowd loves strong men," he once told the writer Emil Ludwig. "The crowd is like a woman." He had a reputation as a duelist, an intrepid soldier, and a man with intellectual interests. He liked to persuade American journalists, for instance, of his great admiration for William James and Mark Twain. (His English biographer, Denis Mack Smith, doubts that he had ever read either.) There was more validity to the rumor that he had a penchant for American comedy films, especially those of Laurel and Hardy. He had a projector installed for private screenings.

On this first meeting, Hemingway unfortunately bought a good deal of the carefully contrived legend that had grown up around the thirty-nine-year-old Italian leader. (He was not alone; Churchill, George Bernard Shaw, Lincoln Steffens, and Pound were early admirers. The philosopher Benedetto Croce at first espoused Fascism and later recanted. So did Toscanini. Mussolini was one of the first of the modern dictators to recognize the usefulness of the media in propagating the lies and the hatred that eased the march to power.) Hemingway's interview, published in the June 24 issue of the *Daily Star,* contained a few errors of fact — Mussolini's age, his place of birth — perhaps derived from propaganda sources.

His glowing account of Mussolini's rise to power was more revealing. Hemingway claimed that when the war broke out, Mussolini's fight for Italy's intervention on the Allied side had cost him his editorial job at the Socialist newspaper *Avanti.* He also repeated the myth that Mussolini had promptly enlisted as a private in the crack Bersagliere corps. In glowing terms, he added, "Severely wounded in the fighting on the Carso plateau and several times decorated for valor, Mussolini, a patriot above all things, saw what he regarded as the fruits of Italy's victory being swept away from her in 1919 by a wave of communism." He concluded that Mussolini had had "a very good reason" for his renunciation of the Socialist party.

But that favorable interpretation of Mussolini's career had been largely fictionalized from fact by Mussolini and his promoters. At first, following the Socialist party line, Mussolini had denounced the war as a capitalist venture, then dramatically shifted his political stance when he realized there was more to be gained by supporting the Allies. He had not, in fact, enlisted when Italy declared war against Austria in May 1915 but had waited five months until he was conscripted in September. Mussolini's "valorous" war wounds were the result of an accident during training exercises in 1917, when a grenade thrower had blown up. Having a flair for self-dramatization, he embellished the official legend. The explosion, he claimed, was "the most beautiful moment in my life." Mussolini's forty wounds were mostly superficial, but he improved the story by claiming that he had stoically refused any anesthetic while they were treated. He left the army as an invalid a few months later without medals.

His career, up to the moment Hemingway interviewed him, had been a matter of dramatic about-faces, from pacifist to interventionist, from radical socialist to ambivalent right-wing opportunist who courted capitalist financing for his newspaper and his political campaigns. As Mussolini himself admitted, he was an "adventurer for all roads." His career, patterned after the braggadocio tactics of D'Annunzio, was an opportunely stage-managed affair. But Hemingway, unlike other journalists and statesmen, had an early awakening; within a year, he would be denouncing Mussolini as a well-practiced fraud.

III

"And for Christ's sake dont ever go back Horney — not under any circumstances — because it is all gone," Hemingway wrote Bill Horne about his pilgrimage to the scenes of his Red Cross service. He and Hadley had taken a circuitous route, traveling from Milan to Vicenza, then by bus to Schio. He had imagined that Schio would be wonderful to revisit after the war. That was his first disappointment. The Due Spadi had shrunk to a small inn; the old Country Club barracks had been newly reconverted into a busy factory. From Schio, they traveled north by car to Trento, then circled down along the Lago di Garda to Sirmione, the "beautiful point that runs out into the lake that you can see from Dezenjano — the station where we saw the Czechs, remember?"

At Verona they boarded the train to Mestre, and then by car toured the towns along the Piave where Hemingway and Horne and their friends had been stationed. Fossalta di Piave, heavily bombarded during the war, was now "a brand new ugly town with nothing to remind you of the war except the scars in the trees. . . . Not a sign of the old trenches." Nevertheless, he found the spot where he'd been wounded: "It was a smooth green slope down to the river bank." The Piave, the once muddy river that would haunt his fiction, was now running clean and blue; a team of horses on the riverbank was pulling a huge cement barge upstream. "We can't ever go back to old things," he wrote Horne, "or try and get the 'old kick' out of something . . . the old things are nowhere except in our minds now."

That was his brisk account to a friend. In an article for the *Toronto Daily Star,* "A Veteran Visits the Old Front," Hemingway chronicled his growing disappointment step by step. It was useless to return to the old front, he warned other veterans. They would feel only "the supreme, deadly, lonely dullness" of the place. What had once been great events in their lives would seem little more than "fever dreams or lies you had told to yourself." Time, he realized, was obliterating his personal past. The battlefield where he had been wounded had "gone back into a green smugness." The trenches were filled in, the pillboxes had been blasted out and smoothed over. The dead soldiers, whose graves had made the site "both holy and real," had now been removed to cemeteries miles away. He had wanted to "recreate something for my wife and had failed utterly," he wrote. The past "was as dead as a busted Victrola record. Chasing yesterdays is a bum show."

Hemingway's dismissal of the past, however, was a tactical ploy. The article was another instance of his ability to create a public persona for himself. It read well and was self-serving. With heroic modesty he described his own wounding — the blood-soaked puttee, the "squidge" of the blood in his boot as he limped to the dressing station — making it clear to the readers of the *Star* that he was a bona fide hero. But in his journalistic apprenticeship, he could do more than that; in his cleverness, he managed to appropriate a past that was not his. In reporting on Schio, Hemingway described, as if it were an authentic eyewitness account, the battalions of the Brigata Ancona and Brigata Tuscana, trudging through the white dust of the Schio road in 1916, on their way to check the Austrian offensive. "They were good troops in those days and they marched through the dust of the early summer, broke the offensive along the Galio-Asiago-Canoev line, and died in the mountain gullies, in the pine woods on the Trentino slopes." At the time that historic incident took place, however, Hemingway was still a high school boy in Oak Park.

Truth, for Hemingway, was becoming a malleable property, both in his fiction and in his supposedly nonfictional accounts. "A writer's job," Hemingway would claim, was "to tell the truth," a practice that required the probity and honesty of "a priest of god." High-sounding phrases. Hemingway would also claim, "If you make it up instead of describe it you can make it round and whole and solid and give it life. You create it, for good or bad. It is made; not described."

The past, despite Hemingway's disclaimers, would become for him a no-man's-land between dream and reality, where distinctions blurred and enemies, friends, lovers, moved at risk. Hemingway would become proficient at making it over, making it plausible and habitable. (Over the years, his personal reminiscences, as his letters reveal, would be transformed and reshaped for better literary effect.) "A Veteran Visits the Old Front" represents one of the more controlled and emphatic successes of his years of apprenticeship as a journalist. He had managed to convey the poetry of loss even in a hard-boiled journalistic piece. He had learned — a dangerous lesson — that he could *mindfully* recreate and reshape his personal past — and his public persona — until it cast a satisfactory shadow.

Paris in the doldrums: he and Hadley had returned in the swelter of late summer. It was a dull time for news. Hemingway scratched around for material for the *Star:* a brief anecdote about Sinclair Lewis in London, horseback riding — in poor form — in Rotten

Row. Lewis complains to the groom about the shortness of the run; the groom tells the celebrated American author that he shouldn't expect "bloomin' prairies" in London. (The story had been making the rounds of the envious crowd at the Dôme.) Hemingway filled in with reports on pesty rug vendors in Paris and on the political embarrassments of Premier Poincaré, who, under the scrutiny of the camera eye in the age of modern political coverage, had — or hadn't — laughed during a solemn ceremony at the Verdun cemetery.

That summer in Paris, Hemingway suggested to William Bird that Ezra Pound, who had returned in early July, would be the ideal editor for the series of books Bird wanted to publish under his Three Mountains Press imprint. Pound was agreeable, even enthusiastic. "I shall keep the series strictly modern. One can be more intimate," he wrote to William Carlos Williams, whom he asked to contribute. The printing would be good, Pound promised. The books would be limited private editions. Bird, who had purchased a handpress on the Île St.-Louis and would be doing the printing himself, had offered to pay the authors $50 in advance and perhaps another $50 later. Pound initially suggested some six or seven writers for the series: himself and Williams and, among the other possibilities, Ford Madox Ford, Eliot, Wyndham Lewis, as well as Hemingway. Pound's contribution was to be *Indiscretions,* a reprint of earlier autobiographical articles from *The New Age,* an English magazine. (More importantly, Bird would later publish *A Draft of XVI Cantos of Ezra Pound,* the first official installment of his lifetime poem.) Williams's contribution to the series, which Pound dubbed an "Inquest into the state of English prose," was *The Great American Novel.* Hemingway's contribution, since he had no body of work readily available, was first announced as "Blank." The eventual title was *in our time,* published in 1924.

The Hemingways' vacation that summer consisted of a few weeks in Germany, hiking through the Black Forest with friends — Bill and Sally Bird, Lewis Galantière and his fiancée, Dorothy Butler. They planned to stay at country inns and fish for trout in the local streams. Hemingway and Hadley made the first leg of their journey by air, flying from Paris to Strasbourg. The others took the train. (It was, according to Hemingway, Hadley's first plane trip, and he made it the subject of a comic piece for the *Star* in which Hadley the intrepid slept through the adventure while he worried about everything from the questionable-looking pilot to the dubious name of the company, the Franco-Rumanian Aero Company.)

The vacation proved to be less than agreeable. Hemingway and Hadley got along famously with the Birds, but neither cared much for Galantière's fiancée. With Dorothy Butler, Hemingway took his usual stance toward the undeserving women involved with close male friends. Dorothy, as far as he was concerned, was just a girl from Evanston, Illinois, getting "cultured" in Europe. And when, after the trip, Hemingway wrote Harriet Monroe about the aggravations of Lewis's love affair, he noted that Dorothy had left town "and we have all cheered up." Hadley considered Dorothy selfish, and after some unpleasant episode prior to Galantière's marriage to her, told him so. The result was an aggrieved letter from Dorothy to Hadley, which Hemingway decided to answer. His undated response in the Kennedy Library papers in Boston (it is not clear whether it was ever sent) is a striking example of Hemingway's spleen and but one of the savage letters he could and would write, on occasion, in his lifetime. Hemingway bluntly stated that Dorothy was a selfish bitch and that Lewis would be a good deal better off in the hands of Dr. Fernandez (a psychiatrist, perhaps?) than married to her. "Even though I kissed you Dorothy," Hemingway wrote, "even while I kissed you, I never liked you but I was willing to make the effort to like you for the sake of seeing Lewis occasionally." He advised her not to get "Ritzy" about his letter. As a parting insult, he added, "Hadley says she is very sorry if Lewis came to our house without permission."

Despite the personal animosities, he and Hadley managed to enjoy most of the trip. They hiked through the Black Forest, fished for trout in the Elz River. "We can't afford to leave this country," he wrote to Gertrude Stein, in one of the chummy postcards he regularly sent her when he was away on vacation or on assignment. It would give him heartburn every time he spent a franc in Paris, knowing what it would buy in Germany. Still, he confessed, "I'm homesick for Paris." The devastated German economy was also the subject of a letter to his family. "Because the mark keeps dropping we have more money than when we started two weeks ago and if we stayed long enough could doubtless live on nothing. Economics is a wonderful thing." For the *Star*, he wrote articles on the German inflation and the hostility of German innkeepers toward tourists and "auslanders" who lived cheaply off the devalued mark. A five-course meal, he told his Canadian readers, could be had for 120 marks, about 15 cents, but he had seen a white-haired old gentleman who couldn't afford the 12 marks to buy a few apples.

Even more grim was the tale of a German riot he had mailed to the *Star* from Cologne, where he and Hadley, having left their companions behind, paid a visit to Chink Dorman-Smith, who was stationed there. Protesting the high cost of living, a German mob had tried to pull down a bronze statue of the kaiser, hacking at it with hatchets. A policeman, attempting to quell the disturbance, was thrown into the nearby Rhine. Clinging fiercely to one of the stone abutments of a bridge, he made the mistake of shouting up at the crowd, saying he knew some of the rioters and would report them. The angry mob swarmed down on him and tried to shove him into the swiftly moving current. Hemingway seized on the incident for an article for the *Star Weekly:* "It meant drowning for the policeman to let go — and he hung on. Then the mob chopped his fingers loose from the stone with the hatchet with which they had been attacking the statue."

As a writer, Hemingway tended to avoid self-conscious symbolism and would rankle at symbolic interpretations of his work. ("All the symbolism that people say is shit," he complained. "What goes beyond is what you see beyond when you know.") Yet he was a superbly visual writer. He had an undeniable gift for focusing on some incident from life and shaping it into an image as incisive as a news photograph that carried unstated meanings. Earlier in his *Star* article, perhaps from a story picked up from Chink Dorman-Smith, he gave a graphic report on the hostility of the Germans toward the French soldiers occupying Silesia, telling how, when the French troops departed under the protection of the British, the Germans rounded up the girls who had been seen in public with French officers, stripped them, shaved their heads, and drove them out of town. With the doomed policeman, Hemingway had, after all, created an ultimate symbol of the fate of postwar Germany, clinging desperately to the old order in the swift currents of rising political violence.

⁊ ⁊ ⁊

Back in Paris, Hemingway learned that Bill Bird had arranged to interview Georges Clemenceau at his seaside retreat in St.-Vincent-sur-Jard. The eighty-one-year-old statesman was planning a lecture tour in America. Hemingway, the consummate opportunist in his apprentice years, asked if he could go along. In an earlier article for the *Star,* published in February, Hemingway had written that Clemenceau was politically dead, that he had outlived his usefulness in postwar France. He had based that assumption on the flimsy evidence of a single man-in-the-street interview, or rather a man-in-the-café interview. ("In the cafes the Frenchmen have nothing to gain or lose by the things they say, so they consequently say the things that they believe.") Hemingway's man-in-the-café declared,

"The people are tired of Monsieur Clemenceau, and he will have to wait until he is dead to be a great man again." It made a lively story if not an altogether convincing argument.

Hemingway, nevertheless, was now keen to interview the old war hero. He and Bird took overnight *couchettes* to the fishing village of Les Sables d'Olonne and made the twenty-two-mile trip to Clemenceau's villa by taxi. The interview with the old Tiger (the cab was kept waiting outside) took place in a newly built sun-room. Clemenceau's eyes sparkled under his bushy white eyebrows, his face was "as brown as an Ojibway." Clemenceau conducted the interview in English: during the American Civil War, he had been a French teacher in Stamford, Connecticut. He was cordial and friendly, "as though the whole trip were a matter for pleasant discussion between he, Mr. Bird and myself." In a moment of strange forgetfulness, considering his opinions seven months earlier, Hemingway, in writing up the interview for the *Star,* referred to Clemenceau as "still the most dangerous political power in France." It made a better story.

Hemingway's notes for the interview are a bit more direct than the prose elaboration in his article. In the course of the talk, he asked if Clemenceau would visit Canada. Clemenceau's reply was emphatic. "No," he said, "I will not go to Canada — The Canadians rejected military service to help out France." Besides, he said, his American tour was a definite mission to explain things to the American people. Sensing a lively controversy, Hemingway pressed the issue. Hadn't Clemenceau a message to give to the Canadian people, other than his remark about military service? "No," Clemenceau answered, jerkily. "No. No. I have nothing to say to Canadians. Nothing, whatever!" The interview concluded with the arrival of André Tardieu, Clemenceau's lieutenant and the editor of the *Écho National.* Clemenceau accompanied the two Americans to the door. "It is nice here, eh?" he asked, looking outside. There was a long stretch of white beach, a thin surf crisping toward it, the smell of the sea and rotting kelp. Clemenceau drew a deep breath. "It's nice here," he said once more. He pointed toward a red banner flapping on a flagpole. "That is the Japanese carp," he said. "The symbol of virility. They hoist it whenever a male child is born." It had been given to him by the wife of the Japanese ambassador.

On the return trip to Les Sables, Hemingway wanted the cab driver to stop at the telegraph office so he could cable the story to the *Star* on the spot. But Bird cautioned against it; he thought the story would be offensive to Canadian readers and was not likely to be printed. Hemingway's feature story, including the account of Clemenceau's outburst, mailed on September 14, was in fact turned down, a rejection which Hemingway resented even years later. In a

1935 article in *Esquire,* he recalled the episode more in sorrow than in what must have been his original resentment. Tactfully referring to the "great Canadian paper," which had turned down the interview, he tersely quoted Bone's rejection as follows: "'[Clemenceau] can say these things but he cannot say them in our paper.'" But the circumstances were not so black and white as Hemingway pictured them. Bone did indeed turn down the article but on the grounds of journalistic responsibility. He felt that Clemenceau was ignorant about Canada's Military Service Act, which *had* provided for compulsory service and had been enacted well before the Armistice. Even though Clemenceau's reference to Canada was the most interesting part of the interview, Bone wrote Hemingway, he didn't think they should use it at all, though he hated "to pass up your excellent color . . . throughout the article." He suggested that Hemingway should see Clemenceau again if it were convenient. "If he wants to attack Canada, all right; we can consider whether we will let him stir up bad feelings or not, but we should in no case allow him to do so in ignorance of facts which we ought to be in a position to give him."

Whether it was no longer convenient for Hemingway, or whether Hemingway's apparent reluctance to challenge Clemenceau at the time of the interview now made it embarrassing to reinterview the statesman, is not certain.

The little bubble of controversy which caused the suppression of the article has its interest in the annals of journalism. But far more tantalizing among the buried items of Hemingway's interview with Clemenceau, recorded both in the notes he took at St.-Vincent-sur-Jard and in the unpublished article, is Clemenceau's admission, in September 1922, that he considered the Versailles treaty a failure. Hemingway had asked the former premier if he were planning to write his personal impressions of the war and the treaty. Clemenceau was forthright: "I can only tell the truth about the war and the treaty and if I tell the truth it will cause too many controversies and recriminations. I made the treaty. There is no denying that. It doesn't work. I know why but I'm not going around telling people why. It would only make more enmities." Hemingway's comment in his notes: "Going to America to defend his one remaining illusion — France. The old tiger sharpening his claws."

Bird's offer to bring Hemingway along on an important assignment was a generous one, considering the rivalry among reporters. His friendship with Hemingway would weather the Paris years — the period, significantly, of Bird's greatest usefulness to a young writer. These were the years, as well, in which Bird witnessed Hemingway's contentious breaks with many others who had helped him in his rise to fame. Yet Bird would remember his own special case. "I never had a quarrel with him," Bird recalled. "He never tried to maroon me on a desert island." There were moments, however, when he sensed an uncomfortable strangeness in Hemingway's character. Late in life, Bird recalled that on one of their train trips together (whether to Les Sables d'Olonne or some other destination, he didn't specify) they had discussed homosexuality. Perhaps as a joke or as an attempt to shock his friend, Hemingway suggested that it might be worth experimenting. It was an uneasy occasion — at least Bird remembered it as such — and it left a decidedly unsettling impression on his mind.

IV

In late September, Hemingway was off on another assignment for the *Star,* this time to cover the last phases of the Greco-Turkish war. The slow, strategic advance of the Turkish leader, Mustapha Kemal, and his nationalist troops toward Constantinople, then under Allied protection, had thrown the city's polyglot population — Christians, Jews, White Russians, Greeks, and Turks — into near panic. At the least, they feared the establishment of a rigid Islamic regime, the puritanical banishment of drink and prostitution (though Kemal himself, during moments of stress and depression, had a drinking problem). At worst, they feared a bloodbath in retaliation for the massacre of the Turks at Smyrna three years earlier. Headlines on September 15 blared the news that Smyrna was already in flames, more than 1000 killed in the fire, and 60,000 Greeks and Armenians homeless.

The assignment was a hazardous one. There was the threat of war between Turkey and the Allies; there were rumors of epidemics. The assignment was the cause of a bitter quarrel — the first serious one — between Hemingway and Hadley, who was adamantly opposed to his going. Hadley would not speak to him for the three or more days before his departure. What probably made her more angry is that Hemingway, judging from the evidence, had deliberately proposed the assignment, wiring Bone enthusiastically, listing the expenses — $200, travel inclusive, and $9 a day living expenses — and assuring the editor that it was a "WONDERFUL ASSIGNMENT BUT IF WAR HASTE NECESSARY STOP IF NO WAR GREAT SERIES NEAR EAST ARTICLES ANYWAY." The travel arrangements had to be settled, his visas approved and stamped at the various embassies of the countries he would be passing through — Greece, Serbia, Bulgaria. Then, on September 25, there was the rush to the Gare de Lyon to catch the Simplon-Orient Express with a drunken taxi driver who slammed the luggage around and broke the carriage on his typewriter, making it inoperable. It was not a happy departure. Hadley had been unyielding, letting him go without even a good-bye.

It was a long, uncomfortable trip. From Sofia, Hemingway sent another of his postcards to Stein, who was taking an extended vacation with Alice Toklas in Provence, informing her that the train was six hours late and rapidly getting later, and that the weather was good and hot. "You ought to make it sometime in the Ford," he added. It was Hemingway's first glimpse of Bulgaria, though he had written a lengthy *Star* article about the country and its radical leader, Aleksandr Stambouliski, several months before while attending the Genoa Conference. The article, which appeared in the April 25 issue of the *Daily Star,* was a cautionary example of the strengths and flaws of Hemingway's early journalism, its concentration on personalities, its sometimes doubtful grasp of political complexities. Stambouliski, the brusque, mustachioed premier and agrarian reformer, had caught Hemingway's eye: he stood out among the notable diplomats at Genoa "like a ripe blackberry in a bunch of daisies." Hemingway concocted a colorful fairy-tale version of Stambouliski's rise to power, how he had confronted Bulgaria's King Ferdinand and told him to get out of the country ("Ferdinand being a keen judge of situations, very promptly got out") and how Stambouliski had taken the young heir, Boris, in hand ("'If you attempt to leave Bulgaria I will put you under arrest. . . . You are the new king'"). It all had a Graustarkian ring.

From whatever mysterious sources he drew upon — press handouts? information from seasoned reporters? the Paris edition of the *Chicago Tribune*? — Hemingway managed to work up his own detailed account of the politics and economics of a country he had not then visited. "There are no internal problems in Bulgaria," Hemingway confidently stated, "there are no troublesome minorities." The Farmers' party was in control of the parliament, the Communists had only fifty seats, and the two bourgeois representatives had only "the inalienable right of all minorities — that to endorse." It sounded authoritative and informed. But barely nine months after Hemingway's brisk passage through Sofia, Stambouliski's agrarian government was overthrown by a troublesome "minority" cabal, and Stambouliski, captured outside his village, was executed. As a young journalist, Hemingway's grasp of realpolitik was not always reliable.

He was at his best in feature stories rather than hard-news reports, and his best articles, based on firsthand experiences, would have the vividness of his fiction.

***

Pictures: The Orient Express snakes its way down a rolling, sun-baked, treeless plain that leads to the sea. Along the shore there are glimpses of children bathing in the blue water, then rows of ram-shackle tenements. A Frenchman, looking out the window, comments, "Stamboul." There is a descent into a long culvert that finally opens out to the city and rapidly passing views of dirty white mosques. Then the station, crowded with porters, hotel runners, men in soiled white suits pressing their services as interpreters. Constantinople is hot, grimy, full of British and French soldiers there to prevent any invasion by Kemal's army. The route to the Hotel de Londres in the European quarter is jammed with trams and honking motorcars. Hemingway catches it all in a striding prose. In Galata, the business and entertainment district, men in suits and fezzes amble past shops, banks, and saloons. (The signs are in four languages.) At night, "Old Constans" is dark, smelly, the streets slippery with refuse. Dogs nose at the garbage, rats scuttle out of the way. In the red-light district, blowzy whores proposition British sailors. Constantinople, Hemingway realizes, is not the opulent Middle Eastern city he had seen in movies, posters, paintings — all gleaming white and sinister.

The Hotel de Londres is riddled with fleas and bedbugs; Hemingway's face is speckled with insect bites. (The Hotel Montreal will be no better.) In the morning, minarets rise above the mist that hovers over the Golden Horn. When the mist dissolves with the heat of the day, the harbor is forested with masts. Through his binoculars, Hemingway can see an Italian steamer leaving port, the rails crowded with Greeks fleeing the city. ("I will take up the question of Greek atrocities later when I have evidence and testimony of both Christians and Turks," he tells the *Star* readers.) At the Rumanian and Armenian embassies, there are long lines of people waiting to get passports and visas. The city is full of White Russian officers and civilians who have fled the Soviets (Kemal's allies) and are now trapped in their sanctuary. Many are reduced to selling their jewelry: Hemingway buys an antique necklace for Hadley from a White Russian waiter. Constantinople is a city of fear — "the sickening, cold, crawling fear-thrill" of those who cannot get away. This description, tossed off in a news story, is nonetheless revealing: fear, for Hemingway, is a thrilling state of mind. At the American consulate on October 1, he renews his passport for another eight months.

His initial stories consist of a flurry of unsigned spot news reports that read like wire pieces — brisk and informational. (John Bone cables him on October 6 that his dispatches are duplicating those of the International News Service. True: Hemingway had made a double-dealing arrangement with Frank Mason to cover the assignment for the INS as well.) Amazingly, within a few days, he has picked up a knowledgeable vocabulary and a widening background in Middle Eastern politics. He begins to assume that voice of authority which will characterize much of his journalism: "The Mudania Conference will determine the question of peace or war." But there is little firsthand news to report on the conference because the British have banned all correspondents from the site of the armistice treaty between the Turks and the Greeks. Hemingway has his problems with the official censors, posted at the wire service in Constantinople. They disappear for three or four hours at a time, while "urgent" cables pile up. His story on the Mudania Conference, such as it is, is cut drastically, eliminating even such banal details as the population of the little town on the coast of the Sea of Marmara. (He writes about the censorship, reverting to some old ploys, making it seem that he had been an old hand in Constantinople when the official notice of censorship was posted on September 20.)

His political instincts serve him well. He speculates on the likely outcome of the Allies having ceded Eastern Thrace to the Turks: "Eliminating the Greeks from Thrace will unite Bulgaria and Turkey, making a dangerous wedge of pro-Soviet countries that thrust into the center of the Balkans." Writing about the patchwork of shifting alliances and power struggles in the volatile area, he compares the edgy peace of the Balkans — which for him means the peace of Europe — to a percussion stick of dynamite between a mattress and a bedspring: "It may not go off, of course, for some time. Still, it is not oversecure."

As always (it is a symptom of his luck) he makes useful contacts: Charles Sweeny, a soldier of fortune, savvy on matters of military strategy; a Captain Wittal, a former officer in the Indian Cavalry, and a Major Johnson, both of whom are serving as British liaison officers with the press at Constantinople. Both had been official observers during the Greek defeat in Anatolia in early September. The Greek soldiers, they tell Hemingway, were an efficient fighting force during the Anatolian campaign but were betrayed by bungling politicians and by criminally negligent officers, some of whom had worn face powder and rouge, a detail Hemingway finds important enough to report. In one "show" in Anatolia, the artillery had massacred its own infantry by mistake. Witnessing it, Major Johnson had cried as he watched, powerless to do anything because British officers had to observe strict neutrality. Later, Hemingway would also meet an American newsreel cameraman, Shorty Wornall, who let him in on the tricks of the trade, telling him how he managed to shoot a burning village from two or three different angles so that it had all the drama of a huge conflagration, a journalistic improvement on reality.

Hemingway would make good use of Captain Wittal's story, both in an article for the *Star,* and even more importantly in "The Snows of Kilimanjaro," where the dying Harry Walden remembers the "newly arrived Constantine officers, that did not know a god-damned thing, and the artillery had fired into the troops and the Britsh observer had cried like a child." In that summing-up of a man's bitter experiences in the modern world, Hemingway would add a fictional recollection of how Harry, after a fight with his wife in Paris, had whored throughout his stay in Constantinople and, following a brutal fight with a British officer, won a hot Armenian slut who was "rose-petal, syrupy, smooth-bellied, big-breasted and needed no pillow under her buttocks" — a story that biographers have tended to take as either pure autobiography or a fantasy wish fulfillment on Hemingway's part. (It does read like another version of the tall tale about the insatiable hostess of his Sicily trip, which Hemingway told to Chink Dorman-Smith.) Yet Hemingway would later convince Bill Smith that during his early years of marriage he had been unfaithful to Hadley only once and that had been in Constantinople.

At Muradli, in mid-October, doctoring himself with quinine and aspirin for the case of malaria he has picked up in Constantinople, Hemingway witnesses the evacuation of the Greek army, the grim aftermath of the political maneuverings at the conference table. There is a stream of tired, unshaven soldiers in ill-fitting American uniforms, trudging along the wearying roads that lead to Western Thrace and Macedonia; wagon trains of baggage carts drawn by mud-flanked water buffalo being goaded forward. He focuses on the cut telegraph wires, dangling from the poles like Maypole ribbons, creating an instructive image of the futility of communication. He travels by car, horseback, and foot (so he will tell Bill Horne), following the route of the dispossessed. Somewhere in Thrace he manages to shoot twenty-two quail with a borrowed shotgun. ("Nice open country with sort of sage brush and they seemed easy to hit.")

At Adrianople, where he actually arrives by train near midnight on a rain-soaked night, he meets Shorty Wornall and his crew and puts up in a lice-ridden hotel run by a heavyset, slovenly Croatian woman. Madame Marie is one of those earth mothers for whom he would always feel a certain brusque admiration. When he complains about the lice, she tells him off: "It is better than sleeping in the road? Eh Monsieur? It is better than that?" At Adrianople, in the driving rain, he sees a twenty-mile column of refugees, a "ghastly, shambling procession" of the homeless, leaving their villages and farms behind them: peasants in brightly colored costumes bedraggled by mud and rain, bearing their worldly possessions on their backs; an old farmer carrying a pig, a chicken dangling from his scythe; families in bullock-drawn carts loaded with mirrors, mattresses, sewing machines, oddments of furniture. In one of them, a woman is giving birth under a blanket while her little daughter looks on, frightened, and begins to cry. (Later, in one of the vignettes for *in our time,* Hemingway will make something more out it: a child's startled glimpse of the mystery and terror of birth.)

Amid the stream of stumbling peasants, bobbing camels, Greek soldiers in motorcars, pushing toward Karagatch, he sees a thin file of oxcarts traveling in the opposite direction: ragged Turkish farmers commandeered by the Greeks to pick up more refugees and goods in the back country. In each cart, a Greek soldier, cloak pulled round his shoulders against the rain, sits guard, his rifle ready between his knees. There is an incident: a frightened Turk, having taken the wrong turn, is struck by the soldier with his rifle butt with such force that he falls from the cart and runs like a scared rabbit along the road. Hunted down by a cavalryman and two soldiers, he is beaten bloody in the face and returned to the wagon. The episode goes unnoticed by the others in the line of march. But for Hemingway it is another brief synopsis of the human condition: misery travels in both directions on the Karagatch road. The lesson is reinforced by Madame Marie, who has seen it all before — the Greeks, the Turks, the Bulgars. "They've all had Karagatch," she tells Hemingway. She quotes a Turkish proverb: "It is not only the fault of the axe but of the tree as well." In his lifetime Hemingway would witness more than his share of experiences like the road to Karagatch. They give credibility to his later, ambitious claim that as a writer, he was "trying to make, before I get through, a picture of the whole world — or as much of it as I have seen."

By October 21, traveling by way of Sofia and Trieste, he reaches Paris, bug-bitten and tired. He and Hadley make up, make love, are happy together once more. He writes to Gertrude Stein that the weather in Paris is cold and rainy: "Why don't you come back and cheer up this town?" He adds, "I've given up my other pursuits and sleep all day. Sleep is a great thing. I've just discovered it." Hadley, too, writes Stein about Hemingway's return and the gift he brought her ("I have a necklace to show you from there. A wonder") and the new Baghdad coverlet for their bed. She thanks Stein for the huge candied casaba melon she has sent them.

By October 27, he concocts a story for John Bone about the duplication of his dramatic Thracian refugee piece, which had been "pirated" by the INS. He had been out of funds and had used the INS charge account to transmit it to Paris, but the INS had stolen it. "At any rate, I have had it out with [Frank] Mason," he wrote Bone. "It was a personal matter and a question of ethics," he said. Perhaps he believed it.

V

It was probably the travel involved and the heavy writing assignments that turned Hemingway against journalism. He found little time for his own writing and was all the more concerned about publication. Writing Harriet Monroe from Paris on November 16, he asked when she intended to publish the poems he had sent her. The Three Mountains Press, with Ezra Pound editing, he told her (truthfully or untruthfully), was bringing out a book of his stuff and he wanted permission to include the poems. It is possible that Hemingway may have considered reprinting the poems; but his letter may also have been a ploy to prod Monroe into publication. None of the poems would appear in Bill Bird's 1924 edition of *in our time*. Hemingway's letter to Monroe contained a fund of gossip: Dave O'Neil, a wealthy lumberman and sometime poet, a friend of Hadley's from St. Louis, was in town with his wife and children, planning to stay in Europe indefinitely, "but that usually means two years," he wrote. And Ford Madox Ford was expected to arrive on the following day for a month's visit — an indication that Hemingway kept himself well informed on arriving celebrities.

Ford, a prolific writer and novelist, author of an earlier overlooked masterpiece, *The Good Soldier*, and the editor of the defunct *English Review*, had published Thomas Hardy, Henry James, H. G. Wells, as well as promoted D. H. Lawrence and Pound. He was traveling with his current mistress, the Australian painter Stella Bowen, en route to the Riviera. During his brief stay in Paris, Ford attended the funeral of Marcel Proust on November 21, at the church of St.-Pierre-de-Chaillot. Among the crowd of mourners were Diaghilev, the writers François Mauriac and Maurice Barrès, the rabble-rousing conservative politician Léon Daudet, the son of novelist Alphonse Daudet — the mix of artists, academicians, the waning old-guard society that Proust had made the subject of his multivolume novel. It was a solemn occasion at which, symbolically perhaps, a frightened little dog belonging to one of the mourners took refuge under the hearse, then darted off, never to be recovered. Ford attended as the self-elected "representative of English letters." He seems to have viewed the event as a kind of laying on of hands; at any rate, he later claimed that it had inspired him to begin work, at St.-Jean-Cap-Ferrat, on his novel sequence, *Parade's End.* With his multifarious connections, Ford was a man with a reputation and a following, a man worth knowing.

But Hemingway had little time to cultivate the acquaintance of the tall, portly, watery-eyed man with the walrus mustache and the man-of-letters manner he subsequently met in Pound's studio. (He would claim he had disliked Ford on sight.) In fact, on November 21, the day of Proust's funeral, Hemingway was on his way to Switzerland to cover the Lausanne Conference, convened to settle the territorial questions of the Greco-Turkish conflict. Overworked, he had come down with a bad cold and a sore throat. (In another under-the-table arrangement, he had agreed to run the wire services for the INS and Universal News Service, both of them Hearst operations, as well as cover the conference for the *Toronto Star.*) Hadley, who had remained behind in Paris but was scheduled to join him later for a vacation in Chamby, was also sick with a bad cold and felt too miserable to make the trip. Hemingway sent her sentimental cables and letters urging her to join him: she was "Poor dear little Wicky Poo" and his "sweet little feather kitty"; he was her "little wax puppy." Evidently they were practicing the rhythm method, and Hemingway rationalized that since they were both laid up with colds "we haven't lost so much time on the time of the month because you've probably been too sick." He hated for her to miss "what is the most comfortable and jolly time for mums." But he promised, "Won't we sleep together though?" But few marriages are quite as convincing or as banal as the endearments on paper may appear. Hadley had some doubts that he was eager to have her come; Hemingway had to reassure her that he was still "crazy" for her to be with him and that he wasn't stalling. In the margin, he wrote "Dear sweet Mummy!" Then he asked if she had written to some other marital couples: the "Steins" and the "Ford Madox Fords," who were staying at the Hôtel de Blois on the rue Vavin. If Hemingway maintained that he had spotted Ford as a phony from the beginning, he was, nonetheless, eager to pursue the acquaintance.

There were, possibly, other reasons for Hemingway's reluctance about Hadley's arrival. He was disgruntled about his workload: "I'm so sick of this — it is so hard. Everybody else has two men or an assistant, and they expect me to cover everything by myself — all for one of Mason's little baby kike salaries." Running the news service for both the morning and afternoon Hearst papers turned out to be grueling. Many nights he filed his last dispatch at around three in the morning. Since reporters were not allowed to cover the actual sessions at the Hôtel du Château at Ouchy, they had to rely on prepared statements and press briefings held at the delegation headquarters in the various hotels scattered around Lausanne. With every country wanting to present its own version of what was happening and the caucuses following in rapid succession, Hemingway had to step very fast to get them all in. "Mason has kiked me so on money," Hemingway complained to Hadley, "that I can't afford taxis and have to take the street car and walk."

Under the circumstances, Hemingway wrote little for the *Star*, and the two feature articles he did write did not appear until months after the conference had first convened, hardly the kind of up-to-date coverage his editors had expected. But the articles were notable. Hemingway's scathing coverage of Mussolini's press conference at Lausanne was remarkably prescient. The Italian leader was riding high; his March on Rome the month before was widely regarded as a historic event. In fact, as later historians have shown, it was a media event, a stage-managed demonstration of violence which created an aura of inevitability. It proved politically effective. But the truth was that the Italian government had already yielded to Mussolini's demands, and the "historic" march on the capital, whatever its show of force, had been hastily contrived to give the appearance of a spontaneous seizure of power.

At Lausanne, Mussolini made the most of his opportunities: demanding spurious concessions in advance, delaying the opening session by his lateness. His press conference was another demonstration of the theater of politics. According to Hemingway, Mussolini was sitting at his desk, poring over a book and frowning as the reporters were ushered into the room. He was "registering Dictator" and already calculating the headlines in tomorrow's papers. Slipping round the desk, Hemingway discovered that the Italian leader was studying nothing more than a French-English dictionary — and holding it upside down. Where five months before, Hemingway had given a glowing account of Mussolini's dramatic rise in Italian politics, he now called him "the biggest bluff in Europe." Hemingway went on, "Study his past record. Study the coalition that Fascismo is between capital and labor and consider the history of past coalitions." (Before, Hemingway had seen that coalition as a mark of the shrewdness of Mussolini's economic strategies.) Mussolini, he now claimed with more accuracy, had a "genius for clothing small ideas in big words," although that did not diminish the dictator's skills as an organizer.

Hemingway made much of Mussolini's haughty indifference to a group of peasant women who tried to present him with a bouquet of roses. When one of the women stepped forward to give a little speech, he scowled at the group with his "big-whited African eyes" and turned abruptly on his heels and went back into his room. But half an hour later, he had given a private interview to Clare Sheridan, an attractive, internationally known sculptor and journalist who had, in Hemingway's resentful phrase, "smiled her way into many interviews." It would perhaps have galled Hemingway even more if he had known that Mussolini had invited Sheridan, who was covering the conference for the *New York World,* to continue the interview on his train trip to Milan and Rome following his dramatic appearance at Lausanne. Sheridan, who had "smiled" her way into interviews with Lenin and Mustapha Kemal, found Mussolini the least impressive leader of the three. But she had the opportunity to assess a more dangerous private man than the strutting public figure Hemingway reported on. In Rome, she found Mussolini more communicative, less theatrical, than he had been at Lausanne. When she asked him what he cared for most, Mussolini answered, "Power!" with a special emphasis; power, he told her, to ameliorate the conditions of the masses. She reminded him that he had once said he despised the people. Mussolini responded that the people should have good wages, an eight-hour workday, decent food and education, "but they must in no way interfere in the political life of the nation." What Clare Sheridan remembered particularly was Mussolini's parting advice on what it took to succeed in life. "Above all, keep your heart a desert!" the dictator told her.

Most biographers attribute Hemingway's abrupt about-face on the subject of Mussolini to the influence of his new acquaintance with the young South African journalist William Bolitho Ryall, another of the swashbuckling newspapermen in the tradition of Lionel Moise and Richard Harding Davis for whom Hemingway had an expressed admiration. A correspondent for the *Manchester Guardian* and a pro-British propagandist, Ryall had been wounded by a mine at the Somme. He had served as a liaison officer to the French press at the Versailles Peace Conference. Caustic, brilliant, antidemocratic, he made a specialty of debunking the legendary celebrities of international politics. Later, under the byline William Bolitho, he worked for the *New York World* and produced a best-selling book, *Twelve Against the Gods*. Ryall, thin, redheaded, with a self-deprecatory grin, deplored the lack of daring in modern life, promoted the adventurer against the social man: "The adventurer must be unsocial, if not in the deepest sense anti-social, because he is essentially a free individualist." (Among the adventurous heroes and heroines of his book were Alexander the Great, Casanova, Isadora Duncan, and Woodrow Wilson.) He was the newsman's Nietzsche.

Under the influence of Ryall, Hemingway, in his *Star* articles, began demoting his former, easily acquired, heroes. Paying as much attention to dress codes as to political dialectics, he noted that Stambouliski had taken to wearing silk socks and drinking champagne (but avoided riding in capitalist limousines for fear of political repercussions at home). Chicherin, the brilliant diplomat with an inhuman capacity for work, was now wearing fancy uniforms, even though he had never been a soldier. Following a brilliant passage in which Hemingway described Chicherin's indifference to public opinion, his dislike and distrust of women, his lack of fear concerning assassination ("but he would turn pale if you shook your fist under his nose"), he passed on a bit of backstairs gossip: Chicherin's mother had kept him dressed as a girl until late in his childhood. Hemingway drew a glib psychological conclusion from that revelation: "The boy who was kept in dresses until he was twelve years old always wanted to be a soldier. And soldiers make empires and empires make wars."

It is one of the eerie facets of Hemingway's character — the putting down of some admired figure who disappointed his expectations — that he could so abruptly turn derisive toward men with whom he might have felt some sense of identification: Mussolini, the self-dramatizing soldier and newspaperman who courted publicity; Chicherin, the boy kept in dresses by his mother and the man who had his uniforms specially tailored in Berlin. Had he forgotten that his own uniform had been tailored by the fashionable Spagnolini in Milan? But the more powerful source of Hemingway's disillusionment with heroes was probably his regrets about his father.

Hemingway regarded his evenings spent with Ryall drinking brandy and discussing politics as valuable. He later acknowledged that Ryall had told him things "that were the beginning of whatever education I received in international politics." What especially impressed him were Ryall's views on "the malady of power," an updated version of Lord Acton's dictum that all power corrupts and absolute power corrupts absolutely. In Ryall's diagnosis, the symptoms were recognizable; it began with the suspicion of one's associates and it ended with the absolute conviction of one's own indispensability.

Ryall also was disdainful of journalism. That perhaps was one source of Hemingway's dissatisfaction with the fourth estate. Ryall encouraged younger colleagues like Hemingway to quit the profession before they became burnt-out reporters, too long at the trade, "cadging drinks and dead-dog assignments" from more successful friends. Those views reinforced the advice Gertrude Stein would give Hemingway in the course of their conversations that winter. Stein had evolved a theory of concentration as the necessary effort a true writer made to find the exact word or words that matched his or her emotional experience of an event. She had developed the idea in the course of writing *The Making of Americans,* the elephantine, unpublished novel that she regarded as her neglected masterpiece and "the beginning, really the beginning, of modern writing." While writing it, she kept a series of notebooks in which she wrote character sketches of the people she met or knew, in an attempt to analyze what she called their "bottom natures." Like artists' sketches, these were intended to serve in the creation of the characters that would make up, in her grand ambition, the "history of every kind of them, every kind of men and women." Hemingway, too, adopted the practice of making such brief character profiles of the people he met in Paris.

Stein's opinion was that newspaper writing, because it was topical and directed toward an audience — the newspaper readership — was a threat to the serious writer. "If you keep on doing newspaper work," she told Hemingway, "you will never see things, you will only see words and that will not do, that is of course if you intend to be a writer." Hemingway's views on serious writing would sometimes improve upon Stein's ideas. He once claimed, "You must be prepared to work always without applause" — a dictum he never quite sustained in practice. In newspaper writing, he maintained, "you told what happened and, with one trick and another, you communicated the emotion aided by the element of timeliness." But for serious writing, he developed a code of his own that was a refinement of Stein. "Remember what the noises were and what was said," he told an aspiring writer. "Find what gave you the emotion; what the action was that gave you the excitement. Then write it down making it clear so the reader will see it too and have the same feeling that you had. That's a five finger exercise." He had learned that valuable lesson during his Paris apprenticeship when Stein and Pound were his great sources of encouragement — a term far more significant than the bland word implies. For what that unlikely pair of American mentors had given Hemingway, by their example, was the courage to be himself as a writer, to discover his own way. Whatever his differences with Stein in later years, he was still willing to admit that her advice to quit journalism "was the best advice she gave me."

He had already begun to put some of Stein's theories to work in one of his earliest stories, one that owed, besides the encouragement of Stein and Pound, a debt to Sherwood Anderson. "My Old Man," written in Paris, is a story of American innocence abroad and a boy's disappointment in the jockey father who was his idol but is progressively revealed as a crook — to the reader, if not to the boy, Joe Butler, who narrates the story. It is a story done with the concentration that Stein had advised, from the tawdry racetrack settings in Italy and France with which Hemingway was thoroughly familiar, and which are rendered with a photographic precision, to the awareness of the boy's double loss when the father is killed in a racetrack accident. The boy's illusions about his hero are stripped bare when he overhears a bit of racetrack gossip that his father "had it coming to him on the stuff he's pulled." The whole life episode, with its visual immediacy, is cleverly set inside the frame of the boy's — or young man's — later recollections. And the inescapable ending, when Joe admits to his loss ("But I don't know. Seems like when they get started they don't leave a guy nothing"), makes it clear that Joe blames the world that has exposed his father as a fake more than he blames his former hero. Hemingway would write other stories about a boy's disillusionment with his father, but few would be as ambivalent as this first one.

⸙ ⸙ ⸙

Despite the overwork, Hemingway managed a good deal of drinking and fraternization with the other reporters at Lausanne. Aside from the educational sessions with Ryall, he was often in the company of Lincoln Steffens, as well as George Slocombe and Guy Hickok. Steffens was deeply impressed by Hemingway's cabled report on the Greek exodus from Thrace. It was so vivid, Steffens remarked, that "I was seeing the scene and said so." It was one more bit of evidence that made him feel that Hemingway had "the surest future" among the young writers and artists he was meeting in Europe. Encouraged, Hemingway showed him "My Old Man," which Steffens liked so much he sent it to Ray Long, the editor of

Cosmopolitan, for consideration. During his first week in Lausanne, Hemingway also found time to take a short trip to Chamby and make reservations for the vacation he and Hadley were planning. They were expecting a little convention of friends to join them: Chink Dorman-Smith planned to spend Christmas with them, and a neighbor of Hemingway's from Oak Park, Isabel Simmons, also intended to visit. So did the lumberman-poet Dave O'Neil and his family.

It was Hemingway's good fortune that he usually made a good impression on the older professionals whom he courted. Energetic, active, shadowboxing along the street as he walked, he was the picture of youthful ambition and spirit. "He was gay, he was sentimental, but always at work," Lincoln Steffens recalled. But there were other reporters who thought him too confident, with "a certain overbearing attitude that did not go down well with the rather friendly atmosphere of more seasoned newspapermen." Hemingway's behavior in a sparring match with G. Ward Price, a much respected correspondent for the *London Daily Mail,* shocked several members of the press corps. Price, who had covered the retreat from Caporetto for *Century Magazine,* had been badly shot up during World War I, was blind in one eye and wore a monocle in the other. He and Hemingway indulged in a few friendly sparring matches at a Lausanne gymnasium. During one of their bouts — with the same kind of sudden belligerence he had exhibited with the bespectacled Galantière — Hemingway mauled Price badly. After the match he was heard to say that he "hated" men who wore monocles.

Years later, in one of those quixotic gestures that continually surprise in Hemingway's behavior, he rearranged the story, claiming it was Price who regularly battered him during their sparring matches. Until, that is, with the assistance of Ryall, who served him as trainer, he called for a rematch and managed to break a couple of the Englishman's ribs. So Hemingway depicted the episode thirteen years later, characterizing Price, with gratuitous sarcasm, as "The Monocled Prince of the Press." But he also paid tribute to his sparring partner as "one of the best newspapermen of his time." It was a typical Hemingway performance, part compliment and part put-down. Price, with gentlemanly aplomb, some thirty years later, would recall Hemingway as a "good-looking dark young man" and remembered the punch as not quite so disastrous as Hemingway described it, though painful enough that he thought it might have splintered a rib. He knew nothing of Hemingway's past, Price admitted, wasn't even aware that Hemingway had published anything, "and, to be perfectly frank, I should have been surprised, at the time, if anyone had told me that he would found a new school as a fiction writer." Price did not see Hemingway again until the closing phases of World War II, when he was "hailed" in the Ritz Bar in Paris "by a mysterious figure with an enormous iron-gray beard, who said, 'You need not cut your old friends like that' — upon which I recognized — with difficulty — my former sparring-partner who had now become one of the world's masters of English prose." It was also typical of Hemingway that he would remember for the rest of his life any man — and there were many — with whom he had once had a vital contact.

8

Memory Is the Best Critic

IT WAS at Lausanne that Hemingway suffered, supposedly, one of the most dramatic losses of his career. The episode would have been a nightmare for any writer. When Hadley, early in December, packed for her trip to join her husband, she had the happy thought that Hemingway might want to show Lincoln Steffens some of his recent work. She packed whatever manuscripts she could find in a small valise. At the Gare de Lyon, she gave the luggage to a porter. But when she got to her compartment, she was horrified to find that the valise with the manuscripts was missing. Frantic, she checked the other compartments, made a search with the conductor — but without success. The valise had all too evidently been stolen.

What horrified her most was that she had packed the manuscript pages for Hemingway's unfinished first novel along with virtually all his other manuscript material, including the carbons. The overnight train trip was one of mounting anguish. When Hemingway met Hadley at the Lausanne station on December 3, she immediately broke down and sobbed so uncontrollably she couldn't tell him what was wrong.

In *A Moveable Feast,* Hemingway, with insidious credibility, made a legendary episode of the scene, describing Hadley's fright and his own consoling affection: "I told her that no matter what the dreadful thing was that had happened nothing could be that bad, and whatever it was, it was all right and not to worry." When he learned what had been lost, he was stunned, but certain that Hadley could not have packed all the carbons as well. As Hemingway recalled it in his dramatic scenario, he had immediately hired someone to take over his assignment. "I was making good money then at journalism, and took the train to Paris. It was true all right and I remember what I did in the night after I let myself into the flat and found it was true," thus leaving all his biographers to speculate on the revengeful act — a binge? a night with a whore? — by which he relieved his anger and frustration.

The evidence, however, suggests that little about the story, except the loss of his manuscripts, or some of his manuscripts, was true. Hemingway did not make a hurried return to Paris, nor, as some biographical accounts have reconstructed the story, did he spend the following day with Gertrude Stein and Alice B. Toklas, having lunch and reading over Stein's recent writings, talking all afternoon, before he took the train back to Lausanne. Stein and Alice Toklas were still in St.-Rémy in Provence and did not return to Paris until early February 1923. (In a letter to her friend Etta Cone, dated February 6, Stein speaks of being "just back" at the rue de Fleurus.) The available evidence, in fact, indicates that it was not Hemingway but his friends Hickok and Steffens who, within a few days, returned to Paris, where they went at once to the Bureau of Lost and Found, told Hadley's story to the official there, and searched through the three days' worth of items. Having no good news to report, Steffens wrote to Hemingway on December 9 that the valise was still missing and had most likely been stolen. In the meantime, Hemingway had also written to Bill Bird, asking if he could manage to get a free advertisement, by way of his newspaper connections, offering a reward of 150 francs (about $12). But Bird, as Steffens reported back to Hemingway, thought Hemingway would have to offer more of an inducement. "No use, I think, and Billy said so," Steffens reported. Hemingway should wire them whether he wanted to offer more money. "I am afraid the stuff is lost, Hem," Steffens added. "I am sorry, but I guess you will have to rewrite your 'early works' or do better things hereafter to make up for them." On December 11, Bill Bird wrote Hemingway to corroborate the fact that he would have to offer a larger reward, suggesting that Hemingway use an agency that would put up posters around the Gare de Lyon area.

Even then, Hemingway did not return to Paris to check whether Hadley had perhaps left some of the carbons in their apartment. In fact, he waited until after his Christmas vacation with Hadley and Chink Dorman-Smith at Chamby. There, the three enjoyed a pre-holiday week or more of skiing and bobsledding, with shopping expeditions to nearby Montreux. Nor did the loss dim the jolly Christmas day celebrations of the three friends, who opened their presents and Christmas stockings at breakfast time in the Hemingways' rented chalet. They spent the day skiing, taking lunch in an empty cattle barn on the steep slope of a mountain. Hemingway — a year later, on the first anniversary of the purportedly disastrous loss of his manuscripts, in a nostalgic article for the *Toronto Star* — described his holiday as "the kind of Christmas you can only get on top of the world."

It was not until mid-January 1923 that Hemingway finally made his return to Paris. (Whether, after that lapse of healing time, he committed the drastic act he hinted at in *A Moveable Feast* is uncertain.) Writing to Ezra Pound about the loss of his "Juvenilia," on January 23, he reported his dismay at finding, on a trip to Paris the week before, that Hadley "had made the job complete by including all carbons, duplicates, etc." All that remained of "my complete works," he wrote, consisted of three pencil drafts of a "bum poem which was later scrapped," some correspondence with John McClure, the editor of *The Double-Dealer,* and some carbons of his *Star* articles. Pound, no doubt, would say "Good," Hemingway thought. "But don't say it to me. I ain't yet reached that mood. 3 years on the damn stuff. Some like that Paris 1922 I fancied."

Pound's answer was what Hemingway expected: Hemingway should regard the loss as an "act of Gawd." No one, Pound claimed, had ever been *known* to have lost anything by the suppression of early work. "The *point* is: how much of it can you remember?" What Hemingway was out of pocket, he maintained, was the time it would take to rewrite the parts he could remember, no doubt "a bloody sweat." Pound went on to give a remarkably cogent analysis of the intimate connection between a writer's style and his memory. If the form of a story was right, he claimed, one ought to be able to reassemble it from memory, otherwise not. "As hez been remarked: memory is the best critic. If the thing wobbles & wont reform, then it had no proper construction & never *wd* have been *right.* All of which is probably cold comfort." Hemingway took the lecture with droll equanimity: "I thank you for your advice to a young man on the occasion of the loss by stealing of his complete works. It is very sound. I thank you again."

Yet the inventory of Hemingway's "complete works" lost at the Gare de Lyon remains hazy and somewhat exaggerated: Hemingway's recollections varied over the years. "My Old Man" had been saved because Steffens had sent it to Ray Long. "Up in Michigan," which Stein had claimed was a good but unpublishable story, had been stowed away in a drawer. The most painful loss — "What was going to be my first novel" — was definitely lost, as were some twelve or more poems, aside from the six that Harriet Monroe had in her keeping. And there were, in one of Hemingway's recollections, an undetermined number of stories that he had spent "a whole winter in Petoskey and later in Toronto writing."

But the manuscript versions of some three dozen poems written in Chicago and during his first year in Paris have subsequently been recovered and posthumously published. Several early manuscripts, among them "The Mercenaries," "The Woppian Way," "The Ash Heel's Tendon," "Portrait of an Idealist in Love" and "Cross Roads — An Anthology," mostly written during his winter stint in

Petoskey and in Chicago, have surfaced among his voluminous papers at the Kennedy Library, a few of which have been published. Hemingway had left them, along with several of his Chicago poems, in a box with his parents before his trip to Paris only the year before. It seems unlikely that he could have forgotten about that cache when he blithely claimed in his letter to Pound that his complete works, the productivity of three years, had been lost. The "Paris 1922" sketches that he grieved the loss of may well have been among the stolen works — in which case, Hemingway did manage to rewrite them very effectively, thereby confirming Pound's opinion.

In fact, it is difficult to believe that Hemingway, no matter how industrious, could have accomplished a great deal of serious writing that first year abroad. His journalistic activities and the necessary backgrounding they required — the Genoa Conference, the travels in Germany, the Clemenceau interview, his coverage of the Greco-Turkish war, the Lausanne Conference — were extensive. ("I've traveled nearly 10,000 miles by R.R. this past year," Hemingway boasted to his father.) There were also the vacation travels — the two ski trips to Chamby, the sentimental journey to Italy, the fishing expedition in the Black Forest. The enormity of his literary loss is definitely open to question.

There is no doubt, however, that Hemingway brooded over it, however compassionate and concerned he might have been about Hadley at the Lausanne train station. Lincoln Steffens, who had witnessed the scene, felt that Hemingway had been remarkably patient and far less upset than his wife. But Hemingway must have entertained some suspicions that Hadley's accidental loss of his work had been, at least, a matter of carelessness on her part. Knowing how valuable it was to Hemingway, why hadn't she kept the small valise in her possession instead of giving it to the porter? (In another version of the story, she had left the valise on her seat, then stepped outside the car for a few moments.) Perhaps Hemingway also suspected she had had some deeper psychological motivation.

Neither Hemingway nor Hadley would ever forget the episode. Indeed, they had little chance of escape; it was kept alive by the queries of later biographers and scholars. Hadley was convinced that Hemingway had been deeply damaged by the loss. In 1952, she told one biographer that Hemingway had put himself so deeply into the writing of his first novel (it was the "truly wonderful chapters" of the novel that she most remembered) that he "never recovered from the pain of this irreparable loss." She complained to another biographer in 1965, "That painful subject again!" But Hadley's testimony is contradictory. In 1970, she admitted to another biographer, Michael Reynolds, that she had never read the manuscript of the novel because Hemingway had not discussed it with her. "It was sacred to himself — consequently the loss, through my misadventure, was deadly to him." What she remembered were some stories about Nick Adams. At that point she was convinced that it wasn't a novel but rather chapters of an autobiographical work that had been lost. Asked if Hemingway had tried to reconstruct the lost material, she thought that he did "strive to dig parts of it out of the back of his mind. How successfully I do not know as I never saw a completed work about this young man Nick Adams."

Hemingway would give this much-discussed episode in his life an ominous interpretation in *The Garden of Eden,* the posthumously published novel that he began writing in 1946. There, Catherine Bourne deliberately burns her husband's stories in an incinerator, stealing the notebooks in which he had been writing them from his Vuitton suitcase and dousing them with gasoline to make a real blaze of it. Under the cover of fiction, he turned Hadley's accidental loss into a deliberate and vengeful act by a possessive, jealous wife who laid claim to her husband's stories because she had paid for them with her financial support. Hemingway had a tenacious memory even where long-buried events were concerned, and his depiction of David Bourne's realization of his loss has all the freshness of a recent event: "He closed and locked the suitcase and searched all of the drawers in the armoire and searched the room. He had not believed that the stories could be gone. He had not believed that she could do it."

In Hemingway, the mere spark of experience could ignite grievances that burned long years in his fiction. The fact that in the stories that Catherine Bourne destroyed, David had been trying to recapture and redeem the image of his dead father, a white hunter in Africa (as well as his own collapsing literary reputation), gives the episode an added irony. The murderous rage that Bourne supposedly feels — but does not convey with any real conviction in the edited and published version of the novel — may be only the pale reflection of the hurt and anger Hemingway had felt but never expressed to Hadley.

As late as 1951, Hemingway would tell one of his biographers that the pain of that loss had been so bad that he had tried "to forget it and put it out of my mind almost with surgery." And in *A Moveable Feast,* he would picture himself as having been nearly destroyed, unmanned, by the loss, that it had taken him months to recover: "It was a bad time and I did not think I could write any more then." But memory was a volatile agent in Hemingway's character. In fact, the loss of his manuscripts acted as a spur. It marked the real beginnings of his career as one of the most recognized writers of his time.

✓✓✓

Hemingway's depression over the loss of his manuscripts could hardly have been relieved by his growing squabbles with the International News Service. His complaints to Frank Mason about the extent of his work and his meager salary, however, did bring prompt relief in the form of a $35 increase, making his weekly salary $95, as of November 29 — in 1922, hardly the miserly amount he complained of. When the early checks failed to reflect the full increase, he promptly wrote the firm asking that the error be rectified. To keep his identity secret in wiring his reports to the INS, Hemingway was using the name John Hadley, and Hadley may have been further caught up in the conspiracy by keeping the INS informed of Hemingway's address in the Balkans. (She would later admit that her husband's double-dealing had seared her "puritan soul.") But when the INS New York bureau cabled that "Hadley" had been scooped on an announcement involving Lord Curzon, Hemingway at first scribbled an angry reply on the back of the cable, saying that the story had broken at eleven P.M. and if Mason wanted twenty-four-hour service, he should "Pay for it." For the cabled message, however, he softened the language to say rather innocuously that twenty-four-hour service was "costly." The euphemism defeated his purpose. Mason replied, saying that the Curzon story was certainly worth paying the necessary tolls: "DONT UNDERSTAND WHETHER COSTLY REFERS TO TOLLS OR WHAT."

The real break came in mid-December when Hemingway sent an urgent request for expenses due him amounting to 800 Swiss francs, and Mason countered that the sum did not seem justified according to their bookkeeping records. He urged Hemingway to submit his receipts as soon as possible so they could settle the account. He signed the wire with kindest regards. Hemingway, furious, sent a blunt reply in cablese: "SUGGEST YOU UPSTICK BOOKS ASSWARDS." In an angry follow-up letter he complained that Mason's refusal to send the money he needed to pay his hotel bills and other expenses had caused him a great deal of extra expense and inconvenience and had smashed up all his vacation plans. "I can only regard it as an unfriendly and insulting gesture," he said.

✓✓✓

"Mussolini told me at Lausanne, you know, that I couldn't ever live in Italy again," Hemingway wrote Ezra Pound in a January 23 letter, giving it as one of the several reasons for his delay in making a proposed visit to Rapallo. Were Pound's "fascist pals," he asked, liable to give Hadley castor oil? But his real reluctance, it appears, was that Pound was proposing a walking tour of the Romagna, the country of Sigismondo Malatesta, the Renaissance condottiere, power broker, and patron of the arts. (Pound was then in the process of researching and writing his Malatesta cantos.) Hemingway, enjoying the skiing in Chamby, felt no inclination "to eat bad food and sleep in poor inns in Italy," particularly following in the footsteps of a historical personage about whom he had little knowledge and less interest.

How plausible was Hemingway's claim that Mussolini had threatened him? The insolent shadow of the Italian dictator and the violent riots, street beatings, and political murders that accompanied his rise to power had begun to touch the lives of many American expatriates and literary figures. Mussolini was, indeed, touchy and peremptory in his dealings with the foreign press. Once he had consolidated his power base, foreign reporters who wrote critically about him were in danger of being roughed up or expelled, or worse. In 1925, George Seldes, for instance, was deported — and barely escaped being beaten at the border town of Modano — for publishing, in the Paris edition of the *Chicago Tribune,* an article on the brutal murder of the outspoken Socialist leader Giacomo Matteotti which implicated Mussolini in the crime. Hemingway, in the first of his articles on the Lausanne Conference, having called Mussolini the biggest bluff in Europe, had gone on to brag, "If Mussolini would have me taken out and shot tomorrow morning I would still regard him as a bluff. The shooting would be a bluff." It was a risky, if rhetorical, challenge.

But the fact is that the Italian dictator, after a mere week in office as prime minister, had spent only two days at the Lausanne Conference, November 20 and 21, making his theatrically late appearance at the inaugural ceremonies on November 20, and disdainfully participating in the public sessions. In that brief span, Mussolini had kept up a busy schedule of receiving delegations and giving out press statements. Since Hemingway's passport reveals that he crossed the Swiss border at Vallorbe on November 21, presumably in the morning, it seems highly questionable that he had managed a private interview with the busy dictator, and most likely that he had only attended the crowded press conference of November 21 along with all the other reporters on the last day of Mussolini's attendance. Hemingway's jealous reaction to Clare Sheridan's private interview with Il Duce suggests that he was granted no such favor. More telling is the fact that Hemingway, who in all of his other published articles made a point of citing every personal encounter he had with celebrities and statesmen, never mentioned any private interview in his articles for the *Star.*

If Mussolini had read Hemingway's scathing characterization of him as a bluff, he might well have been furious enough to make such a threat. But the article was neither written nor published until well after Mussolini, surrounded by his Blackshirts, had staged a dramatic departure at the Lausanne station. Hemingway's article appeared two months later, in the January 27, 1923, issue of the *Toronto Daily Star.* (That is, four days *after* Hemingway had written Pound about Mussolini's edict.) Was it possible, if not probable, that Mussolini had read and angrily responded to Hemingway's more admiring Milan interview, five months earlier? Even so, Hemingway was far too opportunistic a reporter not to have made use of his supposed confrontation with the Duce at Lausanne. The probability is that the confrontation never took place.

Pound, however, seems to have taken the news as fact. "You musn't tease Benito," he wrote Hemingway, from what he jokingly referred to as Fascisti Headquarters in Rapallo. "Otherwise the climate is *perfectly lovely,* perfectly lovely." Pound was still pushing for their walking tour of the Malatesta sites, all the more so because he was planning a trip to Calabria. But Hemingway remained reluctant. He was working on "new stuff" and had enough "grub money" for six to eight months. He and Hadley hadn't planned to get to Rapallo until the end of February when, it seemed, Pound would be gone.

Hemingway hinted that he might rather go to Calabria, if, that was, Pound wasn't planning on making the trip with Nancy Cunard. "Drop this unbecoming delicacy," he joked, suggesting that Pound might have plans to celebrate the rites of spring while on the road with the notorious heiress. "I aims to cramp no man's stride on the Road," he added. Pound, however, preferred to meet in Rapallo, where he was staying with his wife. "The Fascio is very quiet and well behaved here. I can't answer for Calabria."

The Hemingways did manage, after all, to get to Rapallo while the Pounds were still there. They made the trip in response to one of Ezra's antically capitalized and heavily marked-up letters, with the words "COME NOW" underlined four or five times with blue pencil, indicating that Pound "was feeling the limitations of language," so Hemingway reported in an undated manuscript item. They had begun the journey within twelve hours of receiving the letter, "a tribute to Ezra's prose style," leaving the slush of a mountain winter behind and taking the train to Italy, catching the postcard glimpses of blue sea and damp, walled gardens in between the camera-shutter clicks of the many tunnels en route. The two couples made their walking tour, though in the confused chronology of the correspondence between Pound, Hemingway, and various third parties, the exact date is nowise clear. (It may well have been on a second meeting sometime between mid-February and early March.) Hemingway, so the legend goes, used his knowledge of military strategy to outline the tactics of Malatesta's battle campaigns in Piombino and Orbetello for Pound's benefit. ("I tried to explain to him how they would, more or less, have to have been fought.") Hadley remembered their picnic lunches of bread and wine, with figs for dessert, and the fact that Pound was more agreeable than usual. She suspected that the expedition was more fun for Hemingway than it was for her. She also wondered whether Hemingway wasn't a bit in love with Dorothy Pound.

II

The necessary constructs of biography, when certainties are hard to come by: "I've been working hard and have two things done," Hemingway wrote Gertrude Stein in a letter from Rapallo tentatively dated February 18, 1923. That letter provides an opening but uncertain date for the Hemingways and the Pounds' trek to the sites of Sigismondo Malatesta's military campaigns. It was in that letter that Hemingway told Stein that the Pounds had left Rapallo three days after he and Hadley had arrived there. A final date for that excursion seems to be March 10, when Hemingway wrote to Ezra Pound from Milan, recounting some details from their visit to Orbetello. ("That guy who tried to stop us that night was Della Rossa a millionaire archeologist.")

It is possible, though by no means certain, that one of the two things Hemingway had written was the poem "They All Made Peace — What Is Peace?" a trendy, vanguard satirical poem about the Lausanne Conference, written in a Steinian vein. Hemingway had a particularly vivid recollection of writing the poem. He remembered (or misremembered) that he had written it following a return visit to Paris (not, obviously, the famous overnight trip to Paris after the loss of his manuscripts but a later visit, perhaps, after February 6) when he had spent an entire day with Gertrude Stein and Alice Toklas before catching the evening train to Lausanne. On the train ride, he claimed, facing the prospect of opening the wire service on the following morning, he consoled himself with a bottle of Beaune in the dining car. Apparently under the influence of the wine and the example of Stein's recent work, he wrote his caustic poem on the conference. Its twin themes were politics and sex, as indicated by the bawdy ambiguity of its title. Cast in the form of the disjunctive word plays and poems Stein had been writing in St.-Rémy ("A Saint in Seven," "Saints and Singing," etc.), Hemingway's poem ran along in blunt disconnected statements:

> Baron Hayashi gets in and out of the automobile.
> Monsieur Barrere gets telegrams. So does Marquis
> Garroni.

Clearly intending to shock, Hemingway depicted the major statesmen (among them some former heroes) as pederasts:

> Lord Curzon likes young boys.
> So does Chicherin.
> So does Mustapha Kemal. He is good looking too.
> His eyes are too close together but he makes war. That
> is the way he is.

He repeated his little anecdote about Mussolini, with his "nigger eyes," reading his book upside down. And he made jocular references to Steffens and the American ambassador, Richard Washburn Child. "Lincoln Steffens is with Child. The big C. makes the joke easy." With a final topical reference to Mosul, the oil-producing city on the border of Turkey, which hinted at secret oil deals and the territorial dispute that had arisen between Turkey and Great Britain, and a passing reference to the Greek Orthodox patriarch of Smyrna, who had been hanged by the Turks, Hemingway nailed down the high talk of the peace tables to the more murderous realities. Far from being bereft of inspiration, he had created one of his more sophisticated and successful poems.

Gertrude Stein, however, would remember Hemingway's all-day visit to the rue de Fleurus that spring under very different circumstances:

> He and his wife went away on a trip and shortly after Hemingway turned up alone. He came to the house about ten o'clock in the morning and he stayed, he stayed for lunch, he stayed all afternoon, he stayed for dinner and he stayed until about ten o'clock at night and then all of a sudden he announced that his wife was enceinte and then with great bitterness, and I, I am too young to be a father. We consoled him as best we could and sent him on his way.

Hemingway, years later, acknowledged the validity of the episode when Stein published her maliciously funny version of it in *The Autobiography of Alice B. Toklas,* but he clearly disagreed with Stein's interpretation. In an angry letter to Ezra Pound, he claimed that when Bumby was going to be born, he was merely "crabbing" to Stein about the fact that he didn't have enough money to head a family and try to write. Yet, even that late he seems to have unconsciously associated the event with something drastic. "Pero no hay remedio" (But there is no remedy), he told Pound, misquoting the caption of one of Goya's *Disasters of War* etchings. Stein had said he said he was "too young to be a father." But he added scornfully, "Had been a father considerable time." Guy Hickok, too, would recall Hemingway's dismay at the time. He and a friend had been discussing birth control methods in his *Brooklyn Eagle* office. Hemingway, who had been silent throughout the discussion, then spoke up with bitter finality, "There is no sure preventative." Hickok passed the story on to Steffens; that was how Steffens learned of Hadley's pregnancy. It would not be one of the stranger ironies of biography if the solution to the tangled chronological problems of the trip to Rapallo, the walking tour with the Pounds, the visit to Stein, even the stories and poems Hemingway was writing at the time — and their subliminal motivations — could only be determined by the date of Hadley's pregnancy and the date that she had informed her husband.

⁂

But there is still the question of the "two things" written. Hemingway had presumably already begun work on some of the vignettes from *in our time* which would first appear in the Spring 1923 "Exiles" issue of *The Little Review,* along with "They All Made Peace." He seems also to have begun the preliminary sketches for a later story, "Cat in the Rain." A few of the vignettes, those dealing with the fighting around Mons, may have been begun at Chamby when he was seeing Chink Dorman-Smith. In his Rapallo letter to Stein, Hemingway frankly, and a bit fawningly, expressed his indebtedness to her: "I've thought a lot about the things you said about working and am starting that way at the beginning. If you think of anything else I wish you'd write it to me. Am working hard about creating and keep my mind going about it all the time. Mind seems to be working better." His tone sounds as if he had had a fairly recent conference with Stein on the problems of writing.

He had also been reading Stein's new book, *Geography and Plays* (published at her own expense by the Four Seas Company), a collection of short pieces and plays, most of them in her difficult, gnomic style. Nonetheless, Hemingway assured her, "I had a wonderful time with the book." There is evidence, in fact, that Hemingway liked the book quite well, indeed. When, in his story "Soldier's Home," Hemingway came to write about the souvenir photograph of Harold Krebs and the German girls on the Rhine, he consciously or unconsciously lifted and adapted a line from Stein's play-poem "Accents in Alsace": "In the photograph the Rhine hardly showed."

Whether at Stein's request or on his own volition, he tried his hand at writing a review of *Geography and Plays* for the Paris edition of the *Chicago Tribune.* It appeared in the March 5 issue of the paper in "Notes on New Books," edited by Stein's friend W. Dawson Johnston. Hemingway had sent the review to Stein, giving her carte blanche to edit it as she saw fit. "You can cut out any or all of it and if you don't like it I'll do another one. That's the liberalest offer I know how to make." It was his first published book review, a statement of his new literary alliances since his arrival in Paris, and it served as an occasion for a boisterous attack on what he regarded as the literary establishment of the moment, including Sinclair Lewis, *The Saturday Evening Post,* and "the unbelievably stupid but thoroughly conscientious young men who compile the Dial."

> Gertrude Stein is a sort of gauge of civilization. If you think Mr. Sinclair Lewis is a great writer and Babbitt a great book you probably won't like Gertrude Stein. If you think Mr. Lewis is doing the best he can employing a *Saturday Evening Post* technique to prove an H. L. Mencken theory with masses of detail and occasional interjected shots of BEAUTY . . . and somebody ever lends you a copy of Geography and Plays, or if you buy one, you will be very happy for a number of hours.

Not content with that salvo, he sent off another:

> Gertrude Stein is probably the most first rate intelligence employed in writing today. If you are tired of Mr. D. H. Lawrence who writes extremely well with the intelligence of a head waiter or Mr. Wells who is believed to be intelligent because of a capacity for sustained marathon thinking . . . you ought to read Gertrude Stein.

Hemingway recommended that interested readers should also read her *Three Lives,* particularly the story "Melanctha," which he deemed "one of the three best short stories in English," leaving readers free to choose the other two themselves. He also gave faint praise to Sherwood Anderson's introduction to the Stein volume (though he had liked it very well when he had first read it a year earlier). Now he called it "a little restrained," attributing the flaw to Anderson's having been the recipient of the first annual Dial Award. (It carried with it a sum of $2000.) Undoubtedly, Hemingway claimed, "the new respectability was still on him" when he wrote the introduction. It was the first public notice of Hemingway's growing attempt to disengage himself from Anderson's example and reputation.

Stein, sending Hemingway a copy of the review, said she was delighted with it and so was Dawson Johnston. It had evidently been cut; she regretted that it "was mutilated." "You see," she added, "I would make a rotten editor. I have such a strong feeling about the sanctity of the written word and the typewritten more than I have for the printed, but then there is diplomacy. What was it that our great and good president said, open covenants openly arrived at, wasn't that it?" Paris was nice and quiet, she said. "Incidentally, have a new Picasso and a new somebody else." She and Alice were looking forward to seeing him in Paris.

Hemingway and Hadley were planning to go skiing at Cortina d'Ampezzo at the end of the month, so Hemingway informed Stein. Rapallo was disappointing; the tide rose and fell only about an inch, he said, and they had had seven days of muggy weather. "The place aint much," he added. Rapallo was disappointing in other ways, as well. He had planned to play tennis and do some sparring with a "nice guy," the painter Mike Strater, but Strater had sprained his ankle, so that was off. Hemingway had first met Henry "Mike" Strater and his wife, Maggie, at Pound's studio in Paris after his return from Constantinople. A tall and lumbering six-footer with a stutter when he got excited or nervous, Strater had studied and painted in Spain and Paris. He was a Princeton friend of F. Scott Fitzgerald's, who, in fact, had used Strater as the model for Burne Holiday, the pacifist and philosopher of his best-selling novel *This Side of Paradise*. At Rapallo, Strater painted a portrait of Hemingway (he had made an earlier one of Hemingway in a gray sweatshirt in Auteuil) and what Hemingway deemed a "corking portrait" of Hadley.

Also at Rapallo, Hemingway met Edward J. O'Brien, the editor of the annual *Best Short Stories* volumes, published by the Boston firm Small, Maynard and Company. O'Brien was boarding in a monastery in nearby Montallegro. Hemingway's forceful effect on others might be judged by the fact that when O'Brien read "My Old Man," he decided to include it in his forthcoming 1923 anthology, even though the story had not yet appeared in print. Hemingway told O'Brien, as he frequently did with people he met during this period, about the loss of his manuscripts. The editor, it seemed to him, was "hurt far more than I was." Remembering Chink Dorman-Smith's advice never to discuss casualties, however, Hemingway felt he should ease O'Brien's sorrow by feeding him "all that stuff you feed the troops" about how he intended to go on and bravely start writing stories again. Beneath the sardonic humor of his remark, there is also a sense of pride in being able to manipulate the sympathies of well-wishers and friends. His soulful tale and stiff upper lip were effective. When the *Best Short Stories of 1923* appeared, O'Brien dedicated the volume to his young "discovery." Unfortunately, he spelled the name as Hemenway.

111

In his early stories, Hemingway did not stray far from autobiographical terrain. He made use of every advantage life presented, and it was not strange that Hadley's pregnancy — and his response to it — provided him with the leverage for a series of stories on marital discord. Hemingway's mood is reflected in a circumstantially related story written a year later. In "Cross-Country Snow," Nick Adams and a younger friend, George, nicknamed Gidge, are mournfully completing a day's skiing excursion in a Swiss mountain resort. George is slated to return to school on the late train from Montreux. Nick and his wife, Helen, are due to return to the States. Helen's pregnancy, the precipitating cause of their return — and the hidden motivating force of the story — is not revealed until near the end of the tale. At several points, the story is autobiographical. The George of the story, for instance, has been based on young George O'Neil, who had been skiing and bobsledding with Hemingway at Chamby and Les Avants. The mentions of Montreux and the Dent du Lys fix the place and suggest the time as that of Hemingway's long Christmas vacation, though Hemingway may not have known yet that Hadley was pregnant. Nick and George commiserate on the loss of their life-without-consequences; they mourn the opportunities for skiing and fishing they are now being forced to give up. George, in unabashed youthfulness, complains, "Gee . . . don't you wish we could just bum together? Take our skis and go on the train to where there was good running . . . just take repair kit and extra sweaters and pyjamas in our rucksacks and not give a damn about school or anything." The "anything" should be taken as an oblique reference to Nick's coming fatherhood. Hemingway firmly establishes his characters' camaraderie, a relationship free from the distractions of marriage: "George and Nick were happy. They were fond of each other. They knew they had the run back home ahead of them." The good friends try hard to put the best face on this last episode of their mountain idyll. George wishes they could make a promise that they will go skiing together in the future. But Nick sullenly concludes, "There isn't any good in promising." The premise of the story is thin, the boyish sentimentality not quite credible. Yet its very weaknesses, in a strange way, mark it as one of the quintessential Hemingway stories in praise of male companionship — the belief in the dubious idyllic life of masculine Edens so often compromised by the intrusion of women.

Two other stories relating to the period of Hadley's term suggest a certain sourness of mood. Only obliquely do they refer to a pregnancy. But they represent Hemingway in faultless command of his subjects, drawing every nuance from the intermittent use of dialogue. "Cat in the Rain" reads like a scenario for one of the better foreign films. A young wife looks out a hotel window at the sodden landscape of an Italian seaside resort. She is restless, dissatisfied. Her young husband, reading on the bed, pays scant attention to his wife's boredom. She spies a cat huddling from the relentless rain under one of the green patio tables and decides that she wants a kitty — that kitty. But when she goes out, under a protective umbrella held by a solicitous hotel maid, she discovers that the kitty is gone. In her hotel room, sitting in front of the mirror, she is unhappy with the way her hair looks. (Like Hadley, she has bobbed her hair.) When her husband says that he likes it the way it is, she complains, "I get so tired of it . . . I get so tired of looking like a boy."

In an exasperated litany (it is one of Hemingway's perfect sequences) the young woman itemizes her wants. "And I want to eat at a table with my own silver and I want candles. And I want it to be spring and I want to brush my hair out in front of a mirror and I want a kitty and I want some new clothes." Her husband's response is blunt: "Oh, shut up and get something to read." In the end the wife has at least one of her wishes; the overly attentive *padrone* sends up a big tortoiseshell cat for her. Her inattentive husband continues his rainy-day reading in bed.

Hemingway, not very convincingly, denied any autobiographical element in "Cat in the Rain." He maintained that the models for his story were a young American couple he had met in Genoa. (Ironically, Agnes von Kurowsky had written him about her "thrilling rescue" of a kitten out in the rain when she had been stationed in Florence, adding another thread to the autobiographical circumstances of the story.) At the same time, he noted that the attentive *padrone* was the hotel keeper in Cortina d'Ampezzo, where he and Hadley vacationed after their stay at Rapallo — which rather contradicts his claim that the story had been written at Rapallo when Hadley "was 4 months pregnant." He seems instead, really, to have made notes for the story at Rapallo and completed it later at Cortina.

About the second story, "Out of Season," there was no question in Hemingway's mind that the story, definitely written in 1923 at Cortina, was based on an actual experience, a fight with Hadley. The story was, he claimed, "an almost literal transcription of what happened. Your ear is always more acute when you have been upset by a row of any sort, mine I mean, and when I came in from the unproductive fishing trip I wrote that story right off on the typewriter without punctuation."

Structurally, "Out of Season" is the most masterly and subtle of the three stories. Everything is suggested, nothing examined in detail, yet it is a mordant character analysis of the principals in a marriage. On the surface, it is a straightforward account of an illegal trout-fishing expedition. Though it is off season, the young husband of the story is conned into making the trip by the hotel gardener, an alcoholic older man named Peduzzi. Peduzzi has promised excellent fishing, and the too compliant husband — much to the wife's disgust — agrees to go along with it, though he does not want to do anything illegal. His wife tags along, fuming at his cowardice. "Of course," she says, "you haven't got the guts to just go back. . . . Of course you have to go on." The husband is plainly fearful but prefers to assert himself against his wife rather than the wheedling Peduzzi.

Peduzzi also cons the husband into buying a bottle of Marsala for their excursion. When they reach the muddy river, the old gardener indicates that they still have a half hour to go to find the best spot. That provides the husband with the excuse to suggest that his wife go back to the hotel — the weather is cloudy, there is the threat of rain, they are not likely to have much fun; he is being overprotective of her but for unspecified reasons. She leaves. Peduzzi, pleased by the wife's departure, convinces the young husband that the spot they are in is perfectly good for fishing. The husband is still uneasy: "He felt uncomfortable and afraid that any minute a gamekeeper or a posse of citizens would come over the bank from the town." When it turns out that neither of them has any lead for a sinker (Hemingway is deft at using such innocuous symbols of male inadequacy), the fishing party is called off, much to the relief of the young husband. They drink up the Marsala, Peduzzi refusing until the husband has taken two swigs at the bottle and then craftily finishing it off himself. He next cons the young man out of four lire for another try the next morning, though it is clear that the husband is not going to risk another illegal adventure or a squabble with his wife. (Peduzzi had asked for five, but the husband only gives him four: Hemingway's recognition of the minor ways men restore their self-esteem in losing encounters.) Out of mere bits of dialogue and spare descriptions, Hemingway manages to create a subtle examination not just of marital discord, but of the wars of character that prompt and provoke the discord.

Often, in the more complex Hemingway stories, some central event, like a stone cast into the middle of a pond, ripples outward toward the edges of the story. In "Out of Season," it is clear that the real quarrel between the young couple is not the illegal fishing trip but some more intimate agenda. Midway in the story, Hemingway reveals that the couple has had a prior nagging and still unresolved quarrel. It is one of Hemingway's masterstrokes that this item of information connects up with the very beginning of the story. There, as if in passing, he supplies the information that the young couple were just going to lunch when Peduzzi first approached the husband. In the time frame of the story, their luncheon quarrel becomes the motivating factor for the action:

> "I'm sorry you feel so rotten, Tiny," he said. "I'm sorry I talked the way I did at lunch. We were both getting at the same thing from different angles."
>
> "It doesn't make any difference," she said. "None of it makes any difference."
>
> "Are you too cold?" he asked. "I wish you'd worn another sweater."
>
> "I've got on three sweaters."

The presumption is that the young woman may be pregnant (the reason for her husband's concern about her health). But the husband's solicitousness is also a backhanded reminder that her condition has jeopardized their freedom, sentiments Hemingway was beginning to feel on facing fatherhood for the first time. The illegal fishing expedition has become a convenient arguing point for other more intimate dissatisfactions. The suggestion is that the earlier argument was brought on by the young husband's broaching the subject of an abortion.

"Out of Season" has other hidden, perhaps unconscious, allusions that relate to Hemingway's life and recollections: Peduzzi's taste for Marsala wine, for instance. When the subject of the wine is first mentioned, the young man thinks, "What in hell makes him say marsala? That's what Max Beerbohm drinks," a gratuitous remembrance of Hemingway's visit to the aged writer in Rapallo. Peduzzi also has a disagreeable habit of calling the husband "*caro,*" with unwarranted familiarity. Hemingway makes the reader sense there is something a little sinister about the way Peduzzi manages to manipulate the young man. The episode of the wine, therefore, stirs up the queasier biographical connection of Hemingway's account — whether true or a later invention — of the homosexual Englishman with the beautiful manners who visited him in the Milan hospital and brought him a bottle of Marsala, but got "wet" about wanting to see his wounds dressed.

III

Robert McAlmon, the American writer and publisher, was certain that he had first met Hemingway in Rapallo in 1923, soon after the Pounds had left town. Hemingway, however, could not remember when they had first met; it was, perhaps, a memory he preferred to forget. McAlmon had been traveling in Italy on one of his periodic escapes from Paris. (In Rome, McAlmon had seen Mussolini in a histrionic public appearance, standing on a balcony, reaching out and crushing something in his powerful fist, declaring, "I hold Rome in the hollow of my hand.") In Venice, Nancy Cunard had first mentioned to him the man she mistakenly referred to as the "innocent young Canadian" who was visiting the Pounds. As with many memoirs of the period, McAlmon's lively recollections in *Being Geniuses Together* (and in an unbridled private letter to the Yale scholar Norman Holmes Pearson) represent the convergence of fact, misinformation, true accounts slanted by personal prejudice, and moments of posing for posterity which make up the authorized materials from which substantial biographies are constructed.

En route from Venice to the French Riviera, McAlmon recalled, he stopped off at Rapallo and met the Hemingways on his first night at the Hotel Splendide. He was clearly impressed by Hemingway, three years younger than he, but in an ambivalent way. He remembered Hemingway as, at times, "deliberately hard-boiled, case-hardened and old" — a nice evaluation; and at other times, "the hurt, sensitive boy, deliberately young and naive, wanting to be brave, and somehow on the defensive" — an estimate that seems equally apt. During the day, he and Hemingway wrote in their hotel rooms. But when the sun went down, Rapallo was dismal and depressing. At night, they both managed to drink "moderately." (When Hemingway met him, McAlmon already had a reputation as a hard drinker. "If the world's going to hell," McAlmon claimed, "I'm going there with it, and not in the back ranks either.") Hemingway talked a lot, perhaps too much, about Gertrude Stein, Harriet Monroe, and Sherwood Anderson. McAlmon also heard the distressing tale of the lost manuscripts.

In McAlmon's recollection, both Hadley and Maggie Strater, Mike Strater's wife, were pregnant at the time. Strater was not particularly perturbed about being a father a second time; McAlmon characterized him as having a roving eye, in any event, but with little chance of indulging it in his wife's presence. Hemingway, on the other hand, frequently complained "in a boyish way" that he and Hadley "couldn't have any fun anymore" because of her condition. McAlmon would, in fact, remember that confession in referring, rather derisively, to one of Hemingway's stories — undoubtedly "Cross-Country Snow" — in which the young hero stated, as he remembered it, "It isn't fun any more if you can't ski." McAlmon would have been on target if he had mentioned any of Hemingway's three stories of the period. The lack of "fun," in fact, forms a minor leitmotif in the stories drawn from Hemingway's early experience of imminent fatherhood. In "Cross-Country Snow," George suggests that maybe they will never go skiing again, and Nick says, "We've got to. . . . It isn't worth while if you can't." The young American wife in "Cat in the Rain" declares, "If I can't have long hair or any fun, I can have a cat." And the young gentleman in "Out of Season" sends his wife back to the hotel with this consoling remark: "It's a rotten day and we aren't going to have any fun, anyway."

McAlmon's recollections of Hadley, both at Rapallo and later, were devastating. He was embarrassed by her adoring pronouncements: "Sometimes when I wake up in bed and see my young husband next to me, his beautiful young face, I think I'm sleeping with Christ." Recounting that bit of testimony, McAlmon at least admitted, "Now that's not verbatim, but like it." He also recalled that Hadley had an embarrassing habit of producing telegrams Ernest had sent her with such forlorn messages as "I can't sleep for thinking of you sweet feather kitty." At those moments, Hemingway would snatch up the wire, telling Hadley that their company probably wasn't interested "in our love." McAlmon's nastiness may not have been all invention: Chink Dorman-Smith would also recall that at Chamby the Hemingways would "disturb my bachelorhood" with blow-by-blow accounts of the events of their lovemaking.

Hadley's effusiveness, perhaps, reflected not only her pregnancy but the fact that Hemingway, sometime after his return from Constantinople, had made a brash attempt to recapture his past by furtively writing to Agnes von Kurowsky. Agnes's warm reply, written around Christmastime, had followed them to Chamby. "I never was more pleased over anything in my life," Agnes wrote Hemingway, after she had gotten over the initial surprise. She referred to the "little bitterness" over the way their "comradeship" had ended. "Anyhow, I always knew that it would turn out right in the end & that you would realize it was the best way," she continued, "as I'm positive you must believe, now that you have Hadley." And she went on, "Think of what an antique I am at the present writing," a remark that may have reminded Hadley that she was no younger than

Agnes. After giving a brief account of her interim career, she added,

> It is so nice to feel I have an old friend back because we were good friends once, weren't we? And how sorry I am I didn't meet & know your wife. . . . How proud I will be some day in the not-very-distant-future to say, "Oh yes. Ernest Hemingway. Used to know him quite well during the war." I've always known you would stand out some day — from the background.

Among the italicized memory fragments in Hemingway's "The Snows of Kilimanjaro," that anthology of Hemingway's real and fictional or otherwise adulterated memories, Harry Walden reflects on the mistake he made in writing to his old girlfriend and of the moment of truth when her letter arrived at the breakfast table: "But his wife said, 'Who is that letter from, dear?' and that was the end of the beginning of that."

⁂

"McAlmon came and stayed a long time," Hemingway reported to Pound on March 10, 1923. "I read nearly all his new stuff. Some 16–18 stories, a novel or so. He wrote seven or nine new stories while at Rapallo." Whatever Hemingway's later views, he was, at first, both admiring and envious of McAlmon's talents as a writer. If he were a tipster, Hemingway told Pound, he would whisper into the shell-like ear of a friend, "Go and make a small bet on McAlmon while you can still get a good long price." McAlmon, sober, had an undeniable personal magnetism. "Both men and women were strongly attracted to McAlmon," Sylvia Beach remembered. (For a time she thought she was in love with him and his "Irish sea blue eyes," but decided, much to McAlmon's relief, that it was an affection she had dreamed up while on a lonely seaside vacation with nothing much else to think about.) He was also a fund of entertaining and caustic gossip. "McAlmon has given us the dirt on everybody," Hemingway wrote Pound. "It is all most enjoyable."

Pound tried to temper Hemingway's too enthusiastic discovery of McAlmon: "Re: Robt. I dare say the price is still a bit long — However there is this — he's yr. bloody contemporary." He cautioned, "Of course 7–9 new stories in a week is a little *too* much, even for the young." Nonetheless, he was glad Hemingway and McAlmon had had a "rapprochement"; he had been hoping for it for some time. On the subject of the younger generation, Pound was encouraging: "You're it," he said. "Go to it." Yet Pound's relations with the two young men were quixotic. He had chosen Hemingway, not

McAlmon, as one of his candidates for the "Inquest into the state of English prose," which Bill Bird was publishing. Over the years, he would keep up an avuncular friendship with both men. But in time, he became increasingly critical of their neglect, as writers, of what he considered the crucial social and economic issues of the time. Late in life, Pound would claim, despite Hemingway's reputation in the field, that it was really the acerbic McAlmon "who was much more courageous."

No doubt, Hemingway's initial appreciation of McAlmon's talents was self-serving. When they first met, McAlmon had already published a volume of poetry, *Explorations,* and his collection of short stories, *A Hasty Bunch.* In 1923, under his Contact Editions imprint, he was in the process of publishing his plotless young-man novel, *Post Adolescence,* derived from his Greenwich Village experiences, and a second collection of short stories, *A Companion Volume.* He was a sympathetic and published author at a time when Hemingway was, himself, eager for publication. Having read the few stories and poems Hemingway had on hand, McAlmon generously offered to take Hemingway on as one of his Contact Editions authors. That was one version of McAlmon's story; another was that, out of sympathy for Hemingway's lost stories, McAlmon had asked him to send some manuscripts on to Paris before he made the decision: "He had some stories he had written, and mourned because . . . his love Hadley had left a sheaf of other MS. on the train somewhere. Ezra's idea was that she was jealous of his writing and did it deliberately. I dunno." (The most widely published version, perhaps derived from Bill Bird, has it that McAlmon announced his intentions of publishing Hemingway in the late spring, leaving Bird bereft of material for the Hemingway volume he was planning to print.) The result, in any event, was Hemingway's first book, *Three Stories and Ten Poems,* a slender volume that appeared in late summer 1923, several months earlier than Bird's edition of *in our time.*

The three stories chosen included "Up in Michigan," the Cortina d'Ampezzo story, "Out of Season," and "My Old Man." The poems were a reprint of the six Harriet Monroe had already published, with an additional four, "Oklahoma" and "Captives," two Chicago poems that somehow miraculously survived the manuscript loss, and "Montparnasse" and "Along with Youth," both presumably written in Paris. McAlmon, as a writer, preferred a hard-bitten sense of reality, but chose to publish "My Old Man," even though he considered it too much in the vein of Sherwood Anderson's folksy, false-naive style. The other two stories, which he regarded as sketches rather than full-fledged stories, he felt, "were fresh and without derivation so far as I could detect."

Hemingway, eager for publication, had accepted McAlmon's offer with alacrity and even a touch of gratitude. And for a few years afterward, he kept up an active campaign, praising McAlmon as a writer and publisher. In 1924, he was promoting McAlmon with Edward J. O'Brien: "He has written a really fine long poem and some really promising prose in a thing called Village." When *Village,* McAlmon's second novel, was published, Hemingway wrote the author in expansive terms, "Village is absolutely first rate and damned good reading. . . . You've probably had so many people tell you that by now that you're tired of it." Hemingway would also write Pound that McAlmon's "stuff," including *Village,* a number of poems, and a series of stories about homosexuals in Berlin, was "damn important. It is god damn important." But there was a note of qualification regarding McAlmon's callousness: "He jumps in and out of the story, he throws grammar and syntax overboard . . . christ, how he philosophizes and soliloquizes but three of the stories are among the best short stories ever wrote. Take it or leave it." A bit later, following the 1925 publication of *Distinguished Air (Grim Fairy Tales),* McAlmon's Berlin stories, Hemingway recanted a bit, confessing to Ernest Walsh, a poet and editor he had met through Pound, "I have never yet succeeded in re-reading anything by McAlmon. On the other hand I remember all of McAlmon I've ever read," a nice distinction. McAlmon, Hemingway also told Pound, was, at his best, a documentary writer. "His interests," he claimed, "are all those of a scientist. He just happened not to be born with a good enough brain to be a scientist. Village is a splendid document. So are a couple of the Distinguished Air stories." Whatever McAlmon remembered, Hemingway said, was nearly always interesting: "What he creates is just awful."

By then, Hemingway had, in his own way, begun to separate himself from the realist tradition. He had begun "inventing" from experience, as he called it, drawing upon not only his own experiences and knowledge but from that of others, as well. Referring to his hospital stay in Milan, for instance, Hemingway once claimed it was sometimes a matter of listening to the men talk while convalescing. "Their experiences get to be more vivid than your own. You invent from your own and from all of theirs. The country you know, also the weather." Ideally a writer would know everything but would avoid parading his erudition.

That was the case, in fact, with the six vignettes, which, along with "They All Made Peace," Jane Heap and Margaret Anderson would publish in the Spring 1923 "Exiles" issue of *The Little Review.* In terms of his career, the vignettes were the most important writing Hemingway accomplished during his winter excursions. Done in the manner of his Paris 1922 sketches, they were sharper and more incisive, had more significance and impact as writing. Yet only one had been taken from Hemingway's own experiences: the dramatic memory of the Greek evacuation along the Karagatch Road which had been used in Hemingway's *Toronto Star* dispatches and revised to the barest essentials as the vignette beginning, "Minarets stuck up in the rain out of Adrianople across the mud flats." The enigmatic opening episode ("Everybody was drunk"), a brief exchange between a kitchen corporal and a drunken officer en route to the Champagne, seems to have been developed from some story Hemingway may have heard but is otherwise untraceable. Two sketches ("We were in a garden at Mons" and "It was a frightfully hot day") written in a clipped British-style narrative were based on Chink Dorman-Smith's experiences during the Belgian campaign. Hemingway based a detailed bullfight episode on information from Mike Strater and from accounts by Gertrude Stein and Alice Toklas, who had become aficionados of the bullring during earlier trips to Spain. It was written before Hemingway had ever witnessed a bullfight. Yet somehow he had managed to visualize the scene: "The kid came out and had to kill five bulls because you can't have more than three matadors, and [with] the last bull he was so tired he couldn't get the sword in." Impotence and disgrace — already Hemingway's theme. The young matador finally succeeds: "He sat down in the sand and puked and they held a cape over him while the crowd hollered and threw things down into the bull ring."

The most vivid episode — as striking as any bit of newsreel footage — a graphic story of the shooting of the six Greek cabinet members of the discredited Constantinian government on November 28, 1922, had been adapted from newspaper accounts of an event Hemingway had not witnessed in person. ("They shot the six cabinet ministers at half-past six in the morning against the wall of a hospital. There were pools of water in the courtyard. There were wet dead leaves on the paving of the courtyard.") It was from such "invented" eyewitness recreations, a mix of fact and fiction, that Hemingway evolved as a writer.

⁂

A routine assumption is that Hemingway's separations from Hadley were caused by John Bone's rapid-fire assignments. But, often enough, Hemingway personally requested the assignments that took him away from her. On February 18, around the time, presumably, that he might have learned of Hadley's pregnancy, Hemingway wrote Bone proposing a series of articles on the French occupation of the Ruhr in retaliation for Germany's failure to meet its reparations payments. Bone replied by cable and letter on March 7; the letter did not reach Hemingway until he and Hadley were already settled in Cortina. Bone thoroughly approved of Hemingway's proposal for the trip ("Excellent," he said) and suggested a series of eight to twelve articles over a four-week period. He assumed Hemingway would want to be paid on a salary and expense basis. The assignment meant leaving Hadley behind in Cortina while he hurried back to Paris to do background research before beginning the German trip.

Hadley did her best to keep busy, though she was plainly at a loss. "Your Tiny was pretty near in despair before she got your first letter this morning," she wrote Hemingway in Paris. Her companions during her enforced skiing vacation at Cortina were the visiting Isabel Simmons and Renata Borgatti, a concert pianist of some fame at the time. Borgatti, who had a reputation as a lesbian femme fatale, was a former lover of the expatriate American painter Romaine Brooks, who did a striking portrait of her seated at a piano. She was a demonic pianist who made up in fire what she sometimes lacked in control. Borgatti looked like Franz Liszt and played like "a man of undisciplined genius." She was one of the more identifiable members of the Natalie Barney–Radclyffe Hall set, whom the English writer Compton Mackenzie depicted in his novel of lesbian affairs, *Extraordinary Women.* Hadley seems to have gotten on well with her; they became friends, discussed music and men. Hemingway, with his odd attraction to lesbian women, viewed Borgatti, blandly, as another one of the boys. She, in turn, was convinced that Hemingway was a young man one would definitely be hearing about. What astonishes is the freedom of Hemingway's discussions about sexual matters with lesbian women. He and Borgatti, for instance, had chummy discussions about the lesbian amours of Natalie Barney, or the lack of them; gossip that Hemingway, with surprising frankness, passed on to Stein and Toklas. According to Borgatti, Hemingway informed Stein, Barney no longer had much sexual attraction and this was the explanation for her habit of lolling about on polar bear rugs or in polar bear pajamas "and such like beauty aids." Barney's mind, Hemingway said, had "all the charming quality of a dog's in heat."

✓ ✓ ✓

"To write about Germany," Hemingway announced in the first of his articles for the *Daily Star,* "you must begin by writing about France." He was making a virtue out of necessity, since he was still in Paris at the time. Part of his coverage was pure homage: "France is a broad and lovely country. The loveliest country that I know."

But most of it was devoted to a painstaking explication of the French political scene: the decline of the Liberals precipitated by the strong-willed Clemenceau, the disarray of the French Communist party, recently "purified" by Russian party leaders on the grounds that it was too mawkishly patriotic and weak-willed. In a second article he outlined the rising power of the Royalist party under Léon Daudet, editor of *L'Action Française* and the writer of what Hemingway termed an "obscene" novel. (Rather hypocritically, Hemingway, who would make a career of trying to get words like *cocksucker* past timid editors, described Daudet's *The Procuress* as a novel "whose plot could not even be outlined in any newspaper printed in English.") And in a third article, he gave a lengthy account of the corruptions of the French press, which could be bought by foreign agents and governments to print articles favorable to their special causes. (William Ryall, though unnamed, was one of the principal proofs and sources for these assertions.) Hemingway also gave a reasoned account of the economic failures of French policy in the Ruhr, including the huge costs of maintaining a standing army and hired laborers in Germany.

Hemingway's coverage of French politics ("It is a very intimate politics, a politics of scandal") represented the best and most analytical moments of his career as a journalist. His articles seem to have benefited from his background research and his interviews with Parisian officials. In the Kennedy Library collection, there are several pages of detailed notes tracing the current political problems of France back to the political machinations surrounding the Versailles treaty. The bare notes (gathered from what sources?) indicate Hemingway's assiduousness: "Military intrigue by the French to encourage a rebellion in the Rhine provinces, particularly on the Left Bank of the river and obtain by coup d'état what they had not succeeded in getting at the peace conference." "Attempts outside the peace conference to secure more sweeping economic control of the Left Bank and incidentally cripple Germany." Oddly, little of this information, including the efforts of French general Charles Mangin, a hard-line Royalist, and a cabal of Wiesbaden conspirators to create an autonomous Rhineland Republic with its capital at Coblenz in May 1919, found its way into the published articles. Perhaps it was dated news, or still considered a libelous accusation. Or, perhaps, Hemingway was applying to his journalism the theory he was evolving for his fiction, that the writer, so long as his knowledge was accurate, did not need to provide all the details, that they would still carry a kind of subliminal weight and authority.

Hemingway's articles on France were enterprising, a mix of dutiful research and lucky guesses. (He predicted, correctly, that Édouard Herriot would be the likely dark-horse winner as premier in the scheduled 1924 elections.) The articles combined wit with cynicism: "You have only to hear M. Viviani pronounce the words 'la gloire de France' to want to rush out and get into uniform."

By contrast, his reports from Germany, though briskly written and informative, lacked the analytical approach of his three French stories. They were more like the colorfully written pieces on situations and personalities he had been sending the *Star* for some time. But his account of the French takeover of the rail lines at Offenburg and the refusal of the German mining companies to ship coal to France, his scathing remarks about German industrialists who sold on the market for pounds and dollars but paid the workers in useless marks, and his reporting on the economic hardships of the German people did make it clear that his sympathies lay with the victims of the political and economic manipulation that was a consequence of the Versailles treaty.

Hemingway had good reason to feel proud of his accomplishment. Writing to his father, who had complimented him on the series, he said with some modesty, "Lord knows I worked hard on them. . . . They handle the show pretty well, at least make it an actual thing to people instead of simply a name on the map." It was, after all, his aim as a writer, to create something more than a name on a map.

It was not until sometime in April that Hemingway returned to Cortina, by way of Paris, to complete his vacation with Hadley. And it was there, on May 9, that John Bone wired him proposing, once more, a trip to Russia, where conditions seemed exceedingly interesting. But Hemingway, this time, cabled immediately, "RUSSIA UNFEASIBLE FOR ME AT PRESENT UNLESS EMERGENCY STOP LETTER FOLLOWING."

There is little doubt that Hemingway felt some resentment over Hadley's pregnancy. It had, indeed, precipitated a family crisis at a time when he was coming into his own as a writer. His bitterness, at least, registers subliminally in the stories of marital discontent he was writing at the time. It was expectable that Hadley might want to have the baby in America or Canada because she believed that the doctors and hospitals would be better there than in Paris. So Hemingway, the story goes, was obliged to return to Toronto and resume work at the *Star*.

The detailed evidence, however, makes it clear that Hemingway had already committed himself to returning to Toronto well before he learned of Hadley's pregnancy. Almost from the beginning of

Hemingway's stay abroad, in February 1922, John Bone was encouraging him to think about taking a staff job in Toronto at a promised $75 a week when he returned from Europe. Despite his continuing praise of Hemingway's coverage of the Genoa Conference and the continental scene, Bone wrote in August, "The articles you are sending are valuable and of course add to the interest of both the Daily and the Weekly but we are of the opinion that if you were here, both you and we would now be making ever greater progress." Before early November, Hemingway had evidently accepted the offer but had left the time of his return open. On November 2, Bone was asking, "Can you let me know anything definite as to when you expect to come to us on the Star staff in Toronto?" By December — that is, well before the news of Hadley's pregnancy — Hemingway told Bone, much to Bone's disappointment, that he would not be returning before the fall of 1923. By February 18, in the same letter in which Hemingway proposed covering the French occupation of the Ruhr, Hemingway had given him the definite date. Bone's response was enthusiastic: "Delighted to know from your last paragraph that you expect to be in Toronto ready for work in September. That will be splendid."

IV

It was Robert McAlmon who offered Hemingway the opportunity to attend his first bullfight. Back in Paris in the late spring of 1923, sometime in May, McAlmon mentioned that he was planning a trip to Spain. Hadley had immediately responded, "Oh Hem would like to go there too. He does want to see a bullfight." Her plaint became so persistent, McAlmon claimed, that out of sheer exasperation, he suggested that Hemingway join him, that he would help out a bit with the expenses. Although, in his memoir, *Being Geniuses Together,* McAlmon got the year wrong — 1924 instead of 1923 — he rather accurately suspected that Hemingway's "need to love the art of bullfighting came from Gertrude Stein's praise of it, as well as from his belief in the value of 'self-hardening.'" There had been other English and American bullfight enthusiasts before Hemingway, McAlmon acknowledged, but Hemingway had "made it into a literary or artistic experience." According to McAlmon, there had been a week of discussions with friends (Bill Bird planned to meet them later in Spain) before he and Hemingway made their trip. There had been loving farewells between Hadley and Hemingway ("Beerypoppa" and "Feather-kitty," McAlmon acidly recalled) at the station. Both he and Hemingway, he remembered, were "well lubricated with whisky" when they boarded the train.

⁂

Ever since Hemingway had first learned about the ritual drama of the bullring from Mike Strater and, more importantly, from Gertrude Stein, he had been enthralled. Recounting the history of his involvement in *Death in the Afternoon* (1932), Hemingway remembered a day at the rue de Fleurus when Stein had spoken of her admiration for Joselito, one of the most famous of matadors, who had been fatally gored in the ring in May 1920. Stein had shown Hemingway pictures of herself and Alice Toklas at the bullfights during their 1915 wartime visit to Spain. In one of the photos, Stein and Toklas were sitting in the first row of the wooden barreras at Valencia, with Joselito and his brother Rafael, "Gallo," standing in front of them. Stein had used another of her heroes, the equally celebrated matador Juan Belmonte, as the subject of an odd little narrative poem, "I Must Try to Write the History of Belmonte," which Hemingway had read in *Geography and Plays*. Belmonte's failure to appear at a corrida Stein and Toklas had attended had been the inspiration for the poem. What Hemingway may have appreciated in that poem were the flashes of color, the gossip of the aficionados in the cafés: "A Mexican is to take his place. The man at the Cafe Artistos after much experience likes him better and says that though not good looking has better technique." In its stream of dialogue and domestic episodes involving Stein and Toklas, the poem caught some of the edginess and excitement of the corrida. It ended with Stein's ringing endorsement of Gallo: "I forget war and fear and courage and dancing. I forget standing and refusing. I believe choices. I choose Gallo. He is a cock. He moves plainly."

Hemingway's recollection of his urge to visit Spain was more than a contrived bit of personal propaganda. It was one of those episodes in the life of the creative artist when everything — his intuitions, the circumstances of his life, a chance occasion, his unspecified ambitions — converged. Everything is connected in the life of a writer; Hemingway associated his yearning to go to Spain with his ambitions as a writer — and with his need to escape from journalism. Bullfighting, his initiation into the ritual, was presented as a kind of epiphany in which much that had happened to him in Europe — his still unassimilated wartime experiences, his hard-earned political education as a reporter, his apprenticeship as a creative writer — was profoundly involved. Hemingway gave this account in *Death in the Afternoon*: "I was trying to write then and I found the greatest difficulty, aside from knowing truly what you really felt, rather than what you were supposed to feel and had been taught to feel, was to put down what really happened in action; what the actual things were which produced the emotion that you experienced."

In retrospect, he explained his rationale: "The only place where you could see life and death, i.e., violent death now that the wars were over, was in the bull ring and I wanted very much to go to Spain where I could study it." This remark may seem casual, but it offers the most candid evidence for Hemingway's urge to court danger and violence as a literary device. It is also an admission of the traumatic effect his wounding had had upon his life. "I was trying to learn to write, commencing with the simplest things, and one of the simplest things of all and the most fundamental is violent death." He had gone to Spain, he said, to find the definitive action that would give him "the feeling of life and death that I was working for."

These were, admittedly, the thoughts of the mature Hemingway, the seasoned writer of a decade later, the man who would conceive of writing as confrontation: part risk, part performance, an attempt at proving one's self again and again, and in the process, acquiring a more daring identity than that of the sedentary man at his writing desk. But the occasion for those later notions seems, honestly, to have begun in Spain. In the sun-drenched arena of the bullring, Hemingway discovered for himself and for his writing a focal metaphor. Even the sun, he claimed in *Death in the Afternoon,* was a participant. He quoted a Spanish proverb, "*El sol es el mejor torero.*" The sun was the best bullfighter, and without the sun, Hemingway added, even the best bullfighter was not there: "He is like a man without a shadow."

⁄ ⁄ ⁄

But literary epiphanies, admittedly rare, have their origins in the mundane world, in the banalities of dusty journeys, cheap hotels, sweltering nights, noise, crowds, personal animosities. How otherwise and ordinary the circumstances of Hemingway's initiation into bullfighting might have been for another observer, one learns from Robert McAlmon's recollections, keeping in mind the obvious conflict of the personalities involved. Their differences had begun on the train trip to Madrid. At one of their stops, after a heavy night of drinking, McAlmon and Hemingway noticed a dead dog, its skin pulsating as if it were breathing, the effect of swarms of maggots feeding inside the carcass. McAlmon, badly hung over, turned away in disgust. Hemingway gave his patron a lecture on facing up to reality, though he followed McAlmon to the dining car for a whiskey: "Hell, Mac, you write like a realist. Are you going to go romantic on us?"

Nor did McAlmon measure up to Hemingway's exacting standards when they saw their first bullfight. As an antidote to witnessing the possible goring of the horses, they had had several preliminary drinks. They had also taken along a bottle of whiskey. When the first bull charged head-on into one of the picador's horses and tossed it, McAlmon rose to his feet with a yell. He liked it even less when he saw another horse trotting around the ring dragging its entrails. McAlmon's memories of that first bullfight were of the unreality of the scene and the insensitive crowd daring the matador from the safety of the stands, the cruelty of the kill. Hemingway was struck by the whole ceremonial approach to the event and by the performances of the chubby-faced Chicuelo, a favorite in Madrid, and Nicanor Villalta, who walked like a young wolf and had a reputation as a "great one." In Hemingway's mind, the ritual killing of the bull would acquire a tragic significance. "Only thing that brings man [appreciation?] of life and death," he scribbled in the notes he made of his days in Spain.

The tour of the corridas from Madrid (where Bill Bird joined them) to Seville, Ronda, and Granada grew progressively sour. At night, the trio made the rounds of bars and nightclubs, drinking heavily. In Seville, Hemingway, suffering through another flamenco performance, growled, "Oh, for Christ's sake, more flamingos!" Bird was annoyed because Hemingway intermittently badgered and insulted McAlmon along the way. McAlmon, however, maintained a stoic reserve, even paid for a black lace mantilla Hemingway had looked at, complaining he hadn't money enough to buy it for Hadley. Bird told McAlmon he was a sucker, that Hemingway had more money than he pretended to have. He also took Hemingway aside and complained about his behavior, reminding him that McAlmon was paying the bills and buying the scotches. Hemingway gave him a bitter laugh. "You know," he said, "I'll take anything from *you*." Later, in Paris, Hemingway had the bad grace to complain to Sylvia Beach that McAlmon had kept him from serious observation and work by wanting to stay out all night. But as McAlmon caustically observed, when he and Bird did the night spots either one of them was free to leave when he got bored; Hemingway could have done the same.

What plausible truths were there in the later, acrid recollections of either McAlmon or Hemingway? McAlmon, for instance, nastily recalled "a beauty of a dream scene" that had occurred one night when he and Hemingway were sharing a hotel room: "I was Vicky, the buxom, tough and beautiful tart of the cabaret of the night before." If Hemingway had pawed McAlmon after a boozy night on the town, it might explain his belligerence during the trip (as well as McAlmon's later charges that Hemingway had homosexual inclinations). But whatever Hemingway's surly behavior in Spain, there is no evidence of a break in the friendly and flattering letters he wrote McAlmon during the ensuing months when he was courting him as a publisher.

Back in Paris, Hemingway's enthusiasm about his Spanish trip was certainly apparent. "I am very anxious to talk about toros y toreros with you," he wrote Stein, inviting himself to the rue de Fleurus. He and Hadley were planning a trip to Pamplona to take in the bullfights in early July, before their mid-August voyage to Canada. "I don't think it would hurt Hadley," he said. Hemingway joked that in Canada he would buy a bull calf and practice veronicas. It was, he said, too late for him, "but we may be able to do something with the kid." In the meantime, he was busy with friends. Renata Borgatti was in town; he and Hadley had gone to the boxing matches with Ezra Pound, Jane Heap, Mike Strater, and McAlmon. "Swell fights," he wrote Isabel Simmons. Tiny was in good shape, he told Simmons, and they were going down to Pamplona. Bullfighting ought to be "a stalwart pre-natal influence," he thought.

The *feria* at Pamplona with Hadley proved to be more enjoyable than his trip with McAlmon. They arrived on a sultry summer night, the city alive with riau-riau dancers, fireworks, the shrill music of bands. The sound of the fifes, Hadley said, "made blood-red stripes across your heart." For Hadley there was the constant excitement of the running of the bulls through the narrow streets in the early mornings, the crowds of young men and boys rushing ahead into the brilliant sunlight of the arena. Hemingway was struck by the faces of the Spaniards, straight out of Velázquez and Goya and El Greco. During the fights, he would tell Hadley to look away whenever a horse was gored. She featherstitched baby clothes during those times, "embroidering in the presence of all that brutality," she recalled.

Hemingway was especially impressed with Maera, "dark, spare and deadly looking, one of the very greatest toreros of all time," he wrote in a later article for the *Star Weekly*. He recalled the afternoon that Maera had been tossed by his bull when placing the banderillas and was badly injured and how he had managed, still, to give the death thrust to the bull with a wrist swollen to twice its normal size. Maera ("*Era muy hombre*") was a man he could admire: blunt-spoken, a bit arrogant, a fighter. "He was generous, humorous, proud, bitter, foul-mouthed and a great drinker. He neither sucked after intellectuals nor married money" was Hemingway's tribute.

Hemingway poured out his enthusiasm and passion for bullfighting in his letters. Writing to Greg Clark at the *Toronto Star,* he gushed that it wasn't a sport but a tragedy, "and God how it's played. The tragedy is the death of the bull, the inevitable death of the bull — the terrible, almost prehistoric bull." He was also, at the time, well aware of the literary possibilities of his new experience. He wrote his father, "It will make some very fine stories some day."

⸸ ⸸ ⸸

Back in Paris by July 17, Hemingway had kinder thoughts on his coming fatherhood. Hadley had not been sick a minute or even nauseated much of the time, he wrote Bill Horne. "We're both crazy about having the young feller." They were planning to sail for Montreal on the Cunard liner *Andania,* on August 17, he said.

There was still time for him to put the finishing touches on the proofs and the cover design of McAlmon's edition of *Three Stories and Ten Poems.* Bill Bird had suggested that he use the titles of the stories and poems on the cover for a more effective design. Hemingway liked the look of it, but he would defer to McAlmon's decision: "You are the publisher," he wrote McAlmon on August 5. But by way of adding some pointed encouragement, he mentioned that he had taken the cover and proofs to Gertrude Stein, asking her opinion. She thought that putting the titles on the cover "made it any amount stronger and better looking." She had even given him some suggestions about the typography. He was, it appears, no less concerned about his first publication than he was about his first child. He worried about the slimness of the volume, suggesting that it should be padded with a few more blank pages: "Nobody will buy a book if it is too goddam thin."

Hemingway also put in time writing and revising additional vignettes for Bird's volume, *in our time,* the title taken from the Book of Common Prayer: "Give peace in our time, O Lord." The same title had been used for the six vignettes, previously published in *The Little Review.* A few of the new sketches dealt with his recent visits to Spain, including a masterly composition on the fictionalized death of Maera, the matador he had so admired in Pamplona. The bullfighter, gored, has been hurried to the infirmary: "Maera felt everything getting larger and larger and then smaller and smaller. Then it got larger and larger and larger and then smaller and smaller. Then everything commenced to run faster and faster as when they speed up a cinematograph film. Then he was dead." Eerily, Maera *would* die — but of consumption, not from goring — the following year.

In all, there would be eighteen sketches. "When they are read altogether," Hemingway assured Pound, the editor of the volume, "they all hook up. . . . The bulls start, then reappear and then finish off. The war starts clear and noble just like it did, Mons, etc., gets close and blurred and finished with the feller who goes home and gets clap." The book would end with a sketch of the king and queen of Greece in their garden, which he had just written. (The king and queen of Greece, oddly enough, had made an appearance in Stein's "History of Belmonte," as well.) The final vignette was based on an anecdote told to him by Shorty Wornall, who had visited the royal couple and was now in Paris. The last sentence, Hemingway said, would read, "Like all Greeks what he really wanted was to get to America." He promised Pound, "It has form all right."

Before sailing (the *Andania* was delayed until August 26), there was a final meeting with Pound, who gave Hadley an odd parting gift, his old velvet smoking jacket. (She kept it for years.) Pound also gave her some advice, telling her never to try to change her husband. Then he announced that he might as well say good-bye because in his view a woman inevitably was completely changed when she had a baby: "You just won't be the same again at all," he warned her.

That Hemingway had glum feelings about his return to Canada was obvious from the letter he wrote to Isabel Simmons. "Christ I hate to leave Paris for Toronto the City of Churches," he said, adding an ironic qualification, "But then all of life is interesting." His years abroad had given him a large purchase on life. He was an author with two books being readied for publication. He would soon be a father. He was a man who had begun to cast his shadow.

9

The Perpendicular Pronoun

TORONTO was one of those occasional periods in purgatory which Hemingway suffered in his lifetime. He and Hadley had a pleasant enough apartment on Bathurst Street, small, with a sun-room that looked out over a ravine, a bedroom with a Murphy bed, wall space enough to hang their collection of paintings by Masson and Dorothy Pound. But Toronto was dull and provincial. On his free evenings, they saw his friends the Connables, and Greg Clark and his wife. But not often; Hemingway frequently worked until two in the morning. His boss, Harry Hindmarsh, city editor and son-in-law of the owner of the *Star,* disliked Hemingway, thought him too cocksure, and sent him out on assignments in the provinces. "Absurd assignments," Hadley called them; she thought Hindmarsh's treatment of her husband "an ugly case of mean jealousy." Morley Callaghan, an aspiring young Canadian writer, then working part-time at the paper, recalled Hemingway's blunt four-letter words and white face when he checked the daily assignment sheet. Callaghan was stunned when he saw the inconsequential assignments Hemingway was given.

Feeling uprooted, Hemingway comforted himself with thoughts of Paris and bullfighting in Spain; he kept up his correspondence with Stein and Pound. "I have understood for the first time how men can commit suicide simply because of too many things in business piling up ahead of them that they can't get through," he wrote Stein. He confessed to Pound, "I am now undertaking the show on a day by day basis. Get through today. Then get through tomorrow tomorrow. Like 1918." He was reading *Ulysses* at night to cheer himself up (not too thoroughly; his presentation copy, given him by Sylvia Beach, reveals that he cut the pages for only the first half of the book and for Molly Bloom's soliloquy at the end). As a favor to Sylvia, he had smuggled in several copies for distribution to American bookstores. He assured Pound, "Someday someone will live here and be able to appreciate the feeling with which I launched Ulysses on the States (not a copy lost) from this city."

On October 11, Hemingway wrote his "Dear Friends," Stein and Alice Toklas, the news that his son had been born the day before at two in the morning. The baby weighed seven pounds and five ounces and was already nursing. The birth had taken three hours. Hadley, he said, was convinced that the childbirth business was greatly overrated. In his letter, the baby was dubbed "young Gallito." Actually they would name him John Hadley Nicanor Hemingway, combining Hadley's name (and Hemingway's wire service pseudonym) with that of the bullfighter Nicanor Villalta, whom Hemingway had admired at Madrid. But Hadley's nickname Bumby clung to the boy throughout his childhood. Hemingway had not been present when the baby was born. "Felt dreadfully about Hadley having to go through the show alone," he wrote Stein and Toklas. He had been on assignment in New York, covering the arrival of Lloyd George ("a cantankerous, mean, temperamental and vicious man who never shows it in pooblic"). He gave Pound a much more savage version of his resentment. He had been on the train coming back to Montreal, engaged in a smut session with reporters and coal barons, when the baby had been born. When he learned of it, he was in a mood to kill Hindmarsh. "Compromised by telling him would never forgive him of course and that all work done by me from now on would be with the most utter contempt and hatred for him and all his bunch of masturbating mouthed associates."

There were other frustrations. He complained to Sylvia Beach that it was impossible to do any writing of his own. "The paper wants all day and all night. Much longer and I would never be able to write anymore. Also the people are all merde." He had been kept so busy that he hadn't had time to mail out the review copies of his "#3 sturries and ten pums." Writing to Edward O'Brien, he discussed his frustration in suggestive terminology. At night he was too tired to think, let alone write; then "in the morning a story starts in your head on the street car and have to choke it off because it was coming so perfectly and easily and clear and right and you know that if you let it go on it will be finished and gone." He was ready to chuck journalism, he wrote Stein: "You ruined me as a journalist last winter. Have been no good since."

Pound wrote him that Ford Madox Ford was starting a new magazine. "Do knock off something of premiere ordre and send it on," he told Hemingway. Ford, keen on "les jeunes," was "going to knock s::t out the Dial and the mags." The magazine would be "neither gaga lunatic" like *The Little Review* nor "dead" like Eliot's review *The Criterion.* "GET to it," Pound advised. Hemingway promised to send something, but he was hardly in the mood: "Feel that

I'm so full of hate and so damned bitchingly, sickeningly tired that anything I do will be of little value. Still the diseased oyster shits the finest pearl as the palmist says." It was a garbled message. In December, when Hemingway failed to produce anything in time for the first issue, Pound sent him one of his crank letters: "See here Ole Bungo WHHHHHere's your copy?" What was the use, he asked, of "pore ole grampa Ford" producing a review in which the young could express themselves, "IF you aren't goin ter come across wif de PUNCH!" Pound added, "I think, meself, you'd better come bak here and direk the policy of the damn thing. I want a little leisure for composition."

Despite Pound's involvement with Ford's *Transatlantic Review,* he had managed to complete the cantos that would make up the first published edition of his lengthy epic poem. After the Malatesta cantos, Pound informed Hemingway, he had written five more "chants," making sixteen in all. Two of these represented his depiction of Hell, an excremental realm to which he consigned his personal enemies, politicians and profiteers, money lusters, bishops, Fabians, and the English: "Above the hell-rot / the great arse-hole / broken with piles." Pound told Hemingway, "After Hell, I have said a few chaste words on the war." Canto XVI recounted the wartime experiences of friends, Wyndham Lewis and Richard Aldington. A brief passage commemorated the wounded Hemingway lying buried by the debris of the mortar explosion: "And Ernie Hemingway went to it, / too much in a hurry, / And they buried him for four days." One day longer, it seems, than it took Christ to resurrect himself.

⸙ ⸙ ⸙

What angered Hemingway was that he had been "decoyed" back home to do a little feature writing and put the *Star*'s cable department in order. Instead, he found himself covering the drilling operations of the British Colonial Coal Mines Ltd. in Sudbury, interviewing Canadian survivors of the recent Japanese earthquake, querying Lord Birkenhead on Prohibition and the possible marital plans of the Prince of Wales, who was touring the provinces. ("Prince Charming, the Ambassador of Empire, the fair haired buggar," Hemingway described him in one of his salty letters to Pound.) There was a lengthy interview with Count Apponyi, a seventy-seven-year-old Hungarian statesman, "one of the few surviving idealists in Europe."

Hemingway's blowup with Hindmarsh had had its consequences. Not long after it, he was writing exclusively for the *Star Weekly* under his old boss, J. Herbert Cranston, doing feature stories (signed, unsigned, or under his John Hadley byline) on Lloyd George's brief whistle-stop meeting with the eighty-four-year-old son of Abraham Lincoln, Robert Todd Lincoln; the water level of the Great Lakes; the iodine treatment for goiter; and the recent award of the Nobel Prize in Literature to William Butler Yeats, who "has written, with the exception of a few poems by Ezra Pound, the very finest poetry of our time." There is little evidence that prior to the award, Hemingway had paid much attention to Yeats, but two years later he would lay claim to Yeats, Pound, and Anonymous as his favorite poets: "If Yeats hasn't written swell poems then nobody else ever has or ever will."

Hemingway was keeping himself informed on events in Europe, intrigued by the news reports of Adolf Hitler's rash attempt to take over the Bavarian government in early November. ("The paper is full of the Hitler and Ludendorff fiasco," Hemingway wrote Stein. "It sounds very funny. The early dispatches so far.") The failed putsch had its grim, comic-opera elements. With a small force of storm troopers, Hitler, the most fanatical of the right-wing German leaders, had — astonishingly — managed to arrest the major Bavarian government officials at a huge beer hall meeting. Wielding a revolver, he harangued and pleaded with them to join his Nationalist Revolution, hysterically threatened to kill them and himself if they refused, and boldly announced his plans for a march on Berlin. In his fumbling rush to glory, he made no plans to take over the radio and telegraph offices, failed to gain control of the state police or military barracks. His hostages, released on their word of honor by war hero General Erich Ludendorff, mounted a reprisal as soon as they were freed. On the following day, in an ill-timed show of power, the Nazis paraded to the center of Munich. The state police opened fire on Hitler and his supporters and the one-day revolution collapsed in disarray. Hitler ignominiously fled the scene, suffering a dislocated shoulder from a fall. Hiding out in the attic of a friend, he made a halfhearted attempt at suicide. Three days later he was arrested. But out of that debacle and the ensuing trial, he emerged a national hero, the Führer. As Hemingway later remarked to Pound, lecturing the poet on twentieth-century politics, "The great qualification to hold office is to have been in jail." He asked, "Have you ever been in jail?"

⁂

In the *Star* office Hemingway found some relief from his dissatisfactions by writing a series of Steinian character studies of his fellow journalists: "[Bobby] Reade and [Greg] Clark sit around and talk. Talk is cheap . . . Reade is dry inside his head like the vagina of an old whore. Dry and futile . . . Greg is very romantic. But I can never understand all the way inside of him because he is romantic." Morley Callaghan was impressed by the terse authority of Hemingway's verbal comments on his colleagues: one of them had no shame, Hemingway claimed, another had a homosexual style. They also talked literature. Callaghan remembered Hemingway declaring that when it came to fiction Joyce was the greatest writer in the world, and *Huckleberry Finn* was a very great book. Hemingway asked to see one of Callaghan's stories, but when Callaghan neglected to bring it in as promised, saying he had been too busy, Hemingway abruptly wheeled on him. "I see," he said, "I just wanted to see if you were another goddamned phony." When Callaghan did show him the story, Hemingway did an about-face, generously told him that he was a real writer. "All you have to do is keep on writing," he advised.

In the meantime, he had begun promoting his own reputation. Having read in one of Burton Rascoe's gossipy literary columns in the *New York Tribune* that the critic Edmund Wilson had recommended Hemingway's sketches in *The Little Review,* Hemingway wrote Wilson, sending him a copy of *Three Stories and Ten Poems.* Gertrude Stein, he said, had told him she had written a review of it, but he didn't know whether it had been published yet. "You don't know anything in Canada," he complained. If Wilson liked the book, he asked, would he send him the names of four or five people who might review it?

Wilson acknowledged the book warmly, suggesting that he might do a review for *The Dial.* Hemingway replied in flattering terms, "As far as I can think at the minute yours is the only critical opinion in the states I have any respect for." He disagreed with Wilson's opinion that "My Old Man" derived from Anderson, offering a somewhat obscure distinction. His story was about a boy and his father and racehorses. "Sherwood has written about boys and horses. But very differently . . . I know that I wasn't inspired by him." Putting further distance between himself and Anderson, he added, "His work seems to have gone to hell, perhaps from people in New York telling him too much how good he was. Functions of criticism." Hemingway was, he said, nonetheless, very fond of Anderson. He suggested that if Wilson was planning to review *Three Stories and Ten Poems* in the "Briefer Mentions" of *The Dial,* it might be better to wait until *in our time* came out; Wilson would get a better idea of what he was trying to get at. In sharp contrast to his feelings about

Anderson and his influence, Hemingway was more willing to admit his debt to Gertrude Stein: "She is where Mencken and Mary Colum fall down and skin their noses."

Stein's review of *Three Stories and Ten Poems* did appear in the Paris edition of the *Chicago Tribune* on November 27, 1923. Her praise was brief, personal, and prosy in its approval:

> Three stories and ten poems is very pleasantly said. So far so good, further than that, and as far as that, I may say of Ernest Hemingway that as he sticks to poetry and intelligence it is both poetry and intelligent. Roosevelt is genuinely felt as young as Hemingway and as old as Roosevelt. I should say that Hemingway should stick to poetry and intelligence and eschew the hotter emotions and the more turgid vision. Intelligence and a great deal of it is a good thing to use when you have it, it's all for the best.

It is difficult to tell how pleased Hemingway was with Stein's review and her casual reference to the hotter emotions of "Up in Michigan." But it was, after all, the first published review of Hemingway's first book. His thanks edged on ambivalence. "It seems very sound to me. I liked it," he wrote her in early December in an apparently misdated letter. What bothered him, he said, was why, with his fine intelligence, he had ever come to Canada. He sent her a weather report on her own reputation: the younger critics were turning on her and Sherwood Anderson. "I can feel it in the papers etc.," he wrote. But he tempered the news with flattering encouragement. In Paris, he had read portions of Stein's long, unpublished novel *The Making of Americans* and had been deeply impressed. Now he reassured her: "Oh well you will get them back again. Wait till the History of an American Family is published." He told Stein he was planning to quit the *Star* on January 1. "I have some good stories to write — will try not to be turgid," he added, in pointed response to her criticism.

There are a number of unanswered questions about the actual circumstances under which Hemingway resigned from the *Star.* Years later, he claimed that it was a bitter fight with Hindmarsh over the Count Apponyi incident which had triggered his decision. (Hindmarsh had carelessly thrown out with the trash some of the count's papers that Hemingway had submitted with the article, expressly asking to have the documents returned.) The evidence, however, is ambiguous: a letter to John Bone, dated circa December 26 (and possibly misdated), indicates that a run-in with Hindmarsh was a possible factor. Hemingway's letter is a lengthy diatribe on Hindmarsh's dishonesty, his inability to admit to a mistake, his fits of temper, his exhibitions of wounded vanity. ("Mr. Hindmarsh *says* that I think I know more about assignments he gives me than he does. I have given him no cause to think this.") It is possible that this letter was never delivered. A second letter, dated circa December 27, is a mere two paragraphs, tendering his resignation from the "local staff of the Star" as of January 1, if convenient.

Chronology does not always substantiate Hemingway's versions of his life. His interview with Count Apponyi appeared in the October 15 issue of the *Daily Star,* a full two months and more before his supposedly angry December resignation. Nor does it appear that he worked under Hindmarsh after the Apponyi interview; his remaining articles were all written for the *Star Weekly.* Early in November, in fact, he had already informed his father, "From now until Christmas I will work on the Weekly Star altogether." Also his November letters to Pound, Sylvia Beach, Edmund Wilson, and Edward O'Brien all indicate that his plans for quitting the paper in January were well in hand by then. And his December letter to Stein makes it clear that he intended to sail on the Cunard liner *Antonia,* leaving New York on January 19. Possibly, Hemingway, having planned his escape to Europe, engineered some later incident with Hindmarsh to provide himself with an excuse to resign. In any event, there are several reasons for regarding Hemingway's recollections of his dramatic departure from the *Star* as dubious.

Among the other correspondents Hemingway alerted about his departure for Europe was Jim Gamble. Not having heard from Gamble for two years, he was surprised and delighted by a letter from his old friend. There was no doubt about the enthusiasm of Hemingway's December 12 reply; it was gushy. He was, in fact, hoping that they might have a reunion in New York before he sailed. Gamble, he was sure, would like Hadley tremendously. "She is a corker Jim," Hemingway wrote, fumbling for words, "and I should know because we have been married over two years and I have practically no friends, as I imagine you have, who are happily married." He launched into a summary of his newspaper assignments at the Genoa conference and in Constantinople, his trips to Spain, the fact that he had two books being published in Paris. "All this is frightfully full of the perpendicular pronoun," he apologized, "but I was so excited to hear the small amount of news I got from you that I've run on at great length."

✓✓✓

Since Hadley did not feel up to making the Christmas trip to Oak Park with the baby, Hemingway went alone. His parents, eager to see their grandson, were plainly disappointed. Hemingway's sister Marcelline, now married and living in Detroit, had returned home for the occasion with her husband, Sterling Sanford. One evening, Hemingway surreptitiously handed her a copy of *Three Stories and Ten Poems,* warning her, "Don't show this to the family, Marce." He advised her to read it after she left. When she read it on the train to Detroit, she was shocked by the sexual explicitness of "Up in Michigan." What disturbed her even more was Ernest's "lack of any decent consideration" in using the first names of people they knew in a "vulgar, sordid tale" that he had invented. "My stomach turned over," she said.

Grace was unexpectedly thrilled by her son's new maturity. In an evangelical letter, written on the day that Hemingway left, she affirmed that Ernest's view of the world now seemed very like her father's, "a big world vision that cannot place any arbitrary boundary lines to the mercy and justice of God." She went on to assure him, "You will never know the joy it is to a mother to find her son is a thorough-bred." Ironically, among the Christmas gifts Grace sent to Hadley and her new grandson was a short little dress in keeping with the fashion in which she had dressed Ernest. Hadley, in her thank-you letter, said it would bring back Christmas pleasures "way out of season." She added, "Right now, for dress up, he fits just a tiny bit loosely into the beautiful silk stockings and adorable pink shoes."

They were planning to leave Toronto for New York on January 14, Hadley told Grace and Clarence, so it would be best not to write them after January 12. For obvious reasons, she did not tell her in-laws that she and Hemingway were planning to break their lease, which had another seven months to run. (Hadley, in fact, felt so guilty that it was not until the *Antonia* was well at sea that she felt safe from the authorities.) Shortly before their departure, they had a brief note from Clarence, mourning his lost opportunity to see his grandson: "I feel like running away from here and going to Toronto and New York to see him. Wish I had the chance." He enclosed a check for $10 for the steamer trip.

II

A week or more after their ten-day crossing to Cherbourg, Hemingway wrote Ezra Pound, who was wintering in Rapallo, "I have about 7 stories to write. Don't know when or where able to write." They had found a semifurnished apartment at 113 rue Notre-Dame-des-

Champs, not far from the Pounds' studio at 70 bis and only a few blocks from the rue de Fleurus. It was a warren of small rooms, adjacent to a sawmill, fragrant during the day with the smell of fresh-cut wood but noisy with the piercing whine of the saw. Hadley was not feeling well; her insides were all "haywired," Hemingway told Pound, and she wasn't sleeping well. The weather was dreary, and the town seemed full of "an enormous number of shits." Hadley had rehired her old *femme de ménage,* Marie Rohrbach ("Marie Cocotte"), to help with the housework and with Bumby. In good weather, if Hemingway was trying to write in his boxy workroom off the dark hallway, Hadley took the baby out for long sessions in the Luxembourg Gardens in a carriage borrowed from the Straters.

Hemingway had, in fact, begun writing soon after they settled into their apartment. Hadley wrote her in-laws on February 20, "Ernest has written two dandy stories this week and is at his third this morning." Hemingway, however, kept up the fiction of hardship. They were still "experimenting" with living with a baby, he told Pound. "Have tried to write but couldn't bring it off. Have written a few stories in cafes and one place and another."

On March 16, the baby was christened at St. Luke's Episcopal Church, where Joyce's son, Giorgio, sang in the choir. Bumby wore the little christening clothes that had once been his father's. The baptismal certificate listed Captain E. E. Dorman Smith and Miss Gertrude Stein and Miss Alice Toklas as the sponsors. Afterward, there was a little fete at the apartment with champagne and sugared almonds. Chink had vowed he would stand godfather to the baby even if "he was a triple deformity." And Gertrude and Alice had been pleased; on Bumby's six months' birthday in April, they brought their "Goddy" a silver christening mug and rubber toys. Photographs of the pair (Alice in a threatening hat, hovering, inquisitive and maternal, over the baby carriage in a Parisian park) testify to their taking their duties seriously at first. Bumby would fondly remember them as "the two giant women gargoyles" of his childhood.

The Hemingways that spring were feeling strapped for cash. George Breaker, Hadley's St. Louis friend and broker, had mismanaged her funds through poor investments, with a loss of several hundred dollars. (Her trust funds were still intact.) At Pound's urging, Hemingway had taken a position as editor for Ford Madox Ford's *Transatlantic Review,* the first issue of which had appeared in January. Hemingway's duties consisted of reading and editing manuscripts. It was Ford's stated policy to encourage the young and the daring, but the first issue had carried only Robert McAlmon's story "Elsie" and an experimental prose piece by Jean Cassou, along with two of Pound's recent cantos. It also resurrected a short novel, *The Nature of a Crime,* on which Ford and Joseph Conrad had collaborated some fifteen years earlier. There were congratulatory letters from more traditional-minded writers like H. G. Wells and T. S. Eliot, the latter questioning Ford's policy of promoting the young: "Good literature is produced by a few queer people in odd corners: the use of a review is not to force talent, but to create a favourable atmosphere."

It was a sign of Hemingway's dedication to Stein that once on the staff of the *Transatlantic,* he wasted no time in promoting her novel *The Making of Americans.* By February 17, he had already propositioned Ford with an early segment of the manuscript and written to Stein, "Ford alleges he is delighted with the stuff and is going to call on you. . . . He wondered if you would accept 30 francs a page (his magazine page) and I said I thought I could get you to. (Be haughty but not too haughty.)" Quite possibly, he had misrepresented what the publication would involve. Stein's novel, begun in 1903 but not completed until 1911, had started out as a family saga, with as many longueurs as the "simple middle class monotonous tradition" it was attempting to depict. In its later unabridged book form it would run to 925 pages, long enough to sink any magazine, even one like the *Transatlantic,* which carried its brave logo of a ship cresting the waves and the motto *Fluctuat.* In the magazine it would run for nine installments, amounting to 111 pages.

Stein was thrilled by Hemingway's effort to promote her work. She considered the book proof of her rightful place in the vanguard of the modern movement, the precursor of Proust and Joyce. ("So for the first time a piece of the monumental work which was the beginning, really the beginning of modern writing, was printed.") It was her "eternal hymn of repetition." Struggling within the Laocoönic coils of the novel, it was not unusual for Stein to break into the narrative with mournful asides to the reader about the difficulties of the task: "I am all unhappy in this writing. I know very much of the meaning of the being in women and men . . . and now I am telling it and I am nervous and driving and unhappy in it." (Hemingway, too, during his apprenticeship, would occasionally resort to such authorial asides, most notably in "Big Two-Hearted River." There he used a more stylish stream-of-consciousness mode for Nick Adams's commentaries on such writers as Joyce and Cummings and Stein herself.)

Since Stein had only one bound copy of her manuscript, both Hemingway and Alice transcribed the segments for publication. Hemingway's reward for his efforts, Stein was convinced, was that in copying the manuscript, and subsequently proofreading the galleys, he had benefited from the close study of her style. One might easily dismiss this as the expression of Stein's magnanimous ego, except that Hemingway, at the time, had seconded the notion. Writing to Edward O'Brien about the installments in the *Transatlantic,* he claimed, "I think it is wonderful stuff, but to get it, really, you have to read it as hard and concentrated as tho you were reading proof on it."

There is little doubt that Hemingway was genuinely impressed by Stein's novel. He must have been struck by the book's opening paragraph: "Once an angry man dragged his father along the ground through his own orchard. 'Stop!' cried the groaning old man at last, 'Stop! I did not drag my father beyond this tree.'" The contest between father and son, the sense of the parental burden dragged to the point of final recognition and reprieve, must have caught Hemingway's attention, given his own troubled relationship with his father. And it is clear that Hemingway recognized the effectiveness of Stein's use of gerunds in conveying a sustained sense of immediacy: "As I was saying every one has in them . . . their own way of sleeping, their own way of resting, of loving, of talking, or keeping still, of waking, their own way of working, of having stupid being in them."

In Hemingway's posthumously published story "Summer People," probably written not long after his return to Paris in 1924, Nick Adams's ruminations on sex and love are clearly derived from Stein's run-on style: "It wasn't just love. . . . It was liking, and liking the body, and introducing the body, and persuading, and taking chances, and never frightening, and assuming about the other person, and always taking never asking, and gentleness and liking, and making liking."

Even after the tedious chore of proofreading the *Transatlantic* installments, Hemingway continued to tout Stein's novel in the most enthusiastic terms. Publication in the *Transatlantic* had stirred up some hopes of book publication in America by way of Hemingway's friend Harold Stearns, who was serving as Paris agent for the New York publisher Horace Liveright. When that attempt fell through, Hemingway wrote Stein in the most consoling terms, "I feel sick about it but don't you feel bad, because you have written it and that is all that matters a damn. It is up to us, i.e. Alice Toklas, Me, Hadley, John Hadley Nicanor and other good men to get it published. It will all come sooner or later the way you want it. This is not Christian Science." As late as 1926, when Stein's long unfulfilled dream was finally realized and Robert McAlmon published the complete version of *The Making of Americans,* Hemingway referred to it as "one of the very greatest books I've ever read."

Three Stories and Ten Poems had not created a stir, and the long-awaited publication of the Paris edition of *in our time* was delayed by one setback after another at the bindery. ("Fuck Literature," Hemingway wrote Pound on the day after his son's christening because copies still had not arrived.) The fine thrill of success was too long in coming. There were favorable puffs in the April issue of the *Transatlantic,* to be sure. Marjorie Reid, reviewing *in our time,* wrote, "He projects moments when life is condensed and clean-cut and significant, presenting them in minute narratives that eliminate every useless word. Each tale is much longer than the measure of its lines." Young Kennon Jewett's two-line review of *Three Stories and Ten Poems* in the same issue praised Hemingway's "sensitive feeling for the emotional possibilities of a situation. His method is realistic, but unlike most of his school he has not killed his work on the shallow hardness of photography." But they were both staff writers for the magazine. Burton Rascoe's mention of *in our time* in another of his "A Bookman's Day Book" columns for the *New York Herald Tribune* was no more satisfactory for Hemingway than Rascoe's earlier reference to *Three Stories.* Hemingway wrote Pound, "Burton Rascoe said In Our Time showed the influences of who the hell do you think? — Ring Lardner and Sherwood Anderson! There it is. Oh well." Actually, although Rascoe had made a passing reference to Lardner and Anderson, he praised the vignettes as having "here and there a sentence or a paragraph of genuine power."

The most important notice would come from Edmund Wilson but not until the October issue of *The Dial,* in which he reviewed both *Three Stories and Ten Poems* and *in our time.* Wilson dismissed the poems as negligible but had high praise for the brief, compressed vignettes. Quoting Hemingway's description of the shooting of the Greek cabinet ministers, Wilson commented that the young writer was "remarkably successful in suggesting moral values by a series of simple statements of this sort." He described Hemingway's cool, objective style as "a harrowing record of the barbarities of the period in which we live."

But the review was, perhaps, a mixed blessing since Wilson saw Hemingway as "the only American writer but one — Mr. Sherwood Anderson — who has felt the genius of Gertrude Stein's *Three Lives* and has evidently been influenced by it." Wilson maintained that the three American writers formed a school whose characteristic was "a naiveté of language, often passing into the colloquialism of the character dealt with, which serves actually to convey profound emotions and complex states of minds. It is a distinctively American development in prose."

Hemingway wrote Wilson, thanking him for the review: "You are the only man writing criticism who or whom I can read when the book being criticized is one I've read or know something about." If he had known that Wilson had written his review in April and had had to write the editor Alyse Gregory in September, reminding her ("I wish you would print my little notice of Hemingway's books sometime soon . . . so that he can get the benefit of it"), Hemingway would have had one more excuse for his continuing anger against *The Dial.* He blamed Scofield Thayer for Pound's dismissal from the magazine. For a lifetime, without cause, he also accused Gilbert Seldes of having turned down his poems. In February, Hemingway had informed Pound, in scatological terms, "Seldes, his sphincter muscle no doubt having lost its attractive tautness, has left the Dial. An aged virgin has his place, There is no doubt a similarity." The "aged virgin" was Alyse Gregory, who remained managing editor until Marianne Moore took over the post a year later. (From the beginning to the end of his career, Hemingway, in writing about his male rivals and enemies, would imagine a hell as obscene as anything to be found in Pound's cantos; Scofield Thayer would be the perennial bugger and Gilbert Seldes, always, the butt of that particular metaphor.)

Hemingway would have additional charges for his long-term indictment of the magazine. On the strength of Wilson's favorable review, he submitted a short story (probably "Soldier's Home") but heard nothing until he received a letter from Gregory, dated December 4, returning the story "which we do not find wholly suited to our present needs." Still persistent, in January 1925 Hemingway sent another, possibly his bullfight story, "The Undefeated," another of his major early stories. This time Thayer approved but the publisher, J. Sibley Watson, declined. Since neither could come to a meeting of the minds, it was left up to Marianne Moore to cast the deciding vote, and she turned it down.

That *The Dial* should have turned down "Soldier's Home," a Hemingway masterpiece, might seem incredible if it had not already been turned down by the *American Mercury,* along with "The Three-Day Blow." H. L. Mencken and George Jean Nathan could not agree on these and, presumably, other Hemingway stories, though the letters of rejection Hemingway received in May and August and again in September 1924 made encouraging suggestions that he try again. In September, Nathan admitted, "Mencken and I cannot agree on the enclosed pieces of your work. . . . But we shall continue to read with utmost sympathy anything that you send in to us."

Hemingway was even more disappointed — in fact, deeply wounded — by the response of his family when the copies of *in our time* they had ordered arrived at Oak Park. According to Marcelline, her father had been mortified by the vignette "One hot evening in Milan" ("A Very Short Story"), in which the rejected soldier contracts gonorrhea from a salesgirl while riding in a taxicab through Lincoln Park. Clarence believed that no gentleman should mention venereal disease outside a doctor's office. He was adamantly opposed to allowing such "filth" in his house. He grimly returned the books to the publisher, even though, according to Marcelline, Grace had pleaded with him to keep at least one copy of what she assumed was her son's first book. Marcelline, visiting at the time, thought the offending vignette much milder than "Up in Michigan." She warned the family that Hemingway would know that the copies had been returned and would resent it bitterly. Hemingway did: "I wonder what was the matter, whether the pictures were too accurate and the attitude toward life not sufficiently distorted to please who ever bought the books or what?" he wrote his family when he learned that five copies ordered by his parents had been returned to the publisher. He conveniently blamed the insult on Grace.

III

It did not take long for Hemingway's initial courtship of Ford Madox Ford to turn to animosity. Nothing about the blustering, oversized, pink-faced writer, editor, and womanizer with the wheezing voice and officious manner pleased Hemingway. Predictably, Ford's talk about his wartime service, aggrandized in the figure of Christopher Tietjens, the hero of *Some Do Not,* which was running serially in the *Transatlantic,* aggravated Hemingway: "I'm going to start denying I was in the war for fear I will get like Ford to my self about it." At the age of forty-two, Ford had held a commission in the Ninth Welsh Battalion and served in the line transport, behind the lines, at Becourt woods in France. Though not wounded or gassed, he was knocked to the ground by nearby shellfire and seriously damaged his front teeth. The result was a traumatic shell shock — he lost his memory for a brief time while he was in the hospital. For several years after, he suffered from periodic nervous disorders.

Like Hemingway, Ford tended to fictionalize his wartime service. Hemingway, who may never have known the true story, maintained that Ford had never recovered from the miracle of his having been a soldier, and he followed Tietjens's progress in Ford's novel-sequence with a good deal of scorn. "Down with gentlemen," Hemingway wrote Pound. "They're hell on themselves in literature." He also suspected that Ford, under one of his various pseudonyms, was writing letters to the editor of the *Transatlantic* in praise of his own books, a claim that was quite possibly true.

As a subeditor, Hemingway was soon taking a hand in directing editorial policy at the magazine. He was bent on dragging Ford, who *was* old enough to be his father, further along on his own editorial path than Ford was prepared to go. Ford, Hemingway wrote Pound, was "running the whole damn thing as compromise." Except for "Tzara and such shit in French," Ford was too willing to publish the kind of writing the editors of the *Century* or *Harper's* would accept. "That's the hell of it. Goddam it he hasn't any advertizers to offend or any subscribers to discontinue why not shoot the moon?" He contributed, with some regularity, to the gossipy "Chroniques" columns, in which, in his best subversive manner, he countered Ford's choices of the turn-of-the-century memoirs of Luke Ionides and the more intellectual contributions of Tristan Tzara, André Salmon, and René Crevel, with manly, lowbrow notes on the virtues of bull-fighting, the health of the racehorse Epinard, and praise for the boxer Eugène Criqui, "in the contemplation of whose work I experience a certain ecstasy which is not given me by reading the works of my contemporaries." He also rigorously promoted his friends and acquaintances. He plugged the first exhibition of André Masson at the Galerie Simon ("Two of his paintings hang in Gertrude Stein's studio with something like thirty of the best Picasso's in the world and do not lose by the comparison") and the departure of Mike Strater for the United States. The presence in Paris of Djuna Barnes gave rise to an odd comment on the "legendary personality" who, according to her publishers, had dominated European nightlife for a century. "I have never met her," Hemingway noted, "nor read her books, but she looks very nice." His interest, however, may have been sparked by her appearance in the April issue with a first-class story, "Aller et Retour," or by the fact that Barnes was another of the lesbian women of Paris who piqued his curiosity, along with Natalie Barney and the "Little Review girls," Margaret Anderson and Jane Heap, as well as Janet Flanner and her friend Solita Solano — the Nip and Tuck of Barnes's later, scandalous guidebook of Barney's lesbian circle, *Ladies Almanack.* With Flanner, whom he met before she became Genêt, the celebrated Parisian correspondent for *The New Yorker,* Hemingway developed a long and remarkably untroubled friendship.

Writing to Edward O'Brien about his services for the magazine, Hemingway presented himself as a coach for some of the younger contributors and staff members, notably Nathan Asch, Kennon Jewett, and Ivan Beede. "They are three kids with plenty of talent — Asch the most, Jewett the least." Hemingway claimed to have "discovered" Asch, the son of Sholem Asch, the popular Yiddish novelist; on his way to the W.C. one day, he picked up a batch of manuscripts and became so excited reading one of Asch's stories that he forgot to button up his fly. He showed the story to Ford, who was also impressed. Beede, a subeditor at the *Transatlantic,* hailed from David City, Nebraska. Jewett, a twenty-year-old critic and reviewer for the magazine, was an easterner, a Harvard boy with an interest in Rimbaud, Laforgue, and Flaubert. Hemingway's encouragement of his protégés may not have been as generous as he implied. He told O'Brien, "It is discouraging to try to help people do something in their own way and then just have them imitate." This was not the case with Asch or Beede, he said, but Jewett was too young and too facile.

Ford's confidence in Hemingway's talents as a writer shone brighter in his remarks than in practice. In the pages of the *Transatlantic,* according to Ford in his role as the editorial "we," Hemingway was "the admirable American prose writer" or "the man whose tastes march more with our own than those of most other men." In one of his charming and questionable memoirs, *It Was the Nightingale,* Ford claimed that he had read no more than six words of Hemingway's before he decided "to publish everything that he sent me." But that was hardly the case. To be sure, Hemingway's important early story "Indian Camp" appeared in the April 1924 issue, but the other stories, "The Doctor and the Doctor's Wife" and "Cross-Country Snow," appeared only in the final issues of the magazine's yearlong existence, when Hemingway had more leverage in the magazine's editorial policies. For Hemingway, impatient for recognition, the April appearance was hardly strong evidence of Ford's commitment. Writing to Pound, he complained that Ford had several more of his stories but obviously couldn't or wouldn't publish them. "The only stories I've got that I know the St. Nicholas Mag. wont publish I know damn well Ford wont too. So where the hell do we get off at." Despite his anger, Hemingway was circumspect. "Don't let any of this get back to Ford because then it would just mean a row with me and no good done." Nonetheless, he told Pound, "I am fond of Ford. This ain't personal. It's literary." It was one of his fine rationalizations of the kind he often made when he felt duty-bound (for high-minded reasons) to bite the hand that helped him.

Hemingway had his opportunity very shortly after his letter to Pound. The *Transatlantic* was in financial trouble. Late in May, Ford, who had no gift for financial management, made a trip to the United States in hopes of persuading John Quinn, a major patron of the magazine, to invest more money. Unfortunately, Quinn, dying with cancer, was too ill and discouraged to discuss the matter. (Ezra Pound, well aware of the magazine's financial problems, warned his father, "Ef yew see Ford; feed him; but don't fer Gawd's sake put any money into the Transatlantic Review." When Ford sailed to New York, he left Hemingway in charge of the magazine, with the responsibility for finishing up the July volume (for which Ford had already commissioned most of the editorial material) and editing the entire August issue. It was an inconvenient time for Hemingway. He was hard at work on a story he considered important, "Big Two-Hearted River," and he was making plans for a trip to Spain with Hadley and friends in late June.

Still, he set to work putting his signature to Ford's magazine with what must have been a perverse pleasure. For the July issue he took editorial credit for reprinting a nonsense play by Ring Lardner, "I Gaspari." By way of introducing the piece, he added a gratuitous slur on Tristan Tzara for translating Romeo and Juliet without benefit of knowing the language, a passing slur on Cocteau, and a caustic reference to Gilbert Seldes. Since Donald Ogden Stewart was credited as one of the obtaining agents of the Lardner piece, it is probable that Hemingway was also responsible for the inclusion of Stewart's dull collegiate satire in the July issue's "Literary Supplement." Hemingway had met Stewart, a Yale man and a former *Vanity Fair* staff writer, the year before in Paris, admired Stewart's wit and nonchalance and touted his comic novel, *Mr. and Mrs. Haddock Abroad.* Lardner and Stewart — it was the point of his plodding preface — were Hemingway's proof "how very much better dadas the American dadas, who do not know they are dadas, unless, of course, Mr. Seldes has told them, are than the French and Roumanians who know it so well."

In the August issue, John Dos Passos's story "July" had quite probably been commissioned by Ford. But no doubt Hemingway was eager to use it in an issue that would be weighted with American contributors. Hemingway, who thought Dos Passos's 1921 war novel, *Three Soldiers,* was "a swell book," may have met the author for the first time during the summer of 1924. (Besides thinking, erroneously, that they had previously met in Italy in 1918, Dos Passos also had a vague recollection of having met up with Hemingway again in Paris in 1922. He seemed to remember a lunch with Hemingway and Hadley at Lipp's, at which he found Hemingway's "acid estimates" of Clemenceau and Lloyd George and Litvinov highly invigorating.) But it was during the summer of 1924 that Hemingway became exceptionally friendly with both Dos Passos and Stewart: "both great guys, you know the old stuff," Hemingway informed Howell Jenkins. Dos, in fact, reminded him of Bill Smith "before he started to go haywire." Hemingway went on to assure Jenkins, "All the men are drinkers." He and Dos Passos, however, were put off by Stewart's social ambitions; Stewart was insistent that both of them should get to know "people that mattered."

Probably as a favor to Robert McAlmon, Hemingway published two poems by Bryher in the poetry section. It was no favor that he also included two poems by the Baroness Elsa von Freytag Loringhoven, a genuine eccentric whose appearance was the epitome of dadaism: she was as likely to wear two metal tea balls pendent from her breasts as to shave her head and paint it vermillion. In her Greenwich Village phase the baroness terrorized male poets with her amorous intentions. Wallace Stevens, it was said, was afraid to go below Fourteenth Street for fear of meeting her. Having conceived a grand passion for William Carlos Williams, the baroness relentlessly pursued him, suggesting that he needed to contract syphilis (through her) as the highroad to suffering and serious art. According to Ford, Hemingway had been trying to get the baroness's poems into the *Transatlantic* for months, but Ford had managed to remove them from the table of contents before publication. Now that Ford was in New York, Hemingway made his move. It is also possible that he published the baroness's poetry out of devilment, as an embarrassment to Williams, then in Paris with his wife, Floss. The July issue had carried Williams's essay "Voyage of the Mayflower," perhaps another of Hemingway's choices. McAlmon had introduced Hemingway to the poet, who was a practicing doctor. On June 4, in fact, Dr. Williams performed a circumcision on Bumby in the Hemingways' apartment. (Williams would later claim, with some relish, that Hemingway nearly fainted at the sight of his son's blood.)

If Hemingway had planned no other confrontation with Ford's editorial authority and tastes, he would have succeeded just as well with what he had decided to omit from the August issue. He discarded the next installment of Luke Ionides's Pre-Raphaelite memoirs and he dropped the poems of J. J. Adams to make way for the baroness. The unkindest cut of all, no doubt, was that Hemingway deleted both Ford's pseudonymous Daniel Chaucer essay and the latest installment of *Some Do Not.*

That it was a calculated insult seems certain. But Hemingway did not stay around to witness the effect. After setting up the August issue, late in June, he took off for Spain as he had intended. When Ford returned in July it was too late to make substantial changes. He could only add a few bland comments to his New York editorial, acknowledging that the August issue, with few exceptions, was "entirely of Mr. Hemingway's getting together." It was Ford's turn for a bit of sarcasm: "It must prove an agreeable change for the Reader and it provides him with an unusually large sample of the work of that Young American whose claims we have so insistently — but not with such efficiency — forced upon our readers," a neatly turned sentence that cut both ways. Ford was left in the awkward position of promising that "should any large body of readers so demand," the next issue would include another installment of *Some Do Not.*

IV

A small company of congenial friends at Pamplona: Bill Bird and his wife, Sally, McAlmon, Dos Passos and his fiancée, Crystal Ross, Don Stewart, young George O'Neil, Chink Dorman-Smith, Hadley and Hemingway. (Bumby was being cared for by Madame Rohrbach in Paris.) On the surface, the seven-day fiesta of San Fermín was a happy occasion. Hemingway took charge of the arrangements: rooms at the Hotel Perla, the most comfortable hotel in town, tickets each morning for the amateur fights, block of seats for the corridas in the afternoons. At night, riau-riau dancing in the streets, fireworks, bouts of absinthe-and-pernod-drinking in the night spots, or else the cold drafts of Spanish *cerveza* served at the Café Iruña. For the first two days it had been windy, making the cape work hazardous in the afternoon fights. But Maera had performed wonderfully. Otherwise the weather had been good, only one hot day. Hemingway, writing to Howell Jenkins, touted it as "the godamdest wild time and fun you ever saw."

Except for Bill Bird and Dos Passos, the men were in the crowded arena by seven in the morning when the young or defective bulls were let loose and the amateur bullfighters tested their mettle. "I appeared in the bull ring on 5 different mornings — was cogida [tossed] 3 times — accomplished 4 veronicas in good form and one natural with the muleta," Hemingway boasted in a letter to Pound. Writing to Edward O'Brien, he claimed he had been "gored," a very different thing. Actually it was Don Stewart who had been hurt; a young bull had charged him full-force, fracturing two of his ribs. Even the accidents of others were lucky for Hemingway. The *Chicago Tribune* headlined a front-page story of the incident, "BULL GORES 2 YANKS ACTING AS TOREADORS." The *Toronto Daily Star* captioned a photograph of Hemingway and Hadley with the same misinformation: "Bull Gores Toronto Writer in Annual Pamplona Festival," although Hemingway had only come to Stewart's rescue and neither had been gored. Stewart, despite his injuries, was still game. He did not allow them to "spoil the last frenzied night of drinking and dancing," though they were painful enough to send him back to Paris the next day. Still, he maintained, it had been "a memorable week, a male festival, a glorified college reunion."

From Pamplona the remaining company of friends traveled to Burguete, high in the Pyrenees near the French border. It was a small village with only one inn. Herds of sheep and goats grazed in the hills; peasants, riding mules along the narrow roads, carried bundles of cordwood or bloated wineskins. Hemingway would remember the countryside vividly: the white houses, the forests of thick-trunked beech trees, and at the higher reaches, the pines. It was Bill Bird who had suggested the side trip; he had wanted to see the ancient monastery at nearby Roncesvalles, the setting of the twelfth-century epic the *Chanson de Roland*. On an excursion several miles from Burguete, near an abandoned mine shaft, they fished the Irati River for trout in an ice-cold pool beneath the falls. "We butchered them this summer. Big trout," he wrote Jenkins. "Hadley caught six in less than an hour out of one hole." McAlmon, however, had other memories; while they were fishing, Hemingway, annoyingly, took notes for his story "Big Two-Hearted River." McAlmon remembered, "He was so intent thinking about what it was that a man who was fishing would be thinking about, and what Bird and I would be thinking about, that he didn't catch many trout." He was convinced that, as a writer, Hemingway used rather than wondered about people. If, as McAlmon suspected, there had been something pretentious or desperate about Hemingway's note-taking, it is confirmed by Hemingway's mid-July letter to Pound from Burguete. He was still bearing a grudge against Ford: "I've tried and tried and can't go on with the thing that was 2/3 done and running smooth when he said I had to run the magazine." Nor did he admit he had tried to sabotage Ford in his editing of the July and August issues. Hemingway complained that he had written two letters to Ford from Pamplona and received no answer. "I suppose he is sore at me though Christnose I tried to run his paper the way he would have liked to have it run." He had, he told Pound, been "thoroughly gypped."

The friends disbanded at Burguete; Bill and Sally Bird returned to Paris. Chink, George O'Neil, McAlmon, and Dos Passos left for a hiking expedition through the Pyrenees. Hemingway accompanied them for five miles or more along the way, but his leg bothered him and he decided to return to Hadley.

⁂

Despite his exuberant letters to friends, Hemingway clearly felt that at Pamplona the male contingent had let him down. Bill Bird, who had seemed a promising aficionado the year before, avoided the amateur fights in the morning. Hemingway was convinced that his absence was Sally Bird's doing. Dos Passos, too, had disappointed him. In the weeks they had chummed together in Paris before the Pamplona trip, they had hit it off well, discussing writing and writers over drinks at the Closerie des Lilas. At Pamplona, however, Dos had attended only one of the amateur fights. (Dos Passos, in fact, had disliked the whole idea of having to prove himself *muy hombre* in the arena.) Hemingway blamed that, too, on another interfering woman, Dos's fiancée Crystal Ross.

Dos Passos saw it differently. In a letter to a friend, Dos described the vacation week in disparaging terms: "I found myself I dont know how at a lot of bullfights in Pamplona at a ferocious fiesta with a lot of fake bohemians." (Forty-two years later he gave a slightly softened version in *The Best Times:* "It was fun and we ate well and drank well but there were too many exhibitionistic personalities in the group to suit me.") Neither did Chink Dorman-Smith have a wonderful time. Hemingway recalled that his friend "suffered sincerely and deeply at what happened to horses at first bullfight — said it was most hateful thing he had ever seen." McAlmon recalled that among the little company of friends, there had been a good deal of muttering about Hemingway's taking over all the arrangements — as a commissioned tourist guide — because "he knew the ropes." Since Dos Passos spoke Spanish fluently and Bill Bird knew a little and all of them were experienced travelers "all of us thought we might have been left to handle our own expenses rather than paying him to pay for us." Particularly since Hemingway gave the impression that it was work that he had "bravely" assumed for their benefit.

But one of McAlmon's most souring recollections of the trip, whether truth or supposition, was that Hadley was pregnant for the second time. "It was one of those secrets everybody knew," McAlmon claimed. One night at Roncesvalles, Hemingway, in a complaining mood, was mumbling about being too young to have more children and burdens. Nor would Hadley be the good playmate anymore. "He was tragic about it, and Hadley, too, became upset." (Hadley, he noted, "was taking aspirins.") Finally, when the discussion went on too long, Sally Bird blurted out, "Stop acting like a damn fool and a crybaby. You're responsible too. Either you do something about not having it, or you have it." Perhaps McAlmon invented Hadley's pregnancy and Sally's outburst out of sheer malice. Yet, if in his memoirs he is often the embittered man, ready to give any incident a cynical interpretation, he seldom strikes the reader as a practiced liar. The truth appears to be that at Roncesvalles Hadley had missed her period, giving rise to Hemingway's gloomy behavior. Only after their departure did it prove to be a false alarm.

111

That summer, Hemingway had begun to think of himself as a victim. In May, he had been full of hopeful plans for publishing a book of fifteen or twenty short stories that would be interwoven with the vignettes or interchapters from Bird's edition of *in our time.* He wanted to bring out "a good fat book in N.Y. with some good publisher who would tout it." He had ten stories in hand, he informed Edward O'Brien, hoping O'Brien might help him place some of the stories with a literary agent or a magazine editor. But by July, his ambitions thwarted, Hemingway's anger and frustration erupted in a letter to Pound: "The Transatlantic killed my chances of having a book published this fall and by next spring some son of a bitch will have copied everything I've written and they will simply call me another of his imitators." That was his real grievance. (Was he worrying, perhaps, about Asch or Jewett?) Another was that he was hard up financially. "Now we haven't got any money anymore, I am going to have to quit writing and I never will have a book published. I feel cheerful as hell. These god damn bastards." His financial woes were a subject of complaint in letters to Pound and to Edward O'Brien: "In the meantime, if I could sell some of the stories it would help out as I have quit newspaper work." Considering that he could afford a week's trip (without Hadley) to the Gard that spring, catching the bullfights at Nîmes, and that they were vacationing in Spain that summer, was he merely talking up his financial woes for good effect? In response to his dejection, McAlmon, Stein, even Don Stewart, lent him money or sent small sums as gifts over the remainder of the year.

Whatever the later, casual generosity of friends, Hemingway, that summer, definitely felt he had been "bitched financially and in a literary way by my friends." (These enemies, other than Ford, went unnamed.) In his discontent, Hemingway fastened on bull-fighting rather than writing as a far more satisfying and honorable profession. He told Pound, "I take great and unintellectual pleasure in the immediate triumphs of the bull ring with their reward in ovations, Alcoholism, being pointed out on the street, general respect and the other things Literary guys have to wait until they are 89 years old to get." Curiously, in his new philistinism, he vented his bitterness on the unoffending James Joyce: "In all the other arts the more meazly and shitty the guy, i.e. Joyce, the greater the success in his art. There is absolutely no comparison in art between Joyce and Maera — Maera by a mile — and then look at the guys. One breeds Georgios the other gets killed or breeds bulls . . . I wish to hell I was 16 and had art and valor."

V

The troubles began, soon enough, after Hemingway's return from Spain in late July. To start with, the *Transatlantic*'s patron John Quinn had died and with him the major hope of keeping the magazine afloat. Ford's solution, Hemingway wrote Gertrude Stein, who was then vacationing in the Ain, was to stay up all night sending *pneumatiques* or spending 100 francs in taxi fares in hopes of soliciting 500 francs from wealthy prospects like Natalie Barney.

Hemingway himself stepped in and solved the immediate problem by getting his Chicago pal Krebs Friend, then in Paris and recently married to a wealthy older woman, to put up the money. Local gossip had it that Krebs, who had been badly shell-shocked during the war, was feeling morose, and that Mrs. Friend, reportedly forty years older than he, was buying the magazine to give her young husband a reason for living. The Friends, through Hemingway's agency, were ready to put up $200 a month to keep the magazine going with an option to buy at the end of six months, with Ford staying on as editor. Hemingway wrote Stein that with help now in sight, Ford was on his high horse, claiming the magazine as a good money-making proposition and treating Friend, condescendingly, as the enemy. Ford wasn't too far from being wrong. Krebs and his wife, determined to make the magazine a paying proposition, had ideas of their own. In the time-honored fashion of amateur publishers, Mrs. Friend decided to drop any contributions that had to be paid for. And Krebs was suggesting that it would be a good idea for younger contributors to show their loyalty to the magazine by drumming up ads. Hemingway suspected (he was exactly on target) that the magazine would "go to hell on or about the first of Jan."

There were other grievances in Hemingway's bill of particulars. Ford had badgered Hemingway into providing a "Pamplona Letter" for the September issue. Hemingway did so with bad grace, making an invidious comparison between journalism and creative writing. Journalism, one did for money, and he liked to be well paid for it. (He complained, in print, that the meager 30 francs a page he received from the *Transatlantic* was "only a supplementary reward.") Writing journalism, he said, destroyed the real value of an experience like bullfighting. Creative writing had to be done religiously. "Once you put a thing into words, unless you 'do it on your knees,' you kill it." For good measure, he added a few perfunctory sentences on the *feria* but confessed that to write about it too well might be a mistake: Cook would begin running tours to Pamplona and ruin it. "Practically all the people that deserved to be at Pamplona were there this year," he added. To which Ford inserted a wounded "Merci!" by way of editorial comment.

Hemingway's truculence found further expression when Ford asked him, as a representative of the younger generation, along with Robert McAlmon and others, to contribute to a memorial supplement on Joseph Conrad, who had died on August 3. The fact that younger writers like Hemingway and McAlmon might admire Conrad but regard him as representative of the old guard literary establishment (in which Hemingway included Ford himself) did not deter Ford's sense of the appropriateness of the gesture. In his homage, written for the September issue, Hemingway noted Conrad's declining reputation, admitted that he could never reread anything of Conrad's, but said he nevertheless got from Conrad's books something he got from nothing else he ever read. The tribute, unfortunately, offered Hemingway a perfect opportunity to air a few of his grievances about the vanguard establishment. It was fashionable among his friends to disparage Conrad, he said; it was even necessary in the tight little world of expatriate Paris. Most of the people he knew agreed that Conrad was a bad writer and T. S. Eliot a good one, but he disagreed: "If I knew that by grinding Mr. Eliot into a fine dry powder and sprinkling that powder over Mr. Conrad's grave Mr. Conrad would shortly appear . . . I would leave for London early tomorrow morning with a sausage grinder." In a subsequent issue, Ford apologized for the bloodthirstiness of the unnamed chronicler who had attacked Eliot. It was a question of ethics not to censor a writer in the magazine. "We were besides convinced that Mr. Eliot does not mind. He does not. . . . We take the opportunity of expressing for the tenth time our admiration for Mr. Eliot's poetry." The public apology infuriated Hemingway, and for a while he and Ford were not on speaking terms.

Ford, however, was an inveterate party giver, and during the year of the magazine's existence his parties were famous in the quarter. At first they were afternoon teas held at the *Transatlantic* offices, then at Ford's studio apartment on the boulevard Arago. Harold Loeb, whom Hemingway met, with his girlfriend Kitty Cannell, through Ford, recalled one of the wild parties. The main room at the boulevard Arago, crowded with "dancers, expounders, strollers, music, and smoke," erupted into minor violence when a pair of young Americans began a fistfight. ("There was blood but no body.") Loeb, dancing with a tall, elegant Swedish girl, saw Berenice Abbott fall on her back in the middle of the floor as the painter Waldo Peirce looked on. "Some of the guests seemed confused," Loeb remembered, "but Ford was quite calm." When the boulevard Arago parties became too boisterous for "at homes," Ford moved them to the *bal musette* near Hemingway's old apartment on the rue du Cardinal-Lemoine.

Since Ford was at the center of the expatriate social life, it was difficult for Hemingway to avoid him. Especially because Ford was publishing two more of Hemingway's stories in the *Transatlantic*. Their relationship evolved into a kind of armed truce, at least on Hemingway's part; Ford was too bumbling in his affections to bear a grudge for long. Burton Rascoe, then in Paris with his wife, Hazel, remembered the odd spectacle of attending one of Ford's parties at which Hadley sat with the guests while Hemingway stood at the bar, pointedly not attending the party. Glaring at the company, he warned his wife, "Pay for your own drinks, do you hear! Don't let him [nodding toward Ford] buy you anything."

Hemingway continued his vilification by writing to Stein about the situation at the magazine: "There are a good many other angles to it that we can talk about when you all get back. Ford is an absolute liar and crook always motivated by the finest synthetic English gentility." What he said about Ford to Pound, at the time, is not clear, since Pound was then in Paris closing up his studio for his final move to Rapallo. But as an expert in playing off rivals, Hemingway wrote Stein, giving her a caustic account of Pound: "Ezra goes to Italy for good on Sunday. He has indulged in a small nervous breakdown necessitating him spending two days at the Am. Hospital during the height of the packing." Hadley had more intimate family news for the "Steins." Ezra and Dorothy had taken them out to dinner and that night "E[rnest] had AWFUL dreams. He was alone and he had to creep in and stay with me to be sure everything was alright. At times so big and important and then so small." There was, perhaps, truth to Hemingway's remark to Stein, "The town isn't much fun with you all gone. All the gossip dries up inside me and poisons my enjoyment of my friends' misfortunes."

VI

Despite his summer rantings, Hemingway managed to complete his projected book of stories by the fall of 1924. "I've worked like hell most of the time and think the stuff gets better," he wrote Edmund Wilson. He had achieved his goal of fourteen stories, which, with the intervening vignettes, would make up the book he had planned. He explained his artistic intentions: to give a picture of the whole and, in between, examine it in detail. "Like looking with your eyes at something, say a passing coastline, and then looking at it with 15× binoculars. Or rather, maybe, looking at it and then going in and living in it — and then coming out and looking at it again."

That basic declaration of the method of *In Our Time* has been a source of puzzlement for critics attempting to discover some rigorous architectural plan for the book. There is no doubt that Hemingway intended *In Our Time* to be a structured book rather than a mere collection of stories. Under the influence of Paris and its vanguard writers like Joyce and Pound and Stein, he meant it to be modern in style. Yet the choice of the stories and the intervening vignettes was more a found structure than a rigidly ordained scheme. Two of his earlier vignettes were recast and titled as stories ("A Very Short Story" and "The Revolutionist"), perhaps to round out the number of stories needed, and with his persistent hopes of defeating the censor, he intended to publish "Up in Michigan" as the second story in the book. Themes, names, identities, passing references, to be sure, are threaded, fugally, through the book from vignette to story; the violence of war and the ritual violence of the bullfight are juxtaposed. *In Our Time,* the capitalized version, was to be Hemingway's most experimental book. Hemingway, however, would never be the formalist that Joyce was — or Proust, the earlier hero of vanguard Paris. His tough, ironic style certainly would speak for a new generation of writers and influence many who followed. But his later novels, following *In Our Time,* would revert to the narrative techniques of the nineteenth century. There was some justice to Gertrude Stein's biting remark that Hemingway "looks like a modern and he smells of the museums."

Hemingway's reference to the passing coastline does suggest a plausible influence for his narrative method and it seems to have been Pound. *Periploi* was the ancient term for the accounts of seamen on exploratory voyages — like those of Odysseus, the hero of Pound's opening cantos — a cartography based on passage along a coastline. Pound used the term to characterize his poetic method and the structure of the *Cantos*. As he later defined it in Canto LIX, "Periplum, not as land looks on a map but as sea bord seen by men sailing." It was, as Hemingway's stories and vignettes were intended to be, not an overview but a narrative form in which seemingly disconnected episodes and events made up a chronicle of things seen, the report of a journey, the record of a life in time.

That *In Our Time* is one of Hemingway's masterpieces is all the more surprising, since it is the work of a young man at the outset of his career. It is definitely a book rather than a collection of stories. Through the character of Nick Adams, the hero of many (though not all) of the stories of *In Our Time,* Hemingway created a fictional persona for himself and for his time. He announced themes that would carry him through a lifetime of work: the disappointments of family life, the disaffections of early love, the celebration of country and male comradeship, a young man's initiation into the world of sex, the consequences of marriage. In the interchapters, Hemingway recreated the destructive violence of battle and the ritual violence of bullfighting intended to give the larger chronicle of his times — the world of war and politics, of crime and punishment — that were juxtaposed with the more personal circumstances of the stories.

The invention of Nick Adams was one of the most vital inspirations of Hemingway's career. The character appears first as the wounded Nick Grainger of the early story written in the hospital in Milan and as the soldier named Adams who is killed in battle in an unused vignette, "Did You Ever Kill Anyone?"

> The advance was going like clockwork. We'd shelled the shit out of everything. Adams and I and two men were on the extreme right of C. Company.
>
> Cra-pung.
>
> Adams went down like a batter that has been beaned.

Adams was given permanent status in the childhood Nick of "Indian Camp," who poignantly believes he will live forever. In that story, published in the April issue of the *Transatlantic,* as well as in two of the earlier vignettes in *in our time,* the resurrected Nick Adams began an important career in Hemingway's fiction. Chronologically, his life would roughly parallel but not necessarily intersect with the circumstances of Hemingway's life up to the culminating masterpiece of that particular mode, "Fathers and Sons," published in 1933.

That Nick Adams — in some ways the better self — had a less bitter life, was a different persona in which Hemingway could acknowledge fear and failure, lust and tenderness, a more measured resentment against his mother. It was as if, in the fictional alter ego of Nick Adams, Hemingway had created the sensitive, ironic, perhaps even more intellectual, persona he would seldom allow himself to be in life. In the fiction, he risked a different self.

No story, perhaps, among the fourteen that make up *In Our Time,* would have the persistent interest of "The Doctor and the Doctor's Wife." Written in Paris in the spring of 1924, it is one of the essential documents in any critical account of Hemingway's long and wayward relationship with his parents. As a major story, it illustrates the dialogue between fact and fiction that is the benchmark of Hemingway's approach as a writer and his remembrance of the past. We have a time: the summer of 1911, the summer that his sister Carol was born and Ernest was twelve. At Walloon Lake, when Hemingway was young, it frequently happened that the logs from the sawmill escaped from the boom. When they became waterlogged and sank just below the surface, they were a hazard to boats and swimmers. Often enough, they drifted ashore. It was Clarence Hemingway's habit to hire one or two of the local Indians, usually Dick Boulton or Billy Tabeshaw, to saw up the big logs for firewood. Perhaps in that summer of 1911 there was an argument between Dr. Hemingway and Dick Boulton. That, at least, is how Hemingway construed the situation when, thirteen years later, in the spring of 1924, he was living in the cheap apartment above a sawmill at 113 rue Notre-Dame-des-Champs in Paris. In the story, Dick Boulton, truculently, and once too often, refers to one of the logs as being "stolen" property. He insists on cleaning the sand off the log so that he can determine the name of the company — White and McNally — before he begins cutting. Boulton insists, too, on calling Nick Adams's father "Doc" once too often, and Dr. Adams, becoming more and more irritated, finally tells the Indian that if he thinks the log is stolen he should pack up and leave:

> "Take your stuff and get out."
>
> "Listen, Doc."
>
> "If you call me Doc once again, I'll knock your eye teeth down your throat."
>
> "Oh, no, you won't, Doc."

Faced down by the Indian, a big, scrappy man, Dr. Adams turns his back and walks up the hill to the cottage.

He receives little comfort from his wife, who calls to him from her bedroom, where she is resting with the blinds down. After asking what the trouble is, she gives her husband a pious sermon. (Hemingway pointedly explains that she is a Christian Scientist, that her Bible, her copy of *Science and Health,* and her *Quarterly* are on her bedside table.) "Remember," she tells him, "that he who ruleth his spirit is greater than he that taketh a city."

The doctor, sitting on his bed, presumably thinking about retaliation, is cleaning his shotgun, jamming shells into the magazine, then pumping them out; they lie scattered on the bedspread. At this point, Mrs. Adams's solicitude is only slightly irritating. She asks, once more, what the real trouble is: "Tell me, Henry. Please don't try and keep anything from me. What was the trouble about?"

The doctor has a down-to-earth explanation for the confrontation: Boulton owes him money for having treated his "squaw" (there is just the edge of condescension in the doctor's use of the word) when she had pneumonia. The likelihood is that Boulton has picked the quarrel in order to avoid working off his debt. Hemingway's depiction of the doctor's reactions, his fussing with the shotgun, is one of suppressed hostility, resignation, and, as usual in Hemingway's treatment of male attitudes, disguised allusions to the sexual: "The doctor wiped his gun carefully with a rag. He pushed the shells back in against the spring of the magazine. He sat with the gun on his knees. He was very fond of it." Mrs. Adams's reaction is disbelief: "Dear, I don't think, I really don't think that anyone would really do a thing like that."

Defeated, Dr. Adams puts the gun behind the dresser and goes out, letting the screen door slam behind him. He hears his wife catch her breath at the sound of the slamming door; he makes a sheepish apology. Outside, on the path to the hemlock woods, he finds his son Nick reading. Although Mrs. Adams has asked the doctor to tell Nick that "his mother" wants him, the two go off to look for the spot where Nick has seen some black squirrels. As in any first-rate Hemingway story, the language, the sense of character, and the action are so well engineered that it takes pages of explication to point out the underlying sense of the deviousness of human relationships, the hidden motivations, that the writer has compacted into a mere five pages of carefully honed dialogue and simple declarative sentences.

"The Doctor and the Doctor's Wife" is not an exact, photographic portrait of Clarence and Grace Hemingway, but the clues, both overt and subliminal, do point to autobiographical elements. Clarence Hemingway had a gun that he was extremely fond of, nicknamed "Old Ed"; he *was* in the habit of hiring Dick Boulton and Billy Tabeshaw to saw up the stray logs that had drifted ashore at Walloon Lake. And although Grace was an Episcopalian, not a Christian Scientist, she did, because of her poor eyesight and migraine headaches, frequently retreat to her darkened room when she was tired from the children or the bright reflected light at the lakeside cottage. Such details, together with Hemingway's careful buildup of proper names within the story — the real Indians, the name of the logging company, etc. — introduced the technique that Hemingway adopted early in his career, one that was meant to establish the authenticity of the scene but which inevitably suggested an autobiographical context that could hardly have been overlooked by his family and friends.

Yet, when Clarence Hemingway, by chance, came upon the story in the December issue of the *Transatlantic Review,* he incredibly overlooked or, like some primitive tribesman confronted by his photograph, appears not to have recognized himself in the denigrating portrait of Dr. Adams. Writing his son on March 8, 1925, he praised the story's verisimilitude and his son's power to call up a scene: "I know your memory is very good for details & I surely saw that old log on the beach." He had even brought out the old family album "and showed Carol and Leicester the photo of [Dick] Boulton and Billy [Tabeshaw] on the beach sawing the big old *beech* log." He expressed his regret that his son had not seen see fit to have sent him a copy of the story: "Wish, dear boy, you would send me some of your work more often."

Hemingway thanked his father. "I'm so glad you liked the Doctor story." Immediately, he took up the issue of verisimilitude, said that he had put in Dick Boulton and Billy Tabeshaw "as real people with their real names because it was pretty sure they would never read the Transatlantic Review." (By implication he would be more cautious about using the names of people who might read the *Transatlantic,* including his parents.) The reason he had not sent home any of his work was "because you or Mother sent back the [Paris] In Our Time books. That looked as though you did not want to see any." He made an earnest effort to explain his ambitions as a writer: "You see I'm trying in all my stories to get the feeling of the actual life across — not to just depict life — or criticise it — but to actually make it alive. So that when you have read something by me you actually experience the thing. You can't do this without putting in the bad and the ugly as well as what is beautiful." It was a touching attempt. "If I write an ugly story that might be hateful to you or to Mother," he added, "the next one might be one that you would like exceedingly." The rationalizations of a son who knows the guilty secret that fiction is bound to hurt.

From its inception, Hemingway clearly regarded "Big Two-Hearted River" as the climactic story in *In Our Time* and the culminating episode in the Nick Adams adventures that he included in the book. He had begun it in May, then, stalled by his work at the *Transatlantic*, had put it aside. In mid-August, at work on it again, he wrote Stein, saying that, in the story, he was "trying to do the country like Cézanne." He was having a hell of a time at it and sometimes getting it a little bit: "It is about 100 pages long and nothing happens and the country is swell. I made it all up, so I see it all and part of it comes out the way it ought to . . . but isn't writing a hard job though? It used to be easy before I met you. Certainly was bad, Gosh, I'm awfully bad now but it's a different kind of bad."

Stein answered that she was glad he was doing a good fishing story; she wanted "awfully to read it." Quite likely she was flattered by Hemingway's remarks and by his admission that nothing happened in his story. It was one of Stein's contentions that modern writing was not concerned with traditional narrative forms, with the conventional beginning, middle, and end of a story. Magnanimously she claimed that of the three most important novels of her generation (she included Proust's *Remembrance of Things Past* and Joyce's *Ulysses* with *The Making of Americans* in that favored number), "There is, in none of them, a story." On the surface, "Big Two-Hearted River" is a simple and straightforward account of a young man's solitary two-day fishing excursion in the woods of upper Michigan. It opens abruptly, as many Hemingway stories do, with the protagonist, Nick Adams, standing on the railroad tracks; his bedroll and gear have just been pitched out from the baggage car. Nick watches as the train disappears around a hill. The landscape is starkly defined; Nick has been set down in "burned-over country" in Seney, Michigan, a ghost town destroyed by fire. But beyond the town itself, there is a beckoning wilderness. In the long trek to his fishing spot, the wasteland is absolved by stretches of meadow and growths of sweet fern.

Hemingway, strangely enough, often used the anxiety-provoking moments of waiting in a train station, or the sense of vulnerability that accompanies a traveler on train trips or journeys, as the context for a number of important stories: "The Light of the World," "Hills Like White Elephants," "Homage to Switzerland," "A Canary for One." Curiously, too, the opening paragraph of "Big Two-Hearted

River" would be echoed in the opening sentences of another *In Our Time* story, one with threatening homosexual intimations. "The Battler" is about Nick's encounter with a battered ex-prizefighter and his Negro companion, encamped in the woods. In the opening of that story Nick picks himself up after having been brutally thrust out of the train by a vicious brakeman. There, too, Hemingway creates a profound sense of isolation and apprehension as Nick watches the train move out of sight around a curve.

Little happens in "Big Two-Hearted River." There is only the slow motion of description; moments of tedious, compulsive detail followed by moments of surprising lyricism — and the sense of ongoing immediacy, of the continuous present that Stein claimed was another condition of modern writing. As the story gets under way, there is the hint that Nick Adams is existential man — Adam, without a past, psychological or otherwise, and with only, perhaps, an unforeseeable future. While it is clear that Hemingway does not intend the reader to know the circumstances that have brought Nick to this particular adventure, there is a subtle hint that Nick has suffered some psychological wound or misfortune, that his pilgrimage to the Big Two-Hearted River is meant to be a form of rehabilitation. Nick is a man escaping his past, a man with the need to leave everything behind him, "the need for thinking, the need to write, other needs." (Hemingway, there, pointedly buries one of the vital clues to Nick's past: Nick is a writer.) In one of the most important and idyllic moments in the story, Nick peers down into the river as it runs beneath the railroad bridge. He catches sight of the trout working their way upstream. It is one of those brilliant, symbolic descriptions of the natural world that Hemingway was always able to manage, one of those stylistic achievements he sustained even late in life, when his talent began to fail him: "Nick looked down into the clear, brown water, colored from the pebbly bottom, and watched the trout keeping themselves steady in the current with wavering fins. As he watched them they changed their positions by quick angles, only to hold steady in the fast water again. Nick watched them a long time."

In meticulous detail, Hemingway records the progress of Nick's journey through the landscape: "Ahead of him, as far as he could see, was the pine plain." He keeps the river, the Big Two-Hearted, to his left, catching glimpses of the water through the trees. Eventually, he sets up his camp within sight of the river, on a rise above a meadow. There is an almost too persistent, hypnotic sense of the ritual care with which Nick puts up his tent, shaping the pegs with his ax ("He wanted them long and solid to hold in the ground"), and prepares a meal — a can of pork and beans and a can of spaghetti heated together in the frying pan. (He is oddly self-defensive: "I've got a right to eat this kind of stuff, if I'm willing to carry it.") He brews some coffee. The numbing detail, somehow, makes the sense of security Nick feels credible, at least as credible as a man is likely to feel in the world of violence beyond the forest: "Nothing could touch him. . . . He was there, in the good place. He was in his home where he had made it."

The next day (installment II of the story), Nick sets out to fish the Big Two-Hearted. He fixes a breakfast of buckwheat flapjacks; he assembles his fishing rod, threading the line, selecting the gut leader and hook with the same finical care. Hemingway's language itself acquires a mad insistence; he has set himself the challenge of accounting for all those ordinary moments and actions, in slavery to obdurate time, that clever writers avoid with dazzling transitions. Little wonder the writing of the story was problematic, time-consuming, from the outset. The moments of real action, however, stand out sharply. Nick loses a big trout in deep water: "There was a heaviness, a power not to be held, and then the bulk of him, as he jumped. He looked as broad as a salmon." Nick feels suddenly shaky. "The thrill had been too much. He felt, vaguely, a little sick." He climbs onto the bank to rest: "He did not want to rush his sensations any."

In a story presumably without climax, the incident is the climactic moment. After it, the narrative winds down. Nick catches two large trout and studies the course of the river through a deep cedar swamp. But he feels a reaction against wading up to his armpits there, trying to hook big trout in places where it would be impossible to land them. In the fast, deep water, in the half light, he thinks to himself, the fishing there would be "tragic." The word has an ominous ring. "Nick did not want it." Instead, he cleans his trout beside the river before returning to camp. Hemingway emphasizes the fact that they are both males — the "long gray-white strips of milt" are smooth and clean — and he tosses the guts onto the shore for the mink to eat. The story ends, then, with a dying fall. Nick returns to the security of his tent. "There were plenty of days coming when he could fish the swamp."

✓ ✓ ✓

But that was the ending of the published story. In the first typescript version of "Big Two-Hearted River," completed in September, Hemingway had ended the story with an eleven-page rumination, written in the stream-of-consciousness vein, comprising the thoughts of Nick Adams, aspiring writer. That, presumably, explains the function of the preliminary hint that Nick Adams was a writer — a hint left stranded when Hemingway cut his original ending and wrote a new one. The differences between the two versions are instructive. In the early version, Nick Adams the writer heads back to his tent in the pine woods, intent on writing the story that becomes "Big Two-Hearted River." The last lines of that original story read: "He went on up the trail to the camp. He was holding something in his head."

What Nick Adams is holding in his head is the story of a solitary fishing expedition on the Big Two-Hearted River, including an eleven-page coda of Adams's reflections on life and letters — an unsuccessful but daring hodgepodge of personal reminiscences, all of which were the property of Ernest Hemingway, author, but which he assigned outright to his fictional persona, the writer Nick Adams. Nothing reveals the autobiographical dependency of Hemingway's fiction more openly than the manuscript versions of "Big Two-Hearted River." In the earliest manuscript fragment, Hemingway had begun the story as a first-person narrative in which he was traveling with two companions, Jock and Al — Jock Pentecost and Al Walker, who had made the expedition with him to the Fox River in the summer of 1919. In another manuscript version, Helen, Nick's wife, was originally Hadley. The eleven pages of manuscript deleted from the final version included more autobiographical material: Hemingway's recollections of summer storms on Lake Walloon ("holding an umbrella over the engine to keep the waves that came in off the spark plug, pumping out"); the fishing expeditions with Bill Smith ("Everyplace they had been together. The Black, the Sturgeon, the Pine Barrens, the Upper Minnie, all the little streams"); the misalliance of Katy Smith and Odgar and the breaking up of the old gang ("Helen thought it was because they did not like her. . . . Gosh, he remembered the horror he used to have of people getting married"); the bullfights that summer of 1924 with Chink and Don Stewart and how Maera, "the greatest man he'd ever known," had waved to them and waited for Helen/Hadley to see him and waved again. In a blatant, incriminating transfer of life to fiction, aiming for that higher ground, literature, Hemingway was writing a story about a writer, Nick Adams, who is in the process of writing a story about Nick Adams, a fisherman-writer, whose stories carry the titles of stories by Ernest Hemingway. Adams speaks of himself as the author of "My Old Man" and "Indian Camp," stories in the volume *In Our Time.* Nick's thoughts are Hemingway's thoughts. Against the contradictory evidence of this particular story,

Left: Newly discovered photograph of Hemingwa in his Section Four ambulance, 1918. *Middle:* Hemingway and friends, with captured Austrian helmets and weapons, at Schio, after the June 1918 offensive. The photograph was taken by Milford Baker. *Bottom:* The first Red Cross ambulances to cross the Piave, 1918

Opposite page
Top: The recuperating Hemingway with Agnes von Kurowsky (on his right) at the San Siro racetrack. The nurse on Hemingway's left is probably Elsie MacDonald. *Bottom:* President Woodrow Wilson and King Victor Emmanuel during Wilson's January 1919 tour of Italy

4
1
2

Above: Hadley and Hemingway on their wedding day, September 3, 1921, with Carol, Ursula, Leicester, and Hemingway's parents. *Below:* The groom among his bachelor friends. From the left: Jock Pentecost, Charles Hopkins, an unknown friend, Dutch Pailthorp, Hemingway, Bill Smith, Bill Horne, Carl Edgar, another unknown friend

Bobsledding at Chamby-sur-Montreux, winter 1922–1923. "If you want a thrill of the sort that starts at the base of your spine in a shiver and ends with you nearly swallowing your heart . . . try bobsledding," Hemingway advised the readers of the *Toronto Daily Star.*

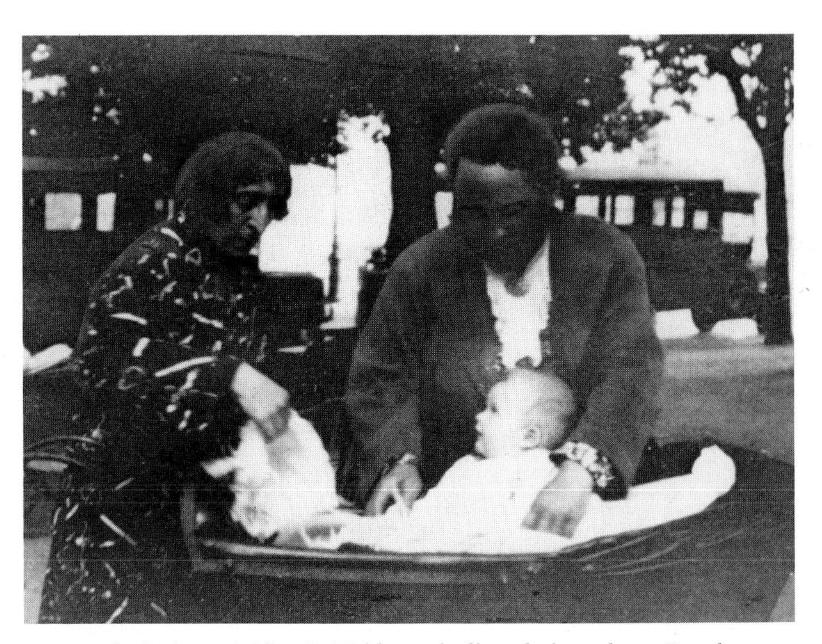

Gertrude Stein and Alice B. Toklas, minding their godson, Bumby, 1924. Jack Hemingway remembered the pair as "the two giant women gargoyles of my childhood."

Above left: F. Scott Fitzgerald, Zelda, and Scottie in Paris, Christmas 1925. *Above right:* Robert McAlmon at Shakespeare and Company, photographed by Sylvia Beach. *Below:* Sylvia Beach and James Joyce at Shakespeare and Company

Nick Adams is evolving the Hemingway theory of invention rather than raw transcription from life: "Everything good he'd ever written he'd made up. None of it had ever happened." That was what Nick's family couldn't understand: "They thought it all was experience."

Nick assesses his contemporaries: Joyce's weakness was that he was too damn romantic and intellectual about his hero. Stephen Dedalus in *Ulysses* was Joyce himself, "so he was terrible." But Bloom and Mrs. Bloom had been made up — Bloom was "wonderful" and Mrs. Bloom was "the greatest." It was easy to write if you used tricks. And Joyce had invented hundreds of new ones. But that didn't make the tricks any better. "They would all turn into clichés." Smart stuff was easy to do; like E. E. Cummings with his "automatic writing," that was easy. But not *The Enormous Room,* that was "one of the great books. Cummings worked hard to get it." Young Asch had something "but you couldn't tell. Jews go bad quickly. They all start well . . . Don Stewart had the most next to Cummings." But, "they weren't after what [Nick] was after."

In the cleverest bit of his interior monologue, Hemingway has Nick Adams the writer turn his sights on Nick Adams the protagonist: "Nick in the stories was never himself. He made him up. Of course he'd never seen an Indian woman having a baby. That was what made it good. Nobody knew that." Hemingway's Nick knows that he will become a great writer. "He knew it in lots of ways." Nick is, in fact, a bit maudlin on the subject: "It was hard to be a great writer if you loved the world and living in it and special people. It was hard when you loved so many places." The great hope of Nick Adams the writer — and of Ernest Hemingway — was to write stories as objective and real as the paintings of Cézanne, to do the country as Cézanne had done it. ("You had to do it from inside yourself.") Nick/Hemingway remembers the Cézannes he has seen; the portrait of Madame Cézanne at Gertrude Stein's, the two paintings he had seen at the Luxembourg, and the pictures he had seen every day at a loan exhibition at Bernheim's, the gallery near the Closerie des Lilas: "the soldiers undressing to swim, the house through the trees, one of the trees with a house beyond, not the lake one, the other lake one. The portrait of the boy." Nick Adams, it is clear — except, perhaps, to his creator — is more romantic about his hero than Joyce ever was.

But no story or poem completely leaves its author behind, abandons him in the orchard. Every nuance, prejudice, every innocent detail of a fiction bears the genetic imprint of the writer. If a writer borrows experiences, situations, uses the gossip of other people's lives, creates characters of his own, what he does with them is his choice, reflects his character and imagination. If he tries to creep into the mind of another, probing, exploring, explaining, it is his purview that he gives the reader — not the mind of another. Nick Adams observes himself: "He always worked best when Helen was unwell. Just that much discontent and friction." It is a damaging admission; if Ernest Hemingway did not react precisely that way in relation to Hadley, he had entertained that notion, found it serviceable for Nick.

///

Although Hemingway claimed his friends had "bitched" him in "a literary way," he did not want for friends concerned about his career. In September he sent his book of stories, including the original version of "Big Two-Hearted River," to Don Stewart in New York. Stewart gave the manuscript to his publisher, George Doran. (Other friends, Dos Passos, Harold Loeb, Sherwood Anderson, would also try to get a publisher for *In Our Time*.) In October, Hemingway recommended the book again to Edmund Wilson: "I think you would like it, it has a pretty good unity. In some of the stories . . . I've gotten across both the people and the scene. It makes you feel good when you can do it. It feels now as though I had gotten on top of it."

But when Gertrude Stein and Alice Toklas returned to Paris in the fall, Stein read his fishing story and what she referred to as his "little story of meditations" on writers and writing, and told him, "Hemingway, remarks are not literature." This, despite the flattering remark he had made about her editorial wisdom in the story: "She'd know it if he ever got things right." She had, indeed, been right that Nick's reflections on writers and writing did not work. They were awkward and intrusive. But perhaps she had been wrong in discouraging the attempt. Had Hemingway been capable at this stage of his career of bringing together the two streams of narrative, the objective account of the experience on the river and Nick Adams's subjective ruminations on writing (as, say, Proust had done in the final pages of *Remembrance of Things Past*), he would have accomplished a tour de force in modern writing. As it was, he had lacked the talent to bring it off, lacked the style to accomplish the tricky merger of fact and fiction. It would be twelve years before he was to accomplish that peculiar narrative feat with a masterpiece, "The Snows of Kilimanjaro."

Hemingway took Stein's criticism to heart. In early November, he wrote Don Stewart telling him to delete the original ending and substitute the new one he was sending: "I have discovered that the last eleven pages of the last story in the book I sent you are crap, i.e.

faecal matter, to wit shit, either bovine or equine. It don't matter." Around the same time, he wrote Robert McAlmon in the same scatological terms, saying that he had cut all the "mental conversation" in the story. "I got a hell of a shock when I realized how bad it was and that shocked me back into the river again and I've finished it off the way it ought to have been all along. Just the straight fishing."

10
The Dangerous Friend

IT WAS one of the stranger coincidences in Hemingway's life that he had had Bill Smith so much on his mind throughout 1924. In April, drunk in Arles, he happened to read a story in a Marseilles paper about a former Chicago assistant district attorney, Wanda Stopa, who had attempted to murder the rich "publiciste" Y. K. Smith. In due time, Hemingway's family sent him the *Tribune* accounts of the scandal ("BOHEMIA GIRL ENDS LIFE IN DETROIT HOTEL; Slayer Takes Poison as Her Way Out"), embellishing them "with suitable moral comments." It was a raucous story. Stopa, who had been having an affair with Y.K., had invaded his home at Palos Park, intent on killing him and his wife. Y.K. was not at home, but Stopa had fired three shots at Doodles, ill in bed, and missed each time. She then turned the gun on Henry Manning, the sixty-eight-year-old caretaker, who had come to Doodles's rescue, and shot him dead. Doodles escaped through a window. The distraught Stopa, whom Y.K. had been supporting for months, fled to New York and then Detroit, where she committed suicide in her hotel room.

The whole tabloid affair, which Hemingway probably read with some amazement, must have started up nagging memories of Bill and Katy Smith and the Horton Bay and Chicago days. Possibly, it may have prompted a steamy, incomplete Nick Adams story, "Summer People." (The gerund passages in the Stein manner suggest the story was written that year.) In "Summer People," Hemingway, as Nicholas Adams (nicknamed Wemedge), indulges in a sexual episode with Kate, so named. In a nighttime scene in an isolated woodlot — Kate has brought two blankets — Nick indulges in anal intercourse with the passionate Kate:

> "Is it good this way?" he said.
> "I love it. I love it. I love it. Oh, come, Wemedge. Please come. Come, come. Please, Wemedge. Please, please, Wemedge."

It was a story far more *inaccrochable* than "Up in Michigan," and it was never published during Hemingway's lifetime. At about the same time, Bill Smith cropped up in a brace of stories, "The End of Something" and "The Three-Day Blow," which Hemingway had completed that spring. Then, in August, in the coda to "Big Two-Hearted River," his recollections of Bill and their fishing expeditions, their friendship, had returned like some ghost from the past.

It could only have been a surprise, then, even a shock, when late in November or early December, Hemingway got a letter from Bill asking to resume their friendship. "Is my arm long enuf to reach an olive branch clear acrosst the Atlantic? If so grasp it," Bill wrote him on November 21. He did not want to stir up Hemingway's old quarrel with Y.K. nor deal with the problem of Doodles. ("No use tho to go into that muck by mail.") Bill apologized for the angry letter he had sent Hemingway two years earlier: "I realize quite well . . . that my last scroll was a savage, bitter thing and if you care to fling it into the division of dead letters (from dead writers) perhaps we can again capture some of what was once ours."

Hemingway was stunned and delighted: "You could have KO'ed me with the proverbial pinion," he wrote Bill on December 6. "I haven't felt so damned good since we used to pestle them on the Black." There was no doubt about Hemingway's enthusiasm; he felt "almost too swell to write." Smith's mention of what they had once had together struck a responsive chord. Hemingway's reply was emphatic:

> I know how damn good all our old stuff was Bird because everything, almost everything worth a damn I've written has been about that country. It was the whole damn business inside me and when I think about any country or doing anything it's always that old stuff, the Bay, the farm . . . and the wonderful times we had with the men and the storms in the fall and potato digging and the whole damn thing.

It was as if he and Bill were now sharing the legacy of their past. "And we've got them all and we're not going to lose them."

In the first rush of enthusiasm and in subsequent letters — long letters, written every week or so — Hemingway urged Bill to join him and Hadley in Europe. There were cheap lodgings in Paris, he said. Bill could have his meals with them; three could eat as cheaply as one. "I'll stake you to second class home," he promised. He was full of suggestions for jobs; Bill could work as a secretary for W. Dawson Johnston at the American Library in Paris, or as a bartender or a taxi driver. Another possibility was that they could work as bootblacks in Spain, touring the bullfights. Bill would make a good bullfighter, Hemingway suggested. "You got the intelligence, the coordination and the looks. I'm too big."

He was as ready as ever with advice on sexual matters; Bill seemed to be having problems. Celibacy was swell for a man, but only up to a point. Bill ought to "yence"; it was a great conditioner for a male, made a man see clearer. Since Bill had mentioned his landlady as a serious possibility, Hemingway advised, "If she's married and wants it they ain't no harm." His next pronouncement seemed to be Hemingway's private credo: "Now serious yencing should be devoid of consequences and entanglements. Entanglements are what ruin yencing." Paris was full of young college girls wanting "to have it happen to them." Bill ought to come to Paris and get in on some of the free college yencing. If he himself weren't married or was married but not in love, he would yence if there were no entanglements.

Hemingway filled Bill in on his new friends: Stewart ("Get Mr. and Mrs. Haddock Abroad") and Dos Passos ("He's a guy you'd like"). Harold Loeb and Paul Nelson, new friends, were both Princeton men. "Loeb is really good. He and I play doubles together all the time." Nelson was studying architecture, gave swell drinking parties with all the French painters as guests. Hemingway brought Bill up to date on his writing; the manuscript for *In Our Time* was in New York; he had a story, "Mr. and Mrs. Elliot," coming out in *The Little Review:* "Should rate a laugh even from a graham cracker addict." (Bill was on the popular Graham diet.) When Bill mentioned that Hemingway's mother was proud of him, Hemingway contradicted, "The reason the maternal speaks of the enditer with pride is because of the care with which I keep my printed works from the family fireside."

Beneath the wisecracks, the bawdiness, the brag, there was a genuine sense of Hemingway's affection and his relief at having regained a needed friendship. He had clearly regretted the loss; he and Bill were on a new footing. "But now I know there's always a new deal of some sort — and now here we are back on the old basis of the best days." Having learned that Bill had had a breakdown and suffered from manic-depressive episodes, Hemingway was sympathetic: "This gets complicated as hell. But Boid I feel so damn strongly that you're coming through like a ton of the papered ones. I don't know. Just got the hunch. This is no religion."

⁂

From Paris, on December 10, not long before leaving for Austria, Hemingway wrote Robert McAlmon (in Italy) a letter that had its own tabloid aspects. "I dreamt night before last you were dead," he said. "Hope this finds you well . . . I dreamt I read it in the papers with a big full page layout, picture of you and Bryher and the Ellerman Castle in Scotland etc. Is there one?" In dreams as in fiction, Hemingway had an imaginative way of disposing of an envied rival with an undeserved wealthy wife. Half seriously, he advised McAlmon to watch his step in Italy, not get himself "bumped off" by some wild adolescent fascisti.

His real problem with McAlmon was having failed to come up with a suitable story for McAlmon's anthology, the *Contact Collection of Contemporary Writers,* scheduled for publication in 1925. The new stories he had on hand were too long, and one of them was unpublishable. With his letter, Hemingway mailed "The Doctor and the Doctor's Wife," saying, "This is the best short story I ever wrote so am sending it. It's short enough anyway." But McAlmon objected: hadn't it appeared in the current, December, issue of the *Transatlantic*? Djuna Barnes, Joyce, H.D., were all sending work that had not appeared anywhere else, McAlmon told him. "You'd better too." McAlmon, privy to what Hemingway had been writing, asked, "How about the Smith story, or O'Neil, or Krebs? They're around 5,000 words aren't they?" Within the week, Hemingway sent the Krebs story, "Soldier's Home," another of the *In Our Time* stories. It was a hurried replacement; he and Hadley were in the throes of packing for their December 20 departure for Schruns. "Anyhow," he wrote, "this story is as good as I've got and conforms on length." He added, "Gertrude thinks it's a good story anyway."

Wanting to escape the bone-chilling cold of the Paris winter, Hemingway had chosen Schruns, in the Vorarlberg, for his winter vacation. He discovered that it had its advantages. Austria was cheaper than Switzerland; the rooms at the Hotel Taube were big and comfortable; the food was hearty and inexpensive; there were thirty-six kinds of beer. The Hemingways hired an attractive young nurse for Bumby, now an active toddler able to say "auto" and "Dada." They could leave the baby with the nurse and take five-day ski trips, living in a hut in the upper reaches of the mountains. At night, gale winds blew the snow across a bright moon. It turned out to be a dangerous season on the slopes, with sudden avalanches. Four men had been killed, Hemingway wrote Gertrude Stein. A fifth, buried in snow, had been rescued by shouting for help every three minutes.

In early January, Hemingway, reporting on the generosity of his friends, wrote Harold Loeb from Schruns that Don Stewart, who had taken the manuscript of *In Our Time* to the publisher George Doran in New York, had sent him "an enormous check." At first, mistakenly, Hemingway had thought the check was an advance from Doran for the publication of his book, since there was a letter from Doran enclosed. The check, however, turned out to be a Christmas present from Don, "to keep up our morale I think. He's a swell guy." The news from Doran, who had held on to the manuscript for months, was disappointing. "Every body had read it 4 times etc.," Hemingway complained. "But Mr. Doran felt they couldn't go all the way with me on the matter of sex in a book of Short Stories." It would have been different had it been a novel. Stewart had then given the manuscript to H. L. Mencken in hopes that he would recommend it to Alfred Knopf. Hemingway was not optimistic: "Well as Mencken doesn't like my stuff and [George Jean] Nathan does that will probably end in horsecock too." If that failed, Stewart would take the book to Boni and Liveright.

Hemingway remembered that he was at the Madlener-Haus, high in the mountains, when he got the good news that Boni and Liveright had accepted *In Our Time.* Cablegrams had arrived from both Stewart and Harold Loeb, who was then in New York, overseeing the publication (by Boni and Liveright) of his first novel, *Doodab.* That night, Hemingway was so excited that he was unable to sleep. At the Hotel Taube, Horace Liveright's March 4 cable, waiting for him, was something of an anticlimax: "WANT TO PUBLISH YOUR SHORT STORIES THIS FALL TWO HUNDRED DOLLARS ADVANCE AGAINST USUAL ROYALTIES ANSWER." Liveright's follow-up letter suggested a few problems. There was a questionable passage in the story "Mr. and Mrs. Elliot," Hemingway's sardonic tale of a sexually inept American couple with artistic pretensions. ("Mr. and Mrs. Elliot tried very hard to have a baby. They tried as often as Mrs. Elliot could stand it.") Liveright also considered "Up in Michigan" unpublishable because of its sexual explicitness. Back in Paris in mid-March, Hemingway wrote, or finished, "The Battler" as a substitute. His story about "a busted down pug and a coon," he wrote Dos Passos, "is a hell of a swell story and better than Up in Mich."

In his March 31 letter to Liveright, returning the signed contract and the new story, Hemingway showed no intention of playing the obliging novice. He combined reasonable compliance with brusque self-assurance. The new story, he admitted, made the book a good deal better. But he wanted it understood that no alterations of words would be made without his approval. "This protects you as much as it does me as the stories are written so tight and so hard that the alteration of a word can throw an entire story out of key." It was an accurate assessment of his method. He made the needed concessions to Liveright and his literary editor, T. R. Smith; they were on the spot and better informed than he about what was "unpublishably obscene," and he would leave that to their judgment. More revealing was the fact that at the real start of his literary career, he distanced himself from "modernists" like E. E. Cummings, whose *The Enormous Room* was a classic example of a "fine book" that did not sell because it "was written in a style that no one who had not read a good deal of 'modern' writing could read. That was hard luck for selling purposes." He had targeted his audience more carefully: "My book will be praised by highbrows and can be read by lowbrows. There is no writing in it that anybody with a high-school education cannot read." He ended the letter with just the right touch of flattery and assertiveness: "I do not need to tell you how pleased I am to be published by Boni and Liveright and I hope I *will* become a property. That's up to both of us."

His confidence may have been prompted by the fact that, out of the blue, he had had a letter from a sympathetic editor, Max Perkins, of Scribner's. In fact, there had been two. The first, dated February 21, 1925, was misaddressed, and Hemingway seems not to have received it. Egged on by F. Scott Fitzgerald, Perkins had managed to obtain a copy of the earlier Three Mountains edition of *in our time* and was very impressed. Perkins's letter was flattering and astute, noting "the power in the scenes and incidents pictured, and by the effectiveness of their relation to each other." It revealed Perkins's sharpness as an editor in approaching a new author; he mentioned that he had had some difficulty in getting a copy of Hemingway's book, a subtle reminder of the disadvantages of small-press publications. He also acknowledged that, much as he had liked *in our time,* it was too slender a volume for a commercial publisher to bring out. Booksellers would not be able make a substantial profit on such a book, and therefore the trade would have little interest in it. "This is a pity because your method is obviously one which enables you to express what you have to say in very small compass." Perkins wondered whether Hemingway might have something else without "these practical objections." The second letter was written five days later when Perkins had gotten a proper address from John Peale Bishop, who had stopped by his office. In it, Perkins, having heard that Hemingway did have a book ready, expressed interest in seeing it. "We would certainly read it with promptness and sympathetic interest if you gave us a chance."

When he answered Perkins, Hemingway had already accepted the offer from Liveright. He made a point of explaining that under the terms of the contract, Liveright held an option on both his second and third books. The only way he could get out of that obligation was if the firm failed to exercise their option on the second book within sixty days. Still, he said, he was "very excited" to get Perkins's letter. An experienced angler, Hemingway offered what he supposed was an attractive lure. He was not interested in writing a novel (despite the fact that his contract stipulated that he write one) because he considered it "an awfully artificial and worked out form." He preferred the short story. But he hoped, someday, to do a very big book on bullfighting. "If I am ever in a position to send you anything to consider," he told Perkins, "I shall certainly do so."

The notion that the novel was an artificial form was something Hemingway had only recently evolved for himself in reviewing Sherwood Anderson's autobiography, *A Story Teller's Story*. (Both he and Gertrude Stein had done double-feature reviews of the book for the March issue of *Ex Libris*.) Stein's brief review of Anderson's book was full of warm praise. Anderson, she said, was a writer who did not "reflect life or describe life or embroider life or photograph life." Rather, he expressed life, "and to express life takes essential intelligence." That might not be the most important thing for a writer to do, but it was "the most permanent thing to do." Her published praise, however, was more cautious and measured than her personal response. In an earlier letter, she had told Anderson that the writing in *A Story Teller's Story* was "far and away, the best you have ever done."

The waltz of recommendation: Hemingway's lengthier review was equally guarded. The book was good, Hemingway admitted. "There are very beautiful places in the book, as good writing as Sherwood Anderson has done and that means considerably better than any other American writer has done." But Hemingway took the occasion to put down Anderson's most recent novel, *Many Marriages*, and set out, rather officiously, to analyze Anderson's problems as a writer. "He is a very great writer and if he has, at times, in other books been unsuccessful, it has been for two reasons," Hemingway said. "His talent and his development of it has been toward the short story or tale and not toward that highly artificial form, the novel. The second reason is that he has been what the French say of all honest politicians, *mal entouré*." The latter charge was that Anderson's reputation had been piped up by unreliable New York friends and critics ("They called him a 'phallic Chekhov' and other meaningless things"). The predictable result was that in trying to live up to his New York reputation, Anderson had become worried and uncertain and had written a poor book. Still, as a final concession, Hemingway advised readers that *A Story Teller's Story* was a book they ought to read and "a wonderful comeback" after the failure of Anderson's last novel.

Anderson, at about the same time, had read Hemingway's *In Our Time* stories and wrote Stein that he had liked them — "all of them."

He was just in the process of changing publishers, moving to Boni and Liveright with his latest novel, *Dark Laughter.* As a helpful gesture, he had written a "crackerjack" blurb for Hemingway's new book. He was also planning, he told Stein, to review *In Our Time* when it was published: "Have already asked one of the bigger reviews to save it for me." Anderson's blurb was brief but unqualified in its praise: "Mr. Hemingway is young, strong, full of laughter, and he can write. His people flash suddenly up into those odd elusive moments of glowing reality, the clear putting down of which has always made good writing so good."

It is not clear what other services Anderson may have performed by way of encouraging Boni and Liveright to take Hemingway's book, but Hemingway wrote him rather effusively, as if he had: "I can't write letters and so I can't tell you how grateful I am for your getting my stuff published. It means a such a hell of a lot." He apologized in an offhand manner for his critical comments on *Many Marriages:* "Sure, probably I was wrong about the Many Marriages. I will read it again some time when I can give it a better break. . . . All criticism is shit anyway. Nobody knows anything about it except yourself." Professional critics made him sick; they were the camp-following eunuchs of literature. "They won't even whore. They're all virtuous and sterile. And how well meaning and high minded."

/ / /

Ever since January, Hemingway had been actively assisting Ernest Walsh and Ethel Moorhead with their plans for a new magazine, *This Quarter,* which was patently intended to rival *The Dial* and replace the defunct *Transatlantic Review.* Hemingway had first met Walsh in Ezra Pound's studio in the summer of 1922. A talkative young American poet in failing health, Walsh had been an aviator during the war. He had been seriously hurt in a plane crash that had damaged his lung and he was suffering from tuberculosis. Living on a small disability pension in Paris, he had twice been hospitalized and was subsequently taken up by Ethel Moorhead, a wealthy Scotswoman who jealously guarded and cared for him and furthered his career by setting him up as coeditor of their proposed magazine. They made an odd couple: Miss Moorhead, middle-aged, plain, tense-mouthed, wearing a pince-nez; Walsh, years younger, painfully thin and lanky, hair tousled, favoring the raffish look, wearing his English overcoat over his shoulders like a cape. Hemingway was, at first, put off by Walsh's flair — and no doubt, by his tragically romantic wartime service.

But in response to their request for a contribution to their magazine, Hemingway sent them "Big Two-Hearted River." From the beginning, when Walsh and Moorhead were in residence in the Hôtel Vénétia in Paris and later when they were taking a leisurely journey (because of Walsh's ailing health) from Pau through Grasse in their new De Dion-Bouton motorcar, Hemingway bombarded them with suggestions for worthwhile contributors and the editorial content of the magazine. Having learned that the couple planned to pay for contributions and pay on acceptance, Hemingway congratulated them on their wisdom; that was "the absolute secret of getting the first rate stuff." Serious writers knew that their best work would never get into purely commercial magazines, but they were reluctant to give it to magazines that paid nothing. Obligingly, Walsh and Ethel Moorhead sent him a check for 1000 francs (about $50) for "Big Two-Hearted River," which made him even more receptive. Hemingway responded with one of his odd, temporarily heartfelt, compliments: "The Editors of This Quarter are a couple of white men."

Hemingway spread the word about the new publication to both Stein and Evan Shipman ("great news spreaders," he assured Walsh). Shipman was one of the ingratiating failures whom Hemingway cultivated in Paris, a young American poet and racetrack aficionado with a deprecatory smile and bad teeth, who made a career out of expecting a modest inheritance of a few thousand dollars. (A heavy drinker, he had a habit of writing notes to Hemingway from the Sélect, explaining that he was in difficulty, and asking to borrow 1000 francs until next month.) Hemingway also informed McAlmon, Nathan Asch, and John Herrmann, the young writer from Michigan whom he had met in Paris with his writer girlfriend, Josephine Herbst, the year before. In his letter to Walsh, Hemingway promoted all his current friends: Harold Loeb, who was in New York, he said, and could write a vivid New York letter; Don Stewart; William Carlos Williams; Edmund Wilson ("He does first rate criticism"); Lewis Galantière ("Writes excellent criticism of French books and could do you very damned well as Paris correspondent"). It says something of Hemingway's powers of persuasion that many of the writers he touted appeared in the first and second issues of the quarterly.

Walsh dedicated the first issue of the magazine to Ezra Pound for, among other services, "his creative work, his editorship of several magazines, his helpful friendship for young and unknown artists." Hemingway, asked to contribute one of the homages, wrote promptly from Schruns on March 9, not long before his return to

Paris. His tribute would appear in the first issue, accompanied by a solemn acknowledgment from James Joyce ("I owe a great deal to his friendly help, encouragement and generous interest in everything that I have written") and an exuberant tribute by Walsh ("He keeps to his hill. He will not come down. He will outlive those who have been fingered overmuch by the crowd"). Hemingway's praise was more direct: "There is only one living poet who ranks with Pound and that is William Butler Yeats." Pound, he said, was a major poet as distinct from minor poets like T. S. Eliot, Wallace Stevens, and Marianne Moore. Eliot, he acknowledged, had a fine talent; "He never takes chances with it and it is doing very well thank you. Whitman on the other hand, if a poet, is a major poet." But, Hemingway complained, Pound, the major poet, was devoting only one fifth of his time to poetry; the rest of his time "he tries to advance the fortunes, both material and artistic, of his friends. He defends them when they are attacked, he gets them into magazines and out of jail. He loans them money. . . . And in the end a few of them refrain from knifing him at the first opportunity."

Back in Paris, Hemingway found himself saddled with the editorial and production work of bringing out the first issue of the magazine. Hemingway's attentiveness to his new and unpaid editorial assignments, quite probably, derived from the fact that Walsh and Moorhead planned to reward excellence in the form of an annual prize of $2500 to the contributor whose work in *This Quarter* was judged the best. A second, lesser prize of $1200 was to be given to the best young contributor. At some point in Hemingway's dealings with the pair, Walsh confidentially informed Hemingway that the prize, or one of the prizes, was to be awarded to him. He urged Hemingway to keep up on further contributions. "Don't worry," Hemingway told him, "there's going to be more literature produced." He also assured him that he would not say anything about the prize to anyone, even to himself. "I don't want to figure on anything that would be so damned wonderful and then maybe lose out on it. Money is so important to us that I can't play around with the idea of it."

Yet it was clear that he was spending too much time at editing, reading copy and proofs, sending out galleys, taking crowded buses to the printer (Herbert Clarke's on the rue St.-Honoré, the same printer he had worked with on the *Transatlantic*). It was hardly unnatural that he should voice some complaints to the still absent Walsh. "I'm glad as hell to do this now to help you out," he wrote Walsh, "but I've found out how damned much time it takes . . . I'm not complaining about it or trying to tell you what a fine guy I am to do it." Aside from having to earn a living, there were other considerations: "If I'm not creating I'm absolutely miserable and ugly and I have to have my mind clear to write the stuff I'm working on now."

Hemingway proposed what was a reasonable solution. Ever since hearing from Bill Smith, he had been trying to talk Bill into a trip to Paris. When he finally heard that Bill was planning to join him and Hadley in April ("Jo-esus Bird, the thought of you as a male cross Atlantic ticketed perhaps by now sets a male upwards"), Hemingway wrote Walsh suggesting that Bill take over his assignments. Bill could see to editing the copy, take over the printing and distribution of the magazine, make sure Walsh and Moorhead got their money from sales. He could get Bill to take on the job for 1000 francs a month. But Walsh balked at the idea, thought that Hemingway was meddling, implied that he was trying to get money out of Moorhead on a pretext. The rebuff did not sit well with Hemingway; he had only suggested that they hire someone to do a job he had been doing for nothing. The air of camaraderie between Hemingway and Walsh, however, continued for a year or more. They both had cause to keep the relationship going.

II

Like many of the stories in his life, Hemingway's account of his first meeting with F. Scott Fitzgerald is a tangle of altogether plausible and equally questionable details. According to *A Moveable Feast,* it took place at the Dingo bar on the rue Delambre one day in late April 1925. Hemingway was drinking with some "completely worthless characters" (in some interpretations, Lady Duff Twysden, an English aristocrat, and her lover and cousin Pat Guthrie). Fitzgerald was with a stalwart and amiable companion, Dunc Chaplin, a former varsity hero of the Princeton baseball team. This is the prologue to what has come down to us as a sometimes comic, sometimes savage, account of the meeting of two great American writers, the chronicler of the Jazz Age and the creator of the Lost Generation.

Hemingway's recreation of the meeting thirty years later still has an air of credibility. Fitzgerald was drinking steadily, talking nonstop at Hemingway, praising his writing in extravagant terms. On the second bottle of champagne, he began asking obnoxious questions (Had Hemingway slept with his wife before he had married her?) and persisted even though Hemingway did his best to deflect the personal queries. Hemingway was put off by Fitzgerald's looks: he was too pretty for a man, his legs were too short for his body, he was too well tailored in his Brooks Brothers suit. Without warning, Fitzgerald suddenly passed out, falling into a dumb stupor, his face taking on a death's head expression. Chaplin reassured Hemingway that Fitzgerald did not need medical attention: "No. That's the way it takes him," he said. The two managed to get Fitzgerald to a cab and send him home. (It makes a nice episode except for the fact that Chaplin denied ever having taken part in the meeting between the two; he was not even in Europe in 1925.)

A few days later Hemingway supposedly met Fitzgerald again, sober, at the Closerie des Lilas. The talk, on this occasion, was about writing. Fitzgerald asked Hemingway to read *The Great Gatsby,* which had just been published. He spoke about the book with a modesty and diffidence that convinced Hemingway that Fitzgerald must have actually written something quite good. ("He had the shyness about it that all non-conceited writers have when they have done something very fine.")

On the basis of the second meeting, Hemingway agreed to accompany Fitzgerald to Lyons, where Fitzgerald's Renault had been garaged on his trip to Paris with his wife, Zelda. Hadley, Hemingway claimed, was happy to have him take the trip, though she had never been impressed with anything she had read by Fitzgerald. Hemingway's account of the journey is telescoped to within a few days after their meeting at the Closerie des Lilas, though it may not have taken place until late in May or early June. It provides a comic interlude in *A Moveable Feast,* chiefly at Fitzgerald's expense, a story of missed connections, cross-purposes, a boozy drive in a decrepit open car in a succession of rainstorms (Zelda had insisted that the top of the Renault, which had been damaged in transportation, should be cut away), with repeated stops in bistros along the way. At a hotel in Châlon-sur-Saône, Fitzgerald came down sick with a cold and was convinced that he was dangerously ill and possibly close to death. Hemingway recommended that he take to his bed while their wet clothing was being dried and pressed. He ordered a pair of stiff whiskeys with lemon. He also managed to rustle up some aspirin and, belatedly, a bath thermometer.

In the meantime, the talk turned personal. Fitzgerald revealed (or Hemingway claimed that Fitzgerald revealed) that he and Zelda had never spent a night apart since they were married; therefore he had to call her in Paris. While waiting for the call to be placed, he told Hemingway about the tragic love affair Zelda had had with a French aviator on the Riviera. (The aviator supposedly had died in a crash all for the love of Zelda.) When Hemingway finally took Fitzgerald's temperature (placing the bath thermometer under his arm), he managed to convince the patient that his temperature was normal. Fitzgerald, pleased, told Hemingway that he had remarkable recuperative powers. But at dinner that night, he suddenly passed out and had to be put to bed. The next day, on the final leg of their journey, Fitzgerald cheerfully related the plots of all the novels of Michael Arlen. That the trip involved a good deal of heavy drinking was quite probably true. In a letter to Pound, Hemingway boasted, "Didn't miss one vintage from Montrachet to Chambertin. Elaborate trip."

It is another of the Hemingway legends, proof of his acuity in sizing up women, that on first meeting Zelda Fitzgerald, he was aware that she was insane and that she was fundamentally jealous of her husband's talents as a writer. In *A Moveable Feast,* Hemingway made a distinctive episode of the meeting. After the trip to Lyons, he and Hadley had been invited to lunch at the Fitzgeralds' stuffy bourgeois apartment on the rue de Tilsitt. Aside from having her beautiful dark blond hair ruined by a bad permanent, Zelda was suffering from a hangover and did not look her best. Hemingway pointedly mentioned that Scottie, the Fitzgeralds' three-year-old daughter, had a strong Cockney accent, acquired from an English nanny they had hired under the illusion that their daughter would learn to speak like Lady Diana Manners. The lunch was very bad and the wine was only a little better. During the course of the meal, Zelda's hawkish eyes would go blank every once in a while as she remembered some episode from the previous evening. She smiled whenever Fitzgerald, playing the good host, took a drink of wine. It was clear to Hemingway, then and later, that she was bent on ruining Fitzgerald's efforts to write. What is amazing in Hemingway's account is how much of the destructiveness of a relationship he managed to convey in the few paragraphs of his carefully contrived luncheon episode.

Yet, an earlier manuscript version of this same episode presents a different but equally vivid and credible picture. On the Sunday after Hemingway's first meeting with Fitzgerald at the Dingo, he and Hadley met Scott and Zelda for drinks, not at the Closerie des Lilas but at the Dingo again, a mistake Hemingway readily realized because, like any small bar and bistro on a Sunday afternoon, the Dingo was an empty, stale-smelling, dismal spot that could not be enlivened even by drinking champagne. From there, the two couples — and Bumby, then a year and a half — had proceeded to the Fitzgeralds' apartment, which was as thoroughly depressing as Hemingway described it in the published version. Fitzgerald insisted on showing Hemingway his ledger books, indicating how much money he had made from writing year by year. He also brought out his stereopticon slides, "horror pictures, executions, the corpses, burned roasted aviators and the like."

In this version of the first meeting with Zelda, Hemingway admitted she might have once been the beauty she was reputed to be. Although she was badly groomed, her face too drawn, she nonetheless had a certain "golden blowsiness," with tawny, smooth skin and lovely colored hair (unfortunately ruined by the bad permanent). Her legs were light and as long as "nigger legs." Hemingway thought her very spoiled. Still, she had a memorable effect on him: "I did not like her but that night I had an erotic enough dream about her. The next time I saw her I told her that and she was pleased. That was the first and last time we ever had anything in common." Perhaps. There is one bit of documentary evidence that refutes Hemingway's differing accounts of his first meeting with Zelda, indicating that it did not take place at the rue de Tilsitt apartment at all but at the Hemingways' humble flat. And while Hemingway, in *A Moveable Feast,* described Zelda as looking dissipated, sly, and certifiably insane, the evidence suggests that his erotic-dream version of the meeting, at least, had plausibility. He was, in fact, impressed enough by Zelda to want to show her off as a newfound trophy. "Dear Friends," he wrote Gertrude Stein and Alice Toklas, "Fitzgerald was around yesterday afternoon with his wife and she's worth seeing so I'll bring them around Friday afternoon unless you warn me not to."

⁄ ⁄ ⁄

In that fourth year of his marriage, Hemingway did have women on his mind. There were two new and interesting women in his life. Robert McAlmon introduced Hemingway to Lady Duff Twysden, who was in Paris with Pat Guthrie: "The title seemed to electrify him," McAlmon remembered. For weeks, he claimed, Hemingway was up in Montmartre escorting Duff and Pat, even paying for drinks for the couple. In *The Sun Also Rises,* Duff would become Brett Ashley, the most elusive, gratifying, and perverse of Hemingway's fictional heroines: "damned good-looking," stylish rather than fashionable in her jersey sweaters and tweed skirts, her hair brushed back like a boy's ("She started all that"). Hemingway, using his "power of invention," describes Brett as sleekly attractive, "built with curves like the hull of a racing yacht." A heavy drinker, promiscuous, she frequents the Sélect and the Coupole but travels with an entourage of young homosexuals ("Aren't they lovely? . . . And when one's with the crowd I'm with, one can drink in such safety, too"). Independent, callous, she cadges drinks from friends ("I say, give a chap a brandy and soda"), picks up and leaves when the party becomes boring.

But that was the fictional woman, not necessarily the daughter of a Yorkshire wine merchant, twice married, estranged from her second husband, Sir Roger Twysden, tenth baronet, naval officer in the late war, and a nasty alcoholic. Duff, waiting out her divorce in Paris, and her young Scots lover and cousin were a noteworthy pair in the Quarter. Parisian expatriates remembered the couple in wildly contradictory terms. Jimmie the Barman, impressed by Duff's upper-class manners and her condescending chumminess at his bar (he regularly put her bills for food, drink, and cigarettes on the cuff), considered her the thoroughbred British aristocrat: "At all times the perfect lady." Guthrie, a remittance man with a history of alcoholism, was rumored to be bisexual. (Scholars now suggest that Guthrie may have been the drawing card for Duff's homosexual cadre.) In life, in any event, Hemingway treated the rumor as unfounded, blamed Duff for the "fairies." Planning the annual trip to Pamplona that year, Hemingway, having learned that Pat and Duff would also be joining the crowd, wrote Loeb, "As far as I know Duff is not bringing any fairies with her. You might arrange to have a band of local fairies meet her at the train carrying a daisy chain."

But fiction allowed further complications. In the first draft of the *The Sun Also Rises,* in a segment describing his Paris personae and using real names (it was deleted from the published version of the novel), Hemingway seemed to intimate that Guthrie had homosexual as well as alcoholic problems: "various habits that Duff felt sorry for and did not think a man should have and cured him by the constant watchfulness and the exercise of her then very strong will." That good deed may have been pure invention; it would be hard to explain how Duff "cured" Guthrie by surrounding him with a homosexual entourage.

Don Stewart found Duff "enormously attractive to look at or to be with." Harold Loeb, trying to break off his three-year relationship with Kitty Cannell, was patently stuck on Duff, and she was, for a time, taken with him. Their brief affair (Loeb described it in unbelievably maudlin detail in his memoir, *The Way It Was*) would cause a quarrel between Hemingway and Loeb. But it also provided a dramatic moment in Hemingway's novel.

McAlmon thought Duff was an "awful mess and tramp." He resented the way she and Hem came up to him at the bar at Zelli's: "The primary idea, I gathered, was that I'd buy the drinks, Duff pulling the 'Good old Bob, he's really one of us' line." Others wondered why Hadley, tagging along for the evening, put up with Hemingway's infatuation with another woman. Years later, however,

Hadley would remember Duff, with some equanimity, as "lovely, a very fine lady, and very much of a man's woman. . . . She was fair and square." By then she had subscribed to the legend of Duff's code of honor that husbands were off limits. At the time, it may have been another matter. McAlmon, who took pleasure in setting a record straight, recalled a night at Zelli's when Hadley was crying in a corner, and Hem and Duff had asked him and another regular of their crowd, Josephine Brooks, to take Hadley home.

Scott Fitzgerald cared little for either the original Duff or the imagined Lady Brett Ashley, maintaining that they were both replays of Iris March, the feckless heroine of Michael Arlen's *The Green Hat.* Berenice Abbott claimed that Hemingway, even though smitten by Duff's old-world breeding, had not understood the woman at all. "His portrait was superficial. . . . He made her out to be a tramp — that was crazy. But he looked at women only sexually not as people."

Somewhere in that mix of myth and questionable identities, there was, perhaps, a real woman. Duff Twysden had some talent as a musician: at the age of twelve she reputedly gave a piano recital at the Trocadero. She had some gift as an artist: "They were good paintings," Berenice Abbott asserted. She had married as she chose, and in her independence and self-will had abandoned a son by Twysden, leaving him in the care of relatives. But she was a woman not terribly different from other expatriate women in Paris in the twenties — perhaps less interesting than a score of other women Hemingway had met and possibly undeserving of the fame his fictionalization brought her. In a certain sense, Hemingway did create her.

⁂

Pauline Pfeiffer: it was Kitty Cannell who introduced the Hemingways to the Pfeiffer sisters, Pauline and Virginia, small and exotic-looking, so Kitty thought, and rather like a pair of Japanese dolls with their hair cut in dark bangs, although they hailed from Piggott, Arkansas. Pauline, the elder of the two, was four years older than Hemingway. They first met, presumably, soon after he and Hadley had returned from their winter vacation in Schruns. At that first meeting, so legend has it, Hemingway was more struck by Virginia, or "Jinny," the more sociable and vivacious of the two. He is supposed to have said that he would like to date Jinny on the condition that she would wear her sister Pauline's stylish fur coat. Pauline, at first, was disdainful of Hemingway, finding him crude, a loafer who remained reading, unshaven, in a rumpled bed, when she and Jinny paid a first visit to the Hemingway apartment. She wondered why Hadley put up with such behavior.

The Pfeiffer family was wealthy. Pauline's father had started out with a chain of drugstores in Missouri, then bought some 60,000 acres of rich farmland in northeastern Arkansas, with tenant farmers producing lucrative harvests of wheat, corn, and cotton. Pauline's mother was devoutly Catholic; Paul Pfeiffer had converted one of the rooms of their Piggott farmhouse into a small chapel. Uncle Gus Pfeiffer (Pauline was his favorite) held controlling stock in Warner Pharmaceuticals and in the Richard Hudnut Company, the cosmetics firm. Pauline had attended the Visitation Convent in St, Louis, where she had met Katy Smith. She had majored in journalism at the University of Missouri, for a time worked as a reporter at the *Cleveland Star,* then at the *New York Daily Telegraph. Vanity Fair* hired her as a fashion reporter and publicist. In New York, she had reluctantly become engaged to one of her cousins, Matthew Herold, a lawyer for Richard Hudnut, an engagement she was trying to escape from when she took on a job as an assistant to Mainbocher, the Paris editor of *Vogue.* Rumor had it that she was in Paris on a husband-hunting expedition. Jinny Pfeiffer, who had accompanied her sister, had little interest in men other than as social companions. Later in life, Hemingway would claim that Jinny had tried to convert Pauline to the lesbian cause.

III

When Bill Smith arrived in Paris in the spring of 1925, Hemingway was overjoyed. It was as if there had been no break in their friendship at all. The circumstances were not the most auspicious. Hemingway had not been able to persuade Ernest Walsh to hire Bill to take over the editorial and production duties on *This Quarter,* and a job at the American Library had fallen through. Flat broke, Bill moved in with Hemingway and Hadley in their apartment for several weeks, an act of generosity Bill would always remember. Later in life, he would loyally remind interviewers, "There's a lot of that aspect of Hemingway that doesn't come out."

For Smith it was a crowded and memorable summer. Hemingway introduced him to the assembled characters who would make up the personae of *The Sun Also Rises:* Duff Twysden and Pat Guthrie, Harold Loeb and Kitty Cannell. Don Stewart was in town with his friend, the Algonquin Hotel wit Robert Benchley. Stewart, that summer, had taken up with a girl from the Quarter, Josephine, a dancer at Zelli's, whom he settled in a little hotel on the rue Lepic. (It was his first kept woman, he remembered.) In the evenings, he would take in the prizefights and bicycle races with Hemingway and Bill, then wend his way home to Josephine. Stewart and Bill Smith would share the honors of becoming the composite character Bill Gorton in Hemingway's novel. (Stewart, proud of the fictional union, would later address letters to Smith as "Dear Better Half of Bill Gorton.")

Hemingway also introduced Bill, or clued him in, to others in his circle: Harold Stearns, who would play a minor role as Harvey Stone in *The Sun Also Rises;* Evan Shipman, in whom Smith developed an avuncular interest, referring to him as E. Shipmale ("Tell the lad hello for I," Smith would later write Hemingway). Bill, an interested observer, soon became aware of Hemingway's absorbing interest in Duff Twysden and Pauline Pfeiffer's reluctant but growing interest in Hemingway, and noted Pauline's ploys for catching Hemingway's attention. ("I was talking to someone about you just the other day," she would tell Hemingway. "Oh? And what did he say?" Hemingway would respond.) Bill was impressed with how Hadley had kept open house for Ernest's friends during that consequential summer: Stewart and Benchley, Pat Guthrie, the Fitzgeralds. A rivalry developed between Smith and "F. Scatt," as Bill called Fitzgerald. Smith willingly admitted that Scott had "quite a bit of stuff" as a writer. "Though it perhaps would please me more if he didn't," he confessed to Hemingway. "My opinion of the lad always being colored by his of me. Or rather what I felt his was." Smith had an easier time with Harold Loeb, with whom he developed a real and lasting friendship, not altogether to Ernest's liking. Despite Bill's unobtrusive ways, Loeb discovered that he "had a wit which expressed itself in cynical wisecracks and that he was loyal, discreet, and reliable. We became good friends." Smith also struck up easy relationships with Kitty Cannell and with Pauline Pfeiffer, who referred to him, enigmatically, as H. Gug.

⸙ ⸙ ⸙

"He was then the kind of man to whom men, women, children, and dogs were attracted. It was something." So Hadley would record the effect Hemingway made on others during the early years of their marriage. It was true that many men were impressed by the youthful Hemingway — the aggressive grin, the opportunities he offered for brusque man-to-man talk, the sense, finally, of a literary man who was completely down-to-earth. Loeb, for one, had been fatally struck: "I admired his combination of toughness and sensitiveness, his love of sport and his dedication to writing. . . . It was a good sign that men like Hemingway were taking up writing."

It was hardly true that all women liked Hemingway. Kitty Cannell claimed that he was "in every way a man's man. I think he disliked women heartily; and in most cases they disliked him — excluding sex, of course. But many very clever men seemed to idolize him." Zelda Fitzgerald considered Ernest a "bogus" male. Reportedly, she had told him to his face, "Ernest, nobody is as male as all that." Hadley, who thought Zelda essentially frivolous, recalled Zelda's saying to her, in front of Ernest, "I notice that in the Hemingway family you do what Ernest wants." Hadley did not dispute the fact; she nonetheless decided that Hemingway was "too assured a male" for Zelda. But it was certainly true, in the fourth year of his marriage, that Hemingway, as a writer burgeoning into success, acquired a new circle of wealthy and influential friends who would be helpful in the immediate years ahead. He had the indispensable knack of attracting what he needed for the furtherance of his reputation and career. It would always be his luck.

That year, Hemingway met Gerald and Sara Murphy, a unique couple who would be swept up into the legend of the period. Gerald was in his late thirties when they met. Sara, five years older than her husband, was a woman of astonishing, old-fashioned beauty, content to be the perfect wife and helpmate. Their children, Patrick, Baoth, and Honoria, were handsome, well mannered, golden, children fresh from a James Barrie play. Murphy's money came from the Mark Cross Company in New York. (In those early years, he had little concern or interest in business, preferred the expatriate life.) The Murphys had a house in St.-Cloud; another, the Villa America, in Antibes on the French Riviera, was in the process of being renovated. They had taste as well as style, a gift for creating an ambiance of pleasure and good breeding which intrigued their friends. They knew everyone it was necessary to know in Paris, were friendly with Picasso and Léger, took up with principals in Diaghilev's *corps de ballet,* gave a fabulous party on a houseboat on the Seine for the premiere of Stravinsky's ballet *Les Noces.* On the Riviera they feted their friends with cruises on their yacht, gave beach parties on their private beach, La Garoupe, and intimate dinners at their villa. The house, with its terraced gardens of exotic trees and flowers, would serve as one of the recognizable settings for Fitzgerald's novel *Tender Is the Night.*

Gerald had studied with the Russian artist and stage designer Natalia Goncharova. He painted in a meticulous, modern, hard-edged style. "Before I die," he promised, "I'm going to do one picture which will be hitched to the universe." But he would give up painting in 1929, the year he learned that his son Patrick was suffering from tuberculosis.

It was clear, to Gerald at least, that Hemingway preferred Sara, although he seemed to admire both the Murphys. For years, Hemingway had what amounted to a crush on Sara. During later periods of stress or depression, he would write her woebegone letters. She would answer, full of ready sympathy: "You are a stimulus and an ideal for your friends." Sara's loyalties, once formed, were transfixed and framed tastefully in silver, like cherished family photographs. Gerald, however, knew that Hemingway had certain reservations about him. Murphy was not, after all, athletic, nor the usual sportsman; he did not fit the pattern of Hemingway's male friends. Gerald felt at home in social situations where wealth dominated, though he did not exactly court the rich. And there was, perhaps, an undercurrent of disapproval on Murphy's part which Hemingway sensed. Like many of Hemingway's male friends, Murphy fell easily into the habit of giving in to or agreeing with Hemingway's opinions and prejudices. He disliked it in himself. He remembered, for example, a conversation in which Hemingway brought up the subject of male homosexuals. "He was extremely sensitive to the question of who was one and who wasn't." Casually, Hemingway said, "'I don't mind a fairy like so and so, do you?' For some reason, I said, 'No,' even though I had never met the man. I have no idea why I said it, except that Ernest had an ability to make it easier to agree with him than to not . . . I wondered later if he had laid a trap for me." Murphy noticed that Hemingway "is never difficult with people he does not like, the people he does not take seriously." On occasion, Hemingway had crossed swords with Sara or with Dos Passos but never with him; "the line has been drawn very definitely between the people he admits to his life and those he does not. I have never felt for a moment a claim to his affection and do not receive it."

There are few positives, black or white, in human friendships; they depend as much on the weather of circumstances as on the force of emotion. Mere slights, a casual indifference, may shape their course as well as the grander passions. Habit is their stabilizing influence. Gerald Murphy was not the least perceptive of Hemingway's friends — and critics. Late in life, after years of puzzled study, intermittent correspondence and reunions, he gave his own peculiar assessment of Hemingway's career: "Ernest will have given his life *one* thing, and that is scale. The lives of some of us will seem, I suppose by comparison, piddling. . . . For me, he has the violence and excess of genius."

⁂

Among the friends of the Murphys whom Hemingway met that summer was Archibald MacLeish. There were several reasons for Hemingway to like MacLeish. A Yale graduate (like Gerald, a Skull and Bones man), MacLeish had gone on to Harvard Law School and was a practicing lawyer with a prestigious Boston firm when, in the summer of 1923, he gave up the legal profession, sold his Cambridge house, and, with an allowance from his father, moved to Paris with his wife, Ada, a professional concert singer, and two children. His ambition was to become a recognized poet. During World War I, he had served in a hospital unit, then transferred to the field artillery, taking part in the second battle of the Marne. For Hemingway, it was another mark in MacLeish's favor.

Although he and his family would remain in France for some five years, with occasional trips to America, MacLeish did not consider himself an expatriate. "I never met or heard of an American expatriate in Paris in those years," he maintained. MacLeish thought of Paris as the vantage point from which American writers could discern their true subjects. But he did see himself as reacting against the lack of values in the new generation whom he admonished in an updated version of *Hamlet,* rather portentously called *The Hamlet of A. MacLeish*: "We have learned the answers, all the answers: / It is the question that we do not know. / We are not wise." Like Hemingway, though less successful at it, MacLeish wanted to avoid symbolism and rhetoric in his writing. As he announced in his poem "Ars Poetica" early in his career, "A poem should not mean / But be," a definition that would haunt all his later work. In Hemingway, MacLeish discerned a brotherly spirit and commemorated their early meeting in Paris in memorial lines:

> Veteran out of the wars before he was twenty;
> Famous at twenty-five: thirty a master —
> Whittled a style for his time from a walnut stick
> In a carpenter's loft in a street of that April city.

IV

The well-organized trip to the fiesta of San Fermín which Hemingway had planned for that summer was hampered by delays and complications. Hemingway was still arranging affairs for *This Quarter.* Almost the last thing he did in Paris, late in June, was to alert Ernest Walsh that the segment of Joyce's new work in progress (*Finnegans Wake*), promised for the Autumn-Winter issue, would be forthcoming in ten days. (Joyce, at first reluctant to send anything at all, was now not sure where to send it, as Walsh's whereabouts seemed so uncertain.) Then the planned fishing expedition at Burguete which he and Hadley and Bill had been looking forward to had to be put off for several days because of the late arrival in Paris of Hemingway's Boni and Liveright editor. It was not until June 25 that they were able to get away. Two days later they were in Pamplona, where Bill Smith's fishing permit was issued and dated. When they reached Burguete, they met another disappointment: the stream that had been so full of trout the year before had now been ruined by logging operations. "Fish killed, pools destroyed, dams broken down. Made me feel sick," Hemingway wrote his father.

The more serious problem proved to be the friends assembled in Pamplona. The chemistry was somehow all wrong during the week of festivities in early July. Harold Loeb, who had canceled out of the fishing expedition, arrived with Duff and Pat Guthrie. Guthrie, annoyed by the lovesick Loeb, turned drunk and nasty. Don Stewart sensed rancor in the air. He conceded that women — or more accurately the complications of sex — managed to ruin what should have been a purely "male festival." Duff was an extremely attractive woman; Hemingway was certainly the handsomest man of the group. It would have been natural, Stewart thought, that the two would have been attracted to each other, though he hadn't actually observed anything. It hadn't occurred to him then, he admitted, that Hadley and Hemingway might not be as perfectly happy together as they seemed.

Day by day, the occasion turned sour. Stewart began to notice a mean streak in Hemingway's character. Somehow, he connected it with Hemingway's rise to fame. Although there was no large audience yet, Hemingway's "little Paris books" and short stories had begun to create "a critical ground swell." Whereas before Hemingway had been companionable, smiling his aggressive smile, now he was assertive: "You were not to disagree with the Master in any way from then on." It began to cross Stewart's mind that Hemingway could be "a dangerous friend to have."

Loeb's initial offense, in Hemingway's view, was that he was not interested in bullfighting. He made it plain that he disliked the whole affair, considered it shoddy, disapproved of the tawdry ceremonies and the worn, comic-opera costumes of the matadors. He found it hard to look at the bull's death agony: "It seemed, in some obscure way, shameful." Then, too, when Hemingway learned that Duff and Loeb had had a secret rendezvous at St.-Jean-de-Luz, he had a noticeable attack of jealousy. Aware of Hemingway's foul mood, Loeb asked Bill Smith about it. Bill, taking evasive action, dryly answered that Hemingway's anger focused on the fact that Loeb and Duff had gone off together in a wagon-lit: "He went off muttering the foulest string of curses I ever heard. 'In a *wagon-lit,*' he said at every other step."

At Pamplona, Harold added to his crimes by hovering around Duff on every occasion until it became annoying to everyone. One night he kept Duff out on a drinking spree, which she continued even after Loeb had returned to his hotel. The next day she turned up at lunch slightly bruised and with a black eye. When Loeb asked about it, Hemingway brusquely interrupted, telling him Duff had fallen on a railing. That night at dinner, the last night of the *feria,* Guthrie, drunk and in a bitter mood, told Loeb he should have sense enough to leave when he wasn't wanted. Hemingway joined in, accusing Loeb of spoiling the party. When Loeb asked Duff if she wanted him to leave, she pointedly remarked, "You know that I do *not* want you to go." Hemingway blasted Loeb: "You lousy bastard. . . . Running to a woman." The two stepped outside to fight. But when Loeb, having taken off his glasses and put them in his pocket to protect them, looked for a safe spot to hang his jacket, Hemingway jokingly asked if Loeb wanted him to hold the jacket for him. He then broke out into a boyish smile. Both admitted that neither one wanted to fight, and the two of them walked back to the café together. The following morning Loeb received an apologetic note from Hemingway: "I was terribly tight and nasty to you last night and I dont want you to go away with that nasty insulting lousiness as the last thing of the fiestas. I wish I could wipe out all the meanness and I suppose I cant but this is to let you know that I'm thoroly ashamed of the way I acted and the stinking, unjust, uncalled for things I said."

Hints, intimations, a tangle of psychological speculations, have gathered around the squabble at a café table in Pamplona on a July night in 1925 and Hemingway's abrupt backing out of a fistfight he had done his best to provoke. (In *The Sun Also Rises,* the scene takes place at the Café Suizo, and Robert Cohn knocks out Jake Barnes, an even more demeaning reversal.) The actual event has been given stature, strangeness, by its fictionalized treatment. There is, ironically, a photograph — a famous photograph — of the friends (or some of them) drinking beer in a Pamplona café which could serve as a tantalizing illustration of the scene. Hemingway casually looks at the photographer (perhaps Bill Smith). Beside him is Duff, pert, slyly amused, hands in her lap. (Hemingway's description of her in the early draft of the novel might pass as a literal transcript of the photograph: "Her eyes crinkled up as we came up to the table.") Next to her, Hadley, fresh and beaming, a bit too plump and matronly. Three men are unidentified or unidentifiable. Is the bespectacled man, bow-tied, trimly barbered, sitting behind Duff, staring straight at the camera, Loeb? (Don Stewart remembered that Harold was a fanatic about searching out the barbers of Pamplona. Hemingway describes Robert Cohn as bareheaded and bespectacled.) The slightly balding man next to Hadley is most probably Don Stewart. And the man on the right-hand side, opposite Hemingway? Hemingway's foot is resting familiarly on the rung of the man's chair. Like Hemingway, the man is wearing a beret. Pat Guthrie? (In the beer-drinking episode in the novel, Pat Guthrie/Mike Campbell wears a beret.) He looks, oddly, like a male clone of Lady Duff, slightly androgynous, lean-featured, thin eyebrows arched.

Time, in its perverse way, has multiplied the discrepancies in the versions of the quarrel. Yet nothing much (or beneath the surface, perhaps, a good deal) had changed following it. Don Stewart generously paid the hotel bill for Pat and Duff, who were broke, then left Pamplona to visit the Murphys at Antibes. Pat and Duff, along with Loeb and Bill Smith, drove to St.-Jean-de-Luz, bitter feelings, apparently, soothed by the necessary economies of the travel arrangements. Hemingway and Hadley traveled third-class to Madrid, on money borrowed from Stewart, or so Stewart claimed.

ɻɻɻ

Yet, at the time, Hemingway's letters, aside from the disappointment of the fishing expedition, gave no hint of his anger and dissatisfaction. He kept up his press agentry about Spain and his love of bullfighting. Writing at length to Gertrude Stein from Madrid in mid-July, he noted that the weather had been "fine." They had had a bibulous train trip from Pamplona to Madrid with two priests and four members of the Guardia Civil, and that was "very fine." They had had a bull dedicated to them. Hadley had left the bull's ear wrapped in one of Don Stewart's handkerchiefs in a drawer, where it ripened and began to smell. The paintings at the Prado had been rehung and looked "very fine."

Hemingway's enthusiasm, no doubt, came from having said good-bye to the disruptive Pamplona crowd. And to the fact that he had discovered a spectacular new young bullfighter, Cayetano Ordóñez, nicknamed Niño de la Palma. In a *mano a mano* with Belmonte, the young Ordóñez had made the old master look cheap. Ordóñez "did everything Belmonte did and did it better," parodying, in Hemingway's eyes, Belmonte's gestures, flourishes, even his ungainly stances. Strictly by chance, Hemingway had found a new hero, a man who, like himself, was mastering his art and was now in a position to shame his betters — the very image of the young contender.

V

What compulsion leads a writer to fictionalize his experiences, make them over, make them anew, alter them to serve another, more demanding purpose? Seemingly against his will, or out of some interior demand, Hemingway, that summer in Spain, found himself swept up in the writing of a novel, despite the fact that he had only recently told Max Perkins that he had no intentions of writing one. That, however, turned out to be only a manner of speaking, since on June 15, in Paris, Hemingway had launched into "Along with Youth," subtitled "A Novel," with a scene depicting Nick Adams's 1918 transatlantic crossing aboard the wartime transport *Chicago* in the company of his friend the Carper and two Polish officers — a narrative that ended forever on page 27.

In Valencia, he had better luck. Possibly on or in advance of his birthday, July 21, Hemingway abruptly began work on a novel that would sum up his generation for generations of readers, would become the literary monument for the postwar expatriate life of Paris. He would regard the writing of his novel — first named *Fiesta,* then *The Sun Also Rises,* a title derived from a passage in Ecclesiastes — as one of the watersheds of his writing life. During the course of two months (he would later foreshorten the time to six weeks), while traveling in Spain and following his return to Paris in early August, he worked at the first handwritten draft of the book in a burst of creativity:

To Bill Smith (then back in Paris), July 27, Valencia: "I work from lunch until the bullfight starts. The story is fairly funny. Have Ford in it as Braddocks. The master goes well as Braddocks."

To Sylvia Beach, circa August 3, Valencia: "I've written six chapters on a novel and am going great about 15,000 words done already. It's going to be good but will be harder to write when there aren't any bull fights."

To Bill Smith, August 5, Madrid: "Have 8 chapters done on novel — averaged 2000 words a day since we left Pamplona. Going like wildfire. Ought to be swell novel. . . . If I'm still going good Hash may come up alone about Mon. or Tues. August 10th or 11th. . . . I don't want to come to Paris while I'm going so damn good. This book is going to crack right through."

To Gertrude Stein and Alice Toklas, August 20, Paris: "I just got back yesterday . . . I have been working very hard and done about 50 some thousand words on a novel. I want to get it finished now and then put it away and come back and work it over. . . . Never worked so hard. . . . It certainly is funny how your head, I mean my head, can go most of the time like a frozen cabbage and then it can give you hell when it starts going."

To Ernest Walsh, circa August 1925: "I am working all the time and thinking all the time about this novel and don't seem to be able to think about anything else. Have around 68,000 words done I should think. It is going to be a swell novel with no autobiography and no complaints."

⸙ ⸙ ⸙

Hemingway may have assured Ernest Walsh that his novel would contain no autobiography and no complaints, but it would involve both. With a few admittedly important exceptions, the story line of the novel would follow the sequence of events in Hemingway's life in the summer of 1925. *The Sun Also Rises* is about a group of Paris friends attending a *feria* in Pamplona, Spain. The cast of characters includes a promiscuous titled English lady, Brett Ashley, and her lover cousin Mike Campbell; an American writer and former boxing champion at Princeton, Robert Cohn; the narrator, Jake Barnes, a newspaper correspondent who had been so severely wounded in the war that he has been rendered impotent, a man manqué; and Jake's longtime friend, a highly successful writer, Bill Gorton. The catalyst of the novel (Hemingway, at first, had some difficulty in determining who was to be the hero, if indeed there was to be one) is Pedro Romero, a handsome young bullfighter at the start of his career, adored by the public, regarded by the critics as the white hope of an art that, like writing in a disordered age, is in a phase of decadence.

The lady of the story, promiscuous and a dipsomaniac, although in love with Jake Barnes, is engaged to marry her alcoholic cousin. She has had a willful passing affair with Robert Cohn, whom she subsequently abandons. She is the queen bee in a circle of randy males. Predictably, she falls in love with the bullfighter (she is thirty-four; he is nineteen) and precipitates a fight between Robert Cohn and Jake, whom Cohn, in a bitter scene, accuses of pimping for Lady Brett. Barnes, who prides himself on his friendship with the aficionados of the bullfight, particularly Montoya, the proprietor of the hotel where the friends are staying, finds himself in disgrace with Romero's supporters. Brett, however, has a change of heart, gives up her bullfighter as a redemptory gesture in her otherwise wasteful and self-indulgent life. ("I'm not going to be one of these bitches that ruins children," she explains to Jake. She has had to telegraph him to rescue her from a hotel in Madrid which she cannot leave for lack of funds.) "You know it makes one feel rather good deciding not to be a bitch. . . . It's sort of what we have instead of God," she says in another of the well-remembered exchanges in the novel. In the taxi on the way to catch the Sud Express back to Paris, Brett, resting in Jake's comforting arms, complains of their fate: "Oh, Jake . . . we could have had such a damned good time together." And Jake, in the perfect rejoinder, answers, "Yes. . . . Isn't it pretty to think so?"

⁂

Like the red-pigmented *sinopia*, the initial sketch hidden under the finished version of a Renaissance fresco, there is a ghost version of *The Sun Also Rises.* (By chance or by deliberate design, Hemingway preserved the original, "Fiesta" version, an opening draft of thirty-one loose pages continued over into seven schoolboy copybooks.) In the early version Hemingway did not stray far from the actual people and the incidents on whom he based his novel. With a few noticeable exceptions, he began with the real names: Niño de la Palma, Hemingway himself, Loeb, Duff, Pat Guthrie, Bill Smith, Don Stewart. Even Hadley made an appearance in the novel-to-be. (Unlike Hemingway's final version, *Fiesta* began with Niño de la Palma dressing for the corrida in his hotel room.) Hadley, however, would be an early casualty, discarded altogether, a wife who became a hindrance to the plot and the dramatic possibilities of Jake's unrequited love affair with Lady Brett.

Later, in the process of writing — and evidently concerned about the risk of libel suits — Hemingway, like an Indian covering his trail, dropped most of the real names, tried out new ones. Harold Loeb became, first, Gerald Cohn (a neat combination of Hemingway's mild antipathy toward Gerald Murphy and his feelings about Loeb) and then, finally, Robert Cohn. (At one point in the manuscript, Cohn is referred to as Leopold — a curious slip on Hemingway's part, connecting Loeb's name with the celebrated and much-publicized Leopold and Loeb case in Chicago, involving the homosexual murder of Bobby Franks by a pair of rich young college students.) Hemingway — "Hem" in the first draft — eventually became the narrator, Jake Barnes; Bill Smith and Don Stewart merged to become, first, Bill Grundy, then Bill Gorton. (Slack editing left the name Grundy, at one point, as a vestigial error in the published version.) Pat Guthrie became Mike Campbell. And Duff, after a stint as Duff Anthony, settled into the novel as Lady Brett. Dos Passos, who made a brief appearance in his own name, became Alec Muhr, and subsequently disappeared from the text. From the very beginning, Henry Braddocks was clearly intended as a caricature of Ford Madox Ford, and the rather obtuse Mrs. Braddocks was his mistress, Stella Bowen. Juanito Quintana, proprietor of the Hotel Quintana in Pamplona, became Montoya.

Kitty Cannell did not attend the fiesta, but she appeared in the Paris chapters as the unfortunate Frances Clyne. Cannell, not keen on Hemingway to begin with, thought that Loeb had such a "terrific case of hero worship on Hemingway" that he was blind to the way Hemingway manipulated his friends. She considered him an opportunist, disliked the clever Tom Sawyerish way Hemingway got money and favors from people, then made it appear that he was embarrassed by friends forcing favors on him. Nor did she like Hemingway's obvious anti-Semitism, or the way he talked down Ford Madox Ford, who was a friend of hers. She also deplored Hemingway's lack of consideration for Hadley, letting her live in the mean quarters they had, letting her dress the way she did: "She never had any new clothes." A predictable response, perhaps, considering that Cannell, blonde and statuesque, was very fashion-conscious. (She would serve as the Paris fashion editor for the *New York Times* for a number of years.) From time to time, Cannell took Hadley out shopping with her, bought her little gifts — earrings from an antique shop, perhaps — which, she intimated, gave her pleasure and annoyed Hemingway.

Hemingway's revenge came in the form of a scathing characterization of her both in the early draft and the later published version of the novel — despite the fact that, in a confidential moment, according to Cannell, Hemingway had told her, "I've taken your advice. I'm writing a book full of plot, drama and everything. I'm tearing those bastards apart (referring to Bill and most to Harold.) I'm putting everyone in it. But you're a wonderful girl, Kitty, I've always liked you and I wouldn't do anything to annoy you, for the world!" But Hemingway, by then back in Paris, had already savaged Kitty in a devastating fourteen-page episode written in Madrid (an episode condensed and honed to a deadly sharpness in the final revisions). In it, Frances Clyne, with ruthless persistence, shames Robert Cohn in front of Jake by analyzing Cohn's method for breaking up their affair: "Yes that's the way it's done. Gerald's sending me [to England]. He's going to give me two hundred pounds and then I'm going to visit friends. Won't it be lovely? The friends don't know about it yet." What Hemingway did delete was a vicious sketch of the Cohn-Clyne relationship: "During this time he had 'lived with' a woman who lived on gossip and so he had lived in an atmosphere of abortions, doubts and incidents, confirming these doubts as to the sex of different friends, dirty rumors, dirtier reports, still dirtier suspicions, and a constant fear and dread, by his companion that he was going with other women and was on the point of leaving her." Even so, his treatment of the pair in the final version of *The Sun Also Rises* was devastating enough.

There were, as well, a number of incidental characters who were sketched in acid. Glenway Wescott, whose novel *The Apple of the Eye* had been having a considerable success, puts in a brief appearance first as Ralph Severn, then as the too readily identifiable Roger Prescott. Changed finally, at the publisher's request, he is Roger Prentiss, the supercilious young man Jake is introduced to in a bar scene. Jake later confesses that the meeting was enough to make him want to vomit. In real life the reasons for Hemingway's wrath were twofold, literary and sexual. Hemingway, taking the measure of a rival writer, claimed Wescott's stuff was "fundamentally unsound," considered his prose a "literary fake." In private, he referred to the writer with disdain as "Glenway Weskit the author of the pineapple of the eye and the fairies best bet in literature." The mincing pair of homosexuals who enter the *bal musette* with Brett ("I do declare. There is an actual harlot. I'm going to dance with her, Lett. You watch me") were clearly identifiable as Cedric Morris and his companion Arthur Lett-Haines, both minor painters and well known to the expatriate crowd. The singer Georgette Leblanc (Margaret Anderson's lover) comes in for a slur when Jake introduces his fictional *poule,* Georgette Hobin, to the crowd at the restaurant, Le Nègre de Toulouse, as Georgette Leblanc. (In private Hemingway referred to Leblanc even more scurrilously as "Georgette Mangeuse le Blanc.")

Few of Hemingway's friends or passing acquaintances would escape the hardship of his characterizations. It was therefore not at all surprising that mere changes of name did not dissuade readers in Paris who knew the entire cast of characters from recognizing that the book was, indeed, a vicious *roman à clef* when it was published in 1926. As Janet Flanner, "Genêt," announced in a brief mention in *The New Yorker,* "All these personages are, it is maintained, to be seen just where Hemingway so often placed them at the Sélect."

A writer's contacts with life, no matter how ephemeral or minor, are seldom lost. It may be only a remembered anecdote or a piece of information picked up in the morning paper, but it will, sometime, have its irresistible use. Fiction is that complex weave of life circumstances, stray knowledge, unbidden psychological motivations, old hurts, new fears, grievances real or imagined, mere coincidences, suppressed rivalries, the constructive urge. *The Sun Also Rises,* like its failed predecessor, *Along with Youth,* marked the convergence of persistent themes in Hemingway's fiction: the ills of the world, a young man's romantic conception of love, the waywardness and promiscuity of women, the almost sensual arousal-state of fear, the essential tests of a man's courage, the unwarranted conviction of one's own immortality. (Nick Adams's pledge: "Other people can get killed but not me.") There is, perhaps, some justice to Fitzgerald's remark that after the psychoanalysts have been forgotten, "E.H. will be read for his great studies into fear."

Suppressed rivalries: as if the writing of the novel were Hemingway's attempt to prove himself, to break away from his mentors, to compete with rivals. In some respects, particularly in the early version, the writing was an exercise in spleen. Hemingway, seeing himself as a contender, had begun to take the measure of his mentors and contemporaries with critical and acerb asides in both his novel and his private life. Both during the initial writing of the novel and during the crucial revisions that winter, his comments about his betters were sharp and sometimes contradictory. Openly critical of Sherwood Anderson's *Many Marriages,* he was even more so of Anderson's *Dark Laughter,* telling his mother that it was a "pretentious fake with two or three patches of real writing in it." In a letter to Fitzgerald on the importance of subject matter, Hemingway panned Dos Passos's *Streets of Night,* claiming that what made it "lousy" was its subject matter — Boston. (On the other hand, "What made 3 Soldiers a swell book was the war.") He could seldom pass up a chance to put down Ford Madox Ford and, in the first draft of *Fiesta,* complained about Braddocks's novels: "In them there was always a great deal of passion but it took sometimes two and three volumes for anyone to sleep with anyone else." In his letters to Pound, it was always Hemingway's complaint that Ford took an interminable time to get his heroes to battle or to bed. ("You may recall my prediction that Teecheegins would never actually face the Boche because if Ford had any confidence that he could handle combat he would . . . not have taken 2 vols. to get his hero back to the lines?") About *Finnegans Wake,* when he read the installment in *This Quarter,* he wrote Walsh, complaining slyly about its obscurity: "Joyce is swell. I would always rather know what it is all about but I like Joyce straight, with orange juice, with Liffey water or what have you."

In some respects, Gertrude Stein escaped his irritability. Hemingway definitely made use of her ruminative technique in *The Making of Americans* of writing about the process of the writing while engaged in writing. It proved consoling, apparently, during his writing sessions on the novel. At times, Hemingway's use of the device is instructive: "I wanted to stay well outside of the story so that I would not be touched by it in any way. . . . But I made the unfortunate mistake, for a writer, of first having been Mr. Jake Barnes." But mostly, as when Hemingway explores his difficulties in trying to settle upon a hero, it is muddling and awkward. ("Gerald Cohn is the hero. When I bring myself in it is only to clear up something. Or maybe Duff is the hero." At one point, in exasperation, he recalls Stein's advice: "Gertrude Stein once told me that remarks are not literature. All right, let it go at that. Only this time all the remarks are going in and if it is not literature who claimed it was anyway." Fortunately for *The Sun Also Rises,* Hemingway followed Stein's advice rather than her example. Most of his intrusive authorial asides were deleted before publication. In the completed novel, a fine cynicism would undercut the maundering sentimentality of the earlier drafts.

Stein's most helpful gift to Hemingway came in the form of a brusque remark about himself and his expatriate friends: "You are all a lost generation." Hemingway later used it as the first of the two epigraphs for the published volume. There, he countered it with a quotation from Ecclesiastes: "One generation passeth away, and another generation cometh; but the earth abideth forever . . . The sun also ariseth, and the sun goeth down, and hasteth to the place were he arose." Stein's remark proved very useful in the media, giving reviewers a convenient peg for their criticism. In the end, it became the epithet for an entire generation, including the innovative writers and artists, Hemingway's contemporaries, who came of age between the two World Wars of the twentieth century.

Hemingway, fussed by the attention the phrase received, later claimed that his novel was a refutation of Stein's remark. Yet at one point in the ongoing composition and revision of *The Sun Also Rises,* he had actually intended to use *The Lost Generation* as the title for his book. He had even written a short foreword to explain the circumstances of the remark: how Stein, during the previous summer, had stopped at a garage in the Ain to have a valve fixed in her old Ford, how quick and skillful the young mechanic had been, and how pleased she was with his work. Stein had asked the garage keeper where he had gotten boys like that; she had heard that you couldn't get young men to work anymore. The garage keeper (actually, in Stein's account of the incident, it had been the proprietor of the Hôtel Pernollet, where she and Alice were staying) told her that it was only those who had gone off to the war, "the ones between twenty two and thirty that are no good. *C'est une génération perdue.*" They were spoiled, no good, the garage keeper said. "A little hard on them," he added.

In his discarded foreword, Hemingway went on to make some sweeping generalizations of his own which tended to confirm, however, the fatalistic view of a lost generation that he later wanted to deny. His generation in France, he said, had sought salvation in the Catholic Church, Dadaism, the movies, Royalism, and, once again, the Catholic Church — in a two-year span. "There may be another and better war," he added, "but none of it will matter particularly to this generation because to them the things that are given to people to happen have already happened."

ɻ ɻ ɻ

What raised *The Sun Also Rises* beyond a merely trendy, topical novel was the symbolic merger of the art of bullfighting and the art of writing that Hemingway made a presiding metaphor of the book. Oddly enough, the account he gave Stein in his July 15 letter of the contest between the young Niño de la Palma and the aged Belmonte would become the critical encounter (not the expectable one of the love affair between Lady Brett and Jake Barnes) in the novel. And it was relevant that he had written his account of the real event to the one person — a woman — who would be sure to appreciate his feelings. Hemingway had clearly been impressed; his letter catches his excitement at watching the contest of the young contender and the aging professional. Cayetano Ordóñez, Niño de la Palma, had been dazzling:

> Then he stepped out all by himself without any tricks — suave, templando [moderate] with the cape, smooth and slow — splendid bandilleros and started with 5 Naturales with the muleta — beautiful complete faena all linked up and then killed perfectly. He comes from Ronda and everybody in Spain is crazy about him — except of course those that can't stand him.

The description of the brash young man that many people were crazy about — "except those that can't stand him" — was easily, wishfully, that of Hemingway himself.

Within a week of his letter to Stein, Hemingway (in Valencia) set to work on his novel in full force. The first chapter began with the young man who had inspired him, and it was titled after him, "Niño de la Palma." The opening sentence read like the entrance of a hero: "I saw him for the first time in his room at the Hotel Quintana in Pamplona." Ordóñez, too, like the other characters, would go through several name changes, introduced first by his nickname, Niño, and finally as Pedro Romero, the name of a legendary eighteenth-century bullfighter. Romero becomes the indirect hero of the novel, the man who conducts himself most honorably. The day after he receives a brutal beating from Robert Cohn in a fight over Brett, Romero acquits himself magnificently in the bullring. Early on in the first draft of the book, Jake/Hemingway, as narrator, declares, "Nobody ever lives their life all the way up except bull fighters."

For structural and dramatic reasons, Hemingway made the contest between Ordóñez and Belmonte a climactic episode toward the end of the first draft, repeating some of the phrases he had used in his letter to Stein:

> It was like a course in bull fighting, all the passes linked up, all completed, all slow, templed, and smooth. They were all sincere, there were no tricks and no mistifications and each pass as it reach[ed] its summit . . . gave me that ache inside that only comes from greatness.

Refined a bit more, the account was carried over into the published text:

> It was like a course in bull-fighting. All the passes he linked up, all completed, all slow, templed and smooth. There were no tricks and no mystifications. There was no brusqueness. And each pass as it reached the summit gave you a sudden ache inside. The crowd did not want it ever to be finished.

In one of the most masterly sections of the book, Hemingway described the ritual in exacting detail: the blistering sun, the sword handlers opening their cases, the blood-stained muletas being unfolded, Romero scuffing the wet edge of his cape in the sand to give it weight in the wind, the studied look of a bull before it charges. Hemingway imbued all this, the sense of the excitement and danger of the bullfight, with a near physical quality. But in some ways the most interesting aspect of the contest between the older man and the younger is the charity (a rare moment in the text) with which Hemingway treated Belmonte: "In bull-fighting they speak of the terrain of the bull and the terrain of the bull-fighter. . . . Belmonte, in his best days, worked always in the terrain of the bull. This way he gave the sensation of coming tragedy."

But Belmonte, suffering from a fistula that makes it painful for him to move in the ring (another offense against his dignity), no longer works in the territory of the bull. Once the most famous matador of his time, he has sold out to fame and safety, the praise of the rich, has become an adjunct of fashionable society. He can no longer measure up to the legend he has created, and the crowd insults him, tosses bread and cushions into the ring. So graphic is Hemingway's command of the scene that the reader has, if only for the moment, the actual sense, as in a newsreel, of the historical man — but in an admittedly fictional context: "His jaw only went further out. Sometimes he turned to smile that toothed, long-jawed, lipless smile when he was called something particularly insulting." Belmonte, Hemingway notes, "no longer had his greatest moments in the bull ring. He was not sure that there were any great moments."

No less masterly are Hemingway's descriptions of Pedro Romero's grace, the sense of exigency in his performance. "Romero smiled. The bull wanted it again, and Romero's cape filled again, this time on the other side. Each time he let the bull pass so close that the man and the bull and the cape that filled and pivoted ahead of the bull were all one sharply etched mass." If it was never quite clear, in the personal complicity that exists between a writer and his fictional characters, whom Hemingway intended to be the hero of *The Sun Also Rises,* the underlying sense of Hemingway's admiration of Romero, who proves himself a man in his test of courage, is evident in the writing. When, in a scene in which Brett reads Romero's palm and tells him he has a long life line, Romero, like the young Nick Adams in "Indian Camp," sees his life stretching ahead: "I know it," Romero says. "I'm never going to die."

⁊⁊⁊

Against the dissipated life of the Paris crowd, Hemingway clearly intended to contrast the heroism of the bullring. It was chance, again, the arrival of Bill Smith in Paris that spring, the exuberant renewal of their friendship, that provided another of those fortunate circumstances that allowed Hemingway to develop his theme further. The fishing expedition on the Irati, in which Bill and Jake take part, is (as it was intended to be) Hemingway's depiction of a male idyll, or Eden, bereft of women. (Hadley, now excluded from the novel, was no deterrent.) They are boisterous and bawdy during their meals at the rustic inn at Burguete; they fish together along the Irati, the wine bottles chilling in the stream. The fishing is good (unlike the real experience that summer of 1925). The two men are on their old friendly basis, reminiscent of Bill and Nick Adams in "The Three-Day Blow," and of Hemingway and Bill Smith in the long summers in upper Michigan. They discuss literature and politics, H. L. Mencken, William Jennings Bryan, the reputed accident that made Henry James impotent. They joke about sex. True, the account of this male idyll bogs down a bit from Hemingway's boyish sentimentality and his heavy hand with rude humor, but the episode is one of Hemingway's unabashed paeans to male camaraderie. Even the bad jokes come across as authentically bad in the scene.

In the published text, there is an interminably long-winded joke about irony and pity in literature. (It is a disguised slam at Gilbert Seldes, who in a review of *The Great Gatsby* had cited Fitzgerald's command of irony and pity in depicting a tiny section of life with a consuming passion.) Bill intones a little ditty that goes, "Irony and Pity. When you're feeling . . ." The discussion turns into a slur against the New York critics and the New York literary establishment as well as an ironic bill of particulars against the expatriate life. Bill cites Jake as a classic example: "You're an expatriate. You've lost touch with the soil. You get precious. Fake European standards have ruined you. You drink yourself to death. You become obsessed by sex. You spend all your time talking, not working. You are an expatriate, see? You hang around cafés."

Suddenly the talk turns sentimental. Bill announces that Jake is a good guy, and then, in a moment of guarded affection, says, "Listen. You're a hell of a good guy and I'm fonder of you than anybody on earth. I couldn't tell you that in New York. It'd mean I was a faggot." The whole conversation is suddenly brought down to what one might read as Hemingway's edgy admission that the greatest threat to his treasured male idylls was the taint of homosexuality, whether actual, or latent, or imagined by others. Bill suddenly covers up this brisk admission of affection — even, perhaps, love — with an intentionally outrageous monologue: "That was what the Civil War was about. Abraham Lincoln was a faggot. He was in love with General Grant. So was Jefferson Davis. . . . Sex explains it all. The Colonel's Lady and Judy O'Grady are Lesbians under their skin."

The early draft version of the novel was less cautious, more suggestive, in its treatment of this scene: Jake asserts his personal distance from what Bill is going to say. He ruminates, "It is funny that a thing that ninety nine times out of a hundred you yourself never even think about, other people should mind so. It is imagination I suppose." He asks what the dope is on Bill himself in New York circles. Bill answers, "I'm crazy. Also I'm supposed to be crazy to get married. Would marry anybody at any time. Then I'm tight. And I get all my best stuff from Alice in Wonderland. Since Charley Gordon and I had an apartment together last winter, I suppose I'm a fairy. That probably explains everything." Continuing his diatribe against the New York establishment, Bill says, "My God it would make you sick. They don't talk about complexes anymore. It's bad form. But they all believe it. And every literary bastard in New York never goes to bed at night not knowing but that he'll wake up in the morning and find himself a fairy. There are plenty of real ones too."

/ / /

Critically, it may not matter whether Hemingway's construction of the fictional truth was accurate to the life and letter. But the author, until proven otherwise, is guilty of everything he intimates, imagines, or invents. In *The Sun Also Rises,* Jake, in a moment of spitefulness, confesses, "I have a rotten habit of picturing the bedroom scenes of my friends." Whether this was a personal admission of Hemingway's (one suspects that it might have been; *The Sun Also Rises* is, among other things, a novel about the varieties of bedding down) may not be a critical issue. But the various constructions the author puts upon his experiences from life belong to biography. They are part of the thicket of circumstances that surround any great work of literature.

11

All Things Truly Wicked

FEW THINGS in Hemingway's career astonish more than his abrasive reaction to the publication of the Boni and Liveright edition of *In Our Time* on October 5, 1925. It marked his American debut. A masterpiece by a twenty-six-year-old, barely known writer, it certified his connections with the literary vanguard. The fourteen stories (several of them among Hemingway's best, beginning with "Indian Camp" and ending with "Big Two-Hearted River") were interleaved with the reprinted vignettes from the Paris *in our time* and several new ones. The vignettes and the stories counterpointing one another offered an innovative structure that impressed the critics, as did Hemingway's distinctive declarative style. In fact, with his brusque syntax and the words as crisp as new bills, Hemingway had given the short story a fresh currency. That fact was recognized by nearly all the more perceptive critics. "His language is fibrous and athletic, colloquial and fresh, hard and clean, his very prose seems to have an organic being of its own," the unsigned reviewer in the *New York Times* commented, adding, "He makes each word count three or four ways." "Make no mistake," *Time* magazine claimed, "Ernest Hemingway is somebody; a new, honest, un-'literary' transcriber of life — a Writer." The anonymous reviewer in the *Cleveland Plain Dealer* admitted that the construction of the book "may puzzle the reader for the moment, but its final effect will be satisfying enough to justify its strange method." Singling out the descriptive passages in "Big Two-Hearted River," the reviewer went on to state, "To write like this is to be a supreme artist." According to Mary Plum in the *Chicago Post,* "The characters are alive; they are as honest and human creations as any in fiction. In fact, it seems absurd to speak of this book as fiction or its characters as fictitious. They are too obviously drawn from life." The stories were unusual, brutal, trenchant, and terse, she noted; Hemingway was likely to become "one of the most original and vital short story writers in America." Hemingway was nothing if not autocratic about his reviews: the *Chicago Post* review, he wrote Fitzgerald, "says all of it obviously not fiction but simply descriptive of passages in life of new Chicago author. God what a life I must have led."

He began to regard his affiliation with the vanguard, his reputation in Paris, as a liability. Six months earlier, he had assured Horace Liveright that his book would be praised by the highbrows but readable enough for the lowbrows. Now he was annoyed that critics were too ready to associate his work with that of Stein and Anderson. Herbert J. Seligman, in the *New York Sun,* made a telling point about the structure of the alternating passages: "The flat, even banal declarations in the paragraphs alternating with Mr. Hemingway's longer sketches are a criticism of the conventional dishonesty of literature. Here is neither literary inflation nor elevation, but a passionately bare telling of what happened." In passing, he associated Hemingway with the modernists, Joyce, Stein, and Anderson. Still Seligman claimed there was something lacking that might be chalked up to inexperience: "Varied though his experience, [Hemingway] has not yet the big movement, the rich content of such a book as *Dark Laughter.*"

Paul Rosenfeld's long and appreciative review in *The New Republic* also cited Hemingway's vanguard affinities, claiming that his short stories "belong with cubist painting, Le Sacre du Printemps, and other recent work bringing a feeling of positive forces through primitive modern idiom." There was something of Anderson in the clear medium of Hemingway's style, and, "There is Gertrude Stein equally obvious; her massive volumes, slow power, steady reiterations. . . . Wanting some of the warmth of Anderson and some of the pathos of Gertrude Stein, Hemingway's style nonetheless in its very experimental stage shows the outline of a new, tough, severe and satisfying beauty related equally to the world of machinery and the austerity of the red man." Grace Hemingway sent her son the copy of the Rosenfeld review as well as a recent article on Anderson in *The Atlantic Monthly* by Hemingway's new friend Archibald MacLeish. Hemingway thanked her but commented, "What a lot of Blah Blah that N. Republic review was. Still I'm always glad to read them."

Ernest Walsh, in his review of *In Our Time* in the Autumn-Winter issue of *This Quarter,* expectably praised it highly. "Hemingway," Walsh wrote, "has always been ripe. He began life as a ripe force. . . . There are lines in Hemingway's stories *that come at one reading them as if they had grown in the reader's heart* out of an old memory or an old wish to remember." Hemingway was one of the elect, Walsh claimed. "He belongs." Hemingway, it appears, may have thought the review overripe: "I have to be restrained about yr. review . . . but Christ I thought it was a swell review and I only hope I will be able to write the way you say I write." Whatever Hemingway's brag, he exhibited a certain insecurity about his talents; he was never a man on whom the praise of rivals fell lightly. Still, he would claim, "But the hell of it is that I am not in competition with my contemporaries but with the clock — which keeps ticking."

Scott Fitzgerald's review of *In Our Time* in the May 1926 issue of *Bookman* was that of a friend convinced. It echoed its predecessors in some respects, even saw Hemingway as "an augury" of something better in the "dismal record of high hope and stale failure" that characterized the current literary scene. Fitzgerald, praising the Nick Adams stories in the volume, especially "Big Two-Hearted River," "The Doctor and the Doctor's Wife," "The Three-Day Blow," and "The End of Something," recognized in them something "temperamentally new" in American fiction. He gave his review a resounding finale: "Many of us who have grown weary of admonitions to 'watch this man or that' have felt a sort of renewal of excitement at these stories wherein Ernest Hemingway turns a corner into the street."

///

If one were to trace the beginnings of Hemingway's subsequent break with both Anderson and Stein, it would have to begin with the publication of *In Our Time.* There were no ostensible personal confrontations before that. But Hemingway clearly wanted to put a stop to the repeated comparisons of his work with Anderson's; they would irritate for months, even years. His later break with Stein had a more direct cause. Writing to Ezra Pound about the reception of the book, he complained,

> Le Grand Gertrude Stein warned me when I presented her with a copy not to expect a review as she thought it would be wiser to wait for my novel. What a lot of safe playing kikes. Why not write a review of one book at a time? She is afraid that I might fall on my nose in a novel and if so how terrible it would have been to have said anything about this book no matter how good it may be.

Having delivered that diatribe, he nevertheless propositioned Pound: "You might, if you liked the goddam book, and I think you will because it is pretty good and hard and solid and they are all damning it for being hard-boiled and cold and lacking in verbal beauty and felicity, whatever the hell that is, do something for Eliot's thing." The mention of Eliot and his magazine, *The Criterion,* however, aroused another grievance against Stein: "Eliot doesn't know whether I am any good or not. He came over and asked Gertrude if I were serious and worth publishing and Gertrude said it were best to wait and see — that I am just starting and there wasn't any way of knowing yet." He added, "Oh well, what the hell. I'm not asking you to review it and I won't be sore if you don't." Pound, in fact, begged off reviewing *In Our Time,* apparently on the grounds that he had resolved not to write any more prose of any sort. Hemingway responded, "Naturally I regretted saying anything about reviewing as soon as I had mailed same. I get your point perfectly." The only reason he had asked, he said, was "because you are the only guy who ever told me anything sensible and practical about prose." What had made him so sore when he wrote was that his so-called friends regarded him as something fairly scabrous for having published a book with a so-called regular publisher: "It seems to have been the very worst way I could have betrayed them all. Referring to G. Stein, McAlmon et al."

Hemingway's relationship with his publisher would become another of the casualties associated with the publication of *In Our Time.* Harold Loeb, reporting from the States that his novel *Doodab* had done very poorly, also mentioned that Boni and Liveright wasn't making any great attempt to sell *In Our Time.* Hemingway turned surprisingly philosophical: "Evidently they made up their minds in advance that it was not worth while trying to sell a book of short stories whether anyone wanted to buy it or not. Well one learns, supposedly as one lives." He had finished his novel, he informed Loeb, and was planning to rewrite it and type it out in Austria. (He and Hadley and Bumby would be spending the winter at Schruns.) Hemingway claimed that he was telling everyone he was very satisfied with Boni and Liveright, that they had treated him very decently. "It's up to them to keep me happy though and that means they've got to give *In Our Time* a good ride and that I must have a good advance on the novel." It was a relaxed, affable letter. "They are certainly putting Sherwood over big and will evidently make the boy a lot of money," he added with no apparent rancor. "I suppose it all takes time and that they know what they are doing."

Yet in November, in an abrupt turnabout, Hemingway was planning a carefully engineered campaign for breaking his contract with Boni and Liveright and maneuvering to place his novel with Scribner's. The vehicle was a hastily written satirical novel, *The Torrents of Spring,* which was clearly calculated to cause problems with his publisher, since it was a deliberate parody of Sherwood Anderson. Boni and Liveright had the option on his next three books, one of which had to be a novel. If, however, they turned down the book that Hemingway submitted next, he was free of his obligations to the publisher and could go elsewhere. By November 30, Hemingway was writing Ezra Pound with his plans in full operation. He had written "a funny book" of some 28,000 words in only ten days, he announced. It was a satire on America, he claimed, "Probably unprintable but funny as hell." That he considered it "unprintable" was already evidence enough that he suspected Boni and Liveright would turn it down. His reason for writing was equally evident since he boasted to Pound, "Wrote it to destroy Sherwood and various others. It does all write [*sic*]. It's first really adult thing have done. Jesus Christ it is funny." He promised to send Pound a carbon of the book when it came back from the typist. He spelled out his intentions even more clearly for Pound's benefit: "It is a regular novel only it shows up all the fakes of Anderson, Gertrude, Lewis, Cather, Hergo [Joseph Hergesheimer, a best-selling novelist of the twenties] and all the rest of the pretentious faking bastards . . . I don't see how Sherwood will ever be able to write again. Stuff like Gertrude isn't worth the bother to show up. It's easier simply to quote from it." When Pound read the manuscript, in one of his critical misjudgments, he approved: "I prefer 'Torrents of Spring' to the dying torrero ["The Undefeated"] or to the Old Man."

What Hemingway had written in fact was a lightweight satire about the sparse literary life and the litterateurs in the boondocks of Petoskey, Michigan, and one Scripps O'Neil, a bumbling folksy Anderson-style hero given to vagrant trains of thought: "My wife left me. . . . We'd been out drinking on the railroad tracks. We used to go out evenings and watch the trains pass. I write stories." Scripps promptly marries the elderly waitress at Brown's Beanery, who is given to reading the *Manchester Guardian Weekly* and pondering such imponderables as English politics, the cabinet crises in France, *The Dial, Vanity Fair,* Marianne Moore, E. E. Cummings. ("What was it all about? Where was it taking her?") But just as promptly, Scripps takes up with a younger waitress named Mandy, who has a fund of literary anecdotes that stun him. (With tears in her eyes, Mandy recites the last words of Henry James: "Nurse . . . put out the candle, nurse, and spare my blushes." Scripps is responsive, tells himself, "A chap could go far with a woman like that to help him!")

There was, as well, a subsidiary hero, Yogi Johnson, who thinks of the gay life of Paris. (It is the little "fairy tracings" of frost on the windowpanes of the pump factory which bring such thoughts of Paris to his mind.) Yogi has been a soldier in the war, comes home disaffected with American life and American women. Yogi, too, ponders in the fashion of Anderson's male ponderers, "Was he going to pieces? Was this the end?" Interpolated into the text are sardonic commentaries about the improbabilities of the battle scenes in Anderson's and Willa Cather's novels. There are editorial asides about a lunch with Dos Passos ("whom I consider a very forceful writer, and an exceedingly pleasant fellow besides. This is what is known in the provinces as log-rolling") and a drunken visit from

Fitzgerald: "It was at this point in the story, reader, that Mr. F. Scott Fitzgerald came to our home one afternoon, and after remaining for quite a while suddenly sat down in the fireplace and would not (or was it could not, reader?) get up." For good measure he made a passing swipe at Stein in the title for Part 4, "The Passing of a Great Race and the Making and Marring of Americans." ("Ah, there was a woman! Where were her experiments in words leading her?")

Testing the material, Hemingway read aloud chapters from the book to his friends, Fitzgerald, Dos Passos, the popular novelist Louis Bromfield, whom he had met earlier in Paris. They all declared the book was OK, Hemingway wrote Bill Smith on December 3, stretching the truth. He was planning to fire the manuscript off to Liveright as soon as it was returned from the typist. Fitzgerald, eager to place Hemingway with Scribner's, wrote Max Perkins about the book, "I loved it, but believe it wouldn't be popular." He described it accurately as "almost a vicious parody" on Anderson. Hadley thought the book was detestable and found herself in the awkward position of being a "thoroughgoing wet blanket," particularly since Pauline Pfeiffer considered it terribly funny and was so totally for publication. Hadley was convinced that if it hadn't been for Pauline, Hemingway would not have submitted the book. Dos Passos admitted that he laughed when passages were read to him one autumnal afternoon at the Closerie des Lilas, but he considered it a bad move on Hemingway's part to double-cross an old champion like Anderson, who, after all, had been their friend. He tried to argue Hemingway out of publishing it. It wasn't good enough to stand on its own feet, and besides, *In Our Time* had been so "damn good" Hemingway ought to wait until he had something really good to follow it with. Hemingway claimed that Sherwood was the last person he wanted to hurt, but he turned evasive. "Hem," Dos Passos noted, "had a distracting way of suddenly beginning to hum while he was talking to you."

Hemingway's actions argue that he had worked out the whole scenario in his mind. *The Torrents of Spring* was clearly the means for breaking with Boni and Liveright, and Hemingway's conduct of the campaign, from the moment he sent off the typescript to Boni and Liveright on December 7, 1925, to the publisher's cablegram rejecting the manuscript on December 30, was masterly. His letter to Horace Liveright summoned up the honorable tradition of satire from Henry Fielding's *Joseph Andrews* (a parody of Samuel Richardson's *Pamela*) to Donald Ogden Stewart's recent *A Parody Outline of History.* He asked for a $500 advance, the smallest guarantee, he claimed, that the firm would push the book properly. He outlined his grievances on Boni and Liveright's handling of *In Our Time:* the lack of advertising, the massing of all the blurbs on the front cover, "each one of which would have made, used singly, a valuable piece of publicity but which grouped together as they were simply put the reader on the defensive." (He was right on that count; several later reviewers claimed that it was intimidating.) He told Liveright that he should have asked for a $1000 advance because if they pushed the book as they knew how to, they could have 20,000 in sales. The only reason the firm might have against publication, Hemingway said, "would be fear of offending Sherwood. I do not think that anybody with any stuff can be hurt by satire." Then, with a bit of casuistry, he inadvertently admitted one of his underlying reasons for writing the book: "In any event it should be to your interest to differentiate between Sherwood and myself in the eyes of the public and you might as well have us both under the same roof and get it coming and going." He asked Liveright to cable him at the Hotel Taube in Schruns "at once," as he had other propositions to consider.

Not only did Hemingway take this bold approach to his publisher, but he enlisted the help of two obliging friends, Fitzgerald and Louis Bromfield. Fitzgerald, probably at Hemingway's urging, wrote Liveright a timely letter, encouraging publication of *The Torrents of Spring,* calling it "about the best comic book ever written by an American" and comparing it to *Alice in Wonderland.* "Frankly," Fitzgerald told Liveright, "I hope you won't like it — because I am something of a ballyhoo man for Scribners and I'd some day like to see all my generation (3) that I admire rounded up in the same coop." Around the same time, Hemingway had let it be known to Bromfield that he might be in the market for a new publisher as well. Bromfield wrote his own publisher, Alfred Harcourt, who promptly expressed an interest in the satire and, so Bromfield related to Hemingway, in flattering terms claimed, "We shall try to do the young man as much credit as he'll do us, and that's considerable." Harcourt, Bromfield wrote Hemingway, was also ready to make an advance as soon as Hemingway liked, provided he was free of Liveright.

When Liveright cabled Hemingway on December 30 — "REJECTING TORRENTS OF SPRING. PATIENTLY AWAITING MANUSCRIPT SUN ALSO RISES. WRITING FULLY" — Hemingway immediately sprang into action, writing Fitzgerald in Paris. In a letter dated December 31 to January 1, he admitted, "I have known all along that they could not and would not be able to publish it as it makes a bum out of their present ace and best seller Anderson." Although he claimed he did not have this scheme in mind when he wrote *Torrents,* he noted that *Dark Laughter* was now in its tenth printing. Putting the pressure on Fitzgerald, he quoted Harcourt's offer, assuring him that he had no intention of double-crossing him or Max. "It's up to you how I proceed next," he told Fitzgerald with some urgency; he was jeopardizing his chances with Harcourt by offering it to Scribner's first. It was not the most auspicious time for Fitzgerald. Zelda had been ill that winter, and on a doctor's recommendation they were planning a stay at a sanatorium at Salies-de-Béarn. Hemingway applied both flattery and apologies: "You, however, are an important cog in the show and I hate to ask you to write even one letter when I know you are so busy getting away and all." He told Fitzgerald that he planned to wire Liveright the next morning to send the manuscript for *Torrents* to Don Stewart at the Yale Club. Hemingway had, in fact, even worked out the operation down to the timetable Fitzgerald should follow. "Today is Thursday," he wrote. "You will get this letter on Saturday (perhaps). The mail boats leaving are the President Roosevelt on Tuesday and the Majestic and Paris on Wednesday. Mark your letter via one of the latter 2 ships and it will go fastest. . . . Oh, yes. That reminds me that the advance I want is $500." In a postscript, he noted that he hadn't been able to sleep last night for worrying. He asked Fitzgerald's advice on whether he should go to New York himself. "Then I could be on the spot and could settle things without a six week lapse between every proposition." Fitzgerald, eager to be of service, wired Max Perkins on January 8, "YOU CAN GET HEMINGWAYS FINISHED NOVEL PROVIDED YOU PUBLISH UNPROMISING SATIRE. HARCOURT HAS MADE DEFINITE OFFER. WIRE IMMEDIATELY WITHOUT QUALIFICATIONS." Perkins replied the same day: "PUBLISH NOVEL AT FIFTEEN PERCENT AND ADVANCE IF DESIRED. ALSO SATIRE UNLESS OBJECTIONABLE OTHER THAN FINANCIALLY."

In his letter to Liveright, dated January 19, Hemingway did his best to make an ironclad case for his move. Their contract, he said, clearly stated that if Boni and Liveright turned down his second book, they had no claim on his third: "There can be no doubt on this point." He had submitted the manuscript in good faith, he said. What rankled Hemingway was that Liveright had suggested that none of his editors had approved of *Torrents.* Hemingway's response was caustic: "Your office was also quite enthusiastic about a novel by Harold Loeb called *Doodab* which did not, I believe, prove to be a wow even as a *succes d'estime.*" Publishers, he realized, were not in business for their health. He expected to pay his keep and eventually make a great deal of money for his publisher: "You surely do not expect me to have given a right to Boni and Liveright to reject my books as they appear while sitting back and waiting to cash in on the appearance of a best seller; surely not all this for $200."

II

In Hemingway's life, as in many another, the clues to crucial moves came first — even, perhaps, unsuspected; the necessary rationalizations came later. In the midst of quitting his publisher and cutting himself off from his former mentors, he was also in the process of taking leave of his wife. Was it merely coincidence that in Paris in late November, Hemingway should have been writing about a man, waffling, in the process of leaving one older literary-minded wife for a younger one? In *The Torrents of Spring,* Diana Scripps, waitress, trying to hold on to her husband in competition with a vital and attractive younger woman, has a moment of bitter reflection: "She was no better than a slut, that Mandy. Was that the way to do? Was that the thing to do? Go after another woman's man? Come between man and wife?" Hadley may not have been entertaining such thoughts; but Hemingway certainly was, even if only in a fictional way. The supreme irony, of course, was that Hemingway was reading aloud his little domestic satire for both women.

Yet, in the fall of 1925, the Hemingways' marriage seemed to be on stable ground. That fall, in Paris, Hemingway made the final $100 payment on what was intended to be Hadley's birthday present, Joan Miró's seminal painting *The Farm,* a late example of the artist's hard objective style, a picture of a Spanish farm about which Hemingway, in a loving moment, claimed, "It has in it all that you feel about Spain when you are there and all that you feel when you are away and cannot go there." Hemingway's grand story about the purchase of the painting was that Evan Shipman, who had arranged to buy it for 5000 francs, had eventually said to him, "Hem, you should have 'The Farm.' I do not love anything as much as you care for that picture and you ought to have it." He and Shipman had rolled dice to decide and he had won. Hemingway bragged to Pound about his new acquisition, "Will doubtless be referred to at death as Famous collector, lead adventurous youthful life and at one time wrote several very promising short stories." He had been hoping to get down to Italy for a visit, but the final installment on the painting had ruled that out. He had gone to Chartres instead, he told Pound. Though it seems not to have been altogether true, he bragged that, having just finished his novel, he had "staid drunk for a week getting rested inside and out. Think it is a hell of a fine novel."

Perhaps there was a hint, at least, of Hemingway's straying affections in a Paris letter to Bill Smith. "Pauline and I," he wrote Bill, "killed on a Sunday two bottles of Beaune, a bottle of Chambertin and a bottle of Pommard and with the aid of Dos Passos a quart of Haig in the square bottle and a quart of hot Kirsch." (Hadley, down with the grippe for a week, presumably was not much company.) Hemingway, by then, had already invited Pauline to spend the Christmas vacation with them at Schruns. From Schruns, where he was still recuperating from a sore throat caught in Paris but reading voraciously (Turgenev's *Fathers and Sons* and *A Sportsman's Sketches,* Thomas Mann's *Buddenbrooks;* he had several volumes of Trollope on hand), he kept the MacLeishes and the Fitzgeralds informed on his reading list. *Fathers and Sons,* he told Fitzgerald, "isn't his best stuff by a long way. Some swell stuff in it but it can never be as exciting again as when it was written and that's a hell of a criticism for a book." He told MacLeish, "Turgenev to me is the greatest writer there ever was. . . . War and Peace is the best book I know but imagine what a book it would have been if Turgenev had written it." Writing to Fitzgerald, near Christmas, he sang the praises of his Paris friends: "I think MacLeishes and Murphys are swell. Also Fitzgeralds." Pauline Pfeiffer, he informed Scott, was expected the next day to stay for Christmas and New Year's.

There is little evidence that Hemingway and Pauline openly indulged in an affair during the Christmas holiday at Schruns. In fact it is very improbable, given Hadley's apparent trust and the closeness of the quarters. They skied together (photographs show Hadley and Pauline, each beaming broad smiles, posed with Hemingway; the two women sitting affably together, resting against the ski lodge, smiling like aging sorority sisters). There were the evenings when Hadley played the piano at the inn for Hemingway and Pauline. There was a good deal of drinking. When Pauline returned to Paris, she wrote with noticeable frequency, giving the vacation a somewhat monastic gloss. "Oh my soul, I wish I woz in Schruns," she wrote them in mid-January. "I miss you two men. How I miss you two men!" Another clue? During this period when Hemingway was awaiting word on the fate of *The Torrents of Spring,* he kept up his correspondence with Ernest Walsh. In answer to Walsh's question, he made a declaration of his religious faith that may have been prompted by his growing interest in Pauline. "If I am anything I am a Catholic," he told Walsh. He had had extreme unction administered to him when he was wounded in Italy in 1918, he claimed, "So I guess I'm a super-catholic. . . . It is most certainly the most comfortable religion for anyone soldiering. Am not what is called a 'good catholic'. . . . But cannot imagine taking any other religion at all seriously." In a follow-up letter dated January 2, he elaborated in more sarcastic terms:

> Although I am catolic have never had much admiration for martyrs or Saints. . . . One of the good things about the Church, correct me if I'm wrong, is that they make a definite time limit before we can become Saints. . . . Of course on the other hand it lets in people like Jeanne D'Arc who were the shit of life but developed wonderful publicity organizations after their death.

Hemingway's profession of faith, his recollection of having received extreme unction years before, has been one of the more problematic matters of his life for critics, scholars, and biographers. Certainly it would prove to be convenient a year and a half later when, having divorced Hadley, he was able to marry Pauline. As a Catholic, his previous marriage to Hadley outside the faith was not an obstacle for his marriage to Pauline. The odd feature of his conversion was that it had a bearing upon his fiction. In Chapter 12 of the first manuscript version of *The Sun Also Rises,* Hemingway first designated Bill Gorton as a Catholic, then changed his mind, making Jake a member of the faith instead. But in that first version, Jake is an ineffectual believer who goes to Mass with some regularity, but when Brett, on one occasion, accompanies him to church and wants to hear him go to confession, Jake discourages her. Among the episodes that Hemingway wrote early on, one describes Jake at the Pamplona cathedral, praying for his friends and for himself, though in the latter case he prays for rather venal things like making a lot of money. His thoughts turn to ways of making it. "Then starting to think all that made me not feel very religious any more," he explains as he leaves the cathedral.

In the final revisions, however, after his affair with Pauline had begun, Jake's thoughts after prayer suggest a much more serious change of heart, a sense of *mea culpa:* "I was a little ashamed, and regretted that I was such a rotten Catholic, but realized there was nothing I could do about it, at least for a while, and maybe never, but that anyway it was a grand religion, and I only wished I felt religious and maybe I would the next time."

✓✓✓

Hemingway had decided, after all, on a trip to New York to settle his affairs with Boni and Liveright and to meet with Max Perkins at Scribner's. Pauline, ever helpful, back in Paris, was full of enthusiasm, encouraging Hadley to make the trip with her husband, even suggesting that she would go with him to New York if Hadley did not. She also encouraged Hadley to come to Paris, where, presumably, they might comfort each other while Ernest was away. When she learned that Hemingway alone would be stopping in Paris before taking the *Mauretania* on February 3, she counseled, "I feel he should be warned that I'm going to cling to him like a millstone and old moss, and winter ivy." It may have been what she preferred to do, but during Hemingway's brief stay in Paris, there was little time. Pauline was busy covering the spring fashion shows for *Vogue,* but she and Hemingway did manage to see some art exhibitions and dine together. If Hemingway's account of the affair in *A Moveable Feast* is accurate, it was not until after his return from New York that they had sex together. Writing to Ernest Walsh from Paris on February 1, he claimed that he had "rediscovered" that "The Undefeated," which had appeared in the second issue of *This Quarter,* was a grand story, and he was very proud of it. He was eager to get back to Schruns, he claimed. "I miss Hadley and Bumby terribly and always drink too much when I'm not with them."

The heavy drinking certainly proved to be the case during his New York adventure. (He stayed at the Brevoort in Greenwich Village.) Hemingway had drinks with Horace Liveright, and the two had parted on amicable, first-name terms. His meeting with Max Perkins was cordial and highly successful. Perkins welcomed him warmly, professed to like *The Torrents of Spring,* and offered Hemingway a $1500 advance on the satire and the forthcoming novel, with 15 percent royalties. Perkins, he acknowledged, "wrote an awfully swell contract and was very damned nice." The reception at Scribner's had set him up so well that, in a bravado mood, visiting Alfred Harcourt — whom he liked a great deal, he told Bromfield — he played the bad boy and, after the usual amenities, informed Harcourt that his author Glenway Wescott was fundamentally unsound as a writer.

He met "hells own amount of people" on his New York visit: Robert Benchley and Dorothy Parker (who would be traveling companions on the return voyage); the poet Elinor Wylie, with whom he fell in and out of love. ("Great love at first sight on both sides," he said at the time. Three years later, learning of her death, he referred to her as a "lecherous cat." Wylie, however, remembered that Hemingway was "playing the butcher's boy" when they met.) Hemingway saw the Owen Davis adaptation of *The Great Gatsby,* starring James Rennie and Florence Eldridge, at the Ambassador Theater. ("Would have paid to get out a couple of times but on the whole it is a good play.") It was during this visit that he may have renewed his friendship with John Herrmann and Josephine Herbst (though they were living in New Preston, Connecticut, at the time), and at a party praised E. E. Cummings's *The Enormous Room* in exactly the same terms he had used for Herrmann's novel *What Happens,* wounding both Herrmann and Herbst deeply. Through them, quite probably, Hemingway met the sassy, outspoken, midwestern-born novelist Dawn Powell. Their long-term friendship may have been assured by the fact that they saw each other infrequently. (Hemingway would become the distant Andy Callingham, the internationally known, publicity-seeking, self-involved novelist who makes intermittent appearances in Powell's Manhattan-based novels.) Somehow he managed to visit with his Oak Park friend Isabel Simmons, now married to the classical scholar Francis Godolphin. On his final day in New York, the city he would forever claim he hated, he had late-morning cocktails (three shakersful) at the apartment of the critic Ernest Boyd and his wife, Madeleine, had a bibulous lunch with friends, attended a matinee and then a dinner party at the Hotel Merley, where everyone was as cockeyed as he, was invited by Marc Connelly to attend his play *The Wisdom Tooth* but had to return to the Brevoort to pack. It was understandable that, writing Isabel Godolphin from the *Roosevelt,* three days from Cherbourg, he asked her to please pick up the gold-mounted Waterman fountain pen, large size, that he had left behind in Room 344 at the Brevoort.

In *A Moveable Feast,* Hemingway gives a terse account of the beginning of his affair with Pauline, of how, when he reached Paris, he should have taken the first train to Austria, "But the girl I was in love with was in Paris then, and I did not take the first train, or the second or the third." That was the published version of the episode. But the far more dramatic version was in a deleted clause: "and where we went and what we did, and the unbelievable wrenching, killing happiness, selfishness and treachery of everything we did gave me such a terrible remorse [that] I did not take the first train." When finally he reached Schruns, in the published version, and saw Hadley waiting at the station, "I wished I had died before I ever loved anyone but her." Hadley was smiling, the sun on her tanned face and her hair red-gold in the sunlight, and Bumby was beside her "blond and chunky and with winter cheeks looking like a good Vorarlberg boy." Hemingway's account, with and without the deletions, is as beautiful as the elegant closure of a short story and as vivid as the truth, though it may not have been precisely either. And the lesson of his affair with Pauline, written in his last years when he was more inclined to sacrifice the truth for the greater rewards of fiction, had the heightened verity of cold type: "All things truly wicked start from an innocence."

Life in Schruns after Hemingway's return was not quite so dramatic — or melodramatic. His letter to Max Perkins on March 10 was businesslike and cordial. He had had lunch and dinner with Scott and Zelda in Paris before they left for the Riviera. He was anxious to see proofs of *Torrents,* scheduled for publication in May. He seemed resigned on learning that his story of a crooked boxing match, "Fifty Grand," which Perkins had sent to *Collier's* for him, had been turned down: "It is quite hard in texture and there is no reason for them to take something that is not absolutely what they want." He assured Perkins that *The Sun Also Rises* would be completed by May, in time for fall publication. He had only five more chapters to do over and then would set it aside to gain perspective. He was expecting Dos Passos that night or the next day. He had planned a skiing expedition with Dos and the Gerald Murphys in the higher mountains above Schruns. When he finished with the *Torrents* proofs, he would be returning to Paris and after that he and Hadley were planning to go to Spain and Antibes.

In the passing references of a correspondence, sometimes the bare armature of more complicated situations in a life reveals itself. Yet, nothing in Hemingway's letter to Perkins, nor in his subsequent correspondence with others, hints at the dark fable he would make out of that spring in Schruns, the spring in which he completed *The Sun Also Rises.* Dos Passos would remember it as "the last unalloyed good time" he spent with Hemingway and Hadley. Gerald and Sara had joined them. "Everything was fantastically cheap. We stayed at a lovely old inn with porcelain stoves called the Taube. We ate *forellen im blau* and drank hot kirsch." They made an excursion to the Madelener Haus, where there were roaring fires and hot food. "The people were as nice as they could be. Everybody cried 'Grüss Gott' when they met you. It was like living in an old fashioned Christmas card." Gerald Murphy remembered Hemingway's patience in teaching him and Dos the rudiments of skiing, particularly once when they went through a forest: "Ernest would stop every twenty yards or so to make sure we were alright." When Murphy reached the bottom, Hemingway asked if he had been scared. Murphy said yes, he guessed that he had. Hemingway "said then that he knew what courage was, it was grace under pressure. It was childish of me, but I felt absolutely elated."

It would be a far different story that Hemingway would tell in his last, bitter years. In *A Moveable Feast,* Dos Passos would be the "pilot fish" that had steered the sharks (the Murphys) to Schruns, thereby corrupting him and his work with their wealth. Though Hemingway was twenty-seven and a man far more experienced in the world than most, the picture he painted of himself at the time was totally unconvincing. He and Hadley, it seems, were the proverbial innocents, happy in their love. "Those who attract people by their happiness and their performance," Hemingway moralized, "are usually inexperienced. They do not know how not to be overrun and how to go away." But the Murphys — "the good, the attractive, the charming, the soon-beloved, the generous" — had all the insidiousness of the rich. What made it worse was that they gave each day a festival quality. "Under the charm of these rich I was as trusting and as stupid as a bird dog." He had even read aloud the revised part of his novel, and they had praised it, telling him it was great, truly great: "You cannot know the thing it has." Had he been professional enough, he would have wondered, "If these bastards like it what is wrong with it?" That was how it was at the time, Hemingway claimed. But it was far from what he thought at the time and how he acted.

⁂

Literary affairs: Hemingway was back in Paris when he sent the revised typescript of *The Sun Also Rises* to Max Perkins on April 24. There were plenty of small mistakes for the reader to catch, he said — misspelled words, punctuation, etc. "I want the Mss. back with the proofs." Perkins's response was more than enthusiastic. "'The Sun Also Rises' seems to me a most extraordinary performance," he replied on May 18. "No one could conceive of a book with more life in it." He was especially impressed with the bullfighting scenes and with Jake and Bill's fishing expedition. "You have struck our pet phrase, 'pity and irony,' to death so I can't use it," he added, "but the humor in the book and the satire . . . are marvelous, and not in the least of a literary sort." Apropos the humor, however, there was "one hard point" he felt it necessary to raise: the comic passage referring to Henry James and James's purported bicycle or tricycle accident, which had left him permanently injured and probably impotent. "I swear I do not see how that can be printed." It was not something that could have been published if James were alive (James had died in 1916), and in some ways "it seems almost worse to print it after he is dead." He assured Hemingway that he was not raising the issue because Scribner's was James's publisher. "The matter referred to," as Perkins described in the gingerly fashion that would remain true of his later dealings with Hemingway, "is peculiarly a personal one." But as far as the book as a work of art was concerned, it seemed to Perkins "astonishing, and more so because it involves such an extraordinary range of experience and emotion, all brought together in the most skillful manner . . . I could not express my admiration too strongly."

Despite the high praise, Hemingway's novel was a subject of some debate at Scribner's. The reference to James's accident and more importantly its analogue in Jake Barnes's emasculating war wound and his impotence were matters of concern among the Scribner's editors. Oddly, William C. Brownell, who had vetoed Fitzgerald's first novel, and John Hall Wheelock, both old-timers on the staff, argued for accepting the book. Brownell did not find Jake's condition a problem: "Also the tragedy is real and *impressive* as an incident of war that must often happen and that few have ever thought of as one of war's inevitable horrors." Wheelock, much to Perkins's amazement, felt there was no question whatever but that Scribner's should publish the book. Hemingway may have thought Scribner's acceptance was a sure thing after his New York visit, but Max Perkins's May 27 letter to Charles Scribner reveals there had been second thoughts: "Dear Charley, You wanted to know the decisions on Hemingway: We took it with misgiving." One of the important considerations was that the firm had a reputation among young writers of being ultraconservative, a reputation that would have been confirmed if they declined Hemingway's book and the word got around, as Perkins was sure that it would. "That view of the matter influenced our decision largely," Perkins reported. "I simply thought in the end that the balance was slightly in favor of acceptance, for all the worry and general misery involved." Perkins told Scribner, "But you won't see Hemingway. He's in Spain. Bullfights, I suspect."

Hemingway had, in fact, made plans for his annual tour of the bullfights that season and then for a trip to Antibes for the month of August at the invitation of the Murphys. They had offered the Hemingways the guesthouse at the Villa America. But nothing that spring and summer would be as planned. In late April or May, Hadley, invited by Pauline and Virginia Peiffer on a tour of the Loire Valley, found Pauline snapping at her for unexplained reasons. Jinny, by way of apology, said that her sister had been given to moody spells ever since childhood. When Hadley, intuitively, asked if Ernest was somehow involved, Jinny answered that she thought the two were very fond of each other. Hadley had no inclination to discuss the subject further. But back in Paris, miserable and uncertain, she confronted Hemingway. He turned on her for bringing up the matter. "What he seemed to be saying to me," Hadley remembered, "was that it was my fault for forcing the issue." Hemingway preferred to leave the matter undiscussed, and Hadley, for the time being, left it that way. She had been suffering for weeks with a bad cough, and to make matters worse Bumby had one as well. (Hemingway suspected Bumby had whooping cough.) As late as May 4, when he wrote to Fitzgerald, Hemingway was still planning on the family trip to Spain. Perhaps Hadley had not yet asked the incriminating question. Still, Hemingway told Fitzgerald he was feeling "low as hell," but attributed it to the long spell of rainy weather in Paris. "Haven't seen the Bromfields, Edith Wharton, Comrade Bercovinci [Konrad Bercovici] or any other of the little literary colony for some time," he added. The Murphys had arrived the day before. "I wish to hell you had come up with [the] Murphys — I've not had one man to talk to or bull shit with for months."

In the end, Hemingway made the trip to Spain alone. Perhaps he and Hadley had it out before he left. A week or so after he arrived in Madrid, he wrote Fitzgerald, then in Paris. "You'll be seeing Hadley today," he told Scott, perhaps with a guilty conscience. "Wish the hell I were." He hadn't yet heard from Max Perkins about *The Sun Also Rises* but was hopeful. He had the carbon with him and promised to let Fitzgerald read it when they were together on the Riviera. (Scott and Zelda had rented a villa at Juan-les-Pins for the summer.) But it was to be a summer of interrupted plans, mishaps, and recriminations. Hadley did not join him in Spain, instead went to Cap d'Antibes to stay with the Murphys, presumably to recuperate with Bumby, sunning on the beach. There, at least, she might relax, relieved by the company of the MacLeishes and the Fitzgeralds.

In Madrid, Hemingway was lonesome but busy. It was during this stay in Madrid, he claimed, that he shut himself up in his hotel room and, in one day, wrote two of his more important stories, "The Killers" and "Ten Indians," as well as "Today Is Friday." ("I was in love and the girl was in Bologna and I couldn't sleep anyway, so why not write," he explained years later.) It was from Madrid, before the May 28 publication of *The Torrents of Spring*, that Hemingway wrote a blustering, self-important letter to Sherwood Anderson, explaining how and why he had come to write his satire: "You see I feel that if among ourselves we have to pull our punches, if when a man like yourself who can write very great things writes something that seems to me, (who have never written anything great but am anyway a fellow craftsman) rotten, I ought to tell you so." And it was from Madrid on May 23 that he wrote his father about the forthcoming publication of his two novels and the news that he had just learned from Hadley that she could not join him in Spain that day because Bumby had come down with whooping cough. (The Murphys, concerned about their own children, had called in their doctor and

Bumby had been quarantined.) Hemingway was planning to join Hadley on the Riviera, and when Bumby was well they would return to Spain, he told his father. Hemingway, full of confused and confusing plans, talked up a proposed visit to his parents at Oak Park for two or three days in the fall. Hadley also wanted to visit her relatives in St. Louis, though Hemingway wanted to stay only one day at the most in St. Louis. Then, since he planned to work on a new novel ("and some gents when they are working on a novel may be social assets but I am just about as pleasant to have around as a bear with sore toenails"), he would then go on to Piggott, Arkansas. For his father's benefit he explained the Piggott connection: "Pauline Pfeiffer who was down in Austria with us and is going to Spain this summer lives in Piggott." Pauline was getting them a house there. It was also time for a bit of recrimination. "I heard that you were upset about my wanting to winter at Windemere so decided not to bother you on that score." For his father's benefit (and out of what guilty feelings?), he added, "Having been to mass this morning, I am now due at the bull fight this afternoon. Wish you were along."

⸙ ⸙ ⸙

At the Riviera, life and literary concerns dogged Hemingway. He finally heard good news from Max Perkins. "I was very glad to get your letter and hear that you liked The Sun a.r. Scott claims to too," Hemingway wrote Perkins on June 5 from the Villa Paquita in Juan-les-Pins. (Bumby was still under quarantine, and the Fitzgeralds, finding their villa uncomfortable, offered it to the Hemingways for the remainder of the lease.) Hemingway took issue with Perkins's worries about the Henry James mentions. James was as historical a figure as Byron or Keats or any of the great writers whose lives, personal and literary, had been written about. He didn't have the second part of the manuscript — it was over at Scott's — but the conversation between Bill Gorton and Jake Barnes about James was intended to be a humorous talking around the subject of Jake's mutilation. "Scott said he saw nothing off-color about it."

Fitzgerald, however, did have a great deal else to say about the novel, and in an interminably long and detailed written critique complained about the "sneers, superiorities, and nose-thumbings-at-nothing" that he encountered in his reading. He also felt that Hemingway hadn't made Jake's impotence dramatic enough: "I felt the lack of some crazy torturing tentativeness or insecurity — horror, all at once, that she'd feel — and he'd feel." Barnes wasn't like an impotent man, Fitzgerald said. He was a man "*in a sort of moral chastity belt.*" One of Scott's more useful criticisms was that in the important opening pages of the book Hemingway spent too much time filling in the biographies of his characters and that that whole section of the book ought to be cut. It was an indication of Hemingway's insecurity in the important matter of his first serious novel that he was willing to take Fitzgerald's advice and his somewhat condescending praise. ("But remember this is a new departure for you," Scott wrote him, "and that I think your stuff is great.") Writing to Perkins, Hemingway alerted him to the fact that he intended to cut the opening section of the book in proof (though he made it seem that it was his own idea: "Scott agrees with me," he said).

Perkins, sending the proofs of *The Sun Also Rises,* disagreed: readers not used to Hemingway's style might find such biographical information helpful. "But you write like yourself only, and I shall not attempt criticism. I couldn't with confidence." What worried him more was Hemingway's references to real people: "*I* know who Roger Prescott [Glenway Wescott] is quite well. . . . Why not call him Prentiss. You don't want to harm him." A mention of Hilaire Belloc, though admittedly harmless, might still be a problem: "An Englishman will actually sue for libel on the slightest provocation." Perkins suggested that Hemingway disguise the name in some way. Then there was the question of what Perkins delicately referred to as "a particular adjunct [the "balls"] of the Bulls referred to a number of times by Mike." Wouldn't it be better not to spell it out but to use a blank? ("The bulls now without appendages," Hemingway wrote in an answering letter.) Perkins was still fussing about the Henry James matter. He knew Hemingway felt that James was a historical character, "But in truth, this town and Boston are full of people who knew him and who cannot regard him as you do. There are four right in this office who were his friends, two his close friends." In the end, the Henry James of the unfortunate accident was reduced to just Henry, whom Bill conceded was a good writer. Perkins's cautionary letter was prompted by his conviction that Hemingway's bold language would divert attention from the intrinsic quality of the book by starting up the "howls of a lot of cheap, prurient, moronic yappers." Hemingway perhaps didn't appreciate the possibilities because he had been too long abroad. Nevertheless, Perkins was conciliatory; he recommended doing nothing that "would *really harm* the text in this matter of words, but I urge reducing so far as you rightly can the profanity, etc."

It was an uneasy summer. The good fortune of his career at the moment was being eroded by other, more personal concerns, the pleasures of the Riviera spoiled by Hadley's unhappiness, Bumby's illness. When the Murphys threw a welcoming party for Hemingway at the Casino with champagne and caviar, Fitzgerald, jealous, made disparaging remarks about the affectation of the affair. Gerald had walked out, disgusted by Scott's behavior. Throughout the summer, drinking heavily, Fitzgerald made a persistent nuisance of himself at the Murphys' parties — throwing Sara's favorite Venetian glasses over the garden wall, getting into a brawl with Archie MacLeish. The Murphys banished him for a period of two or three weeks. For Hadley, the most difficult part of that summer was the arrival of Pauline in advance of the proposed trip to Pamplona. Pauline stayed with them at the Villa Paquita. "Here it was," Hadley remembered, "that the three breakfast trays, three wet bathing suits on the line, three bicycles were to be found. Pauline tried to teach me to dive, but I was not a success. Ernest wanted us to play bridge but I found it hard to concentrate." Unhappy days.

Nor was it better in Spain, where Gerald and Sara accompanied the three of them to the fiesta. Pamplona marked the end of a year of irreversible changes. They stayed, as the custom was, at the Hotel Quintana; they were photographed, as Hemingway and Hadley had been only the year before, sitting at table in a sidewalk café, perhaps the same one. But this time, the cast was not the cast of *The Sun Also Rises*. Sara and "Dow-Dow" (Hemingway despised Sara's nickname for her husband) sit prim and well dressed. Hadley, who had had a relaxed and beaming smile the year before, can summon up only the barest one this time. Only Hemingway, wearing a beret, a tie, and tweedy jacket (perhaps a more expensive one), looks much the same. Pauline, center stage, manages a weary grin. The expressions of the three bootblacks in the foreground are positively feral.

Pictures of life seldom conform to the shapes and shades of the private unhappiness of others. What did the Murphys remember of the *feria*? Gerald recalled the sight of the matadors in their rooms at the Quintana, waiting for the hour of the corrida, stretched out on their beds, surrounded by flowers and candles, staring at the statues of their saints — a funerary glimpse. He remembered the night Hemingway put the crowd up to challenging Sara and him to do the "*Dansa Charleston*" and how they danced in the floodlights to a jazz band. At the first corrida, Sara had left in disgust at the sight of the broken-down horses being gored by the bulls but returned the following day.

The Murphys left with Pauline, who was taking the train to Paris while they returned to the Villa America. Pauline, writing to Hemingway and Hadley from Paris in the phrases of the dissatisfied wife in Hemingway's "Cat in the Rain," chanted, "I'm going to get a bicycle and ride in the bois. I am going to get a saddle too. I am going to get everything I want. Please write to me. That means YOU, Hadley." It was not until Hemingway and Hadley stopped at the Villa America on their way to Paris that the Murphys learned that they intended to separate. The Murphys were generous and sympathetic, though Sara privately thought Hadley had been terribly mistaken in bringing up the affair to Hemingway. Gerald offered Hemingway the use of his Paris studio at 69 rue Froidevaux. And on their stopover in Paris before returning to America, Gerald deposited $400 in Hemingway's bank account. He and Sara acted on the hunch, Gerald wrote, "that when life gets bumpy, you get through to the truth sooner if you are not hand-tied by the lack of a little money. I preferred not to ask you, so Sara said, 'Deposit it, and talk about it after.'"

The Murphys' generosity proved costly. In his last years, in one of the paranoid moods that destroyed the probity of the art he had so painstakingly created as a young man, Hemingway found it convenient to blame the Murphys for his desertion of Hadley and his marriage to Pauline. In a murderous passage deleted from the published version of *A Moveable Feast,* he wrote that the Murphys "collected people then as some collect pictures and others breed horses and they only backed me in every ruthless and evil decision that I made . . . I had hated these rich because they had backed me and encouraged me when I was doing wrong." With at least a glimmer of the youthful integrity that made him the writer he was, he conceded, "But how could they know it was wrong and had to turn out badly when they had never known all the circumstances? It was not their fault. It was only their fault for coming into other people's lives. They were bad luck for people."

III

After the publication of *The Sun Also Rises* on October 22, 1926, there was no longer any question that Hemingway was an American writer to be reckoned with. The major reviews were highly favorable. The critic for the *New York Times Book Review* claimed that no amount of analysis could convey the quality of the book: "It is a truly gripping story, told in a lean, hard athletic narrative prose that puts more literary English to shame." Conrad Aiken in the *New York Herald Tribune* praised the dialogue as brilliant: "If there is better dialogue being written today I do not know where to find it." In *The Atlantic,* Bruce Barton noted that Hemingway "writes as if he had never read anybody's writing, as if he had fashioned the art of writing himself." It was true, Barton admitted, that Hemingway's people were immoral, drank too much, had no religion or ideals (that would be a familiar critical demurrer in many of the reviews), but, he asserted, "they have courage and friendship, and mental honestness. And they are *alive.* Amazingly real and alive." Hemingway's recent acquaintance Ernest Boyd, in the *Independent,* found the technique "fascinating." When the reader was not swept along by the astonishing dialogue — "subtle, obvious, profound, and commonplace — but always alive" — there was the careful enumeration of little facts "whose cumulative effect is to give them the importance of remarkable incidents."

Even the adverse criticism gave Hemingway's book the status of importance and seriousness. Alan Tate, writing in *The Nation,* argued that Hemingway's novel was successful but at some cost to "the integrity achieved in his first book" (*In Our Time*). Rather ingeniously, Tate claimed that Hemingway's "hard-boiled" style disguised a characteristic sentimentality, which did not show up in the shorter form of his stories and vignettes but had been laid bare in the longer form of a novel. "It is not that Mr. Hemingway is, in the term which he uses in fine contempt for the big word, hard-boiled; it is that he is not hard-boiled enough in the artistic sense." The reviewer for the *Chicago Daily Tribune,* in the sensitive territory near Oak Park, was angered by the book, not because of the "utterly degraded people" of the story, but because Hemingway's book showed such "immense skill." Hemingway could be a distinguished writer. "He is, even in this book, but it is a distinction hidden under a bushel of sensationalism and triviality."

Having drawn upon the expatriate life of Paris as the subject of his novel, Hemingway inevitably found himself caught up in more personal consequences of publication. Kitty Cannell, when she read the book, was so angry, "I took to my bed for three days." At the Dôme, people came up to her and asked, "Did you really shake Harold down for 2000 bucks?" After that, whenever she saw Hemingway, she looked right past his ear "with perfect detachment." Hemingway, writing to Fitzgerald, claimed that it was rumored that Loeb was out to shoot him, so he had put out the word that he could be found unarmed sitting at Lipp's brasserie. "No bullets whistled." He also told Scott he had run into Duff in a bar and that she wasn't sore at all, "said the only thing was she never had slept with the bloody bull fighter." Bill Smith wrote to congratulate him, "You certainly wrote out a nice book." But wasn't he worried that Loeb would slip poison into his aperitif one day? "You doan leave the lad precisely untouched." The reviews he had read, Bill added, gave Hemingway "a nice play," and he had heard the book had gone into a second printing. By mid-December the sales of the book had reached 7000, according to Max Perkins. He had ordered a second and third printing, expecting the book to do well into the spring. What irked Hemingway, however, was that having used Gertrude Stein's pronouncement "You are all a lost generation" as an epigraph, he had, in the critics' minds, become the spokesman for the expatriates, a prophet if not an apologist for the Lost Generation. He now did his best to dissociate himself from the epithet. He had intended, ironically, to "play off against that splendid bombast (Gertrude's assumption of prophetic roles.) Nobody knows about the generation that follows them and certainly has no right to judge." He didn't mean the book to be a hollow or bitter satire, he told Perkins, "but a damn tragedy with the earth abiding for ever as the hero."

Grace Hemingway wrote her son in far stronger moral terms than the reviewer for the *Tribune.* She was glad to see that *The Sun Also Rises* was a success, but it seemed a doubtful honor to have produced "one of the filthiest books of the year." Surely he knew other words besides *damn* and *bitch.* It was the standard litany of high-mindedness with which she had often tried to rescue her son. She wondered if he was having domestic problems or if drink had "got" him. "I love you dear," she assured him, "and still believe you will do something worthwhile to live after you." Clarence wrote him in gentler terms, "You surely are now famous as a writer and I shall trust your future books will have a different sort of subject matter. You have such wonderful ability and we want to be able to read and ask others to enjoy your works."

Among his other private irritations with the reception of the book was the critical review by Dos Passos in the *New Masses.* He acknowledged that the book was well written. "I mean that anywhere I open it and read a few sentences they seem very good; it is only after reading a page that the bottom begins to drop out." Dos Passos, much involved at the time with issues like the Sacco and Vanzetti case and dissatisfied with American writing in general, took the preferred *New Masses* line. He scored the decadence of the characters in the book. "What's the matter with American writing anyway?" he asked. "The few unsad young men of this lost generation will have to look for another way of finding themselves than the one indicated here."

What ought to have caused a serious rift between them was somehow averted. Dos sent Hemingway a carbon copy of the review and a letter of apology. "I've written a damn priggish mealymouthed view of it that makes me sick. The book makes me sick anyway, besides making me very anxious to see you, and homesick for good drinks and woodcock and Pamplona and bullfights and all that sort of thing." He was clearly in a depressed frame of mind. "I feel thoroughly sore about everything. Everything I write seems to be crap and everything everybody I like writes seems to be crap. They're going to kill Sacco and Vanzetti . . . and everything is inexpressibly shitty." Remarkably, Hemingway took Dos Passos's review very calmly. Writing to Perkins, he claimed, "I think it was fine about his not liking the book and wanting it to be better, but a poor criticism that Pamplona in the book wasn't as good as Pamplona in real life."

What did arouse his anger to an exceptional degree was a belated review of *The Torrents of Spring* by Ernest Walsh, which had appeared in the October 1926 issue of the *New Masses.* Headlined "The Cheapest Book I Ever Read," Walsh vilified Hemingway's satirical thrusts at Sherwood Anderson and Ford Madox Ford, both of whom had praised his talents and helped to further his career. "The fact that Mr. Hemingway meant it to be cheap doesn't make it funny. Or readable." For a writer as intelligent and self-aware as Hemingway, there could be "no such excuse as stupidity or innocence" for producing a book like *The Torrents of Spring.* A practiced opportunist himself, Walsh had cudgeled Hemingway in highly knowledgeable fashion, even to a sarcastic reference to the medals Hemingway had received for his service during the late war, in which, Walsh noted, a number of Italian citizens had also participated: "It is not from Mr. Hemingway that we learn about the assistance he received from the number of Italian citizens." Walsh's review, certainly, was enough to have earned Hemingway's enmity for a long lifetime except for the fact that Walsh, hemorrhaging severely, died of tuberculosis in Italy in the same month that his review was published.

Ezra Pound, who was thinking of starting a literary magazine of his own (*Exile*), became the unwitting recipient of Hemingway's frustrated anger. He was not sorry that Walsh was dead, Hemingway told Pound in one of his letters, "Except in the sense of being sorry for anybody dead. And I have known too many good guys die to be able to sweat much from the eyes about the death of a shit." In the pages of Pound's magazine, Hemingway suggested, they might include an insulting list of his peeves: "ALL FAIRIES. The dead Mr. Walsh. The living Carnevali." Pound attempted to maintain his own views in the continuing spate of Hemingway's mentions of the dead publisher and poet. "I am sorry Mr. Walsh is dead," Pound wrote Hemingway, referring to the fact that no obituary of Walsh had appeared in the Paris edition of the *Herald Tribune,* "an he shudn't have writ that article about you, but that's no reason for a little goat turd like Moss, to keep a two inch obit out of the Herald. Wot te hell, the paper's there to print the news."

IV

In late August, back from Italy, they had decided to live apart, Hemingway taking Gerald Murphy's studio at the rue Froidevaux and Hadley, at first, putting up at the Hôtel Beauvoir. Eventually, she found an apartment at 35 rue de Fleurus, not far from Gertrude Stein and Alice Toklas. The more important condition that Hadley imposed, the one that proved most difficult, was her requirement that Hemingway and Pauline agree to a separation period of one hundred days. After that, if they were still certain about their feelings for each other, she would agree to a divorce. Pauline, though apprehensive about the separation, returned to the States, planning to wait out the three months with her family in Piggott. She was equally apprehensive about the response of her family, particularly her mother. In New York, where she stopped for a week, she saw the Murphys and Robert Benchley. She was already counting the days. (Dos Passos, who had seen Pauline in New York with the Murphys, wrote Hemingway that he wanted to knock Hemingway's and Hadley's heads together, but he also admitted that Pauline was "an awfully nice girl." So "Why don't you get to be a Mormon?" he asked.) In Piggott, Pauline told her mother. Mary Pfeiffer felt terrible and immediately asked, "And how does she feel?" meaning Hadley. She advised Pauline not to mention the matter anymore and not to tell her father until later, thereby making the situation easier — and worse. In Piggott, Pauline settled into a siege of remorse over Hadley. She wrote Hemingway about her guilty feelings: "Ernest and Pfeiffer, who tried to be so swell (and who were swell) didn't give Hadley a chance. We were so . . . scared we might loose [*sic*] each other — at least I was — that Hadley got locked out."

Hemingway, for his part, tried to keep busy with work; amazingly, he managed to complete three or four major stories during the separation period. But he was tormented by doubts about whether Pauline would be able to hold firm under the pressure of her mother's disapproval and her own guilty feelings. In mid-November, there was a period of two or more weeks when he didn't hear from her. In the meantime, her sister, Jinny, who was in Paris, had heard from home that Pauline had gone to pieces because of nerves. He wrote Pauline what he admitted was "a lousy terribly cheap self-pitying letter just wallowing in bathos etc. etc. etc." All that he could think now, he wrote her, was "that you that are all I have and that I love more than all that is and have given up everything for and betrayed everything for and killed off everything for are being destroyed and your nerves and your spirit broken . . . and that I can't do anything about it because you won't let me." It seemed to him that Pauline had given herself and her heart as hostage to her mother and the whole thing was absolutely hopeless. He had been having thoughts of suicide, he told her. (In his confused letter it was not clear whether he was referring to similar thoughts he had had the winter before when they were, the three of them, at Schruns, and he had vowed he would kill himself if the situation wasn't cleared up by Christmas but then promised that he wouldn't.) "But now it is getting all out of control again." He was not a saint, he said, nor built like one, and "I'd rather die now while there is still something left of the world than to go on and have every part of it flattened out and destroyed and made hollow before I die." But he wouldn't, he promised again. "And all I want is you Pfife and oh dear god I want you so. And I'm ashamed of this letter and I hate it."

Only a few days later, on November 16, Hadley wrote him from Chartres, where she had gone off alone to think over her situation. (Hemingway had agreed to take care of Bumby.) By then she had decided "The entire problem belongs to you two — I am *not* responsible for your future welfare — it is in your hands and those of God (a pretty good scout and a *swell* friend.)" She no longer would hold them to their three-month separation. She now felt free to seek a divorce, but asked Hemingway to get valid information about the legalities. "Please for the sake of peace and on account of Bumbie put all discussion and arrangements of these matters into letters unless of course it is something that can be said in a few words and need not involve a quarrel."

With the perverse awkwardness of all human relationships, Hemingway had managed to see Hadley before receiving her letter and the two had had an uncomfortable meeting going over the situation. On November 18 he wrote her a letter, apologizing for making her go through again everything that she had painfully spelled out in her letter. With relief and generosity, he told her, "I think your letter like everything that you have ever done is very brave and altogether unselfish and generous." He had realized only in the last week — "and the horror of it was very great" — how he and Pauline had been pressuring her to divorce him, "a pressure that came from a sort of hurried panic fear that we should lose one another," a reaction that Hadley must have regarded with suspicion or looked upon as a poor basis for two people to marry on. He was instructing Scribner's, he told her, to turn over all the royalties for *The Sun Also Rises* to her. "Will you please just take it as a gift without any protestations or bitterness," he told her, "because it is really your right and due and it would make [me] terribly happy if instead you would be very generous and take it as a gift." But somehow in his relief about Hadley's agreeing to the divorce, he was confused about whether he was allowed to write Pauline that the waiting period was over.

Hadley, replying the next day, was a bit ruffled: "Haven't I yet made it quite plain that I *want* to start proceedings for a divorce from you — right away. Thus the three months separation between you and Pauline is nil as far as I am concerned." She needed to think out the money considerations, but the gift of the royalties from *The Sun Also Rises* was very acceptable. "I can't see a reason just now why I should refuse it." She would send him a list of things, including furniture, she wanted from the old apartment. For the two of them, there remained that proof of the end of something, the settling of the bills: "You paid out 300 francs to Marie and 80 something for gas — (can't find bill at moment) and I gave you 200 for coal." She was enclosing what seemed somewhere near the difference. "Eat well, sleep well, keep well and work well," Hadley said.

The final act of closing out their marriage, the transfer of Hadley's possessions and some of the household goods to the new apartment on the rue de Fleurus (including the Richardson family silver that had been given them as a wedding present, Hadley's favorite Dresden china, and Miró's *The Farm*) was difficult. Hemingway's penance consisted of several long trips with a handcart, at the end of which, so Hadley recalled, he was "weeping down the street and I know he was very sorry for himself." She felt sorry for him as well.

A few days later, Hemingway wrote Scott Fitzgerald at Juan-les-Pins on the state of his affairs. He had had a grand spell of working, he said, had sold two stories to *Scribner's* and written two more that he couldn't sell but which would be suitable for a book. Hadley, he announced, was divorcing him. Starting off life anew poorer than he had ever been since the age of fourteen was interesting. "Anyway I'm now all through with the general bumping off phase and will only bump off now under certain special circumstances which I don't think will arise. Have refrained from any half turnings on of the gas or slitting of the wrists with sterilized safety razor blades. Am continuing my life in original role of son of a bitch sans peur et sans rapproche" — an interesting slip of the French tongue, using the word for reconciliation instead of the intended *reproche* (reproach). Both Hadley and Bumby were well, he told Fitzgerald. He had had

Bumby for ten days while Hadley was away on her trip to Chartres. One morning he had taken the boy to a café for a *glace*. Bumby, holding the new harmonica his father had bought him and eating his ice cream, had commented, "La vie est beau avec papa."

⸙ ⸙ ⸙

While Hadley was filing for a divorce in Paris, Hemingway, on Christmas night, was on a train for Switzerland. He, Pauline, Jinny, and the MacLeishes began the New Year skiing in Gstaad. For a month or more Hemingway had been staving off his parents' queries. Having learned the knack of implication by omission, he implied that Bumby was still living with his parents in a comfortable, well-heated apartment, stressing the fact that the studio on the rue Froidevaux, which they knew about, was merely for work. Unfortunately, in Oak Park, the Loomises, the family's neighbors there and at Walloon Lake, had been circulating stories; Clarence was anxious to settle them. "The gossip is about a serious domestic trouble," Clarence wrote Hemingway in mid-December. "Please write to me the truth so I can deny the awful rumors that you and Hadley have had a break. I cannot believe a word of such gossip until I hear from you direct."

Hemingway, however, still angry over his mother's remarks about *The Sun Also Rises,* put off writing until early in February, when Grace, who had taken up painting, sent him the catalogue for an exhibition of paintings at Marshall Field, the department store, in which her picture of Jim Dilworth's blacksmith shop at Horton Bay had been reproduced. Hemingway explained to Grace, "I did not answer when you wrote about the Sun etc. book as I could not help being angry and it is very foolish to write angry letters; and more than foolish to do so to one's mother." He understood that the book might be unpleasant, "But it is not *all* unpleasant and I am sure is no more unpleasant than the real inner lives of some of our best Oak Park families." He was clearly not inclined to give any quarter. "Besides," he added — it was one of his more insidious points — "you, as an artist, know that a writer should not be forced to defend his choice of subject but should be criticized on how he has treated that subject."

Even then, he was evasive about his divorce and made no mention of Pauline. He wrote his parents that he and Hadley had been separated since September and that by now — the time of his letter, February 5 — "Hadley may have divorced me." (On March 11, the *New York Times* carried a page 2 report that Hadley had been granted a divorce from Hemingway on the grounds of desertion.) They were, however, still the best of friends, he told his parents. Hadley,

Hemingway wrote, would be traveling in the States with Bumby and was planning to visit them in Oak Park. He was writing them now because he knew they were worried. He had "been leading a very monastic life" and trying to write as well as he was able. He had never been a drunk or a steady drinker. ("You will hear legends that I am — they are tacked on everyone that ever wrote about people who drink.") All he wanted was tranquillity and a chance to write. He finally delivered himself of his real quarrel with Grace. "Dad has been very loyal and while you, mother, have not been loyal at all. I absolutely understand that it is because you believe you owed it to yourself to correct me in a path which seemed to you disastrous. So maybe we can drop that all." It was not until several months later that Hemingway told them the details, and only after Clarence had written him a pathetic letter about how grieved they were at the idea of a divorce. "Our family has never had such an incident before and trust you may still make your get-away from that individual who split your home. Oh Ernest, how could you leave Hadley and Bumby? . . . Put on the arrows of God and shun evil companions."

Hemingway answered with the necessary sympathy and the necessary lies. His father had been fortunate, having been in love with one woman all his life. He still loved Hadley; "I did not desert her nor was I committing adultery with anyone." But for over a year he had been "in love with two people and had been absolutely faithful to Hadley." Clarence in one of his letters had expressed an angry wish that all "Love Pirates" were in hell. (He had picked up the term from Sunny.) Hemingway offered a tempered reply: "I have seen, suffered and been through enough so that I do not wish anyone in Hell." He was writing them now because he did not want them to suffer any feelings of shame and disgrace. But Hemingway was ready still to put the blame for his silence on Grace. "The reason I haven't made either of you a confidant was because I was so upset about Mother accusing me of pandering to the lowest tastes etc. in my writing that I shut up like a hermit crab." He would write them often, he said, "if we can lay off of literary criticism and personalities."

12

The Master of Indirection

In that winter of discontent, Hemingway was also arranging to take his leave of Sherwood Anderson and Gertrude Stein. The break with Anderson had begun, in truth, with his Madrid letter giving his reasons for publishing *The Torrents of Spring*. Anderson, responding, complained about Hemingway's patronizing tone: "You always do speak to me like a master to a pupil. It must be Paris — the literary life. You didn't seem like that when I knew you." He also called Hemingway on his remark about not pulling punches between friends, interpreting it as a passing threat. "Come out of it man. I pack a little wallop myself. I've been middle weight champion. You seem to forget that." Anderson tried to put a good face on Hemingway's satire. "Tell the truth I think the Scribner book will help me and hurt you. Spite of all you say it's got the smarty tinge. You know it." Hemingway answered that Anderson was probably right: "the book will do you good (publicity) and I am sure it will hurt me with a lot of people." Nonetheless, Hemingway claimed, he had had a grand time writing it in only six days. He thought it was funny and he had gotten $500 for it, compared to the $200 advance for *In Our Time*. Anderson, mindful of the meager amount, just about half the $300 difference, he had gotten for *Winesburg, Ohio*, commented, "They're a swell lot, the publishers and the reading public." Still, he was disposed to turn a compliment Hemingway's way: "What I always felt in you is a sense of vitality — the ability to take it. Most so-called artists haven't enough juice to get through the first few years."

Hemingway and Anderson would meet in Paris at the end of the year. Anderson, traveling with his third wife, Elizabeth Prall, and his son John, was in a funky, self-pitying mood, suffering from a prolonged writer's block. Irritable, keeping to his room, drinking by himself, he begged off from a party given in his honor by Gertrude Stein, and a dinner with Joyce, pleading a bad case of the flu. Anderson's report of his meeting with Hemingway in his memoir is brisk: Hemingway, one day, showed up at his hotel suggesting they go out for a beer. No sooner had they been served than Hemingway lifted up his glass, said, "Well, here's how," drank it down, then turned and walked hurriedly away.

Hemingway's account of their meeting, one more addition to the fugue of misconstructions that evolve out of any factual incident, is more extended. Hemingway wrote Max Perkins that he and Anderson had spent two fine afternoons together. They had discussed the *New Masses* and its editors; Anderson had spoken fondly of *Scribner's* magazine and the $750 fee he had received for his short story "Another Wife," which had appeared in the December issue. "He was not at all sore about Torrents," Hemingway assured Perkins, "and we had a fine time." Yet, in a cryptic report on his Paris visit, Anderson wrote dejectedly, "Sherwood Anderson — / A man's name. / You hearing it around. / Presently a kind of deep sickness . . . / Hemingway made a damn fool by it; Joyce, too. I saw it popping in them both. / I am Joyce. / I am Hemingway. / Christ!"

Gertrude Stein, in *The Autobiography of Alice B. Toklas,* would give a reasonably accurate accounting of the implications, if not the substance, of Hemingway's patronizing letter to Anderson, presumably having heard about it from Anderson himself:

> Hemingway had at one moment, when he had repudiated Sherwood Anderson and all his works, written him a letter in the name of american literature which he, Hemingway, in company with his contemporaries was about to save, telling Sherwood just what he, Hemingway, thought about Sherwood's work, and, that thinking, was in no sense complimentary.

But her conclusions were wide of the mark: "When Sherwood came to Paris, Hemingway naturally was afraid. Sherwood as naturally was not." That Hemingway would have been afraid of Anderson seems unlikely; embarrassed, perhaps, ashamed of his behavior, more likely.

The break between Hemingway and Stein had a different, undetermined etiology. In the loose chronology of her "autobiography," Stein does not acknowledge any specific quarrel, notes only that, at a party, Hemingway had "explained" his reasons for not being able to review *The Making of Americans,* which McAlmon had published in the fall of 1925 and that at some point following that — presumably after the publication of *Torrents* or Hemingway's break with Anderson — she and Hemingway did not see one another for some years. Whenever Hemingway was in Paris, Stein noted that when she went out for a walk, Alice would admonish her, "Don't you come back with Hemingway on your arm." But of course she did, and they resumed their talks. It was then that she accused him of having "killed a great many of his rivals and put them under the sod." Hemingway denied it.

For months, and then for years, Hemingway fired a barrage of insults in letters and in public print. But the serious rift did not come, as he would have it, after the publication of *Torrents,* when Stein broke with him because he "had attacked someone that was a part of her apparatus." Nor did it occur for the unlikely reason that one day when he was at the rue de Fleurus, he had overheard, from upstairs, a humiliating, lesbian quarrel between Alice and Gertrude in which Gertrude had so abased herself in his eyes that he could no longer stand listening to it. That was the way it ended for him, he maintained, "stupidly enough, although I still did the small jobs, made the necessary appearances, brought people that were asked for and waited dismissal with most of the other men friends when that epoch came and the new friends moved in."

Among the Hemingway papers, there is a thin trail of slighting remarks, explaining how, if never quite why, he had broken with Stein, some written around 1925 and 1926 during his first spell of disaffection, and others perhaps roughed out in the late 1950s when he was working up the sketches for *A Moveable Feast.* An early bit of doggerel proclaims, "Gertrude Stein was never crazy / Gertrude Stein was very lazy." In the fall of 1926, Hemingway sent *Scribner's* a heavy-handed satirical piece titled "My Own Life," suggesting that if the magazine was not interested, Perkins might turn it over to Edmund Wilson at *The New Republic.* A parody version of Frank Harris's autobiography, *My Life and Loves,* it purported to tell how Hemingway had broken with a number of mentors and friends, including Gertrude: "Miss Stein was always charming. 'Hemingway, why do you always come here drunk?' she asked me one afternoon. 'I don't know, Miss Stein,' I answered, 'Unless it's to see you.' 'All you young men are alike,' Miss Stein said." On one of his visits he finds a padlock on the door and a sign reading, "KEEP OUT. THIS MEANS YOU." It was then that he had broken with Stein, he said, adding drolly, "Needless to say I have never ceased to regret it."

Stein's name, at the time, was also on his list of possible insultees for the pages of Pound's *Exile.* But Hemingway reconsidered: "I would be glad to insult Gertrude Stein but would prefer to do it through a more widely circulated medium," he wrote Pound at just about the time he was sending "My Own Life" to Perkins. Pound was responsive: "Somewhat contented to see from yr. hand script, that Gertie Stein is losing her hold on what we used a few years ago to call 'the younger generation.' Does this come under caption: Personality tells."

⁊⁊⁊

Early in March, Hemingway was again in Gstaad with Pauline and Jinny. This time he brought along Bumby for a ten-day visit. Pauline looked after the boy while Hemingway went off on his daytime ski runs. (Bumby, an inquisitive child, had taken to calling her "Paulinose" because Hemingway's answer to all his questions was "Pauline knows.") Pauline, who had written Hemingway during their separation, "I am going to look out for you and after you and I won't have anything else to do but try to please you," fell readily, if not altogether willingly, into the role of the dedicated housewife even before the marriage. In spite of his recent bout of misery because they were separated, and in spite of his vow that he would never return to Italy while Mussolini was in power, Hemingway, as early as February, began making plans for a tour of Fascist Italy with Guy Hickok. "Hickok and I are demarring in H's motor propelled vehicle for Rimini and San Marino on or abt. March 20. Should encounter enroute or at Milan or way back or at Rapallo," Hemingway wrote Pound. He planned to be back in Paris by April 4. (Pauline, accurately, referred to the trip as the "Italian tour for the promotion of masculine society." It was a repeat performance of the male-rites-before-marriage trip, like the fishing expedition he took with his friends before his wedding with Hadley.) After Hemingway's departure from Paris with Hickok, Pauline was left with the task of finding an apartment. With the help of Jinny and Ada MacLeish, she located one at 6 rue Férou, near the Church of St. Sulpice and the Luxembourg Gardens. Newly painted, it had a large bedroom, a salon and dining room, a good kitchen, as well as a separate study for Hemingway. It was also left up to Pauline and Jinny to make the arrangements for the wedding ceremony.

In late March, in Hickok's battered Ford coupe, the two travelers crossed the border into Italy at Ventimiglia, traveling down the Riviera to Genoa. At Rapallo, Hemingway had a fortuitous meeting with the Italian priest Giuseppe Bianchi, who had purportedly baptized him in 1918. (According to one scholar, he may have obtained a "sworn declaration of fact" that he had been converted, thus nullifying his marriage to Hadley.) In a village twenty kilometers above La Spezia, a self-assured young Fascist, disdainful of foreigners, commandeered a ride down to the seaport, standing on the running board, looping his right arm inside the car. "That's a young man who will go a long way in Italy," Hemingway told Guy. In one of the more curious feats of his career, Hemingway described the young man in sardonic terms in an article, "Italy, 1927," first published as a straight journalistic account in *The New Republic* (May 18, 1927) and five months later as a short story, retitled "Che Ti Dice la Patria?" abolishing the boundary line between nonfiction and fiction by fiat. Both as reportage and as fiction, it is an effective piece of writing. Whether the itinerary and the events of his ten-day tour of Mussolini's Italy followed exactly the course described in the article, from Ventimiglia to Pisa, Florence, across the Romagna to Rimini, and back up through Forli, Imola, Bologna, Genoa, and Ventimiglia again, is questionable. (A postcard to Pound from Rimini — "Forli last night. Gave your card to Sigismundo [Malatesta] and the Elephant. Heading North. Visited San Marino today. Tea-ed with Minister of foreign affairs" — suggests that Hemingway had taken some literary liberties with the routing.)

But in the three vignettes that made up the article or story, Hemingway gave a chilling portrait of the new Fascist society. In the comic second sketch, the two men dine in a restaurant — presumably a bordello before Mussolini abolished prostitution. A chummy whore assaults the uncomfortable Guy Hickok with her obvious charms, and a young man with pomaded hair, apparently the establishment pimp, tells her, "Listen . . . let them go. These two are worth nothing." In the final sketch, driving along the coast from Ventimiglia to the French border, a surly Fascist policeman with a revolver fines them twenty-five lire for traveling with a dirty license plate, then, in what was obviously a well-practiced bit of extortion, ups the fine to fifty lire when they complain about the dirty state of the roads in Italy. The entire piece can be read as Hemingway's reply to the propaganda effort claiming that Mussolini had restored order and efficiency in Italy. Little wonder that when he and Hickok reached Menton, across the French border, Hemingway would describe it as "very cheerful and clean and sane and lovely." The final irony of Hemingway's travelogue is, perhaps, predictable, but effective. "The whole trip had taken ten days," Hemingway remarks in answer to the title question. "Naturally, in such a short trip, we had no opportunity to see how things were with the country or the people."

Hemingway's marriage to Pauline Pfeiffer took place on May 10, 1927, in Paris at L'Église de St.-Honoré-d'Eylau on the place Victor-Hugo, in the fashionable sixteenth arrondissement. Jinny was Pauline's attendant; Ada MacLeish, who did not believe Hemingway's story of his baptism as a Catholic and resented the implication that his marriage to Hadley was invalid, nevertheless gave the couple a small luncheon. Hemingway and Pauline honeymooned at Grau-du-Roi, an unpretentious village at the mouth of the Rhône. Writing to Max Perkins, he praised the landscape: "This is a fine place below Aigues Mortes on the Camargue and the Mediterranean with a long beach and a fine fishing port. . . . Am healthy and working well and it ought to be a good summer." With his letter, Hemingway sent Perkins two stories he had been working on, the first, "Ten Indians," begun nearly two years earlier at Chartres but for which he now found the satisfactory conclusion: Nick Adams's resigned acceptance of his broken heart and Prudy Mitchell's infidelity. The other story quite probably was "Hills Like White Elephants."

Every story has a basis in the writer's life, and "Hills Like White Elephants" may have had its inception around the time that Hemingway wrote to Fitzgerald on March 31, telling him about his relief that Pauline had returned to Paris: "I've been in love with her for so damned long that it certainly is fine to see a little something of her." On the letter, Hemingway had written the sentence "We sat at a table in the shade of the station," and then explained, "This is the start of something or other." Revised, it would crop up in the first paragraph of his story. In the story, a young American woman named Jig and her rather selfish and worried boyfriend are waiting at a train station for the express from Barcelona which will take them to Madrid. The title of the story and the prevailing image is that of the distant line of hills, white in the sunlight. "They look like white elephants," Jig says. Her boyfriend is moody, coercive, trying by one argument or another to convince her to have an abortion. By the end of the story, after the verbal sparring ("Doesn't it mean anything to you? [she asks.] We could get along." "Of course it does. But I don't want anybody but you. I don't want anyone else. And I know it's perfectly simple"), the boyfriend seems to have succeeded, though the outcome is not altogether conclusive. It is a classic, understated Hemingway story of the failure of communication between the sexes. But one of the oddities is that he should have written a story about abortion when he was on the verge of marrying Pauline, of "converting" to the Catholic faith to do so. Odd, too, that it may have reflected his feelings when he suspected, in Spain — the setting of the story — that Hadley was pregnant a second time. And even more odd that on his manuscript copy of the story he should write the enigmatic note "Mss. for Pauline — well, well, well." Another oddity is that in the earliest manuscript fragment relating to the story, written in 1925, it is Hemingway who remarks to Hadley, "*Look* at those god-dam white mountains," and Hadley answers, "They are the most mysterious things I have ever seen."

Hemingway's divorce from Hadley and his marriage to Pauline and the convergence — a man, for a time, with two women in his life — would have a long reach into his fictional life. The honeymoon at Grau-du-Roi would provide the setting for the newlywed couple David and Catherine Bourne in the posthumously published version of Hemingway's uncompleted novel, *The Garden of Eden* (1986). Hemingway, as if transcribing the ultimate male fantasy, would give an idyllic account of the lovemaking, the nude bathing, the eating, and fishing of the early phases in the marriage of his young American couple, the husband a writer, author of a successful novel, his wife an attractive, exciting, and wealthy young woman. "He had many problems when he married but he had thought of none of them here nor of writing nor of anything but being with this girl whom he loved and was married to and he did not have the sudden deadly clarity that had always come after intercourse." And Catherine Bourne would have the additional virtue of leading her husband into a destructive but erotic maze of gender transmutations and sexual experiments and a highly sensual ménage à trois with another attractive young woman named Marita. But it would be nineteen years before Hemingway would begin to ring his fictional changes on that fantasy.

Another series of manuscript pages — attempts perhaps at another novel dealing with the experience — relates the story of James Allen, a failed writer turned failed painter, and/or Philip Haines, a writer, both of Paris, and in the process of divorcing his wife of five years to marry a young woman named Dorothy Rogers, a friend of his wife. In both versions of the tale, Dorothy, like Pauline, has returned to the States to wait out the divorce from the wife, Harriet, leaving the man to suffer through the experience. In both versions of the tale, the man is a writer of "delicate things on the fantastical side," thus clearly differentiating him from Hemingway's clean-cut declarative style. In what may have been a fantasy wish — or revenge — on Hemingway's part, James Allen sleeps with his wife during the interim of their separation. It is an odd and telling encounter but one which Hemingway seems to have intended to cut from the story. Hemingway describes the scene with the obsessional detail that signifies something more than mere necessary description. The bed is set low on the floor with no head or foot to it. "In the daytime there was some sort of a Persian figured cover that he had never understood properly." (In the mind of a writer, every item is warehoused for future use: in their apartment on the rue du Cardinal-Lemoine, the Hemingways had had "a new Bagdad bed cover.") It is raining, the large French windows are open, and the rain makes a pool on the waxed floor. "He saw the upthrust curve of her chin and her arms held him always too tight; his own weight lightly removed by elbows. There was no change." James Allen wakes with "a hollow feeling of unfaithfulness" for having had sex with his estranged wife. Otherwise, the details of the separation follow the pattern of Hemingway's own unhappy months of waiting to divorce Hadley. Even the geography pertains: James Allen, separated from Harriet, takes a studio off the avenue du Maine. (Gerald Murphy's studio on the rue Froidevaux was off the avenue du Maine.) Philip Haines's first realization of his love for Dorothy Rogers occurs following one of her visits to the apartment where he and his wife live. One night, as usual, he walks Dorothy to the corner of the rue d'Assas to catch a cab. He puts his arm around her and kisses her "and she kissed him there on the sidewalk in the dark and he told her that he loved her." (The Hemingways' apartment, during Pauline's visits, was of course on the rue Notre-Dame-des-Champs, around the corner from the rue d'Assas.) In the early phases of a manuscript, Hemingway kept to the streets of actuality.

⁂

Back in Paris, he was invalided for a week or more by an anthrax infection he had picked up at Grau-du-Roi, after cutting his foot on rocks while swimming. But it did not interfere with his plans for another summer in Spain. As usual, he planned to attend the *feria* of San Fermín in Pamplona early in July. This time, he and Pauline were joined by a new friend, the bearded and blustery Maine painter Waldo Peirce, a man full of gusto, whom Hemingway immediately took a liking to. (Peirce had served with the ambulance service in France during the war.) In Pamplona, the two made a vivid picture in the midst of the revelry. One of Hemingway's recent acquaintances, Harry Crosby, staying at the Hotel Perla with his wife, Caresse, caught a glimpse of the pair which he recorded in one of the run-on entries in his Lost Generation diary. Crosby had spent a night of absinthe-drinking and wandering the rain-wet streets (with a visit to a bordello, where six women were selling for five pesetas each, and thirty men were clamoring for them; he did not partake), then somehow managed to find his way back to his hotel and his wife. The next morning, breakfasting in the bright sunlight at a café: "eggs and beer cold beer in tall glasses (later on cold absinthe in tall glasses) and Hemingway of the Sun Also Rises drove past in a carriage and shouted at us and Waldo Peirce was with him looking like Walt Whitman and everyone began rushing off for the Bullfight (one last round of absinthe)."

Hemingway had met the Crosbys just before New Year's in St.

Moritz, where he and MacLeish and Crosby talked shop and did some heavy drinking in the "hof bar": "And they both think Cocteau is an ass and so do I and all three of us despise the English. . . . And we drank. And H. could drink us under the table." That spring, in Paris, they met again at Ada MacLeish's concert in the Conservatoire and Hemingway had introduced Crosby and his wife to James Joyce. Hemingway and Crosby would never be close friends; they went once to the circus together and drank with the Spanish clowns, and afterward Hemingway brought him and his wife back to the rue Férou to meet Pauline. (The truth was that Hemingway disapproved of Crosby's wealth and ready dissipation, and, in moments of self-righteousness, he despised him.) But it was a useful literary relationship; the widowed Caresse would later publish editions of *In Our Time* and *The Torrents of Spring* under her Black Sun imprint.

In Valencia, Hemingway wrote Waldo Peirce, back in Paris, thanking him for a set of drawings he had made for Bumby and apologizing for the fact that the Spanish trip had cost more than Peirce had planned on. In August, he said, they planned to move on to Madrid and then La Coruña and Bilbao. The heat was sweltering. He also wrote Bill Smith, acknowledging that his one appearance in the bullring, even with the bull's horns blunted, was not a success. The whole season had gone sour, Belmonte had been badly gored, and Marcial Lalanda as well. Niño de la Palma, a bridegroom of a week, was also wounded. From Santiago de Compostela, on August 31, Hemingway wrote Max Perkins, advising him that he had mailed the corrected galley proofs for the new collection of stories first-class registered mail. "It was very hard convincing them in the post office that there was anything in the world worth that many Spanish stamps." And in mid-September, from Hendaye, France, where he and Pauline were spending the last of their honeymoon trip, Hemingway wrote Scott Fitzgerald, thanking him for the loan of a hundred dollars. He would pay it back as soon as his "new monumental work" came out, not later than October, he hoped. He told Fitzgerald that he had had some difficulty deciding on a title for his new collection of stories — even the Bible had failed him, "So I called the book Men Without Women hoping it would have a large sale among fairies and old Vassar Girls."

II

A divorce; a wedding; the nagging persistence of the literary life. Whatever his frame of mind at the time of his separation from Hadley, Hemingway kept interested parties — Max Perkins, Scott

Fitzgerald, Archibald MacLeish — informed as to his capacity for work in hard times. It was in December 1926 that he had first informed Max Perkins that a collection of stories should be the next order of business — "and I think it's very important that it should be awfully good." If *The Sun Also Rises* proved to be a success, "there will be a lot of people with the knife out very eager to see me slipping." Of his recent stories, *Scribner's* magazine elected to publish "The Killers" in its March 1927 issue and "In Another Country" and "A Canary for One" the following month. His typewriter was broken, and he was using a borrowed one with so many problems he had to keep his mind on the "malignancy of the machine" and hadn't been able to rewrite one of the new stories he intended to send. In a letter to Pound, Hemingway boasted, "Scribner's don't know it but am going to make them publish old Up in Michigan story with the fucking in it. If they won't I won't publish book at all." (Ironically, he would himself drop it, perhaps because it did not fit his schema for the book.) Pound, picking up on the idea of a book of stories, was dictatorial: "Now, mong cher ami. You will do no such GOD DAMND thing. You will publish ANOTHER NOVEL next, and *after* that, and NOT UNTIL AFTER THAT you will make them pub. the sht. stories. Wotter yer think yer are, a bloomink DILLY-tanty ?????"

Hemingway did not take Pound's advice. In February, from Gstaad, he sent Perkins a list of proposed stories, including those that would be appearing in *Scribner's* magazine, along with "Fifty Grand," which was being circulated to other magazines, and "An Alpine Idyll," which Pound was considering but felt needed fixing up because it was too "licherary." Hemingway listed his long bullfight story, "The Undefeated," and included two that he had just finished, "A Pursuit Race" and "A Simple Enquiry." The first he described as "about the advance man for a burlesque show who is caught up by the show in Kansas City." And the other he said was "a little story about the war in Italy." In both cases, he played down the nature of the stories. Yet the first was about a dope addict who had run to ground and was beyond reclamation, the other about a homosexual Italian officer who half-heartedly attempts to seduce his orderly. "Banal Story," another of the proposed stories, had appeared in *The Little Review* the year before, though in an abridged version. (Jane Heap, with Hemingway's permission, had deleted the Rabelaisian instances of the narrator's farting while reading *The Forum.*) Its virtue, in Hemingway's eyes, was that Edmund Wilson had thought highly of it when it appeared in the magazine. Hemingway took the time to explain the significance of the title of the collection: "In all of these, almost, the softening feminine influence through training, discipline, death or other causes, being absent." He was, at the same time, planning a book about bullfighting that would not be just a history or textbook or an apologia but would have a certain permanent value itself.

Men Without Women, published in October 1927, was at best a piecemeal collection of stories, not the structured work nor the masterpiece that *In Our Time* was. There were fine and important stories among the fourteen collected in the volume, some of them certified masterpieces: "The Undefeated," "Hills Like White Elephants" and "In Another Country." The last story dealt with the war and relationships with women. An unnamed young wounded American is undergoing physical therapy in a Milan hospital. He has established a kind of camaraderie with other wounded and even badly disfigured young Italian officers who each afternoon have their therapy session in the new wing of the hospital. There is an element of political duress in Hemingway's story which binds the men even more closely together. Passing through the city's Communist quarters on the way back from their sessions, they are subjected to the insults of working-class citizens shouting at them, "*A basso gli ufficiali!*" ("Down with officers," a popular antiwar taunt at the time).

The young American has a girlfriend and plans to be married. He is taken up by an embittered Italian major, who, before the war, had been the country's greatest fencer and now is also undergoing physical therapy for a badly damaged right hand. (The major does not believe in the efficacy of the new machines or the therapy; he thinks it an idiotic idea, calls it "a theory, like another.") His young wife is ill. When the American mentions that he hopes to marry, the major, unaccountably, lashes out at him: "The more of a fool you are. . . . A man must not marry. . . . If he is to lose everything, he should not place himself in a position to lose that." His wife dies suddenly of pneumonia, and the major, a difficult, off-putting person, apologizes for his rudeness. He breaks down, devastated, repeating, "I am utterly unable to resign myself," revealing the vulnerability of the human condition.

The title of the story was derived from Marlowe's *The Jew of Malta* — "Thou hast committed / Fornication: but that was in another country, / And besides, the wench is dead" — though it is probable that Hemingway picked it up from the epigraph to T. S. Eliot's "Portrait of a Lady." The title alone, in the way of all mysterious and devious literary connections, offers a whole cabinet of curious allusions, probable false alarms and possible clues to the life of "old Hemingstein," who *had* committed fornication with Pauline, was about to lose his first wife, was having second thoughts about marrying a second time — and to the younger Hemingway who, in another country, probably had not committed fornication but wished he had, with Agnes von Kurowsky, who, in her betrayal, had mentioned in her letters to Hemingway a thirty-year-old Italian major of the Alpini with a paralyzed right arm who had been in the hospital for forty months of his five-year service.

Equally important to the collection was the story "Now I Lay Me," in which Nick Adams, recuperating from his wounds, fearful that his soul might leave his body if he falls asleep, whiles away the hours recalling the streams he has fished in boyhood and his mother's callous, perhaps vindictive, burning of his father's Indian artifacts and medical specimens. Hemingway, at one point, had considered naming the story "In Another Country-II." He had begun it, too, in the woebegone period when he was separated from Pauline and, perhaps (though the timing of the early manuscripts and false starts may not be definitively right), when he was bitter over his mother's letter with its burning rejection of his writing. Still, in one of the early drafts, Nick's mother (read: the author's) makes one of the slips that reveals the glaring connection between literature and the life that fashioned it: "I've been cleaning out the basement, dear," Mrs. Adams calls to her husband, "and [Ernie's] Nicky's helped me burn the things." That Hemingway wrote his story of the wounded Nick Adams and his sleepless nights and dire thoughts of death, repeating his prayers ("on those nights I was cold-awake and said my prayers over and over and tried to pray for all the people I had ever known") during the time he was tormented by worries over his affair with Pauline suggests his state of mind at the time. "You lie all night half funny in the head," he wrote Pauline then, "and pray and pray and pray you won't go crazy. And I can't believe it does any good and I do believe it does hell's own amount of harm." He was not, he assured her, "a depressed rat naturally."

Hemingway would give this story an ironic twist — perhaps too ironic, since in the end, he did not place it directly following "In Another Country" but as the final story in the collection. In "Now I Lay Me," Nick's Italian-American orderly is convinced that Nick, who is not married, should get married. "A man ought to be married," he tells him, in direct contradiction to the Italian major. "You'll never regret it. Every man ought to be married." But Hemingway's ironies, often enough, cut both ways. The orderly's marriage is pretty routine, and his advice that Nick should marry a nice Italian girl with plenty of money is crass. As a writer, particularly as a writer of short stories, Hemingway eschewed easy answers. In all Hemingway stories, the reader has to make a commitment, considering the weight and importance of each sentence as carefully as if he were alone in a wood, listening for every rustling in the underbrush, making note of the repetitions as if they were footfalls, nearing.

Though Hemingway's caustic remark that the title of the collection was intended to be a lure for fairies and old Vassar girls was a joke, it did characterize the nature of several of the stories. Not that the female presence was absent from the stories — that was hardly the case — but so many of the stories involving women were about failed relationships or marriages, and others, like "A Pursuit Race" and "A Simple Enquiry," touched on the theme of homosexuality. The minor stories in the collection were "An Alpine Idyll," "Banal Story," and "Today Is Friday," a playlet about three Roman soldiers on the day of the crucifixion: *First Soldier* — "I tell you, he was pretty good in there today."

ɤɤɤ

The more timid critics of *Men Without Women* deplored the people and the subjects Hemingway wrote about. Lee Wilson Dodd in the *Saturday Review of Literature* claimed, "The people he observes with fascinated fixation and then makes live before us are . . . all very much alike: bull-fighters, bruisers, touts, gunmen, professional soldiers, prostitutes, hard drinkers, dope-fiends." And Joseph Wood Krutch in *The Nation* lamented the spiritual weariness of the work: "In his hands the subject-matter of literature becomes sordid little catastrophes in the lives of very vulgar people." In general, the favorable reviews pointed out the distinctiveness of Hemingway's style. The unnamed reviewer in *The New Yorker* pronounced the collection "a truly magnificent work . . . I do not know where a greater collection of stories can be found . . . Hemingway has an unerring sense of selection." Percy Hutchinson in the *New York Times Book Review* declared that Hemingway had carried the art of the reporter to the highest degree. His facts might be gathered from experience or compounded solely from the imagination, "but he so presents them that they stand out with all the clearness and sharpness (and also the coldness) of pinnacles of ice in clear frosty air. To sum up in a figure, Hemingway's is a stark naked style."

English reviewers were less kind. Cyril Connolly in the *New Statesman* offered a summary judgment that the book was "a collection of grim little stories told in admirable colloquial dialogue with no point, no moral and no ornamentation." But the English reviewer who would rankle Hemingway most was Virginia Woolf in a lengthy front-page essay in the *New York Herald Tribune Books* section. It was as much a discourse on the practice of book reviewing as it was a review of *Men Without Women.* Woolf took up the issue of Hemingway's reputation as an "advanced" writer and then, using *The Sun Also Rises* as evidence, proceeded to dismantle it, having decided that "this rumor of modernity must have sprung from his subject matter and from his treatment of it rather than from any fundamental novelty in his conception of the art of fiction." With the perceptiveness of a major writer, she fixed on one of the climactic moments in Hemingway's novel, the account of Pedro Romero in the bullring, and using Hemingway's own metaphor, delivered, first, some stinted praise: "Mr. Hemingway's writing, one might paraphrase, gives us now and then a real emotion, because he keeps absolute purity of line in his movements and lets the horns (which are truth, fact, reality) pass him close each time." But then she delivered the fatal blow. There was something wrong with Hemingway's people: compared to Chekhov's people they were as flat as cardboard; compared to Maupassant's they were as crude as photographs; compared to real people, they were of an unreal type.

> They are the people one may have seen showing off at some cafe, talking a rapid high-pitched slang; because slang is the speech of the herd; seemingly much at their ease, and yet if we look at them a little from the shadow not at their ease at all. . . . So it would seem that the thing that is faked is character; Mr. Hemingway leans against the flanks of that particular bull after the horns have passed.

It takes a major writer to do such a job on another major writer. And Woolf, reacting to the blustering masculinity of the writer and the title of his book, proved that she could handle the sword and muleta as well as any man. She did him the honor of placing him in what would be considered distinguished company, though not necessarily so distinguished to the Bloomsbury mind:

> Thus Mr. Lawrence, Mr. Douglas and Mr. Joyce partly spoil their books for women readers by their display of self-conscious virility; and Mr. Hemingway, but much less violently, follows suit. All we can do, whether we are men or women is to admit the influence, look the fact in the face and so hope to stare it out of countenance.

Hemingway's talent, she conceded, might develop along other lines. "It may broaden and fill out; it may take a little more time and going into things — human beings in particular — rather more deeply." Her review, one of the little masterpieces of the reviewing trade, noted his gifts and failures. Woolf complained, for instance, about Hemingway's overuse of dialogue — a danger, she felt, for a writer, since the reader had to supply the intonations. In one of the neater sallies, she turned Hemingway's prose against him: "At last we are inclined to cry out with the little girl in Hills Like White Elephants, 'Would you please please please please please please please stop talking?'"

> Mr. Hemingway, then, is courageous; he is candid; he is highly skilled; he plants words precisely where he wishes; he has moments of bare and nervous beauty; he is modern in manner but not in vision; he is self-consciously virile; his talent has contracted rather than expanded; compared with his novel his stories are a little dry and sterile. So we sum him up.

But, as she had the good grace to acknowledge, her summing up also revealed "some of the prejudices, the instincts and the fallacies out of which what it pleases us to call criticism is made."

It would take another major writer, Edmund Wilson, reviewing *Men Without Women* in the December 14 issue of *The New Republic,* to redress the balance. Wilson felt that Hemingway had received very little intelligent criticism. Critics like Dodd, "with his usual gentle trepidation in the presence of contemporary vitality," and Krutch, who contended that Hemingway dealt with very vulgar people, had missed the mark. In what way, Wilson asked, could the fate of Hemingway's bullfighter in "The Undefeated" be called "a sordid little catastrophe"? It was true, Wilson noted, that "A Pursuit Race" was a story about a dope fiend, but what was more important was that it was "a story about a man who has just lost a desperate moral struggle." The story was given more point by the fact that the manager of the burlesque show, understanding that the struggle has been lost, leaves without waking him up. And while "A Simple Enquiry" was "a glimpse of one aspect of army life: that strange demoralization that may bring with it a kind of stoicism," the significance of the incident lay in the fact "that the major refrains from dismissing the boy who has just refused his advances." What Wilson detected in such tales was one of Hemingway's absolute gifts as a writer, "his masterly relevance in indirection." For what happens in the corners of Hemingway's stories — the orderly's Italian wife in "Now I Lay Me," who doesn't read English but cuts out the editorials and the sports pages to send to her husband; the insolent waiters in a restaurant remarking about the bullfighters ("Look at that bunch of camels," one of them says) — serves as counterpoint or confirmation for what is taking place at the center of the story. And the implication, in the stories, always, is that there is a larger, implacable life that extends beyond the frame. In his review, Wilson went on record:

> It would appear, then, that Hemingway's world is not quite so rudimentary as Mr. Krutch or Mr. Dodd represents it . . . I do not say

> that the world that Mr. Hemingway depicts is not, on the whole, a bad world; it *is* a bad world, and a world where much is suffered. Mr. Hemingway's feelings about this world, his criticism of what goes on in it, are, for all his misleadingly simple and matter-of-fact style, rather subtle and complicated.

⁊⁊⁊

After publication, the regrets, recriminations — the rationalizations. "The Virginia Woolf review was damned irritating," Hemingway wrote Max Perkins. He chalked it up to the Bloomsbury crowd living for their "Literary Reputations" and believing that the best way to keep them up was to slur off or impugn the honesty of anyone coming up. "Well God be with them though I would have enjoyed taking the clothes off Virginia Woolf this noon and permitting her to walk down the Avenue de l'Opera letting every one, truth, reality, whatever she liked — pass close each time." He asked Perkins to hold off on the clippings for a while; he was working hard and the damned things "are irritating and make you self conscious."

He made the same complaint in a letter to Fitzgerald, noting that "friends" would send him 2000 copies of any review that said the book was "a pile of shit." He was rabid on the subject of Burton Rascoe, who in his review in the *Bookman,* "hadn't read a damn thing in the book but knew it contained 50 G and so reviewed it on that alone and dismissed the unread stories with a few well placed kisses on Miss Wescott's sphincter muscle." He was happy to report, however, that the book had sold seven thousand–plus and that on the proceeds he and Pauline were planning to spend a week at the six-day bicycle races in Berlin as well as see his German publishers and drink a little beer.

For a writer, each story has its history of acceptance and rejection. Fitzgerald wrote Hemingway that Zelda had liked the book better than anything he had written and that "Hills Like White Elephants" was her favorite. Fitzgerald's was "Now I Lay Me." The story about the Indians, however, had left him cold. He was glad, too, that Hemingway had left out "Up in Michigan," saying, "They probably belong to an earlier and almost exhausted vein."

Hemingway admitted that he hadn't liked "Ten Indians" either and wouldn't have published it except that Scribner's wanted enough for a book. "Did like White Elephants and In Another Country — I suppose that last is a swashbuckling affectation too." He was working on a new novel, Hemingway said, and had about 50,000 words done on it, but what with the "bloody damned reviews" coming in and a case of the piles he was all knocked to hell on working.

Archibald MacLeish, who had read several of the stories in manuscript form, claimed that "A Pursuit Race" took him all wrong: "I thought the first paragraph sounded like a parody of your stuff & had nothing honest to do with the story. And I thought the story itself missed fire by that narrow fraction of an inch which is the difference between failure & success in work as close to the bone as yours." On the other hand, MacLeish was full of praise for "A Simple Enquiry": "I think it's in your real manner, a fine, cool, clean piece of work, sure as leather, & hard and swell." For good measure, he added a marginal commentary: "Ten things 'said' for every word written. Full of sound like a coiled shell. Overtones like the bells at Chartres. All that stuff you can't describe but only do — & only you can do it." Whatever the public response to his work, Hemingway had definitely reached an audience of his peers.

III

For Hemingway, accidents seemed to become a way of life. At Montreux that winter, he picked up Bumby one night to put him on the potty, and the boy, putting his hand up, cut his father in the eye with his fingernail. Altogether unromantic, Hemingway described it, but it troubled him for weeks. The local doctor gave him a cocaine wash to relieve the pain. During his "blind spell," he wrote Pound, Pauline read aloud Henry James's *The Awkward Age.* "It sounds like the most puerile drool. Leave me know. My impression is that he knew NOTHING about people." In Paris, in mid-March, going to the toilet at two A.M., he mistakenly yanked the chain for the skylight instead of the flush box; the skylight fell, giving him a severe gash on the head. Pauline, six months pregnant, anxiously tried to stanch the bleeding with thirty thicknesses of toilet paper and a makeshift tourniquet made of a dish towel and a stick. With the help of Archibald MacLeish, Hemingway managed to get to the American Hospital at Neuilly in a cab. There, it took nine stitches to sew up the wound, which left a permanent scar. "How the hellsufferin tomcats did you git drunk enough to fall upwards thru the blithering skylight!!!!!!!!" Pound wrote him. Hadley, having learned of the accident, wrote him with more sympathy, "You poor dear old thing! What rotten, rotten luck . . . I expect you are both a bit discouraged about how life *is* one damn thing after another."

As Hemingway explained to Perkins in a March 17 letter, he had been held up on the novel he had been working on. Variously titled *A New-Slain Knight* or *Jimmy Breen,* it was intended to be a modern version of *Tom Jones,* and although Hemingway had already done twenty-two chapters, he had put it aside. (The young protagonist of the never-completed novel, twelve-year-old Jimmy Breen (or on occasion, Crane) is on his way from Michigan to Paris with his father, where they plan to meet his mother. Although Jimmy's father shares some of Clarence's puritanical views on kissing and masturbation, he is vastly different in other respects, a revolutionist and a heavy drinker. Oddly, Hemingway would also speak of it as his Oak Park novel.) He well knew, Hemingway assured Perkins, that Scott, who was struggling with a new novel, ought to have published his a year or two ago. He would not fall into that kind of alibi-making himself. "But this next book *has* to be good. The thing for me to do is write. But it may be better not to publish until I get the right one."

He was beginning to have serious doubts about the subject. "There is a *very very* good chance that I don't know enough to write that yet and whatever success I have had has been through writing what I know about." In the meantime, he had begun a second novel that had started first as a story but now seemed more promising. "I should have gone to America two years ago when I planned. I was through with Europe and needed to go to America before I could write the book that happened there." He was more confident about his second option; he was now, suddenly, getting "a great kick out of the war and all the things and places and it has been going very well."

Late in March 1928, he and Pauline, who wanted to have her baby in the States, sailed from La Rochelle aboard the RMS *Orita* for Havana and there transferred for a boat to Key West. Although Hemingway supposed that he was unable to write his American novel abroad, ironically, he was no more successful with it after he returned home. It remained abandoned after twenty-two chapters. But caught up in his enthusiasm for his second project, he had few troubles in settling down to work on a novel (*A Farewell to Arms*) about two lovers in wartime Italy. But those troubles would be serious.

✓✓✓

It may well have been John Dos Passos who had told Hemingway about Key West. Dos Passos had first visited it in 1924 during a walking tour through Florida. Key West was then a coaling station with a busy harbor and not a tourist attraction. Life moved at a relaxed pace, nonetheless, with one or two drowsy stopover hotels for passengers on their way to Cuba or the Caribbean. The frame houses and shady streets had a vague New England look. There were few automobiles because there was, then, no highway to the mainland, only the single-track railroad on the viaduct. There was a creditable Spanish and Cuban population considering that it was linked by car ferries to Havana. Dos Passos admired the Cuban cigar rollers, "interesting people to talk to, well informed and often surprisingly well read," who hired someone to read to them from the Socialist newspapers or Spanish novels, as they worked at their long tables in the cigar factories. The larger population was English-speaking: railroad men and mainlanders from Florida, descendants of New England whaling fishermen, and the local Conchs. "Nobody seemed ever to have heard of game laws or prohibition."

Hemingway and Pauline, since they planned to stay six weeks or more, took an apartment on Simonton Street. It was not long before Hemingway met the regulars who would form his circle of Key West friends. Chief among them were Lorine and Charles Thompson, whose family constituted much of the local business: a hardware store, fish house, ship's chandlery, cigar box factory, and tackle shop. Charles Thompson, about Hemingway's age, was a devoted sportsman and fisherman and would become a longtime friend and persistent competitor. (Strangely, in letters to others, Hemingway, always fluent with chummy nicknames, would never refer to Thompson as anything other than the formal Charles.)

And Hemingway soon found the saloon that would become his home away from home during his years at Key West, Sloppy Joe's on Green Street, a dark cave with a bar and a picture of Custer's last stand above it. The proprietor was Josie Russell, whose fast cabin cruiser, the *Anita,* routinely used for rum-running trips between Cuba and the Keys, Hemingway often chartered for expeditions, fishing for sailfish and amberjack and tarpon. (At first, however, Hemingway claimed to be working steadily on his novel and fishing in the afternoons.) He also befriended Eddie "Bra" Saunders, an elderly fishing guide, whose boat Hemingway rented when Josie Russell's was otherwise occupied. It was from Bra Saunders that Hemingway heard the story of the *Valbanera,* a Spanish ship that years before had run aground in quicksand during a hurricane, and how Bra, having been the first to discover her, had risked his life trying to salvage something from the wreck without success and how, through one of the portholes, he had seen a woman floating in one of the cabins, her outstretched hand covered with valuable rings. Out of that tantalizing, climactic image — the unattainable, bejeweled woman, her once-tied hair loosened and floating out in the water — Hemingway conceived one of his more mysterious, wide-ranging stories, "After the Storm." The contrapuntal narrative is that of a greedy, vicious barroom brawler who, try as he might, cannot break the porthole glass to salvage the prize and gives up, only to have a crew of Greeks blow the ship open: "They picked her clean. First there was the birds, then me, then the Greeks, and even the birds got more out of her than I did."

Dos Passos was one of the first guests that Hemingway enticed to Key West. Disgusted after the execution of Sacco and Vanzetti, discouraged by a long siege of unsuccessful theater work with the struggling New Playwrights Theatre in New York, making plans to go to Russia, Dos took Hemingway up on his invitation, though he was not sure why. "At the moment I'm in a little jerkwater boat full of seasick passengers being conveyed (I hardly know why) to Key West," he wrote one of his friends. No sooner had he checked into the Overseas Hotel than Hemingway had him out fishing for tarpon. (In Key West, the tides would be a determining factor in life; on that first day, according to Hemingway, the tide was right.) The daily excursions would last until the gaudy sunsets gave way to moonlight. In the little Spanish restaurants, there was good food well furnished with Rioja wine. But the most important event of Dos Passos's vacation was his first meeting with Katy Smith, who came to visit Hemingway and Pauline a few days before Dos Passos left. In his memoir, Dos Passos would telescope the brief first meeting with the longer second, in the spring of 1929, a plausible mistake since the same cast of friends who arrived the second year — Katy's brother Bill, Waldo Peirce, and Mike Strater — had showed up days after he left in 1928. But, from the beginning, it was clear that he appreciated Katy's spunk, her droll wit, and her lively gray-green eyes.

It was in Key West that spring that Hemingway had an unexpected, brief visit with his parents, who had been vacationing in St. Petersburg. He met them on the dock on their return from an Easter trip to Havana. They lunched together and took a tour of the island. Clarence was in poor health and worried; he had been depressed and irritable for months, was suffering with diabetes as well as angina pectoris. On this trip, too, he learned that his Florida real estate investments had not appreciated at all, but he allowed himself to be convinced by an agent that it was only a temporary lull in the market. Grace, expansive as ever, told Ernest and Pauline about her recent painting expedition in the Southwest with her brother Leicester. Clarence, it seemed, had appreciated the opportunity to meet Pauline; at least there were tears in his eyes when he told Marcelline about the family reconciliation.

But the memory of the meeting must have been dampened for Hemingway. On June 1, rather late in Pauline's pregnancy, writing from Piggott, Arkansas, where he and Pauline were staying with

Pauline's parents, he wrote his father in Oak Park about the prospects of having the baby in Michigan. Clarence, responding on June 4, said the family would not likely be getting to Windemere until sometime after the Fourth of July. "You would best consider having your new baby in Kansas City or St. Louis," Clarence advised, "as the Petoskey Hospitals are really only best for local emergencies. Nurses & maids are very scarce up there. . . . If you want to have me attend your wife at the Oak Park Hospital, I am glad to offer you my services." Through June, there were nervous queries from Oak Park: "We are anxious to hear what you are planning — Will you be here for the 27th June Stork Party?" Clarence wrote on June 18. "Let me know at once, as we can make no plans to go to Windemere until I hear from you." In the end, Hemingway and Pauline decided on Kansas City because it was a known medical center.

On June 27, in a sweltering heat wave, Pauline began labor, entering the Research Hospital in Kansas City. It was a protracted delivery, lasting eighteen hours, and the baby was delivered by cesarean section. It was a nine-pound boy, whom they named Patrick. The specialist, Dr. Carlos Guffey, advised that Pauline should not become pregnant for another three years. "Pauline had a very bad time — cesaerian (can't spell it) and a rocky time afterwards. I was worried enough," Hemingway informed Max Perkins, from Piggott, on July 23. The baby was "very big dark and strong seeming." In spite of the worry and the heat, Hemingway had continued on with his novel: "Am now on page 486 — it must average 180 words to a page." He hoped to get out to Wyoming with Bill Horne for a spell of hunting and fishing and to finish work on *A Farewell to Arms.* Pauline planned to leave the baby, by then on a bottle, with her family and join him in Wyoming in September for a month. Writing to Guy Hickok several days later, Hemingway gave a more graphic account of the ordeal: "They finally had to open Pauline up like a picador's horse to lift out Patrick."

❦❦❦

As in a Hemingway story, motivations may remain hidden. After the difficulties of fatherhood, the need to get away: "If [Patrick] keeps on yelling it is a cinch I won't be able to write and support him," Hemingway wrote Hickok, though jokingly. At the end of July, in the yellow Ford runabout (a gift from Uncle Gus Pfeiffer), Hemingway had picked up Bill Horne and the two set out for Wyoming. (Was it mere coincidence that he had arranged to spend the time with Horne, a ghost from the war years he was writing about?) The Bighorn Mountains, Hemingway wrote Waldo Peirce, looked like the Guadarramas in Spain, only bigger. The jackrabbits were as big as mules, the nominal hyperbole. As usual, he felt it necessary to justify to friends his hours of work and play:

> 1st day — worked four pages, fished with Bill Horne, caught 12.
> 2nd day — worked 4½ pages, fished with two girls, caught 2.
> 3rd day — worked zero, fished by self alone, caught 30-limit.

Whether intentionally or not, his inventory also carried a moral as to the virtues of fishing by oneself. He was ready to give up novels, he told Peirce, though he now had 548 pages. "As it is have been in a state of suspended something or other for 3 or 4 months."

Still, he had, during that time, kept Max Perkins regularly informed about his progress on the book. And of his criticisms about his publisher's failure to advertise: "I think I will have to get a large advance on my next book . . . to assure it being advertized in florid and gigantic manner . . . Glenway Wescott, Thornton Wilder, and Julian Green have all gotten rich in a year in which I have made less than I made as a newspaper correspondent." They were bachelors all, Hemingway emphasized, "and I'm the only one with wives and children to support."

He was alone in Sheridan in mid-August when Pauline arrived. "She is strong as a goat again," Hemingway assured Peirce. "Pat weighs 18 lbs now, parked with his grandparent." He had finished the first draft of his novel — finally. The rest of that summer was given over to hunting and fishing, traveling in Wyoming and Montana. In Shell, Wyoming, Hemingway met Owen Wister, the novelist, author of *The Virginian* and an admirer of *The Sun Also Rises*. ("Were I thirty," Wister had written a friend of Hemingway's, "that's the way I should wish to write.") He and Pauline shot prairie chickens on the Crow Indian Reservation near the Bighorn Mountains, made a wide tour west, south of Yellowstone and past the Grand Tetons, eventually making their way back to Arkansas. From Piggott, Hemingway wrote Perkins that he was eager to start rewriting his book but thought it better "to let it lie until we get settled in Florida." The encouraging thing was that he believed the novel was pretty good and he had a good start on the earlier one to follow it. "Have never felt better or stronger or healthier in the head or body — nor had better confidence or morale." It was probably a sign of his confidence that he held off accepting Perkins's offer of a $5000 check as an advance on the new novel, saying that he had promised the first look at it to Ray Long for possible serialization in *Cosmopolitan*. He frankly preferred to serialize it in *Scribner's* even if it made a difference of a few thousand less. His hesitations proved successful. Perkins offered $10,000, the going rate that Scribner's paid Edith Wharton and John Galsworthy for serialization. In the end, Hemingway received $16,000.

⁂

"Where are you going to be the end of Oct.?" Hemingway wrote Scott Fitzgerald earlier that month. "How's to get stewed together Fitz?" The Fitzgeralds, back from Paris with Scottie's French governess and, in one of their recent brave extravagances, a French taxi driver named Philippe, whom they had hired as a combined chauffeur and butler, were installed in their Greek Revival mansion, Ellerslie, in Edgemoor, Delaware. Scott, despite many stalls and promises, had managed to send Perkins only the first two chapters of his protracted novel, *Tender Is the Night.* Hemingway, having heard, by way of Perkins, that Scott claimed he was putting in eight hours a day of writing to the eleven that Joyce spent, used his letter as an occasion for an extended razz: "How does it feel old fellow? . . . I look forward with some eagerness to seeing the product. Will it be like that other great worker and fellow Celt? Have you gone in for not making sense?"

Hemingway was himself on a busy schedule of traveling before getting back to the revisions on his novel. In late October, he and Pauline made a dutiful visit to Oak Park. Clarence's mood had worsened since his Florida visit; he was irritable and suspicious, was given to locking his bureau drawers and clothes closet, spent hours in his office behind closed doors. Grace was hurt by his behavior. (Marcelline remembered, "It was agony for my mother, who shared the bedroom with him, to think he must be distrusting her.") Clarence had also become extremely possessive of thirteen-year-old Leicester, wanting the boy to ride with him on his calls, resenting even the time Leicester spent in school. He turned a deaf ear to Grace's appeals that he give up his practice and rest. How much of this family drama Hemingway was aware of on that brief visit (he and Pauline were staying at the Whitehall in Chicago) is not clear, though he was perhaps as worried as Grace by his father's behavior. It was some relief, probably, when he and Pauline went to spend a few days with the MacLeishes in Conway, in western Massachusetts, and decided to remain a week. Back in New York he conferred with Perkins, saw Mike Strater and Waldo Peirce.

Before returning to Piggott to pick up Patrick, there was, after all, a reunion with the Fitzgeralds, as bibulous as Hemingway had suggested. The occasion was the Princeton-Yale game at Palmer Stadium on November 17. Hemingway, Pauline, and Strater took the morning train to Princeton to meet Scott and Zelda, who were staying at Cottage, Fitzgerald's old undergraduate eating club (in lieu of fraternity buildings). Hemingway paid a solo visit to Isabel and Francis Godolphin, stayed about an hour for drinks, and left before game time. (He had written them in advance, telling them he didn't want to meet any professors or publishers' representatives.) At the game, which Princeton won 10–2, Fitzgerald had behaved himself. But on the train trip to Philadelphia, he began drinking and became obnoxious, referring to another of the passengers, a medical intern, as a clap doctor.

At Philadelphia, Philippe was waiting with the Buick to drive them to Ellerslie. Hemingway, according to one of the several versions of his overnight stay, had found the Fitzgeralds' rented mansion, with its wide views of the Delaware River, impressive: "It was a beautiful mansion, right on the water, rolling green lawn, but the big trees made it kind of melancholy." Throughout the visit, Scott and Zelda were being dressy and grand and bearing down heavily on the sauce. Playing the perfect host at dinner, Scott had uncorked six bottles of Burgundy for Hemingway alone, knowing it was a wine he liked, but, disastrously drunk, he made insulting remarks to the attractive young black maid serving dinner: "Aren't you the best piece of tail I ever had? Tell Mr. Hemingway." The next morning, clean and spruce in blue blazer and white flannels, Scott had wanted to play "forced games" like croquet, while Hemingway was anxious about catching the train. (True enough, croquet was one of the prescribed pastimes on the wide lawns at Ellerslie.) Hemingway became insistent on the subject of catching the train. In his brisk thank-you note, written aboard the Spirit of St. Louis en route to Piggott, Hemingway apologized. "I am sorry I made a shall we say nuisance of myself about getting to the train on time — We were there far too early." At the station, there had been some mishap involving the police. "When you were in the hands of the Cop," Hemingway added,

> I called on the phone from our platform and explained you were a great writer — the Cop was very nice — He said you said I was a great writer too but he had never heard of either of us. I told him rapidly the plots of some of your better known stories — He said — this is absolutely literal — "He seems like a Dandy Fellow" — thats the way Cops talk.

Whatever the incident was, it has become a lost episode in time. In Fitzgerald's November entry in his journal, the whole gaudy visit of the Hemingways has been reduced to "Yale & Navy games. Ernest down. Delplangue [the French governess] gets on our nerves."

⸙ ⸙ ⸙

In Key West, Hemingway and Pauline moved into a white frame house on South Street, found for them by Lorine Thompson. Sunny Hemingway, dissatisfied with her work as a dental assistant, had come to Florida with them, at her brother's urging, to serve as a typist while Ernest made the revisions on *A Farewell to Arms.* According to her memoir, Sunny felt unwelcomed (by Pauline) and a bit like a servant, having been instructed in the care and feeding of Patrick. Patrick's bed — as well as the typewriter and typing table — was in her room at the opposite end of the house from Hemingway and Pauline's bedroom. "What Pauline did, when she was not planning meals with the Negro maid, Olive, I really don't know," Sunny recalled. "I was pleased to be with my adored brother and could never even intimate that I felt put upon by his wife. He adored her, and they were happy together, planning fishing trips and social times with friends."

But she had been in Key West a little more than two weeks when Hemingway had to go off on another of his junkets, this time to New York to pick up Bumby, who was arriving from France to spend the holidays with his father. Hemingway and Bumby had lunched with Perkins that afternoon and were on the train to Florida that night, when Hemingway, at the Trenton stop, received a telegram from his sister Carol, telling him that his father had died that morning. Having done some Christmas shopping in New York, he had only $40 in his pocket. Hemingway wired Max Perkins, as well as Mike Strater and Fitzgerald, for money. Fortunately Scott managed to get $100 to him at the Philadelphia station. Leaving Bumby in the care of the Pullman porter on the train to Miami, he caught the night train to Chicago.

As Hemingway learned later, that morning — the morning of December 6 — Clarence had awakened with a severe pain in his foot. For a doctor, it could only have raised fears of arterial problems and, probably, the dread worry of gangrene and possible amputation because of diabetes. He told Grace about it but did not follow her advice to see a colleague. Clarence had been in a depressed state of mind over his financial difficulties, though they were not as terrible as he allowed himself to believe. He and Grace had taken out a mortgage on their house in order to buy the real estate properties in Florida and a payment on a promissory note was coming due. His brother George had advised them to sell off some of their Florida lots and cut their losses. "But I don't see how I *can* sell those lots," Clarence had insisted. "They are for our family and our future."

He was also beset by other family worries. He had become overprotective of Leicester, who at the time was at home sick with a cold.

Only recently, Clarence had refused to allow the boy, or any other member of the family, to ride with him in the car. (It was only later that Grace learned that Clarence had become fearful that he might have an angina attack while driving and lose control of the car.) When Clarence came home at lunchtime that day, he asked Grace how Leicester was and was told that he was feeling better but was sleeping. He went down to the basement and burned some personal papers in the furnace. Then, mounting the stairs, he went to his bedroom, closing the door behind him. Taking out his father's Smith and Wesson revolver, he sat on the bed and placed the barrel against his right temple and fired a single shot. In the grim terminology of the medical report, "The bullet pierced the brain looping under the skin, after shattering the bone of the skull in the left temple 5 cm. above and 7 cm. posterior to the external auditory meatus. There were powder burns at the point of entrance of the bullet. Blood was oozing from the bullet wound." It was Leicester who hurried to the bedroom and, pushing open the door, found his father lying crumpled on the bed.

The coroner's inquest convened the next day — Hemingway, presumably, had not yet arrived — and determined that the death was a suicide. Grace, heavily sedated, did not appear. But Leicester, the only other family member on the scene (Carol had been at the high school) gave an account of the events. Uncle George testified as to the victim's health, stating that his brother was suffering from diabetes and a bad heart, a "hopeless case," in his judgment. Given the family sense of propriety — Clarence's suicide had been reported in the *Chicago Tribune* — it was understandable that Hemingway, as Leicester remembered it, told him, "At the funeral, I want no crying. You understand, kid? There will be some others who will weep, and let them. But not in our family."

After the funeral, Hemingway wrote Fitzgerald a brief thank-you note from Oak Park: "You were damned good and also bloody effective to get me that money. . . . My Father shot himself as I suppose you may have read in the papers . . . I was fond as hell of my father and feel too punk — also sick etc. — to write a letter but wanted to thank you."

BOOK

THREE

The Artist's Reward

13

Fathers and Sons

And in that prolonged conjunction, life, fathers die and sons grieve. When, in the fall of 1926, Anson Hemingway died, his son Clarence wrote to his son Ernest in clinical detail, "My dear father died this morning at Seven o'clock. . . . The day before he had written several letters and paid up all his bills. . . . He was eighty-two and one month and eleven days, his birthday was August 26th 1844." The exactness of the details substantiated the truth of the event and, perhaps, the authenticity of Clarence's feelings — a stratagem of style for which his son would become justly famous. Ernest, then in the midst of his marital difficulties, replied with consoling words, "Dear Dad, I am dreadfully sorry to learn of grandfather's death. It makes me very sad not to have seen him again before he died, but it is good he died so happily and peacefully." It was a troublesome period in Clarence Hemingway's life; he and Grace were attempting to sell the North Kenilworth Avenue house, and there was the question of what to do with Ernest's effects. Ernest, thinking of his own son, was concerned about his military souvenirs: "As for my war trophies I hope you can put them all in a trunk or box and store them if you sell the house as I value them very much for Bumby."

And two years later, Clarence Hemingway, repeating his father's tidiness, burned some of his personal papers in the basement furnace, then went upstairs and shot himself with his father's revolver. "My father shot himself," Hemingway wrote Max Perkins after the funeral. "I was very fond of him and feel like hell about it. Got to Oak Park in plenty of time to handle things. . . . Realize of course that thing for me to do is not worry but get to work — finish my book properly so I can help them out with the proceeds. What makes me feel the worst is my father is the one I cared about."

Archibald MacLeish, whose father had died earlier that year, wrote Hemingway with warm understanding, "I know how the death of your father changes him in your mind and he becomes what he was when you were very young and your heart is destroyed with tenderness for him. . . . You are walking in your own boyhood and everyone is very far away." But those, quite probably, were MacLeish's sentiments about his own father's death. More to the point, he offered Hemingway sensible advice: "You must not let your mind work over and over the way it happened. I know how your mind works round and round your pain like a dog in cover going over and over the same track and what a torment it is to you. But now you must not. It is too serious."

After the initial shock, Hemingway adopted, with friends, a hard-boiled, sometimes callous response to his father's death. "My father shot himself in December," he wrote Sylvia Beach, "so now — after having left my family when I was 14 and never taking anything from them I now finally have the responsibility of them. He left practically nothing except my mother and two children still in school. Poor old boy he had tough luck investing money . . . and then got sick." Privately, in the sanctuary of his writing, Hemingway would regard Clarence's death as an act of cowardice. In a canceled passage of The Green Hills of Africa, he would give vent to his feelings. Talking about personal courage, he assessed a few of his contemporaries. Dos Passos was as "brave as a damned buffalo," while Fitzgerald was "a coward of great charm." A brave man had a certain pride, he maintained, even if a coward claimed that pride was of no importance. Hemingway went on to contrast his pride against Clarence's lack: "My father was a coward. He shot himself without necessity. At least I thought so. I had gone through it myself until I figured it in my head. I knew what it was to be a coward and what it was to cease being a coward. Now, truly, in actual danger I felt a clean feeling as in a shower."

In time, Clarence's suicide would even serve as a justification for Hemingway's sardonic rebuttals to later Marxist critics who claimed that he had it easy as a writer. Citing the difficult time when he was writing A Farewell to Arms, Hemingway sarcastically argued in a letter to Max Perkins that "outside of Patrick being born, only incident was my father shooting himself and me acquiring 4 new dependents and mortgages. Then some shitfaced critic writes [that] Mr. Hemingway retires to his comfortable library to write about despair."

At times, he viewed the death of one's father as a usable experience; so he suggested in a letter to Scott Fitzgerald. "Remember us writers have only one father and one mother to die," Hemingway claimed. Fitzgerald's father had recently died, and Fitzgerald had made a lonely, boozy voyage back to America (Zelda was in a Swiss sanatorium at the time) to stand at his father's grave in Rockville, Maryland. "But don't poop away such fine material," Hemingway advised, especially not in the pages of The Saturday Evening Post. (Fitzgerald did use the experience, but in a flip, mediocre story, "On Your Own," that was turned down by seven magazines including the Post and was never published in his lifetime.)

But Clarence Hemingway's suicide was a subject Ernest gave a good deal of ambivalent thought to over the years. Sometimes, he could be amazingly callous. Writing to Ezra Pound, he saw it as an inconvenience during the writing of A Farewell to Arms: "I would have been glad to pay my esteemed father a good sum or give him a share in the profits to postpone shooting *himself until the book was completed — Such things have a tendency to distract a man." In the mid-thirties, when he was suffering through a bout of depression and sleeplessness and getting up in the small hours of the morning to write, he confided to his mother-in-law, "Had never had the real old melancholia before and am glad to have had it so I know what people go through. It makes me more tolerant of what happened to my father." It was not exactly true that he had never felt real depression before his father had died, but it was true that Clarence's suicide, an unlooked-for literary property, would haunt him for years.*

It was in his fiction that Hemingway, over the years, tried the case of his father's betrayal. In A Farewell to Arms, *the hero, Frederic Henry, does not even mention a father, as if, perhaps, Clarence, because of his action, had been wiped clean from memory. But there is a passing reference to a step-father, which, curiously, crops up in a bit of dialogue between Catherine and Lieutenant Henry, who, learning that Catherine is pregnant, asks her,*

> *"Have you a father?"*
> *"Yes," said Catherine. "He has gout. You won't ever have to meet him. Haven't you a father?"*
> *"No," I said. "A step-father."*
> *"Will I like him?"*
> *"You won't have to meet him."*

Equally curious in this gratuitous dismissal of the father is the fact that neither Catherine nor Lieutenant Henry mention the related subject of their mothers. But in a passage deleted from the next to the last chapter of the novel, Henry, ruminating on love and faith, the things of this world and the next, asks himself,

> *But if you were born loving nothing and the warm milk of your mother's breast was never heaven and the first thing you loved was the side of a hill and the last thing was a woman and they took her away and you did not want another but only to have her; and she was gone, then you are not so well placed and it would have been better to have loved God from the start. But you did not love God and it doesn't do any good to talk about it either, nor to think about it.*

One wonders, then, why the issue of parentage was raised at all, unless it had some deeper subliminal significance for the author rather than for his hero or his heroine. Lieutenant Henry does, however, mention his grandfather in warm but oblique fashion. He has picked up his mail at the hospital: "There was a letter from my grandfather, containing family news, patriotic encouragement, a draft for two hundred dollars, and a few clippings." Hemingway, it seems, in erasing his father, had nonetheless transferred to his fictional grandfather certain of Clarence's kindnesses and added a few qualities that were lacking. Frederic Henry is, in fact, at odds with his family. When Catherine, later in the novel, asks whether he has written them, Frederic admits that he hasn't. "Don't you care anything about them?" she asks. Frederic answers: "I did, but we quarreled so much it wore itself out."

⁂

In the months following his father's death, Hemingway played the dutiful son, assuring Grace that her future was secure. He sent her $578.93 for unexpected tax assessments and promised to send her $100 a month for the next year or more. If Grace would send him the necessary information and a description of all the Florida properties, he would, through the Pfeiffer family connections, see about selling them off. "Never worry," he told his mother, "because I will always fix things up — can always borrow money if I haven't it — So don't ever worry, but go ahead with good confidence and get things going." Marcelline and her husband, he said, should also contribute because they had the money and because they (he could not resist airing one of his family grievances) "have always been great friends of the family while I live by my pen and have been more or less of an outcast." Hemingway vented his spleen against Uncle George, whom he blamed for his father's financial predicament. George should do something about the mortgage on the North Kenilworth Avenue house, even if he had to pay for it himself. "He did more than anyone to kill Dad and he had better do something in reparation. I know his sanctimonious tightness and he is going to do what he ought to do about that house or I will have his hide." It was neither the first nor the last time that Hemingway would think of literature as a medium for revenge: "Have never written a novel of the H[emingway] family because I have never wanted to hurt anyone's feelings but with the death of the ones I love a period has been put to a great part of it and I may have to undertake it."

Grace kept up the fiction that she wanted to believe, that her son was carrying on the tradition of the Hall males, that he was the man she expected him to be. Her letters were full of praise and thanks. "How wonderful of you to want to do this for me — Surely God will bless you when you have such a generous heart," she wrote him late in February, after he made the offer of a hundred dollars a month. "Why Ernest! it's like being reprieved when you expected to hang." Although Hemingway gave out the impression to friends that Clarence had left very little in his estate, Grace's letter made it clear that Clarence's life insurance amounted to $21,000, with another $1000 in their joint checking accounts, and that she had now invested the sum in stocks and bonds, allowing her $100 a month in coupons.

(Hemingway, wanting to take a firm hand in his mother's financial affairs, had requested that she give him an accounting.) But Grace, too, was experienced in the manipulation of guilt and reprimand, sympathy and the rewards of affection that families indulge in privately. "An income of $200.00 a month instead of $100.00 is all the difference between comfort and poverty," she wrote him. "I haven't dared to attend a church dinner, or renew a magazine subscription, or have a shoe-shine or a soda, and have walked to save carfare etc., etc." She made it clear that she was doing her part, taking on pupils, planning to take in boarders. She had saved money from the sale of her paintings to pay $400 in taxes on the Oak Park house. She thanked him, too, for offering to help in getting attention for her painting.

On March 7, Grace sent Hemingway a package by Railway Express (prepaid, $2.78, she noted) containing a roll of her two best desert paintings. "Any honors you could get for me — with them — will help me to be more self-supporting," she told him, "but I know you understand the whole situation, and I love and thank you for wanting to help me." Ernest was to have a free hand in deciding, though she hoped he might get them exhibited in Paris. Plain, hand-carved gilt frames three inches wide were what they needed, she said.

The package containing the paintings would give rise to one of the legendary stories about Hemingway's relationship with his mother: how the unthinking mother had callously sent him the weapon with which his father had killed himself. In that same package she also sent cookies for Sunny, a cake for Pauline, and a book for Bumby, as well as the Smith and Wesson revolver, which Hemingway had wanted. (She had just gotten it back from the county coroner.) "Les wants you to leave it to him, when you are thru with it — but you have first choice," she wrote. "Old Long John was the pistol I learned to shoot with when you were a baby in my arms. You always loved to cuddle into my neck when the gun fired." But within days she heard from Hemingway that he wanted her to keep the revolver for him at Oak Park. On March 11, she wrote him to return it. "I will take care of it for you — I waited as long as I dared to hear from you, and then sent it." On March 24, she suggested that he pack it well in the clothes Sunny would be sending home "because Leicester says it is agin the law to send it."

Katy Smith, who was visiting Key West at the time, remembered the package very well: "For Heaven's sake, Ernest," she complained, "haven't you opened your mother's box yet?" When Pauline finally opened the box, it was discovered that the cake, gone moldy, had seeped into the paintings. Since Grace had carefully itemized the contents of the package in her letter, it would seem that the callousness was Hemingway's.

Yet Hemingway, for all his concern, would never be the dutiful son that Grace dreamed of, or imagined; his recriminations against his mother were nonstop. In one of his cheeky, awkward poems, titled "Poem, 1928," he classed himself as one of the young men of the generation that had fought in foreign wars and buried their friends and "Buried our fathers, when these did shoot themselves for economic reasons — / An American gesture to replace bare bodkins with the Colt or Smith and Wesson / Who know our mothers for bitches." He would keep up his vendetta for years.

II

Wanting companionship, Hemingway began enticing his male friends to Key West for fishing expeditions. Writing Max Perkins on January 8, he promised, "The Gulf Stream is alive with fish — really — it's like the old wild pigeon and buffalo days." All Max needed was old clothes and tennis shoes. The principal inducement was that, with Sunny and Pauline typing for him, he had twenty chapters of *A Farewell to Arms* redone and about fifteen or twenty more to do. "It's the only way you can get this Mss." He had been working six to ten hours every day, he said, and would be glad to have an excuse to lay off for a while. He had been expecting Archibald MacLeish, but those plans had fallen through. However, Waldo Peirce was due shortly. Hemingway had laid in a stock of fourteen bottles of Château Margaux, salvaged from a boat that had struck a reef recently, plus a stock of prewar absinthe. "It makes too crazy dreams, so am saving it for you and Waldo." Temporarily, at least, Hemingway had begun writing to Max the filial letters about fishing and hunting that he had written to his father, though Perkins was not quite fifteen years older than Hemingway. Along with the assurances that he was working steadily, Hemingway also sent Perkins occasional reports that he was dutifully attending Mass on Sundays.

Hemingway also badgered Dos Passos: "For God's sake come down. . . . Tarpon are in and have caught two." He was absolutely broke, he said, but Waldo, who was scheduled to arrive next week, "has some jack. His mother died." (Hemingway made the mean comparison: "My old man shot himself but it was no help financially — on the contrary!") His eagerness to have Dos Passos at Key

West may have had ulterior motives. Sunny was convinced that her brother was trying to fix her up with the writer. "He built him up to me at every opportunity. I began to look forward to his arrival and had a fine mental picture of him." When Dos Passos arrived, she was expectably let down: "I was shocked to see a bald man with nervous, jumpy movements." She made no effort to play up to Dos Passos, who was nine years older than she, and Hemingway was put out by her behavior. She was relieved that Dos Passos was far more interested in Katy Smith.

Fishing was not Max Perkins's sport. In a joking letter to Fitzgerald, written on January 23, the week before he left for Key West, he tried to persuade Scott to join him on the trip: "I will have you back inside of nine days. I would feel much safer with you too. Without you I may leave a leg with a shark, or do worse." Fitzgerald begged off, pleading work on his novel. Perkins, however, enjoyed himself during the time that he spent with the Hemingways in Key West, rising early in the mornings for his fishing expeditions with Ernest. (As a good host, Hemingway made sure Perkins caught at least one tarpon by handing him the rod and reel when he had had a strike.) In the evenings, Perkins read the revised manuscript of *A Farewell to Arms.* Max was enthusiastic, keen to have Scribner's serialize it in the magazine, though cautionary about some of the language. On February 13, after his return to New York, he wrote Hemingway that Scribner's would pay $16,000 for the serialization rights and that the first installment was already being set in type. It was the highest fee the magazine had ever paid for a serialized novel. On February 14, Hemingway wired his response: "AWFULLY PLEASED PRICE OK ERNEST HEMINGWAY."

/ / /

In a blustery letter to Guy Hickok, Hemingway referred to his book as a "long tale of transalpine fornication including the entire war in Italy." He was feeling his oats. In a subsequent letter, he assured Hickok that Scribner's "don't know what the hell it's about or they wouldn't touch it. But it's a swell book — I'm damned if it's not." There was something in Hemingway's nature when young, some sense of embarrassment, that made him resort to irony or cynicism whenever he put forth his best effort at being human, his best achievements as a writer, particularly when he was searching for the approval of male friends. *A Farewell to Arms* was a far more complex piece of work than the randy blurb he gave it in his letter to Hickok. It was the story of a tragic love affair in the midst of war, of individual loss in a sector of the broader history of World War I, and perfectly representative of Hemingway's theory that the smaller picture has all the authenticity needed to define the shapeless whole. Ten years after his youthful bully-boy participation in the campaign on the Piave, Hemingway was giving voice, eloquently, to his disillusionment with war through Frederic Henry's dissatisfaction with cant and wartime propaganda: "Abstract words such as glory, honor, courage, or hallow were obscene beside the concrete names of villages, the numbers of roads, the names of rivers, the numbers of regiments and the dates."

Hemingway's novel, in fact, was a novel of such particularities: the bloody graphics of death in the trenches; the muddy roads of retreat; swollen rivers; place names like Caporetto and Gorizia that had, by the time he wrote his book, become part of an ignominious history. Instead of glory, he wrote about the cynicism of foot soldiers; instead of victory, he pictured the bewilderment of the displaced, like the two frightened adolescent sisters traveling with the caravan of cars which Lieutenant Henry and his men are driving to Pordenone. When the cars break down on one of the side roads, Henry gives the girls ten-lire notes, telling them to join the civilians on the main road of the retreat: "I watched them go down the road, their shawls close around them, looking back apprehensively at us. The three drivers were laughing."

A Farewell to Arms was the novel that placed Hemingway, early, among the American masters. That he recognized its importance is evident from the complicated brag and modesty with which he later referred to his use of the conjunction *and* in the five paragraphs that constitute Chapter I — the opening descriptive passages in Hemingway's prose that are, usually, a sign that he is contemplating the serious business of literature:

> In the late summer of that year we lived in a house in a village that looked across the river and the plain to the mountains. In the bed of the river there were pebbles and boulders, dry and white in the sun, and the water was clear and swiftly moving and blue in the channels. Troops went by the house and down the road and the dust they raised powdered the leaves of the trees.

It is a justly famous bit of writing, the image of later troops trudging along the muddy road in a fall rain, their capes bulging forward, covering their ammunition clips, marching "as though they were six months gone with child," a jarring premonition of Catherine Barkley's fatal pregnancy. And then the brief concluding paragraph of the chapter: "At the start of the winter came the permanent rain and with the rain came the cholera. But it was checked and in the end only seven thousand died of it in the army."

The "permanent rain" of the passage is a foretelling of the long rain that runs like a murmuring leitmotif through the book, from the account of the muddy retreat from Caporetto to the final rain in which Lieutenant Henry walks back to the hotel from the hospital after Catherine's death. Hemingway had mastered the technique so well that he could carry it off with a single sentence, as in his description of a cloud coming over a mountain: "It came very fast and the sun went a dull yellow and then everything was gray and the sky was covered and the cloud came on down the mountain and suddenly we were in it and it was snow."

Years later Hemingway would boast that he had used the repetitive *and* in "conscious imitation of the way Mr. Johann Sebastian Bach used a note in music when he was emitting counterpoint." *A Farewell to Arms,* in fact, is the most satisfying and most sustained, the consummate masterpiece, among Hemingway's novels. Its range, its themes, are broader, more complex, than those of *The Sun Also Rises.* It bears the mark of Hemingway's best gifts as a writer — the careful observation of nature, the clinical use of dialogue as the revelation of character, the faith that exactness of language was all the philosophy a writer needed in the practice of his art.

⸙ ⸙ ⸙

In Hemingway's novels, the hero usually has one serious relationship with a woman, but there are always the many men. In a war novel like *A Farewell to Arms,* it is expectable that there would be a host of male characters, and they are depicted, however briefly, with the verve Hemingway maintained in his short stories. Whether it was a distinct need in Hemingway's character or a fact of life in his relationships with men that was transferred to his fiction, there is always a cadre of men, old or young, who instantly befriend, admire, or want to do for the Hemingway hero: solicitous headwaiters, hotel managers, barkeepers. In *A Farewell to Arms,* there are the four ambulance drivers who are trapped in the dugout with Lieutenant Henry when the trench mortar hits. (The brassy, sarcastic Passini dies, horribly, his legs blasted off above the knee: "Oh Jesus shoot me Christ shoot me mama mia mama Mia.) There is the cheery English driver who gets Lieutenant Henry to the "medical wallahs" at the dressing station. ("Lift him very carefully about the legs. His legs are very painful. He is the legitimate son of President Wilson.") Each of these characters is well defined, crackling with life. Hemingway never failed when it came to describing men in action or in the company of other males; he had the palaver, the brag, the randiness, down pat.

Lieutenant Henry's two principal male friends are a gentle, unnamed priest from the Abruzzi and Captain Rinaldo Rinaldi, the Italian doctor and Frederic Henry's self-proclaimed "blood brother and roommate." That the novel opens with them is not fortuitous. Hemingway does not overdo the symbolism, but they are the representatives of sacred and profane love. Critics have routinely regarded Lieutenant Henry's relationship with the young priest as the more significant. At the beginning of the novel, Henry disappoints the priest, who had suggested he take his winter leave visiting his family in the Abruzzi. Instead Henry spends his time in the cities, "nights in bed, drunk, when you knew that that was all there was, and the strange excitement of waking and not knowing who it was with you, and the world all unreal in the dark." Henry tries his best to explain that he had genuinely wanted to go to the Abruzzi but, for one of those inexplicable human reasons, had not: "and we were still friends, with many tastes alike, but with the difference between us. He [the priest] had always known what I did not know and what, when I learned it, I was always able to forget. But I did not know that then, although I learned it later." The import of that message is never quite clear. Was what the priest knew the secret of grace, perhaps? Or love of God? In the dual time of fiction — the time of the action and the time of the narrator's remembrance, which run parallel and may not converge until the end of the story — what Lieutenant Henry has learned and learned to forget is still cloaked in ambiguity. Perhaps it was the nature of real love rather than the plainly sexual affair he had in mind when he first met Catherine.

There is the hint of that in a scene in which the priest, who has been the butt of jokes by the men in the mess hall, visits the wounded Henry in the field hospital. But Rinaldi, equally eager to see Henry, pays a visit in advance of the priest. (It is of some significance that Hemingway regularly pairs Henry's scenes with the priest and with Rinaldi). He alerts Henry to the priest's forthcoming arrival. "He makes big preparations," Rinaldi says dryly. In the teasing way he has adopted in his relationship with Henry, Rinaldi even suggests that there is something going on between Henry and the priest: "I think you and he are a little that way. You know." When Henry tells him to go to hell, Rinaldi jokes, "Oh I love to tease you, baby. With your priest and your English girl, and really you are just like me underneath."

Henry's talk with the priest turns to the love of God. Henry confesses he does not love God:

> "You do not love Him at all?" [the priest] asked.
> "I am afraid of Him in the night sometimes."

"You should love Him."

"I don't love much."

"Yes," he said. "You do. What you tell me about in the nights. That is not love. That is only passion and lust. When you love you wish to do things for. You wish to sacrifice for. You wish to serve."

When the priest tells him that one day he will love and then he will be happy, Lieutenant Henry tells him that he has always been happy. The priest's reply seems a calculated response to Henry's earlier ruminations. "It is another thing," the priest tells him. "You cannot know about it unless you have it."

The thread of religion, of religious faith, runs through *A Farewell to Arms.* Knowing the circumstances of Hemingway's life at the time of writing the novel, his conversion to Catholicism and his marriage to Pauline, one can't avoid the suspicion that Hemingway was both trying to explore the subject as a literary property and exploit it personally, justifying his knowledge of his new faith. As author, he is fluent with both prayers (the desperate begging prayers of wounded men) and blasphemy (the soldiers refer to the local brothel madam as Mother Superior). There is a very pointed reference to Mantegna's *Dead Christ* in Milan ("Very bitter," Catherine remarks, and Lieutenant Henry echoes, "Very bitter . . . Lots of nail holes"), which may be a bit of mockery. But it would not have been beyond Hemingway's talent to have intended it to be self-serving or sarcastic and, at the same time, as symbolic as any referent in Eliot's *The Waste Land.* Even Catherine's saying to Lieutenant Henry, "You're my religion," is not to be taken lightly in the religious context of the novel. (It was another of Hemingway's transferences, casting his own experience in a feminine role: it was Hemingway, in a letter to Bill Horne, who had moaned, "and Bill, I forgot all about religion and everything else because I had Ag to worship.") One of the personal religious references is to the St. Anthony medal, which Catherine gives to Lieutenant Henry for good luck just before he goes off to the front. (He loses it when he is wounded.) Ironically, in life, it was Hemingway who sent Agnes von Kurowsky a St. Anthony when she went to Florence for her extended stay. ("But do you think you should have given me your good luck, dear boy? Suppose you should go back to the Front while I'm here, & have it not to guard you?" Agnes wrote him.) It is, then, a meaningful, desperate prayer that Henry utters when Catherine lies dying in the Swiss hospital, "God please make her not die. I'll do anything you say if you don't let her die. You took the baby but don't let her die."

Feminists might balk at the character of Catherine, her passivity or abject submissiveness to her lover. True enough, her constant repetitions of "darling" are grating; her startling admissions — "You're my religion. You're all I've got" — may seem a bit craven. But there is a strangeness, an abruptness, that Hemingway intended in Catherine's character that makes her memorable. Her submissiveness is meant to be another symptom of her craziness, her waywardness, the element of desperation in her makeup. She is not simply, after all and only, the gratifying fantasy of the male ego.

There is something ambivalent, even queer, in Hemingway's depiction of the couple's game playing after Frederic Henry's desertion and their escape to Switzerland, a thread of strangeness that runs through Hemingway's treatment of male-female relationships. In fiction, at least, Hemingway seems willing to entertain the notion that love and sex are a merger of sexual identities. Catherine wants Frederic Henry to let his hair grow long while she has hers cut shorter, "and we'd be just alike only one of us blonde and one of us dark. . . . Oh, darling, I want you so much I want to be you too." Frederic Henry responds, "You are. We're the same one."

That bit of experimentation, perhaps, has more to do with Hemingway's obsessions than with Catherine's character. It crops up elsewhere in his writing, and it may have been initiated by Hadley — at least Hemingway attributes the same bit of game playing about hair length to her in a fragmentary sketch in the Hemingway archives, labeled "worthless sketch, discarded," that was probably intended for *A Moveable Feast.* Hadley says:

> "In a month you wont be able to keep it from coming over your ears. Are you getting frightened?"
> "Maybe.
> "I am a little bit too. But we're going to do it aren't we?"
> "Sure."

That underground stirring of ideas of sexual transference, androgyny, the merging of identities, however, though buried in Hemingway's work over the years, would only become readily apparent with the posthumous publication of the edited version of *The Garden of Eden,* the sprawling, 1500-page manuscript Hemingway began in 1946. In it Catherine Bourne, "crazier" than Catherine Barkley, insists, pleads, badgers her husband, David, into adopting the same coiffure as hers and the same hair color as well, the color of "the bark of a young white birch tree," so that they are twins, summer-tanned and androgynous. In the heavily edited published version, the game playing at sexual transference appears to take a Krafft-

Ebing turn when David, in some unnamed fashion, allows himself to be sodomized by his wife: "and he helped with his hands and then lay back in the dark and did not think at all and only felt the weight and the strangeness inside." Catherine, with eerie satisfaction, declares, "Now you can't tell who is who can you?"

⸻

In *A Farewell to Arms,* it is Rinaldi who plays the seemingly obligatory role in Hemingway's fiction of the male counterbalance, the comrade, to the Hemingway hero's involvement with a woman. In his relationship with Lieutenant Henry, Rinaldi represents the equally dominant hold of the masculine secular and profane. Like Agnes von Kurowsky's Italian suitor, Enrico Serena, on whom he was modeled, Rinaldi has made a stab at courting Catherine before yielding to his American friend. When Henry visits Rinaldi at Gorizia just prior to the retreat from Caporetto, he finds him depressed by the war, by the carnage of the failed summer offensive that has brought a heavy round of operations. Rinaldi has been drinking heavily and is convinced that he has a case of syphilis. Hemingway's handling of the episode is masterly. Rinaldi reverts to his usual teasing camaraderie, but there is an edge of difference in their relationship all the same. (The reader learns that Rinaldi has kept Henry's toothbrush glass as a mordant souvenir of mornings after the nights before at the officers' brothel, when Henry, as Rinaldi reminds him, tried to "brush away the Villa Rossa from your teeth . . . swearing and eating aspirin and cursing harlots.") Knowing how his overtures annoy Frederic Henry, Rinaldi comes over to the bed, where he is sitting, and says, "Kiss me once and tell me you're not serious." Henry responds, "I never kiss you. You're an ape." (Hemingway intimates that Henry's absence has been a precipitating factor in Rinaldi's depression.) When Rinaldi tries to joke about Henry's affair with Catherine Barkley, he is put off, told to shut up, albeit in a joking way. He turns suddenly glum: "Oh, yes. All my life I encounter sacred subjects. But very few with you. I suppose you must have them too." The break between them is the result of Henry's now serious affair with Catherine, and it is clear that Rinaldi is jealous, a possibility he admits. He has no married friends, Rinaldi claims; married friends don't like him. When Henry asks why, he says, "I am the snake. I am the snake of reason." But Hemingway has subtly infused this scene with the implication that Rinaldi's earlier insinuations about the priest might also be the result of jealousy and that there is probably a touch of homosexuality in Rinaldi's feelings toward Lieutenant Henry.

There is a remarkable evenhandedness about the sexuality of the principals in this novel. Nurse Ferguson, Catherine's devoted friend, is also jealous of Lieutenant Henry. At Stresa, where the two nurses are on leave, and Henry, having deserted (he has made his "separate peace"), joins them, Ferguson becomes increasingly moody and unreasonable. She knows that Catherine is pregnant and is angry with Henry for having gotten her friend in trouble. But the truth is, she is emotionally involved with both of them. At one point, Ferguson and Henry squabble; she tells him, employing Rinaldi's metaphor, "You're like a snake. A snake with an Italian uniform." In her nervousness and anger, she breaks down in tears. Catherine tries to comfort her but makes the mistake of smiling, knowingly, at her lover. "Don't you smile at him with your arm around me," Fergy tells Catherine. Later, Catherine asks Henry to be nice to Ferguson: "Think how much we have and she hasn't anything." Henry says he doesn't think Ferguson wants what they have, but Catherine's reply suggests otherwise: "You don't know much, darling, for such a wise boy."

For all their importance in the early stages of the novel, Ferguson, Rinaldi, and the priest disappear in the quickening pace toward the final pages of the novel recounting the escape to Switzerland and Catherine's death. There is a brief moment in Switzerland when Lieutenant Henry wonders about Rinaldi and the priest and other people he knows. He tells Catherine, "But I don't think about them much." Nor does he want to think about the war. "I'm through with it," he says. But in one of the several endings that Hemingway proposed for the novel — and discarded — Rinaldi and the priest appear among the cast of characters whom Henry, looking back in time, tries to account for in his attempt to come to terms with his past. They are the casualties of time, perhaps, along with other seemingly transient figures in the hero's life:

> I could tell how Rinaldi was cured of the syphilis and lived to find that the technique learned in wartime surgery is not of much practical use in peace. I could tell how the priest in our mess lived to be a priest in Italy under Fascism. I could tell how Ettore became a fascist and the part he took in that organization. . . . Many things have happened. . . . Everything blunts and the world keeps on. You get most of your life back like goods recovered from a fire.

Not topflight Hemingway, at least in Hemingway's mind. But the discarded ending is better than many a writer would have been satisfied to publish. And a revelation, too, of how the novel — in Hemingway's mind — was meant to extend beyond its frame.

⁊⁊⁊

Ever since his visit to Key West, Max Perkins had been keeping Hemingway posted on Fitzgerald and the progress of his novel. Scott had also informed Hemingway that he was planning to leave for Europe around March 1 but wouldn't go unless his novel was finished. Perkins, who had already read two preliminary chapters, was eagerly awaiting the manuscript. But on March 8, Perkins wrote Hemingway, "Scott sailed last Saturday, and without finishing his novel. You will see him in Paris. I am going to write him a long letter. I am afraid of his losing his nerve, but if he does not, he will come out all right. And in spite of his faith in youth, he will do better in age if he will only keep out of trouble enough." Perkins's information may only have added to Hemingway's growing disdain for Fitzgerald's waste of his talent. Hemingway was himself on the verge of a trip to Europe, a troublesome voyage that entailed trundling his family — Pauline, Patrick, and Sunny, who was making her first trip abroad, and Bumby, who was being returned to his mother in Paris. The first leg of the journey was the trip to Havana, where they boarded the North German Lloyd liner *Yorck* on April 5.

The prospect of being saddled with Fitzgerald in Paris weighed on Hemingway's mind, particularly since he was planning to make revisions in his novel (he would later claim that he had revised the ending thirty-two times) as well as read galley proofs for the serial publication in *Scribner's*. Before sailing, he sent off an emphatic letter to Perkins: "Please don't under any circumstances give Scott our Paris home address. Last time he was in Paris he got us kicked out of one apartment and in trouble all the time, (insulted the landlord, peed on the front porch — tried to break down the door 3–4 and 5 A.M. etc.)." He preferred to see Scott in public places. "When I heard he was going to Paris it gave me the horrors," Hemingway added.

But once in Paris, in the circle of gossipy Americans, most of whom knew one another or knew about one another, there was hardly any tactful way Hemingway could avoid meeting Fitzgerald or avoid telling him where he was living without its being an obvious snub. What course Hemingway took is not clear, but it is certain that Fitzgerald was aware that Hemingway was not as warmly disposed toward him as he had been in the past. "Certain coldness," Fitzgerald wrote in his ledger book after a dinner with the Hemingways in June. More than likely, Fitzgerald had been hurt by the fact that Hemingway had not let him see the manuscript of *A Farewell to Arms* until after it had begun appearing in *Scribner's* magazine, beginning with the May-June issue. (That slight may have accounted for the officious thoroughness of Fitzgerald's letter of suggestions and advice.) Fitzgerald, for example, recognized a certain laxity in Hemingway's portrayal of Catherine Barkley. He had, in effect, cannily noted one of the curiosities in Hemingway's work: that he was more adept at capturing the character of his women in his short stories than in his novels. "In Cat in the Rain . . . you were really listening to women — here you're only listening to yourself," Fitzgerald said of an episode involving Catherine. He recommended that Hemingway cut it thoroughly or rewrite it. He was, he recognized, treading on dangerous ground: "Our poor old friendship probably won't survive this but there you are — better me than some nobody in the Literary Review that doesn't care about you & your future."

Despite the impertinence, Fitzgerald's advice, his criticisms, were at times well taken. As a master of fiction, Fitzgerald was well aware of the use of coexistent time in Hemingway's novel — the time of the love affair and Frederic Henry's remembrance of it a decade later: "I mean — you're seeing him in a sophisticated way as now you see yourself then — but you're still seeing her as you did in 1917 thru nineteen yr. old eyes." Fitzgerald's complaint about the hero and heroine was pointed: "either the writer is a simple fellow or she's Eleanora Duse disguised as a Red Cross nurse." It is clear that Hemingway had discussed his characterization of the heroine with Fitzgerald sometime before he allowed his friend to read the manuscript (commentators seem not to have noticed this point) since Fitzgerald asked, "Where's that desperate, half-childish dont-make-me-think V.A.D. feeling you spoke to me about? It's there — here — but cut to it! Don't try to make her make sense — she probably didn't."

Hemingway's blunt private response to Fitzgerald's critical letter was a bold marginal scribble: "Kiss my ass."

✓✓✓

Hemingway had other reasons that summer in Paris for his irritation with Fitzgerald, who participated in an ignominious episode involving Morley Callaghan, the young reporter Hemingway had known at the *Toronto Star.* Callaghan, then twenty-six, was in Paris with his wife, Loretto. Callaghan's novel *Strange Fugitive* had recently been published, and critics had begun to link Callaghan's name with Hemingway's. In Paris, Callaghan — and more especially, Loretto — felt there was a certain amount of resistance from the Hemingways to any developing friendship between the two writers, particularly on the part of Pauline. Loretto told her husband that Pauline was not about to put herself out in any way. "She's read all that silly Scribner stuff about you and Hemingway. . . . Nobody's edging in on Ernest while she's around. It's a very big thing for her to be Ernest's wife, you know."

During that summer, Hemingway and Callaghan boxed three or four times at the gymnasium in the American Club. "You would not believe it to look at him," Hemingway wrote Max Perkins, who had published Callaghan's novel, "but he is a *very* good boxer. . . . He is fast, knows a lot and is a pleasure to box with." But one of their afternoon matches would be the source of a later controversy that further damaged their relationship — and did even more damage to Hemingway's relationship with Fitzgerald. Hemingway had had a heavy lunch that day at Prunier's with John Peale Bishop and Fitzgerald. He knew he would be in poor shape by the time of the match, which was set for five o'clock. He and Fitzgerald, who had agreed to be official timekeeper, went round to get Callaghan, persuading him to fight an hour or so earlier. Because of Hemingway's condition, the two agreed to one-minute rounds with two-minute rests in between. In the first round, according to Hemingway, Callaghan managed to cut him on the lip and mushed up his face in general. Moreover, the round began to seem the longest Hemingway had ever fought until Fitzgerald, ashamed and embarrassed, confessed that he had let it go on for three minutes and forty-five seconds. ("So interested to see if I was going to hit the floor!" Hemingway commented in his letter to Perkins. Moreover, he did. "I slipped and went down once," he acknowledged in his letter.) Callaghan recalled that Hemingway had been furious with Fitzgerald and berated him, "If you want to see me getting the shit knocked out of me, just say so. Only don't say you made a mistake." It had been an awkward scene: Fitzgerald, shamefaced, having been scolded by his one of his ready-made heroes; Hemingway storming out to the locker room to clean up before returning to the match.

One of Callaghan's more indelible memories of that summer in Paris was of a late afternoon at a sidewalk café when Hemingway, fishing out the proofs of the first two chapters of *A Farewell to Arms* from the bag in which he carried his boxing gloves, asked Callaghan to have a look at them. Callaghan noticed a change in style from *The Sun Also Rises:* "the magic was in the way the words came cleanly together; the landscape was done with his painter's eye, not Cézanne's eye, his own." But he was also aware of another less satisfactory trait, Hemingway's tendency to identify with his heroes. In the beginning, Callaghan acknowledged, he had felt sure that Hemingway would be "a broad objective writer like Tolstoy." Now it seemed he was becoming "an intensely personal writer, each book an enlargement of his personality in the romantic tradition." When Callaghan tried to express his admiration for the descriptive passages, saying that the new book was a bigger book than *The Sun Also Rises,* Hemingway laughed. *The Sun Also Rises* was the kind of book you wrote in six weeks, he said. Callaghan objected; the book had been very warmly and rightly praised by the critics. Hemingway, now serious, began talking with the conviction of a man with some vast store of wisdom about writing. "Always remember this," Hemingway told Callaghan as they sat together in the dimming light of early evening in Paris. "If you have a success, you have it for the wrong reasons. If you become popular it is always because of the worst aspects of your work. They always praise you for the worst aspects. It never fails."

III

In late June, just before the annual pilgrimage to Spain, Hemingway learned that the *Scribner's* issues carrying the second and third installments of *A Farewell to Arms* had been banned from the newsstands in Boston. ("Hey you old pornographer," Dos Passos wrote him. "They've nailed Scribner's family journal in Boston. Gee I hope you cash in on it as you certainly should if Scribner's doesn't get cold feet.") Only two weeks before he had been negotiating with Perkins on the words *balls* and *cocksucker,* disguised as b——ls and c——ks——r in the book version. ("Certainly those letters cannot corrupt anyone who has not heard or does not know the word. There's no proof it isn't cocksure.") Writing to MacLeish from Montroig, Spain, where he and Pauline were visiting Miró, he complained about the "emasculation" of the text by the "literary gents" on the magazine. "I think you'll like it as a book," he told MacLeish, who had been following the serial version. If the book was emasculated — "a tiny operation with a great effect" — it would be because the reaction in Boston had frightened Scribner's, Hemingway contended.

In Madrid, late in the summer, Hemingway met another of the unique characters who crossed his path, the American bullfighter from Brooklyn, Sidney Franklin. Trained in Mexico, Franklin, born Sidney Frumpkin, had made his debut in Seville earlier in the summer. Hemingway, however, did not catch up with him until September, at the urging of Guy Hickok, who was hoping to get a feature on Franklin for the *Brooklyn Daily Eagle.* Hemingway wrote Hickok that he had heard that Franklin, in another of his triumphs, had been "carried out on the shoulders again," this time in San Sebastián. "Will write something for you if I meet him but not under my name. You see I could sell an interview with him by me (signed) for a thousand seeds."

Franklin's account of his first meeting with Hemingway in his gossipy memoir, *Bullfighter from Brooklyn,* is a marvel of condescension. Franklin confesses that when they first met in a Madrid café, he had never heard of Ernest Hemingway. He was, at first, put off by Hemingway's appearance: seedy-looking, wearing a battered pair of bedroom slippers. (A peculiar detail, but accurate. In another of his untimely accidents, Hemingway had cut his foot.) Still, Franklin was impressed by the fact that Hemingway had worked up his own glossary of bullfighting terms, which he himself had difficulty translating into English. He invited Hemingway to a fully described sumptuous lunch at home. In the course of the meal, Franklin learned, too, that Hemingway was a connoisseur of wines. The two proceeded to talk about bullfighting with gusto. The lunch lasted five and a half hours.

Franklin, whose bullfight entourage included a Spanish duke, an uncle of King Alfonso's who was, he claimed, "one of my most outspoken admirers," traveled with a caravan of some twenty-odd automobiles. He agreed to take Hemingway on tour for a month and a half. They got so involved in their long nightly conversations on the road that Franklin had Hemingway's bed or cot moved into his room, and, according to his memoir, they shared the double bed when nothing else was available. In their talks, Hemingway made a point of asking Franklin to describe and demonstrate the technical points of each of the maneuvers in the various passes. While discussing the great matadors, Hemingway suggested that Franklin, in his routines, resurrect some of the passes the greats had performed but which were now no longer used. Franklin did, much to the acclaim of the critics and the crowd. In his memoir, he had the grace to admit that Hemingway's suggestions were partly responsible for his own meteoric rise that season in Spain.

✓✓✓

Hemingway was back in Paris when the reviews of *A Farewell to Arms,* published on September 27, 1929, began to arrive. They were superb. Henry Hazlitt, in the *New York Sun,* wrote, "In depth, in range, in drama, *A Farewell to Arms* is the finest thing Hemingway has yet done" and labeled Hemingway's account of the retreat from Caporetto "unforgettable." Percy Hutchinson in the *New York Times Book Review* found it "a moving and beautiful book" but wondered if the extreme to which Hemingway had developed his declarative style was not "a sort of protective covering for a nature more sensitive than he would have one know." Malcolm Cowley, in a perceptive review in the October 6 *New York Herald Tribune,* thought the title was symbolic — "Hemingway's farewell to a period, an attitude, and perhaps to a method also." He considered it "more colored by thought" than Hemingway's previous work. "Perhaps even Hemingway may decide in the end that being deliberately unsophisticated is not the height of sophistication."

Even Fanny Butcher, the *Chicago Tribune* reviewer and one of Grace Hemingway's local mentors in things cultural, declared it "the most interesting novel of the year. . . . Anyone who thus has watched American writing cannot but find in it a blossoming of a most unusual genius of our day." She detected the influence of Stein's *Three Lives* but argued that Hemingway did it "in a longer, more complicated medium and with more certain power." The final pages had caused her to sob uncontrollably. Grace clipped out the review and sent it to her son with the marginal comment, "Yay, Fannie." Her own words were approving: "I'm sure I *personally* greatly appreciated the closing numbers of 'The Farewell to Arms.' It is the best you have done yet — and deserves the high praise it is receiving."

For Hemingway, the critical praise was gratifying, and for the most part the book was the success that he hoped it would be. The initial printing of 31,050 copies sold promptly. There were two new printings in October and three in November. Within a year, a stage version of the book appeared on Broadway, adapted by Laurence Stallings and starring Elissa Landi and Glenn Anders. It had a brief run of only twenty-four performances. Considering the shortness of the run, Hemingway wondered about the fifteen curtain calls on opening night, and decided, "They must have all been by people who wanted to sleep with either Mr. Anders or Miss Landi." He netted $24,000 from the sale of the movie rights to Paramount, but Hemingway was never to be impressed by or satisfied with play or movie versions of his work.

Despite the aura of success, Hemingway took umbrage at the critics. Late in the summer, he had written Fitzgerald from Hendaye in a philosophical mood, genuinely trying to console Scott, who was in a depressed state over his failure to bring off *Tender Is the Night.* "That terrible mood of depression of whether it's any good or not is what is known as The Artist's Reward," he said. Summer was a discouraging time to work. "You don't feel death coming on the way it does in the fall when the boys really put pen to paper." But in a later letter to Fitzgerald, he scored the critical reception of his own book: "Look what tripe everything is — In plain talk I learned to write from you — in Town and Country from Joyce — in Chic Trib from Gertrude — not yet reported the authorities on Dos Passos, Pound, Homer, McAlmon, Aldous Huxley and E. E. Cummings —

Then you think I shouldnt worry when some one says I've no vitality."

Hemingway had good reason to be satisfied with the English reviews. Arnold Bennett, in the *London Evening Standard,* found it "hard, almost metallic, glittering, blinding by the reflections of its bright surface, utterly free of any sentimentality. . . . A strange and original book." The *Times* reviewer claimed that Hemingway had "found in the War a finer scope for his very powerful talent than he has ever found before." He singled out the portrait of Rinaldi as "the most brilliant achievement in a brilliant book." Hemingway boasted to Perkins, "The book has stirred up a hell of a business in England — V. Sackville West broadcasted about it from the official British Broadcasting and the head of the B.B.C. raised hell and she, Walpole, etc. replied." He added, "It's had much better reviews in England than U.S. Damned funny."

The private appraisals were rewarding. John Peale Bishop wrote him, "I should need to be strong and well fortified to give it all the praise I think it deserves. But let me at least say that no contemporary could have done better, and few in the past have surpassed its best stretches." Dos Passos informed him, "Dear Hem, do you realize that you're the king of the fiction racket?" Two different publishers, having heard that Hemingway was dissatisfied with Scribner's, took Dos aside, eager to know if it was true. "Looks like you'll be able to have any number more dependents if this keeps up," Dos told Hemingway. "I have a theory that the whole fiction market will go belly up in a couple of years — so now is the time to cash in." (Ironically, Dos's letter was written five days before the stock market collapse on October 29.) He, Dos Passos, was in the process of completing the manuscript version of *The 42nd Parallel,* the first volume of a trilogy, *U.S.A.,* that would become, quietly and patiently, one of the landmark works of the period. He had other reasons to rejoice as well. On August 19, in Ellsworth, Maine, he had married Katy Smith. Hemingway's letter of congratulations was ebullient: "Damned glad to hear you men are married. Best love from us to Kate. I'm happy as hell about it!" But his jocular commentaries had an edge of irony: "Bishop was ruined by Mrs. Bishop's income. Keep money away from Katey. Eternal youth has sunk the Fitzes — Get old, Passos — Age up Kate — Old Hem ruined by his father shooting himself — Keep guns away from Katherine's old man."

⸙ ⸙ ⸙

That fall of 1929, by chance or fate, several troublesome strands of Hemingway's life converged in a not altogether agreeable way. The stock market crash proved to be a worry. "I hope to Christ you weren't caught in the market," he wrote Perkins. It was probably a sign of his concern that he asked Perkins to wire him what the sales on the book were. Perkins, with sidewise logic, writing Fitzgerald and perhaps wanting Scott to pass on the information to Hemingway, told Fitzgerald that *A Farewell to Arms* had sold about 36,000 to date, adding "the only obstacle to a really big sale is that which may come from the collapse of the market — what effect that will have nobody can tell." Fitzgerald passed on that troublesome bit of news to Hemingway, causing more worries and more cables. Once again, Perkins wrote Fitzgerald explaining that it was difficult to give an accurate accounting, that he particularly didn't want to give an overstatement. "In reality, between ourselves, the sales must now be 50,000 and perhaps more, but only 47,000 show on the card." Eventually, reassured that the sales were continuing (the book would be a best seller despite the economic failure), Hemingway wrote his apologies to Perkins: "I only write when Scott gets me stirred up. I know he does it only because that is his idea of the sort of thing that is exciting to a writer. But it's not exciting — only annoying."

It was but one of the instances that would put a strain on Hemingway's relationship with Fitzgerald that fall. Hemingway had earlier written Perkins alerting him to the fact that Robert McAlmon would be in New York searching for a publisher and suggesting that Perkins ought to see him. Much to Perkins's amazement — so Perkins confided to Fitzgerald — when he took McAlmon to lunch, "what does McAlmon do but start in to say mean things about Ernest (this is absolutely between you and me) both as a man and as a writer." He supposed that McAlmon was jealous. Fitzgerald had a ready response; McAlmon was a failed writer and a rat. A few years ago, he assured Ernest that Fitzgerald was a fairy. Next he was telling Callaghan that Ernest was a fairy. "God knows he shows more creative imagination in his malice than in his work. . . . He's a pretty good person to avoid."

Perkins apparently disclosed the details of McAlmon's story to Morley Callaghan, who saw Perkins in New York shortly after the McAlmon visit. It turned out to be the same "scandalous story of something" that had happened on their trip together in Spain which McAlmon had told Callaghan earlier in Paris in the spring (evidently the episode in which Hemingway had mistaken him for Vicky, the beautiful and buxom tart, in the room McAlmon and Hemingway had shared for a night). Callaghan, in his memoir, gives an account of Perkins's disgust. "I tell you this because McAlmon is your friend," he told Callaghan. "I don't care if you tell McAlmon why we're not publishing his book. I hope you do tell him." But Perkins, it seems, was not that emphatic about not publishing McAlmon's book. Writing to Fitzgerald at about the time of the incident, he was thinking of publishing McAlmon all the same: "I was impressed with McAlmon's 'Village'. . . . Some of the passages in it are very fine, but he does not seem to have any attractiveness of style, but rather the reverse." If McAlmon was patient, he said, Scribner's might publish a book of some of the better things in *Village* combined with other suitable material. "I would certainly like to do this even on his own account because he is entitled to publication."

At first, Fitzgerald, gossipy at his best and more so when drunk, held off telling Hemingway about McAlmon's tale telling, but finally revealed that McAlmon "was at his old dirty work around New York." Both Hemingway and Pauline were irate. Hemingway vowed vengeance.

It was understandable then that Hemingway's patience might be wearing thin when Gertrude Stein, having met him one evening in late November, invited him to a Wednesday evening party and lecture (of her own) at 27 rue de Fleurus. She asked Hemingway to invite Fitzgerald, as well. Stein, Hemingway wrote Fitzgerald, "claims you are the one of all us guys with the most talent, etc. and wants to see you again." Stein had also asked Hemingway to invite the poet and critic Allen Tate, whom Hemingway had met a few months earlier, and his wife, the writer Caroline Gordon.

Allen Tate, in his droll and not altogether trustworthy memoir, "Miss Toklas' American Cake," would recall that Hemingway had waited until the very morning of the party to issue the invitation, saying, "Gertrude has taken me back into favor." The implication is that, after his earlier break with Stein, Hemingway had only recently reestablished contact with her. Plausible enough, but a handful of dated and undated notes, invitations, and a pneumatique from Pauline to the Stein household — one dated February 27, 1928, acknowledging Gertrude's note telling them of the death of her old friend Mildred Aldrich — indicate that Stein and Hemingway were on reasonably good terms again well before the winter of 1929. (The news of Aldrich's death must have brought back memories of the cold March day, six years earlier, when Hemingway and Stein, fast friends then, had stood with Aldrich on the battleground near Meaux.)

The party that Wednesday evening turned out to be a memorable occasion, the last time — had any of the principals realized it — that Stein, Hemingway and Fitzgerald would be together. It was one of those events that can be reconstructed only from faulty memoirs and passing references in scattered documents, the stuff of time past. The lecture, according to Tate, was pure farce, Stein sitting in an overstuffed chair at the end of the room near the fireplace, while the gentlemen, seated in a half circle of chairs confronting her, listened attentively as the oracle spouted out her theories on the development of American literature, dismissing Henry James and Ford Madox Ford (both of whom, in fact, Stein admired) as irrelevant to the abstractionist trend of American literature of which, of course, she was the culminating fixture. The wives and ladies of that evening, meanwhile, at the other end of the salon, had been enjoying tea and chocolate cake. It was Tate's conviction that on this occasion of Hemingway's restoration to favor, neither Stein nor Hemingway had exchanged a single word.

But letters, explored in detail, are in the main a more reliable source, and the letter Hemingway felt obliged to write Fitzgerald the morning after the Stein party tells a different story. The evidence is that he and Stein and Fitzgerald had had a spirited discussion in which Gertrude had complimented Fitzgerald, and Fitzgerald, who had a history of perversely taking praise amiss, inexplicably had taken her comments as a slight. The next day, Fitzgerald sent Hemingway a hurried note evidently apologizing for his behavior. Hemingway, suffering a "good hangover" and a bad stomach, was in the odd position of having to apologize for himself and testify to Stein's good intentions: "I cross myself and swear to God that Gertrude Stein has *never* last night or any other time said anything to me about you but the highest praise. That is absolutely true." He retraced the scene: "She was praising her head off about you to me when you came up she started to repeat it and then at the end of the praise to spare you blushes and not be rude to me she said that our flames (*sic*) were maybe *not* the same — then you brood on that." What was remarkable in Hemingway's morning-after letter was his equanimity and patience under Fitzgerald's unwarranted assault.

From the letter, it is clear that Hemingway had been eager to hear what Stein had to say about *A Farewell to Arms* and had received only measured praise. "I like to have Gertrude bawl me out," he told Fitzgerald, "because it keeps one['s] opinion of oneself down — way down — She liked the book very much she said — But what I wanted to hear about was what she didn't like and why — She thinks the parts that fail are where I remember visually rather than make up — That was nothing very new."

⁂

The climax of the whole concentrated series of aggravations with Fitzgerald came when a story about the boxing match between

Hemingway and Callaghan was circulated in the *Denver Post* by gossip columnist Caroline Bancroft and was repeated in Isabel Paterson's "Turns With a Bookworm" column in the *New York Herald Tribune Books* section. The story claimed that Hemingway, to his chagrin, had been knocked out by Callaghan in one round. It was just the kind of story that would delight everyone who bore Hemingway a grudge, and Callaghan knew immediately that "a legend very important to Hemingway might be destroyed." He promptly wrote to Paterson, denying that he had ever knocked Hemingway out and denying that they had ever had an audience during their matches. "Once we had a timekeeper," he admitted in a sly aside without mentioning Fitzgerald's name. "If there was any kind of a remarkable performance that afternoon the timekeeper deserves the applause."

In the meantime, the story had begun circulating in Paris, and Hemingway, furious, certain that Callaghan was the source of the slander, badgered Fitzgerald into cabling Callaghan, "HAVE SEEN STORY IN HERALD TRIBUNE. ERNEST AND I AWAIT YOUR CORRECTION." At the same time, Fitzgerald, with renewed feelings of guilt about the episode, began pestering Hemingway with letters harping on the subject and seeking reassurance. Hemingway wrote him, "If you remember I made no cracks about your time keeping until after you had told me over my objections for about the fourth time that you were going to deliberately quarrel with me." It was clear that Fitzgerald was harping on the subject, and Hemingway was embroiled in one of those wrangles that become more entangled with each exchange. "You'll remember though," Hemingway wrote Scott, "that I did not, sore as I was about everything in general, accuse you of any such time juggling, I only asked you if you had let the round go on to see what would happen." Faced with the need to go on assuring and reassuring Fitzgerald, Hemingway tried to finalize the argument: "I know how valuable your sense of honor is to you, as it is to any man, and I would not wound you in it for anything in the world."

To clinch his case, he told Fitzgerald that two of his friends had died recently. The first he did not name; the second was Harry Crosby, who, on December 10, in a suicide pact, in a borrowed apartment at the Hôtel des Artistes in New York, shot his former mistress, Josephine Bigelow, as they lay in bed, fully clothed. Some two hours later, he turned the gun on himself. Hemingway had last seen Harry and Caresse Crosby in Paris in October, first at the races at Longchamp and then when the Crosbys had come to dinner at the rue Férou. Crosby's diary entry for October 10 noted the good wine, the book of Goya etchings (*The Disasters of War*) that Hemingway had shown him, and an album of photographs of a fishing expedition off Key West taken by Waldo Peirce, "one remarkable one of a man's arm (intact) taken out of the belly of a shark." He also noted that Hemingway had given him an autographed copy of *A Farewell to Arms.*

Did Fitzgerald know Crosby? Hemingway asked. "He told me about this girl before he went to N.Y. . . . He was a hell of a good boy and I feel awfully bad today about him . . . and I'll be damned if I'm going to lose you as a friend through some bloody squabble." He signed the letter "yr. affectionate friend, Ernest."

14

A Thousand Intangibles

LIKE MANY an American in Paris following the crash, Hemingway returned to America. He and Pauline, Patrick, and a French nursemaid, Henriette, sailed on *La Bourdonnais* on January 10, 1930. Stopping en route at New York, then on to Havana, they reached Key West early in February. Their friend Lorine Thompson had found them a large house on Pearl Street. Back in the States, Hemingway was not exactly at home either. He preferred to live on the outskirts of mainland America — in Key West and, later, in Cuba, fishing for sailfish and marlin — with occasional trips to Wyoming and Montana, where he hunted elk and bear and grouse. He still ruminated on art and life, but he seemed to be making a case for the active life, defending himself in letters to friends. "A man can be a hell of a serious artist and not have to make his living by it — see Flaubert, Cézanne and Co. And it implies no criticism of the seriousness of a guy's work to take it for granted that he would be more willing to knock off work for a trip than a guy who doesn't eat if he loses his job through knocking off."

Even in his active life, however, Hemingway was in touch with his literary and artist friends. Dos Passos and Katy, Josie Herbst and John Herrmann, Max Perkins, Archie MacLeish and Ada, Mike Strater, and Waldo Peirce were invited to Key West to keep up the reality and the myth of old friendships. Whether intentionally or unconsciously, Hemingway set about creating a new persona and a new program for himself as a professional writer. He plainly did not want to be considered an aesthete. In the thirties, his views on writing and writers were blunt and often vulgar in print and in private, all part of his effort to stress his masculine pursuits in the literary world, particularly among the New York intelligentsia. He would pepper his published texts and letters with slurring references to homosexual writers. "Nobody but Fairies can write Maspertieces or Masterpieces consciously," he assured Fitzgerald, to whom he liked to make teasing innuendos about homosexuality in their relationship. (He sent Fitzgerald an inscribed 1931 photograph of himself, "To Scott from his old bedfellow," signing it Richard Halliburton, the name of the then celebrated travel writer, whom they both considered homosexual.) Fitzgerald, who at times liked to play the caricature of a fairy in his letters to Hemingway, was unhappily then struggling against fears that others thought he was homosexual — including Zelda, whose life had degenerated into madness and intermittent stays in mental institutions, and one of whose aberrations was the belief that her husband and Hemingway were having a homosexual affair.

⸙ ⸙ ⸙

Strange, then, that in that new decade when Hemingway was intent on creating a public persona for himself, chance should supply him with an alter ego, an impostor, who presented himself as the real Ernest Hemingway, traveled the circuit Hemingway traveled, laid claim to the books Hemingway had written, even signed copies in bookstores. Hemingway, at first, took it as one of the misbegotten badges of fame, boasted about it to a reporter in an interview for the *Kansas City Star* in the fall of 1931, referring to the impostor as "my other self." Over the years, he embellished upon the details a bit, but it was an intriguing tale nonetheless. According to Hemingway, his doppelgänger was a psychopathic case, the son of an American admiral who traveled the same routes that Hemingway traveled in Europe and in America, lectured coast to coast on the ladies' club circuit, even turned up in Hollywood.

This shadow, a consequence of his growing fame, was not a figment of Hemingway's imagination; according to Leicester, the impostor had turned up at Grace's doorstep as late as 1933. T. R. Smith, Hemingway's former editor at Boni and Liveright, alerted Hemingway that an impersonator claiming to be Hemingway was staying at the Explorers Club, entertaining young men in his hotel room, reading them passages from his works, taking them to breakfast. In 1935, the editor of *Esquire* magazine, Arnold Gingrich, reported that Ernest's doppelgänger was active in Chicago. Hemingway was convinced, so he informed Gingrich, that the impostor, with his obvious sexual proclivities, was the source of the "ineradicable" rumors that Hemingway was "a phony and a buggar." Later, he would tell his biographer Carlos Baker, "When you have a phony around who lectures on his life and works and the life is yours and not his and the works are your own, and you try never to talk about them, it makes things complicated." A strange predicament for a man as concerned about his identity as Hemingway was. Other writers — Kafka, perhaps, or Borges — might well have turned the situation into a metaphysical fable for modern times, but that was never to be a direction that appealed to Hemingway.

Yet the irony — superb in its way — was that Hemingway was himself creating a sometime impostor, a public persona whose reputation preceded him in his travels or whose fame attracted the curious and the embittered like a magnet. The media Hemingway proved to be a nuisance. He was the boastful sportsman, the he-man, the user of four-letter words in print — the creation of Hemingway's active life as well as his literary fame — whom tourists and belligerent drunks sought out in Sloppy Joe's in Key West, or in the Floridita in Havana and the Stork Club in New York. A misguided lawyer, for instance, tested Hemingway's mettle in the swank Manhattan nightclub, trying to push him in the face; Hemingway retaliated by knocking him out. The incident made the "People" column of *Time*. The *Sunday Mirror* headlined its story "Hemingway by K.O. in Big Night Club Card." He was becoming "the 'tough guy' of American letters."

⁂

Hemingway published little in 1930, the year of his return to the States. In Paris, he had written a brief preface for *Kiki's Memoirs,* a racy autobiography by the popular Montparnasse model, who, in her memoir, remembered Hemingway's boyish charms: "I saw Ernest again, looking more like a first-communion lad and friendlier than ever; I wondered if he was still a virgin." Kiki, otherwise, itemized the men she had loved and left, from Modigliani to Man Ray, whom she was in the process of leaving ("He has an accent I like and a kind of mysterious way with him"). For Hemingway, it was an opportunity to praise, unreservedly, the lush womanhood of "an Era that is over" while paying off the unnamed Virginia Woolf for her nettling review of *Men Without Women:* so far as he knew, Hemingway remarked, Kiki was a woman who "never had a Room of Her Own." For good measure, he added, "If you ever tire of books written by present day lady writers of all sexes, you have a book here written by a woman who was never a lady at any time."

Back in Key West, he seems to have begun the mysterious story-in-dialogue, "The Sea Change," about the breakup of a couple having a conversation in a bar, the woman planning to leave the man for her lesbian lover, though promising to come back. He uses the word "perversion"; she objects, "There's no necessity to use a word like that."

> "What do you want me to call it?"
> "You don't have to call it. You don't have to put a name to it."
> "That's the name for it."

"No. . . . We're made up of all sorts of things. You've known that. You've used it well enough."

"You don't have to say that again."

Some critics suspect that that cryptic bit of dialogue indicates that the man is a writer who ought to, and probably does, know human nature well enough to be understanding. In those terms the story could easily be a case of Hemingway's exploring the implications of human sexuality at a time when Robert McAlmon was spreading the scandal that Hemingway was a secret homosexual and Pauline a lesbian. Yet, at various times, Hemingway claimed that the story was completely invented or else that it was based on a couple he had seen in the Basque Bar in St.-Jean-de-Luz — "and I knew the story too too well." Another late explanation, this one given to Edmund Wilson, was that he had written it as a result of a three-hour conversation with Gertrude Stein about lesbianism, "the mechanics of it, why the act did not disgust those who performed it." As a result, "I was so sold on her theory that I went out that night and fucked a lesbian with magnificent result; i.e. we slept well afterwards." It was the knowledge gained from Stein, he claimed, that had enabled him to write "The Sea Change."

Another of the stories he worked on that spring was a dry little Prohibition tale that he had begun earlier, based on his 1928 trip to Wyoming. "Wine of Wyoming" is a local-color tale of Prohibition America, about a French couple, the Fontans, selling homemade bootleg wine and beer in a roadhouse operation. The story, he informed Perkins, "is nothing but straight reporting of what [I] heard and saw when was finishing A Farewell to Arms out in Sheridan and Big Horn." But time has been kind to what, in its time, had been an ordinary little tale, giving it the status of a bit of Americana, a report from the interior, circa 1930. Perkins arranged for its publication in the August 1930 issue of *Scribner's* magazine, and it was reprinted in *Winner Take Nothing*.

The preoccupations of a writer: the real challenge, as Hemingway once defined it, was "the necessity to put a thousand intangibles into a sentence." He knew the necessity for economy of effect: his famous dictum of the iceberg with seven eighths of the real subject lying beneath the surface — further intangibilities. He also understood the devious, nearly impossible task of weaving narrative time into a piece of fiction, merging the past and the present together with the ruminations of the mind — the author's or the character's — and the hazards of confusing the two. In a work of fiction, there was the luggage from the past that a character brought with him and that made him seem credible — even though the author might find the extra baggage cumbersome. Any character, and more so the hero, must arrive from somewhere, leaving behind parents or a lover or, perhaps, a wife whose absence must be explained. Perhaps, too, the hero is withholding secrets that the author pretends not to know and the reader pretends to believe the author does not know.

It was, however, a lean year for short stories. Hemingway seemed to be cleaning out the larder. That spring he resurrected another borderline tale, part fiction, part nonfiction, which he had begun the year before, "A Natural History of the Dead." In his little anthology of death and dying, he recounted his first horrendous brush with death at the Milan munitions factory in 1918, while lugging off the bodies and the pieces of bodies. (It was an experience he did not let go of easily; he later inserted the story with some additions, title and all, in the ongoing narrative of his bullfight book, *Death in the Afternoon.* It would also be reprinted as a short story in *Winner Take Nothing.*) It was clearly Hemingway's intention to shock the reader with his powers of detached observation, his dismissal of sacred notions of glory and honor in battle. In grisly detail, he pictured the corpses in the field after the Austrian offensive of June 1918: "The dead grow larger each day until sometimes they become quite too big for their uniforms, filling these until they seem blown tight enough to burst. The individual members may increase in girth to an unbelievable extent and faces fill as taut and globular as balloons." In even more thoughtful detail he describes death as a result of Spanish influenza: "In this you drown in mucus, choking, and how you know the patient's dead is: at the end he shits the bed full."

It was to his bullfight book that Hemingway gave most of his attention — when not distracted by his many visitors. Josephine Herbst and her husband, John Herrmann, were in Key West at the time, but, strangely enough, had not sought Hemingway out, though they had heard he was there. They were living by the "code" of Paris, Josie recalled. "We didn't begin by looking him up. It wasn't the way you did things in Paris in the special, good days, when we had all lived there, and when it was the custom to run into people, casually, on the street, or in a cafe, but not to hunt them out in their houses or apartments or wherever they might be working. There was a code which respected work beyond anything else and we were still living in it." They were also put off by the fact that Hemingway had become a Catholic in order to marry Pauline. But one day John came back to the house with Hemingway in tow: "Hem came up in a rush, like clean air. . . . That's the kind of eager, fresh way he had, of coming up close, looking you straight in the eye," and they were all reconciled.

That spring of 1930 was also the spring of the "grand venture to the Dry Tortugas." The visiting Max Perkins and Mike Strater, together with John and Hemingway, made an adventurous all-male trip to the Dry Tortugas, some seventy nautical miles from Key West. Bad weather stranded them for more than two weeks on Garden Key, where they sheltered in a shed near old Fort Jefferson. Josie, left behind with Pauline at Key West, was plainly worried. "They were going to fish there four days and return," she wrote her friend Katherine Anne Porter. "It is over 2 weeks and a northwest wind has been blowing so hard they can't make the passage back. I laughed my head off when they went, taking 24 cans of spaghetti and 12 of beans for a 4 day trip but I guess they knew what they were about." What Herbst remembered most about the visit to Key West was "the dreaminess of the place, its island completeness" and the awkward way that Hemingway, just as they were leaving, thrust a manuscript at John, telling him to sell it in New York for whatever he could get. It was the manuscript for one of the articles he had written for *Esquire.* They sold it for $180 and used the money toward the trip they took to Russia that fall.

"Have been working hard," Hemingway assured Max Perkins on April 11. "Have caught three tarpon since you left — now another North Easter blowing like the devil." And in mid-May, with the tarpon running heavy and Dos Passos and Katy visiting, he wrote to Mike Strater, "Dos lost one that looked like 200 [pounds]. It jumped 7 times . . . Kate lost some big ones too." He told Strater, "I have 74 pages done on the book am working on but it gets so damned hot hell to work." Bumby would be arriving in New York within a few days. He was expecting Uncle Gus Pfeiffer, too: "His arrival delayed by purchase of 4 million dollar business."

Wanting to escape the heat, Hemingway spent a long summer in Wyoming after an obligatory visit to Piggott. Pauline had left earlier with baby Patrick and the nurse, Hemingway making the long drive to Arkansas with Bumby. In Wyoming, they rented a cabin with a view of the mountains on the Nordquist Ranch near the Clarks Fork Branch of the Yellowstone. Hemingway set to work, with interruptions for trout fishing. By mid-August he was going over the copy for the new Scribner's edition of *In Our Time,* still pushing, without success, to get "Up in Michigan" published, changing the name of Ag to Luz in "A Very Short Story" to avoid any possibility of libel action. *In Our Time,* Hemingway told Max Perkins, was "a hell of a good book — the stories, when I read them now, are as good as ever." He also informed Perkins that he had some 40,000 words done on his bullfight book. By early September, he was up to page 174, he wrote Mike Strater, whom he was trying to convince to come out for the hunting season. Pauline and Bumby would be leaving on September 13 for New York, where Bumby was scheduled to take ship back to France. Hemingway was planning to stay on through October. "So far I've killed two damned big old cattle eating bear," he wrote Strater.

But the bear hunting and the writing came to an end on the first of November. Late in October, Dos Passos had joined him for a hunting trip in the high country. Dos, it turned out, was too near-sighted for the sport, but he took pleasure in the scenery and the animals. Hemingway, however, was in his element. Dos noted that he already had the ranch hands under his thumb; they thought he was the most wonderful guy they had ever met. "He had the leadership principle all right," Dos Passos conceded. "It occurred to me that he would make a first rate guerrilla chief."

After their ten-day trek in the wild, driving back toward Billings, Montana, they had an accident. Hemingway, blinded by the headlights of an oncoming car, drove his car into a ditch, where it rolled over. Dos Passos and a ranch hand crawled out, unharmed, but Hemingway was seriously hurt, with broken bones, his right arm pinned in back of him. They managed to get him to a hospital in Billings. Dos called Pauline, who arrived in time for the operation and stayed with him during the weeks of recovery. The doctor had had to bind the broken bones with kangaroo tendon, then sewed up the nine-inch incision. "The inside of the arm looked like the part of an elk you have to throw away as unfit for human consumption when you butcher it out," he wrote Guy Hickok later. His right hand was paralyzed, and it was a question of whether a nerve could be restored to normal. In torturing pain much of the time, he was as irritable as one of the black bears he had been hunting. When Archie MacLeish went to the trouble of paying him a visit at the hospital, Hemingway was in a foul mood. "The most hair raising flight of my life," MacLeish remembered, "only to find Ernest in bed with a magnificent black beard, full of suspicion of my motives [in coming] and convinced — so he said — that I had come out to see him die." It was a considerable relief when, shortly before Christmas, Hemingway was able to leave the hospital for Piggott.

II

A thousand intangibles: what impulses drive a writer — above all, Hemingway, one of the most traveled of authors — to choose the locales in which he manages to write a particular work? Why write about the Michigan woods in a Parisian café, or a war in Italy in the heat of Key West? Certainly, Spain, in the summer of 1931, was the appropriate locale for finishing a study on bullfighting. When Hemingway returned to Key West early in the year, his progress on the book was slow, and it was several months before he could write with any ease. Even then, he wrote Fitzgerald, "can only write about 400 or so words still before arm poops out and am putting those 400 or so into reducing our national debt to Max." (Still, in March, he managed another expedition to the Tortugas and boasted of shooting twenty-seven out of thirty clay pigeons, holding the shotgun with his left hand against his right shoulder.) Hemingway planned to spend the whole summer in Spain, finishing his book, he told Fitzgerald. He hoped to visit Scott in Switzerland in the fall if Scott was still there. He was sorry to hear that Zelda was having such a rotten time. She was undergoing treatment at the Prangins Clinic at Nyon, after a series of mental breakdowns. One of the precipitating factors had been her frantic desperation over her failure to make a career as a ballet dancer. Hemingway offered consoling advice, suggesting that Zelda should not feel any worse about it than she already felt. She had not, after all, started soon enough. "She wouldn't have wanted to start late and be the Sidney Franklin of the Ballet would she?" Hemingway joked, then conceded, "You know us word merchants Fitz — always ready to give comforting advice to others while pewking with the other hand about our own troubles."

Hemingway had other intangibles to consider: Pauline was pregnant again. (This time, they were both hoping for a girl.) He would be traveling to Spain from Havana and landing at Vigo. Pauline and Patrick and the nursemaid would leave from New York for Cherbourg late in May. Hemingway planned to meet her at Hendaye Plage for a brief holiday, then make a trip to Paris to pick up Bumby. Pauline, with her usual efficiency, had taken on the task of having the stored furniture from their apartment on the rue Férou shipped back to the Key West house that Uncle Gus had bought for her that spring for $8000. (The house at 907 Whitehead Street was in need of renovations. Two stories high with a wrought-iron verandah on the second floor, it stood on a corner lot with a run-down garden of date palms and banyan trees.)

Hemingway made the voyage on the SS *Volendam* on May 4. There was a group of Spanish priests aboard, returning from Mexico. "It looks like a dull voyage," Hemingway wrote Waldo Peirce from aboard ship, "all sacerdotes so far."

⁄ ⁄ ⁄

In Madrid, in the late spring, Hemingway met up again with Sidney Franklin, who was still recuperating from a series of operations after being seriously gored in Madrid in the 1930 season. Hemingway and Franklin took in the early bullfights. In keeping with the aim of his book, Hemingway had come back to Spain to size up another, younger generation of bullfighters, to see how they measured up to his heroes — and how well they died. At Aranjuez, he had seen a much-vaunted new bullfighter, Ortega, and found him "lousy" and then decided he was no better in Madrid a day or two later in his full presentation as a matador. On that same day, he had witnessed the tragic goring of a far better young prospect, the bullfighter Gitanillo de Triana, the "bravest and most honorable" of the younger gypsy bullfighters, who was horribly gored in the spine. Gitanillo would lie in a hospital through the heat of the summer, dying, painfully, of spinal meningitis.

Hemingway's trip that summer provided unexpected material for a minor essay on the Spanish temperament, delivered in a letter to Dos Passos, outlining the growing political unrest in Spain. In April 1931, King Alfonso XIII had fled the country and a new government — the Second Republic, more liberal and, at the same time, more dogmatic than the first — had been established. The political change, however, had hardly healed the violent factionalism of the country. In Pamplona, where radical and anarchist factions had burned convents in the early weeks of the unrest, there had been a huge protest rally by monarchist and Catholic groups bent on subverting the newly proposed government. Hemingway had arrived in time for the election of the new Cortes. "Chances for Marxian revolution nil," he wrote Dos Passos. "May yet have a terror though." But he was cynical of all reformist governments: "If worst comes to worst history of 1st Republic will repeat." His analysis of the situation was surprisingly accurate. He had arrived in time for the early rehearsals of the bitter and bloody civil war that would engulf the country five years later.

In his book, he made a few generalizations about the character of the Spaniards: "If the people of Spain have one common trait it is pride and if they have another it is common sense and if they have a third it is impracticality." He scolded the new government for its hostility toward bullfighting. He nonetheless predicted the survival of the art "in spite of the great wish of [Spain's] present European-minded politicians," who wanted "no intellectual embarrassments at being different from their European colleagues that they meet at the League of Nations, and at the foreign embassies and courts."

⸙ ⸙ ⸙

In *Death in the Afternoon,* what Hemingway termed, in translation, "the moment of truth," the moment of the final sword thrust when the bull is killed, would become a password for a generation or more of writers, litterateurs, aficionados, as well as a cliché for journalists. Hemingway backed away, rather grumpily, from critics — Pound, for instance — who assumed there was something "mythic" or symbolic in his love of bullfighting. He assured Pound, who had dredged up Mithraic associations, "Leave us get bulls straight. I have never regarded bulls as anything but animals. I have never been a lover of animals. I have never heard of Mithra — lacking a classical education." No, the matador played with death, Hemingway maintained, daring it, bringing it closer and closer in the course of performing a work of art. "He gives the feeling of his immortality, and, as you watch it, it becomes yours."

So that there should be no question that bullfighting was the most dangerous form of art, Hemingway described the deaths of some of the more famous matadors of his time. Although he had not actually witnessed it, he related the story of the goring of Varelito, who, wounded in Seville, in much the same manner that Sidney Franklin had been gored, while being carried to the infirmary, spent his rancor on the fickle audience who had jeered him: "Now I've got it. Now you've given it to me. Now you've got what you wanted." It had taken Varelito weeks to die. There were other bullfighters who caught a frightening glimpse of death but for whom death did not come — old Luis Freg, for example, gored many times in the ring and for whom death seemed certain often. Once, lying delirious in a hospital bed, he shouted, "I see death. I see it clearly. Ayee. Ayee. It is an ugly thing." But Freg was not, after all, marked for death. In the summer of 1931, broke, he was giving a series of farewell performances.

Treating death, Hemingway did not intend to be the romantic elegist. His was the pose of the unsentimental naturalist or the battlefield photographer. "All stories, if continued far enough, end in death," Hemingway tells the tiresome Old Lady, one of his fictional devices in *Death in the Afternoon,* "and he is no true-story teller who would keep that from you." The convergence for Hemingway was a demonstration of his skills as a writer and his attempt to make sense of death — "the feeling of life and death that I was working for." He had seen violence and death in his time, he informs the reader in the opening pages of the book. But under the pressure of writing about them as a journalist, he felt he had never been able "to study them as a man might, for instance, study the death of his father or the hanging of some one, say, that he did not know." That, he claimed, was why he had gone to Spain to study the bullfights.

There is little doubt that this anatomy of death (and its obverse side: courage in facing it) had been prompted by the most recent and meaningful death in Hemingway's life, his father's suicide. "Courage comes such a short distance: from the heart to the head," Hemingway claimed, "but when it goes no one knows how far away it goes."

Sidney Franklin figures pertinently in the final, impressionistic chapter of *Death in the Afternoon*, one of those peremptory bits of experimental writing Hemingway often indulged in and which critics seldom gave him credit for. Franklin was intimately connected to Hemingway's sketch of the idyllic masculine rites that were an inescapable feature of his view of life and literature. For much of that summer, Franklin, recuperating from his wounds, appears to have had little to do with bullfighting itself. But he played host, often, to Hemingway and the local aficionados and the out-of-work bullfighters of his circle. Sidney's circle spent much time, that summer, on the banks of Madrid's Manzanares River in the section called La Playa, just outside the city. The beach, as Franklin describes it in his memoir, was made up of sandy and grassy areas bordering the twenty- to thirty-foot-wide and shallow river. "We used to bring the makings and cook our afternoon meal right there on the beach," he explained. "Most of the fighters who weren't busy fighting accompanied us. There never was a day when we had fewer than ten fighters with us."

There are photographs of those summer picnics that lack all the structure of Cézanne's idylls of male bathers, exposing the differences between art and dumb reality. Taken in the glare of noon, they show a little band of men, the bullfighters and aficionados Franklin spoke of, unidentifiable now except for Sidney himself and Hemingway, both of them taller than little Luis Crovetto, Franklin's devoted *mozo*, his valet. The scene is dappled with hard shade; the men, nude or wearing loincloths or covering themselves with some hastily snatched item of clothing, are lined up in front of the camera. Franklin stands tallest, covering his private parts with a copy of *A.B.C.*, the influential Madrid monarchist newspaper. Hemingway, the only one modestly dressed, is wearing belted shorts, has an elastic support bandage around his knee. He seems fully at ease in the scene, laughing, as if at some quip from the photographer, his arm resting lazily on Sidney's shoulder. A *paella* pan is settled on the stones of a makeshift campfire; in one of the snapshots, one of the men, squatting in the foreground, raises a wineskin to his mouth with a wise-guy smile.

Strangely, the photographs deny Hemingway's later claim that he never liked the touch of other men: "I have never cared for any man and dislike any tactile contact with men except the normal Spanish *abrazo* or embrace which precedes a departure or welcomes a return from a voyage or a more or less dangerous mission or attack." Displays of affection between men, then, were acceptable in situations of danger — a reasonable explanation for the camaraderie of war; the freedom of affection and loyalty between men in battle — no excuses needed. In the lyrical passages of the final chapter of *Death in the Afternoon,* Hemingway would make something different out of the incident, though the setting was the same caught by the unknown photographer. There he stresses the approved masculinity of the event by adding a few whores to the written version of his *fête champêtre,* recalling

> the unsuccessful matadors swimming with the cheap whores out on the Manzanares along the Pardo Road; beggars can't be choosers, Luis said; playing ball on the grass by the stream where the fairy marquis came out in his car with the boxer; where we made the paellas, and walked home in the dark with the cars coming fast along the road; and with electric lights through the green leaves and the dew settling the dust, in the cool at night.

The whores do not appear in the photographs preserved in the Hemingway archives. Understandable, perhaps, since Hemingway, with his wife in Hendaye or Madrid, would hardly have wanted incriminating photos of himself posing with prostitutes. Nor do they appear in Sidney Franklin's narrative. Were the whores real, or an invention? Perhaps they were introduced into Hemingway's narrative to offset the appearance of the fairy marquis, who more than likely was not an invention.

"Make all that come true again," Hemingway wrote in that final chapter of the book. He might have been invoking the muse in what was essentially a remarkable nine-page ode to the thousand intangibles. There is no discernible pattern, only the associations that occur in the mind of the writer, a sequence of seeming non sequiturs. It is the grammar of immediacy: place-names and remembered episodes, caustic remarks about bullfighters. (In the book, Hemingway was as libelous about certain matadors as he was about French homosexual writers like Gide and Cocteau, targets of his special venom. Of the matadors, Miguel Casielles was "a complete coward" in the ring, he claimed. Cagancho "has not the courage of a louse.") In a superbly catty run-on passage, Hemingway catches the nasty inflections, the emptiness of the conversations, of the failed matadors, aficionados, hangers-on in the cafés at night. (Is it a portrait sketch of Sidney and the conversations in his entourage? Most probably.)

> Then you could walk across the town to the cafe where they say you get your education learning who owed who money and who chiselled this from who and why he told him he could kiss his what. . . . Who wouldn't fight with who and when and why and does she, of course she does, you fool you didn't know she does? Absolutely and that's all and in no other fashion, she gobbles them alive, and all such valuable news you learn in cafes. In cafes where the boys are never wrong; in cafes where they are all brave; in cafes where the saucers pile and drinks are figured in pencil on the marble table tops among the shucked shrimps of seasons lost and feeling good because there are no other triumphs so secure and every man a success by eight o'clock if somebody can pay the score in cafes.

There are incidents, too, that seem to have no recognizable bearing in the drift of the prose but which, nevertheless, are strikingly vivid. It is a picture of Spain, a Spain existing in the mind and memory of a writer:

> cider in Bombilla and the road to Pontevedra from Santiago de Campostella with the high turn in the pines and blackberries beside the road; Algabeno the worst faker of them all; and Maera up in the room at Quintana's changing outfits with the priest the one year every one drank so much and no one was nasty. There really was such a year.

⁂

What lies concealed beneath the surface details, nearly unspoken, in *Death in the Afternoon* is the worrisome undercurrent of Hemingway's relationships with men in his life and in his work, and the nagging question of the threat of homosexuality. In Hemingway's fiction, women often seem cast for a role, tailored for some typical male presumption, adoring or flattering, their conversations apt to be cloying, submissive, simpering. His women, fairly often, beg the question of reality in order to convey some masculine idea of the feminine. A Lady Brett may escape the stereotype but not the Maria of *For Whom the Bell Tolls*.

Hemingway was more exacting, often more affectionate and sometimes even maudlin about his male characters — that is, the all-important comrades and acquaintances of the Hemingway hero: Cohn and Mike Campbell in *The Sun Also Rises,* Rinaldi and the young priest of *A Farewell to Arms,* the Bill of the Michigan stories. He has fewer preconceptions about his male characters, seems to have studied men more carefully, more intimately, out of easy friendship or potential rivalry. He was, it seems, more demanding in his male relationships, quicker to anger, fiercer in his resentment of anything he could interpret as a slight or a case of disloyalty. And the men who didn't count in his life, didn't count. He was often moved to generosity, ready to help a friend out with a loan in times of need.

Yet, over the years, Hemingway pursued the suspicion of homosexuality. In "The End of Something" and "The Three-Day Blow," it is Bill who, for unquestioned motives, has encouraged and helped engineer Nick's break with his girlfriend Marjorie. There is the strong suggestion of a homosexual relationship between the prizefighter Ad and Bugs, his black caretaker, in "The Battler." The homosexual major in "A Simple Enquiry," with obvious intent, questions the nineteen-year-old soldier Pinin about his sexual affairs and then decides not to pursue his opportunities. Still, the major wonders how truthful the soldier has been about having a girl and being in love: "The little devil . . . I wonder if he lied to me."

In the notes and drafts for an unpublished story or sequence of sexual vignettes called "Crime and Punishment," written around the time Hemingway was working on *Death in the Afternoon,* there is a blistering account of the activities of a recently released convict, a sailor. (Random descriptive passages in the manuscripts crop up in Chapter 20 of the book.) The narrator, originally from Petoskey and riding the rails, is waiting to catch a freight train with a sailor whom he has just met. The sailor, originally from Traverse City, has been released from a twenty-year sentence at San Quentin for having buggered (with a companion) another younger sailor. The narrator hears out the sailor's tale with increasing impatience and a growing awareness of how it is likely to end, how the sailor and his buddy had been unjustly accused. "[The damned kid] took it all right the first time. I swear to Christ he took it and he liked it." But when they wanted it the second time, the kid had squealed on them. Only later did they learn that the master-at-arms who had charged them was also involved with the kid and got only seven years. Released from prison, the sailor finds the country gone to hell in the Depression: "You can't make enough to buy a cup of coffee let alone a piece of tail." When the narrator asks him what he is going to do, the sailor says that he'll ride the freight and bum a meal wherever he gets kicked off "and I'll jack off here in the open air with old mother five fingers and be goddamned glad I'm out." (Hemingway is clearly demonstrating his command of the male vernacular.) Predictably, the sailor adds, "Unless you've got something better to suggest." Predictably, the narrator answers that, no, he doesn't have anything better to suggest.

The most enigmatic of Hemingway's published stories of homosexuality is "The Mother of a Queen." Complex and tightly written — only four and a half pages long — it was, according to Hemingway, one of the reported, as opposed to invented, stories in his 1933 collection *Winner Take Nothing*. ("I write some stories absolutely as they happen.") Hemingway claimed that it was based on the bullfighter José Ortiz. In the story the Mexican bullfighter, Paco, had lost his father early in life. His youthful career was under the supervision of his manager, who was also his lover. The manager had provided a permanent burial plot for the father, but when Paco's mother died some years later, the manager, considering that he and Paco might not be together much longer, paid for her burial plot for only a five-year period. Paco does not pay his bills, squanders his earnings on expensive matador costumes (then, perversely, packs them so carelessly that they are ruined by seawater on the voyage from Spain to Mexico). He also pays out money to a young "punk" from his hometown whom he has taken a fancy to.

A friend, Roger, the narrator of the story, has taken charge of the cashbox and the management of Paco's affairs while the bullfighter is away on his Spanish tour. Roger, whose precise relationship to Paco is purposely shadowy, has a bitchy tongue, is bossy and self-assured. It is he who, when payment comes due on the mother's burial plot, insists that Paco pay it promptly, even offers to attend to it himself. "Keep out of my business," Paco tells him; he will take care of it himself. But Paco stalls and stalls. Having taken money from the cashbox, he still does not pay the bill. The result is that his mother is exhumed and her bones thrown out on the public ash heap. "What kind of blood is it in a man," Roger asks, "that will let that be done to his mother?" It is the contrapuntal question of the story, repeated in the final paragraph, where Roger's diatribe might represent Hemingway's more rabid views on "the mincing gentry":

> There's a queen for you. You can't touch them. Nothing, nothing can touch them. They spend money on themselves or for vanity, but they never pay. Try to get one to pay. . . . What kind of blood is it that makes a man like that?

Yet the story is not simply an expression of Hemingway's disgust with homosexuality, as it might easily appear on the surface. How is one to demonstrate the welter of connections it had with Hemingway's life and experiences, his frame of mind? There is the whole begged question of the narrator, Roger, and his relationship with Paco. There is the presumption among some critics — a highly reasonable one — that Roger is based on Sidney Franklin because it was likely that Franklin had told Hemingway the story about Ortiz, the Mexican bullfighter. An equally pertinent indication of Franklin's role in the character of Roger is Hemingway's ear for the conversational style of his characters. Roger's assurance that Paco is homosexual — "sure he's a queen, didn't you know that, of course he is" — is very similar to Franklin's manner in *Death in the Afternoon:* "and does she, of course she does, you fool you didn't know she does? Absolutely and that's all and in no other fashion, she gobbles them alive."

But there is equal reason for believing that Paco, too, may have been modeled, in part, after Franklin. For Franklin, a bullfighter trained in Mexico, was definitely costume-conscious. In *Bullfighter from Brooklyn,* he inventoried his extensive purchases down to the incidentals and boasted of his personally designed special outfit: "Immediately after the accident I had ordered a salmon or coral-pink uniform embroidered in ivory coloured silk." Franklin was superstitious about the traditional black costume, believing it bad luck. No doubt, he took some pride in having brought a measure of haute couture to the bullring. Franklin, too, had had his luggage and swords "ruined by sea water" in the hold of a ship during a particularly unfortunate tour in Mexico.

And what of Hemingway's connections with the circumstances of "The Mother of a Queen"? Is it, perhaps, strange that four years after his father died, Hemingway should write a story about a son's negligence and a mother who would not stay permanently "buried" after five years? While Grace had tactfully praised *A Farewell to Arms,* had acknowledged her gratitude for her son's financial help, for a trust fund established by Ernest, Pauline, and Uncle Gus, she had not yet earned Hemingway's forgiveness. He was still of the mind that it was Grace who had been responsible for his father's suicide. Strange, too, that in April 1932, during the period in which Hemingway had probably written "The Mother of a Queen," he had so far neglected to write his mother that she had sarcastically reminded him, "I won't bother you with any more letters after this; as it will take you some time to answer the last six that I have written you."

Granting that the facts of the case may be that the bullfighter Ortiz actually did refuse to bury his mother in proper fashion, still a writer is responsible for what he picks up on from life, whether the experience is that of another or his own. ("The good parts of a book," Hemingway advised Fitzgerald, "may be only something a writer is lucky enough to overhear or it may be the wreck of his whole damn life — and one is as good as the other.") "The Mother of a Queen" may be an instance of both cases. If so, Paco's blatant rationalization for his negligence toward his mother, as Hemingway ironically presents it, is devastating: "Now she is all about me in the air, like the birds and the flowers. Now she will always be with me."

⁂

In reflecting at one point in the book on the finality of one's life, Hemingway makes one of those curious associations that suggest there is something suspect in his flat observations. He raises the issue of marital fidelity. There was no lonelier man, "except the suicide," than a monogamous man who has lived happily with a good wife and has outlived her. From that brisk assertion, whether one agrees with it as true or as one of Hemingway's sentimental truisms, he goes on to make a personal confession. "I would sooner have the pox," he claims, "than to fall in love with another woman loving the one I have." ("What has this to do with bulls, sir?" the Old Lady, his fictional interlocutor, asks with good reason.) Ambiguity is a superb tactical device; whether Hemingway was remembering his first marriage or his second is not quite clear. If "another woman" was Pauline, it was hardly flattering.

But there is, at least, a possibility that Hemingway had a third woman in mind. Returning to America that September on board the *Île de France,* the Hemingways encountered Don Stewart and his wife. Like Pauline, Beatrice Stewart was pregnant. Through the Stewarts, Hemingway and Pauline were introduced to an attractive and vivacious twenty-two-year-old socialite named Jane Mason, the wife of G. Grant Mason, the head of Pan American Airways in Cuba, who had a luxurious estate west of Havana. Slender, a strawberry blonde with blue eyes, Jane was an irresistible attraction for the two soon-to-be fathers. She had a scattering of interests, enjoyed deep-sea fishing and shooting, and had a wide circle of wealthy friends. She had had some training in art at Briarcliffe, dabbled in sculpture and painting. There was a wild, awesome streak in her nature that Hemingway would come to understand later in their relationship. She was subject, as Hemingway was, to mood swings, shifting from enthusiasm to a black despondency, and had apparently made one or two ineffectual attempts at suicide, though her husband had not taken them too seriously. Was it Jane Mason whom Hemingway had in mind when he spoke of "another woman," or was he merely entertaining the notion of another woman?

III

"My bloody book is finished except for one piece of translation in the appendix," Hemingway wrote Guy Hickok on December 12, 1931. "Am getting Mss copied in Key West and sending it to Scribner. To be out in the fall." It was a good book, he assured Hickok. "Really maybe best one yet." Hemingway's letter was a passel of newsy items. His son Gregory Hancock Hemingway had been born in Kansas City in November and was built like the Battling Siki, the West African fighter — all shoulders, long arms, big feet, weighing in at nine pounds at birth. "Very black hair. Solemn pan. Hope the bastard has a talent for business." It had been a difficult birth. Pauline had gone into labor at six P.M. on Armistice Day and was in labor for twelve hours when the doctor decided on a cesarean section.

Prohibition was a nuisance, he noted, drugstore prescription whiskey was generally phony; druggists were cutting it with grain alcohol and distilled water. The best brands were Briargate and Golden Wedding. The Depression, strangely, had made everyone a damned sight more polite and easier to get along with. Despite the economy, Uncle Gus was doing better in Kansas than he had the year before, and his business dealings with Germany were highly successful. "I imagine Hitler will come into power in Germany. What do you think?" Hemingway asked. "Well all this going haywire in Europe has re-established the foreign correspondent's job, just after the papers had all decided there was nothing news except airplanes and divorces out of Europe."

Hemingway was keen for Dos Passos's appraisal of *Death in the Afternoon.* Dos had read a good part of the manuscript during a rushed four-day visit to Key West with Katy. (He and Katy were on an extended trip that would take them through Mexico and to the West Coast and back through the Southwest.) In a follow-up letter, he was full of praise: the book was "an absolute model for how that sort of thing ought to be done." The accounts of the fighters, the Spanish towns, were a "knockout," he wrote Hemingway. But Dos had some critical reservations: "I'm only doubtful, like I said, about the parts where Old Hem straps on the longwhite whiskers and gives the boys the lowdown." He objected to much of the literary talk, the secrets of the profession, the explanations of why Hemingway liked living in Key West, and so on. "The volume is so hellishly good. (I'd say way ahead of anything of yours yet) and the language is so magnificently used — (why right there sitting in Bra's boat reading the typewritten pages I kept feeling I was reading a classic . . .) — that it would be a shame to leave in any unnecessary tripe." Hemingway took Dos Passos's advice to heart. When he replied, Hemingway admitted that he had gone over the book some seven times and cut "4½ galleys of philosophy and telling the boys." He had also cut all of Chapter 20, except the lengthy homage to Spain. He left in the Old Lady because it was O.K. or, at least, "necessary as seasoning."

With Max Perkins, Hemingway had a burst of temper prior to publication. When Scribner's sent him galley proofs that a compositor had tagged "Hemingway's Death," the irony was lost on the man who had written an elegy on death in the bullring. With a vehemence that was no joke, he fired off a telegram to Perkins demanding, "DID IT SEEM VERY FUNNY TO SLUG EVERY GALLEY HEMINGWAY'S DEATH OR WAS THAT WHAT YOU WANTED?" The next day he bawled Perkins out in a letter. "You know I am superstitious and it is a hell of a damn dirty business to stare at that a thousand times. . . . If I would have passed out would have said your goddamned lot put the curse on me." He was dissatisfied as well with Scribner's advance publicity, which ballyhooed material he had cut from the galleys. With measured sarcasm, he said that if Scribner's continued to advertise the book as a kind of miscellany, readers would be disappointed because it didn't have "a cook book and a telephone directory as well." Nor did he like the photos of himself chosen by the publicity department: "for christ sake no more of those open mouth open collar wonders. Promise me that. And NIX on that one of me lying with the sick steer."

Death in the Afternoon was published on September 23, 1932. The reviews were more favorable than might have been expected, considering he was writing about a blood sport that was of little interest to most Americans. Even H. L. Mencken, Hemingway's bugaboo, writing in the *American Mercury,* found *Death in the Afternoon* "an extraordinarily fine piece of expository writing," but he complained that it "often descends to a gross and irritating cheapness." The narrative was "full of the vividness of something really seen, felt, experienced," Mencken acknowledged, but the language was "often bald and graceless." He suggested that if Hemingway had cut out "the interludes behind the barn," it would have been a first-rate book.

Quite generally, the reviews stressed the sense of the author's personality. Herschel Brickell, in the *New York Herald Tribune Books* section, thought it "excellent reading, full of the vigor and forthrightness of the author's personality, his humor, his strong opinions — and language. . . . In short it is the essence of Hemingway." Granville Hicks, in *The Nation,* decided that people would read the book because of their interest in Hemingway rather than in bullfighting. "Fortunately the author, fully aware of the interest in his personality, has made a vigorous effort to put as much of himself as possible into this book." Lincoln Kirstein, in *Hound & Horn,* gave the book the roundest praise, considered it both a "spiritual autobiography" and a "tragic masterpiece." Kirstein zeroed in on the book's peculiar, irritating quality: "It also defines in a way which has perhaps never before been attempted, at least in the English language, the ecstasy in valor." While noting Hemingway's foibles, his cult of his own personality, Kirstein concluded that the book "stands head and shoulders above his worst self; it is his best self. . . . Hemingway, whether he likes it or not, is at once a reformer of literature and a violent reactionary. He has made it almost impossible for anyone to write loosely of a certain portion of physical experience again."

Robert Coates, one of Hemingway's former Paris associates, however, complained in *The New Yorker* of Hemingway's often harsh opinions of readers, writers, and things in general: "There are passages in which his bitterness descends to petulance (as in his gibes at William Faulkner, who has done him no harm save to come under his influence, T. S. Eliot, Aldous Huxley, Jean Cocteau, and others, living and dead), there are also passages of bright, appealing honesty." Coates's criticism elicited a speedy response from Hemingway in a letter published in *The New Yorker.* He claimed innocence of any such intent. "There weren't any cracks against Faulkner," he asserted, even though in one of his asides, he had gratuitously remarked, "you can't go wrong on Faulkner. He's prolific too. By the time you get them ordered there'll be new ones out." Hemingway did, however, admit that the other gibes had been intended. "The Eliot thing has been back and forth for a long time. [Waldo] Frank is a twirp (pen in hand), no matter how admirable politically." (Frank had had the temerity to write a book called *Virgin Spain.*) Hemingway claimed that he had plenty of respect for Faulkner and wished him luck. Still, he would feel free to make a joke about Faulkner if he chose. There were, he boasted, no subjects he would not joke about if the jest was funny enough. He was very fond of wing shooting, he said, and "I would shoot my own mother if she went in coveys and had a good strong flight."

IV

Although he plainly distrusted the New York literary critics, in the early thirties Hemingway was still on good terms with Edmund

Wilson. Wilson, in fact, had written the introduction for Scribner's 1930 reissue of *In Our Time.* Hemingway himself had suggested to Perkins that Wilson write it: "He is, of all critics or people, the one who has understood best what I am working at." He also approved of Wilson's new Scribner's book, *The American Jitters,* a political report on Depression America. Hemingway considered it "*wonderful* reporting," though he thought Wilson's move to the political left a handicap. As he wrote Dos Passos, Wilson "is sometimes boring because, like any convert, he hasn't the necessary elasticity, but he is damned good. . . . You and Bunny Wilson are the only consistent guys among all the word chaps." Hemingway cast a cold eye on the current political scene: "I suppose I am an anarchist — but it takes a while to figure out." It was the practice practice now to "poop" on anarchists like Enrico Malatesta in Italy, but Malatesta's name "will sound honester in 20 years than Stalin['s] will . . . I don't believe and can't believe in too much government — no matter what good is the end."

Fortunately, Wilson had not reviewed *Death in the Afternoon.* His private opinion, in a letter to Fitzgerald, was that it was "pretty maudlin — the only thing of his I haven't liked." Bullfighting was probably a good clean sport, but Hemingway, he felt, had made it "disgusting." There was, however, no overt cause for friction when, on a short visit to New York in January 1933, Hemingway had dinner one night with Wilson and Scott Fitzgerald. The three men, none of them the worse for drink, met for what turned out to be an even boozier dinner at the Aurora Restaurant. Hemingway arrived in a horse-drawn cab, explaining that he wanted to do something for the horse — compensation for the horses that died in the bullring. He was in good spirits throughout the meal. For the benefit of the waiters, he sang a chorus or two of a bawdy Italian song he had learned during the war. Scott, already drunk when Wilson arrived, fixed him with a "basilisk stare" and became immediately hostile. "What happened to you?" he asked, and then "Where's Mary Blair?" (Blair was Wilson's first wife, whom he had divorced some years earlier. Wilson was, in fact, suffering the aftermath of the accidental death of his second wife, Margaret Canby, who had died a few months before.) Wilson was annoyed not only by Fitzgerald's behavior but by his evident hero worship of Hemingway: "Hemingway was now a great man and Scott was so much overcome by his greatness that he embarrassed me by his self abasement."

Early in the evening, Scott announced that he was looking for a woman, and Hemingway told him he was in no condition for one. Thereupon Fitzgerald said he was done with men, saying perhaps he really was a fairy. Hemingway explained to Wilson that he and

Fitzgerald were in the habit of kidding around like that, but he warned Fitzgerald "not to overdo it." Fitzgerald's behavior went from bad to worse. At first he put his head down on the table like the dormouse at the Mad Hatter's Tea Party; then he lay down on the floor "pretending to be unconscious but actually listening in on the conversation and from time to time needling his hero, whose weaknesses he had studied intently, with malicious little interpolations." At times, Wilson and Hemingway had to take Fitzgerald to the can, holding his hands while he vomited. Meanwhile Fitzgerald alternately insulted them and asked if they really liked him.

During the quiescent periods, as Fitzgerald lay on the floor, Wilson and Hemingway carried on a rambling conversation at the table. Wilson remembered Hemingway's telling him that Fitzgerald was worried that his penis was too small — a story that Hemingway would repeat on several occasions to other listeners and to biographers and work up as one of the demeaning revelations in *A Moveable Feast.* (Wilson had already heard the report from John Peale Bishop, who told him that Scott was in the habit of making that assertion to anyone he met, including, once, a woman who sat next to him at a dinner party.) Hemingway went on to explain that this was because Fitzgerald was looking at his penis from above, while he should have been looking at it in a mirror. Wilson, who didn't quite understand the point, was of the opinion that ideas of impotence were very much on people's minds in those days because of the Depression. "I have the impression," he noted, "that various kinds of irregular sexual ideas are feared or become fashionable at different times: incest, homosexuality, impotence."

Wilson remembered, too, Hemingway's mentioning a recent car trip he had made with his son Bumby (they were en route from Key West to Piggott), and how they had stopped overnight in a hotel in Mississippi, and how Hemingway realized they were in Faulkner territory. He told Wilson — "with the utmost seriousness," Wilson recalled — that he had put Bumby to bed and then sat up all night with a gun on the table in front of him, the assumption being that Faulkner was a serious rival who might well send dangerous characters, of the kind who turned up in his novels, to do Hemingway harm. Wilson admitted, "I thought this was rather queer, but no queerer, perhaps, than some other things that came out in drinking conversations."

At the end of their evening out, Hemingway and Wilson managed to get Fitzgerald back to his room at the Plaza. Wilson stayed on with him for a while, thinking Scott might open up:

> but he simply took off his coat, vest, pants, and shoes and put himself to bed and lay looking at me with his expressionless birdlike eyes. I had asked him what he did in Baltimore — he replied truculently, The usual things! I said I'd heard the theory advanced (by Dos Passos) that he was never really drunk but used the pretense of drunkenness as a screen to retire behind — this only made him worse if anything in order to prove that he was really drunk — though his answers to questions and remarks suggested he was in pretty good possession of his faculties.

The next day, Fitzgerald called them both to apologize. When Wilson remarked on the cold eye Fitzgerald had given him, Fitzgerald, still in a belligerent mood, said "No confidence, eh? Well, you'll have to learn to take it." In his call to Hemingway, he had merely asked Hemingway to repeat some remark that he had made. He also wrote to Max Perkins, admitting that he had been on "a terrible bat. Ernest told me he concealed from you the fact that I was in such rotten shape." He was making his confession, he said, by way of explanation for his not having called his editor while in town, "thus violating a custom of many years standing." Perkins answered on January 27, "You did call me up, by the way. I was out and did not get back until after five, and then I called up the Plaza but you were out. I left a message that you were to get in touch with Ernest at the Brevoort." Like the dinner at the Aurora, a story of missed connections.

⸙⸙⸙

Given Hemingway's touchiness on the question of his masculine image, there is little wonder that when Max Eastman, belatedly reviewing *Death in the Afternoon* in *The New Republic* (June 7, 1933), questioned Hemingway's he-man posture, Hemingway would bear him an enduring grudge. To begin with, the article was titled "Bull in the Afternoon"; it set the tone of the piece. Eastman, readily enough, extolled Hemingway's virtues as a writer, maintaining that there were "gorgeous pages" in the book, "big humor and reckless straight talk of what things are, genuinely heavy ferocity against prattle of what they are not." Eastman admired Hemingway's bitterness as a writer, a bitterness that would not let him settle for the Cult of Unintelligibility, or the new Bohemianism, or the cheap moral decorum practiced by the conservative critics, led by Irving Babbitt, known as Humanism ("that shallow cult so admirably exterminated root and branch by Ernest Hemingway in a paragraph of this book)." But there was, Eastman claimed, "an unconscionable quantity of bull" poured and plastered all over whatever Hemingway wrote about bullfights. Why, Eastman wondered, did Hemingway indulge in such clouds of juvenile romanticism whenever he crossed the border into Spain?

Eastman's denigration of bullfighting was bad enough, but the fatal blow was this pointed observation:

> It is of course a commonplace that Hemingway lacks the serene confidence that he *is* a full-sized man. Most of us too delicately organized babies who grow up to be artists suffer at times from that small inward doubt. But some circumstance seems to have laid upon Hemingway a continual sense of the obligation to put forth evidences of red-blooded masculinity. It must be made obvious not only in the swing of the big shoulders and the clothes he puts on, but in the stride of his prose style and the emotions he permits to come to the surface there.

Hemingway's problematic manner, Eastman asserted, had begotten a veritable school of new fiction writing, "a literary style, you might say, of wearing false hair on the chest." Eastman had picked up that particular critical gibe from Hemingway himself. In *Death in the Afternoon,* Hemingway delivered his opinion that in the ring, Ignacio Sánchez Mejías's bravery was laid on with a trowel: "It was as though he were constantly showing you the quantity of hair on his chest or the way in which he was built in his more private parts."

Eastman's critique raised the hackles not only of the author but of his friend Archibald MacLeish, who, fastening on the sentence that Hemingway lacked the confidence of knowing he was a full-sized man, wrote a hasty letter to *The New Republic,* calling the assertion scurrilous. Rather innocently, MacLeish offered evidence of Hemingway's power and potency, not from personal knowledge, to be sure, but by alluding to Hemingway's three sons, advising Eastman to study "the birth records of the cities of Paris and Kansas City where he can satisfy his curiosity in secret."

Stirred up by Eastman's article and by MacLeish's reading of it, and by the fact that Bruce Bliven of *The New Republic* declined to publish MacLeish's letter, Hemingway mounted his own campaign, first drafting a letter or two to the magazine, one asking that "Mr. Max Eastman elaborate his nostalgic speculations on my sexual incapacity," another of which characterized Eastman as a "groper" sexually and a traitor in politics. In a letter to Bliven himself, Hemingway wanted to know just what constituted a full-sized man: "Is it a matter of numbers or of measurements? When did I first lose confidence or have I never had it?" In the official letter to the editors, as a parting shot, Hemingway wrote, "Mr. Alexander Woollcott and the middle-aged Mr. Eastman having both published hopeful doubts as to my potency is it too much to expect that we might hear soon from Mr. Stark Young?" There was more than simple sarcasm in his query. Max Eastman had a reputation as a ladies' man and was therefore above reproach so far as Hemingway's gender slurs were concerned, but, in New York literary circles, Woollcott, with his high-pitched voice, was rumored to be impotent (or even thought to be a hermaphrodite), and drama critic Stark Young was known to be homosexual. (It is of some consequence, too, that Young had reviewed the stage version of Hemingway's *A Farewell to Arms* during its short run in New York. In *The New Republic,* Young had praised Laurence Stallings's adaptation, particularly the second-act hospital scene, as "every bit as good as the novel, and to my mind much better.")

Hemingway's letter did not appear in the pages of *The New Republic,* though Eastman published one denying any innuendos in his article. He also wrote mollifying letters to both Hemingway and MacLeish. Hemingway, still fuming, wrote MacLeish about Eastman's gesture. "What a slimy lying shit he is. He wrote me a sucking letter too. What a thing the literary man is." In a letter to Max Perkins, Hemingway, expectably, vowed revenge. If he ever saw Eastman anywhere or anytime, "I will get my own redress myself." They were a nice lot, he charged, "the professional male beauties of other years."

A little more than a month later, he was defending himself against similar charges made by a disloyal woman-friend, Gertrude Stein, in her book *The Autobiography of Alice B. Toklas.* Stein's book was one of the earliest first-person accounts of expatriate American life in Paris, and, of course, featured her role in it from the invention of Cubism and the First World War through the arrival of the Lost Generation writers. It was, in its lively fashion, Stein's announcement that she now considered herself sufficiently historical to warrant an autobiography and, for all her complacent egotism, this was true enough. Her book did, indeed, make a place for herself, her friends, enemies, and rivals in cultural history, a task made easier by the fact that the book became a best seller.

Stein had hit upon a novel device in the literature of autobiography: writing her own memoir, so to speak, by ghostwriting the autobiography of her lifelong companion, Alice Toklas. Aside from the novelty of it, the device proved to be useful, allowing her, in many instances — and certainly in the case of Hemingway — to wield a double-edged sword, giving her own supposedly benign appraisals of her contemporaries and then undercutting them with the more acerbic observations of Alice.

Hemingway had not been feuding with Stein at the time, but he was probably apprehensive about what she might say. In April 1933, before the book was published, he confided in Janet Flanner, who had mentioned Stein's forthcoming book in one of her Paris letters for *The New Yorker.* Among the people who had already read the manuscript, Flanner said, there was some question about which of the various merits of the book was the most "meritorious." She listed, among a handful, "the Picasso part, or the analyses of Hemingway." In his letter to Flanner, Hemingway was more revealing than he perhaps intended:

> Gertrude S. I was very fond of and god knows I was loyal too until she had pushed my face in a dozen times. Last time I saw her she told me she had heard an incident, some fag story, which proved me conclusively to be very queer indeed. I said You knew me for four or five years and you believe that? Oh it was very circumstantial, she said. Very circumstantial indeed. She wouldn't tell me what it was.

"Poor old Papa," Hemingway groaned. He would probably read all about it in her autobiography. The likelihood is that Stein had heard such a story; it was not the kind of thing she would invent to confront Hemingway with — and the probability was that Hemingway had enemies in Paris who would have been happy to spread such gossip. The guilty party may well have been Robert McAlmon, who perhaps told Stein his shady story about the night he and Hemingway had spent together in Spain after a bout of heavy drinking. "I never cared a damn about what she did in or out of bed," Hemingway wrote Flanner, "and I liked her very damned much and she liked me. But when the menopause hit her she got awfully damned patriotic about sex."

Stein, however, did not reveal the teller or the tale in her gossipy book. Still, it must have been on Hemingway's mind when he read the final installment of the book in the August issue of *The Atlantic Monthly.* There, he confronted himself and his relationship with her in the inevitably distorted mirror of Stein's prose. He learned that as a writer he had been "formed" by Stein and Sherwood Anderson; that both of his mentors were "a little proud and a little ashamed of the work of their minds." Both considered him a good pupil. Alice, however, protested, saying that Hemingway was "a rotten pupil." Stein also trimmed his macho image a bit by pointing out what she and others regarded as Hemingway's peculiar frailty. "Ernest is very fragile, whenever he does anything sporting something breaks, his arm, his leg, or his head." It was clear that Stein had been apprised of most of his recent accidents. Having wounded his vanity as a man, she next attacked his pride as an artist. She compared his success as a writer to that of the painter Derain: "He looks like a modern and he smells of the museums," she said.

But Hemingway was not, perhaps, prepared for the devastating way that Stein gave the considered opinions of Stein and Anderson on the subject of Hemingway:

> They admitted that Hemingway was yellow, he is, Gertrude Stein insisted, just like the flat-boat men on the Mississippi river as described by Mark Twain. But what a book, they both agreed, would be the real story of Hemingway, not those he writes but the confessions of the real Ernest Hemingway. It would be for another audience than the audience Hemingway now has but it would be very wonderful.

If he could not ignore Eastman's innuendos, Hemingway was even angrier at Gertrude's calling him yellow. Given Stein's suspicion that he was homosexual, what else could she have been referring to when she remarked, "But what a story that of the real Hem, and one he should tell himself but alas he never will. After all, as he himself once murmured, there is the career, the career."

Later that year, Hemingway paid her back in kind. In an essay written for *Cahiers d'Art* on the painter Joan Miró, Hemingway had an opportunity to remark that Miró's painting *The Farm* had taken him nine months to create whereas "a woman who isn't a woman can usually write her autobiography in a third of that time." He, too, could handle a riposte as easily as Stein. "If you have painted 'The Farm,'" he said, "or if you have written *Ulysses,* and then keep on working very hard afterwards, you do not need an Alice B. Toklas."

That was his more tempered public response. Only a few days after reading the installment in *The Atlantic Monthly,* Hemingway vented his anger in a letter to Pound. He had learned more about how to write and not to write from Pound than any son of a bitch alive, he said.

> Learned from her too — in conversation. She was never dumb — in conversation. Damned smart — in conversation. But it seems she and old mother hubbard Anderson made me in their spare time. Well by Jesus that will be something for them to be remembered by if its true. I stuck by that old bitch until she threw me out of the house when she lost her judgment with the menopause but it seems that I'm just a fickle, brittle brain-picking bastard. She gave me some damned good advice many times and much shit to boot. . . . Read the damned piece. She disposes of you too. There is nothing like a self appointed legendary woman.

"Well gents," he threatened, "It will be a big day when [I] write my own bloody memoirs because Papa isn't jealous of anyone (yet) and have a damned rat trap memory and nothing to prove. Also the documents."

15
The Green Hills of Africa

"We have a fine house here and the kids are all well," Hemingway wrote Janet Flanner from Key West in the early spring of 1933. "Also four coons, a possum, 18 goldfish, three peacocks and a yard with fig tree, lime tree. Very fine the way Pauline has fixed it. We have been (and are) damned happy." But that was in a manner of speaking: he was nevertheless going to Cuba in three days, leaving Pauline behind. He planned to stay several months for the fishing. After that, he was planning on a trip to Spain and then Africa. He was, he said, "homesick for Spain and want to go and see the animals and hear the noises they make at night." He was plainly restless. "Look, why don't you come to Havana?" he asked Janet. There were miles and miles of beaches with hard white sand, and the Gulf Stream ran almost black, coming right in to the shore. Pauline was in the habit of coming out to Cuba for two or three weeks at a time, Hemingway told Flanner, "then goes back to K.W. to check up on the children and the house. Finest life you ever saw."

For Pauline, it seems to have been less than a pleasure. Hemingway had been romancing Jane Mason since he had first met her on the *Île de France*. She had visited the Hemingways at Key West in 1932. (And had given them two flamingos for the growing menagerie.) Hemingway saw Jane more often in Cuba, where the Masons had their estate at Jaimanitas. Jane was a frequent companion on his fishing expeditions. (An entry by an unknown hand in the ship's log of the *Anita,* Josie Russell's cabin cruiser, read "Ernest loves Jane.") But Bumby, who visited with his father in Havana in May of 1933, accompanied by his half brother Patrick, later tended to discredit the idea that very much of an affair could have been conducted, on the boat at least: "Too much was going on, and Papa would not carry on in front of the crew. They were his buddies." Still, Hemingway boasted that Jane would crawl into his hotel room at the Ambos Mundos through the transom, a feat that almost certainly must have been far more noticeable than sneaking in by way of the door. Pauline, in Key West, had reason for concern, as one of her plaintive letters to her husband makes clear. She had been experimenting with new hairstyles and new hair colorings, it seems, in an attempt to make herself more attractive, considering the beautiful competition. And in a joking mood, she wrote Hemingway, "Am having large nose, imperfect lips, protruding ears and warts and moles all taken off before coming to Cuba. Thought I better, Mrs. Mason and those Cuban women are so lovely."

But that spring there was a break in the increasingly fugal relationship between Hemingway and Jane Mason. In late May, while driving Bumby, Patrick, and her adopted son Antony to Jaimanitas, she was forced off the road by a bus and her large Packard rolled off a soft shoulder and down a forty-foot embankment, finally settling in a gully. Fortunately she had thought to turn off the ignition as the car went over the side. No one was hurt, but Jane was bruised and badly shaken. Bumby, with considerable cool, remarked, "Don't worry Mrs. Mason, I'll get you right out."

Then, several days later, in a fit of depression, Jane fell or jumped from the second-story balcony of her home and broke her back. Grant Mason, who considered it another attempt to gain sympathy, nonetheless decided it was serious enough to ship his wife back to New York for treatment, with a nurse in constant attendance and bars on the porthole windows. She was hospitalized for five months and had to wear a back brace for a year. Hemingway, rather grimly, referred to her as the girl who had fallen for him, literally.

It was in that same troubled spring, in late May or early June, that Hemingway, still at the Hotel Ambos Mundos, met the twenty-nine-year-old photographer Walker Evans, then on assignment in Cuba, taking photographs for Carleton Beals's forthcoming book, *The Crime of Cuba,* an indictment of the poverty and terrorism under the dictatorship of Gerardo Machado. Evans's photographs of grimy dockworkers, of Havana prostitutes and street vendors, of the back streets, the mean poverty and teeming life of Cuba (his photos of the political murder victims, however, were appropriated from newspaper files) on the eve of a revolution against the U.S.-supported Machado regime, focused more on the human aspect of the Cuban situation than did Beals's polemical tract.

Whether Evans met Hemingway through an introductory letter or through another source (Beals had given him letters to newsmen and friends in Havana) is not clear. As a photographer, he had been living a hand-to-mouth existence for some time, and in Cuba he ran out of cash. Hemingway lent him what Evans referred to as a small amount of money to stay on and finish his assignment. The two spent time drinking together in the local bars at night. As Evans remembered it, Hemingway "was at loose ends . . . and he needed a drinking companion." Evans, who had an aversion to photographing celebrities, took no pictures of the famous author. "I refused to do Hemingway and E. E. Cummings and all those people," he once remarked. "Much to Hemingway's delight I might add. I think he felt I wanted to be coaxed." But by way of commemorating the occasion, it appears, Evans did take photographs of one of the downtown Havana theaters with a poster blazoning the Hollywood version of *A Farewell to Arms.* The encounter in Havana was the only occasion that Hemingway and the photographer met.

⸙⸙⸙

"Leave for Europe Aug. 7 — will be there Aug. Sept. Oct.," Hemingway informed Ezra Pound, in a July 22 letter from Key West. From there he was going to East Africa. He had spent several months fishing the Gulf Stream for marlin, he said. "I weigh 187 now," he told Pound, "weighed 211 when started on the trip, fished 97 days (Probably do it as an affectation)." The African trip had been long in the planning. It had been on his mind since the spring of 1930, when he had run into his old Red Cross companion Milford Baker in the elevator at Abercrombie and Fitch. In the gun shop, the two had talked about the proper rifles for big game in North America and Africa. Since Uncle Gus had proposed underwriting $25,000 for the expenses of an African safari, Hemingway took Baker up on his offer to oversee the making of a custom-made Springfield rifle with a telescopic sight. ("No kick to gun," Hemingway boasted to Mike Strater in June when the rifle arrived in Key West. "One shot with the 22 grain bullet that went through about a foot and ½ thick palm tree tore out a place the size of your head and shoulders — hell — my head and your shoulders.")

At first, Hemingway had hoped that Strater and Archie MacLeish as well as Charles Thompson would join him and Pauline on the proposed African venture. But MacLeish had had to postpone, and Mike Strater, too; then there was the accident in Montana and Pauline's pregnancy, and Hemingway had put the trip aside. (In the meantime, Hemingway, in a generous gesture, had made a $1000 loan from the trip money to Dos Passos, invalided in a Baltimore hospital with a serious bout of rheumatic fever.)

It was not until 1933 that the plans were finalized. "I may have become a naturalist," Hemingway informed Pound not long before his departure. But Pound was less than impressed. "An if you are going to be a nacherlist//thass O/K/ but ef yew air goin to Afrik fer to annoy a tranquil family of man eatin lions etc /// I reprobate you." Hemingway had, in fact, planned the trip with more than his usual seriousness and attention to detail. During one of his jaunts to New York, he had even visited Clyde Beatty, the lion tamer, who was appearing in Madison Square Garden. During a rehearsal, Hemingway studied the action of the animals, fascinated by the lithe movement as they crouched and sprang, impressed by Beatty's use of a kitchen chair as a defensive weapon.

But by then the makeup of the long awaited safari had changed. Hemingway had had some intermittent quarrels with both MacLeish and Strater during the course of fishing expeditions, and both men decided against making the trip for various reasons, important among them the fact that Hemingway was likely to spoil it with his competitive behavior. The final plan now was that he and Pauline would make the safari with Charles Thompson, who planned to meet them in Paris in the late fall. They had arranged to sail from Havana on the *Reina de la Pacifica* in early August, with Hemingway stopping at Santander to take in the bullfights while Pauline and her sister, Jinny, went on to Paris. Young Patrick would be traveling with them. (Gregory was staying with his nursemaid, Ada.) Accompanying them, also, was Bumby, who would be returning to his mother in Paris. Hadley, after a cautious five-year courtship, had married Paul Scott Mowrer in London on July 3.

⁂

In Spain, Hemingway had a spell of freedom from family concerns, following up on the bullfights, mostly disappointing. Marcial Lalanda had succumbed to success and was no longer interesting to watch. Domingo Ortega still dominated his bulls but was monotonously theatrical. In Madrid, Hemingway met up with Sidney Franklin once again. Franklin, considerably buoyed up by the boost in his reputation from Hemingway's *Death in the Afternoon,* was obliged to undergo another operation for the rectal wound he had suffered in the bullring three years earlier. Hemingway generously paid the hospital bill. With equal generosity, he also helped edit, cut, and rewrite a "trashy" Spanish bullfight novel that Sidney was translating for an American publisher. Despite the regular attendance at the disappointing bullfights, Hemingway had also begun a long Cuban story, "One Trip Across," the adventures of Harry Morgan, rumrunner, that would eventually become the novel *To Have and Have Not.*

If Hemingway was disappointed by the bullfights that season, he was equally disappointed with the three-year-old Spanish republic. The idealists of the revolution were in power, he felt, with their fingers in the pie, and the plums were now getting pretty small. When the pie ran out, he predicted in a letter to his mother-in-law, Mary Pfeiffer, there would be another revolution. He was less prophetic in his second article for Arnold Gingrich's *Esquire.* (His first, "Marlin off the Morro," had appeared in the August issue of the new men's magazine.) There was money around, Hemingway noted, but it seemed to be in the hands of the innumerable functionaries of the government. "While the peasants are as bad off as ever, the middle class is being taxed more than ever, and the rich certainly will be wiped out, although there is no sign of it yet." Nor was he happy with Madrid: the Cafe Fornos, one of his old haunts, had been torn down to make a new office building, and the customers had moved next door to a new café called the Aquarium. A swimming pool had now been built on the banks of the Manzanares River, on the site where he and Sidney and the out-of-work bullfighters used to swim and drink and cook their *paella*. It was a thoroughly modern establishment with an artificial beach with real sand and water that was cold and remarkably clean.

Paris turned out to be equally disappointing when Hemingway arrived there late in October. The visit was a big mistake, he told the readers of *Esquire*. He heard of old friends who had shot themselves or taken overdoses of drugs. "All I do is go out and get depressed and wish I were somewhere else. It is only for three weeks but it is very gloomy." Montparnasse, he found, had been discovered by the French bourgeoisie, and the big cafés were doing a steady business. The only foreigners to be seen were Germans: "The Dôme is crowded with refugees from the Nazi terror and Nazis spying on the refugees." He had gone to the very big retrospective exhibition of Renoir but would have preferred a show of Cézanne or Van Gogh. Food was as good as ever, but expensive. Hemingway was not the only one to find Paris depressing that year. A few months before, Wambly Bald, the journalist whose column, "La Vie de Bohème," had been a regular feature in the Paris edition of the *Herald Tribune*, penned his good-bye column, "Farewell to Montparnasse" ("As I write this valediction I see the parade of silhouettes. What became of Flossie Martin, Harold Stearns, Homer Bevans, the Countess Eileen?"), complaining, "I am tired of jiggling a corpse."

In his "Paris Letter," Hemingway had managed to sum up his disillusionment with the situation and get off another of his periodic insults to Stein, again without naming her: "People must be expected to kill themselves when they lose their money, I suppose, and drunkards get bad livers, and legendary people usually end by writing their memoirs." But that was not the cause of his real depression: "What makes you feel bad is the perfectly calm way everyone speaks about the next war." Whatever his personal grievances and disappointments, he managed to see them in a proper perspective.

Hemingway saw old friends. He visited Janet Flanner and Solita Solano in their rue Bonaparte apartment. Solano offered to type up

Hemingway's Harry Morgan story and send it off to *Cosmopolitan.* (The magazine published it in its April 1934 issue, paying Hemingway $5500, the highest fee he had ever received for a short story.) Sylvia Beach welcomed him with warm affection. "He and I are good old friends," she wrote her sister the day of his visit. "He looks fine and handsome. His new book of short stories, *Winner Take Nothing,* will be soon out and he has finished a new novel and is writing another." But that was a rosier view than actually proved to be the case. The book had already been published in America, and Hemingway was irritated by the reviews Perkins was forwarding to Paris: "A fool like [H. S.] Canby thinks I'm a reporter — I'm a reporter *and an imaginative writer.*" As usual, he made a careful study of the Scribner's advertisements for his book and scolded Perkins for the lack of follow-up. Dorothy Parker's new book of stories was being well advertised in the major papers. Another of his irritations was the way "after a wonderful start [Scribner's] dropped *Death in the Afternoon* absolutely cold. You know yourself." He did not intend to be taken for granted, "Especially as I have always paid my way."

On his last night in Paris, Hemingway and Pauline dined with James and Nora Joyce, feasting on game (pheasant and venison) that he had shot on a hunting expedition with a friend in Sologne the day before. Joyce, aside from his physical disabilities, had been under a strain. His family life was being torn apart by his daughter Lucia's tortuous decline into schizophrenia. She had been undergoing a series of treatments in various clinics without much success, including a brief stay at the Rives de Prangins, near Geneva, where Zelda Fitzgerald had been a patient two years earlier. For the moment Lucia was at home with a nurse companion.

The night of the dinner party, Hemingway and Joyce took their drinking seriously. Joyce was an admirer of Hemingway's adventurous lifestyle. During the earlier, soberer, phase of the meal, Joyce, in a gloomy mood, asked if Hemingway didn't think Joyce's books were too "suburban." Joyce confessed that it got him down sometimes. Nora spoke up, "Ah Jim could do with a spot of that lion hunting." But Joyce was not so sure: "The thing we must face," he said, "is I couldn't see the lion." Nora had a ready answer: "Hemingway'd describe him to you, Jim, and afterwards you could go up and touch him and smell of him. That's all you'd need." Joyce would remember the evening well: Hemingway "promised us a living lion. Fortunately we escaped that." He considered Hemingway, flatteringly, as a modest giant, ready to live the life he wrote about. "He's a good writer, Hemingway," Joyce claimed. "He writes as he is . . . there is much more behind Hemingway's form than people know." It was an accurate assessment of a fellow writer. Hemingway, too, had some fond remembrances of Joyce in his moments of strange acuity. It was either on this or perhaps some earlier occasion that Joyce, with Jesuitical precision, told him, "Hemingway, blasphemy's no sin. Heresy is the sin."

On November 22, at Marseilles, Hemingway, Pauline, and Charles Thompson boarded the *General Metzinger* for a cold, rainy trip through the Mediterranean to Port Said. The *Metzinger* was a disreputable and dirty vessel, the food unpalatable. When they reached Egypt, the weather had turned hot and fine. On December 2, Hemingway wrote Patrick about their trip through the Suez Canal, the ship coasting past the flat desert, a soldier on a camel racing alongside almost as fast as the ship was going. He wrote about the birds — snipe, hawks, a scattering of black cormorants, a blue crane. As they approached the Indian Ocean, before disembarking at Mombasa, they saw schools of porpoises. Hemingway gave his five-year-old son some fatherly advice: "Go easy on the beer," he said, "and lay off the hard liquor until I get back."

Africa surprised him. "Nothing that I have ever read has given any idea of the beauty of the country or the still remaining quantity of game," Hemingway wrote in the first of the African letters he sent back to *Esquire*. The landscape reminded him, at times, of the western reaches of Nebraska; the country washed green after the rains, blue hills rising in the background. On the Serengeti Plain, there were migrating wildebeests in the millions. It was one of the largest herds in years. Traveling with it, on the fringes, were jackals and hyenas, and vultures circling overhead — companion populations caught up in the forward movement of the herd, an ecosystem on the drift. But chiefly it was the lions that engaged Hemingway's study: tawny, dark-maned, lifting their heads out of the tall grass, or resting in the shade of a tree, lying asleep on the high knolls not half a mile away from the black sea of grazing animals.

It was at Machakos that they met up with their white hunter, Philip Percival, at his farm at Potha Hill. Percival was an experienced professional, one of the best in the field. As a young man he had hunted with Teddy Roosevelt, who had considered him a fine rider and good shot. Hemingway was immediately impressed with Percival, who had served in a British intelligence unit during World War I. The white hunter reminded him of an older, slightly heavier Chink Dorman-Smith, with the same dry humor, the same good company, though perhaps more tolerant for his years. He was a crack shot, knew the animals, was an expert student of their behavior.

Their first expeditions were in the nearby Kapiti Plains, shooting gazelles and impalas and guinea fowls. Then on December 20, they began the safari proper with two lorries for the equipment, a white mechanic named Ben Fourie and a Kikuyu driver, gun-bearers and porters and kitchen help. They made the two-hundred-mile trek to Arusha in Tanganyika, arriving in time to spend Christmas day camping on the Serengeti Plain.

The hunting began badly with the first lion, which everyone agreed would belong to Pauline ("P.O.M.," Poor Old Mama, as Hemingway would identify her in *Green Hills of Africa*). They had come upon it late in the evening, a fine specimen. But Pauline, shooting with a Mannlicher, had missed, and Hemingway, taking the second shot with his big Springfield, had caught it on the run, just below the spine. M'Cola, the black gun-bearer, who had taken a fancy to Pauline, immediately claimed it as Pauline's hit. "Mama *piga Simba,*" he shouted, and stuck to the claim as they entered camp, where the natives lifted Pauline up in celebration, circling round and round the fire, chanting "*Hey la Mama! Hey la Mama!*" Hemingway let it go at that, though everyone knew that it was his shot. Pauline acknowledged it in her diary: "Very splendid; wished I had shot the lion. Gave everybody a shilling."

For Hemingway, much of the trip would be a run of bad luck. He came down with amoebic dysentery, trying to fight it off at the outset of the safari. But it brought him down in mid-January. He had contracted the disease earlier, probably from the terrible food on the *General Metzinger,* or perhaps from a meal at Port Said. None of the remedies he tried was successful. As he explained in one of his extended physiological disquisitions for the benefit of the *Esquire* readership, there had been a day, while out shooting sand grouse, when he experienced an intestinal prolapsus that made him feel that he had been "chosen as the one to bear our Lord Buddha when he should be born again on earth." He found himself wondering, he said, "how much Buddha at that age would resemble Gertrude Stein." For all the sardonic joking, it had been a painful experience and he had been passing blood for several days. Percival insisted he go for treatment in Arusha or Nairobi. For the next day or two, Hemingway willingly remained in camp, invalided, reading the English papers and resting until a plane could be summoned by wire at the nearest station at Lake Victoria.

It was two days before the plane arrived, a silver two-seater with a tiny pilot, Fatty Pearson, whom the diminutive Pauline described as "belonging to the weasel family." In her diary, Pauline recorded that Hemingway had gone off "very gay and handsome." The cramped flight took Hemingway to Arusha for a fueling stop and then on to Nairobi, northward past the high, snowcapped Mount Kilimanjaro. It proved to be one of the more important episodes in Hemingway's career; the African safari, the worried wife, the ailing writer, the flight in the *Puss Moth,* would be transfigured in Hemingway's greatest short story, "The Snows of Kilimanjaro," written two years later.

At Nairobi, Hemingway put up at the New Stanley Hotel while being treated with injections of emetine, the specific for amoebic dysentery. It was while recuperating at the hotel that he wrote the first of his *Esquire* pieces. And it was there that he met another celebrated white hunter, Bror Blixen, and his young client, Alfred Vanderbilt, a wealthy socialite and sportsman, a friend of Jane Mason's. Even in Africa, Hemingway managed to make connections of one kind or another with legendary women. Blixen's former wife (they were divorced) was Karen Blixen, the writer Isak Dinesen. (She had recently auctioned off her coffee plantation in the Ngong Hills and returned to Europe.) While Hemingway was recuperating in Nairobi, in fact, Dinesen's first book, *Seven Gothic Tales,* a Book-of-the-Month Club selection, was having a stunning New York success. And it was while he was in Nairobi that Hemingway probably first met the tall and beautiful aviator Beryl Markham, whom Hemingway would later catapult into belated fame by praising her book *West with the Night.* At the time, however, he found her "very unpleasant," probably too self-aware and independent for his tastes. He later admitted that he never once suspected that "she could and would put pen to paper except to write in her flyer's log book."

When Hemingway returned to the new base camp, near the Ngorongoro Crater, late in January, the hunt was for rhino and kudu in the hill country. Unfortunately, Hemingway's bad luck continued. When he shot his first rhino at a distance of three hundred yards, Percival congratulated him, told him it was the best shot he had made. But the glow of satisfaction faded when Charles Thompson brought in a rhino whose smaller horn was bigger than the big horn of Hemingway's specimen. Hemingway acknowledged in *Green Hills of Africa* that he felt like someone who had suffered a heavy financial loss. He also found it difficult to congratulate Thompson: "We had not treated him badly, but we had not treated him too well," Hemingway acknowledged. In one of those efforts of humility that often read like acts of contrition in Hemingway's nonfiction (but seldom appear in his private letters), Hemingway claimed, "I was, truly, very fond of [Thompson] and he was entirely unselfish and altogether self-sacrificing. I knew I could outshoot him and I could always outwalk him." Still, Hemingway admitted, "he beat me on all the tangible things we had to show." And so it continued until the final days before the long rains ended the safari, when Hemingway, camping out at a salt lick with his driver and gun-bearers, tried to better his record with a prize greater kudu bull. (Pauline and Percival had remained in camp, hoping for the best.) Hemingway, at last, bagged a pair of fine specimens, the heads stripped down to the cleanly picked white skulls with ample horns: "They were the color of black walnut meats and they were beautiful to see." Returning to camp, triumphantly sounding the Klaxon and shooting off his gun as they arrived, he discovered that Thompson had bested him again, with "the biggest, widest, darkest, longest curling, heaviest, most unbelievable pair of kudu horns in the world." He was, he admitted, suddenly poisoned with envy. The next morning, though, it was gone.

Percival counseled him: "We have very primitive emotions," he said. "It's impossible not to be competitive. Spoils everything, though." Hemingway assured him, "I'm all through with all that . . . I'm all right again. I had quite a trip, you know." Percival agreed: "Did you not," he said.

⸻

The Hemingways were in Paris in March, just before returning to the States. Hemingway and Pauline invited Janet Flanner and Solita Solano to dinner at Michaud's. They also invited James Joyce. It was a dismal occasion. Joyce, drinking heavily, barely spoke. At midnight, Janet and Pauline became so bored they left. Hemingway, according to Solano, had sat through the meal "in a stupor of silent worship," which may have meant that he too had been drinking heavily, since he was well past the hero-worshiping stage in his relationship with Joyce. When Hemingway excused himself for a moment to go to the john, Joyce clutched at Solano's hand, imploring, "Don't go." Then he said nothing to her for the remainder of the night. After a wild bout of waltzing with the *patronne,* Joyce fell back against a table; Hemingway and Solano had to take him home to his apartment on the rue Galilée.

On a visit to Shakespeare and Company, Hemingway came across a recent essay on himself in *Life and Letters,* by Wyndham Lewis, provocatively titled "The Dumb Ox." In it, Lewis played up, disparagingly, Hemingway's debt to Gertrude Stein: "One might even go so far as to say that this brilliant Jewish lady had made a *clown* of him by teaching Ernest Hemingway her baby talk!" — a charge made more convincing by a very apt comparison of lengthy passages from Hemingway's "Soldier's Home" and Stein's "Melanctha." Lewis condescendingly suggested that Hemingway's art was "an art of the surface — and, as I look at it, none the worse for that," while scoring its matter-of-fact acceptance of violence and its lack of political insight. Gesturing in anger, Hemingway knocked over a vase of tulips Sylvia Beach had placed on a table full of new books, spilling water all over them. Sylvia and Pauline hastily sponged off the wet books. Hemingway gave her 1500 francs for the damage, taking the spoiled books with him, four of which were by Virginia Woolf, another of his English foes. "Poor Ernest," Sylvia wrote her sister, "he is really a very good boy, but primitive, which doesn't interfere with his writing, on the contrary."

The voyage home on the *Paris,* in late March, was the occasion for Hemingway's meeting with another legendary lady, this one the screen star Marlene Dietrich. One evening the actress entered the dining room for a dinner engagement but stopped short of allowing herself to be seated. As she explained, years later, in a Sunday supplement article, "The men rose to offer me a chair, but I saw at once that I would make the thirteenth at the table. I excused myself on grounds of the superstition, when my way was blocked by a large man who said he gladly would be the fourteenth. The man was Hemingway." The two would engage in an intermittent correspondence following that first meeting. Over the years, they met occasionally — Hemingway referred to her affectionately as "the Kraut" — usually when they both happened to be in New York.

On their arrival in New York, Hemingway occasioned as much interest among the waiting news reporters as the famous star. Interviewed by the *Times* and the *Herald Tribune,* Hemingway was ebullient on the subject of lion hunting. He told them that he was going to settle down to a season of intensive writing at Key West in order to earn enough for a return trip to Africa. However, that may have been only a publicity release on his part.

The fact was that he was eager to buy a fishing boat of his own, and he had already made plans to place an order for a thirty-eight-foot cabin cruiser at the Wheeler shipyard in Brooklyn. It cost $7500, and the down payment of $3300 had come from Arnold Gingrich as an advance against Hemingway's future articles in *Esquire.* Although the boat would not be delivered for another thirty days, Hemingway had already decided to christen it the *Pilar,* after the shrine of Nuestra Señora del Pilar, Our Lady of the Pillar, at Zaragoza, and the secret name Pauline had used in her cables to Hemingway at the time of his separation from Hadley.

While in New York, Hemingway had another unsatisfactory

meeting with Fitzgerald, who was celebrating the publication of his novel *Tender Is the Night* — celebrating it too vigorously, since Hemingway recalled that it was impossible to talk with him because he was so drunk. The novel, which explored the disintegration of the marriage of an alcoholic psychoanalyst, Dick Diver, and his beautiful patient, Nicole, was set largely on the Riviera and in Paris. It had been serialized (with romantically appropriate illustrations by Edward Shenton) in *Scribner's* magazine. If Hemingway had read portions of the book by then, he did not attempt to discuss it with Fitzgerald in New York. Instead he complained to Perkins in an April 30 letter, criticizing the book as unsound because Fitzgerald, having obviously taken Gerald and Sara Murphy as the models for his hero and heroine, had made them act in ways the couple would not have behaved; he had transformed them into Scott and Zelda. "The hell of it," Hemingway scoffed, "is that you can't write Prose after you are thirty five unless you can think straight. And it is the flashes where he *does* think straight that carry this book in spite of the worn Christmas tree ornaments that are Scott's idea of literature." Scott's problem was that he "has so lousy much talent and he has suffered so without knowing why, has destroyed himself so and destroyed Zelda, though never as much as she has tried to destroy him."

Nearly a month after their New York meeting, Fitzgerald, waiting for some word, finally sent Hemingway a letter asking for his opinion: "Did you like the book? For God's sake drop me a line and tell me one way or another. You can't hurt my feelings. I just want to get a few intelligent slants at it to get some of the reviewers' jargon out of my head." Two weeks later, Hemingway answered with a long and critical letter. He did and he did not like the novel, he said. "If you take real people and write about them," he told Fitzgerald, "you cannot give them other parents than they have (they are made by their parents and what happens to them) you cannot make them do anything they would not do." He brandished a few labored compliments: "There were wonderful places and nobody else nor none of the boys can write a good one half as good reading as one that doesn't come out by you," he said, but added, "but you cheated too damned much in this one. And you don't need to."

Hemingway launched into a critique of Fitzgerald's character as a writer. "In the first place I've always claimed that you can't think. All right, we'll admit you can think," Hemingway conceded for the sake of argument. "Second place, a long time ago you stopped listening except to answers to your own questions. . . . That's what dries a writer up (we all dry up. That's no insult to you in person) not listening." The book was a lot better than he was saying, "But it's not as good as you can do."

In his lecturing mood, he diagnosed Fitzgerald's problem: "Of all people on earth you needed discipline in your work and instead you marry someone who is jealous of your work, wants to compete with you and ruins you." He claimed that he knew that Zelda was crazy the first time he met her "and you complicated it even more by being in love with her and, of course you're a rummy." He offered, at least, the consolation that Fitzgerald was no more of a rummy than Joyce or than most good writers were. "You can write twice as well now as you ever could. All you need to do is write truly and not care about what the fate of it is." He concluded, "Anyway, I'm damned fond of you."

Fitzgerald answered Hemingway's deflating letter with considerable aplomb. "The old charming frankness of your letter cleared up the foggy atmosphere through which I felt it was difficult for us to talk any more." He did, however, want to go to the mat with Hemingway on the subject of composite characters, a topic they had discussed once in Paris. "Now, I don't entirely dissent from the theory but I don't believe you can try to prove your point . . . in the case of this book that covers ground that you personally paced off about the same time I was doing it." How, Fitzgerald wondered, could Hemingway trust his own detachment? "If you had never met any of the originals then your opinion would be more convincing."

Like Perkins, Fitzgerald recognized that Hemingway was at best "touchy" about any form of criticism; it was best to proceed with caution and compliments. He offered a few soothing remarks, both genuine and generous, considering the circumstances. "I think it is obvious that my respect for your artistic life is absolutely unqualified, that save for a few of the dead or dying old men you are the only man writing fiction in America that I look up to very much. There are pieces and paragraphs of your work that I read over and over." Hemingway was right to claim "that I no longer listen. . . . But I listen to you and would like damn well to hear your voice again."

Ironically, Hemingway, in time, would temper his criticisms of *Tender Is the Night.* Only a year later, he admitted to Perkins, "A strange thing is that in retrospect his Tender is the Night gets better and better. I wish you would tell him I said so." Scott was so pleased with the message that he pasted it in his scrapbook. He wrote Perkins that his friendship with Ernest was one of the high spots in his life, "But I still believe that such things have a mortality, perhaps in reaction to their very excessive life, and that we will never again see very much of each other."

II

"If I ever write anything about [Africa] it will just be landscape painting until I know something about it. Your first seeing of a country is a very valuable one." So Hemingway cleverly announced in a late passage of the book he had been writing about Africa. *Green Hills of Africa* was written in Key West in 1934, mostly over a period of several months, with interruptions for fishing expeditions in the Caribbean and another trip to Cuba. Published in October 1935 after serialization in *Scribner's* magazine, it was indeed a book about landscape, though Hemingway referred to it in more magical or mystical terms as "country," equating it with the love of a woman, an old equation popular among poets and patriots. But Hemingway took it further, making it a trope for sexual intercourse. He described it in passionate terms. "I loved the country so that I was happy as you are after you have been with a woman that you really love . . . and you want more and more, to have, and be, and live in, to possess now again for always, for that long, sudden-ended always; making time stand still, sometimes so very still that afterwards you wait to hear it move."

But even more than country, *Green Hills of Africa* is a book about writing and writers. Hemingway was not ashamed to air his grand ideas on the subject. As a writer, he wanted to see "how far prose can be carried if any one is serious enough and has luck," to see if prose could attain a fourth and even a fifth dimension. Contrary to the usual critical opinion, what he had in mind was a prose that was much more difficult than poetry. "It is a prose that has never been written. But it can be written, without tricks and without cheating. With nothing that will go bad afterwards." His view of the writing profession even outmastered his view of country.

> A country, finally, erodes and the dust blows away, the people all die and none of them were of any importance permanently, except those who practiced the arts, and these now wish to cease their work because it is too lonely, too hard to do, and is not fashionable. A thousand years makes economics silly and a work of art endures forever.

As with *Death in the Afternoon,* the further Hemingway left the literary world behind him, the more the subject of literature crept into his nonfiction narratives. *Green Hills of Africa* is riddled with literary pronouncements, obiter dicta, opinions about Rilke, Paul Valéry, Thomas Mann. It begins, in fact, with a significant literary idyll, flattering to Hemingway and drawn from a chance meeting in the African bush with a cultured Austrian businessman and amateur ethnologist named Kandisky (Hans Koritschoner, in real life). Kandisky knew Hemingway by reputation as a poet through the pages of *Der Querschnitt* — one of the neat coincidences in the literary life. In their campfire conversations, Hemingway does most of the talking, expatiating on American literature — about which Kandisky has a certain curiosity — bandying the names of such respectable classics as Emerson, Hawthorne, Whittier, and company, men who had "minds, yes. Nice, dry, clean minds," or romantics like Poe who were skillful as stylists but dead as writers. It is in this conversation that Hemingway makes his famous and often quoted published pronouncement that "all modern American literature comes from one book by Mark Twain called *Huckleberry Finn,*" with the qualification that a reader must stop with the episode in which Nigger Jim is stolen from the boys: "That is the real end."

Contemporary American writers, Hemingway claims, are either destroyed by making money or end up by writing slop, or by reading and believing the critics. "At present," he assures Kandisky, "we have two good writers who cannot write because they have lost confidence through reading critics." One of the unnamed writers Hemingway had in mind is definitely Fitzgerald, the other is probably Max Perkins's protégé, Thomas Wolfe, whom Hemingway took to referring to as the "World Genius" in his letters to Perkins. ("When is your World Genius going to publish again? Or is he so worried about living up to his press notices that he'll never be able to put it out?") Hemingway had a special gibe for the unnamed Sherwood Anderson, assuring Kandisky, "At a certain age the men writers change into Old Mother Hubbard. The women writers become Joan of Arc without the fighting." Hemingway's anger had a long reach: he had some special criticisms for Gertrude Stein, whom he referred to as a bitch. But at Max Perkins's urging, he later removed the term and deleted some of the other offending phrases: "Woman of letters. Salon woman. What a lousy stinking life." In *Green Hills of Africa,* Hemingway was well on the road to becoming the white hunter in American letters.

⁂

Where the book excelled was in its account of the animals. When it came to describing the natural life, Hemingway had achieved a prose style that animated the bare description. His animals moved; the rhinos crashed through the tall grass of the hidden watercourses, the lions lazily roared, tails flicking the camel flies, as they rested under the mimosa trees in the noon heat. Even a clutch of guinea fowls crossing a dusty road is rendered with the precision and economy of a Japanese haiku: "quick-legged across the road running steady-headed with the motion of trotters . . . they rocketed up, their legs tucked closed beneath them, heavy-bodied, short wings drumming, cackling."

The prize specimens of his African safari, the rhino head, sable, and impala, preserved and stuffed by a New York taxidermist — solid proof of his African safari and of his skills as a big-game hunter — now hung in the dining room of the Key West house (along with Miró's *The Farm,* which Hemingway had wheedled back from Hadley on a five-year loan but never returned during his lifetime). The lion and leopard skins, open-mouthed and glaring, had been turned into rugs. But, in truth, the dead trophies, glassy-eyed, would never be as alive as they were in Hemingway's prose: "It was a cow rhino with a calf and as I lowered the gun, she gave a snort, crashed in the reeds, and was gone. I never saw the calf. We could see the reeds swaying where the two of them were moving and then it was all quiet."

In the book, he captured the ordeal of a hunt by night, sliding down a steep ravine, clinging to vines and "hearing the rustle of night things and the cough of a leopard hunting baboons." Nor, in that prose moment in a nighttime jungle, was Hemingway afraid to mention his private fears: "me scared of snakes and touching each root and branch with snake fear in the dark." Snakes, he admitted, "scare me sick. . . . They always have." There were moments when he too — not the fictive celebrity — came alive in the narrative.

One species did not grace the walls at Whitehead Street: "*Fisi,* the hyena, hermaphroditic, self-eating devourer of the dead, trailer of calving cows, ham-stringer, potential biter-off of your face at night while you sleep." In Africa, he took a special vengeance on the hyena, shooting them at will, not out of sport, but in an attempt to annihilate the offensive species. His description of one of them running, "obscenely loping, full belly dragging," reveals a distinct animus. Hemingway's accounts of shooting the beast are routinely brutal: "There was that comic slap of the bullet and the hyena's agitated surprise to find death inside of him. It was funnier to see a hyena shot at a great distance, in the heat shimmer of the plain, to see him go over backwards, to see him start that frantic circle, to see that electric speed that meant that he was racing the little nickled death inside him."

It was not an incidental aside that Hemingway made when he claimed that hyenas were hermaphroditic (a mistaken claim, but an ancient one, based on the fact that the female hyena, the dominating member of the tribe, carries an appendage shaped like a male penis in addition to its otherwise female genitalia). Sexual oddities were, for Hemingway, matters of curiosity. In one of his articles for *Esquire*, "Out in the Stream: A Cuban Letter," written while he was still working on the text of *Green Hills of Africa*, Hemingway speculated on the sexual identities of the various types of marlin that bred in the waters off Cuba. He also remarked on the sexual odyssey of the jewfish (or jewelfish), which, like the grouper, in its old age, turns female. Without foundation, Hemingway speculated, "Are not the white marlin, the striped marlin and the black marlin all sexual and age variations of the same fish?" What prompted this investigation into the species was the fact that the summer before, Hemingway had caught a striped marlin that had roe in it, spurring a series of caustic suppositions: "It wasn't much of a roe it is true. It was the sort of roe you would expect to find in certain moving picture actresses if they had roe, or in many actors." Given the sexual oddities of the ocean depths, was it implausible, then, considering the greater and lesser sexual peculiarities of the literary life, that Hemingway would ponder on the strange metamorphosis by which the aging Sherwood Anderson, in his dotage, might turn into Old Mother Hubbard?

⁊⁊⁊

Hemingway could hardly have been pleased by the contradictory reviews that *Green Hills of Africa* received. The critics, however, had responded to the clues and stratagems he had presented in the book. As John Chamberlain put it in the *New York Times*, the book was "pretty evenly divided between big game lore and salon controversy." Chamberlain found memorable passages here and there, but complained that the book was "all attitude — all Byronic posturing." That judgment was contradicted by Charles Poore in the *Times*'s Sunday *Book Review*. Poore found it "the best-written story of big-game hunting" he had ever read. Others, like Bernard DeVoto, considered it a step down from Hemingway's earlier work, "A pretty small book for a big man to write." And after Hemingway had taunted the left-wing critics with the unimportance of economics compared with art, it was little wonder that Granville Hicks in the *New Masses* would ask, "Would Hemingway write better books if he wrote on different themes?" Hicks suggested that Hemingway ought to write a novel about a strike, "not because a strike is the only thing worth writing about, but because it would do something to Hemingway. If he would just let himself look squarely at the contemporary American scene, he would be bound to grow."

With the run-of-the-mill left-wing critics, Hemingway could write the criticisms off as strictly party-line carping; but it was a different story with Edmund Wilson's lengthy essay in the December 1935 *New Republic.* Wilson's article, "Letter to the Russians About Hemingway" (it was reprinted in the Russian magazine *Internatsionalnaya Literatura*), took issue with Hemingway's growing Russian reputation, not on political grounds but on aesthetic and moral ones. Wilson started off by proclaiming *Green Hills of Africa* as far and away Hemingway's weakest book, aside from *The Torrents of Spring.* It was precisely on Hemingway's literary judgments that Wilson made his strongest points. "He inveighs with much scorn against the literary life and the professional literary men of the cities; and then manages to give the impression that he himself is a professional literary man of the most touchy and self conscious kind." Borrowing a quip from another reviewer, Wilson noted that Hemingway "went all the way to Africa to hunt, and then when he thought he had found a rhinoceros, it turned out to be Gertrude Stein." Wilson added that *Green Hills of Africa* was "the only book I have seen that makes Africa and its animals seem dull."

Wilson suspected that Russian critics reading the book would find the usual Marxist confirmation that the author of *In Our Time* was becoming more sterile in proportion to his detachment from the great social issues of the day. It was true that one of the most depressing aspects of Hemingway's book was the apparent drying up of the author's "interest in his fellow-human beings." Animals, Wilson claimed, were an interesting topic, but he did not find that Hemingway had made them interesting (a clear case of critical misjudgment). Nor did he think Hemingway had done justice to the natives: "the principal impression we carry away is that the Africans were simple people who enormously admired Hemingway."

Complaining about the "rubbishy" articles Hemingway was writing for *Esquire,* Wilson tried to put his finger on the source of Hemingway's problems as a writer.

> But for reasons which I cannot attempt to explain, something dreadful seems to happen to Hemingway as soon as he begins to write in the first person. In his fiction, the conflicting elements of his nature, the emotional situations which obsess him, are externalized and objectified; and the result is an impersonal art that is severe and intense, deeply serious. But as soon as he speaks in his own person, he seems to lose all his capacity for self-criticism and is likely to become fatuous or maudlin.

It was clear that Wilson still admired the artist, admired the "perfected" style of Hemingway's fiction, which he assessed as "without question one of the finest we have had in America and one of the finest in the world today." But Wilson's complaint that the public author seemed to be overtaking the private artist in Hemingway's promising career was accurate enough. It would, in fact, become one of the credible truths of Hemingway criticism.

Hemingway could hardly have been pleased by Wilson's review. He tried to keep his equanimity about it in writing to Ivan Kashkin, a Russian critic with whom he had recently begun a friendly correspondence. He pointed out that of the "rubbishy" articles he had recently written for *Esquire,* two had been warnings about the prospect of war. About Wilson's comments on *Green Hills of Africa,* he said he found them funny. He suspected Wilson had not read the book. "I think he read the criticisms."

III

The justice of Edmund Wilson's criticism that Hemingway's fiction far outdistanced his nonfiction prose would never be more clearly established than in "The Short Happy Life of Francis Macomber" and "The Snows of Kilimanjaro." Wilson, in fact, had predicted them when he remarked: "One can imagine the material of *Green Hills of Africa* being handled quite successfully in short stories or as a background to one of Hemingway's novels." Both stories were published in 1936 (though Hemingway seems to have made a start on "The Short Happy Life" in late 1934), when Hemingway's reputation was suffering at the hands of critics who complained of the effect of the Hemingway legend on his work and style.

The first was a tale of a wealthy man's rank cowardice in the face of danger. Francis Macomber is thirty-five, a sportsman who has kept himself fit. He is still youthful, good at court games, has a number of big-game fishing records to his credit. But tracking a wounded lion in the bush, he suddenly loses all nerve as the lion springs. His wife, Margot, and the hired white hunter, Robert Wilson, watch as Macomber bolts. "The next thing he knew he was running; running wildly, in panic in the open, running toward the stream." Margot, disgusted by his show of cowardice, taunts him in front of Wilson and finally revenges herself by sleeping with the white hunter that night, confident that her husband, as with her past infidelities, will do nothing about it. She is almost right. The white hunter, disgusted with Macomber as well, sees little reason not to make it with her. (He has a special double cot as part of his camping arrangements to accommodate such windfalls.) Margot Macomber is the type of beautiful American socialite that Hemingway, ordinarily, appeared to detest, with the exception, perhaps, of

Jane Mason. Still, it was Jane who, with her perfect oval face and strawberry blond hair parted in the middle and drawn back, was the principal model for dark-haired, beautiful, and bitchy Margot Macomber.

One or two critics of *Green Hills of Africa* admired the candid, delicate way Hemingway had expressed his love for his wife in the book ("She was always lovely to look at asleep, sleeping quietly, close curled like an animal"). But whatever the impressions Hemingway had given of his marriage in *Green Hills,* the principle behind the two African stories was a complete reversal, a blistering exposure of marriage and mismating. In "The Short Happy Life," Macomber is a man who will become wealthier still without working for it. He hangs on to his money, and to his wife, passively accepting her infidelities. In a devastating phrase, Hemingway focuses on one of Macomber's ambiguous virtues: "He had always had a great tolerance which seemed the nicest thing about him if it were not the most sinister."

It is a weakness his wife feeds on. Margot Macomber, at one time, commanded $5000 for endorsing beauty products she never used. Hemingway informs the reader that she is no longer attractive enough to divorce her husband and so better her position in life, suggesting, perhaps, that she is older than her husband. As a couple, the Macombers have settled into a demeaning accommodation, both of them knowing where they stand with each other. "All in all," Hemingway comments sardonically, "they were known as a comparatively happily married couple, one of those whose disruption is often rumored but never occurs."

Robert Wilson, the third party in the awkward triangle, decides that if he can get Macomber through the buffalo hunt on the next day and the rhino shooting on the day after, he will have fulfilled his obligations as a guide and that will be the end of an uncomfortable situation. But Margot makes the most of it. Archly, she asks about the eland her husband had shot for supper ("They're not dangerous, are they?") and taunts Macomber about the next day's shoot, commenting on how much she is looking forward to it. Macomber realizes that his one chance to redeem himself in his own eyes and in those of his wife is a good showing on the buffalo hunt. This he manages to do with a burst of bravery when they come upon three large bull buffalo. Macomber shoots well enough to earn compliments from the white hunter. But Margot Macomber, aware of her husband's new assertiveness, turns hesitant and sour. The men have used the car to herd the beasts before shooting them, and Margot asks pointedly, "What would happen if they heard about it in Nairobi?" Wilson admits, "I'd lose my license for one thing. Other unpleasantnesses." Macomber, for the first time, smiles. "Now," he tells Wilson, "she has something on you." Wilson, it has already been established, is no admirer of wealthy American women; he has had some experience with them. ("They are, he thought, the hardest in the world; the hardest, the cruelest, the most predatory and the most attractive and their men have softened or gone to pieces nervously as they have hardened.") He has begun to feel sympathy for the man he earlier despised, one of Hemingway's sharpest commentaries on the conspiracies involved in the war of the sexes. Wilson feels a fine disdain for the woman he has slept with and a condescending sympathy for the man he has cuckolded.

Unfortunately, during the hunt, one of the buffalo has not been killed outright, only badly wounded, and has gone off into the woods. Macomber is faced with the same threat he had with the wounded lion. But this time his courage is buoyed up, partly by his hatred for Wilson and by his revenge on his wife. Eager to go in after the wounded beast, he overrides his wife's complaints about the danger involved. She no longer wants him to take chances. As a precautionary measure, Margot Macomber is left behind in the car with her Mannlicher. In the bush, suddenly, the wounded buffalo, in a final gasp, charges the hunters. Macomber, in his excitement, shoots too high as the beast bears down on him. "Macomber, as he fired, unhearing his shot in the roaring of Wilson's gun, saw fragments like slate burst from the huge boss of the horns, and the head jerked." He corrects his aim, just in time to feel "a sudden white-hot, blinding flash explode inside his head and that was all he ever felt." As Hemingway describes it in the most precise terms, "Mrs. Macomber, in the car, had shot at the buffalo with the 6.5 Mannlicher as it seemed about to gore Macomber and had hit her husband about two inches up and a little to one side of the base of his skull."

Of the two African stories, "The Short Happy Life," the deadliest of Hemingway's marital tales, is the one most closely related to the hunting episodes described in *Green Hills of Africa.* The circumstances of the story — the lion hunt, the crashing charge of the wounded bull buffalo, altered for dramatic effect and whatever hidden or unconscious motives a writer uses in transmuting experience into fiction — are almost cinematic reruns of the scenes depicted in the book. Back at camp, after the lion hunting episode, for instance, Macomber allowed himself to be credited with the shooting of the lion and is lifted up by the cook, skinner, and porters, paraded around, and then put down before his tent. (The gun-bearers, having witnessed his shame, take no part in the celebration.) It is a reworked version, another of Hemingway's gender reversals, of the episode when Pauline had missed her first lion — which Hemingway then shot — but allowed herself to be congratulated by the camp crew.

The second instance — Macomber's success in the hunt for the three bull buffalo and the description of the charging of the wounded bull — are restatements of encounters mentioned in *Green Hills* and recalled in more detail in an unpublished African sketch. The differences among the versions are significant. Hemingway gives only a brief recap of the episode in *Green Hills,* but he goes into detail about the shooting of the dangerous second bull that charges out of the bush, merging the two different episodes in the story. In his unpublished African sketch, obviously written later, Hemingway treats the incident of the charging bull in full detail. In actuality, as he describes it, it was Ben Fourie who came running out of the bush to warn the hunters when the bull charged, a role that Hemingway assigned to one of the African gun-bearers in the story — probably to keep the story line from becoming cluttered with characters that would have to be accounted for in terms of plot. In the unpublished sketch, also, it is Charles Thompson, not Hemingway, who aimed too high, "the bits of horn flying from the boss like chips from a slate roof," while Hemingway, "sitting and shooting for the sticking place," manages to put six shots into a patch of hide no bigger than the palm of his hand. The bull, in this account, died with his head in Hemingway's lap — "truly," Hemingway adds. When Percival helps Hemingway up, his trousers are wet with blood. In contrast to the story, Percival did not fire at the charging buffalo, but was covering Pauline: "He said Karl's and my fire sounded like automatic weapons when the bull came out and did not shoot for fear of hitting us — also enjoying the spectacle," a bit of coolness that Hemingway may have admired. The possibility of a fatal accident may well have sparked the idea for the manner of Francis Macomber's death.

Several intangibles from *Green Hills* find their way into "The Short Happy Life," presumably innocent of plot considerations (if anything is ever innocent in fiction or in dreams). Abdullah the native, who is expected to bear witness to the circumstances of Macomber's death, is probably Abdullah the "educated" tracker, whom Hemingway admired in *Green Hills.* There are the references to the book bag and other incidentals from the Hemingways' safari. Some of these referents may be merely the economic use of material by a writer; others, perhaps, unconscious matters of recall. But some coincidences are important. It is clear that Philip Percival (in *Green Hills,* he is designated as Jackson Phillips or more familiarly as "J.P." or "Pop") was one of the models for the fictional Robert Wilson. Hemingway had gotten down Percival's laconic conversational style, using it both in his *Esquire* pieces and in *Green Hills* and continued it in "The Short Happy Life." Percival, in fact, would attest to Hemingway's fantastic recall: "He quoted what I said word for word years later in his letters and in *Green Hills of Africa*." There were, however, elements of Bror Blixen in the Robert Wilson portrait: it was Blixen, for instance, who had the providential double cot. Judging from the characterization of Percival in *Green Hills,* one suspects that Wilson's cynicism and womanizing were derived from Blixen, who was a member in good standing of the Nairobi fast set. The presumption, in fact, is confirmed by Hemingway's note in his African sketch: "Gave White Hunter the appearance of Philip but the habits of Von Blixen."

In one of the nighttime conversations in *Green Hills,* Hemingway asks Pauline whom she would consider a beautiful woman, and Pauline answers Garbo. "Not any more," Hemingway tells her, adding that Margot is. The "Margot" in question is Hemingway's alias for Jane Mason. Pauline agrees, saying "I know I'm not." Hemingway, chivalrously, assures Pauline, "You're lovely." That "Margot" should, in turn, become Mrs. Macomber of "The Short Happy Life" is particularly intriguing since Hemingway, though he denied any connection between himself and Francis Macomber, identifies himself throughout *Green Hills* as B'wana M'Kumba, a native version of a name that sounds too close to Macomber for comfort, whether deliberately or (more telling) an unconscious choice for the name of the protagonist of the short story.

Hemingway's use of Jane Mason (who had posed for cosmetic ads) as his model for Mrs. Macomber seems to have had a particularly virulent etiology. At least, so far as he would remember the circumstances later. In his essay "The Art of the Short Story," written in 1959 and published posthumously, Hemingway claimed that Margot Macomber had been invented "complete with handles from the worst bitch I knew (then) and when I first knew her she'd been lovely. Not my dish, not my pigeon, not my cup of tea, but lovely for what she was and I was her all of the above which is whatever you make of it. This is as close as I can put it and keep it clean" — as close to a complete denial of his actual relationship with Mason as might be imagined, or invented.

But the more important feature of "The Short Happy Life" is that it is one of Hemingway's classic studies of fear. The night before his act of cowardice, Macomber, lying awake in his tent, hears the roar of a lion and finds it more and more unnerving. Hemingway makes it plain that Macomber is afraid of what he imagines, and, since Margot is asleep throughout the ordeal, he has no one to talk it over with. Nor has Macomber ever heard, as Hemingway pointedly states, the Somali proverb that says "a brave man is always frightened three times by a lion; when he first sees his track, when he first hears him roar and when he first confronts him." It is precisely the kind of proverb that Hemingway, as an analyst of the psychology of fear, would pick up. Macomber, after his disgrace, is more troubled by his fears than by his sense of shame. Lying in his cot, listening to the night noises, his fear does not leave him: "more than shame he felt cold, hollow fear in him. The fear was still there like a cold slimy hollow in all the emptiness where once his confidence had been and it made him feel sick." During this dark night of the soul, around three in the morning, Macomber, reawakening, realizes that his wife has left her cot and gone to Wilson's tent. "He lay awake with that knowledge for two hours." When Margot returns, he calls her a bitch. In one of Hemingway's most acrimonious scenes, she responds,

> "Well, you're a coward."
> "All right," [Macomber admits]. "What of it?"
> "Nothing as far as I'm concerned. But please let's not talk, darling, because I'm very sleepy."
> "You think that I'll take anything."
> "I know you will, sweet."

Everything is of consequence in the life of fiction. It matters if Hemingway — as he probably did — had ruthlessly imagined the whole bitter episode between Margot and Francis Macomber, the lethal nastiness honed by terms of endearment, whether it reflected his sense of the bitchiness of women — or of a woman — and their power to demean a man, to demolish his confidence. In that case, the scene is a construct of Hemingway's mind, his sense of marital relationships, of a possible marital relationship. It would matter in another way if the Macombers' conversation had, in fact, been drawn from life, had taken place between Hemingway and Pauline or Hadley — or even Jane Mason — and was only a thinly fictionalized version of a private experience. And, among the possibilities, it is worth remembering that the story was written while Hemingway was still fuming — had reason to fume — about a woman (Gertrude Stein, a decided "bitch" in his mind) who had called him "yellow" in public print.

It matters that Hemingway left unanswered the vexing question of whether Margot Macomber had deliberately or accidentally shot her husband. Henry James, a master strategist, had recognized the tactical advantage of the unanswered question. (His philosopher-brother William James, on the other hand, was a man in search of answers: a question well asked, he claimed, was half answered.) But Henry James knew that a question, once answered, was useless for further fictional purposes. Left unanswered, as in "The Turn of the Screw" — a James story Hemingway admired — the question turns the story in upon itself, opens up continuous possibilities for further speculation and psychological interpretation. "The Short Happy Life of Francis Macomber" is Hemingway's "Turn of the Screw." Robert Wilson, like his author, seems to imply or suspect that Macomber's death was a deliberate act. "That was a pretty thing to do," Wilson tells the sobbing Margot in a toneless voice. "He *would* have left you too." But moments later, he relents, "Of course it's an accident . . . I know that."

Hemingway recognized that, where psychological motivations were concerned, it was better to admit the force of ambiguity in life. In commenting on "The Short Happy Life," he would, on occasion, provide the blunt expectable answer, "Francis' wife hates him because he's a coward. But when he gets his guts back, she fears him so much she has to kill him." Yet, in "The Art of the Short Story," he equivocated: "No, I don't know whether she shot him on purpose any more than you do. I could find out if I asked myself because I invented it and I could go right on inventing. . . . The only hint I could give you is that it is my belief that the incidence of husbands shot accidentally by wives who are bitches and really work at it is very low."

ﾉﾉﾉ

If one is to believe Hemingway's explanation in "The Art of the Short Story," the circumstances involved in the writing of "The Snows of Kilimanjaro" are these: having landed in New York after his African trip, he had told reporters he planned to work and, when he had enough money, return to Africa. As a result, "a really nice and really fine and really rich woman" invited him to tea and suggested that there was no reason Hemingway should wait before making his return visit to Africa. Money, she told him, was only something to be used intelligently and for the enjoyment of good people; she would provide the funds for Hemingway and Pauline to go to Africa and she would accompany them. Hemingway, realizing that it was a serious offer, nevertheless turned it down.

Still, settled once again in Key West, he began to wonder "what would happen to a character like me whose defects I know, if I had accepted that offer." It was that thought that provided the germ of his story: "So I invent how someone I know who cannot sue me — that is me — would turn out." Harry Walden, the protagonist of his story, is, in fact, Ernest Hemingway's double in most of the particulars regarding his career as a celebrated writer and journalist. There is no doubt that Hemingway recognized the importance of "The

Snows of Kilimanjaro"; he referred to it, in the making, as "a major story." ("The Short Happy Life of Francis Macomber" he considered "fool proof.") His recollection was that he had begun writing it in the late summer of 1935. The date was fixed in his mind; he had begun it sometime before the disastrous September hurricane that had swept through part of Key Largo and destroyed much of the Upper and Lower Matecumbe Keys, killing hundreds of veterans stationed in the Civilian Conservation Corps camps there. He had put the story aside and did not read it again until he began rewriting it the following spring. He boasted that he had "put into one short story things you would use in, say, four novels if you were careful and not a spender."

Masterpieces seldom yield up their secrets readily, and Hemingway's "The Snows" is unquestionably the great masterpiece among his short stories. The first intangible is the epigraph he placed at the head of the story, detailing the facts about the nearly 20,000-foot snow-covered Mount Kilimanjaro, the highest mountain in Africa, the western summit of which is called (in Masai) Ngàje Ngài, the House of God. "Close to the western summit," Hemingway added, possibly having heard the story from Philip Percival, "there is the dried and frozen carcass of a leopard. No one has explained what the leopard was seeking at that altitude" — a question that Hemingway obviously preferred to leave unanswered.

Hemingway considered "The Snows" a "difficult" story, though not difficult to read, "because there is so much dialogue." Yet the plot appears a matter of simple construction. A man, the writer Harry Walden, lies dying of a gangrene infection contracted while on safari in Tanzania. It is symbolic of his predicament, and of his character, that he has carelessly allowed a simple scratch on his leg to become infected by treating it improperly. As he lies in his cot, waiting for a plane to take him to a nearby hospital, he drifts in and out of consciousness. The dramatic action consists of his ruminations on his past life as a writer and journalist and his intermittent conversations and quarrels with his wife, Helen, who is trying to keep his spirits up, fending off his spells of bitterness and morbidity. On that skeletal framework, Hemingway hung a complex work of fiction which incorporated the experiences of his own professional career.

The story opens brilliantly with Harry's casual remark, "The marvellous thing is that it's painless. . . . That's how you know when it starts," his offhand acknowledgment that he is facing death. From there, it slips readily into a discordant round of marital carping, a sequence of blame, guilt, and recrimination between two people caught up in an unhappy modern marriage. Helen objects to

Harry's morose frame of mind. "Don't! Please don't," she objects when Harry apologizes for the odor of his gangrenous flesh. Their relationship during the crisis has become one of continuous bickering, broken by a few happy memories that usually have to do with sex.

Harry takes pleasure in rejecting his wife's efforts to keep his spirits up. (It is not quite clear how deeply Helen believes in the hopeful things she is saying. One suspects that she doesn't believe but intensely wants to believe — and Hemingway communicates that suspicion very subtly.) Helen is, in fact, one of Hemingway's more creditable heroines. She is wealthy; her first husband has died; she has lost a child in a plane accident; she has had several unsatisfactory love affairs and has gone through a period of heavy drinking. Her marriage to Harry has brought a needed and welcome focus to her life. She is generous; her money has been put at Harry's disposal for the furtherance of his career — and without complaint, it seems. But faced with death, Harry has moments of ruthless coldness. When Helen asks the usual, complaining question — "What have we done to have that happen to us?" — Harry gives her a clinical reply: "I suppose what I did was to forget to put iodine on it when I first scratched it. Then I didn't pay any attention to it because I never infect. Then, later, when it got bad, it was probably using that weak carbolic solution when the other antiseptics ran out that paralyzed the minute blood vessels and started the gangrene." Where Helen is looking for a simple human expression of hope, Harry spiels out the whole teleological explication down to the fact that their truck has broken down. If they had hired a good mechanic instead of "a half-baked Kikuyu driver," Harry complains, the mechanic would have checked the oil and never burned out a bearing.

It is worth remembering the actual circumstances of Hemingway's African safari. The original ailment had been amoebic dysentery — not, probably, the disease of choice an author might select for a fictional persona who bore some resemblance to himself (though Hemingway had no qualms about discussing it in detail in his *Esquire* pieces). It was Pauline who had fallen into a thornbush and was badly scratched, not Hemingway, and she could write about it with a certain humor ("Very painful taking out thorns from fatty part of anatomy"). They had a good mechanic in Ben Fourie and a good Kikuyu driver, whom Hemingway respected; it was the Austrian's lorry that had broken down. Life experiences in the hands of a master of fiction are extraordinarily malleable. Under the compulsion of some hidden obsession, some necessary perversion of the truth, they become screen memories, or the stuff of dreams, allowing him to choose the patterns he wishes to preserve or distort.

✓✓✓

At his best, Hemingway is a poet of convergences, providing moments of sudden reality, of some deflected vision — an epiphany, perhaps — not altogether recognized or understood, that is nevertheless transfixed in narrative. Harry's premonitions of death, edging in and out of delirium, interrupting, with a kind of cruel beauty, his corrosive squabbling with Helen, are among the most chilling moments in "The Snows." Hemingway ties these premonitions of death to some intangible connection, known only to himself, if known at all: the sight of a hyena crossing in the open space. "It came with a rush; not as a rush of water nor of wind; but of a sudden evil-smelling emptiness." Harry's semiconscious ruminations take on the character of a surrealist movie: "He lay still and death was not there. It must have gone around another street. It went in pairs, on bicycles, and moved absolutely silently on the pavements." At another incursion, Harry imagines, "It can be two bicycle policemen as easily, or be a bird. Or it can have a wide snout like a hyena." The invading presence of death — not its disordered image in Harry's mind — is prefigured in the descriptions of vultures circling in the air, or waiting "obscenely" (the word Harry prefers for them, and the word Hemingway used routinely in describing hyenas, another scavenger) at the edge of the encampment. Hemingway describes one vulture's movement with the kinetic perfection of a nature film: "A fourth planed down to run quick-legged and then waddle slowly toward the others."

"You can't die if you don't give up," Helen tells Harry in one of their squabbles. Harry's response is vitriolic: "Where did you read that?" he says, tearing apart her platitudinous assurances. "You're such a bloody fool," he says, brutally. At his best, Hemingway goes against the grain of sentimentality, emphasizing the constant bickering (unto death, in this case) between the couple, rather than going for the more easily rewarding pathos of their case. (It is important, reading Hemingway's dialogue, to catch the nuances of disdain, disinterest, underlying hostility, he conveys in the simplest retort.) Helen, too, gets off her barbs. If Harry has to "go away," she asks, "is it absolutely necessary to kill off everything you leave behind? . . . Do you have to kill your horse, and your wife and burn your saddle and your armour?" But it offers Harry another opportunity: Yes, he says. "Your damned money was my armour. My Swift and my Armour," a rancorous attempt at humor. Well before the contemporary vogue for novels of marital discord, Hemingway was an accomplished master at the subject. When Harry announces his morbid suspicion that he will die that night, Helen tells him not to be melodramatic, urges him to take some broth. He snaps, "Why don't you use your nose? I'm rotted half way up my thigh now. What the hell should I fool with broth for?" Just as suddenly, he relents, feeling guilty. He takes the broth, though he doesn't want it. In a moment of reflection he turns toward Helen, thinks sarcastically of the wealthy socialite he has married,

> with her well-known, well-loved face from *Spur* and *Town and Country,* only a little the worse for drink, only a little the worse for bed, but *Town and Country* never showed those good breasts and those useful thighs and those lightly small-of-back-caressing hands, and as he looked and saw her well-known pleasant smile, he felt death come again. This time there was no rush. It was a puff, as of a wind that makes a candle flicker and the flame go tall.

The convergence there is meant to tell us something about the author *in* the story, but it tells us, too, about the author *of* the story. In that brief sequence, Hemingway brought together his ambiguous attitudes toward wealth, celebrity, marital relations, sex, love — the fear and stench of death.

Hemingway's couple had come to Africa to escape the easy life of their rich friends. They had planned the safari for the minimum of comfort, no luxuries. It was to be Harry's attempt to get back in training as a writer. When he had, as he considered it, sold out to his rich wife, he told himself he would write about the rich; he would be "a spy in their country." Now, at the point of death, he recognizes that it is too late. He had left behind the people he had known in Paris in the early years when he was a promising new writer. The leisure life has dulled his talents. Worse, "the people he knew now were all much more comfortable when he did not work." Harry blames Helen for his failure, though he knows better: "If you hadn't left your own people, your goddamned Old Westbury, Saratoga, Palm Beach people to take me on —" he complains, then breaks off. (Like Hemingway, Harry knows the geography of affluence.) Helen protests that she loved him, that he is being unfair: "I love you now, I'll always love you. Don't you love me?" Harry's answer is calculated to wound, "No. . . . I don't think so. I never have," echoing the exchange between the mother and the soldier-son, Harold, in "Soldier's Home." Like young Harold, Harry is a man who wants to say — must say — no to a woman's expectations, to her demands. In his need to strike out, Harry calls Helen "You rich bitch," adding, "That's poetry. I'm full of poetry now. Rot and poetry."

✓✓✓

No, Hemingway made clear in "The Art of the Short Story" that he did not intend to explain the leopard. "He is part of the metaphysics," he added, acknowledging, for once, that metaphysics might have some role in his writing. So far as the leopard was concerned, he knew the answer but was under no obligation to tell. Hemingway's metaphysics, it should be said, was grounded in the actual; the frozen carcass of reality was clear evidence enough. He disliked "explainers, apologists, stoolies, pimps. No writer should be any one of those for his own work." Having exhausted the topic, he closed with this imperative: "Put it down to *omertà* [conspiracy of silence]." That was that.

Like a spendthrift, Hemingway had put into the one short story the experiences of a lifetime. "The Snows of Kilimanjaro" is his summing-up at mid-life and mid-career. He could, obviously, sense the bitterness and regret Harry Walden felt realizing that he no longer had time to write the things he wanted to write but had put off doing. He had known, as well as any man, about the finality of death. Hemingway had looked back over his career, remembering the incidents and events — some actual, some borrowed, others invented — in order to broaden the range of Harry's experiences. For Hemingway, like many fiction writers, like Harry Walden, was an autodidact of the self, liked to explore the plausibilities of every situation: What if? Why not? How would it be? He wove the real and its alternatives into Harry's progressive yielding to death. "*No, he had never written about Paris,*" Harry ruminates. "*Not the Paris that he cared about. But what about the rest that he had never written?*" These were the regrets that Hemingway, too, might have felt in mid-life since he clearly imagined them for Harry. Harry had forgone writing about the women he had known and the quarrels they had picked with him, always, he noted, at the wrong time: "*He had never written any of that because, at first, he never wanted to hurt any one and then it seemed as though there was enough to write without it. But he had always thought that he would write it finally.*" True enough for Harry perhaps, but not for Hemingway, who had, after all, committed fictionalized versions of Hadley, Pauline, Duff Twysden, and Agnes von Kurowsky.

For Hemingway, summing up Harry's failure was an act of restating, with crucial accuracy, his own artistic ambitions: "*He had seen the world change, not just the events; although he had seen many of them and had watched the people, but he had seen the subtler change and he could remember how the people were at different times. He had been in it and he had watched it and it was his duty to write of it."* The decisive feat of style in "The Snows of Kilimanjaro" is Hemingway's treatment of Harry's memories. The italicized recollections run through the story like a great fugue: the grim episodes of battle in Anatolia; his night with the hot Armenian slut in Constantinople; the top-story room in which he wrote looking out over the roofs and chimneys of Paris; a Christmas day in Schruns, with the snow so bright it hurt his eyes — all, irrevocably, leading up to that moment in the story when, the *Puss Moth* having finally arrived, Harry makes the ascent toward Mount Kilimanjaro, "as wide as all the world, great, high and unbelievably white in the sun," and knows, certainly in death, where he is going, without, probably, having learned the answer to the leopard's enigmatic climb.

BOOK

FOUR

The Gulf Stream

16

Politics, Women, Drink, Money, Ambition

A man obsessed with writing. He thought of it as the alternative to serving time. When young, you served time for catchword beliefs like society or democracy. In the end, however, you gave up those enlistments to "make yourself responsible only to yourself." Writing was a from of independence: "You exchange the pleasant, comforting stench of comrades for something you can never feel in any other way than by yourself." That something, he conceded, was hard to define, but it was recognizable from the feeling that comes over you "when you write well and truly of something . . . or when you do something which people do not consider a serious occupation and yet you know, truly, that it is as important and has always been as important as all the things that are in fashion."

As nearly as he could describe it, it was like being alone, cruising on the Gulf Stream off Cuba. A circumstance strange enough in itself, like being afloat on a river that takes its course through the wider sea,

> *and when, on the sea, you are alone with it and know that this Gulf Stream you are living with, knowing, learning about, and loving, has moved, as it moves, since before man, and that it has gone by the shoreline of that long, beautiful, unhappy island, since before Columbus sighted it and that the things you find out about it . . . are permanent and of value because that stream will flow, as it has flowed, after the Indians, after the Spaniards, after the British, after the Americans and after all the Cubans and all the systems of governments, the richness, the poverty, the martyrdom, the sacrifice and the venality and the cruelty are all gone.*

It was not the sentimental view of civilization, however, that Hemingway espoused in writing. Instead, his symbol was the image of a garbage scow, piled high and foul-smelling, dumping the refuse of society into deep waters:

> *as the load spreads across the surface, the sinkable part going down and the flotsam of palm fronds, corks, bottles, and used electric light globes, seasoned with an occasional condom or a deep floating corset, the torn leaves of a student's exercise book, a well-inflated dog, the occasional rat, the no-longer-distinguished cat; all this well shepherded by the boats of the garbage pickers who pluck their prizes with long poles, as interested, as intelligent, and as accurate as historians.*

Still, it was the hopeful view of a writer in an age still able to believe that nature, at least, would always survive the depredations of man: "and the palm fronds of our victories, the worn light bulbs of our discoveries and the empty condoms of our great loves float with no significance against one single, lasting thing — the stream."

The past is what has happened in its entirety, the total sum of everything swept away with the moment. It is wider and richer than history. What is remembered and written down, recorded — or salvaged anew like the treasures of the pharaohs' tombs or the fossils of a lost species — what is recoverable in conscious human terms, is history. One man's consciousness, assuming the man is intelligent, alert, curious, concerned, may evoke his piece of the past — a generation, an era, perhaps. Yet facts, details, the perjuries of personal recollection, the innocent or dishonest lies of friends, may not really constitute the life. If one knew everything there was to know about a writer's life at some phase of his or her career (the moment, say, of Hemingway's brooding observations on life and writing and the Gulf Stream), would one know everything that might be known about the writing, its banal origins, its hidden motivations? Or, as in a photograph, is the angle of the light, etched in certainty, simply a matter of the moment, and misleading?

As in a photograph, certainty bleaches out, faces blur, names fade beyond recognition, acquaintances, even close friends no longer identifiable by the curious viewer, linger like ghostly presences in scenes that offer no further clues. Time is irreverent. The biographer (if the subject is famous and salable enough to warrant a biography) retouches the picture, patches up the damages, tries to restore the fixed, fascinating moment out of a once continuous narrative. And the unwilling and, more likely, ambivalent subject — like Hemingway, who became the prey of resolute biographers — might justifiably dismiss the effort as a lost cause, "just one faded snap-shot more compared to what truly happened on a given day."

The given day: suppose that a man in his thirties — Hemingway, shaving in the mirror of a morning — is confronted by the hairy animal in his nature which needs to be suppressed anew each day (through Hemingway, in those years, sported a black mustache and, on occasion, a black beard that made him look more than ever like the photographs of his father in his prime). Six feet tall, he has put on weight, weighs 211 pounds clothed, but, giving himself the benefit of the doubt, imagines that means 200 pounds stripped. He is, by now, aware that he is aging; he wears glasses, plain, steel-rimmed, when he reads or writes. ("Eyes went haywire in Spain. . . . Can't do more than about 4 hours before they go bad.") He cannot ignore the ailments he has suffered in time: recurrent sore throats, a case of bronchial pneumonia brought on by playing a marlin for hours, sweating heavily, and taking chill on the night journey to port; bouts of amoebic dysentery. He is faced with the ravages of accidents along the way: the welt on his head from the falling skylight; the physical damage from the automobile accident in Montana.

("14 stitches in face inside and out — hole in leg — then that right arm — muscular spiral paralysis — 3 fingers on right hand broken — 16 stitches in left wrist and hand.") Imagine that the man, now thirty-six (years having slipped by in the hurrying stream), begins to take stock of his life, the years behind him, the changes made, pleasures ended, mistakes codified, the lies he once told himself and others. Suppose he begins to rationalize, to tell himself and others, as Hemingway did, "A life of action is much easier to me than writing. I have greater facility for action than for writing. In action I do not worry anymore. . . . But writing is something that you can never do as well as it can be done. It is a perpetual challenge." Perhaps he even thinks about that future when he, too, an old man, will look back upon a long life, "And the point of it is that nobody . . . knows how we were then from how we are now. This is worse on women than on us, until you look into the mirror yourself some day." But that is Hemingway at sixty, and time saves its revenge for the end.

⁂

"Along before Christmas I had gotten as gloomy as a bastard," Hemingway wrote Sara Murphy in February 1936. "Thought was facing impotence, inability to write, insomnia and was going to blow my lousy head off." It was not from want of announcing the method of his end that Hemingway's suicide would later come as a shock to his friends. In this case, possibly, he was making a bid for needed sympathy (from a woman who needed sympathy herself: young Baoth Murphy had died the year before of spinal meningitis, and Sara's grief and worry were compounded when Patrick, battling tuberculosis, had a relapse and had to be confined to the Trudeau clinic at Saranac Lake, New York). Hemingway's confession was not a passing remark confirming a moody spell. In a letter to Dos Passos, written the same day, he specified a period of a month and more during which he "felt simply awful, believe as bad as Scott ever felt, about six weeks ago . . . I felt that gigantic bloody emptiness and nothingness, like couldn't ever fuck, fight, write and was all for death."

Still, he reassured Sara that he had gotten himself out of his depression. He had been suffering from overwork and lack of exercise, so he "started going out in the stream and fishing again and in no time was swell." His own condition, then, must have made him especially unreceptive when he received a letter from Fitzgerald, who was, similarly, depressed. Fitzgerald wrote Hemingway an apparently critical letter (now lost) about *Green Hills of Africa.* (Judging from later remarks that Fitzgerald made to Max Perkins, he disliked the "calendar of slaughter" and the "sad jocosity" of Hemingway's references to Pauline as P.O.M., Poor Old Mama.) Fitzgerald's feelings about the book may also have been influenced by Hemingway's slighting reference to him, anonymously, as one of the two American writers "who cannot write because they have lost confidence through reading critics."

Hemingway's personal opinion of Fitzgerald's letter (told to Dos Passos) was that it was both pontifical and "very supercilious." Writing Fitzgerald, Hemingway said he was delighted to see that Fitzgerald didn't know what made a book good or bad any better than he ever had: "That means, anyhow, that you're not having any sudden flashes of insight or intelligence that would mean The End." Fitzgerald, he said, was like a brilliant mathematican who loved mathematics but always came up with the wrong answers. "Also you are like nobody but yourself and in spite of the fact that you think when you meet an old friend that you have to get stinking drunk and do every possible thing to humiliate yourself and your friend, your friends are still fond of you."

Five days later, Hemingway followed up with another ambivalent letter. Referring to his recent bouts with insomnia, he outlined his personal cure: "since I have stopped giving a good goddamn about anything in the past it doesn't bother much and I just lie there and keep perfectly still and rest through it." He offered his diagnosis of Fitzgerald's problems: "You put so damned much value on youth that it seemed to me that you confused growing up with growing old but you have taken so damned much punishment I have no business trying to tell you anything." It was one of the coincidences in their careers that both men should have been suffering from serious depressions at the time. They had, it appears, come to a point in their lives when early success no longer gratified or reassured them. Hemingway, at the moment, was struggling with *To Have and Have Not,* his novel of rum-running and revolution, set in Cuba and Key West. He may have recognized that it had been seven years since his last novel, not quite the length of time it had taken Fitzgerald to write *Tender Is the Night.*

That may have well have been a contributing factor to Hemingway's disgust with the series of essays that Fitzgerald subsequently published in *Esquire,* beginning with the February 1936 issue. *The Crack-Up* was the collective title of Fitzgerald's highly personal confession of the wreck of his life and his career under the influence of alcohol and the high life he and Zelda had been pursuing for the past decade and a half. For all its bitterness and its taint of self-pity, *The Crack-Up* was one of the great triumphs of Fitzgerald's literary career — a sobering indictment, not only of his own wasted life, but those of many of his contemporaries. In his three articles, Fitzgerald looked back on his professional life with an honesty he had avoided in his nonfiction writing. He admitted that he had been "only a mediocre caretaker of most of the things left in my hands, even of my talent." But in all those years he couldn't remember a moment of discouragement. His friends and companions of the gay years had committed suicide or were now institutionalized, but his own morale, he claimed, "never sank below the level of self-disgust when I had put on some unsightly personal show." But he had cracked nevertheless, "like an old plate," and the effect was devastating: "So there was not an 'I' any more — not a basis on which I could organize my self-respect — save my limitless capacity for toil that it seemed I possessed no more."

Fitzgerald had, at least, survived the ordeal. He no longer believed, he confessed, in the old suppositions of his youth — among them, the conviction that "the test of a first-rate intelligence is the ability to hold two opposed ideas in the mind at the same time and still retain the ability to function." He had, sadly, arrived at the rock-bottom realization that the natural state of the sentient adult was "a qualified unhappiness." *The Crack-Up* was Fitzgerald's notice that he had, at least, come through the searing experience of the last few years — his drinking, the waste of his talents, Zelda's madness — with a sense of having learned something of personal value. Certainly, the *Crack-Up* essays gave the lie to Hemingway's condescending suggestion that flashes of insight or intelligence in Fitzgerald's writing would inevitably signal "The End."

Hemingway's refusal to recognize that *The Crack-Up* was one of the masterpieces of American writing was a case of critical failure. He may not have wanted to recognize that art could be contrived from the depths of shameful failure as readily — even more honestly — as from an author's rigorous attempts at self-promotion. On February 7, when he wrote Max Perkins about Fitzgerald's embarrassing performance, he was scathing: "he seems to almost take a pride in his shamelessness of defeat. The *Esquire* pieces seem to me to be so miserable. There is another one coming. I always knew he couldn't think — he never could — but he had a marvellous talent and the thing is to use it — not whine in public." Hemingway wrote Dos Passos and Katy, "My god, did you read Scott's account of his crackup?" He mentioned that he had written Scott, trying to cheer him up, but without success, an odd construction to put on his highly ambivalent letters: "See the reason now. He's officially cracked up . . . Max says he has many imaginary diseases along with, I imagine, some very real liver trouble." He was far more sympathetic writing to Sara Murphy, trying to console her in her troubles. "These are the bad times," he said. "It is sort of like the retreat from Moscow and Scott gone the first week of the retreat. But we might as well fight the best god-damned rear guard action in history and God knows you have been fighting it."

A case might be made for the fact that it was Hemingway's commitment to the active life during the decade of the thirties that kept him from sinking into an ever-deepening depression, beyond recovery. It seemed almost a matter of principle or purpose that after his father's suicide Hemingway chose to distance himself from the cultural pretensions he associated with his mother. He had, it seemed, served his time with the movers and shakers of modern literature in Paris. He no longer depended upon his connections with Joyce and Pound and Stein. It may not have been only a personal break — there were the inner commands of a career, and a writer as aware of literary trends and literary politics as Hemingway must have sensed, if not perceived, that Paris was no longer the creative center it had once been, that he had nothing further to learn there. In the thirties, increasingly, Paris became for Hemingway a stopping-off place on visits elsewhere. After his early success, he needed the unpredictable challenges of people and events, the life of action as well as the trade of the writer. A man with a voracious appetite for experience, he had taken a larger grasp of life and art than many of his contemporaries. He was the celebrated author, the big-game hunter who courted danger, proved his bravery again and again in the public arena, proved himself in his contest with his father's cowardice and his own fears. In the wake of his father's suicide, he made a concentrated, even a desperate, effort to excel in just those aspects of Clarence's life, fishing and hunting, that he could still admire. But at the cost, perhaps, of a certain abrasiveness in his relations with others. It is not unlikely that his drive may have been powered by some inner psychological necessity. And for a decade or more, it seems, the active life proved to be a saving grace in his complicated career.

⁊ ⁊ ⁊

Straight narrative seldom suffices, does not lift the chronicle above the level of dates and hours, does not suggest the intangible ways the past continues to act upon the passing present or hint at what is being prepared for some distant future. It can reveal only, if at all, the convergence of time and circumstances brought to bear on some complex moment or phase of a life. It does not explain, except by mere recitation, the experiences in the unsatisfying year (or, more probably, years) leading up to Hemingway's depression and presumed recovery in the winter of 1935 to 1936. The sales of *Green Hills* had been disappointing; the reviews had not been what he expected. Since the birth of Gregory, his marriage to Pauline had begun to drift toward dissatisfaction. And the purchase of the *Pilar* allowed him to range farther from home on lengthy fishing trips and long stays in the Dry Tortugas and Cuba, while Pauline was tied down to the housekeeping in Key West and family visits to Piggott. Pauline had begun to wish that he would give up fishing and go back to pigeon shooting "because the people are so much nicer." That at least was Hemingway's appraisal of Pauline's attitude: "She likes the fishing but can't stand the fishermen talking about it all night afterwards."

Hemingway would attribute his marital difficulties to Pauline's cesarean operations and the doctors' orders that she no longer conceive and the fact that Pauline, being a practicing Catholic, would not agree to the use of contraceptives. But marriage is a matter of complicity, and only the parties directly involved know the intimate concerns that bring about its failures. ("If I hadn't been such a bloody fool practicing Catholic," Pauline once told Hemingway's fourth wife, Mary Welsh, "I wouldn't have lost my husband.") Hemingway's raw, offhand view in the mid-thirties was that women "break your bloody heart, marry you or give you the clap." But such brags were usually intended to create an impression. "Tell me first what are the things, the actual, concrete things that harm a writer," Kandisky asks Hemingway — or more to the point, Hemingway asks himself, in *Green Hills of Africa.* The ready answer, a bit facetious, is, "Politics, women, drink, money, ambition. And the lack of politics, women, drink, money, and ambition."

Hemingway's on-and-off affair with Jane Mason had begun to go sour in 1934, the summer after the summer of Jane's accidents. Hemingway saw her again in Cuba, frequently enough, while Pauline was in Key West much of the time. But Pauline had made a point of coming over for his thirty-fifth birthday and they celebrated it — with Jane and Grant Mason — in the El Pacifico, the rooftop restaurant in a notorious four-story establishment that included a brothel and a Chinese hash house on separate floors. What may have given Hemingway pause for thought, after that, was that Jane's psychiatrist, Dr. Lawrence Kubie, was engaged in writing up, for the *Saturday Review of Literature,* a series of psychoanalytical interpretations of the works of Erskine Caldwell, Faulkner, and Hemingway. In the case of Hemingway (he managed to suppress the publication of the article), the doctor had analyzed two types of males in his fiction: the seductive father figures who represented the threat of passive homosexuality and the destructive younger males who were in conflict with authority. Bullfighting, and presumably Hemingway's concern with it, represented "the struggle between two fighting males for genital mastery." In the conflict between fathers and sons, "frustration is the only possible outcome," Kubie concluded, with a neat turn of phrase and a borrowed title from Hemingway, "and it is not to be wondered at that in the end, 'Winner Takes Nothing.'"

That winter, the winter of the Kubie problem, Jane Mason made a trip to Africa and was much taken up with a friend, Richard Cooper, an Englishman and an avid hunter who had a coffee plantation in Tanganyika. (Hemingway and Pauline had met Cooper on their safari and liked him.) After which, things were never quite the same between Jane and Hemingway.

What one might add to the account of Hemingway's escape from depression is that over a period of two summers, much of the time spent in Bimini (he first visited the island in April 1935, staying in the home of the millionaire sportsman Mike Lerner), his expeditions on the *Pilar* and the challenges of fishing the Gulf Stream had exerted a beneficial influence. That first time, he had been drawn by the challenge of the big tuna to be caught there. (None, he claimed, had ever been landed intact in those shark-infested waters until he had landed two, proving it could be done: "Have won 350 bucks betting we would with the rich boys. Plenty rich boys. But now no bets.") But the second summer, 1936, the marlin were not running plentifully, and he was disappointed, and Richard Cooper, the elephant hunter and no longer, perhaps, Jane Mason's "My Mr. Cooper," had come over to Bimini from Miami with Jane, who had chartered a boat in competition with Ernest. It was at Bimini that second summer that Jane met Arnold Gingrich (Pauline had helpfully introduced them at the Compleat Angler bar), after which the two began seeing each other in New York. Hemingway had already begun to suspect what was what. In the course of a later argument with Gingrich, Hemingway angrily blurted out "Goddamn editor comes down to Bimini and sees a blonde, and he hasn't been the same since!"

***

Hemingway's relationship with Dos Passos and Katy had also begun to drift in those drifting years along the stream. Dos and Katy had been coming, yearly, to spend time in Key West, occasionally fishing out on the Stream, "a magnificent and mysterious phenomenon, always changing and always present like a range of mountains," Dos described it to a friend. But the old easy camaraderie began to pale as Hemingway became, increasingly, the celebrity. In the fall and winter of 1934 to 1935, when Dos and Katy had stayed at the Hotel Ambos Mundos in Havana and then rented a bungalow in Key West, Hemingway was in a patchy mood, sarcastic about Dos Passos's recent well-paid stint in Hollywood working with the director Josef von Sternberg. (Katy gave Pauline the lowdown on the Hollywood scene: "What they do out here is pound the authors to a smooth paste and mix with rat poison. They use them for flavoring mostly.") Hemingway, complaining of various ailments, took to his bed before supper with a sore throat. Pauline would bring his meal up to him, and Katy and Dos, with their trays, dined with him. (Dos Passos later wrote, "We called it the *lit royale.* I never knew an athletic vigorous man who spent so much time in bed as Ernest did.") By December, Hemingway's mood had passed, or so, at least, Katy wrote the Murphys: "You remember how irascible and truculent (can't spell) he was before. Now he's just like a big cage of canaries, looking fine, too." Still, she noted Hemingway's tendency, of late, to be oracular and thought he needed "some best pal and severe critic to tear off those long white whiskers which he is wearing."

In the spring of 1935, back again at Key West — this time with Dos and Mike Strater — and preparing for the trip to Bimini, there was an accident. Early in April, en route to the island, about five miles out, both Hemingway and Strater had hooked large sharks. In trying to bring Mike's shark up on a gaff so that Dos could photograph it with a movie camera, the gaff had split and hit the pistol Hemingway was holding to finish the shark off with. The gun went off, and the bullet, ricocheting off the brass rail, struck Hemingway in the calves of both legs. They returned to Key West to get a doctor to dress the wounds. They were not serious, having gone through the fleshy part of the legs, but Katy was furious with Hemingway for his carelessness.

Several days later, they started out again, this time reaching their destination. Katy found Bimini fantastical, "a crazy mixture of luxury, indigence, good liquor, bad food, heat, flies, land apathy and sea magnificence, social snoot, money, sport, big fish, big fishermen and competitive passion." Perhaps wanting to avoid the competition (or the stray bullets), she and Dos spent much of their time on the island searching for seashells, rather than on the *Pilar.* But once, at least, Katy had been thrilled by Hemingway's fight to bring in a huge tuna. After several hours, he managed to get it to the boat, only to watch it be demolished by sharks: "They came like express trains and hit the fish like a planing mill — shearing off twenty-five and thirty pounds at a bite," she wrote Gerald Murphy. "Ernest shoots them with a machine gun, *rrr* — but it won't stop them." It was a terrific scene "to see the bullets ripping into them — the shark thrashing in blood and foam — the white bellies and fearful jaws — the pale cold eyes. I was really aghast but it's very exciting."

In February 1936, strangely enough, Dos Passos was also in a depressed mood, fussing over his novel *The Big Money,* which was near completion. "Gosh Hem — this novel business is an awful business. Why the hell did I ever get mixed up in it? I'm in perfectly good shape this winter for the first time in years — but I can feel the old warmish blood running off into ink — the most completely lousy feeling I've ever felt." Hemingway was more sympathetic with Dos Passos than he had been with Fitzgerald. "Don't let the goddamned novel get you down," he wrote Dos, relaying his own remedy for depression: "started fishing and hell in no time felt wonderful and full of juice." But by April he was once again feeling at a loss, urging Dos and Katy to come south for the fishing. He was planning a trip to Cuba and then Bimini and suggested they join him. Pauline was going to Piggott with Gregory, and the only friend he now had who would go anywhere without his wife was Josie Russell. Although, he added sardonically, there was still "Mrs. Mason," who was "almost as apt at going places without her husband as Mr. Josie is without his wife."

Among the gossipy items he had to tell Dos Passos in his letter — but didn't — was a story about the recent visit of the poet Wallace Stevens to Key West. "Have something very funny to tell you about him when see you. I promised Mr. S. not to say anything about it so will have to simply put you in the presence of witnesses." That the story Hemingway did not tell involved a great American poet, a master of cerebration and celebration, and a great American prose writer who had created a style for his time should have so mixed the ridiculous and the sublime, ought to give one pause about the vagaries of the creative life. While visiting friends in Key West in February, Stevens, who did his heavy drinking on business vacations, away from his teetotaling wife, attended a cocktail party in Hemingway territory. Unimpressed by the Hemingway legend, Stevens made some boasting remarks about putting the novelist in his place. Hemingway's sister Ursula, a guest at the same party (she was visiting with her brother and sister-in-law), had gone home in tears. Hemingway, who had been drinking at home, decided to tackle the bear on the spot, arriving at the cocktail party just as Stevens and his friend Judge Powell were leaving. Stevens, as Hemingway learned later, had said his good-byes by announcing, "By God I wish I had that Hemingway here now. I'd knock him out with a single punch."

The squaring-off took place on the rainy street outside. According to Hemingway, who did relay the story to Sara Murphy, he managed to knock Stevens down several times, landing him in a puddle. But then the poet, bigger than Hemingway but some twenty years older, finally managed to deliver a Sunday punch to Hemingway's jaw. Stevens broke his hand in two places, but, miraculously, Hemingway was stunned but not hurt. Hemingway bragged that he

bove: Mussolini's March on Rome, Octo-
:r 28, 1922. "Mussolini was a great sur-
rise. He is not the monster he has been
ctured," Hemingway wrote on his first
terview with the Duce. Seven months
ter, he would call him "the biggest bluff
Europe." *Right:* Hitler in Landsberg
rison following his aborted Beer Hall
ıtsch of November 8–9, 1923. Heming-
ay, lecturing Ezra Pound on twentieth-
ntury politics, later remarked, "The
eat qualification to hold office is to have
en in jail. Have you ever been in jail?"

Left: Hadley, Hemingway, and Bumby at Schruns, Austria, 1926. *Middle:* In a café, Pamplona, 1926: Gerald and Sara Murphy, Pauline, Hemingway and Hadley, and (in the foreground) bootblacks. *Bottom:* At the bullfights with a new wife: Hemingway and Pauline (to the left), La Coruña, Spain, August 1927

Gertrude Stein on her triumphal American tour, 1934–1935, posed by her friend Carl Van Vechten in front of the American flag

Fishing off Key West: Hemingway and Bill Smith, ca. 1928

Although Hemingway met the photographer Walker Evans in Cuba in 1933 and lent him money to complete an assignment, Evans did not photograph him. He chose instead to commemorate the meeting with a photograph of a Havana movie theater then showing *A Farewell to Arms.*

Above: Art and life in Spain a century and a quarter apart: Goya's "Esto es peor" ("This is worse") etching from *The Disasters of War* series. *Left:* From Hemingway's collection of war photo Robert Capa's photograph of a dead soldier in a tree, taken during the Spanish Civil War.

The picnic on the Manzanares River near Madrid, July 1931: unidentified bullfighters and friends with Hemingway; Luis Crovetto, Sidney Franklin's *mozo* (on Hemingway's right); an (on his left) Franklin

Above: Hemingway contemplating dead soldiers, near Madrid. *Below:* Hemingway and sons (left to right), Gregory, John, and Patrick, with Martha Gellhorn on a shoot in Idaho, 1941.

Above: Martha and Hemingway, sailing in the Caribbean. Hemingway's brother, Leicester, was the photographer. *Left:* Ezra Pound in front of the Albergo d'Italia in Rome, where he stayed during his 1941–1943 propaganda broadcasts.

Hemingway as a World War II correspondent in 1944, at work in his London hotel room

had fixed Stevens "so good" that the poet was in his room for five days with a nurse and doctor working on him: "Pauline who hates me to fight was delighted." Having delivered the story to Sara in expansive detail, Hemingway swore her to secrecy. He and Stevens had patched up their differences, he said. He had agreed to say nothing out of consideration for Stevens's reputation in respectable insurance circles (when he wasn't writing poetry, Stevens worked as an executive at a Hartford, Connecticut, insurance company). There was some truth, then, to Hemingway's remark in his April letter to Dos Passos, "As I say am always a perfectly safe man to tell any dirt to as it goes in one ear and out my mouth."

But days afterward, Stevens, too, related the tale in good-humored fashion at another cocktail party with Florida friends, admitting that he had been a fool to get that drunk. Nor did he bear any grudge. Six years later he would take the improbable step of proposing Hemingway as one of the speakers for a series of lectures on poetry at Princeton. "Most people don't think of Hemingway as a poet," he wrote Henry Church, who was organizing the program, "but obviously he is a poet and I should say, offhand, the most significant of living poets." Stevens recognized one of the irreducible elements of Hemingway's genius, his ability to fix a scene or a moment or a revelation of character with a startling sense of urgency, describing it as the poetry of "EXTRAORDINARY ACTUALITY." With a generosity that spoke well for his own character, Stevens claimed that Hemingway was not only the right man for the job, "he is the right man in the sense of being some one who would really create intense interest in what he had to say."

Dos Passos did take Hemingway up on the offer to visit him in Cuba. He brought Katy and Sara Murphy along, but they stayed only a week; Sara, nervous and concerned about Patrick, was anxious to get back to Dr. Trudeau's clinic at Saranac. Dos Passos spent the whole week correcting the galley proofs for the English edition of *The Big Money.* He hardly fished at all. Hemingway, left with the responsibility of entertaining Katy and Sara, groused about Dos Passos's working so constantly. Dos Passos apologized in a letter: "Gosh Hem, it was a tough proposition for you, me bringing all the women folk to Havana, but the trip really did Sara a great deal of good." Hemingway, only slightly soothed, apologized for his behavior, promising, "Will make a good trip soon with lots of exercise and no proof and no bellyaching by old Hem. . . . Would like to have a chance to not mistreat my friends sometime." Hemingway had asked Dos Passos to leave him a set of *The Big Money* galley proofs to read. His reaction was noncommittal: "You must have had hell with that to proofread," he wrote Dos Passos. "It's as long as the Bible but

I can see why you couldn't cut it more." It probably did not sit too well with the rivalrous Hemingway that *The Big Money* sold 7000 copies in advance of publication on August 10, went to four printings by the end of the month, and made several of the best-seller lists; or that Dos Passos was featured on the cover of *Time* magazine, one of the few contemporary American writers to get such publicity. (Hemingway did not make the cover until the following year with the publication of *To Have and Have Not.*)

✓✓✓

"In hunting you know what you are after and the top you can get is an elephant. But who can say what you will hook sometime when drifting in a hundred and fifty fathoms in the Gulf Stream?" Hemingway asked his *Esquire* readers. "There are probably marlin and swordfish to which the fish we have seen caught are pygmies." As an example of those unseen mysteries lying beneath the surface, as the *Pilar* cruised along the deep current of the stream, Hemingway cited two incidents told to him by Carlos Gutierrez, the Cuban mate whom Hemingway had hired. Carlos, then fifty-three, told him how, as a boy, he had been fishing with his father in a skiff and had hooked a small marlin. He had seen it jump twice before it sounded. Several minutes later, he felt a mysterious and terrible weight pulling on the line; it felt, he said, as though he had hooked onto the bottom of the sea. Just as unaccountably, the line slackened and, pulling up his catch, he discovered that some toothless fish had clamped its jaws across his eighty-pound marlin and completely squeezed its insides out as it moved off with the fish in its mouth before finally releasing it. "What size of a fish would that be?" Carlos had asked.

Carlos's second story was about an old man who, fishing alone in a skiff, had hooked a giant marlin that had pulled the boat far out to sea. The old man had stayed with the fish for two days and two nights and had finally managed to lash it to his boat. But then the sharks had attacked, tearing at his catch, while the old man, alone on the Gulf Stream, had fought them off, stabbing at the sharks, clubbing them with an oar, until he was exhausted. Fishermen picked him up, sixty miles eastward. The old man was crying, "half crazy from his loss, and the sharks were still circling the boat." What was left of his marlin, about half, weighed eight hundred pounds. The stories were about the grandeur and superb indifference of the sea, and Hemingway was obviously impressed with both of them. But it was the second story that had the greater meaning for Hemingway, some sixteen years later, when he wrote *The Old Man and the Sea.*

II

In the text of "The Snows of Kilimanjaro" and in the persona of Harry Walden, Hemingway delivered himself of a minor jeremiad against the wealthy. "The rich," he claimed, "were dull and they drank too much, or they played too much backgammon. They were dull and they were repetitious." Still, it was among the rich, in the summer of 1936, not long after he had completed "The Snows," that Hemingway had been spending his time. The wealthy sportsmen whom Hemingway knew and competed with for prize catches, young Tommy Shevlin and his wife, Lorraine, and the Kip Farringtons, had their yachts anchored in Bimini harbor, or off Cat Cay, the small island south of Bimini, dotted with the homes of millionaires.

We have a portrait-sketch of Hemingway at Bimini one summer, his second sojourn on the island, from a sensitive and not critical observer, Marjorie Kinnan Rawlings, another Scribner's author. She was an admirer of Hemingway the writer but had heard distressing rumors about Hemingway the brawler. Having arrived in Bimini in June as a guest on a friend's yacht, Rawlings was astonished and delighted when, one day, Hemingway strode on board to make her acquaintance, grasping her hand in his big paw and telling her how much he enjoyed her work. Instead of the swaggering bully she had expected, she discovered, as she wrote Max Perkins, "a most lovable, nervous and sensitive person." What she saw in Hemingway was the genuine artist and the modest author. A bit awed by her discovery, she noted, "He is so great an artist that he does not need to be ever on the defensive. He is so vast, so virile, that he does not need ever to hit anybody." Sizing up Hemingway's circle of wealthy friends, she remarked, "Hemingway is among these people a great deal, and they like and admire him — his personality, his sporting prowess, and his literary prestige. It seems to me that unconsciously he must value their opinion." But at some cost, she assumed: "He must be afraid of laying bare before them the agony that tears the artist. . . . So, as in *Death in the Afternoon,* he writes beautifully, and then immediately turns it off with a flippant comment, or a deliberate obscenity." The judgment of a serious writer about the society Hemingway had chosen for himself: "They are the only people who would be pleased," Mrs. Rawlings commented, "by the things in his work that distress all the rest of us."

It was not that Hemingway was blind to the risks. For years he had been critical of friends — writers, mostly — who had been caught up in the lives of the rich. Don Stewart had gone Hollywood and was now hanging around with the wealthy on Long Island:

"The Stewarts were ruined by Don getting that 25 thousand contract and meeting the Whitneys," Hemingway told Dos Passos in 1929. He made the same complaint against John Peale Bishop, who "was ruined by Mrs. Bishop's income," an odd judgment considering the fact that it was Pauline's rich uncle Gus who had financed Hemingway's cars and paid for his African safari.

Later in life, he would try to explain his somewhat softened attitude toward the rich in a letter to his publisher, Charles Scribner. He was, he admitted, very snobbish: "Always try not to be and hate all false snobs." What he admired about the gentry, who had their clubs and cliques, was their indifference. "The gentry has always been those who didn't give a god-damn. It has nothing to do with where you went to school (the poor bastards suffer and sweat that out). . . . The real gentry are almost as tough as the really good gangsters."

But in "The Snows," in the guise of Harry Walden, he had reserved his most demeaning criticism for Scott Fitzgerald:

> He remembered poor Scott Fitzgerald and his romantic awe of [the rich] and how he had started a story once that began, "The very rich are different from you and me." And how someone had said to Scott, Yes, they have more money. But that was not humorous to Scott. He thought they were a special glamorous race and when he found out they weren't it wrecked him just as much as any other thing that wrecked him.

No matter that the quote from Fitzgerald's story "The Rich Boy" was inexact; no matter that the bright remark had not, in fact, been made to Fitzgerald but to Hemingway himself. No matter that in the early draft of the story, Hemingway had turned the tables and assigned the smart retort to his stand-in, Harry Walden. It was clearly something more — something more personal — than the effort to show up a rival who was down on his luck which goaded Hemingway into making a fine example of Fitzgerald. Was it an instance, perhaps, of Fitzgerald's having had the courage, the moral honesty, in *The Crack-Up,* to do what Hemingway had failed to do, thus far, in print — to write, as Gertrude Stein would have it, the story of the real Hemingway? "The Snows of Kilimanjaro" may well have been Hemingway's attempt to demonstrate, fictionally, that he was capable of doing so without whining in public.

Nothing indicates Hemingway's lowered estimation of Fitzgerald so much as the fact that in one of Harry's caustic reminiscences of the Paris scene, Hemingway had just as deliberately pilloried the critic Malcolm Cowley: "And there in the cafe as he passed was

Malcolm Cowley with a pile of saucers in front of him and a stupid look on his potato face talking about the Dada movement with a Roumanian who said his name was Tristan Tzara." However, before publication of "The Snows" in the August issue of *Esquire* (it appeared with Fitzgerald's semiautobiographical story of a drunken writer, "Afternoon of an Author"), Hemingway thought better of offending Cowley and substituted "that American poet" in place of Cowley's name. It was open season on Fitzgerald, but it was wiser not to target Cowley, who, as an influential critic and literary editor of *The New Republic,* might still be useful.

Fitzgerald, justifiably, felt wronged by Hemingway's airing his condescending pity in print. Writing from Asheville, North Carolina, where Zelda was in treatment, Fitzgerald was firmer, less compliant, than he had been previously in his correspondence with Hemingway. "Dear Ernest," he wrote,

> Please lay off me in print. If I choose to write *de profundis* sometimes it doesn't mean I want friends praying over my corpse. No doubt you meant it kindly but it cost me a night's sleep. And when you incorporate it (the story) in a book would you mind cutting my name? It's a fine story — one of your best — even though the "Poor Scott Fitzgerald etc.," rather spoiled it for me."

Between competitive authors casual words are not so casual. The "night's sleep" was intended to report that while Fitzgerald might have been wounded, he was not *too* deeply wounded. In a postscript, Fitzgerald tried to set Hemingway right: "Riches have *never* fascinated me, unless combined with the greatest charm or distinction."

Hemingway, for his part, was self-righteous. Writing to Max Perkins about Fitzgerald's letter, Hemingway argued that it was odd coming from a man who had written about his breakdown in the pages of *Esquire.* In response to Fitzgerald (a letter that has been lost), Hemingway played the bully boy, saying that for five years he had refrained from writing about people he knew but was no longer going to play the gentleman; now he would return to being a novelist. Arnold Gingrich, who had seen Hemingway's letter to Fitzgerald, claimed that it was brutal; the language was something one would hesitate to use on a "yellow dog."

Fitzgerald, writing to Beatrice Dance, a friend with whom he had been carrying on a neurotic and guilty love affair, claimed that Hemingway was "quite as nervously broken down as I am, but it manifests itself in different ways. His inclination is toward megalomania and mine toward melancholy." It was obvious that their friendship was wearing thin. In a letter to Perkins, four days later,

Fitzgerald maintained, "Somehow I love that man, no matter what he says or does, but just one more crack and I think I would have to throw my weight with the gang and lay him. No one could ever hurt him in his first books, but he has completely lost his head and the duller he gets about it, the more he is like a punch-drunk pug fighting himself in the movies."

Perkins's role in the affair was hardly admirable. Writing to his cousin Elizabeth Lemmon, he described the actual circumstances of the Hemingway anecdote. Perkins, Hemingway, and the writer Mary Colum were having lunch together in New York, and Hemingway had remarked that he was getting to know the rich. Colum responded, "The only difference between the rich and other people is that the rich have more money." Hemingway appropriated the quip and made Fitzgerald the victim of the humiliating retort. Perkins felt that Hemingway's behavior was "contemptible." He wrote Fitzgerald a soothing letter: "As for what Ernest did, I resented it, and when it comes to book publication, I shall have it out with him." But the actuality was that he was not about to have a serious quarrel with the author who was one of the stars of the Scribner's list.

Early in March 1938, before "The Snows of Kilimanjaro" was to be republished in Hemingway's summary collection, *The Fifth Column and the First Forty-Nine Stories,* Fitzgerald again brought up the subject of deleting his name. "It was a damned rotten thing to do," he wrote Perkins, "and with anybody but Ernest my tendency would be to crack back. Why did he think it would add to the strength of his story if I had become such a negligible figure? This is quite indefensible on any grounds." Perkins again reassured him that his name would be deleted. But it was not as sure a thing as Perkins made it seem. Hemingway, out of some lingering resistance to admit any guilt, revised the passage, but kept the name Scott. Perkins, once more, had to request the deletion in gingerly fashion:

> As to the Scott passage, you amended it very neatly — But I greatly wish his name could come out altogether. If people reading the story do not identify "Scott" as F.S.F., it might as well be some other name (one realizes he is a writer in the very next sentence) and if they do identify him, it seems to me it takes them out of the story for a moment. . . . If his name could come out without hurting, it would be good.

In the end, Hemingway finally changed the name, referring to "poor Julian" instead. But the damage had been done, and the phrase "poor Scott Fitzgerald" became a cultural artifact of the period. As late as 1951, Hemingway was still unwilling to concede the point. Writing to Fitzgerald's biographer Arthur Mizener, he said, "Poor Scott; and didn't he know that the man in The Snows of Kilimanjaro would have spoken of him, or thought of him, exactly as he, Scott, would have mentioned actual things, cars and places?" As a writer — though not a friend — Hemingway was ruthlessly right.

III

Since the late twenties, Hemingway's views on politics might well have been summed up in his feisty, if still undeclared, war with the *New Masses,* the revived Communist version of Max Eastman's earlier *Masses.* The new editors, principally Mike Gold, Joseph Freeman, and James Rorty, adopted the Stalinist party line in opposition to the Trotskyites. Not that Hemingway's stance vis-à-vis the *New Masses* was a matter of pure politics at the time. He was an individualist first and liberal second, a sin in the eyes of Marxist critics, who consistently found his novels and stories lacking in proletarian values. In the twenties, Hemingway's anger at the magazine and its left-wing editors and critics was clearly motivated by their rejection of his writing. In 1926, when the magazine resumed publication with its May issue, the editors had first rejected his bullfight story, "The Undefeated" and then "An Alpine Idyll," claiming that Hemingway's bullfight story had "spoiled us for anything less good." Rorty felt that the "Idyll" had been underwritten in order to prepare the reader for the "stark shocker" of the grim ending, the revelation that the peasant mountaineer, unable to bury his wife in the depth of winter, stood her frozen body in a shed and in time hung his lantern from her open mouth, disfiguring her, when he went to the shed to cut wood. That October, too, the magazine had published Ernest Walsh's slashing review of *The Torrents of Spring.* Hemingway angrily suggested to Pound that jealousy might have prompted the publication of Walsh's review: "They just took the Walsh thing on acct. of hating me," he claimed. "Also they thought I was making money. A widespread delusion. They are just a house organ of parlour, i.e. subsidized by the rich, revolution. You've got no hope there."

Unfortunately, the December issue of *New Masses* contained another irritation, Dos Passos's critical review of *The Sun Also Rises,* which accommodated itself to the Marxist line of literary criticism espoused by the magazine. Also, unexpectedly, a flattering letter to the editors from Pound: "I find five numbers of *New Masses* waiting for me here on my return from Paris, and have read most of the text with a good deal of care. For the first time in years I have even gone so far as to think of making a trip to America; so you can take the blame for that if for nothing else." The editors tendentiously headlined Pound's letter "Pound Joins the Revolution."

Hemingway, writing to Pound from the wintry fastness of Gstaad, steamed, "*The Revolution* — So you joined New Masses," then grumbled about the fact that the publication had glorified "that other noble brother of the Proletariat, the late Rev. Walsh." He plainly intended to set Pound straight: "Listen and Papa will tell you why Messrs. Rorty, Freeman, Mike Gold, etc. etc. want a revolution. Because they hope that under some new order they would be men of talent. *That's all.* Also they are all well paid." The interesting thing about Hemingway's judgment is that it was an opinion lifted directly and recently from Sherwood Anderson during the course of their meeting in Paris following the publication of *The Torrents of Spring.* At the time, Hemingway informed Max Perkins that Anderson "said a very funny thing about the Editors of the New Masses; they, he said, wanted a revolution because they hoped that under some new system of government they would be men of talent." Hemingway, still fulminating against his enemies, told Pound, "FUCK the new masses and their revolution. In case *you'd* mistaken my sentiments."

Pound, contrary to Hemingway's advice, sent the *New Masses* an article on George Antheil, which appeared in the March 1927 issue. And in the Spring issue of *Exile,* he saw fit to comment somewhat favorably on the *New Masses,* acknowledging that Fascism and the Russian revolution were "interesting phenomena," but suggesting that, now that Lenin was dead, he doubted that Russia would soon produce a Utopia. "No country produces two Napoleons or two Lenins in succession."

Pound became the recipient of many of Hemingway's political gripes and certainly the receiver of all his gibes against the Duce and his steady rise to power. In a particularly virulent outburst in one of his letters about the *New Masses,* Hemingway blasted Pound on the subject of Italy: "but what makes you think a gent can't be au courant abt. the state of affairs in the unforchnit country when everyone who knows or cares anything abt. same is expelled into France where they arrive fresh all the time with the DOPE. Not to mention the agents of the govt. itself — chief of Police of Rome — Ricciotti and Co." At one point he claimed that he would no longer mention politics in his letters: "Only don't you ever call me on Dago politics. Yes, I know the lire is stabilized and all about the improvements in the TRAIN SERVICE."

Their arguments did not ease with the years. Pound objected to Hemingway's lack of interest — ignorance, so far as he was concerned — on the subject of economics. When Hemingway, in an *Esquire* article, "The Malady of Power," in November 1935, wrote off his former hero Georges Clemenceau as a man who, having achieved power, "had all his old political opponents jailed, shot, or banished, branding them all as traitors," Pound wrote him exuberantly, "Waal, me deah Hombo / Glad to see you doin man's woik and spillin the dirt on Georges, etc. / wich dont lower me respekk for Benito but raises wot I have fer E.M.H." But it was too good an opportunity for Pound to lecture Hemingway once more: "Now why dont you use yr / celebrated BEAN another 24 minutes and go to it that ALL them buggarin massacres are CAUSED by money what is money HOW does it get that WAY?" Pound's lecture ended in a burst of expletives that might have been near comic if it were not a demonstration of a man out of control about a subject too dear to his heart: "and if the shits didn't want it, and if murder by the million an no fun and no fuckin chance to kill the sonvabitch that profits by hiring some poor simp to likk you first IS ALL godshittering ECONOMICS and to the bottom of that to bitch the bastids IS THE JOB."

No response from Hemingway could have been more effective a rebuttal of Pound's admiration for Mussolini than the article Hemingway wrote for the January 1936 issue of *Esquire* on Mussolini's war in Ethiopia. Pound, who had begun writing propaganda articles for the government-sponsored *British-Italian Bulletin,* after some delay in dealing with the touchy moral issue of an outright imperialist invasion, would claim that Italy needed Ethiopia "to achieve ECONOMIC INDEPENDENCE . . . the MATERIAL WEALTH, the raw materials necessary to feed and clothe the people of Italy. And I hope Italy gets every inch of it."

Hemingway's *Esquire* article addressed itself to the subject of other "poor simps," the common Italian foot soldiers who had been sent to die in Africa while Mussolini's sons "are in the air where there are no enemy planes to shoot them down." In Mussolini's Italy, he claimed, those who remembered and regretted the last war "have been beaten because they opened their mouths, some were killed, others are in prison on the Lipari islands, and some have left the country. It is a dangerous thing in a dictatorship to have a long memory." With the Ethiopians, pathetically unprepared and strategically retreating, Hemingway said, Italy would need at least one decisive military victory before it could arrange "a confidential agreement with the powers to let her alone and remove the sanctions because of the danger of what she will present as 'bolshevism' in Italy if she loses." (Actually, it was the threat of Germany which Mussolini's ministers had already used in their diplomatic negotiations for the formal treaty signed with France in January 1935—one of accommodations that vouchsafed Mussolini's "economic penetration" of Ethiopia.)

In Key West, working without hard evidence, Hemingway mentioned recent dispatches about the sick and wounded Italian soldiers being transported back through the Suez Canal and the probability of the island hospital concentration camps to which they would be sent "in order that their return to Italy shall not depress the morale of their relatives who sent them off." And it was largely Hemingway's imagination, not the strict facts of the case, that conjured up one of his more poetic and moving bits of war reportage, the image of the young Italian soldiers going off to the war in a strange country. No knowledge of the past war, he said, would help these

> boys from the little steep-hilled towns of the Abruzzi where the snow comes early on the tops of the mountains, nor those who worked in garages, or machine shops, in Milano or Bologna or Firenze, or rode their bicycles in road races on the white dust-powdered roads of Lombardy, nor those who played football for their factory teams in Spezia or Torino, nor mowed the high mountain meadows of the Dolomites and guided skiers in the winter, or would have been burning charcoal in the woods above Piombino, or maybe sweeping out a trattoria in Vicenza, or would have gone to North or South America in the old days.

Whatever Pound's opinion about Hemingway's neglect of the topic, it was on the subject of economic theory that Hemingway lectured Dos Passos. Dos Passos's reputation as a committed liberal, if not a Communist, American author, was high at the moment. Hemingway had made a point of warning him against the dangers of letting his politics infect his writing, particularly in the final volume of his *U.S.A.* trilogy, *The Big Money*: "Now watch one thing. In the 3rd volume don't let yourself slip and get any perfect characters in. . . . If you get a noble communist remember the bastard probably masturbates and is jallous [jealous?] as a cat. Keep them people, people, people, and don't let them get to be symbols. Remember the race is older than the economic system." In the early thirties, Hemingway was decidedly against the bureaucrats of political dogma, a stance he tried to press on Dos Passos with suitable irreverence: "Remember our Lord yellowed out on the cross and was only successful because they killed him. Bunny Wilson has forgotten that Christian religion started as violently anti-capitalist jewish system. It is the management that ruins things . . . don't let them suck you in on any economic Y.M.C.A."

When a misguided admirer, Paul Romaine, wrote Hemingway about the hopeful signs of a "Leftward Swing" in his work, Hemingway answered angrily that Romaine's views were "so much horse-shit." There was "no left and right in writing. There is only good and bad writing." When Romaine had the temerity to push the discussion further, Hemingway exploded: "Your idea that I stay on the right but would like to go left but am restrained by 'reasons we both know' is more of the same presumptuous poppycock."

Throughout the thirties, politics coursed through the correspondence of Hemingway and his male friends — and enemies. The network of political commentary that was established vibrated with anger and agreement, registered approval and scorn. In his rant at Romaine, Hemingway was determined to set the record straight on the politics of his friends: "Dos Passos doesn't swing. He's always the same. To hell with all your swingers. E. Wilson is a serious and honest bird who discovered life late. Naturally he is shocked and would like to do something about it . . . I'm no goddamned patriot nor will I swing to left or right."

It was perhaps for the sake of argument that Hemingway cautioned Dos Passos about infectious political views. Although American leftists considered Dos Passos a hero and spokesman for the political Left, Dos Passos himself professed to be a "middle-class liberal, whether I like it or not" and a "'camp follower' of radical parties." He was not, however, an admirer of the *New Masses* cadre. Dos Passos wrote Hemingway, "Anyway as I says to myself writing for N.M. [*New Masses*] we've all got to write a mile of turds before we die." Dos Passos had visited Russia in 1928 and spent several months there meeting intellectuals and writers in Leningrad and Moscow. (Dos wrote Hem, "If you keep away from the newspaper men and foreign correspondents who crepehang considerably, things are pretty swell here.") He had admired the energy and hospitality of the common people he met but was not completely convinced about the success of the system. "Tell us . . . are you for us or against us?" his new friends had asked when they saw him off at the train station on the night of his departure. He found he could not answer. Crossing the border into Poland, he instinctively felt he had been let out of jail.

With the murder of S. M. Kirov, chief of the Leningrad Communist party, in December 1934 and the retaliatory trials and purges initiated by Stalin soon afterward, Dos Passos began to have serious doubts about the Communist party in Russia and the United States. (Historians now believe that Stalin was implicated in the Kirov murder, disposing of a troublesome rival and at the same time using the trials as a convenient means of getting rid of other political opponents.) Arguing with Edmund Wilson, who was planning a trip to Russia (with some misgivings, considering recent developments), Dos Passos was emphatic about his change of mind. The Kirov business, he told Wilson, "has completely destroyed my benefit-of-the-doubt attitude towards the Stalinists — It seems to be another convulsion of the self destructive tendency that began with the Trotski-Stalin row." The Stalin regime, he felt, had entered its "Napoleonic stage." Wilson, however, thought it was a mistake to assume that the victims were innocent because there were so many of them: "I regret that Stalin should have thought it necessary to involve his political opponents in it; but the way they handle those things in Russia has been familiar ever since the Trotsky split." Stalin, Wilson claimed, was a good deal different from Napoleon, who had "megalomaniac imperialist ambitions which one can hardly imagine Stalin entertaining. Stalin, whatever his limitations, is still working for socialism in Russia."

Dos Passos countered, "My enthusiastic feelings, personally, about the U.S.S.R. have been on a continual decline since the early days." He itemized the events that disturbed him: the Kronstadt rebellions, the massacres by Béla Kun in the Crimea, the New Economic Policy, the Trotsky expulsion, the liquidation of the Kulaks — all of which, he contended, left the Kremlin absolutely supreme. "I don't know why I should blurt all this out except that . . . I've been clarifying my ideas about what I would be willing to be shot for and frankly I don't find the Kremlin among the items."

⁂

Hemingway had never visited Russia; nonetheless, by the thirties he had achieved a considerable reputation there. As early as 1928, selections from *The Sun Also Rises* had appeared in Moscow magazines. (So Dos Passos informed him: "The great joker about the USSR for foreign writers is that although you can get jack out of the publishers, you can't take it out of the country, but have to drink it up in vodka and salt herrings.") In 1935 there was a full translation of the novel, followed by *A Farewell to Arms* a year later. In 1937, Hemingway would be named as the favorite non-Russian writer by nine out of fifteen leading Soviet authors. His recognition there owed much to Ivan Kashkin, the critic, translator, and teacher who had edited a 1934 volume of selections from Hemingway's writings, including *Death in the Afternoon.* Kashkin's essay "Ernest Hemingway: A Tragedy of Craftsmanship," based on his reading of Hemingway's work up through the stories of *Winner Take Nothing*, had appeared in the May 1935 issue of *Internatsionalnaya Literatura.*

The article was a sensitive reading (not so insistently political in its conclusions as those of other Russian critics) dealing with Hemingway's moral code and his view of the world and its ills. Kashkin recognized that the fatalism and alienation from society, the indifference to social and political issues, which other Russian critics found so disappointing in a major writer like Hemingway, was something more than a failure — was, perhaps, even a principle. He was particularly insightful on the dark side of Hemingway's imagination as it was reflected in the work: "again and again he was writing of the end — the end of love, the end of life, the end of hope, the end of all."

Hemingway, who received both Kashkin's book and the article in *Internatsionalnaya Literatura* (the Russian critic had sent them by way of William Saroyan, who had been visiting in Russia), was both pleased and appreciative. "It is a pleasure to have somebody know what you are writing about. That is all I care about," he wrote Kashkin from Key West in mid-August 1935. But he did not mince words about where he stood politically — or apolitically — and what he thought of his American critics.

> Here criticism is a joke: The bourgeois critics do not know their ass from a hole in the ground and the newly converted communists are like all new converts; they are so anxious to be orthodox that all they are interested in are schisms in their own critical attitudes. None of it has anything to do with literature which is always literature.

He praised Edmund Wilson as "the best critic we have" and Malcolm Cowley, who "is honest but still very much under the impression of being converted." The others were all careerists, he said.

In the course of his lengthy letter, Hemingway defended himself for his independence from any political creed.

> Everyone tries to frighten you now by saying or writing that if one does not become a communist or have a Marxian viewpoint one will have no friends and will be alone . . . I cannot be a communist now because I believe in only one thing: liberty. First I would look after myself and do my work. Then I would care for my family. Then I would help my neighbor. But the state I care nothing for.

In an inquisitive postscript, he asked, "P.P.S. Don't you drink? I notice you speak slightingly of the bottle. I have drunk since I was fifteen and few things have given me more pleasure. When you work hard all day with your head and know you must work again the next day what else can change your ideas and make them run on a different plane like whisky?"

Hemingway's praise of Edmund Wilson had been a bit premature; soon he would read Wilson's essay "Letter to the Russians About Hemingway" in the December 11, 1935, issue of *The New Republic,* criticizing *Green Hills of Africa.* But much of the essay seemed to be addressed also to Kashkin, whose article Wilson praised circuitously as "what is, in fact, perhaps so far the only serious full-length study of [Hemingway] that has yet been made." Wilson's article was, in fact, a well-reasoned defense of Hemingway against the usual Marxist critiques of his work. Wilson felt that the Soviet critics and the Marxist reviewers elsewhere, caught up as they were in the fight to destroy the "rotten old capitalist world" and bring about a liberation through socialism, tended to underestimate the good qualities of modern, non-Marxist writers, chief among them Hemingway and Marcel Proust. (Strangely enough, Wilson confessed that it was Proust, "that arch-bourgeois, arch-snob, arch-aesthete and arch-decadent," with his dedication to the moral obligations of his art, who had most often come to his mind during his travels in Russia.) Wilson's argument, however, did little to mollify Hemingway. Writing to Kashkin after he had read Wilson's article, Hemingway compared the critic to his grandfather, "who would never knowingly sit at table with a Democrat."

In his letter to Kashkin, Hemingway was both bumptious and personal in his rebuttal of Communism. "You write like a patriot and that is your blind spot," he told Kashkin. "I've seen a lot of patriots and they all died just like anybody else if it hurt bad enough and once they were dead their patriotism was only good for legends." But he also wished that Kashkin would wangle a trip to America so that they could get to know each other. "You know more about my writing than anybody but you do not know anything about me and I have very great pride and a hatred of the shit that will be written about me and my stuff after I am dead." In passing, he made a stunning admission: "I am not so silly but to know that my work will last." Even though Kashkin was a relative stranger, Hemingway was in an extraordinarily confiding mood: "I am truly, and I say this in all humility, very brave . . . I have always been very pleased about this but in the war I was frightened, mechanically, enough times to understand fear and to realize its importance in life." One didn't confess one's bravery in public; everyone would assume you were a liar. But a man could be put down as a coward due to malice by one person or ignorance on the part of another. "Well what the hell," he wrote Kashkin. "But the immortality I believe in is the immortality of what you write." And if your writing lasted you were still subjected to the same shit people wrote about you when you were alive.

It was all silly as hell anyway, "but writing isn't silly and neither is the Gulf Stream and I wish you could go out tomorrow and see it. Am going to fish tomorrow and write the next day."

Despite his feeling about the writers and the editorial policies of the *New Masses,* Hemingway accepted a commission from Joe North to write an article for the magazine on the disastrous Matecumbe hurricane. In private, and justifiably, he complained that the magazine spent the year printing articles about how worthless his writing was and then wired him to get the true story of the disaster. On the night of September 2, 1935, and the following day, the hurricane had torn through the region, hitting particularly hard on the Upper and Lower Matecumbe Keys, where the hard-brawling veterans who were building the highway connecting the Florida Keys to the mainland were stationed. Hemingway exaggerated the number of veterans killed — "between 700 and 1000 dead," where other reports gave a lesser figure — but the tragic loss of lives and the devastation were real enough. Rail lines had been washed away on the Lower Matecumbe Key, the foliage had been stripped clean, and not a building was left standing.

Hemingway visited the area soon after the hurricane was over. In his anger, he blamed the officials of the Roosevelt administration for the delay in getting the veterans off the island in time. Writing to Max Perkins, he asserted, "The veterans in those camps were practically murdered." The sight of the dead left unburied was as devastating as anything he had witnessed in the Lower Piave in June of 1918. Bloated bodies were still floating in the water. Unconsciously, perhaps, Hemingway remembered the explosion at the Milan ammunition factory and fixed upon the dead bodies of two women with a morbid fascination, "naked, tossed up into trees by the water, swollen and stinking, their breasts as big as balloons, flies between their legs." The indignity of death; they had been the two "very nice girls who ran a sandwich place and filling-station three miles from the ferry." Joe Lowe, the model for the rummy Eddy Marshall in Hemingway's story "One Trip Across," drowned at the ferry slip, as well. Hemingway blamed, among others, Harry Hopkins, then head of the Works Projects Administration, and Roosevelt for sending "those poor bonus march guys down there to get rid of them."

Hemingway's article, appearing in the September 17 issue of *New Masses* under the title "Who Murdered the Vets?" demanded, "And what's the punishment for manslaughter now?" It was quoted in

Time magazine and later reprinted in *Internatsionalnaya Literatura.* Marxist critics viewed it as Hemingway's coming-out as a political writer opposed to the villainy of capitalism.

"You have all the luck with hurricanes," Dos Passos wrote Hemingway, having read the piece in *The Daily Worker,* where it had also appeared. "That was a damn fine piece." It was a sign of Dos Passos's growing disillusion with the hard-line politicos that, where others were quick to condemn Hemingway for his tardy espousal of political causes, Dos Passos was ready to defend him. Writing to Malcolm Cowley a year earlier, Dos complained, "I don't think it's entirely because he's a good friend of mine that I am beginning to get thoroughly sick of every little inkshitter who can get his stuff in a pink magazine shying bricks at him." Any movement that made a practice of alienating men of ability, Dos Passos claimed, was in bad hands.

Hemingway would never be quite so generous. In a foul mood, he could be bitter in reprisal. He nursed his doubts about Dos Passos's political commitments. In an undated note, perhaps written in 1933 when Dos Passos was recuperating from his bout with rheumatic fever — vacationing on the Riviera, probably at the expense of the Murphys — Hemingway found an occasion to make a scathing comparison: "Marx the whimpering bourgeois living on the bounty of Engels is exactly as valid as Dos Passos living on a yacht in the Mediterranean while he attacks the capitalist system."

17

The Politics of Desperation

IT WAS a woman — more a companion and lover than a muse or a friend — who provided the change of venue in Hemingway's political and marital life. Hemingway met Martha Gellhorn in December 1936 in Key West. She had been born and raised in St. Louis; her father, only recently dead, had been a gynecologist and professor. Her mother was a spirited and attractive woman, active in social causes and a former Women's Suffragist. Martha had attended Bryn Mawr for three years, then decided she wanted to be on her own. At twenty-eight, she was already a known writer and journalist who believed in hard work and getting ahead. She had written for *The New Republic*, the *St. Louis Post-Dispatch*, and the Paris edition of *Vogue*, and had traveled extensively in Europe: France, Spain, and Hitler's Germany. In her mid-twenties, she had been married briefly to Bertrand de Jouvenel, five years her senior and one of the youthful lovers of Colette, who was, at the time, his stepmother.

In the United States, Harry Hopkins, impressed with her talents and experience, put Gellhorn to work as an investigator for the Federal Emergency Relief Administration. Through Hopkins, she met Eleanor Roosevelt, who introduced her to the president. Gellhorn's work in the FERA resulted in a book of short stories, *The Trouble I've Seen*, based on the tribulations of the out-of-work and dispossessed men and women she had interviewed. Eleanor Roosevelt was so impressed by the book that in advance of publication, she referred to it on three separate occasions in her syndicated column, "My Day." In England, Graham Greene had praised it in *The Spectator*, saying that it was impossible to detect that it had been written by a woman, that Gellhorn had "none of the female vices of unbalanced pity or factitious violence; her masculine characters are presented as convincingly as her female."

Gellhorn's name, oddly enough, had been linked with Hemingway's even before they had met. Her first novel, *What Mad Pursuit*, about a radical young college girl's brushes with convention on moving out into the world, had carried an epigraph by Hemingway, "Nothing ever happens to the brave," and *The Trouble I've Seen* reminded at least one reviewer, Lewis Gannett, of Hemingway. Gannett asked. "Who is this Martha Gellhorn? . . . Hemingway does not write more authentic American speech. Nor can Ernest Hemingway teach Martha Gellhorn anything about economy of language."

Perhaps it was inevitable that when Hemingway met the tall, young, attractive blonde in Sloppy Joe's one afternoon in late December, he would be immediately attracted to her. (Gellhorn, her mother, Edna, and brother Alfred, on vacation in Florida, had stopped in the saloon for drinks.) Pauline, meanwhile, was waiting at home for Ernest's arrival; they had guests for dinner. So attractive was the girl and the conversation that Hemingway delayed and delayed and finally sent word, by way of Charles Thompson, who had been sent to retrieve him, that he would meet his company later at one of the local night spots. Thompson informed Pauline that Hemingway had been detained by a fan, "a beautiful blonde in a black dress."

A woman who knew both when to stay and when to move on, Gellhorn remained in Key West after her mother and brother had left, spending her afternoons with Hemingway and getting to know Pauline, who, if she was aware of how closely the situation approximated her own relationship with Hadley before the breakup of that marriage, did not, at first, allow her fears to show. Martha promptly wrote her friend Mrs. Roosevelt about Hemingway, describing him as an odd bird, "very lovable and full of fire and a marvelous story teller." In a writer, she noted, this would be called imagination, "in anyone else, it's lying. That's where genius comes in."

Hemingway saw her frequently. She read the unrevised manuscript version of *To Have and Have Not* and felt she had been "very smart about it." They were both taken up with the civil war that, as Hemingway had predicted, had broken out in Spain in July with bloody executions and atrocities on both sides. When she and Hemingway met, Madrid was under siege; Hemingway fretted that he was missing the action. Gellhorn's eagerness to see it firsthand created a bond between them; she was determined to get there. Hemingway, to Pauline's dismay, had already had an offer from John Wheeler to cover the war for NANA, the North American Newspaper Alliance. When Martha left for St. Louis around January 10, Hemingway suddenly decided to go to New York the next day. Somehow en route he managed to meet up with Gellhorn in Miami, where, over a steak dinner, they talked more about the situation in Spain. Hemingway accompanied her on the train as far as Jacksonville, where Martha changed trains for St. Louis. She wrote a breezy thank-you letter to Pauline: "My new system of the daily dozen (pages by God) is going to finish this book in no time."

(She was working on a novel.) When the book was finished, Martha said, she might take a cutter and sail around the Horn, "or maybe the Himalayas are the place for an ambitious girl." But it was clearly the trip to Spain that must have been uppermost in her mind.

Matthew Josephson, who met Hemingway in Key West late in 1936, had a chance to study the abrupt but growing relationship between Hemingway and Martha Gellhorn. Because Hemingway had despised the Surrealist crowd with whom Josephson had been associated in Paris, the two men had seen little of each other there. But in Key West, they struck up an incidental friendship. "It was by now visible to most of us in the Key West circle," Josephson remembered, "that the marriage of Ernest and Pauline had reached a delicate stage. She was trying to be patient and also fighting to hold him." Josephson considered Pauline "a peach, both good and intelligent."

Josephson did his best to spark Hemingway's interest in the American political situation but found it hard going. As he wrote the critic Kenneth Burke, "They [American Communists] have certainly gored and maddened him." Hemingway, he noted, was also a bit scornful of Dos Passos for being a bleeding heart for the proletariat while putting up in first-class hotels wherever possible. Nonetheless Josephson claimed he liked Hemingway "more than I ever expected to." The two met frequently, went fishing, swam together, and shared Saturday evenings together at Sloppy Joe's, drinking and listening to the rumba band. Hemingway even asked for Josephson's opinion on the still not final version of *To Have and Have Not.* With some embarrassment, Josephson criticized the second half but praised the earlier segments dealing with Havana and the sea journeys. Hemingway, so Josephson wrote his wife, "received these observations with good grace, though I sensed he was unhappy about them."

Josephson, who had visited Spain two years earlier, had written an article for the *New Masses* warning about the dangers of the republic going under. "We must now protest everywhere," he wrote, "against the crudely conceived intervention by fascist Germany and Italy in Spain." Hemingway, as Josephson remembered it, shared the same sentiment and was clearly disaffected with his life at the moment. He admitted that he had a nice house and boat in Key West, though they belonged to Pauline, he said. "I could stay on here forever, but it's a soft life. Nothing's really happening to me here and I've got to get out."

⸙ ⸙ ⸙

Matthew Josephson had been right in his critical judgment of *To Have and Have Not.* The lengthy final section of the book lacked the unity of the two earlier-published story segments, "One Trip Across" and "The Tradesman's Return." In the long, culminating "Winter" section, Hemingway's tough-minded stoic hero Harry Morgan — now minus an arm, his boat confiscated, after he and his black mate had been shot up in the bootlegging run from Cuba depicted in "The Tradesman's Return" — makes the fatal mistake of ferrying back to Cuba four revolutionary terrorists against the Machado regime. The terrorists have just robbed a Key West bank. It is clear that, having abruptly gunned down Harry's mate, they intend to kill Harry as well, and the ill-fated getaway ends in a bloody shoot-out. *To Have and Have Not,* for all its racy narrative, was freighted with social commentary that remained commentary: diatribes against the bureaucrats of the Roosevelt administration; passing slurs at the FERA; a long, sardonic set piece on the wealthy capitalists in their expensive yachts harbored at Key West. The criticisms of American capitalism, however, have a slightly hypocritical taint, as when Hemingway describes the well-intentioned wealthy man whose money "came from selling something everybody uses by the millions of bottles, which cost three cents a quart to make, for a dollar a bottle in the large (pint) size." (The capitalist was plainly based on Pauline's uncle Gus, who profited — as did Hemingway — from the sales of a popular mouthwash.)

Few writers have left their secrets so exposed to posterity as Hemingway has in the various manuscript versions of his novels and stories: he is the author on the edge of creation. And where he is most vulnerable is in that exercise of anger and attack that seemed, for him, to be so vital a stage in the creative process. Since Hemingway saved this material — the false starts, the buried skeletons of the models for his fleshed-out characters, the splenetic attacks against named friends and companions that would later be deleted from the texts — one can only assume that he intended that inevitably this material would be open to investigation by scholars and critics. (There is, in fact, a vital critical study to be written on this aspect of Hemingway's genius, the relationship of the pressures of the life on the literature.) In one of the early versions of *To Have and Have Not,* Hemingway runs down a list of his "friends" and colleagues. It is delivered in the persona of Tommy Bradley, husband of the sexually promiscuous Helene, who "collected writers as well as their books." (As Arnold Gingrich recognized and warned Hemingway, the Bradleys were far too recognizable as Jane and Grant Mason.) Bradley, thinking back on the writers he has known, has little good to say of any of them. Harry Crosby, whom Hemingway claimed was a real friend when arguing with Fitzgerald, is written off as "a silly ass. He was crazy as a coot half the time and he couldn't write worth a damn." If he had had good sense, he would have killed himself earlier ("Messy about the girl though"). Hart Crane was "an unfortunate buggar, always propositioning the wrong sailors and getting beaten up." Having savaged Fitzgerald once before, Hemingway continued the argument seeking the last word: "He was romantic about money and about youth. Jumped right from youth to senility. . . . Might pull out of it yet if he wasn't so sorry for himself." Only Joyce seemed to fare well: "Wrote two fine books and a very great book and went blind. You cant blame a man for going blind."

The reference to Joyce, possibly, was tribute paid for Hemingway's inclusion of not one but two Molly Bloom monologues in his novel. The first is a surpassingly awkward soliloquy involving Dorothy Hollis, wife of a film director, who takes a sedative and indulges in masturbation when her lover, too drunk, has fallen asleep. ("What can you do but go ahead and do it even though, even though, even anyway, oh . . .") The length of the passage, perhaps, was Hemingway's successful strategy for running it past the censors. The second soliloquy is given to Marie Morgan, Harry's ex-prostitute wife, who, after her husband's death, lying awake, reminisces about their life together. She remembers the time when she dyed her hair blond for Harry. ("And I said, 'You like me blonde?' 'Don't talk about it,' he said, 'Let's go to the hotel.' And I said, 'O.K., then. Let's go.' I was twenty-six then.") But Marie finds no consolations, only wonders, like Dorothy Hollis, how she will get through the nights without sleeping: "I guess you find out all right. I guess you find out everything in this goddamned life."

But the brunt of Hemingway's irritation was reserved for the character Richard Gordon, a phony-radical novelist who is writing a proletarian novel about a strike in a textile factory and is obviously based on Dos Passos. The most scathing indictment is delivered by Gordon's wife, Helen (there are, awkwardly, a Helen and a Helene among the assorted wives in the book). Her dressing-down of her husband should destroy him: "I've seen you bitter, jealous, changing your politics to suit the fashion, sucking up to people's faces and talking about them behind their backs. I've seen you until I'm sick of you." But Gordon is a survivor of abuse — that is what makes him so especially contemptible. Rather predictably, for Hemingway, when Gordon attempts to have sex with the nymphomaniac Helene Bradley, he suffers the humiliation of losing his erection. Tommy Bradley catches the pair in flagrante, but merely smiles and goes out closing the door. ("Don't mind him," [Helene says.] "Don't mind anything. Don't you see you can't stop now?") Gordon, unable to perform, insists on leaving. Helene slaps him hard, twice, in the face: "So that's the kind of man you are," she says. "I thought you were a man of the world."

Left-wing critics would regard *To Have and Have Not,* with its presumed anticapitalist stance and its criticism of the bureaucracy of the new Roosevelt administration, as Hemingway's long-awaited acknowledgment of the proletarian cause. They were content to overlook much that was wrong in the book, its jerry-built structure, its weak and improbable characterizations, and settle for the saving grace of the dying Harry's summary message: "No matter how a man alone ain't got no bloody f——ing chance." Yet, there was enough in Hemingway's treatment of the subject to alert them that he was not quite ready to be gathered into the Marxist fold. It was clear that Harry had no love for the brutal terrorist Roberto, with his acquired taste for sadistic killing. And Harry was more outspoken in his dismissal, in the privacy of his thoughts, of the nice young educated revolutionary who gives him the standard apologetic lecture on the ends justifying the means. "What the hell do I care about his revolution," Harry tells himself. "F—— his revolution."

⁂

It took several months of activity and a good deal of persuasion before Hemingway managed to make his trip to Spain. Despite Pauline's fears, he signed the contract with John Wheeler to cover the war for NANA. Wheeler had offered Hemingway $500 for each cabled story and $1000 for more considered articles up to 1200 words, sent by mail — far more than the $15 to $25 other correspondents were receiving for coverage. To allay Pauline's worries, Hemingway persuaded Sidney Franklin to accompany him as a foreign correspondent, a flimsy tactic that the American State Department regarded as dubious at best. Franklin's passport, therefore, was good only for France and Portugal. Franklin, thoroughly bewildered by the politics of the situation, agreed to make the attempt anyway. With friends on both sides of the conflict, he admitted, "The funny thing was that I didn't have any idea of which side we were going to cover. The political aspect of the war had escaped me entirely." He decided that he was on Hemingway's side.

Dos Passos, too, was eager to get to Spain. He was deeply involved in a project funded by Contemporary Historians, a pro-Loyalist group, the principals of which consisted of Dos Passos, Lillian Hellman, and Archibald MacLeish, who was serving as president. (Gerald and Sara Murphy were among the contributors.) Its mission was to produce a film on the Spanish civil war that would encourage support from the American public. One of its chief aims was to reverse the Roosevelt administration's policy of nonintervention, a refusal to allow the sale of arms to the Spanish Republic, the legally constituted government of Spain. Very early on in the war, Spain had become a proving ground for the weapons and manpower for countries bent on changing the political structure of Europe. The Russians were already sending military aid and advisers to the Loyalists, while Hitler and Mussolini were heavily committed to the rebels led by Generalissimo Francisco Franco.

Hemingway accepted the offer to serve as one of the screenwriters, along with Dos Passos and Hellman, a proposition that, in the end, proved unworkable, since Dos Passos preferred to dwell on the civilian hardships and casualties while Hemingway wanted to stress the heroic military effort of the Loyalist side. The director chosen for the project was Joris Ivens, a young Dutch Communist filmmaker. During January and February 1937, Hemingway was in New York often, consulting with Dos Passos as well as working on another film project, *Spain in Flames,* written by the Cuban novelist Prudencio de Pereda, largely a propaganda effort influenced by the Soviet viewpoint.

Dos Passos was already wary of the strong Communist influence on American efforts to support the Republican government of Spain. On the eve of his departure, he was warned by an old anarchist friend and shrewd political observer, Carlo Tresca, of the dangers of the Communist subversion of the cause. "John," Tresca told him, "they goin' make a monkey outa you . . . a beeg monkey." Dos Passos countered that he and his friends would have complete control of the film. Ivens, Tresca answered, was a Communist; he went on to say that everything Dos Passos would be allowed to do in Spain — the places he would be allowed to go, the people he would be encouraged to see — would be those that furthered the best interests of the Communist party. "If the communists don't like a man in Spain right away they shoot him," Tresca told him. It was a warning Dos Passos would have occasion to remember.

Both Dos Passos and Katy, loyal to Pauline, were uneasy with the noticeable presence of Marty Gellhorn in New York, seemingly at Hemingway's insistence. It had already been worked out between Gellhorn and Hemingway that they would try to get to Spain together. In one of her letters to Hemingway at the time, Gellhorn referred to herself and Hemingway as "conspirators" in their efforts to get her past the restrictions on American travel in Spain. "I have personally already gotten myself a beard and a pair of dark glasses," she joked. "We will both say nothing and look strong." By mid-February, when she wrote to Hemingway from St. Louis, barely two months after they had first met, their plans were well advanced. Hemingway, in the meantime, was trying to dissuade Pauline from accompanying him on the trip, even from traveling with him to Paris. He and Gellhorn, ironically, were conspirators in a double sense. Hemingway had been doing his best to promote Marty's work with Max Perkins. (*Scribner's* magazine accepted one of her stories, "Exile," through his efforts.) It was not, however, until after Hemingway had left for France aboard the *Paris* on February 27, 1937 — accompanied by Sidney Franklin and Evan Shipman, who intended to volunteer — that Martha managed to get fake credentials from Kyle Crichton, an editor at *Collier's*, who provided her with a letter stating that she would be serving as a special correspondent for the magazine. In fact, she had no official assignment.

For months, Hemingway had tried his best to make plausible excuses for the trip to all parties concerned, even promising Pauline that he would take no part in combat. Late in September 1936, with some 55,000 words done on *To Have and Have Not* and having given some thought to a new collection of stories, Hemingway wrote to Max Perkins from the Nordquist Ranch in Wyoming. His letter to Perkins, who was reluctant to have his star author risking his life in Spain, was an attempt to dispel his editor's fears. "When finish this book hope to go to Spain if all not over there," he told Perkins. "Will leave the completed Mss. in a vault so you will be covered on it. I can go over it again when I come back. In case anything should happen to me you would always be covered financially even without this novel by the book of stories."

Writing to his in-laws, the Pfeiffers, he explained his willingness to accept a dangerous assignment in a war zone as a matter of conscience. "This is the dress rehearsal for the inevitable European war," he told them, "and I would like to try to write anti-war war correspondence that would help to keep us out of it when it comes." But he found it necessary to apologize for siding with the Loyalists. The atrocities committed by both sides early in the conflict had been widely reported — newspaper accounts of the murders of priests and bishops and the burnings and desecrations of churches engaged in by the Republicans would certainly have disturbed the devout Pfeiffers and Pauline — and had to be addressed. Hemingway accordingly spoke of himself as the "leader of the Ingrates battalion on the wrong side of the Spanish war." The Reds might be as bad as everyone said they were, "but they are the people of the country versus the absentee landlords, the Moors, the Italians and the Germans."

He was far more forthright about his political allegiances in a letter to Harry Sylvester, a young writer and graduate of Notre Dame (Hemingway referred to him as "a young man high up in the plain clothes jesuits") who wrote him complaining of Dos Passos's support of the Loyalist cause. The Spanish war was a bad war, Hemingway admitted, but it wasn't very Catholic or Christian for the Franco rebels to kill the wounded men in a Toledo hospital with hand grenades or bomb the working-class quarters of Madrid, killing poor people whose politics was "the politics of desperation." He acknowledged the atrocities committed against the clergy by the Loyalists. Still, "why was the church in politics on the side of the oppressors instead of for the people?" His sympathies, he said, were always for "exploited working people against absentee landlords even if I drink around with the landlords and shoot pigeons with them. I would as soon shoot them as the pigeons." He told Sylvester, "I think that's a dirty outfit in Russia now but I don't like any governments. No use to talk about it."

Hemingway's justifications in his letter to the Pfeiffers were as insistently argued but did not escape a taint of the self-serving. He hated to go away, he assured his in-laws, "but you can't preserve your happiness by trying to take care of it or putting it away in moth balls and for a long time me and my conscience both have known I had to go to Spain." It must have also been necessary to ease his conscience in other ways as well, considering the relationship he seemed bent on developing with Martha Gellhorn. Pauline, he told the Pfeiffers, was better off remaining at Key West for the time being. "I would sort of worry about her and I have to work fairly hard and wouldn't let her go into Spain in any event." A sensible attitude, if it weren't from a man clearly contemplating infidelity with another woman. That may have accounted for his need to reassure the Pfeiffers: "I'm very grateful to you both for providing Pauline who's made me happier than I've ever been."

⸙⸙⸙

"After the first two weeks in Madrid [I] had an impersonal feeling of having no wife, no children, no house, no boat, nothing. The only way to function." That was the interpretation Hemingway offered as the necessary psychological state for survival in the capital of a country under the conditions of modern warfare. It had a brave ring to it for the benefit of concerned in-laws, and no doubt, it truly described the sense of alienation, the distance from routine, which he and many another foreign journalist felt in Spain in the midst of a brutal war. But it was also true that by the two-week time span

Hemingway had specified, he had been enjoying the company of Marty Gellhorn for at least a week. She had arrived in Madrid around March 27, accompanied by Ted Allan, a correspondent for the Federated Press. Their transportation from Valencia in a small Citroën had been organized by Sidney Franklin, who had himself only recently arrived in Spain by a dangerous and circuitous underground route. Franklin, on Hemingway's instructions, had bought up a large supply of provisions in Valencia — hams, kilos of coffee and butter, a huge supply of canned jellies and marmalades — minus the hundred-kilo basket of oranges, grapefruits, and lemons which he was forced to leave behind because of the overcrowding in the tiny Citroën. It was a cramped and uncomfortable trip; Franklin, loyal to Pauline, had no great love for Marty Gellhorn, whom he considered too bossy and opinionated.

Hemingway's first cabled dispatch from Madrid was dated March 22. The city had been under siege since the previous October, and a month later the government had been hastily moved to Valencia. Within days of his arrival, in a cold rain, Hemingway was at the Guadalajara front and, at the editors' request, gave a "considered appraisal" of the situation, a grim account of the battle of Brihuega, which had taken place four days earlier, some fifty miles to the northeast of Madrid. Loyalist forces there had routed the Italian troops. Hemingway referred to it as "a major victory after eight months of defensive fighting." It was a generous assessment, since the Republican morale had, until then, been seriously damaged by the disorganized retreats and hard-fought surrenders of its forces, due in large part to infighting among the officers of the militia units. The Loyalist forces were often woefully trained and poorly armed, and the "*causa,*" as Hemingway referred to it, had been weakened by the jealousy and suspicions of its many factions: the Communists against the Trotskyites, the anarcho-syndicalists against the Socialists and liberals. Franco's forces had managed to take advantage of the opposition's weakness and disorder to the extent of reaching the southern suburbs of Madrid, entrenching themselves in the Casa de Campo, the old royal hunting preserve.

A second report on the battle of the Brihuega sector was even more expansive. (Written in Madrid, it was interrupted by a shell exploding on the roof of a building just behind the Hotel Florida, where Hemingway was staying.) Hemingway assured his readers that "the battle of Brihuega will take its place in military history with the other decisive battles of the world," a view that later military historians would hardly credit. He was clearly propagandizing for the Republicans. His sharply focused descriptions of the dead Italian Fascist soldiers looking small and pitiful lying in the bleak rain, however, were no glorification of battle: "They did not look like men, but where a shell burst had caught three, like curiously broken toys." By now, a connoisseur of the brutalities of war, he noted the blasted faces of the dead, lingered over the detritus like one of his discerning garbage pickers on the Gulf Stream, finding scattered letters, official papers, mess kits, useless entrenching tools — souvenirs of lives that had been stopped in death. As he had during his ambulance service in Italy, Hemingway commemorated the Spanish civil war with a collection of photographs: the astonished, agonized look of a sniper, surprised by death, in the bare thorny branches of a tree; the lifeless bodies over which battle had swept like a mindless wave; corpses in disarray.

These were images that held a particular fascination for Hemingway — the moment of truth at the height of battle — as they did for the photographer Robert Capa, whom Hemingway met and befriended in Spain. Capa, in fact, had become famous overnight with a controversial photograph of a Loyalist militiaman descending a hill at the village of Cerro Muriano, near Cordoba. Struck by machine-gun fire and transfixed in the moment of his death, he falls backward, arms outspread in a stubble field in which every blade of grass seems numbered by the camera. The photograph became, for propaganda purposes, *the* decisive image of Republican Spain early in the war — despite persistent rumors and some nagging evidence that it might have been posed.

Throughout his coverage of the Spanish civil war, both in his NANA dispatches and his later articles in *Ken,* the leftist, anticommunist magazine launched by David Smart, the publisher of *Esquire,* Hemingway continued to propagandize for the Loyalist cause, as did many liberal-minded correspondents. Before his arrival in Spain, when Madrid was under siege, Hemingway had admitted that Franco was "a good general but a son of a bitch of the first magnitude and he lost his chance to take Madrid for nothing by being over cautious." Now, with the advantage of being on the scene, he was perceptive about military strategies. In order to win the war, Hemingway claimed, Franco "must either encircle Madrid and cut the line of communications to the coast from Teruel, thus separating Barcelona and Valencia, or come up the coast and take Valencia" — the former proving to be the rebel strategy within the year.

There was no doubt about Hemingway's coolness under fire. With Joris Ivens, whom Hemingway had first met in Paris, and the cameraman John Fernhout, he reconnoitered the battle in the Casa de Campo and, under whizzing rifle fire, crawled back to retrieve one of the cameras left at an earlier position. He was alert, as well, to the savagery of the indiscriminate and constant shelling of Madrid, picturing the graphic horrors of the war: a woman returning from market on a Sunday morning, a sudden victim of an explosion, reduced to a heap of black rags, one leg torn off; the driver of a motorcar, sitting on the sidewalk, his scalp hanging down over his eyes. "This is a strange new kind of war," Hemingway conceded, "where you learn just as much as you are able to believe."

111

Hemingway was to make four trips to Spain: in the spring and again in the fall of 1937, then repeating the pattern in the following year. During that first stint in war-torn Spain, he and Marty Gellhorn shared the life of risk, a circumstance that evidently added to the intensity of their affair. For the moment, for Hemingway at least, it was a life free of the consequences of marriage. And there was an element of daring in Marty Gellhorn's character that Hemingway valued. His women, inevitably, were caught up in his masculine pursuits, but it was Gellhorn who shared the most dangerous assignment, the hardships of wartime Spain and a beleaguered Madrid under lethal and random shellings. Moreover, she shared Hemingway's political beliefs, was an ardent supporter of the Republican cause, and had no patience with those who complained of the subversive effects of the Russian presence in Spain. Even as late as 1959, she could still insist, "I am tired of explaining that the Spanish Republic was neither a collection of blood-slathering Reds, nor a cat's-paw of Russia." Hemingway obviously admired her bravery, her beauty, her willingness to put up with danger and discomfort, and, for the moment, her ambition.

The incongruities of war: Gellhorn and Hemingway were settled in the Hotel Florida in the Plaza del Callao, along with most of the foreign correspondents covering the scene. Martha's room was in what were considered the safer accommodations at the rear of the hotel. To Gellhorn, it seemed slightly crazy to be living in a hotel much like any hotel in Des Moines or New Orleans, with a lobby and wicker chairs in the lounge, while shells burst outside and, every once in a while, windows shattered, making "a lovely tinkling musical sound." Hemingway, according to Sidney Franklin, shared a two-room suite with him on the third floor. But it was evident to the other residents that Gellhorn and Hemingway were having an affair. One night when a shell hit the hot water tank, and the escaping steam made the corridors look like a scene out of the *Inferno*, everyone poured out of the bedrooms in pajamas and nightgowns, exposing "all kinds of liaisons," as Sefton Delmer of the *London Daily Express* remembered, Ernest and Martha among them.

Food was scarce in Madrid, but the ever resourceful Franklin served up breakfasts for friends and favored correspondents in the mornings. According to Hemingway, Franklin was the indispensable aide "who bought us all our food, cooked breakfasts, typed articles, wangled gasoline, wangled cars, wrangled chauffeurs, and covered Madrid and all its gossip like a human Dictaphone." Meals were taken in the shabby basement restaurant of the Gran Vía Hotel and evenings spent at Chicote's bar, formerly an elegant spot, now a mere dugout, where they congregated, nonetheless, for company and conversation. It was not a safe location, but Gellhorn described it as being as crowded as Times Square.

In late April, while the Loyalists were holding firm in Madrid and the Nationalists were making a major assault on Bilbao in the Basque country, Hemingway and Marty made a trip to the Guadarrama Mountains, supposedly gathering information. There was a ten-day gap in Hemingway's war dispatches. (The London office of NANA had been annoying him with reprimanding cables: "NOTIFY HEMINGWAY IMMEDIATELY LIMIT ONE STORY WEEKLY UNLESS OTHERWISE REQUESTED." And then: "REQUEST HEMINGWAY FILE STORY SOON AS EVENTS WARRANT.") In the mountains, they rode horseback up to the high Loyalist-held redoubts. (It was — would be — the setting for Pablo's guerrilla band in *For Whom the Bell Tolls.*) Hemingway considered the Spanish mountain troops the best disciplined and smartest of any he had yet seen. His absence in the Guadarramas probably accounts for the fact that he filed no copy on the bombing of Guernica by the German Condor Legion units on the afternoon of April 26. Relays of Junkers 52s carpet-bombed the city for two and a half hours. It was a market day; farmers had brought sheep and cattle to town; the animals, sprayed by incendiary bombs, ran blazing through the streets until they dropped — a surreal image of the new warfare. Civilians, fleeing the town, were strafed by Heinkel 51 fighter planes. A testing ground for modern weaponry and modern aerial warfare, much of Guernica was destroyed, a third of its population killed and wounded.

Hemingway made no mention of Guernica in his dispatches — a curious omission made even more mysterious by the fact that even two years later he would become vehement about Fascist propaganda efforts to deny that they had destroyed the city, placing the blame on Basque incendiarists. "Well I was not in Guernica," Hemingway said later, "but I was in Mora del Ebro, Tortosa, Reus, Tarragona, Sagunto and many other towns when Franco did exactly what he denies having done in Guernica."

In Madrid, Martha Gellhorn, though in the midst of the turmoil of the war ("It was a feeling I cannot describe; a whole city was a battlefield, waiting in the dark"), was restless with her role as mere traveling companion to war correspondents who had serious work to do. At times she checked over Hemingway's copy, passing it on to Franklin, who then took it to the censorship office in the Telefónica building. It was Hemingway, whom she identified as "a journalist friend" in her 1959 collection of war reports, who encouraged her to write, saying that it was her one way of "serving the Causa." She sent a first report to *Collier's* and was relieved when it was accepted. It was the beginning of a series, written with the same taut phraseology that Hemingway employed. Gellhorn, however, emphasized the civilian angle: the ruined houses looking like scenery in a war movie; the women waiting in line outside the market, clutching their baskets, averting their faces when shells dropped in the square; and how, at night, lying in bed, she could hear the sounds of machine-gun fire only ten blocks away in University City, where the Nationalists were still holding ground.

It was the shared life in Spain which marked the turning point in Gellhorn's relationship with Hemingway. She saw him in a different light than that of the shabbily dressed celebrity she had met in Key West. Accompanying him in Spain, she saw him at his best, a man with more stature than the publicity figure. "I think it was the only time in his life when he was not the most important thing there was. He really cared about the Republic and he cared about that war. I believe I never would've gotten hooked otherwise."

II

It was in wartime Madrid that Hemingway once again found himself in the company of the peers in his profession. Once again, there was the circle of friends and competitors in the trade of writing — and a woman with whom he was in love — the same circumstances that had proved fruitful to his career in Paris. But now it was in a city in a war zone, a city under assault, where one lived, each day, with danger, and with death in the streets. Life under siege gave him little opportunity for despondency. He made friends with Herbert Matthews, the seasoned *New York Times* correspondent. Matthews, one of the more objective reporters on the scene, considered his assignment during the defense of Madrid among the great days of his life. His praise of Hemingway in Spain was generous. Hemingway, he said, represented "much that is brave and good and fine in a somewhat murky world." Hemingway never felt quite so comfortable with Sefton Delmer of the *London Daily Express*, who was less inclined to believe the propaganda handed out by the government press agency. Constancia de la Mora, a highly literate young woman who worked in the censor's office in Valencia and who admired Hemingway unreservedly (he contributed a blurb for her procommunist 1939 autobiography, *In Place of Splendor,* in which he forgot his distaste for legendary women: "She was a legend and this book shows why"), regarded Delmer with suspicion, claiming that he only pretended sympathy toward the Loyalist government, that it was "a piece of fiction he dropped when he went home to London." Mora, who had sent her daughter to safety in Moscow at the outset of the war, loyally followed the party line on the civil war.

In Madrid, Hemingway was equally friendly with Arturo Barea and Ilsa Kulcsar, who directed the censorship office in the Telefónica building. They issued the safe-conduct passes, the petrol vouchers, and made the travel arrangements for correspondents. Although Barea, the forty-year-old Catalan novelist, gave the appearance of being an orthodox Marxist, he could also speak disparagingly of the political infighting on the Madrid front. "Party pride," he noted, "seemed stronger than the feeling of common defense." He would later find himself in trouble with the hard-line Marxists and was removed from his job. In the end, he managed to get out of Spain safely, though not without difficulty.

In the two and more years that Hemingway covered the Spanish civil war, he met many, but not all, of the journalists and writers who converged on the scene. It was clear — to the writers and journalists, at least, if not to the commanding politicians of the time — that the battle against Fascism taking place in that beleaguered country would soon engage the whole of Europe. They were writers whose convictions, largely, were not the official policies of their governments or necessarily the views of the newspapers or the political parties they represented. They were, sometimes, making a personal stand or commitment or investigating the scene, like Antoine de Saint-Exupéry (the correspondent for *L'Intransigeant*) or that most improbable of armed correspondents, Simone Weil, the irritating saint of principle over politics, who attached herself to the troops of the violent anarchist Buenaventura Durruti. (Weil's eyesight was so poor that fellow soldiers would not walk anywhere near her line of vision. "Oh Lord, deliver us from mousy women!" one of her comrades in the field declared.) Other writers were individualists of the *causa* or held to some other persuasion: André Malraux, who had been instrumental in securing French planes for the *causa* and organized the International Brigade's air squadron at Alcantarilla, or the English poets W. H. Auden and Stephen Spender. Auden served as a stretcher bearer in an ambulance unit, and Spender came to Spain on a mission of mercy on behalf of a young friend who had volunteered and then, having become disillusioned, was in danger of being shot as a deserter.

On his third stint in Spain, Hemingway encountered Joe North, editor of the *New Masses.* North admired Hemingway's humanitarian instincts, though not his present politics. In his book, *No Men Are Strangers,* North nonetheless quoted one of Hemingway's more trenchant political distinctions: "I like Communists," Hemingway had said, "when they're soldiers, but when they're priests, I hate them." It was on the same tour of duty that Hemingway also met Vincent Sheean and James Lardner (Ring Lardner's twenty-four-year-old son), both correspondents for the *New York Herald Tribune.* Hemingway took a personal interest in Lardner, who became so caught up in the heroism of the conflict that he decided to join as a volunteer in the Lincoln Brigade. Both Hemingway and Sheean tried, without success, to dissuade the young man. Hemingway found him intractably stubborn: "Of all the pigheaded kids and gloomy superior little snots I think he is way in the lead. . . . He is a nice kid in some ways too, but he is awfully gloomy to make a soldier." Lardner was later killed during the Battle of the Ebro.

The war in Spain may have brought out Hemingway's humanitarian instincts, but it also stirred up his sense of literary competitiveness. He had, for instance, praised André Malraux's 1933 novel, *La Condition humaine* (*Man's Fate*), unreservedly. But after Spain, he blasted Malraux as one of the "pricks and fakers" who deserted the cause early in order to write "gigantic masterpisses" — the book in question being Malraux's 1938 novel, *L'Espoir* (*Man's Hope*). Hemingway accused Malraux of pulling out of the war in February 1937, "before it really started." Ironically, that was seven months into the bloody conflict and a month before Hemingway had arrived in Spain. Malraux, he claimed, was a "phony" who pestered the Soviet-trained Polish general Karol Swierczewski, code-named "Walter," with all sorts of questions until Walter, who had a reputation as a kidder, answered, "*Pense? Moi pense pas. Moi général soviétique. Pense jamais.*" (Think? I never think. I am Soviet general. Never think.)

⁂

What Hemingway brought to Spain was an extraordinary reputation. Even before he had set foot on Spanish soil, he was one of the most visible spokesmen for the Spanish cause, a fact not lost on Marxist propagandists. *Newsweek* had published the story of his fee of one dollar a word as the highest ever paid a war correspondent and noted that he had contributed $3000 for the purchase of ambulances. A *New York Times* article announced his appointment as nominal head of the ambulance committee for the pro-Loyalist

American Friends of Spanish Democracy. *Story* magazine would claim, inaccurately, that Hemingway had contributed $40,000 to the cause. *Time* would repeat the error, giving it even wider circulation. Hemingway's affiliation with NANA meant that his articles would circulate to some sixty newspapers, among them the *New York Times*, the *San Francisco Chronicle*, and the *Los Angeles Times*, as well as his old paper, the *Kansas City Star*. During his two-year coverage of the Spanish civil war, his dispatches were regularly reprinted or excerpted in *The New Republic*, as well as quoted in *Time*. His views on the progress of the war, his comings and goings, were the subjects of reports and interviews in *Life* and *Time* and major American newspapers.

At the Second Writers' Congress at Carnegie Hall in New York, on June 4, 1937 (Earl Browder, secretary of the Communist Party in America, was on the platform with Joris Ivens, who introduced the screening of *The Spanish Earth*, without sound track or the score of Spanish music arranged by Virgil Thomson and Marc Blitzstein), Hemingway spoke out as a writer committed to the fight against Fascism, if not as a man who had embraced Marxism. Standing before a capacity crowd, his steel-rimmed glasses fogging, he addressed, in his rather high-pitched radio commentator's voice, the specific problems of the writer: how to write "truly" and how to project so that the writing would become part of the experience of the person reading it. He scorned those who did not want to work for what they professed to believe in and wanted only to discuss and maintain positions that involved no risk. "Really good writers are always rewarded under almost any existing system of government that they can tolerate. There is only one form of government that cannot produce good writers and that system is fascism. For fascism is a lie told by bullies. A writer who will not lie cannot live and work under fascism." The applause after his seven-minute speech was resounding, but Hemingway hurried off into the wings and did not reappear. Paul Romaine, seated in the audience, was a highly responsive listener. He wondered how the Loyalist cause could lose with Hemingway on its side. Hemingway's brief speech even received the imprimatur of the *New Masses*, which published it in its June 22 issue. Dawn Powell's report to John Dos Passos, who avoided the congress, was less than reverent. The main event of the opening session, she told Dos, occurred around ten-thirty, when "all the foreign correspondents marched on each one with his private blonde led by Ernest and Miss Gellhorn, who had been through hell in Spain and came shivering on in a silver fox cape chin-up." Hemingway's speech, she said in a sardonic summary, was good, "if that's what you like and his sum total was that war was pretty nice and a lot better than sitting around a hot hall and writers ought to all go to war and get killed and if they didn't they were a big sissy."

Hemingway's appearance in New York was followed by an invitation to the White House (arranged by Martha Gellhorn) for a preview showing of *The Spanish Earth.* (By then it had been decided that Orson Welles's orotund reading of Hemingway's script overshadowed the simple eloquence of the action, and Hemingway was persuaded to read his commentary himself.) Hemingway attended with Joris Ivens and Martha. Despite his earlier accusations, he was impressed with Harry Hopkins and liked him. Eleanor Roosevelt, he wrote his mother-in-law, was "enormously tall, very charming, and almost stone deaf." The president was "very Harvard charming and sexless and womanly," reminding Hemingway of some great woman secretary of labor. The food, as he had been warned by Gellhorn, was the worst he had ever eaten: "rainwater soup followed by rubber squab, a nice wilted salad and a cake some admirer had sent in." Both Roosevelts had been impressed with the film, but felt that it should have had more propaganda.

In an attempt to drum up financial support, Hemingway traveled to Hollywood for a showing of *The Spanish Earth* to the film colony. Fitzgerald, working under contract to Metro-Goldwyn-Mayer, attended a special showing at the home of the actor Frederic March and his wife, Florence Eldridge. But he was reluctant about attending the party at the home of Dorothy Parker afterward. Lillian Hellman encouraged him to go, allaying some of his nervousness. Having just arrived in Hollywood, Fitzgerald was painfully trying to stay on the wagon — cause enough to precipitate a lack of confidence. At the party, Hemingway was the center of attention and drinking heavily. Loud and aggressive, his back to the door, he threw a glass into the fireplace, just as Fitzgerald entered. It is not clear whether Scott did in fact talk with Hemingway; he may have slipped out of the party without seeing him. He was, however, impressed enough by Hemingway's fervor for the Loyalist cause to send him a telegram on the following morning: "THE PICTURE WAS BEYOND PRAISE AND SO WAS YOUR ATTITUDE." Fitzgerald also wrote Max Perkins about Hemingway's "whirlwind" visit: "I felt he was in a state of nervous tensity, that there was something almost religious about it." It was the last occasion the two men were together.

In New York, a few days before his return trip to Spain, Hemingway delivered his much delayed comeuppance to Max Eastman. Stopping by Max Perkins's office at Scribner's, he found Eastman in conference with Perkins. After the opening social exchanges, Hemingway got down to business, suddenly ripping open his shirt to show the real hair on his chest, then carefully opening Eastman's shirt to expose the hairless chest beneath. "What do you mean accusing me of impotence," he blurted out. Eastman, picking up a handy copy of *Art and the Life of Action,* in which his "Bull in the Afternoon," was reprinted, thrust the copy at Hemingway, saying "Here. Read what I *really* said." Hemingway, leafing through the pages and steaming in anger, suddenly slapped Eastman in the face with the book. The two men lunged toward each other and began to grapple, falling to the floor. Perkins, rushing to separate them, found Eastman on top, with Hemingway, his anger suddenly spent, lying on the floor and grinning.

The New York press had a heyday with the literary battle of the decade, labeling the pair "the Croton Mauler and the Havana Kid." The *New Masses* found political significance in the affair; Hemingway's shoving a book into Eastman's face was viewed as a "political gesture." (Eastman, regarded as a defector from the Marxist cause, had only recently been branded by Stalin as "a brigand of the pen.") Both men claimed victory, Hemingway asserting, "He jumped at me like a woman — clawing, you know, with his open hands. I just held him off. I didn't want to hurt him." Perkins and the other astonished members of the Scribner's staff refused to comment further on the affair. Perkins did, however, give Fitzgerald a report on the event. Fitzgerald was amused, but saddened: "He is living at the present in a world so entirely his own that it is impossible to help him, even if I felt close to him at the moment, which I don't. I like him so much, though, that I wince when anything happens to him, and I feel rather personally ashamed that it has been possible for imbeciles to dig at him and hurt him."

⸙ ⸙ ⸙

Nowhere was Hemingway's privileged status as a war correspondent more obvious than in his relationship with the Russian-trained staff officers who were headquartered in Gaylord's Hotel, near the Prado, in Madrid. It was Ivens, who considered Hemingway a bit politically naive at the time, who claimed credit for first introducing Hemingway to the Russians at Gaylord's: "I had a plan for Hemingway, and I think I used the right tactics . . . I didn't introduce him to the Russians when he first asked me. But after four weeks, I thought, now, he is ready to make that step and it worked." It was through him, Ivens claimed, that Hemingway was able to get accurate firsthand information. But soon after his first arrival in Spain in 1937, Hemingway struck up a friendship with Hans Kahle, who commanded one of the International Brigades. He was also on the friendliest terms with General "Walter" of the Fourteenth Brigade.

Swierczewski had been born in Warsaw and had served with the Red Army during the revolution. Hemingway would remember, fondly, one of the incidents of war: Walter at a bridge, with nothing to blow it up and the Fascist tanks on the other side, stalled, "thinking it was mined and four of us watching them. Under these circumstances Walter could make jokes." General Walter became the model for the teasing General Golz ("I am *général soviétique*. I never think. Do not try to trap me into thinking"), who briefs Robert Jordan on his mission, the critical blowing-up of a bridge, initiating the action in the opening chapter of *For Whom the Bell Tolls*.

Hemingway had as well a warm relationship with General Paul Lukács, the commander of the Twelfth International Brigade near Madrid. Lukács, a Hungarian Communist, had served with the Austrian army in Italy, opposite Hemingway in World War I. A writer and critic under his real name, Maté Zalka, he was one of the most popular and convivial commanders in the International Brigades. Ilya Ehrenburg remembered Hemingway questioning Lukács about the fighting for the Palacio Ibarra in the Guadalajara campaign, in which two volunteer Italian battalions, Fascist and Republican, were involved in a pitched battle, the two men standing together over the maps and Lukács repeating, "War's a dirty business." The Twelfth Brigade, in fact, was a favorite of Hemingway's. He developed a close friendship with Dr. Werner Heilbrun, the chief medical officer, a quiet and taciturn man, and with Gustav Regler, Lukács's feisty German commissar, a year older than Hemingway. Regler, just before his arrival in Spain, had had a sobering glimpse of the first purge trials in Moscow.

Hemingway had first met Gustavo Durán, a lieutenant colonel in the Sixty-ninth Division, in Paris in the old days when Durán was a musician and composer. Soon after the war began, Durán joined the Communists and was placed in charge of an arms depot. His organizational skills were promptly recognized and he was put in command of a brigade. Hemingway considered him a hero. Dos Passos, too, arriving in Spain shortly after Hemingway, was impressed with Durán, who had taken him to a field headquarters in the foothills near the Escorial. Durán volunteered a bit of his past history, then commented that he was now happier than he had ever been in his life.

There was, however, one officer for whom Hemingway had no respect, General André Marty, short-tempered, insanely suspicious of Fascist treason everywhere, preferring to shoot anyone on suspicion rather than indulge in "petit bourgeois indecision." As a former head of the French Communist party, he was favored by Stalin for having, as a young seaman in the Black Sea fleet, mutinied rather than support the White Russian army in the Russian revolution. Marty was commander of the International Brigades. Placed in charge of the training camp at Albacete, he had a low opinion of the American volunteers of the Lincoln Brigade, regarding them as "spoiled cry babies." Even Ilya Ehrenburg considered Marty "a mentally sick man." Hemingway detested him, claimed that Marty would have been shot if he hadn't become such a bloody symbol.

Among the Russian writers and journalists in Spain, aside from Ehrenburg, Hemingway was much taken up with Mikhail Koltsov, the young, intellectually minded correspondent for *Pravda*. Hemingway would portray him as Karkov in *For Whom the Bell Tolls* and would speak warmly of Koltsov years later:

> He knew I was not a communist and never would be one. But because he believed in me as a writer he tried to show me how everything was run so that I could give a true account of it. I tried to do that when I wrote the book. But I did not start on the book until after the Republic had lost the war and it was over because I would not write anything in the war which could hurt the Republic which I believed in.

At least one military historian of the Spanish civil war believes that Koltsov's function in Spain involved military as well as propaganda activities and that Koltsov "acted as Stalin's agent to spy on the others." If so, having connections with Stalin proved to be hazardous. Late in 1938, Koltsov became one of the victims of Stalin's continuing, megalomaniac purge of suspected military and political leaders.

There was no doubt that Hemingway, wanting to make a good impression, appear savvy, and show himself as a man among men, conformed to the expectable public image he had projected for himself. (His preferential treatment by the Russians — cars, petrol, access to places others found difficult to get to — caused grumbling and resentment among some of the foreign correspondents.) But there were many contradictions in his character, and appearances could be deceiving. With a writer of stature and reputation, Hemingway could, on occasion, relax and carry on a conversation in which he might admit to his artistic intelligence and ideals. Stephen Spender, meeting Hemingway in Spain, expected to find the celebrity figure: "I wondered how this man, whose art concealed under its apparent huskiness a deliberation and delicacy like Turgenev, could show so little of his inner sensibility in his outward behavior." A chance conversation he had with Hemingway about Stendhal's *La Chartreuse de Parme,* a novel Spender had not yet read, revealed the literary man. Hemingway told him that the account of the hero, Fabrice, was the best, deceptively casual description of war in literature. The reality of battle was just as Stendhal had described it, "a boy lost in the middle of an action, not knowing which side will win, hardly knowing that a battle is going on." Spender realized, then, that Hemingway had the kind of literary sensibility that the professional critic, or the don, nearly always lacked. Hemingway "saw literature not just as 'good writing,' but as the unceasing interrelationship of the words on the page with the life within and beyond them — the battle, the landscape or the love affair." Spender would remember one of Hemingway's more intimate admissions. Hemingway told him that his principal reason for coming to Spain was to discover "whether he had lost his nerve under conditions of warfare." All of that sensitivity, however, disappeared when they reached a local tavern and Hemingway, grabbing a guitar, started singing Spanish songs. "He had become the Hemingway character again."

The civil war in Spain would be many a writer's personal challenge. The dangerous circumstances, the conflicts and allegiances, even the suspicions about the political motivations and actions of friends or former friends, would have a telling effect on personal relationships. Josephine Herbst, in Spain when Hemingway was there in the spring of 1937, would write about it with a calculated honesty in a chapter of a later memoir, *The Starched Blue Sky of Spain.* She confessed her bewilderment. "Don't expect an analysis of events. I couldn't do it then, I can't now." She had come to Spain out of a sense of personal dissatisfaction with her life and with the way the world was going, and out of frustration at one's inability to alter the course of events that seemed headed toward a war that should be avoidable.

Herbst had no particular newspaper assignment, but arrived in Spain late in April 1937 with vague commitments to write up the human interest angle for several publications. Like Hemingway, she was sympathetic to the Russian involvement because she felt that Russia, unlike the Western democracies, was fully committed to the Loyalist government. In Madrid, she stayed at the Hotel Florida, dined with the crew of correspondents at the Gran Vía restaurant. Hemingway looked out for her interests. She was often in his company, sometimes at the front on assignments arranged through his goodwill and his useful connections with the Russians. But she also felt irked and uncomfortable about being dependent on his favors.

Thrust into a dangerous and confusing wartime scene, she felt depressed and anxious.

Military actions were a mystery to her, amid the bewildering political factions — the POUM, the CNT, PSUC, and the welter of initials that designated them. "Ask Hem to explain who is fighting where," she noted in her journal. On the surface, her relationship with Hemingway was friendly enough. She was well aware that he was getting favored treatment among the correspondents and was critical of her tendency to be critical of him. At a lunch at brigade headquarters, where Hemingway was the focus of attention, she noted, "Hem good guy but I am going nuts at this fetish business." She asked, "Is it sour grapes?" — and answered, "Perhaps." Her resentment, no doubt, had undercurrents in memories of Hemingway's treatment of her and John Herrmann on one of their trips to the Dry Tortugas. Hemingway had mocked and gibed at Herrmann so unmercifully that she could take it no longer and snapped, "If you don't stop talking that stuff, Hem, I'll take your gun and shoot you."

Living at the Hotel Florida, she saw Hemingway frequently, recognized that he was having an affair with Martha Gellhorn, suspected that it might account for his macho exuberance. At times, when she tried to bring up the subject of her separation from Herrmann, Hemingway would be evasive and misleading. She wondered about Pauline as well.

> When I had finally told him about John who was now gone from my life, and he had answered soberly, "You were a good wife, a very good wife to John," I couldn't resist answering, "That doesn't mean a thing. You ought to know. Hadley was a good wife, too." He had not answered directly but had looked thoughtfully out of the window, and only later that day popped the question "What do you think of Martha?" When I replied that I . . . really knew nothing about her . . . he pounded back with, "But you don't know much about women. How could you? You're always with men."

It was an odd accusation, though probably an accurate reflection of Hemingway's feelings at the time. It was also evidence that Hemingway was less than perceptive in this case — although he was ordinarily sensitive to lesbian tendencies in women. For Herbst, several years before, had begun to have cautious but meaningful affairs with women.

Whatever Josie Herbst might have felt about her conflicted relationship with Hemingway, about her situation in Madrid and her grasp of the politics of the moment, she would look back on her experiences in Spain as extraordinarily significant. Writing to Ilsa Barea, another of the later displaced persons of the Spanish conflict, Josie claimed that Spain had "put iron into me at a moment when I needed iron."

✓✓✓

In Spain, Hemingway, almost as a matter of principle, refused to believe — or, at least in his journalism, refused to believe — in the mounting evidence of the terrorism and treachery with which the hard-line Communists subverted the Loyalist cause. Dos Passos too had his personal confrontation; in Spain, he found it necessary to shed a good many, if not all, of the Socialist principles that had not seen the test of fire. And in Spain, Hemingway and Dos Passos came to the end of their friendship. As Josie Herbst aptly phrased it, Hemingway "seemed to be naively embracing on the simpler levels the current ideologies at the very moment when Dos Passos was urgently questioning them."

The break came as a result of the Robles affair. One of Dos Passos's first acts when he reached Valencia was to hunt up his translator José Robles, whom he had first met in Spain in 1916 and came to know very well later, when Robles was teaching at Johns Hopkins University in Baltimore. Robles, who had translated *Three Soldiers,* was a valued friend. In the summer of 1936, when the military revolt broke out, Robles and his family were vacationing in Spain. He decided to remain, offering his assistance to the Loyalist government. Knowing some Russian, he was assigned to the Ministry of War and later as interpreter for the Russian general Goriev (the code name for Ian Antonovich Berzin, a veteran of the Russian revolution). Goriev, a former head of Soviet military intelligence, was the military attaché in Valencia.

But wherever Dos Passos asked about Robles, he was met with embarrassed silences until, with persistence, he learned that Robles had been arrested by some "special section" and was being held incommunicado. Dos Passos finally located Robles's wife, Márgare, then living in a run-down neighborhood of Valencia with her children. Even after months of inquiry, she was unable to find out where her husband was or why he was being held (despite the fact that her seventeen-year-old son, Francisco, was working as a translator for the press bureau under Constancia de la Mora and had reportedly been told, in secret, that his father was dead). Dos Passos promised to do what he could. He had already been put off by the foreign minister, Julio Álvarez del Vayo, who "professed ignorance and chagrin" and said he would look into the matter. Dos Passos also pressed the pared-down U.S. embassy staff to look into the case. (His friend, the American ambassador, Claude Bowers, had moved to St.-Jean-de-Luz, just over the border in France, shortly after the war began. Though sympathetic to the Loyalist government, Bowers was too far removed from the scene to be of much use.)

The more Dos Passos pressed his inquiry, the more confusing the answers he received. According to one Spanish official, Robles had been kidnapped and executed by some unruly anarchist faction. The chief of the Republican espionage service in Madrid told him that Robles had been executed by a special section that Dos Passos gathered was under the control of the Communists. The execution had taken place, presumably, as late as February or March 1937. Another account was that Robles had been executed as a Fascist spy. An American Communist, Liston Oak, who worked in the propaganda office in Valencia, finally warned Dos Passos that his inquiries were causing embarrassment and could be a source of danger to both Dos Passos and to his friends. (Oak himself would later come under suspicion by the same agencies and asked Dos Passos's help in getting safely across the border into France.) Dos Passos disbelieved the Fascist spy theory; he would later attribute it to "romantic American Communist sympathizers," among whom, quite probably, he included Hemingway. "I certainly did not hear it from any Spaniard," he added.

Dos Passos's theory was that Robles had been the victim of circumstances in the climate of fear and suspicion that was undermining the Loyalist cause. Robles had a brother who had fought on the Franco side, been captured, and imprisoned. Robles had visited him several times in an attempt to persuade him to join the Republicans. That would have aroused suspicion in the volatile political atmosphere. "It was only too likely," Dos Passos reasoned in a letter to the editors of *The New Republic,* written in 1939 when he tried to sort out the probabilities of the case, "that Robles, like many others who were conscious of their own sincerity of purpose, laid himself open to a frameup." But the real reason Robles's case had been pushed to the point of execution, he surmised, was because Robles "knew too much about the relations between the Spanish war ministry and the Kremlin and was not, from their very special point of view, politically reliable." Dos Passos added, "As always in such cases, personal enmities and social feuds probably contributed." It was not the popular view at the time, but it was hardly an unrealistic appraisal, considering that in 1937 Robles's superior, General Goriev, was summoned back to Moscow, with the inevitable results.

Josie Herbst, who became involved in the Robles affair, had a different version of the circumstances under which Dos Passos had learned about Robles's execution. She arrived in Valencia soon after Dos Passos had left for Madrid in the company of André Malraux (in one of the incongruities of war, in a roomy Hispano-Suiza commandeered by Malraux). Josie too tried to hunt up Robles, acting on a suggestion Dos Passos himself had made before she left for Spain. In her case, however, some now unknown official told her that Robles had been executed and made her promise not to tell Dos Passos. In Madrid, seeing Dos Passos daily, she found the promise a burden of guilt she did not want to bear. In Herbst's version, Hemingway had begun complaining to her that Dos's questions were creating suspicions that might get them all into trouble — "After all," Hemingway said, "this is a war." Then, one day, Hemingway told her, with an annoying sense of self-importance, that he had heard from a government source that Robles was safe and would be given a fair trial. Irritated, Josie confessed what she already knew. The two then contrived a story that Hemingway agreed to tell Dos Passos: that a German correspondent whom Hemingway could not name had told him that Robles had been executed, that Josie had also been told and they were not free to say anything more. Hemingway, however, chose to tell Dos Passos in the midst of a crowded luncheon given for the foreign press. From across the table, Josie could see from Dos's expression that he had been told the disagreeable news. The result was an exceedingly uncomfortable drive back to Madrid in an atmosphere full of hostility and guilt. Hemingway leaped from the car as soon as it reached the hotel, and Dos and Josie took a solemn walk in the Plaza Mayor.

But as Herbst's biographer, Elinor Langer, points out, despite all the credible detail, Josie's version contradicts Dos Passos's on several important points, chief among them that Dos Passos had learned of Robles's execution through other sources. There is no evidence that Dos Passos felt any bitterness toward her for her part in the affair. He had, in fact, warm recollections of Josie's conduct in Spain. Two years later, in a letter to her, he recalled a morning when the Hotel Florida was being shelled. Among the guests in pajamas and robes crowding the lobby, Josie had efficiently served coffee. Dos Passos wrote Josie, "Shall always remember how human you looked and acted at the old Florida that morning — amid many depressing circumstances that was one thing that made me feel good." But his experiences in Spain nevertheless had a critical effect. Eventually, he recognized, sadly, that the Robles case was "only one story among thousands in the vast butchery that was the Spanish civil war, but it gives us a glimpse into the bloody tangle of ruined lives that underlay the hurray for our side aspects."

III

It was inevitable that Hemingway was angered by Dos Passos's growing political disaffection with the Spanish situation. To begin with, there had been an ongoing disagreement over the filming of *The Spanish Earth.* Dos Passos had gained a point, at least, in the filming of a water irrigation project in the village of Fuentidueña, near Madrid, that would show the efforts of the Spanish to build for the future even in the midst of the chaos. He was willing to leave to Hemingway and Ivens the blood and guts footage that became the main theme of the documentary. Moreover, Hemingway was becoming increasingly short-tempered with anyone who took an attitude of defeatism or behaved in any way that suggested it. Hemingway had been annoyed by Dos Passos's persistence in pursuing the Robles matter. But what exasperated him even more was Dos Passos's decision — at least as Hemingway construed it — to return to the safety of Paris and Katy, who was waiting for him there. In time, he would work up a spiteful scenario of Dos Passos's cowardice which he told to A. E. Hotchner, relating how Dos, on his arrival in Madrid, sent Katy a cable saying, "BABY, SEE YOU SOON," which Hemingway had had to reassure the censor was not a coded message but only an indication that Dos Passos did not intend to stay long in wartime Spain; how when told about Robles's execution, Dos Passos had turned on him as if he had shot Robles himself; and how the very first time the hotel was bombed, Dos Passos had packed up and hurried back to France: "Of course, we were all damned scared during the war, but not over a chicken-shit thing like a few bombs on the hotel . . . I finally figured it out that Dos's problem was that he had come into some money, and for the first time his body had become valuable."

It was one of Hemingway's stories: Dos Passos did not hurriedly leave Madrid for Paris, but stopped first at Fuentidueña, then went on to Valencia, where he tried, unsuccessfully, to get a death certificate verifying his friend Robles's death from Álvarez del Vayo so that Robles's widow could collect on her husband's American insurance policy. Dos Passos also spent a few days in Barcelona before his departure from Spain. It was there that he met the wounded George Orwell, who had been at the front with the troops of the POUM, the dissident anti-Stalinists whom the Communists were trying to eradicate politically with a stepped-up propaganda campaign. Orwell, who seemed terribly weary, had talked honestly about his own experiences in Spain. Dos Passos guessed that he understood the situation completely. ("Perhaps he was still a little afraid of how much he knew.") While in Barcelona, Dos Passos also interviewed Andrés Nin, the leader of the POUM, who, two months later, under orders from Alexander Orlov, the Russian NKVD agent active in Spain, would be arrested along with forty members of the POUM central committee. (Nin, taken away separately, was tortured and then murdered in secret.) It was in Barcelona, too, that Liston Oak, who had slipped out of Valencia just in time, asked Dos Passos to help him get out of Spain.

It was only when Hemingway again caught up with Dos and Katy weeks later in Paris, just as they were leaving on the boat train, that he delivered the irreparable blow to their friendship. Hemingway showed up at the station in an agitated state and confronted Dos Passos, who admitted that he planned to write what he considered the truth about what was going on in Spain. Hemingway fired back at him, "You do that and the New York reviewers will kill you. They will demolish you forever." Katy, shocked at the way Hemingway had balled up his fist and shaken it at her husband, was appalled. "Why Ernest," she said, "I never heard anything so despicably opportunistic in my life!" Hemingway strode off as the train pulled away.

Hemingway was right about one thing: Dos Passos did have his troubles with the New York critics. In an article in *Common Sense*, soon after his return to the States, he went public with his misgiving about the Spanish civil war, commenting on the violent struggle "between the Marxist concept of the totalitarian state and the Anarchist concept of individual liberty." He conceded that the Communists had managed to organize the various anti-Fascist elements of the Loyalist government but noted that they had also brought their "secret Jesuitical methods, the Trotsky witch-hunt, and all the intricate and bloody machinery of Kremlin policy." Dos Passos's article, titled "Farewell to Europe!" constituted his two cheers for democracy. It caused a stir among the Marxists: Mike Gold, so Dos Passos wrote his old friend E. E. Cummings, accused him of "remaining alas in a state of bourgeois unreconstructed and unliquidated adolescence." Left-wing friends of long standing, like John Howard Lawson, questioned his views, which only furthered the Fascists. ("Fascism," Dos Passos answered, "is nothing but marxism inside out and is of course a worse impediment — but the old argument about giving aid and comfort to the enemy is rubbish; free thought cant possibly give aid and comfort to fascism.") He now thought that foreign liberals and radicals were wrong not to protest against the Russian terror all down the line.

The most insulting communication came from Hemingway, early in 1938, taking issue with another of Dos Passos's articles that had appeared in *Redbook.* Hemingway was sarcastic: "A war is still being fought in Spain between the people whose side you used to be on and the fascists. If with your hatred of communists you feel justified in attacking, for money, the people who are still fighting that war I think you should at least try to get your facts right." Dos Passos had mistakenly referred to General Walter as a Russian, whereas he was, in fact, a Pole. Hemingway then recited the breviary of foreign generals, Lukács, Petrov, Kahle, Copic, none of whom were de facto Russians but Hungarian, Bulgarian, German, and Yugoslav. (A purely semantic distinction on Hemingway's part, since they were, like all the commanders of the International Brigades, favorites of the Comintern.) "I'm sorry, Dos, but you didn't meet any Russian generals." It was clear to Hemingway that Dos Passos could not have found out the truth in ten days or three weeks, "and this hasn't been a communist war for a long time." Hemingway went on, "Then there is Nin. Do you know where Nin is now? You ought to find that out before you write about his death. But what the hell." It could have been only willful or blind ignorance on Hemingway's part as late as March 1938 to hold out the supposition that Andrés Nin was still alive. Nin's arrest the year before had been the subject of inquiries in both the Spanish and international press. The knowledge of his death in official quarters had in fact caused a crisis in the government of Prime Minister Juan Negrín many months before Hemingway wrote his letter to Dos Passos. (Only the extent of Nin's torture at the hands of the Communist-led *cheka,* which had tried to force him to confess to his involvement in a Fascist plot, seems to have been unknown at the time.) Even Josie Herbst, back in the United States, still believing in the necessity of the Communist effort in Spain, found it difficult to raise questions about Nin's murder and the evidence of his complicity in a Fascist plot. Writing to Granville Hicks at the *New Masses,* she complained, "I would like to be able to question without having someone accuse me of disloyalty. . . . There are many things in Spain that are far from simple." Her letter to Hicks was written on September 21, 1937, fully six months before Hemingway questioned Dos Passos on the evidence of Nin's death. The conclusion may be that Hemingway's sources in the Communist camp may have played him false or that his need to sustain his public image had blinded him to the realities.

In his March 1938 letter to Dos Passos, Hemingway's anger escalated until he was repeating his insults. "When people start in being crooked about money," he wrote, "they usually end up being crooked about everything." He reminded Dos of the money still owed him ("not the Uncle Gus money when you were ill. I mean others, just small ones, afterwards"), suggesting that when Dos was paid for one of his articles, he might send him thirty dollars or so — the allusion to Judas being difficult to overlook. "So long, Dos," Hemingway concluded. "Hope you're always happy." But he could not forgo a final thrust: "Honest Jack Passos'll knife you three times in the back for fifteen cents and sing Giovenezza free. Thanks pal."

Nor was Hemingway finished then. In an article for the June 30, 1938, issue of *Ken* magazine, Hemingway, disgruntled by the recent defeat of the Republican forces in the crucial Aragon front, blamed it on the treachery of the Fascists and their Fifth Column supporters, though he maintained he was not at liberty to give the details. But he did give an account of a political commissar he knew who had unexpectedly turned traitor. The querulous article was also the occasion for airing the story of an American writer, "a very good friend of mine," who had turned up in Madrid the year before. The friend was unwilling to believe that a Spanish friend of his who had been shot as a spy had been a traitor. Hemingway wrote this off as "as good an example as any of the good hearted naiveté" of the typical American liberal attitude. "I happened to know," Hemingway assured his readers, "this man had been shot two weeks before as a spy after a long and careful trial in which all the charges against him had been proven." His claim clearly damaged the credibility of his questioning Dos Passos on the point of Robles's death. Yet even so, Hemingway suggested that if his friend the American novelist should read his *Ken* article, he might "admit the possibility" that his friend and translator had been a traitor, after all. "More likely," he conceded, "he will admit nothing." The *Ken* article, "Treachery in Aragon," was the low ebb of Hemingway's coverage of the Spanish civil war.

Perhaps it was the threat of defeat which caused Hemingway to write the article. And perhaps it was the threat of defeat which explained Hemingway's willingness to make his commitment to the Communist effort — and the Communist side — by accepting a commission from *Pravda* to write an article on "The Barbarism of Fascist Interventionists in Spain" for the August 1, 1938, issue. Hemingway, back in Key West for two months and about to leave for the Nordquist Ranch in Wyoming with Pauline and the children, completed the article in a few days, in time for the issue. The article did not have a wide circulation other than in Russia. And it did not surface again until more than forty years later when the manuscript for it was discovered in the Hemingway archives by Professor William Watson, who was researching Hemingway's involvement in the

Spanish civil war. There is the possibility that Hemingway's friend Koltsov may have initiated the request for the article, since in Hemingway's cablegram of acceptance he also sent regards to Koltsov (a message to the winds, it seems, since Koltsov was shortly to disappear into the gulag).

Hemingway's article appeared on page 4 of *Pravda,* surrounded by contributions from Koltsov, Upton Sinclair, Chou En-lai, and Mao Tse-tung — notable company. In it, he announced, "During the last fifteen months, I saw murder done in Spain by the Fascist invaders." He spoke of the murderous Fascist bombings and shellings of the civilian population of Madrid, describing (again), in the usual gruesome detail, the scattered bodies of women who had been waiting in line for soap, a streetcar filled with workers which had been struck by a nine-inch shell, and the hungry dog sniffing about in the wreckage and running off with a large piece of intestine trailing from its jaws. "He was hungry, as everyone else is in Madrid," Hemingway commented. In contrast to the atrocities committed by the Fascists when they took a town, he described the tenderness with which the Loyalist troops took care of the children and helped in the evacuation of the old when they captured Teruel. The Fascists, Hemingway concluded, had not learned that killing a fighting man's wife and children only made of him an implacable enemy. "The crimes committed by Fascism," he predicted, "will raise the world against it."

✓✓✓

On the subject of Spain, Hemingway would be unforgiving with friends and former friends. Still, he was conscious enough of his behavior to recognize his faults. In a later, apologetic mood, he would refer to his involvement in the Spanish civil war as his "great 37–38 epoch" when he had been "self-righteous, no-good and bastardly," having alienated all his friends whom he missed like hell — among them, possibly, Dos Passos. But Dos Passos's drift toward conservatism would annoy him for years to come. "Have you ever seen the possession of money corrupt a man as it had Dos?" he was still asking Edmund Wilson late in life. But the more vindictive of his remarks against Dos Passos — and Katy — lay buried in one of the deleted passages in *To Have and Have Not.* Hemingway had already scored Dos Passos as never repaying his debts to friends when his books came out and claimed (whether true or not is uncertain) that Katy had a habit of stealing from stores and was once arrested in Wanamaker's and taken to court.

Rather pathetically, Katy Dos Passos, who seems not to have noticed the connection between Richard Gordon and her husband

and was never aware of the more vicious remarks in the manuscript, tried to keep up the friendship. Writing to Pauline in 1938, when Pauline's relationship with her own husband was becoming embittered and shaky, Katy remarked how much she regretted the intrusion of politics into the relationship between the Dos Passoses and the Hemingways: "I often wish our husbands were pals as nature intended and feel bitter about all forms of politics and international war-fare — also peace, fascism, democracy and the Kraft Cheese evil. I do not give my views publicly as Dos says he doesn't want a Dorothy Thompson in his home. This hurt me terribly so I don't say much any more, just sit and chew gum."

Hemingway also had his grievances with Edmund Wilson over the Spanish question. Wilson reviewed Hemingway's *The Fifth Column and the First Forty-Nine Stories,* the collection that combined his Spanish civil war play along with an impressive retrospective edition of his previous short stories, including "The Short Happy Life of Francis Macomber," his bullfighting story "The Capital of the World," "The Snows of Kilimanjaro" (in which Fitzgerald's name was changed to Julian), and a poignant story from the civil war, "The Old Man at the Bridge," one of the last he had written. Wilson also took the opportunity to discuss some of Hemingway's Spanish war dispatches, which had appeared in the English magazine *Fact.* In his review in *The Nation,* Wilson praised the recent stories as among the best Hemingway had written, designated "The Short Happy Life of Francis Macomber" as one of his masterpieces, and claimed that the collection represented "one of the most considerable achievements of the American writing of our time." But he discounted *The Fifth Column* as having done little for either Hemingway or the revolution. Wilson's political views had by then turned more to the Trotskyite persuasion, and he questioned Hemingway's too wholehearted acceptance of the Communist or Stalinist party line in his articles about the Spanish conflict. By then, in December 1938, after Munich and Neville Chamberlain's confident claim of "peace in our time," the Spanish civil war was superfluous to nations preparing for the inevitable European conflict. Premier Negrín had already announced the withdrawal of the International Brigades in a speech at the League of Nations. At the farewell parade in Barcelona on November 15, cheering crowds had strewn roses in the streets as the volunteers passed under huge portraits of Negrín and Stalin. The fiery Communist orator La Pasionaria (Dolores Ibarruri) had extolled the troops, "You can go proudly. You are history. You are legend." It was clear that the Republican cause in Spain was doomed, although the fighting would continue for several more months.

Hemingway had only recently returned from his final trip to Spain and one of the most costly of the engagements, the Battle of the Ebro (with the loss of some 70,000 men on the Republican side). The letter he wrote to Wilson, dated December 10, the publication date of Wilson's review, may not have been sent. He began on a soft note: "You were the first critic to take any interest in my writing and I have always been very grateful and have always looked forward to reading anything you write about what I publish." He respected Wilson's judgment, he said, though he could not always agree with it. The dispatches in *Fact,* he said, had been published without his knowledge or consent and he had had no opportunity to correct them. Still, he defended them on the grounds that he was doing his job as a correspondent: "I was paid to write what are called 'eye witness' accounts of fighting in a civil war. (It turned into a foreign invasion)." The tone of the letter became increasingly sarcastic:

> I know that all of you who took no part in the defence of the Spanish Republic must discredit those who did take a part and I understand human beings enough to appreciate your attitude and the necessity for it. The suppression of the POUM, the poor old Poum, was a godsend to all cowards as a pretext for taking no part in the fight against Fascism in Spain, and I hope to live long enough to see John Dos Passos, James Farrell, Max Eastman, and yourself rightly acclaimed as the true heroes of the Spanish War and Lister, El Campesino, Modesto, Durán and all our dead put properly in their places as stooges of Stalin.

Hemingway's diatribe appears to have been the end result of his growing disillusionment. As early as March 1938, along with Edgar Mowrer of the *Chicago News* and John Whitaker of the *New York Herald Tribune,* Hemingway, concerned about the possible defeat of the Loyalists, had alerted the American ambassador Claude Bowers of the need for contingency plans to evacuate from Spanish hospitals American medical personnel and wounded, who might be slaughtered if the Francoists should win. Fortunately, that proved unnecessary when the Republicans managed to hold the Madrid-Valencia line. Then, in late October, writing to Max Perkins from Paris before returning to the front, Hemingway was again in a depressed mood, though he had mentioned that he was working on a new novel and had completed two stories. He was clearly depressed by the events in Spain, "the mess everything's in, the sort of let down and carnival of treachery and rottenness that's going on," and he found it hard to work. Hemingway's letter to Wilson was written after the Battle of the Ebro, which, in mid-November, marked the beginning of the protracted end of the Republican cause. (Hemingway was among the last of the reporters, along with Matthews and Sheean, to make the hazardous crossing to the left side of the river.) The letter represented his bitter private sentiments. His public view would come months later in the elegy to the American dead in Spain which he contributed to the February 14, 1939, issue of the *New Masses* at a time when defeated Republican troops and refugees were making the slow winter trek along crowded roads to the recently opened borders of France. It served as his tribute to that aspect of the conflict which had motivated him most in the war, the fate of men in battle. "The dead sleep cold in Spain tonight," Hemingway wrote, "and they will sleep cold all this winter as the earth sleeps with them." In the spring the rains would come and make the earth "kind" again. "The dead do not need to rise. They are a part of the earth now and the earth can never be conquered. For the earth endureth forever. It will outlive all systems of tyranny." That Hemingway's elegy appeared in the magazine he had hated so virulently years before was a testimony to how much a man's political faith could be eroded in a crucial decade.

IV

"I have bad dreams every night about this retreat," Hemingway wrote Max Perkins on February 7 from Key West. "Really awful ones in the greatest detail." It was strange, he said, because in Spain he never had dreams about anything that happened, only the recurring dream "about getting out of the trucks and having to attack without knowing where the objectives were and no one to explain the positions." Last night he was "caught in this retreat again in the goddamndest detail. I really must have a hell of an imagination." He had temporarily put aside the novel he had begun in Paris but was working on short stories. "I have to know how the war comes out to get that right anyway."

It was an unsettling period in his life. He was spending his time shuttling between Key West and Havana, where he found it more productive to write in his room in the Hotel Ambos Mundos, working from eight-thirty in the morning to two or three in the afternoon. In March, writing to Ivan Kashkin, who had translated his *New Masses* article into Russian, Hemingway confessed that it was difficult to write about the dead: "I would like to be able to write understandingly about both deserters and heroes, cowards and brave men, traitors and men who are not capable of being traitors.

We learned a lot about such people." He might as easily have been describing the novel he was in the process of writing.

Pauline, having suddenly decided to go to Europe on the *Normandy* with friends that summer, had eased the awkward situation of their growing estrangement. Hemingway spent most of his time in Havana, fishing and writing. Martha, who was with him, was also working on short stories and a novel, *The Stricken Field,* based on her relationship with Hemingway (John in the novel) and their experiences as war correspondents. (She was Mary Douglas.) Unhappy with the disorder of the Hotel Ambos Mundos, she managed to find a farmhouse, the Finca Vigía, with a watchtower and swimming pool on fifteen acres of land in the village of San Francisco de Paula, not far from Havana. It was run-down, and Hemingway, inspecting it, considered the $100-a-month rental too high. But Martha took it anyway and renovated it with her own money, and Hemingway gave it the nod of approval by moving in. For the sake of appearances, however, he maintained his mailing address at the hotel. Writing to Hadley in July, he informed her that he had 58,000 words, about 340 manuscript pages, done on his book. He had been jamming it through, trying to finish it before war broke out in Europe: "have never worked harder nor steadier." He was planning to knock off in August, so he could spend part of the summer with Patrick and Gregory and the vacationing Bumby at the Nordquist Ranch. That he was under some self-imposed pressure about the book was clear from an earlier letter to Tommy Shevlin, who had been encouraging Hemingway to join his team in an upcoming fishing tournament. "It is the most important thing I've ever done," Hemingway told Shevlin, "and it is the place in my career as a writer I have to write a real one."

✓ ✓ ✓

Circumstances, then, provided the timely context for the book *For Whom the Bell Tolls,* which was to be, among other things, Hemingway's study of cowards and traitors and brave men in battle, as well as his apologia for supporting the Loyalists in the Spanish civil war. "But remember this," Hemingway's hero Robert Jordan tells himself in a ruminative moment, "that as long as we can hold them here we keep the fascists tied up. They can't attack any other country until they finish with us and they can never finish with us." By the time the book was published in October 1940, World War II was under way, adding a further irony, the recriminating sense of a lost opportunity. The main character in the novel, Jordan, a former professor of Spanish at the University of Montana, has written an unsuccessful book about Spain. ("He had put in it what he had discovered about Spain in ten years of travelling in it.") As a *dinamitero,* he has been given the task of blowing up a mountain bridge behind the rebel lines so that the enemy forces could not bring up reinforcements at the start of a major Loyalist offensive in the mountain region of the Sierra de Guadarrama.

Hemingway had based his character partly on himself and his experiences in Spain and partly on Major Robert Merriman, a Californian and a former professor of economics, who had studied in Russia and was an acting commander of the Lincoln Brigade. (Merriman was later killed in action, giving him heroic status among the Lincoln veterans.) Jordan's assignment takes him to the camp of gypsy guerrillas; the leader, Pablo, is a guerrilla who has turned cautious and cowardly after his early, brutal successes; his *mujer,* Pilar, a forceful earth mother, has begun to assume the leadership of the group, which includes five more men, mostly gypsies. She has also taken under her wing a nineteen-year-old girl, Maria, who was brutally raped by the rebel soldiers after seeing her father, a small-town mayor, and her mother murdered.

In a bit of confused chronology, Hemingway restricted the action of the novel to a period of four days and three nights, presumably early in April 1937. That meant that he had to take certain liberties with the chronology of his own experiences in Spain and with the course of the war itself. (The cynical Karkov/Koltsov, for instance, tells Jordan about the purge of the POUM leaders in Barcelona, although the actual event would not take place until well after Jordan's death. Embellishing the tale with a fiction within a fiction, Hemingway asserts that Nin, though captured, had escaped, probably to Paris.) As in many of Hemingway's novels, the actual and the fictional live side by side. Hemingway used actual names or gave fictional names to identifiable figures, particularly military men, whom he knew in Spain. Gustavo Durán, for instance, remained himself; General Walter became General Golz; Hemingway, inexplicably, gave the name of Kashkin to the Russian *dinamitero,* who had taken part in the train bombing with Pablo and his gang in which Maria was rescued. Kashkin is also, incidentally, the character who introduced Jordan to the Russians at Gaylord's. Pablo, Hemingway claimed, was based on the gypsy bullfighter Rafael el Gallo.

It would be one of the major surprises and one of the fortunate decisions in Hemingway's literary career, considering his propaganda efforts on behalf of the Loyalist government and its Marxist supporters, that in the interests of the accuracy of his fiction or perhaps out of truth to life, he gave an evenhanded account of the atrocities on both sides of the Spanish civil war in his novel. Pilar's account of the massacre of the Fascist officials and sympathizers, organized by Pablo (the men are forced to run the gauntlet of peasants armed with flails and sickles and then are tossed over a steep cliff), is as horrific, in its way, as anything in Goya's *Disasters of War.* In a nearly too clever maneuver on Hemingway's part, Jordan is impressed and envious of Pilar's narrative skills: "That damned woman made me see it as though I had been there."

Although Joris Ivens was convinced that his introduction of Hemingway to the Russians at Gaylord's had been a success, Hemingway's hero was much more ambivalent when Kashkin takes him there for the first time. In the novel, Jordan is put off by the atmosphere at Gaylord's "because it seemed too luxurious and the food was too good for a besieged city and the talk was too cynical for a war." But Jordan admits to being easily corrupted, though he is equally cynical: "In a revolution you could not admit to outsiders who helped you nor that any one knew more than he was supposed to know." He had learned that "if a thing was right fundamentally the lying was not supposed to matter." Robert Jordan freely admits that the Comintern had educated a good many of the Spanish cadre; that El Campesino was no peasant, but an ex-sergeant of the Spanish Foreign Legion who had deserted; that Juan Modesto was one hundred percent a party man. Jordan also admits that although he had disliked the lying at first, he can live with it. "It was part of being an insider but it was a very corrupting business."

Little wonder that left-wing critics and the hardened believers among the veterans of the war were angered by the book. Even more scandalous was the treatment Hemingway gave to the two fanatics of the *causa,* both of whom he despised, André Marty and Dolores Ibarruri, La Pasionaria. Her slogan, "It is better to die on your feet than to live on your knees," turns into a desperate Hail Mary in the mouth of the boy Joaquín, who dies on the hilltop with El Sordo's gang. Before that, one of his older comrades slanders his idol by telling the boy that his La Pasionaria had a fighting-age son hidden safely away in Russia. Hemingway's private sentiments were blunt: "Dolores always made me vomit always." His most vituperative portrait was of Marty, whose blundering suspicions of Fascist spies delay the message Jordan has sent to General Golz to call off the planned offensive. Marty's paranoia provokes a long diatribe by one of his corporals: "We shot French. We have shot Belgians. We have shot others of diverse nationality. Of all types. . . . Always for political things. He's crazy." Josie Herbst, remembering that Evan Shipman, who had joined the International Brigade and been assigned as "some sort of secretary" to André Marty because of his fluent French, suspected that it was Shipman who was the important source of Hemingway's inside information. Only Shipman, she thought, "could have dug up the curious oddments which went into Hem's remarkable account of the Russian goings on at the Gaylord."

There were good reasons for Hemingway's warning to Max Perkins not to talk about the book or his opinions to the "ideology boys" like Alvah Bessie, the writer and later screenwriter, whom he had met in Spain. Bessie's book, *Men in Battle,* published by Scribner's, was a "good, fine straight book," Hemingway told Perkins. "But what was wrong with his outfit was too much ideology and not enough military training, discipline or materiel." It was clear that after the invasion of Poland and the revelation of Stalin's secret pact with Hitler, Hemingway's views on the intentions of the Russians had changed markedly and were of some consequence to his novel. "What do those guys use for Ideology now?" he asked Perkins, referring to Bessie. Martha Gellhorn, on assignment for *Collier's,* had arrived in Helsinki on November 29, the day before Russian bombers attacked the Finnish capital. "I imagine it did not take her long," Hemingway told Perkins, "to realize that those bi-motored Katuskas were no longer our planes."

✓✓✓

The love affair between Robert Jordan and the girl Maria proved to be the weakest link in Hemingway's novel. That the famous scenes in the sleeping bag should bear a certain resemblance to Nick Adams's sexual session with Katy on the blanket in "Summer People" probably testifies to the durability of certain sexual fantasies in the minds of men. Maria, however, is a very docile and compliant heroine, and it is in their duets under the stars that the made-up Spanish idiom Hemingway adopted for the novel begins to wear thin with its *thees* and *thous,* its talk of "la gloria" for the sexual climax. Pilar's lusty interest in the sexual activities of the lovers adds an element of strangeness that Hemingway perhaps meant to offset the blatant sentimentality. Her famous query about whether the earth moved, no doubt was meant to bring the affair down to earth, though that, too, became a cliché. Hemingway hinted, too, at the possibility of a lesbian affection between Pilar and Maria when Pilar confesses she is a little jealous and Maria counters that Pilar had assured her there was nothing like that between them. "Listen, *guapa,*" Pilar answers, "I love thee and he can have thee. I am no *tortillera* but a woman made for men. That is true. But now it gives me pleasure to say thus, in the daytime, that I care for thee." In the end, Pilar confesses that she is a bit in love with both of them. "You please me, *Inglés,*" she tells Jordan. "Now if I could take the rabbit from thee and take thee from the rabbit." It was Arturo Barea who first commented on the implausibility of Hemingway's made-up Spanish and his use of the word *rabbit* as the affectionate term Jordan uses when addressing Maria. (In Spanish, rabbit is *conejo,* also the Spanish slang for "cunt," a fact that Hemingway and Robert Jordan, as a professor of Spanish, must have known.) It is true that Jordan uses it everywhere in the text as a term of endearment, but that does not remove the suspicion that it was intentional. Hemingway was far too well practiced at getting double entendres and obscenities past the censorious eye of Max Perkins and the Scribner's copy editors for it to have been an oversight.

In his efforts to produce a book that would redeem his slipping reputation, Hemingway seemed intent on drawing upon all his personal resources. Even with a subject so far removed from his Oak Park origins, Hemingway could not leave his family drama behind. Robert Jordan's father, like Hemingway's, committed suicide with *his* father's Civil War Smith and Wesson revolver. But unlike Hemingway, Jordan, after the inquest, drops the weapon into a lake. In Chapter 30, Robert Jordan, on the last night before the dynamiting of the bridge, is forced to write his letter to General Golz suggesting that the attack be called off because of Pablo's treachery and the destruction of El Sordo's guerrilla band. Under the circumstances, he thinks that he might be charged with cowardice, a thought that brings to mind his father's suicide.

> I'll never forget how sick it made me the first time I knew he was a *cobarde.* Go on, say it in English. Coward. It's easier when you have it said and there is never any point in referring to a son of a bitch by some foreign term. He wasn't any son of a bitch, though. He was just a coward and that was the worst luck any man could have. Because if he wasn't a coward he would have stood up to that woman and not let her bully him.

Clearly the stream-of-consciousness rumination is tied to Robert Jordan's sense of his own identity — and Hemingway's. "I wonder what I would have been like if he had married a different woman? That's something you'll never know," he thinks.

⁂

Few events in Hemingway's professional career could have been more gratifying than the success of *For Whom the Bell Tolls.* J. Donald Adams, in the *New York Times Book Review,* claimed, "This is the best book Ernest Hemingway has written, the fullest, the deepest, the truest. It will, I think, be one of the major novels in American literature." In *The New Yorker,* Clifton Fadiman wrote, "I do not much care whether or not this is a 'great' book. I feel that it is what

Hemingway wanted it to be: a true book. It is written with only one prejudice — a prejudice in favor of the common human being." Even Edmund Wilson, writing in *The New Republic,* praised it: "Hemingway the artist is with us again; and it is like having an old friend back. This book is also a new departure. It is Hemingway's first attempt to compose a full-length novel with real characters and a built-up story. . . . The author has begun to externalize the elements of a complex personality in human figures that have a more complete existence than those of his previous stories." Lionel Trilling in the *Partisan Review* had a similar opinion: "For here, we feel at once, is a restored Hemingway writing to the top of his bent . . . no one else can make so memorable the events of physical experience, how things look and move and are related to each other." It was Alvah Bessie who spoke for the leftist critics in the pages of the *New Masses,* calling the book Hemingway's "finest achievement," but only in the sense that Hemingway had perfected an extraordinary technical facility and brought an unbearable sense of suspense to the action of the story. "But depth of understanding there is none, breadth of conception is heart-breakingly lacking; there is no searching, no probing, no grappling with the truths of human life that is more than superficial."

For Whom the Bell Tolls was the November 1940 main selection for the Book-of-the-Month Club, with a first club printing of 135,000 copies. By late December, the Scribner's edition had sold 189,000 copies. The book was a runaway best seller. By the following April, 491,000 copies had been sold. When the screen rights were sold to Paramount for $100,000 in January, it could hardly have pleased the *New Masses* cadre. It was certain that Hemingway's version of the Spanish civil war would be *the* version for the American public for years.

⸙⸙⸙

On November 21, 1940, a little more than two weeks after Hemingway's divorce from Pauline became final, he and Martha Gellhorn were married by a justice of the peace in Cheyenne, Wyoming, despite an unexpected visit to Sun Valley from Edna Gellhorn, who tried to dissuade the couple from marrying. Their marriage figured in a two-part photo essay in *Life* by their friend Robert Capa. The second part was a series of quotations from *For Whom the Bell Tolls* accompanied by Capa's civil war photographs. Actually, the photographs of Hemingway and Martha hunting pheasants, dancing together, presumably on their honeymoon, were taken at Sun Valley before the wedding.

The separation and divorce from Pauline (on the grounds of desertion) had not been easy. Though Pauline had lived with the prolonged separations and Hemingway's obvious courtship of Martha, their relationship had eventually descended into the inevitable wranglings and final bitter fights. (They tried to keep it from the two boys, but Gregory would remember the shouting in other rooms, doors slamming, Pauline hurrying out of the bedroom crying — "the usual 'amicable' divorce," as he referred to it later.) Though the custody of Patrick and Gregory, uncontested, went to Pauline, Hemingway would see them frequently, and they spent several vacations with their father and Martha, fishing and hunting. Young Jack, fourteen when he first met Martha as the glamorous blonde at the New York showing of *The Spanish Earth* in August 1937, wondered how his old father could be involved with such a beautiful young woman. Both of Pauline's sons, Patrick and Gigi, twelve and nine when their father married Marty, developed serious crushes on her, liked her frankness and seemingly breezy independence and the fact that her vocabulary was well spiced with four-letter words.

Friends were inclined to wonder about the latest of Hemingway's marital decisions, particularly those who recognized that in Hemingway's wartime play, *The Fifth Column,* the well-tailored woman correspondent, Dorothy Bridges, bore a close resemblance to Martha. The hero, Philip Rawlings, concedes that Dorothy is "enormously on the make," but ironically claims, "I want to make an absolutely colossal mistake." Hemingway's friends had reason to wonder. Martha was the most intelligent and professionally alert of Hemingway's wives, the least willing to be submissive to the Great Man. Scott Fitzgerald wrote Max Perkins, "It will be odd to think of Ernest married to a really attractive woman. I think the pattern will be somewhat different than with his Pygmalion-like creations." Gertrude Stein, in what was probably an apochryphal remark, commented that a man who had married three women from St. Louis couldn't have learned much.

It was to be, from the beginning, a writing marriage. Martha had no intention of giving up her career. Their honeymoon, in fact, was a lengthy tour of the Orient, covering the Sino-Japanese War, Martha writing for *Collier's* and Hemingway for *PM,* the new liberal daily. It was a grueling and uncomfortable journey, spending a month in Hong Kong, then taking in the front at Canton and later flying northward to Chungking, the wartime capital. The seven dispatches Hemingway wrote, mostly from Rangoon, gave an overview of the situation from the Russian-Japanese pact to the Japanese need for oil and rubber in order to win the war and the hint that Japan might go to war with America. In Chungking, Hemingway was the world-famous correspondent, photographed, along with Martha, in the company of Madame Chiang Kai-shek, who served as their interpreter with the generalissimo. It was on their trip to the interior, too, that they met with Chou En-lai, who was living underground, fearful of the generalissimo. It was not the tour Gellhorn had expected. She was appalled at the dirt and disease of China, the drugs, the teenage girls sold into prostitution in a world of venal old men. Yet Hemingway would claim that in China, Martha treated the men like brothers and the women like dogs; it was his little joke — half serious — part of their continuing rivalry as competing correspondents. In many ways Martha's best journalistic writing was a more competent form of journalism — sharper and more observant of the scene — whereas Hemingway, at his poorest, tended to write from his position as a recognized celebrity whose reputation gave him authority. For better or for worse, their marriage was the relationship of two competitive writers. Still, Gellhorn was willing to concede Hemingway's painstaking care as a writer. She would say of him, "He was a genius, that uneasy word, not so much in what he wrote as in how he wrote; he liberated our written language."

18

A Very Lonely Trade

IN HIS early forties he is still the burly, mustachioed man with the wide grin, hunting antelope in Sun Valley, Idaho, with his new young wife and his three sons. He is the man in the buckskin vest and wide-brimmed hat, hunting antelope in the Pahsimeroi valley, or shooting mallards and pintails in the low hills along Silver Creek. (Winter-cold, the flights of ducks hurtle through the pass; a mist rises from the slough; the black Labradors, silhouetted against the reeds, shiver with excitement.) At Sun Valley, in those years, he is in the company of the rich and famous and reports to his editor on the reigning movie stars gathered at Glamour House: Robert Taylor, a miniature man who might photograph up into manhood handsomely except "the actual model that the lens enlarges is neither very gay nor very impressive." Taylor's wife, Barbara Stanwyck, is more to his liking: truly ugly in the flesh but "very nice with a good tough Mick intelligence." Gary Cooper, who was eager to play Robert Jordan in the film version of *For Whom the Bell Tolls,* is fine company to hunt with but "as tight about money as a hog's arse in flytime." They are friends.

The writer in uncertain times: the European war he had predicted as early as 1935 had come with Hitler's Blitzkrieg invasion of Poland on September 1, 1939. Under the secret provisions of the German-Soviet nonaggression pact, Stalin also invaded Poland, and the nation was reduced in a month's time. Countries were disappearing from the map. In the West, there was the stalled waiting of the "phoney War." NANA, Hemingway wrote Hadley at the time, "wants me to cover the war for them as soon as it gets dangerous enough to justify paying me that kind of money. Am very glad to not waste a winter of my life at the sort of war it has been so far."

World War II would give Hemingway even more leverage as a world celebrity. Like most astute journalists, he had seen it as inevitable. "Not this August, nor this September," he told his readers in the September 1935 issue of *Esquire,* nor, he predicted, would it be the next August or September. "But the year after that or the year after that [i.e., September 1938] they fight." He was off by only a year. In 1935 Hemingway was still isolationist: "Never again should this country be put into a European war through mistaken idealism, through propaganda, through the desire to back our creditors, or through the wish of anyone, through war, notoriously the health of the state, to make a going concern out of a mismanaged one."

When the Japanese attacked Pearl Harbor, however, it was an affront to his patriotism. He and Martha had stopped in Hawaii on their Asian trip and Martha had been stunned by the American warships concentrated in the harbor and the Japanese fishing boats anchored all around them ("ideal for Japanese Intelligence") and the planes at Hickam airfield standing wingtip to wingtip. Hemingway had told her that it was the system popular in the First World War: "get everything and everyone packed in one place and get the whole lot wiped out." Hemingway's anger erupted in his letters: Secretary of the Navy Frank Knox should have been relieved of duty within twenty-four hours; the army and navy brass at Oahu should have been shot. "Through our (American) laziness, criminal carelessness, and blind arrogance," he ranted to Charles Scribner, "we are fucked in this war as of the first day and we are going to have Christ's own bitter time to win it if, when, and ever."

But the situation appealed to his sense of adventure. Because Cuba, with its strategic position in the Caribbean, was riddled with former Falangist sympathizers and infiltrated with Fifth Columnists, he decided he should play a part in the war effort. He came up with the idea of a counterintelligence unit, which he would head, to be headquartered in the guesthouse at the Finca Vigía. The proposal, surprisingly, received the support of the American ambassador, Spruille Braden. Hemingway recruited friends from among the waiters in the Floridita and the Spanish exiles from the Loyalist cause, including the local Spanish priest, Don Andrés Untzaín, who had also fought as a gunner on the Loyalist side. Hemingway translated the reports and delivered them to his liaison man at the American embassy, Robert Joyce. (He referred to his operation as the "Crook Factory.") But even that service eventually proved not to be venturesome enough, and he upgraded the scheme to include something more dangerous, outfitting the *Pilar* with bazookas and grenades as a one-ship task force for destroying the German subs that preyed on the cargo ships in the area and harassed and destroyed the local fishing boats. The plan of attack was that the *Pilar,* when detained by some surfaced U-boat, would draw close enough to open fire and speed toward the target, dropping explosives into the conning tower and hatches. The chief of naval intelligence for Central America, Colonel John W. Thomason, who had assisted Hemingway in editing an anthology of war stories, *Men at War* (1942), reckoned that no submarine commander was likely to let Ernest throw so much as a beanbag down his hatch but cooperated in the scheme. "Ernest," Thomason told him, "you are certainly going to have to improvise." Hemingway referred to him, thereafter, as "doubting Thomason." Nevertheless, a Marine gunner–radio operator was assigned to the *Pilar.* Fortunately, during the years that Hemingway was in charge of his improvised attack force, he and the crew (which included his millionaire friend Winston Guest and, on occasion, his teenage sons, Patrick and Gregory) never had a close encounter with a German submarine. Once they sighted U-boats in the distance, and on another occasion trailed a sub as it moved rapidly out of sight.

There were other concerns, aside from the war, seemingly as important to Hemingway. In November 1941, the Limited Editions Club awarded Hemingway a gold medal for *For Whom the Bell Tolls.* Hemingway was not able to attend the ceremony, having promised to make a trip with Martha. But he had specifically wired Scribner's to send a stenographer to transcribe Sinclair Lewis's speech honoring him. When the publisher failed to do so, Hemingway was irate. Four days after Pearl Harbor, he wrote Max Perkins full of bitter complaints, calling Scribner's failure "the most careless, shiftless and callous action I have ever met in civil life." He had it in mind to give the gold medal to the firm as a way of shaming them with their neglect: "I do not ever want to see it. Ever." The reasons for his anger were spelled out the next day in a letter to Charles Scribner: he did not mean to say (though he did, anyway) that if Scribner's had printed Lewis's speech as a pamphlet it might have gotten him the Nobel Prize. "Chances are there aren't going to be any Nobel prizes any more and anyhow this is what I wanted instead." People wanted different things in life, he maintained, "and what I wanted was to read and have, for my kids, that speech."

⸙ ⸙ ⸙

Martha looked askance at Hemingway's Crook Factory operations, though Ernest, eventually, turned the assignment over to Gustavo Durán, who was then living in exile in Cuba; for a time, he moved into the Finca with his wife, which did not please Martha, either. She considered the Q-boat patrols "rot and rubbish," particularly since the crew's activities sometimes descended into drinking bouts at sea with boisterous games of lobbing grenades at buoys. She was also put off by the disorderly life at the Finca Vigía and seems to have given up on the motley servant staff: an alcoholic gardener who seldom appeared for work; a psychotic maid who, at a later date, attacked the cook with a butcher knife and had to be let go; the cook who would pad into the dining room to announce to the already seated luncheon guests, "No lunch today." The housekeeping duties were a burden, Martha conceded: "What drove me crazy was when I had to cope with chauffeurs and servants and loonies, the whole lot, and I never stopped complaining about that."

Fortunately she could put up with the cats, for Ernest was a devoted cat lover. ("Never laugh at a cat," he once scolded Dawn Powell. "Dogs like it because they want to be pals with you. Cats don't want to be pals.") He had turned the house and grounds into an empire of cats: Tester and Dillinger and Tester's kitten ("a wonder cat") and "poor Bates," who died of the same disease as Pony (Hemingway's son Gregory "felt awful about it") and Wolfer (who shared the nickname Hemingway had given to Winston Guest) and Boissy D'Anglas (who would be featured by his other name, Boise, in the posthumously published novel *Islands in the Stream*) and Friendless and Friendless's Brother and Good Will (named for goodwill ambassador Nelson Rockefeller). Hemingway taught Friendless, one of his favorites, to drink milk and whiskey along with him. Friends and favored relatives, like his sister Sunny, who visited the Finca Vigía with her son Ernest (thoughtfully named for his uncle) well after generations of bred and inbred cats had accumulated, remembered the ground-floor room with swinging doors and beds and cushions given over to cats and more cats and marveled at the cases of salmon needed to feed them all and remembered the messes in odd corners. Hemingway pictured the menagerie in other terms: "The place is so damned big it doesn't seem as though there were many cats until you see them all moving like a mass migration at feeding time." It probably only confirmed his worst suspicions about women that Martha, once when he was away, had the male cats neutered to stop the inbreeding and the deformed and blind kittens.

It was hardly a wonder that Martha welcomed the opportunity to escape the occasional circus atmosphere of the Finca Vigía — though she enjoyed the impromptu late-night dinners with guests from the American embassy and the Sunday afternoon swimming parties. "Ernest could be the kindest of hosts," one guest remembered, "but it must have been undiluted hell to try to have any organized life with him." With Hemingway away, busy searching the Caribbean for German subs, Martha took on a *Collier's* assignment, covering the effect of submarine warfare on the Caribbean islands: Haiti, Puerto Rico, St. Thomas, St. Barts, Antigua, among others. Her reportorial tour was hampered by the fact of official censorship on the Allied shipping losses. It was only later that she learned that during the two months she was reporting, August and September 1942, the maritime losses were the heaviest, seventy-one ships in sixty-one days. Hemingway, in Havana, was patronizingly sarcastic about Martha's tour, describing it in a letter to Perkins: "She is at present navigating the Caribbean in a thirty foot sloop with a 4′ × 5′ cabin with a 4′5″ head room, accompanied by three faithful negro followers. I understand that if she is lost at sea, Colliers will pay double for her last article. I expect they will also want me to write a Tribute to their intrepid correspondent."

Were they still in love? At least Martha's letters to Hemingway when they were separated ("I wish we could stop it all now, the prestige, the possessions, the position, the knowledge") give that impression. She wished that, by some miracle, they could return to an earlier time when Hemingway, as in his old Milan photograph, was the dashing young man in uniform, seated in the sidecar of a motorcycle, and she imagined herself as a younger woman, "badly dressed, fierce, loving." She went on, "I would like to be young and poor and in Milan and with you and not married to you. I think that I always wanted to feel in some way like a woman and if I ever did, it was the first winter in Madrid." She still entertained the possibility that they were a plausible couple. But when she took on a hazardous assignment, traveling to England, North Africa, and Italy in 1943 and 1944, Hemingway complained that she should be staying home to take care of him. "What I wanted," he would explain later, "was [a] wife in bed at night not somewhere having even higher adventures at so many thousand bucks the adventure."

She continued to badger him about giving up the idle life, the protracted drinking bouts, the lying stories of his Crook Factory exploits which he told to impress the native population. Their meetings became increasingly antagonistic, particularly on the subject of writing. Young Gregory would remember a quarrel when Hemingway blasted out, "I'll show you, you conceited bitch. They'll be reading my stuff long after the worms have finished with you." The contradictory nature of human relationships: Hemingway was proud to squire Martha, arm in arm, to the Stork Club; proud, too, probably, of his sons' approval of his lucky choice; he nevertheless subjected her to a good deal of verbal abuse and sent angry cablegrams — "ARE YOU A WAR CORRESPONDENT OR WIFE IN MY BED" — trailing after her on her assignments. Martha was becoming more woman than the wife he wanted.

When she got back to Cuba, she was still in hopes that he would return to Europe with her as a war correspondent. She even managed, through Roald Dahl during one of her stops at the White House, to get Hemingway a seat on one of the RAF flights to London. Hemingway's response was to offer his services to *Collier's,* and he was accepted. That meant he had put her out of a job covering the fighting, since the magazine was allowed only one front-line correspondent in the European theater of operations. Hemingway berated her, saying that, doubtless, he was going to get killed; he hoped she would be satisfied. She told him that he was making it impossible for her to go on loving him. When she asked if he could get her on the plane that was flying him to London, he responded that no, he couldn't; the plane was only carrying men. (She later learned that Beatrice Lillie and Gertrude Lawrence were among the passengers on his flight.) A month later, she managed to get passage on a freighter carrying a cargo of dynamite. Hemingway was probably more truthful than he intended when he later commented, apropos of his breakup with Martha after five years of marriage, "I think no one gets a very accurate or credible account from either party to a broken marriage. Certainly I am not giving one." He added, "Anyone confusing a handsome and ambitious girl with the Queen of Heaven, should be punished as a fool."

111

In London he was in the midst of old friends, Lewis Galantière and Robert Capa, then working for *Life.* His brother Leicester showed up, serving in the signal corps. (Martha had been instrumental in getting him assigned to a documentary film unit under George Stevens.) Hemingway, who claimed he couldn't stand to look at Leicester because he looked so much like Grace, finally decided that his brother, in wartime, was a good guy now: "funny, unconceited, over-enthusiastic of course; but a good, civilized guy." Leicester was working with William Saroyan and Irwin Shaw in the same film unit. Hemingway promptly met a new woman, Mary Welsh Monks, a feature writer for *Time* and wife of the Australian journalist Noel Monks. She was well acquainted with the American and English journalists, film directors, and officers in the Office of War Information who lunched at the White Tower restaurant and congregated or lived at the Dorchester Hotel. Small, talkative, opinionated, she had lived through some of the worst of the London Blitz bombings. She and Monks, who was often away on assignment, were at the time drifting apart. Hemingway met her for the first time at the White Tower, where she was dining with Irwin Shaw. "Introduce me to your friend, Shaw," he said. Hemingway promptly asked her to lunch. (It was not until later that he learned that Mary had been involved in a brief but serious affair with Shaw.) After a few dates and in front of two of her friends, Hemingway — in Mary's peppy account in her memoir, *How It Was* — made an unexpected proposal of marriage: "I don't know you, Mary. But I want to marry you." When she objected that they were both married and hardly knew each other, Hemingway countered, "This war may keep us apart for a while. . . . Just please remember I want to marry you." If the chronology of Mary's recollection is correct, Martha had not yet even arrived in London, and the abruptness of Hemingway's proposal could only mean that he considered his marriage to Martha as being in a state of foregone conclusion.

On May 25, barely a week after his arrival in London, Hemingway's marital ambitions had to be put on hold: he suffered one of those formidable accidents that punctuated his career. After an all-night drinking party at Robert Capa's Belgrave Square penthouse, in the small hours of the morning, he was given a ride home to the Dorchester with Dr. Peter Gorer, another of the guests, and his wife. In blackout conditions, Gorer plowed his car into a steel water tank car. He and his wife were badly cut, and Hemingway, whose head had crashed against the windshield, had a deep scalp wound that required fifty-seven stitches and a serious concussion that kept him hospitalized for several days. The wire services carried the story. (In North Africa, Hemingway's son Jack, stationed with a military police outfit, had received a garbled message that his father had been killed and went on a heroic binge, waking the following morning with an equally heroic hangover, to learn that the rumor was false.) Grace promptly wrote her son. "I hope and pray," she said, "you will not have a blood clot on your brain, as I did, for I know what pain that is to bear. No doubt Martha will soon reach you, and be a comfort."

Martha, in fact, arrived three days after the accident and learned of it only from questioning reporters. Though the doctors at St. George's Hospital had prescribed rest and no alcohol, Martha found him in the hospital room, head bandaged, lying prone (he had sustained some serious injuries to his knees as well), and surrounded by visitors and the empty and half-empty bottles of champagne and whiskey with which he had been entertaining his guests. His principal worry, it seemed, was that he would not get out of the hospital in time to take part in the long-expected but still secret D-Day invasion of France. He and Martha quarreled vehemently, and Martha informed him that she was through, she had had enough of his egotism and playacting heroics, his bullying. She moved to another, more exposed, room on the top floor of the Dorchester. From that moment on, she claimed, she considered herself free from Hemingway — so, at least, she told the biographer Bernice Kert. (The vagaries of recollection: Hemingway, several months later, would name Mary Welsh as the sole beneficiary of the wartime insurance policy provided by *Collier's,* claiming that before he had left New York, he and Martha had entered into a mutual property agreement. Martha, he claimed then, had been "fully provided for.") It was a few days after the accident that Mary, learning about it, arrived at the hospital with bouquets of tulips and daffodils and the needed sympathy.

In the early morning hours of June 6, Hemingway, released from the hospital but still not fully recovered from the concussion, was on a landing craft edging toward the French coast, taking part in the historic Normandy landings. (A churning, green, choppy sea: the LCVP moving past the file of low silhouetted cruisers; the concussive booms of the offshore battlewagons, the *Texas* and the *Arkansas;* above the beaches, brown and yellow puffs of smoke drifted in the air. So Hemingway described it.) His account of it in the first of his war articles, in the July 22, 1944, issue of *Collier's,* captured the excitement and the confusion. He gave the impression that the young commanding officers were gung ho but a bit green, particularly Lieutenant Robert Anderson, who commanded the LCVP, and would have fared less well if he hadn't been aboard. Hemingway, however, having studied the maps, was familiar with the sightings, the silhouettes for the Fox Green and Easy Red sectors of Omaha Beach. He recognized the steeple of Coleville church, the heavily wooded valley cutting through the ridge. Through his small Zeiss binoculars, he studied the terrain, knew where the German installations were, and successfully maneuvered the officers away from the murderous crossfire. His description of the landing site is graphic and convincing:

> On the beach on the left where there was no sheltering overhang of shingled bank, the first, second, third, fourth and fifth waves lay where they had fallen, looking like so many heavily laden bundles on the flat pebbly stretch between the sea and first cover. To the right, there was an open stretch where the beach exit led up a wooden valley from the sea. It was here that the Germans hoped to get something very good, and later we saw them get it.

In his element, he is aware of the hazards, the men, the sprawling dead, the small dramas of the larger action. Despite the personal aggrandizement, his account of the D-Day landings, written shortly afterward, is corroborated by later detailed accounts of the invasion: the steep cliffs at either end of Omaha Beach, the vantage points of the heavily fortified German machine-gun emplacements along the lower ridges. The Germans had, in fact, held their fire until the landing troops were most vulnerable. Hundreds of men with their heavy equipment had drowned in the effort to reach the shore under heavy machine-gun fire. From the war diary of the First Battalion of the 116th Infantry Regiment:

> The enemy had waited for the favorable moment. All our boats came at the same time under the automatic weapons' crossfire. Those of the men who jumped instinctively in the sea to escape it went under immediately. . . . Few were those who reached the beach. But the situation was just as untenable there, and they returned to the water, to lay down and let only their heads emerge. Then they crawled on their bellies as the tide was coming in.

Like most of the correspondents on that first day, Hemingway was not allowed to land on the beaches. Once the men and materiel had been discharged, the landing craft turned around and Hemingway was headed back to the attack transport, the *Dorothea L. Dix,* and to England. But later, feuding with *Collier's* over its delays in paying his expense money, he would imply that he had landed on the beaches: "I hit the beaches for you with 57 stitches in my head and still the headaches." And at least one later published story, to which Hemingway probably contributed, had him on the beach, taking command of a combat team and leading them to safety under heavy mortar fire. Hemingway, on reaching London, had told his brother Leicester a very similar tale about his Omaha Beach landing. His *Collier's* article, "Voyage to Victory," however, did not stress the point, though he referred casually to June 6 as "the day we took Fox Green beach."

Unfortunately, it was Martha who had landed on the beaches, though not on the first day. Without permission to take part in the landings, she managed to stow away on board a Red Cross hospital ship by locking herself in a latrine. Anchored offshore, she had helped when the first wounded were brought aboard, acting as an untrained nurse's aide tending to the men. That night, June 7, under skies blazoning with flak, she waded ashore at Easy Red sector to help bring back another contingent of the wounded, most of them Germans. Hemingway never forgave her, tended to discredit her story. In truth, her coverage of the human angle of that historic event was less self-conscious, often more informative, than Hemingway's. Yet, in his irritating, contradictory manner, he would also praise her work when it suited some need. In his argumentative letter to *Collier's* editor Henry La Cossitt, he admitted, "Martha worked as nobody ever worked and my kid brother typed her stuff day and night."

Hemingway could be exceedingly touchy about his reporting. When the columnist Charles Collingwood, on request, told Hemingway that he thought his rather sentimental article "The G.I. and the General" was like somebody's parody of Ernest Hemingway, Hemingway did not speak to him until they got to Paris weeks later. (Part of Hemingway's irritation may have resulted from the fact that on D-Day, Collingwood had landed on Utah Beach with an underwater demolition team.) There are vivid descriptions of combat in the article, but a good part of the piece is devoted to showing that Hemingway the correspondent was a man who could carouse with GIs but was also a familiar of the unnamed general (Major General Raymond O. Barton of the Fourth Infantry Division) who received him in his trailer wearing an old gray woolen union suit. He and the general had, in fact, become friends. Barton provided him with a captured German motorcycle and sidecar and assigned him a driver for reconnoitering the area. Hemingway boasted to Mary that he and the general "lie on same blanket when he is dead, dust, impossible tired at end of day and I give him the gen [lowdown] on how it actually is at all the places we go by motorcycle."

The whole question of Hemingway's exploits during World War II is mined with Hemingway's assertions, many of which have some basis in fact but which are sometimes dubious in the telling. His articles on the battle for Paris are a case in point. For days, he had been held up on the outskirts, having organized a group of "irregulars," French partisans and villagers, in the environs of Rambouillet, some twenty-three miles from the capital. There Hemingway had installed himself in two rooms at the Hôtel du Grand Veneur and, with his partisans (who addressed him as "mon capitaine"), established an informal command force for scouting the enemy territory in advance of the drive on Paris.

General Eisenhower, as a symbolic gesture, had assigned the taking of Paris to General Jacques Leclerc, but Hemingway's irregulars and some of the GIs, and, undoubtedly, Hemingway himself, were impatient with the delay. In the articles he wrote about the drive toward Paris, he registered the complaints of his partisans against waiting for the regular army forces when their scouts and the intrepid villagers in the area were already traveling the roads to Paris, admittedly with serious risks, and reporting on the German tanks and troops along the route. And there were reports of insurrections in Paris itself. Hemingway, in these articles, presents himself in none too convincing terms as deferential to the military police and French army officers who discouraged the efforts of his unofficial liberators. (He met Leclerc, whom he had pictured as totally unimpressed with his reconnaissance activities. "In war, my experience has been that a rude general is a nervous general" was Hemingway's published rejoinder.) Even more unconvincingly, he depicts himself as fearful and overly cautious in combat situations. Encountering German tanks and artillery fire along the route to Paris in what a resistance leader called "*un bel accrochage*" and which Hemingway translated as "what happens when two cars lock bumpers," he depicted his personal response: "It was much too beautiful for me, who had never been a great lover of contact anyway, and I hit the deck as an 88 shell burst along side the road." Since he was not to advance farther with the column, Hemingway joked, "I took evasive action at this point and waded down the road to a bar." Part of this was for comic relief and also, perhaps, to avoid any suggestion that he had disregarded the Geneva Conventions against war correspondents taking part in military actions in any capacity other than as observers. Hemingway had had the foresight to secure a letter from Colonel David Bruce of the OSS, a new friend and the ranking officer in the region, approving of his activities as an intelligence gatherer. The reasonable grounds for his activities were that Hemingway knew French and was very familiar with the territory, at least that was one of the covering defenses he included in his *Collier's* dispatches. But his ebullience, the heavy drinking and rowdiness, the fact that he had removed his correspondent's insignia from his uniform and had amassed a small arsenal of weapons in his room at the hotel, had roused the jealousy of some of the other correspondents. They eventually complained to the authorities that Hemingway was flaunting the Geneva agreements. (At the later hearings convened to consider the case, Hemingway was exonerated, largely due to testimony of his influential officer friends, including Barton and Bruce.)

Fortunately he did not attempt to describe in his *Collier's* articles his triumphal entry into Paris on the afternoon of August 25. (Leclerc's Free French armored division had entered the city in the early hours of that morning.) Hemingway ended the second of the dispatches at the moment that he and his jeep driver, Archie Pelkey, were about to make the descent, Hemingway with a lump in his throat and cleaning his misted glasses, "because there now, below us, gray and always beautiful, was spread the city I love best in all the world."

The rest of the story — the liberation of the Traveler's Club, the liberation of the Ritz Bar, the delirious two-week celebration of the recapture of Paris — was left to the Hemingway legend and his letters to friends. It was a round of conviviality, drinks, dinners at the Ritz. Hemingway did not think it necessary to cover the official ceremony on August 26, when General Dietrich von Choltitz, commander of the German garrison, surrendered at the Gare Montparnasse. Nor did he think it worthwhile to attend the victory parade down the Champs-Élysées; he preferred to celebrate the liberation of Paris drinking brandy at the Ritz. Soon after his arrival, he wrote Mary Welsh, addressing her as "Small Friend," telling her of the "strange life" he had led since his dangerous patrol activities in Rambouillet. He had been scared on one or two occasions. "Some of the patrols we made would scare you worse than Grimm's Fairy Tales even if there had been no Krauts." He might claim that he was very happy, but in the midst of the festivities he was evidently feeling vulnerable, lonely, and nostalgic. "Have strong feeling my luck has about run out," he wrote her, "but am going to try to pass a couple of more times with dice. Have been to all the old places I ever lived in Paris and everything is fine. But it is all so improbable that you feel like you have died and it is all a dream."

For Hemingway, where there was a war, there had to be a woman. ("Funny," he would write Max Perkins, "how it should take one war to start a woman in your damn heart and another to finish her. Bad luck.") Now he was wishing that Mary was with him, that they could be in bed. He was all fought out and wanted something "lovely and touchable or is it tangible, same thing anyway," he wrote her. Should he ask Charles Wertenbaker, Mary's boss at Time-Life, to arrange for her to come to Paris, or would that be indiscreet?

Actually, he had not had to mail the letter; Mary showed up at the Ritz on the morning of August 26, having arrived in Paris the evening before. She found Hemingway in his room with his driver and two of his French comrades, one of them sleeping, dirty boots and all, on the hotel's pink satin coverlets. After a hearty welcome, accompanied by rounds of champagne, she secured a room for herself ("Mary and I lived at the Ritz. You might as well do it in style," Hemingway explained to Hadley, whom he kept informed on his affairs) and went off on her morning's assignment, a brisk sketch of the Parisian fashion scene during the German occupation. That afternoon, still on assignment, she witnessed de Gaulle's victory march, accompanied by his officers, as it paraded from the Arc de Triomphe to Notre Dame, where a Te Deum mass was held. That night she and Hemingway had a wearying and unsatisfying dinner at a Left Bank restaurant with his translator, Marcel Duhamel, after which, crossing the Seine to the crack of sniper fire, she and Hemingway slipped into Ernest's twin bed at the Ritz — the other was occupied by rifles and grenades — and promptly fell asleep.

Hemingway had had only a few free days during that initial visit to Paris, but he made the most of them. His reunion with Sylvia Beach and Adrienne Monnier had been joyous and ebullient. Catching sight of Sylvia, he picked her up and swung her round in a circle. The two women had managed to survive the occupation, though Shakespeare and Company had gone underground, so to speak, its stock of books and memorabilia hidden away in the fourth-floor apartment of their building, for fear of confiscation threatened by a troublesome German officer who wanted to buy Sylvia's last, and personal, copy of *Finnegans Wake*. Sylvia had also been interned for more than six months, though released unharmed through the efforts of a friend in the Vichy government. Hemingway had shown up unexpectedly the day after the German surrender of Paris, concerned that Adrienne might have been implicated as a collaborationist and therefore needing his protection. He had, in a mood of forgive and forget, tried to get in touch with Gertrude Stein but learned she was still in the country. (She and Alice had spent the years in purportedly unoccupied France, living incognito to the Germans, at least, if not to the villagers and shopkeepers of the little towns of Bilignin and Culoz in the Ain. Short on funds, Stein had had to sell her Cézanne, the *Portrait of Madame Cézanne*.) But Hemingway and Mary visited Picasso in his chilly studio on the rue des Grands-Augustins, inspecting his latest paintings and his new young mistress, Françoise Gilot. The four of them had dinner together one evening, and Mary noticed that "Picasso's face, as sensitive as litmus paper, showed a dozen reactions of amusement, concern, delight, at Ernest's accounts of his adventures with the U.S. Army in France, and they reminisced rather solemnly together about the early days in Paris." That was one possible reading of the scene (Mary had a talent for the chirrupy view in her memoirs), but Picasso felt otherwise: "He came to see me after the liberation and he gave me a piece of an SS uniform with SS embroidered on it, and he told me that he had killed the man himself. It was a lie. If he had killed one, he wouldn't have needed to pass around souvenirs." Picasso may have had the correct reading. Hemingway had written Mary about that particular trophy only weeks before but had made no mention that he had killed the officer.

ፈፈፈ

In Paris one night, Hemingway and Mary had their private "wedding night," even though they were both still married and had made no firm commitments to divorce their spouses. Hemingway, according to Mary, was the pursuer. He romanced her when they were together, crooned "I Don't Know Why I Love You Like I Do" and "*Auprès de ma blonde*." (She responded with "This Is the Army, Mister Jones.") He made very clear the kind of wife he was expecting. Having had a wife who was a professional rival, he was not likely to make that particular mistake again. When he began extolling Pauline's virtues as a housekeeper and organizer, Mary understood that what Hemingway was looking for was "the Practical Nurse" for his kids and for him in his old age. He had, in fact, begun to alert Patrick (and Pauline as well) about his marital plans. Marty, he told his sixteen-year-old son, had treated him badly when he was hospitalized in London. "She would not do anything for a man that we would do for a dog." He had made "a very great mistake on her — or else she changed very much — I think probably both." Mary Welsh, whom he was sure Patrick would like, was a "very fine girl. Looked after me in worst time ever had." He had nicknamed her "Papa's Pocket Rubens. If gets any thinner will promote to Pocket Tintoretto. You will have to go to Metropolitan Museum to get the references."

When he and Mary were separated, he seemed to be more affectionate, wrote her frequently and expected letters in return. He called her Pickle, an odd term of endearment, was concerned that she might not be as intent on their affair as he was. He wanted reassurance: "I hope you were quite serious Pickle because I am as committed as an armoured column in a narrow defile where no vehicle can turn and without parallel roads" — as sexually appropriate a metaphor as one is likely to find. His letters, he noted, were getting to be like his son Gigi's, "All small direct statements like I love you."

That fall Hemingway was away often, covering the battles of the north along the Belgian border and the Siegfried Line, where the German armies were making a desperate stand to hold the bridges along the Rhine. Hemingway was in the company of Colonel Charles "Buck" Lanham, who became an inveterate friend. Lanham, three years younger than Hemingway, was a writer and occasional poet, a stubborn and feisty West Point graduate and career man. Hemingway, who had met Lanham earlier in the course of the Normandy breakouts, had taken an immediate liking to him. But it was during the later, hard battles along the Siegfried Line that their relationship was cemented. As commanding officer of the Twenty-second Regiment, he was engaged in some of the hardest-fought, bloodiest battles of the fall and winter of 1944 to 1945 at Schnee Eifel and Hürtgenwald, a discouraging time following the Normandy offensives. Thousands of Americans were killed and wounded, demoralized by the piercing cold and the winter rains that turned the battlefields and support roads into seas of mud.

It was in the field that Hemingway wrote some of the most discouraged and discouraging letters to Mary in Paris. After a day of heavy shelling by German artillery,

> I walked down and back through it to put it in its proper perspective — House rocking quite a lot — up in the lines snow and foggy — woods pretty dropped up — went all over everything trying to get things good and clear in my head and then stayed and ate

> with Buck and we bullshitted and he told stories of when-a-boy certainly made me feel like a cissy — Feel very ashamed how I never fucked my teacher in High School — But was too shy.

He thought ahead to their life together at the Finca Vigía:

> Dearest Pickle my beloved let's think about the boat and the dark blue, almost purple of the Gulf Stream, making eddies at the edge of the current and the flying fish going up in coves and us on the flying bridge steering in shorts and no tops and at night anchored behind the barrier reef down at Paraíso with the sea pounding on the lovely sand.

He had been spooked about the last phases of his assignment; after the capture of Paris, he had felt somehow, as he told Mary, that his luck might have run out. In the battle for Hürtgen Forest, he seemed to experience one of those epiphanies in which all the contradictions of a life — his life — converge, providing no answer, but only the realization of the indefinable complexities. There were the days of waiting, which he found hard to bear. There were the days of heavy fighting, when men looked the color of the drowned and the forest was nothing but the wreckage of trees and the streams were flooded waist-high with yellow mud and a walk through the woods was a walk through heaps of German dead. He had been feeling weary. On the sixth day of the fighting, in a driving thin rain, he had come to some sense of the battle:

> a fight such as has been fought very few times *ever ever* in the world — and the people so damned *unbelievably* wonderful no one could ever believe it — I've seen the flower of the Union and the flower of the confederacy fight so that Pickle it would break your heart — So lovely, and happy and immortal — without this one I would never have known about Americans.

On the eighth day he implied that he had experienced a more personal kind of epiphany, something triggered from the past, which he tried his best to analyze, to fix in the mind.

> But then about yest. and day before just like a gift — stone cold and with nothing to drink — just as though someone were leaving you a million dollars. I get the old feeling of immortality back I used to have when I was 19 — right in the middle of a *really* bad shelling — not the cagy assessment of chances — nor the angry, the hell with it feeling — nor the throw everything away feeling — none of those — just the pure old thing we used to operate on — It doesn't make any sense — But it's a lovely feeling.

The contradictions of the human character: Bill Walton, a *Time* correspondent for whom Hemingway had developed a special affection ("I love Walton very much," he wrote Mary in a sentimental moment) and who acted as a sometime courier for Hemingway's messages to Mary in Paris, remembered Hemingway, during the course of the Hürtgenwald offensive, as "especially gay, without internal conflicts, happily free of the complications of women." But friends and eyewitnesses are not always the shrewdest observers. It was true that Hemingway put up a front of gaiety in the midst of his soldier friends. "I'm cheerful as hell and clown all the time for the guys so don't think I'm walking gloom house," he assured Mary. But it was also true that it was during the battle of Hürtgen Forest that Hemingway had thought to make Mary the sole beneficiary of his *Collier's* insurance policy.

Even in the midst of their love affair under wartime conditions, things did not always go smoothly. During his short leaves in Paris, there had been quarrels. Once, Hemingway brought with him a group of officer friends from Lanham's Twenty-second. (Marlene Dietrich, also staying at the Ritz, was a guest that night.) At first the men were all spit and polish, but as the champagne flowed (Hemingway seemed to have tapped a spring of Perrier-Jouët) they became drunk and offensive. At dinner in the Ritz dining room, one of the officers insulted Clare Boothe Luce, then a congresswoman (on tour) and the wife of Mary's boss, Henry Luce. Mary, angry and a little drunk, with grim self-control, excused herself and left. To make things worse, one of the battalion commanders had vomited all over her bathroom. Hemingway later accused her of insulting his friends. She let him have it, telling him that his friends were "drunks and slobs. . . . They may be heroes in Germany, but they stink, stink, stink here." She had not, she insisted, insulted his "boorish friends." Hemingway, furious, leaned forward and gave her a slap to the jaw — not excessively hard, but hard enough to smart. She recognized immediately that she had touched a vulnerable spot, and she was bantam enough to pursue the advantage. At once she began prancing around the room, chanting, "You poor coward. You poor, fat, feather-headed coward. You woman-hitter." When Hemingway tried to placate her, she became even more irate, pounded her fists against his chest. When he made the ultimate male appeal — "You're pretty when you're mad" — she ushered him to the door, handed him his shirt, tie, and socks and told him good night and good-bye. The following morning, the emissaries arrived, first one company commander and then another, then Marlene, with soothing advice that Papa was, after all, an exceptional and fascinating man. Peace was eventually restored.

In Paris, Hemingway also made peace with Gertrude Stein, if not exactly with Alice B. Toklas. "There wasn't a hell of a lot of time then," he wrote Stein's doughboy friend from World War I, W. G. Rogers, "and so I just told her I had always loved her and she said she loved me too which was, I think, the truth from both of us." In a bold aside, he added, "I always wanted to fuck her and she knew it and it was a good healthy feeling and made more sense than some of the talk." Alice, he said, "was sort of jealous of the friends of Gertrude that were of the same category she was. Picasso had the same theory. He thought we all got flung out into outer darkness on acct. of that and that she did not like Gertrude to be with men who ever worked at that part of their trade."

It was in Paris, at Sylvia Beach's apartment on the rue de l'Odéon, that he attended a literary party of the old familiars of Shakespeare and Company, sponsored by *Life* magazine, which was doing a feature story. Janet Flanner, Louis Aragon, Henri Michaux, and Paul Valéry were among the guests, and Hemingway read aloud to an attentive audience one of the god-awful poems he had written during the recent campaigns on the Siegfried Line, "Poem to Mary": "Now sleeps he / With that old whore Death / Who, yesterday, denied her thrice." And, during one of his recuperative trips to Paris for a couple of weeks (he had a troublesome case of bronchitis), he entertained Jean-Paul Sartre and Simone de Beauvoir at a levee in his Ritz bedroom. Hemingway, stretched out on his brass bed, was wearing a green eyeshade, the bedside table cluttered with liquor bottles. Raising himself up, he clasped the forty-year-old Sartre with a bear hug. Hemingway had been a literary influence for both Sartre and Beauvoir: "Many of the rules we observed in our novels," Beauvoir acknowledged, "were inspired by Hemingway." Sartre, too, had been impressed by Hemingway's declarative style, the way the short sentences remained discrete, intact, each refusing to build upon the next, each one a new beginning, an influence he detected in Camus, as well. Still, Sartre had an even greater regard for Dos Passos, whom he declared "the greatest writer of our time." The talk session lasted for many hours and many drinks, and it was not until the small hours of the morning that Sartre left, while the more resilient Beauvoir stayed on until dawn.

Hemingway, even more so than Gertrude Stein, seldom took advantage of his prestige to acquaint himself thoroughly with French intellectual life and the relentless seriousness of its writers. A few years later, as he did with many of his literary equals, he would give a sour accounting of the two French authors and of the Paris meeting at the Ritz. Sartre he described as "sort of a faintly wormy character; nice, smart, really on the make but just faintly wormy," and Beauvoir was "a dame who all she does is just work and have literary experiences." He would be equally scathing about

Beauvoir's relationship with the American writer Nelson Algren. "If Nelson is as tough a boy inside as he thinks he is how could he have devoted more than one evening to Simone de etc.? Riddle me that?"

⁂

Hemingway would always be wary of the consequences of marriage. But, in Mary, he seemed to have decided he had found a woman who might stay the course, put up with him, sacrifice her career. Whatever else his quarrels with Mary might have engendered, at this point in his life, he must have recognized that when he asserted his independence, fought with her, it was at some cost to himself and his own best interests. Writing Mary from the front, late in November, he did his best to make his point clear.

> I *can't* throw you away. You see because we made a decision on that. We quit that "I can lose anything and you too." That I did it that time before our trouble taught us not to be stupid. I've quit that easy, cheap defense against love. If any bad luck should happen to me please remember, and tell Willie [Walton] because would like to have him know that I have loved you all the time *repeat* all the time, and have fought this one (inside myself) all the time without throwing you away, nor the children, nor the work I have to do afterwards — as sort of a step toward growing up. But I'm a son of a bitch if it's not the hard way."

Why, one might ask, should it have been important that Bill Walton, younger than he by far, should know the intensity, or the validity, of his love for Mary? It is, once more, that strange necessity in Hemingway's relationships with women — oftentimes in the life, and equally so in his fiction — for a kind of unwritten contract, a codicil, stating that his choices of women were sanctioned, approved, endorsed by his closer male friends. In love with Agnes von Kurowsky, he sought the approval of Jim Gamble. (Forced to make a choice between them, he had defied Agnes's disapproval of Gamble and went off with him for the idyllic vacation in Taormina, as he would later, on the verge of marrying Hadley, threaten to take off on a tour of Italy with Gamble.) It was Bill Smith's disapproval that had allowed him to make the break with Marjorie Bump (a decision Hemingway commemorated in "The End of Something" and "The Three-Day Blow"). Jake Barnes's fishing trip with Bill Gorton in *The Sun Also Rises* — as idyllic an episode of male bonding as Hemingway would ever write — is depicted as the emotional counterbalance, a kind of timid declaration of love, to his tormenting affair with Brett Ashley.

In *A Farewell to Arms,* Lieutenant Henry's affair with Catherine Barkley is encouraged, and enviously regretted, by Rinaldi, with whom Henry has as intimate a friendship as that of Jake Barnes and Bill Gorton.

In Germany, Hemingway's conversations with Buck Lanham were not just shoptalk, the business of wintertime battle, and discussions of the Maréchal de Saxe, whom Hemingway was reading with interest. He confided in Buck about the status of his affair with Mary. And Bill Walton was the confidant for both Hemingway and Mary. (Walton felt that Mary in her relations with Hemingway played down the famous writer, treated him "as the hotshot warrior, macho man, great in bed.")

Whatever the tender sentiments he was writing to Mary, he was still angry and irritated about Martha, who early in November had broached the subject of divorce. Having learned of Hemingway's affair with Mary, she felt the timing was appropriate. On Hemingway's part, it may have been a case of wounded vanity that Martha had been so willing to separate. Writing to Patrick, however, he intimated that Marty had wanted a reconciliation. "We don't fight anymore. Once I was gone she wanted back very much." He wanted, it seems, to convince his son that it was he who had had the change of heart. "Going to get me somebody who wants to stick around with me and let me be the writer of the family," he told his son.

With grim irony, he and Martha found themselves thrust together in the battlefield when the fierce German counteroffensive of December 16 began. It was the beginning of the Battle of the Bulge. Hemingway had rushed back to the Fourth Division at Luxembourg, though still feverish with what might have been pneumonia. He and Bill Walton were billeted at Rodenburg with what was left of Lanham's Twenty-second Regiment after the Hürtgenwald campaign. Lanham, not satisfied with Hemingway's physical condition, had the regimental doctor dose him with sulfa pills. Martha, covering the front, arrived unexpectedly for the Christmas Eve and Christmas Day festivities. In a Christmas night letter to Mary, Hemingway tried to give the impression that he had been in control of an awkward situation: "Last night after I sent a message to you so you would know I loved you and that everything was OK., Mrs. M. showed up. (This is just news) I was good and kind on acct. of Christmas. (Explained to Buck I was marrying you if you would have me.) But she came and robbed us of what we should have had together. But the counterattack broke down of its own weight." He assured Mary, "Did not say a mean thing. Nor act one." He wished that she could have been with him instead; he did not care much for his "ration of Bryn Mawr, Bergdorf Goodman and the Lancaster."

Yet another account has it that Hemingway and Martha had appeared at the billet of General Barton for brandies around the Christmas tree. Lanham remembered an uncomfortable and bickering tour of the command posts on the following day, during which Martha, in French, began scolding Hemingway, who was sitting up front with the driver. He recalled how the back of Hemingway's neck grew redder by the minute. When they saw a German V2 rocket speeding across the sky, Martha took notes on the spot. "Remember this, Ernest," Lanham heard Martha say. "That V2 story is mine." The holiday atmosphere worsened on New Year's Eve, when Bill Walton arrived at the Luxembourg hotel and, spotting an attractive blonde in the lobby, realized it was Martha, and introduced himself. Knowing that she and Ernest were separated, he asked her to dinner that evening and she accepted. With some trepidation, he informed Hemingway, who insisted on joining them. Walton could not have been more uncomfortable throughout the entire evening. Both Hemingway and Martha berated each other roundly throughout the meal. When, later, Walton complained to Hemingway about his behavior, Hemingway responded that he couldn't be expected to use a bow and arrow against an elephant. In a childish gesture, using a bucket as a helmet and grabbing a mop for a lance, he laid siege outside Martha's room until, from behind the locked door, she called him a drunk and ordered him to go away.

Hemingway, however, would see Martha one last time. Early in March, on his return trip to the States, when it was apparent that the Allied victory over Germany was assured, he arrived in London to arrange for passage home. (Mary had remained behind in France to carry out one or two more assignments, still reluctant to give up her career to become Mrs. Ernest Hemingway. But she had agreed to move to Cuba when she returned.) In London, Hemingway stopped to see Martha at the Dorchester, where she was laid up with the flu. He had at last agreed to a divorce (though the details were to be worked out later), and Martha was relieved, wanting to get on with her life.

After his return to Cuba, in a long, chatty, and cordial letter to Martha (which Hemingway may not have sent), he filled her in on the home news about Bumby, who had been wounded and captured by the Germans during an OSS mission. "They made one break and were recaptured. Finally they marched them from Nuremberg to Moosberg (200 miles) with the S.S. dealing with those that fell out." He had been liberated shortly before the German surrender: "Not spooked nor nervous. Has grown up terribly in some ways and not at all in others." Hemingway reported on the effects of a recent hurricane ("We lost all the best mango trees; most of the key royal palms looking off toward the Mts."); the sad state of the cats at the Finca Vigía when he returned ("like something out of Dachau. It was heart-breaking. Have them all o.k. now. Blindie drowned in the hurricane"); and the news of the "childries," as he referred to them. Mousie (Patrick) had taken up painting ("reminds you of Van Gogh only it is Mousie and I think it is really good"); Gregory was as good a joker as ever but was now able to joke against himself, "has gotten rid of much of the fierce competitiveness."

He gave Martha his assurances about the reports of their breakup which he had given out. "As filler for scenario should state I'd told columnists what you asked me to in London. Spoken highly of you. . . . No scandal. Two people been married and were busting up. About as dignified as could be." He calmly discussed the divorce arrangements: "Dearest Mook, if you want to marry anyone or have *any* urgency for the divorce will go downtown tomorrow and start it no matter what repercussion on me or others. You have a right to anything you want."

At times, nothing seemed to improve Hemingway's relationship with a wife like the leaving of her. But Hemingway's mood swings were thoroughly unpredictable. Two years later he would remember the battles at the Luxembourg hotel with ripened acrimony. He might still think of Martha as an able journalist, even taking credit for some of her professional skill: "I spent a lot of time trying to help her write well, in her own way, and not like me," he wrote Charlie Scribner. As a journalist, he noted, "She is at her best when angry or moved to pity." Then he gave a devastating critique of Martha's character: "She has hung about enough wars to know something about that but, after Spain, I think she took war to be a sort of very highly organized tribute to her own beauty and charm in which, unfortunately, people were killed and wounded." His recollections of Luxembourg galled him: "I never can think of her with all those glamour clothes and uniforms and remember the smell of the beauty lotions, face packs, etc. in that Hotel at Luxembourg, the last time I saw her on the Continent, without distaste."

Although Hemingway's divorce from Martha, on grounds of desertion (under Cuban law, Hemingway was entitled to everything belonging "to both parties"), was not finalized until December 21, 1945, and Hemingway's marriage to Mary did not take place until the following March 14 in Havana, the news had begun to spread early. Before leaving Europe, Mary found it necessary to warn her parents, "Apparently there are stories circulating that I am going to marry Ernest Hemingway. . . . Until I get home and we can talk it over, please say nothing about it. . . . It is not settled yet." In River Forest, a suburb of Chicago, Grace Hemingway had been alerted. She had not heard from Hemingway for a year, even though she had written to him at both the London hotel and the hospital when she learned about his accident. On March 25, she wrote her son, "And now you are marrying again — so the newspapers tell me. May God's blessing be upon it, this time." With her unerring instinct for saying precisely the wrong/right thing to her son, she added, "I have never lost hope for you, nor ceased to pray that the Great Awakening will come to you, before this life closes." She asked, "What sort of a woman is Mary Welch? Tell me about her."

"Don't know how it is with you," Hemingway had written Martha (in the letter he may not have mailed), "but *terrible* hard for me to write immediately after war. As though all the taste buds were burned off and as though you had heard so much loud music you couldn't hear anything played delicately."

What had the war brought with it besides the avalanche of death, destruction, and ruined cities? In darkened theaters, the flickering newsreels that were fixed in the minds of a generation: the rubble-strewn Führerbunker, where Hitler, suicided at the end of all the misery, disappeared like a nightmare, taking with him his bride of a night and a day; the stacks of corpses, rictus grins, knobby arms and legs piled like bundles of stacked wood waiting for the banked fires of Dachau when liberation arrived too late; the harvest of bodies being bulldozed into the gaping pits of common burial at Auschwitz and Buchenwald; caged men and women, emaciated survivors reaching out between rusted fences; the moon-ash debris of Hiroshima; the image of a limping Japanese diplomat, in striped pants and top hat, hobbling to the surrender table on the deck of the USS *Missouri.* The whole non sequitur album of victory and defeat.

Roosevelt dead, though that image — the draped coffin, the slow-paced caisson, the drum tattoo — would hardly have moved Hemingway, who thought him a "rich and spoiled paralytic who changed our world. As a person I thought he was a bore with endless ill-told anecdotes." And Mussolini captured at Dongo; the brutal picture of the Duce and his mistress Clara Petacci, hanging from their heels, in the midst of a jeering crowd. He the beaten cadaver of swinging flesh, she with her skirt hanging unceremoniously down over her face. That affected Hemingway more: "I hate things like Dongo. But he did not come to too bad an end when you think of his cheap cynicism and how he really hated Italians."

What might have touched him, had he seen it, was the picture of Ezra Pound, the Duce's advocate, the faulted poet of an age, huddling in a cage in the punishment stockade at Pisa, awaiting repatriation and a trial for treason. (The directive cautioned, "*Exercise utmost security measures to prevent escape or suicide. . . . Accord no preferential treatment*"; his cage therefore was constructed with a specially reinforced steel mesh.) "A man on whom the sun has gone down," Pound pronounced himself in the still-continuing opus of the *Cantos.* It was not Pound's poetry, threaded with rabid economic matters, but his polemics, his broadcasts on the Rome radio ranting about his compatriots "now ruled by Jews, and by the dirtiest dirt from the bottom of the Jew's ash can," and the Allied war effort and the "fetish value of metal" that brought Pound to the camp at Pisa, his anti-Semitism a more or less recurrent theme. "I think it might be a good thing," Pound announced on April 27, 1943, in one of his broadcasts, "to hang Roosevelt and a few hundred yidds IF you can do it by due legal process, NOT otherwise. Law must be preserved." (But Hitler had already established a bureaucracy for death, and on July 22, 1942, in the Warsaw ghetto, 6000 Jews a day, by "legal" order, were forced to assemble for resettlement to the East, presumably to work camps. Their real destination was the Treblinka death camp. By May 10, 1943, after the Jewish uprising and two weeks after Pound's talk on the Rome radio, the Warsaw ghetto was a vast burned-over cemetery.)

Early on, Hemingway had foreseen Pound's fate: "Will you please send the photostats of Ezra's broadcasts that you have?" he wrote Archibald MacLeish in May 1943. "Whenever the damned business comes up we will probably be called on, or should be called on. . . . If Ezra has any sense he should shoot himself. Personally I think he should have shot himself somewhere along after the twelfth canto although maybe earlier. . . . But it is a pathological business all the way through and he should not be punished on any other basis."

Hemingway had, like Harry Walden, seen the events and the people. He had seen his share of death. But unfortunately, in time, it brought out the spurious brag in him:

> One time I killed a very snotty SS kraut who, when I told him I would kill him unless he revealed what his escape route signs were said: You will not kill me. . . . What a mistake you made, brother, I told him and shot him three times in the belly fast and then, when he went down on his knees, shot him on the topside so his brains came out of his mouth or I guess it was his nose.

II

He was a man well acquainted with death, the hard, implacable deaths of the battlefields, in Italy, Spain, France, Germany. But even before the war, death had begun to take its toll among his lesser heroes, his friends and rivals. Early in 1939, Yeats, spending his mornings working in a hotel on the Côte d'Azur, his afternoons in a lawn chair gazing out on forever, died. That summer, learning about the death of Ford Madox Ford, Hemingway made a secondhand quip: "People dying this year that never died before," borrowing the remark from Josie Russell. In December 1940, Scott Fitzgerald, age forty-four, was dead of a heart attack in Hollywood. Hemingway claimed, cynically, that Hollywood had done Scott no harm, that he had really died somewhere between the ages of thirty and thirty-five. He conceded that Scott's creative powers had probably lasted a few years beyond that, but he didn't think much of Scott's unfinished novel, *The Last Tycoon,* which Edmund Wilson had edited for publication. Perversely, he now claimed that *Tender Is the Night* was Scott's best book. It had "all the realization of tragedy that Scott ever found. Wonderful atmosphere and magical descriptions and none of the impossible dramatic tricks" that Scott had outlined for *The Last Tycoon.*

Hemingway was down on Bunny Wilson, in any event, because of his 1939 essay "Hemingway: Bourdon Gauge of Morale," reprinted in the critic's 1941 book, *The Wound and the Bow.* Despite Hemingway's disapproval, it would set a standard for later Hemingway criticism and further annoy him. Wilson's long and thoughtful critical study posed the thesis that Hemingway, like the others in the volume (Dickens, Kipling, Joyce, for example) had developed a literature of trauma, working from specified or unspecified Freudian "wounds" that set these writers apart from society, producing a kind of alienation that was a strength and a weakness of their genius. That was a touchy enough secret, but Wilson also scored Hemingway's tendency to publicize himself in his writing, calling the public Hemingway "certainly the worst-invented character to be found in the author's work." Hemingway was irate. Wilson's book was originally scheduled for publication by Scribner's, but the company refused to publish the Hemingway essay and the contract was broken on terms favorable to Wilson. "Hemingway," Wilson claimed, "has been getting worse (crazier) of late years, and they are scared to death that he may leave them." Wilson took the book to Houghton Mifflin, where Hemingway threatened, unsuccessfully, to stop publication by filing an injunction against it. (Ironically, Wilson would himself later resort to threats of legal action because of Matthew Josephson's portrayal of him in his 1962 memoir, *Life Among the Surrealists.*)

For Hemingway, death would never be a simple subtraction; it roused old fires, memories, recriminations. He could be, on occasion, sarcastic, even jocular, on the subject. When Max Perkins wrote him in April 1941, mentioning the deaths of Sherwood Anderson and Virginia Woolf, Hemingway responded, "Writers are certainly dying like flies." He felt some sympathy over Anderson's death from peritonitis in Panama: "It is a damned shame about old Sherwood. He always liked living very much." But he had little to say about Virginia Woolf, never having forgiven her for her remarks about his overemphasized virility. (Fearing another mental breakdown, Woolf had weighted her pocket with a heavy stone and walked into the River Ouse.) Hemingway responded to the announcement with perfect obliquity: "I suppose finally no one will be left alive but the Sitwells." Ironically, at the time of Woolf's death, Hemingway's ardent English admirer, Vita Sackville-West, one of Virginia's former lovers, was writing to Violet Trefusis about *For Whom the Bell Tolls:* "It is just your book and mine. I wish I had written it." She wanted to send Hemingway a copy of her new book, *Pepita,* a biographical study of her Spanish grandmother, and wondered whether Violet knew him. She was in the midst of praising *Death in the Afternoon* when her letter was interrupted. "Darling," she scribbled to Violet when she resumed, "I've just heard the most terrible news which has just put everything out of my head. Virginia has killed herself. It is not in the papers yet but I heard from Leonard."

James Joyce's death, in a Zurich hospital in January 1941 (of peritonitis, following an operation for a perforated ulcer), entailed no personal recriminations, no lingering resentments. Hemingway would remember Joyce, though, as "terrible with his admirers; really insupportable. With idolators: worse. But he was the best companion and finest friend I ever had." Hyperbole? Probably he meant it. Over the years, he would mourn the loss of his literary friends and a few of his enemies. "Writing is a very lonely trade," he wrote Malcolm Cowley, "and with Scott dead and John Bishop dead and having quarreled with Dos (as necessary then as was the civil war; but an awful bore to have quarreled with some one it was always fun to talk with after any war) Jim Joyce dead, Ezra a traitor and his head working very poorly and badly since a long time . . . there is no one to talk with about the metier."

And Gertrude Stein died in 1946, following an operation for cancer in the American Hospital in Neuilly. (Before they wheeled her down the long corridor to the operating room, she roused herself from sedation. "What is the answer?" she murmured to Alice B. Toklas, and when Alice did not respond, she answered for herself, "In that case, what is the question?") Hemingway would for some years more be generous enough to admit to Gertrude's helpfulness when he was a young writer in Paris. But he would finally settle all his old scores in *A Moveable Feast.*

The death that would trouble him most directly, perhaps, was that of Max Perkins in the summer of 1947. Overworked and tired, Perkins came down with pleurisy and pneumonia and then had a final heart attack. In the hospital in Stamford, Connecticut, early on a June morning, he started up from his bed, calling out to his daughters (who were not there). He imagined that an unknown intruder had come into his room. Pointing to a corner, he demanded, "Who *is* that?" then fell back, dead.

Hemingway, who had been sending Perkins progress reports on the novel he had begun (probably the prolonged, never completed *The Garden of Eden,* with its complicated sequence of heroes and heroines, its tangle of heterosexual and lesbian relationships), responded with formal expressions of loss. Max was a "great, great editor," he told Charles Scribner. "One of my best and most loyal friends and wisest counsellors in life as well as in writing is dead." But he could also react with a certain comic diffidence toward Perkins (and his wife, Louise): "Anyway he doesn't have to worry about Tom Wolfe's chickenshit estate anymore, or handle Louise's business, nor keep those women writers from building nests in his hat." Hemingway's references to his former editor would trace an erratic curve. In October, he was comic and cold: "Did I tell you one of Max's womens wrote me and wanted me to be Max to her," he informed Scribner, who became Hemingway's confidant. "But do you think I could get the old hat stretched, clean up my moral precepts, stuff up one ear, and go out with her?" Four years later he would grouse about the burden of the legendary Max. He loved Max very much, he advised Scribner, who was having doubts about filling Max's shoes. "Please bury Max's ghost for keeps and cut out this about he, Tom Wolfe and Scott being gods and you, etc. It makes me ashamed. Max was Max with five daughters and an idiot wife." It was the proper occasion to set the record straight on Max's other star authors: "Tom Wolfe was a one book boy and a glandular giant with the brains and the guts of three mice. Scott was a rummy and a liar and dishonest about money with the in-bred talent of a dishonest and easily frightened angel." In a softer frame of mind, writing to Wallace Meyer, an editor at Scribner's, he took a soberer view: "When Max died I did not think I could stand it. We understood each other so well that it was like having a part of yourself die." Hemingway's dead could never lie in peace; they could be dug up precipitously, their virtues might be praised — but more often, their old sins would be remembered.

Dos Passos was among the survivors of Hemingway's death, though Katy died in 1947 in a terrible automobile accident in which Dos Passos, blinded by the sun, smashed into a parked truck. Katy, asleep on Dos's shoulder, was thrown through the windshield, the top of her head slashed off, the brain lacerated. She died instantly. Dos Passos, badly cut about the face, lost an eye. Hemingway would blame Dos for the accident. Katy's death would leave a legacy of bitterness when Dos Passos published his 1951 novel *Chosen Country,* in which Hemingway figured as the boorish George Elbert Warner. Hemingway was certain, probably correctly, that Katy had supplied Dos with the particulars of his early life that were used against him. (One more reason never to trust one's image to the hands of friends; better to make it one's self.) Dos Passos, thereafter, was the subject of diatribes about one-eyed Portuguese bastards who had Negro blood in their veins.

And Pound, the disgraced poet, would survive, living through his thirteen years of incarceration and treatment as a mental patient, writing at his poem, quarrying history still, translating Chinese odes and Sophocles, more and more the relic of that passing order of modernists who had created an age. A figure of controversy when he was declared of unsound mind (thereby escaping a trial for treason), he became even more controversial when, in 1949, the Fellows of the Library of Congress (Allen Tate, Robert Lowell, Conrad Aiken, T. S. Eliot, W. H. Auden, among them) awarded him the first Bollingen Prize for *The Pisan Cantos,* the highly personal crux of his lifetime poem. ("Give Ezra good wishes and congratulate him on his prize," Hemingway wrote Dorothy Pound, "and tell him how much I admire what he has written since he has been in trouble.")

In the ensuing years, old friends and supporters (among them Hemingway, Eliot, MacLeish, and, belatedly, Robert Frost) mounted the finally successful effort that gained him freedom. After Pound's release from St. Elizabeths in May 1958, Hemingway generously sent him a check for $1000 toward the expenses of his return to Italy, but the poet never cashed it. Pound framed it instead as a memorial to a friend's generosity. In his last years, searching for some concluding metaphor that might illuminate his life, his ambitions and his failure, Pound pieced out the fragmentary ends of that long endeavor, his *Cantos:*

Can you enter the great acorn of light?
　But the beauty is not the madness

Tho' my errors and wrecks lie about me.
And I am not a demigod,
I cannot make it cohere.

Hemingway's old nemesis, Major Eliot, would survive him, too, though by only four years, his place in English literature secured by a plaque in the Poets' Corner of Westminster Abbey, near Tennyson and Browning. A fitting end for the circumspect man who had been quietly building his monument for years. Pound, a frail ghost of himself, journeyed to London to attend the memorial ceremony. ("Who is there now to share a joke with?" he said of the loss.) Still, he lingered on for another seven years, dying in the hospital of SS. Giovanni e Paolo in Venice, at age eighty-seven. After the funeral service at the church of San Giorgio Maggiore, the body was transported by gondola to the burial site in the municipal cemetery on the isle of San Michele.

***

"As you know I was out of business as a writer except for 6 Colliers pieces and the poems . . . from early 1942 to 1945," Hemingway claimed some years after the war. "Then I started, or continued rather, on the long book and interrupted with Across the River when it looked as though I would never get to finish the long book." There were, in fact, two long books on which Hemingway worked during the years after the war, *The Garden of Eden* and the early versions of an ambitious novel that he referred to as "The Sea Book," which was even more grandiosely meant to form one volume of a trilogy embracing the Land, the Sea, and the Air. It was a symptom of his troubles that both projects should have been stalled. So it was hardly strange that Hemingway's next published novel, *Across the River and Into the Trees,* should involve an American army colonel and his love affair with a young Italian countess: it was the combination of love and war that had proved so successful for him in the past. The title was taken from the last words of the feisty Stonewall Jackson, who, mortally wounded in the Chancellorsville campaign, in his delirium said, "Let us cross over the river and rest under the shade of the trees." The setting was Venice, where Hemingway had made a start on the book at the end of an extended visit to Italy with Mary during the winter and spring of 1948 to 1949. (It was his first trip to Europe since the war, and in his big blue Buick, with a hired Italian chauffeur, he made another of his nostalgic pilgrimages to the Basso Piave.)

Hemingway's hero was Colonel Richard Cantwell, a battle-scarred American officer, fifty years old, a veteran of two world wars, observer in the Spanish civil war, who is suffering from high blood pressure and a serious heart condition. In many respects, his vita reads like that of Ernest Hemingway; Cantwell is a heavy drinker, a gourmand of sorts, and is separated from his overly ambitious wife, a former war correspondent. Unlike Hemingway, however, Cantwell is not a writer and has no intention of writing about his war experiences: "I have not the talent for it and I know too much. Almost any liar writes more convincingly than a man who was there."

Cantwell is in love with Renata, nearly nineteen, dark-haired with a "pale almost olive-colored skin, a profile that could break your, or any one else's heart," improbably innocent yet sexually aggressive. (World War II, rather incongruously, is fought in retrospect, in bed or at his favorite table in the bar at the Gritti Palace Hotel in Venice; Cantwell gives the young Renata his personal account of the Normandy breakthrough, the capture of Paris, and the later, bloody battle of Hürtgenwald.) Nor was it particularly strange that Hemingway's protagonist, like several of his late fictional heroes — Harry Walden, Francis Macomber, Harry Morgan, Robert Jordan — should have a rendezvous with death. Cantwell dies of a heart attack in the backseat of his chauffeured army Buick on the way back to his base in Trieste.

Cantwell's affair with Renata was indisputably drawn from Hemingway's more platonic infatuation with a nearly nineteen-year-old Italian girl, Adriana Ivancich, a graduate of a Catholic girls' school and a member of an old family with a palazzo in the Calle di Rimedio in Venice. Hemingway had met her at a duck-shooting weekend at Latisana, northeast of Venice, in December 1948, where he was a guest of the young Barone Nanyuki Franchetti. Having admired her for braving the winter rain during the shoot, he was even more taken with her when later, at the hunting lodge, he caught sight of her drying her long hair in front of the kitchen fire. Learning that she had no comb, he promptly broke his in two and gave her half. Whatever the improbabilities — a wife in tow, the girl's family, particularly her widowed mother, devoutly Catholic and concerned about the proprieties of Venetian society — Hemingway fell headlong in love with Adriana. That she was beautiful — hazel eyes, long black hair, slender and vivacious — that she exhibited some talents as a poet and an illustrator and was obviously flattered by the attentions of a world-famous writer, added to the attraction. Hemingway confessed to Charles Scribner, "Also that I love [Adriana] to die of it and that I love Mary as she should be loved; I hope," though he tried to play it down as one of his "local moral problems" once he was back at the Finca Vigía.

The fact that he should choose a girl so young and protected by her family is a likely indication that, unconsciously at least, Hemingway was creating a situation that made a real affair improbable. He and Adriana, however, kept up a lengthy correspondence, covering some six years, in which Hemingway expressed his ardor, his loneliness for her when he was back in Cuba, and gave her advice on her young suitors, though he was sure none of them could love her quite as well as he did. When he had an accident aboard the *Pilar,* falling on the slippery deck and hitting his head (his fourth concussion), the sight of the blood, he wrote her, made him realize he had to be more careful so he could go on seeing her. He also convinced himself that his deep affection for her was the cause of his renewed enthusiasm for work. Hemingway did his best to further Adriana's career: she would provide the dust-jacket sketches for both *Across the River and Into the Trees* and *The Old Man and the Sea,* and the illustrations for a fable, "The Good Lion," published in the March 1951 issue of *Horizon* magazine. Adriana, though involved, was cautious and correct in her behavior. "I never thought of being in love with him," she claimed, probably truthfully. "I appreciated his kindnesses and his attention. We were friends." The situation — Adriana's youthful evasiveness and opportunism, Hemingway's embarrassing pursuit — and the unlikely fictional romance Hemingway created from it — the aged Colonel Cantwell's mawkish courtship of a teenager and her lusty submission — gave the affair a touch of poignancy not often encountered in the life of the publicized Hemingway. He was all too human in his folly. But it marked a failure of characterization in his novel and was evidence of the long, slow decline in the character of his work. The painful truth of his relationship with Adriana, the demeaning failure of a man unwilling to give up his dreams of prowess and pride, his inability to acknowledge his age, would have served him far better as the subject of a novel.

At first, Mary avoided stating the obvious, that it was a pathetic case of a man with a mid-life crush, making a fool of himself over a teenage girl. (In *How It Was,* she barely mentions Hemingway's fateful first meeting with Adriana. When she reverts to it a few pages later, with that thrust of acerbity which enlivens her often self-justifying memoir, she merely comments that the two "were busily launching a flirtation.") Nor was she much impressed with Adriana's skills as an illustrator. Describing a luncheon, with guests, including Adriana, in a Paris restaurant, she dryly notes, "We were all happy listening to Ernest acclaim Adriana, who had been drawing sketches for the jacket of *Across the River and Into the Trees,* as the girl wonder of the art world."

It was after that luncheon, according to Adriana in her memoir, *La torre bianca* (she was in Paris studying art for a few months), that she and Hemingway took a stroll together to the Café Deux Magots, where they had a drink together, and Hemingway, in an agitated state, told her that he loved her and couldn't do anything about it. When Adriana mentioned Mary, Hemingway claimed that Mary was nice and solid and courageous but that married couples could find themselves on roads that diverged and that it had already happened in their marriage. "From his voice," Adriana remembered, "I knew that he was terribly serious and suddenly I felt paralyzed. . . . It was like waiting for an avalanche, an avalanche that would break from the mountain at any moment." She was considerably relieved when Hemingway finally ended, "I would ask you to marry me, if I didn't know that you would say no."

In another corroboration of Hemingway's strange dependency on male companions when he became involved with a woman (though in this case it was a far younger man than usual), Hemingway befriended Adriana's twenty-eight-year-old brother Gianfranco. Handsome and slender, Gianfranco had been wounded as a soldier with an Italian tank unit in the North African campaign under Rommel. Back in Italy, during the Allied invasion of 1944 to 1945, he and his father had begun working with the partisans. It was a dangerous assignment, and Carlo Ivancich was murdered in an alley in San Michele, his body discovered by his son. The presumption was that he had been killed by Fascist thugs or some member of the Mafia. The family history and Gianfranco's bravery were credentials Hemingway could admire. He took to the young man, invited him to the Finca Vigía — a visit, Mary ruefully noted, that somehow lengthened into a period of several years. When Gianfranco's Cuban job failed, Hemingway lent him money to buy a *finca* of his own. Hemingway seemed to find Gianfranco's presence a consolation or a substitute for the missing Adriana. In some ways, Gianfranco's relationship with Hemingway was more intimate and involved than his sister's. Hemingway's affection for Gianfranco may have had its echo in Colonel Cantwell's admission that he loved only people who fought or had been mutilated by war. The rationale is instructive: "Other people were fine and you liked them and were good friends; but you only felt true tenderness and love for those who had been there. . . . Any son of a bitch who has been hit solidly, as every man will be if he stays, then I love him."

That the intensity of Hemingway's attachment to the Ivanciches introduced considerable disharmony into the Hemingway household was clear when Adriana and her chaperone mother visited the Hemingways and Gianfranco at the Finca Vigía in the late fall and winter of 1950. Hemingway became noticeably more sullen when Gianfranco introduced his sister to the younger people he knew in Havana. One night, when Mary offered to help type up Gianfranco's application for a visa to the U.S. so that he could accompany them on a tour of Florida and the South before they returned to Italy, Hemingway, coming into the room, suddenly became enraged, picking up the typewriter and throwing it on the floor. Their guests sat embarrassed and silent. Later that evening, Hemingway threw a glass of wine at Mary, hitting the white wall of the sitting room.

It was only too clear that Hemingway, in his passion, was trying to precipitate a break with Mary. Although in earlier arguments, Mary had threatened to walk out on him, this time she decided to make a stand. If she had been hesitant about marrying him to begin with, it was in her best interest to remain with him now. One morning she broke the house rule and confronted him at his typewriter. Try as he might to get her to leave him, she told him, it was not going to work: "No matter what you say or do — short of killing me, which would be messy — I'm going to stay here and run your house and your Finca until the day when you come here, sober, in the morning, and tell me truthfully and straight that you want me to leave." Hemingway, she noted in her memoir, never did ask her to leave. Somehow, with her terrier-like insistence, she managed to stick at her marriage, no matter how humiliating the treatment.

Visitors to the Finca Vigía, including Buck Lanham, wondered why Mary put up with Hemingway's behavior. There were times, for instance, when Hemingway was in the habit of mentioning his infidelities (real or invented) in front of Mary and guests. Once, when Mary was entertaining one of her close women friends, Hemingway, arriving drunk and late for dinner, brought along a pretty Havana prostitute whom he had nicknamed Xenophobia. It may well have been sarcasm, rather than bland innocence, that prompted Mary's habit, at this point in their relationship, of referring to herself as the short happy wife of Mr. McPapa.

Mary had begun to recognize a certain slackness in Hemingway's behavior, the routine phrases that cropped up in his conversations with impressionable younger women like Adriana. (There were others, like Virginia "Jigee" Viertel, wife of screenwriter Peter Viertel, who had accompanied Hemingway and Mary on their fall 1949 voyage to Paris on the *Île de France*. At the Ritz, Mary complained to her diary, "It is now one hour and a half since I left Jigee Viertel's room, #94, and Ernest said, 'I'll come in a minute.'") Her criticisms of Hemingway's behavior would have been just as applicable to the novel he was engaged in writing:

> It seemed to me his weariness blurred his personality [she wrote in *How It Was*]. He was making constant repetitions of his philosophies and catch-phrases and jokes . . . I had heard him say "truly" in solemn voice too often, and "daughter," voice benign, and "when the chips are down" and "how do you like it now, gentlemen?" I was also bored with his war.

✓✓✓

Across the River and Into the Trees is the worst of the novels published during Hemingway's lifetime (as distinct from the posthumously published novels edited by other hands). Full of gratuitous slurs against the army brass, several of them men conveniently dead, it reads like a list of Hemingway's pet peeves: Field Marshal Montgomery, "a character who needed fifteen men to one to move and then moved tardily"; General George Patton, "who possibly never told the truth in his life"; and General Leclerc, "another jerk of the third or fourth water." Eisenhower is identified twice as "strictly the Epworth League," then later as "some politician in uniform who has never killed in his life except with his mouth over the telephone. . . . Figure him next as our next President if you want him."

There are a good many of Hemingway's personal gripes: Martha Gellhorn ("the career girl"); the faulty waterproofing of trenchcoats ("Raincoats my ass"); American girls ("They teach them how to count and keep their legs together"). Much of the carping is the flotsam of an author's life, the daily rubbish of the mind. The characterizations are thin; the book is full of obsequious Italian waiters, porters, bartenders, and gondoliers, bowing and scraping in admiration of the colonel:

> "How do you feel about the Russians, if it is not indiscreet to ask, my Colonel?
>
> "They are our potential enemy. So as a soldier, I am prepared to fight them."

There is too much talk of food and drink: "Don't we have fun with food?" Renata asks. "Imagine if we could eat together always." In restaurants and bars, Cantwell is the connoisseur: ordering Roederer Brut '42 and Perrier-Jouët Brut '42. He likes his martinis with garlic olives, knows that the Valpolicella is better when it is new; "putting years on it only adds sediment." Cantwell's snide comment on the *Ladies' Home Journal* (he reads it at the officers' club in Trieste) as a wonderful magazine "because it combines sexology and beautiful foods" might well apply to *Across the River and Into the Trees.*

It is the sexology of the novel that is most at fault, the elaborate fantasy of an aging author and his nineteen-year-old inamorata. The most famous scene and the most infamous in the eyes of the Ivanciches' Venetian friends was the love scene in which Cantwell and Renata indulge in heroic sex in a gondola under an army blanket in a brisk wind.

> He kissed her then and he searched for the island, finding it and losing it, and then finding it for good. For good and for bad, he thought, and for good and for all.
>
> "My darling," he said. "My well beloved. Please."
>
> "No. Just hold me very tight and hold the high ground too."

Once is not enough. "Let's do it again, please, now I am in the lee," Renata says.

Somehow, Hemingway's calibrated style, his dialogue, no longer rang true, as they always did in the stories, where even the briefest bit of conversation managed to reveal some aspect of character. The worst offense is the lengthy conversation that Cantwell, in his bedroom at the Gritti Palace, conducts with the painted portrait of Renata. It threads its way through five chapters: "Here's to you, Daughter. . . . You beauty and lovely. Do you know that, among other things, you smell good always."

Little wonder that neither Mary nor Adriana cared for Hemingway's Renata. "I was unhappy about the middle and later parts of the manuscript," Mary confessed. "It made me feel disloyal, but I was finding Colonel Cantwell's and his girl's conversations banal beyond reason and their obsession with food . . . a mysterious lapse of judgment." Adriana thought Renata's behavior totally out of keeping with her family background. "The girl is boring," she told him. "A girl like that does not exist. . . . Such a girl would not drink all day like a sponge and be in bed at the hotel." Mary recalled that both A. E. Hotchner and Jigee Viertel, at Hemingway's urging, had taken a hand at editing the manuscript at the Paris Ritz, though "with what seemed to me a formidable inattention to style." With Max dead, at this nadir of Hemingway's career, the book needed a firm editorial hand and did not receive it. There are occasional misspellings of place-names in the published version of the book, and a sharp editing would, perhaps, have removed some of the repetitious slurs Hemingway handed out to his private peeves. More problematic were the overlooked mistakes in chronology. At the beginning of the novel Cantwell is fifty; later he is "fifty plus one," though the time span of the book's action is a confused and confusing four or more days. At one point the widowed mother of Barone Alvarito is said to prefer living in the country to Venice because Venice had so few trees; later it is Renata's widowed mother who prefers the country for the same reason, an unconscious slip that tends to suggest that the young *barone* and Renata have the same mother and therefore are brother and sister, clearly not the intention of the novel. But it is an interesting slip, nonetheless. Cantwell has a particular affection for the shy young *barone,* whose smile intrigues him. He rather goes on about it: "He smiled as only the truly shy can smile. . . . It was the strange, rare smile which rises from the deep, dark pit, deeper than a well, deep as a deep mine." It may be only a subconscious slip revealing that the *barone* was based on Gianfranco Ivancich as well as the young Barone Nanyuki Franchetti. Yet it suggests some psychological undercurrent relating more to Hemingway's life than to the fiction. As a pair of scholars has already remarked, Hemingway in his mind and in his letters to Adriana felt that he and Adriana and Gianfranco were in some mysterious way bound together.

From the beginning, Hemingway had a manic faith in the book's importance, its value. In August 1949, he was advising Charlie Scribner, "This is just warming up. In regard to the new medium sized book I want you to get it into the Book of the Month Club and start chopping down trees for the paper now. If it isn't good you can hang me by the neck until dead." Mary clearly had no intention of being disloyal at the time. Hemingway told Scribner he had let her read 121 pages of the manuscript "and she hasn't been any good for anything since. Waits on me hand and foot and doesn't give a damn if I have whores or countesses or what as long as I have the luck to write like that." When the serial version appeared in *Cosmopolitan,* he wrote Arthur Mizener, then working on a biography of Scott Fitzgerald, "I am happy if you like what you have seen of the book. I would like it [to] be better than Proust if Proust had been to the wars and liked to fuck and was in love."

Those were high hopes, considering that he had become stalled on his more Proustian novel, *The Garden of Eden.* In *Across the River* there are none of the developed sexual fantasies (David Bourne's sensual ménage à trois with his wife and mistress, who are at the same time engaged in a lesbian affair; Catherine Bourne's boyish haircuts because she wants to make love to her husband as if she were the boy) that Hemingway would exploit in *The Garden of Eden.* In *Across the River,* there are only passing suggestions of such waywardness. A pair of lesbians turns up at Harry's Bar, and the artist who painted Renata's portrait is described as having been "a little bit *pédéraste*" in his youth. The colonel and Renata playfully think of themselves as Verlaine and Rimbaud.

But it is clear that during the late phase of his life when his creative powers seemed to be waning and he was casting about for new alternatives, Hemingway was, at the same time, mentally entertaining a welter of sexual possibilities. That is one of the odder revelations of *How It Was*. Mary quotes a fantasy interview that Hemingway, not without a hint of cynicism, invented for her amusement:

> Reporter: Mr. Hemingway, is it true that your wife is a Lesbian?
> Papa: Of course not. Mrs. Hemingway is a boy.
> Reporter: What are your favorite sports, sir?
> Papa: Shooting, fishing, reading and sodomy.
> Reporter: Does Mrs. Hemingway participate in these sports?
> Papa: She participates in all of them.

There is the deep suspicion that through some failure of critical judgment, Hemingway half expected that Colonel Richard Cantwell would vindicate him and his life-style in the eyes of the critics. Against those hopes, the broad critical response to *Across the River and Into the Trees* by serious critics was all the more damaging. Maxwell Geismar, in the *Saturday Review of Literature,* found it not only Hemingway's "worst novel" but "a synthesis of everything that is bad in his previous work." Philip Rahv, in *Commentary,* claimed, "This novel reads like a parody by the author of his own manner — a parody so biting that it virtually destroys the mixed social and literary legend of Hemingway that has now endured for nearly three decades." The reviewer in the *San Francisco Chronicle,* Joseph Henry Jackson, also found it a parody, remarking, "I shall wait for the longer, more important novel on which he is reported to have been engaged for some time. It should provide the clue to whether the Old Hemingway is still — as the Colonel might put it — 'operating.'" Cyril Connolly, in the London *Sunday Times,* summed up the novel in one word: "lamentable. . . . If Mr. Hemingway is to turn the corner he will have to cease to be a repressed intellectual, as ashamed of the mind as he is outspoken about the body."

The critical reception may have confirmed, for Hemingway, a nagging premonition that his abilities as a writer and artist might be failing. He had not published a novel for ten years, thereby raising speculative doubts in the minds of the critics to begin with. Queried by *Time* about his personal reactions to the critics' assessments and his personal comments about the Allied commanders in the war, Hemingway cabled a third-person reply: "HEMINGWAY IS BITTER ABOUT NOBODY. BUT THE COLONEL IN HIS BOOK IS." Regarding his sniping at the army brass, he backed down somewhat on Eisenhower, but slyly: "HEMINGWAY HAS NO OPINION IN REGARD TO GENERAL EISENHOWER EXCEPT THAT HE IS AN EXTREMELY ABLE

ADMINISTRATOR AND AN EXCELLENT POLITICIAN. H. BELIEVES HE DID A MARVELOUS JOB IN ORGANIZING THIS INVASION, IF HE WAS ACTUALLY THE MAN WHO ORGANIZED IT."

In an interview with Harvey Breit in the *New York Times Book Review,* he was more direct and defensive: "Sure, they can say anything about nothing happening in *Across the River,* but all that happens is the defense of the lower Piave, the breakthrough in Normandy, the taking of Paris and the destruction of the 22nd Inf. Reg. in Hürtgen Forest plus a man who loves a girl and dies." In *For Whom the Bell Tolls,* he had used straight narrative as his strategy. This time he had done it all "with three-cushion shots." He made a case for himself as an experimental writer ahead of his critics: "In writing I have moved through arithmetic, through plane geometry and algebra, and now I am in calculus. If they don't understand that, to hell with them."

19

The Undertaker Pleases

ABOUT MIDWAY through his career, Hemingway had begun railing against the "fabricated geniuses" promoted by the critics who needed a genius of the season. When such geniuses died, he said, they would no longer exist as writers. There was no sense in writing anything that had been written before unless you could beat it. Serious writers competed only with the dead, not with their contemporaries. It was like a miler running against the clock rather than against the competition. "Unless he runs against time he will never know what he is capable of attaining." That was his high-minded view, and it hardened with age.

The underside of his contest with the immortals was pure Hemingway braggadocio: "I tried for Mr. Turgenieff first and it wasn't too hard. Tried for Mr. Maupassant (won't concede him the de) and it took four of the best stories to beat him." In his "big book," he predicted, he hoped to take on Melville and Dostoevsky. (This was written while he was finishing *Across the River and Into the Trees.*)

He hated the idea of the "shit" that would be written about him and his work after he was dead — so he had told Ivan Kashkin years earlier. But it was inevitable there would be a "Life" or many lives of Ernest Hemingway in the future. He seems to have anticipated it, even collaborated in it to the extent of saving the necessary documentary material for such a life: all the various notebooks, diaries, passports, correspondence, photographs, the drafts of his novels, the early typescripts of his stories — the mass of accumulated papers and memorabilia that had accrued in a highly active lifetime. Despite which, also, in his contradictory fashion, he would announce to the executors of his will, "It is my wish that none of the letters written by me during my lifetime shall be published."

In 1947, however, Malcolm Cowley, the critic he had scorned so vigorously in the early drafts of "Snows," broached the subject of an interview for a full-scale article in *Life,* and Hemingway, with some apparent reluctance, agreed. For two weeks in February 1948, Cowley had come to Cuba, putting up in the Ambos Mundos Hotel with his wife, Muriel, and his son Rob, for a lengthy session of interviews in which he and Hemingway had drunk much, talked more, Ernest filling the critic up with stories of his exploits in the First World War, and his sub-chasing activities in the Second, some lies, some truths, which Cowley repeated or withheld out of discretionary tact probably in order to keep in Hemingway's favor. (Reporting on the interview to his friend, the critic Kenneth Burke, Cowley said, "He overcompensates — he started out by boasting and being a little bit of a four-flusher; now he does his boasting by indirection, and if you call his four-flush you find it's a straight flush.")

Hemingway did not see copy on the highly favorable article, "A Portrait of Mr. Papa," until after it appeared in the January 10, 1949, issue of the magazine. He complimented the writer and then pointed out certain facts that had been misconstrued: "I know how good and friendly and careful you were in that piece just as I know there are lots of things you don't know and things people told you that weren't straight and plenty things I didn't tell you. Other things you draw out a strange interpretation." Cowley had mentioned that in high school Hemingway didn't attend the dances, a bit of information that Hemingway might have interpreted — or, more important, thought a reader might interpret — as his not liking girls. "Do you know how that works? My older sister . . . was not popular until her last year in school and then only with the jerks. I was not allowed to ask any girl I liked to any formal dances until my sister had been asked. [I] was in reserve as her escort."

What would Cowley have made of the bits of misinformation Hemingway did not tell him but which he tended or pretended to believe: that four of his ancestors had taken part in the Crusades and that his great-great-grandmother was a Cheyenne Indian? From the beginning, it seems, Hemingway handled a potential biographer as a skillful angler would, feeding out the line when necessary, reeling it in with care, using his judgment about the strength or wiliness or weight of the catch.

When Cowley later broached the subject of a full-scale biography, Hemingway spelled out his disapproval in a series of letters. "I truly think that we suffer in our times from an exaggerated emphasis on personality," he told Cowley, "and I would much rather have my work discussed than the offence of my life." An interesting interpretation and probably true, except that it came from a man who was a master at promoting his own personality in print. "That's why I don't want any biography," he said. "Literary, yes. I have written it and stand by it, but unless I checked on everything and told you what was true and what was false you would run into all kinds of shit, printed as well as verbal." It was bad for a writer, he maintained, when he started to think of himself as a character.

But, characteristically, he gave a different scenario of the circumstances of the Cowley interview to others, in a sense disowning his collaboration as merely a charitable gesture: "Cowley got a chance of an expense paid vacation with wife and child to Havana contingent on writing a piece about me," he explained to Bill Smith's wife, Marion. "I was sickened of the idea of a piece about me after ten minutes and just gave him the names of my friends that he could ask about me instead of getting a lot of crap from me which would nauseate me to give out and to read."

He was more emphatic about the usefulness of the *Life* piece in a testy letter to his publisher, Charles Scribner. Hemingway was angered when he surmised that Scribner's had let both *A Farewell to Arms* and *Green Hills of Africa* go out of print. He scolded his publisher for the firm's laxity. He reckoned that the Cowley interview in *Life* was worth about $100,000 in publicity, told Scribner that in Denmark alone he had sold 340,000 copies of the books that Scribner's had allowed to go out of print in America.

> So remember, or try to think, that you are a publisher and you have to carry the ball sometimes and just not me who goes to fight in all the fucking wars and gets my brains knocked out and never fake and cheat in writing or write crap for all the dough they offer and waste my expensive time and my one and only life helping Cowley to find out facts and sources for a damned piece that disgusts me to do but is probably necessary historically and from which you will profit plenty more than I will in the long run.

He had early recognized the consequences of publicity, good or bad, and for a few years following the Cowley interview he found it necessary to disprove, say, "Cowley's theory that I was a painfully, self-taught athlete." Before the Cowley article, Hemingway claimed, critics tended to consider him as the simple, shy son of a country doctor "and now, since Cowley, awkward and with bad eyesight." To a later interviewer, he argued, "but think of poor old Cowley who has staked out my whole life of which he knows practically fuck-all nothing." But that wasn't Cowley's fault, he conceded; everything Cowley did had been well intentioned.

Hemingway must have been freshly reminded of the hazards of biography when a woman writer for *McCall's* contacted Scribner's asking to interview his mother for an article about his boyhood years. Hemingway objected violently. (Grace, seventy-seven at the time, and with a badly failing memory, was living with Ruth Arnold as her companion.) Hemingway made it known that he was supporting his mother and that he would cut off her support if she gave out any interviews or provided any information about him. "This is absolute," he told Charles Scribner, whom he enlisted in the battle against "that magazine bitch." His mother was very old, he told Scribner, and because of her age he was playing the devoted son. "But I hate her guts and she hates mine. She forced my father to suicide," Hemingway was still claiming. Once, he said, he wrote advising her to sell the worthless Florida properties that were eating her up with taxes and she had answered, "Never threaten me with what to do. Your father tried that once when we were first married and he lived to regret it."

It may have been only coincidence that about the same time he had gotten out of storage in Key West the photograph albums of his childhood that Grace had so painstakingly put together for all her children. Hemingway must have felt considerably relieved that the photos of him in his pink dresses and the sentimental captions in Grace's handwriting, "Summer girl" and "Sweetie's Dutch Dollie," had not fallen into the hands of the woman from *McCall's*. Writing to his mother, he tactfully mentioned his pleasure in the albums and congratulated her for her "diligence and your lovingness for all of us kids when we were young and must have been great nuisances for you. Your handwriting in the book was lovely to see and the photos that my father took were almost uniformly excellent." Then he informed her about the *McCall's* request and stated emphatically, "I do not care for this type of publicity and will not permit it." He repeated the threat of cutting off his support if the magazine should publish anything without his consent, adding, "Hope this handled that matter." Grace's reply was full of heartfelt thanks for what seemed her son's genuine appreciation of the albums, "which I burned the midnight oil to produce. — How I loved doing it!" But then her letter broke down into telltale repetitions of the same sentences. Making no mention of her son's threats, she ended with "Now goodbye dear Ernest. Always your loving Mother" and an apologetic postscript, "Please excuse my getting mixed and repeating. I am too tired."

It was also in late 1949 that Lillian Ross, who had previously interviewed Hemingway for a *New Yorker* article on Sidney Franklin, asked to interview him again, this time for a "profile" on himself. Hemingway agreed, setting aside a few days from one of his brief stopovers in New York, although, as he told Ross, he didn't plan to see anybody he didn't like or encourage any publicity or even visit Toots Shor's; he wanted to look at El Greco's *Toledo* and the Brueghels at the Met, visit the Modern and the Bronx Zoo, see a fight. "Am going to try to get into town and out without having to shoot my mouth off." Avoiding the news people wasn't just a pose; he wanted time to see his friends. "Time," he added in a penciled note, "is the least thing we have of."

Yet perversely, at the turn of the decade, Hemingway was besieged by biographers, future biographers, and critics seeking information on his personal life or his relationships with the Lost Generation writers. It was in 1948 that he had been first introduced to Aaron Hotchner, who would later become the faithful Boswell of his last fourteen years. Hotchner had arrived in Cuba, a young staff writer for *Cosmopolitan* assigned to interview Hemingway for an article on "The Future of Literature." A former air force officer during World War II in France, he and Hemingway hit it off as friends. Hotchner passed the test. While consuming quantities of frozen daiquiris at the Floridita, they talked about Ted Williams and the Book-of-the-Month Club, Proust, Indians, and aphrodisiacs. The following morning Hotchner was picked up for the usual rite of passage, a fishing expedition aboard the *Pilar.* By the end of their first brief encounter, Hotchner had arranged for Hemingway to write the article on "The Future of Literature" himself, for a sizable fee, $15,000. Though Hemingway signed the contract and received his advance, he never wrote the piece. Instead, he persuaded *Cosmopolitan* to publish the serialized version of *Across the River and Into the Trees.*

Hotchner proved to be an amenable companion. "I really trust Hotchner," Hemingway would tell his publisher. For the next several years, Hotchner made a point of spending time with Hemingway, during vacations, on fishing trips, taking part in Hemingway's later journalistic assignments. From the beginning he had been impressed with the paintings on the walls at the Finca Vigía (Miró's *Farm,* Gris's *Guitar Player,* paintings by Masson, Klee, Braque); the signed first editions by Joyce, Stein, Pound, Fitzgerald, Dos Passos, Ford Madox Ford; Ernest's vigorous tales of his extracurricular sexual activities with Venetian countesses and the mistress of Legs Diamond; the guests who arrived and departed from the Finca. The duke and duchess of Windsor, who had been there the week before Hotchner's arrival, seemed to be overly concerned about the falling ceiling-plaster in the living room. Jean-Paul Sartre and a current girlfriend, Dolores Vanetti, had also been recent visitors. (Vanetti, a former actress, not quite young, was one of the more serious of the principled infidelities in Sartre's long-term relationship with Simone de Beauvoir.) Sartre, Hemingway told Hotchner, had confided to him that it was a newspaper man who had thought up the term *existentialism* and that he had had nothing to do with it. Mary, who had expected Sartre to give the "inside gen" on existentialism (according to her recollection, Sartre claimed the term had been invented by his followers, who then pressed it on him), was disappointed when the two conversationalists carried on like businessmen, talking of publishers and royalties. The only gratifying moment came at dessert, when Sartre "made a small poetic speech about his incapacity to make use of nature for his personal satisfactions as Ernest did with his fishing and bird and animal hunting." It was a loss, Sartre said, "*une privation de mon esprit.*" Mary was relieved when Hemingway, for once, did not offer to take Sartre out in the *Pilar.*

In 1950, when Harvey Breit broached the subject of writing a biography of him, Hemingway turned him down: "Honest, kid, we would both go crazy. I have to get cockeyed to talk about myself and then the next day I have gastric remorse." In the meantime, he was also caught up in a detailed, tricky correspondence with Arthur Mizener, then a professor at Carleton College in Minnesota, for Mizener's biography of Fitzgerald. In his later years — as if Fitzgerald had now taken his place among the honorable dead against whom Hemingway competed — any query about Scott was sure to arouse his old patronizing attitude. He had no respect for Scott except for his "lovely, golden, wasted talent." He told Mizener that he had not been able to read *The Beautiful and the Damned* and thought *Gatsby* was "ok with reservations." He scored Zelda for having undermined Scott's confidence in himself and told Mizener the demeaning story about Scott's fears that his penis was too small to satisfy her. He also made known his distaste for the personal approach by critics and biographers: "I get sick of Bunny Wilson writing about some mysterious thing that changed or formed my life and then dismissing For Whom the Bell Tolls in a foot-note." (He got some satisfaction, he said, though not much, out of a photograph Max Perkins had sent him of Wilson being kicked in the ass by a photographer.)

In a strange request, he suggested that when Mizener introduced him into Fitzgerald's history, he should be treated as if he were dead, along with Scott and Zelda and Max Perkins and John Bishop. At the same time, in the course of his several letters, he seemed intent upon filling in with tidbits from his personal life and glimpses into his daily routine. He was working on the galley proofs of his new novel: "I'd done 42 galleys from 0600 to 1300 and was bored shitless listening to the Cuban election news on the radio. Will put on a mixed program of Fats Waller and Mozart now. They are really very good together." Boredom was also his response to the despairs of the literary life: "Tom Wolfe's interminable flow and his silly love affairs and Scott's aborted virginity and their thirst for fame bored me. But I thought this is the literary life and that's what you are in, boy." Whatever else Mizener may have felt about this extraordinary windfall of gossip and opinion, it must have crossed his mind that Hemingway was a very deserving candidate for a biography.

When Mizener's book *The Far Side of Paradise* was published in 1951, Hemingway backed off. "It is a splendid piece of re-search," Hemingway wrote the biographer, but there were many errors that he would be willing to submit for corrections in future editions. He went into one more of his recitals of the famous Hemingway-Callaghan boxing match. (In this version Scott let the round go thirteen minutes.) It embarrassed him when Scott made him his bloody hero, and he had lost interest in Fitzgerald when the Spanish war came and the war in China, and Scott was so "rum-dumb." Well, the hell with all of it, he added; Scott was dead "and you've buried him for better or for worse and what he wrote that will stand up will stand up."

He told Mizener that he thought Budd Schulberg's novel *The Disenchanted* (based on Fitzgerald) was "grave-robbing," a metaphor that he developed fully for Mizener's benefit, assuring him that his biography was a "good undertaking. Almost as good as the job they did on my father's face when he shot himself. One remembers the face better as it actually was. But the undertaker pleases those who come to the funeral." To others, Hemingway was more scathing about the personal revelations of Mizener's biography and its reliance on anecdote and gossip. "Mizener made money and did some pretty atrocious things (to young Scotty and any offspring she might have) with his book on Scott and every young English professor sees gold in them dirty sheets now." From Mizener's book, it was no large step to his own case: "Imagine what they can do with the soiled sheets of four legal beds by the same writer and you can see why their tongues are slavering (this may not be the correct word)."

Though Mizener's approach was mild enough by later standards of biography, Hemingway was not the only one to be dismayed by *The Far Side of Paradise.* Edmund Wilson, who had also supplied information to Mizener, found it disturbing. Mizener, Wilson wrote his old professor Christian Gauss, "has assembled in a spirit absolutely ghoulish everything discreditable or humiliating that ever happened to Scott. He has distorted the anecdotes that people told him in such a way as to put Scott and Zelda in the worst possible light. . . . On the other hand, he gives no sense at all of the Fitzgeralds in the days when they were soaring — when Scott was successful and Zelda enchanting." He went on, "It is queer, to find one's own day before yesterday turning up as literary history." Both he and Hemingway, it seemed, were experiencing culture shock.

✓✓✓

Having successfully identified the enemy, Hemingway soon found himself besieged by professors intent on delving into his life in one way or another. Charles Fenton, a young Yale professor writing a dissertation about Hemingway's "apprenticeship years," contacted him, asking for information about his early career and trying to verify details received from sources like Herbert Cranston of the *Toronto Star.* On the trail of Hemingway, Fenton had in fact started an extensive correspondence with nearly everyone with whom Hemingway was associated in his early years, among them the high school teacher Fannie Biggs, as well as Hadley and Bill Horne. Hemingway was wary but sympathetic. (Fenton, after all, had served four years with the Royal Canadian Air Force.) "I guess old Cranny has more right to his inaccuracies than you and I have to our attempts to be accurate. He was as badly treated by the *Toronto Star* as a man could be." But when Fenton also began querying his sister Marcelline and his outlawed sister Carol (she had married her college boyfriend, John Gardner, in 1933, against Hemingway's wishes, and he vowed never to see her again), Hemingway gave him a "cease and desist" order: "When you go into my family, etc., it is to me an invasion of privacy." The correspondence developed into angry exchanges. Yet, with each angry response, Hemingway, by way of correcting errors, also began feeding out more tempting bait. Fenton, for example, was wrong when he claimed Hemingway had been tutoring the two Connable children in Toronto. Ralph Connable had been his only student. But it was to Fenton that he gratuitously offered the dubious information that he had had to get the hell out of Petoskey because of troubles with four or five girls.

Meanwhile, Hemingway was also engaged in a lengthy correspondence with Carlos Baker, a professor of English at Princeton, who had written him about a nearly completed twelve-chapter critical study, *Hemingway: The Writer as Artist.* Baker was still in need of answers to some of the vague personal details of Hemingway's life, though he made it plain they related to Hemingway's work. At first, Hemingway balked, using the arguments he had used before and would use again, that he wanted no biography written while he was alive, that his life involved other people whom he did not wish to hurt or implicate. He had led, fortunately or unfortunately, he said, "a fairly complicated life"; there were stories that he did not want to read in some biography:

> the suicide of my father. This is the best story I never wrote. Then comes Pauline moving in on Hadley; which I would never write. Then comes, in a true story, coitus interruptus, with Pauline after the two Caesarians because the doctor said you could not have another and birth control barred. Then Martha moving in on Pauline. Then lots of stuff I don't want to remember and whores and nice girls and whores until I run into Mary. Can you see why I do not want dates and hotel registers, etc.?

To a biographer whom he was trying to dissuade, such a statement — in a first response — could only have been a revelation, something far more personal than the biographer had, edgily, asked for. Hemingway nonetheless laid down a flat ultimatum: "I am resolved to not aid, and to impede in every way, including legal, anyone who wishes to write a story of my life while I am alive. That would include my wife, my brother or my best friend." He made a generous offer: if Baker had already received an advance from his publisher, Hemingway would pay it back, unless it were some outrageous sum. If, however, Baker intended to write only about his work, he would help him in any way he could.

Not wanting to be cut off from the source, Baker agreed to delete much of the biographical material, which was confined to the earlier chapters of his critical study. Fearing that Hemingway was under some misapprehension, he explained that his book focused "directly and analytically" on Hemingway's writing from 1922 to 1950, including *Across the River and Into the Trees.* He wanted to set the record straight, Baker informed him in flattering terms. The thesis of his book was too complex to deliver in a letter, but he outlined it briefly: that Hemingway the writer was regarded as a naturalistic reporter and that he was, in fact, one of the best. But he was more than that: a symbolic writer operating below the surface, using nonliterary and nonderivative symbols, all fully endowed with meanings available to any reader who would take the trouble to read him well and rightly. "You are seen throughout," Baker assured him, "as an eminently practical esthetician."

In his second letter to Baker, Hemingway was more casual and equally informative. Speaking of his reasons for agreeing to the Cowley interview, he maintained that Cowley had told him that the *Life* article would make the difference between whether his son would go to Exeter or not. Though Hemingway disliked academic critics, angered by the unfavorable reviews of *Across the River and Into the Trees,* he seems to have been particularly responsive to the seriousness of Baker's approach and the flattering things he had to say about his work. (He had already begun to call him Carlos.) Eager for an opinion, Hemingway even suggested sending Baker an early typescript version of *The Old Man and the Sea*. Baker welcomed the opportunity. The offer, so early in their correspondence, was surely a significant clue to Hemingway's attitude. In his reply, Baker launched into a lengthy and serious discussion (with flattering queries) about *Across the River* — unwittingly, the perfect move — comparing it, favorably, to Thomas Mann's *Death in Venice*. Hemingway, however, took it in stride, making no allusions to the homosexual implications of the tale. Mann was a writer he admired.

> About the Mann story. I remember liking it very much when I read it but all I remember about it now was a man who was going to die watching a boy. I don't remember the Venice of it at all. Of Mann all that I remember truly is a beautiful story called Disorder and Early Sorrow and Buddenbrooks. I know his Venice was nothing like the town I know.

Baker pointed out the contrast between Mann's sense of decay and the "healthy toughness" of Hemingway's Colonel Cantwell. In passing, Baker noted, giving the quote, that Mann had broached the Hemingway theme of grace under pressure, "to be poised against fatality, to meet adverse conditions gracefully, is more than simple endurance; it is an act of aggression, a positive triumph."

Baker's full, flattering praise of *The Old Man and the Sea* manuscript, which he received promptly enough to suggest that Hemingway was eager for his opinion, caused one of those baffling responses in Hemingway. (In biographies of writers, even the chronology of the letters — when received, how early answered — may have some significance: Baker received the manuscript after May 4, 1951, read it twice, and wrote Hemingway about it on May 6.) Along with his letter of May 6, he sent a copy of his recent article in the *New York Times Book Review* commemorating the twenty-fifth anniversary of the publication of *The Sun Also Rises*. On June 16, having had no response and suspecting that Hemingway neither liked the *Times* article nor his remarks about the novel, he broached the subject gingerly in a letter in which he queried some points about his interpretation of *The Old Man*.

Hemingway wrote him apologetically on June 30. The *Times* piece, which Baker had told him was cut, he understood was more like "a friendly gesture" than an article, but he was as pleased with it as he was with Baker's comments on *The Old Man*. "I love to have people care for my stuff and understand it. The trouble is that I get truly embarrassed (that looks like bare-assed) at praise and the embarrassed thing makes me seem surly . . . I have never learned yet not to be made shy by praise even when I need it the most." The relationship with Baker, thereafter, was steady and cordial. Hemingway assured him that he would be able to quote liberally from his work and made a point of recommending him to Charlie Scribner. They talked the language of writing — one of Hemingway's needs. "A writer has a definite right to select what he will publish," Hemingway told him. "His best friend is the waste basket." He also gave Baker intimate details of his family life; kept him up to date on his various ailments (a bout with bronchitis in March); the general state of his health (blood pressure down to 150 over 65); the surge of visitors — Air Marshal Tedder and his wife, a friendly priest suffering with a heart condition, who had "suddenly gotten afraid to die and I had to cheer him up."

When Grace Hemingway died in a Memphis hospital on June 28, 1951, Hemingway did not attend the funeral. (At the end, before it became necessary to hospitalize her, Grace had been living with Sunny; she did not remember her daughter, hid from her like a child playing hide-and-seek. Yet sitting at the piano in her nightgown, she would play parts of classical numbers with gusto and her own compositions from memory.) Hemingway presented himself to Baker as a dutiful son, saying he had made the funeral arrangements by long distance. In his own little village, he had had the bells toll that morning. "It was really a great relief for all the children and for her too, I should think, since she did not know what was happening for some time now and I do not believe she had the grace of a happy death." And though he had been railing against his mother in the past few years, his account to Baker was that of a man who seemingly had had a change of heart: "I have been thinking about how beautiful she was when she was young before every thing went to hell in our family and about how happy we all were as children before it all broke up."

He was even more circumspect in his remarks to Baker when Pauline died suddenly on the operating table on October 1, the result of a rare tumor of the adrenal gland. Hemingway did not mention Pauline by name, but only as another member of the family, the mother of two sons, and apologized for tardiness in replying to Baker's earlier letter, saying that he had been so tied up with long distance phone calls, "protecting, or trying to protect," the interests of his two sons. He would spare Baker the details, he said. Yet in an earlier letter to Charlie Scribner, written on the day after Pauline's death, he seemed to be a bit overwhelmed, perhaps because he and Pauline had had a bitter quarrel on the phone the night before she died. "The wave of remembering has finally risen so that it has broken over the jetty that I built to protect the open roadstead of my heart and I have the full sorrow of Pauline's death with all the harbour scum of what caused it. I loved her very much for many years and the hell with her faults."

⁂

In his early fifties, then, he was a man negotiating his role in literary history, the broker of his past and private life. Late in 1951, Hemingway learned from Malcolm Cowley of another pending study of his life and work by a professor at New York University, Philip Young. Rinehart and Company had accepted the study for publication on condition of certain revisions. Thomas Bledsoe, an editor at Rinehart, had sent the manuscript to Cowley for his opinion, and Cowley found himself serving as middleman between the publisher and Hemingway. He wrote Hemingway, encouraging publication but also suggesting certain revisions. Hemingway, alerted to the fact that Young had written a book proving that he was all his heroes, including the emasculated Jake Barnes, wanted to discourage Young as early as possible. Writing to Carlos Baker, who had also queried him about Young's book, supposedly scheduled for publication in early 1952, Hemingway said that Cowley had told him the book had been postponed. He suspected it was "some sort of sneak thing" and he had asked Scribner's to refuse Young any permission to quote from his works. (This was about the same time he had granted Carlos permissions.) It was the only means he had of forestalling any attempts at biography. As he explained to his Scribner's editor, Wallace Meyer, "Criticism is getting all mixed up with a combination of the Junior FBI men, discards from Freud and Jung and a sort of Columnist peep-hole and missing laundry list school."

Hemingway complained to Bledsoe that he hadn't been told about the book; that if he had known it was to be a critical study he would have been happy to provide Young with information about his work. But he didn't want any biographical studies written while he was still alive. The Cowley article in *Life* had been a bad thing for him, though that was not Cowley's fault. When he read Lillian Ross's article in proof, it had filled him "with some horror." It made him sound like a "half-breed choctaw," and it didn't give a fair impression of him as a writer who got up at first light and worked hard most of the days of his life. But Lillian was a friend and he was still fond of her.

His letters to Ross, however, suggested otherwise. Mary claimed it was only after friends like Hotchner alarmed him with remarks like "You are ruined!" following the publication of the profile in the May 13, 1950, issue of *The New Yorker* that Hemingway began to take the effect seriously. Mary, who would have her own later quarrels with Hotchner on biographical matters, defended Ross, saying that no single profile could ruin Hemingway. At first Hemingway kept assuring and reassuring Ross that she shouldn't be bothered by the criticisms of her profile. In 1951, he was still writing her, "About our old piece; the hell with them!" Yet at about the same time, he was telling Bledsoe that after *The New Yorker* profile, he had decided he would never give another interview to anyone on any subject. He hated, too, having his personal life presented as a subject of study for college students.

When Philip Young, at a meeting of the Modern Language Association, read a paper in which he took a psychological approach to Hemingway's work, it raised further grave suspicions. Having obtained a copy of the talk from Bledsoe, Hemingway complained that Young's use of psychoanalytical terminology was shocking since he gave no evidence of medical training. Writing to Young himself, he asked for Young's word "that the book is not biography disguised as criticism and that it is not a psychoanalytical study of a living writer." Other than that, he would have no objections to allowing Young to quote from his books. Having made his position clear, he then showered Young with apologies and excuses for having held him up. He even offered money (a bit sardonically, it seems) to help Young financially (Young turned down the offer). As an excuse, Hemingway pleaded the pressures of work and recent personal problems, what amounted to a tide of deaths that had overtaken him in the past year, including the sudden death, from a heart attack, of his publisher.

> No part of this is good for some one who is trying to keep his peace of mind and work well with, in one year, the death of his first grandson in Berlin where his son was stationed as a Capt. of Infantry; the death of his mother; serious illness of his father-in-law with cancer; death of his former wife and mother of two of his sons; suicide of the maid servant of this house (one previous attempt); had kept her on and tried to pull her out of it; then last the death of my last old friend in Africa and then the death of my very dear friend and publisher Charlie Scribner.

In 1952, Hemingway was fielding questions from all three interpreters of his life and reading manuscript drafts from some. As he put it to Fenton in the shrewdest terms,

> I average between fifty cents and a dollar a word for everything that I write and I write you letters between five hundred and fifteen hundred words long which you in-corporate in material which you sell for 2½ cents a word with a royalty deal over 100,000 copies sold. Mr. Fenton I hope you will agree that this is economically unsound.

His correspondence with Fenton, a highly temperamental man himself, turned into bitter quarreling and threats of legal action. But Hemingway, challenged, and responding to financial pleas, relented and allowed Fenton, as well as Young, to quote from his work. Young's book, published in 1952, angered him, with its suggestion that his fiction was inspired by his wounding in Italy, a traumatic experience that had shaped his work and his career. (Quite probably, Hemingway saw it as another, more detailed, version of Edmund Wilson's "wound" theory.) "P. Young: It's all trauma," Hemingway grumbled in an angry survey of his early and diligent biographers in a letter to Harvey Breit. "Sure plenty trauma in 1918 but symptoms absent by 1928 — none in Spain 37–38 — none in China 40–41 — None at sea, none in air, none in 155 days of combat." Malcolm Cowley "thot I was like him because my father was a Dr. and I went to Michigan when I was 2 weeks old where they had hemlock trees." Even Carlos Baker, in his search for symbols, did not escape Hemingway's ranting moods: "Carlos Baker really baffles me. Do you suppose he can con himself into thinking I would put a symbol into anything on purpose. It's hard enough just to make a paragraph." Charles Fenton, "that frustrated F.B.I. character," had run into "the old 'omerta' in Oak Park and that is why no one would give him any Hemingstein gen except jerks."

Years later — the year before Hemingway's death — Fenton committed suicide, jumping from a hotel window in Durham, North Carolina. Hemingway, suffering himself from severe depression in St. Mary's Hospital in Rochester, Minnesota, still had the grim humor to write Baker, "Hope that won't set a bad example to my other biographers."

He wondered what Fenton thought about on his way down.

II

When he was young, in Schruns, not in the year of the avalanches, as Hemingway claimed, but the year after, he was struck by the story Fräulein Glaser told him of a skier killed in an avalanche. When they had found him (by excavating a trail of blood in the packed snow), it was discovered that the man had twisted his neck from side to side until it was worn right through to the bone. Hemingway remembered the grisly story for years. Then, in *A Moveable Feast,* he appropriated it as if he had himself been present: "We became great students of avalanches, the different types of avalanches, how to avoid them and how to behave if you were caught in one. Most of the writing that I did that year was in avalanche time." No one, he claimed, had been able to decide whether the skier had done it on purpose or if he had been out of his head. It mattered little, since the man was refused burial in consecrated ground because the local priest could not be sure the victim was Catholic. For even greater effect, he made the year of this episode 1926, the year in which he had betrayed Hadley with Pauline, the winter in which Dos Passos and the Murphys and Pauline had come to Schruns.

How secure Hemingway makes the reader feel with the exactness of his detail; the famous lean, declarative style, the sense of assurance that it had happened this way and no other. But it was a borrowed story, and the wrong year; for the year in which the skier was refused burial — as he informed Gertrude Stein in a letter — was 1925.

So fiction corrupts history, as the novelist Cynthia Ozick observes. Yet the image, with all its doubtful connections in Hemingway's usage, still serves as an apt metaphor for biography: the rescue of a man buried in the avalanche of his time and circumstances, the dogged attempt at recovery, the wounds of his struggle preserved. The biographer, perhaps — like Hemingway — is a student of avalanches, picking up the trail the subject took to his ending, trying to determine the moment when tragedy struck. Not content with the mere recital of the facts of any historical case, he wants the reader to note the surrendering diplomat's awkward limp, the suddenly interrupted letter, the strains of a waltz coming from the dance at the officers' club on a sultry southern night — the not unimportant details that make or remake the here and now of time past. Perhaps he would like to hear, as in one of those moments in fiction, the accidental tap of a spoon against a plate that evokes the unaccountable moment of happiness in the narrator of *Remembrance of Things Past.* Perhaps he is more ambitious, wanting to reclaim some moment of history with all the authenticity of an old photograph in its corroborating details — the writer's study, the pile of books (with their barely perceptible titles), the stacks of papers, the little bundle of unanswered letters secured by a rubber band, the portable typewriter, the obtrusive cat picking its way through the disorder. He wants to make the reader agree, Yes, that was the way it was on an ordinary day. The ground zero of biography is the incorrigible curiosity that one human being has about another. It is as natural as breathing air.

Hemingway, however, never made it easy. "A major art cannot even be judged," he said in *Death in the Afternoon,* "until the unimportant physical rottenness of whoever made it is well buried." The man who extolled the physical, the life of action, parading his accomplishments, seemed to want the writer to disappear from the work. For him, biography was an obstruction, an invasion of privacy.

Or so he said. It is instructive to follow him in the late years, in his letters, courting and dissuading his would-be biographers. An object lesson in the way a man, subtler, more devious in the manipulation of words than he is given credit for, presents himself to the mirror of posterity, angling, posing, choosing the profile he wants to expose. (His youngest son, Gregory, was alert to his father's gift for "flashing that 'say cheese' smile he sometimes affected," particularly when there was a photographer around.) The letters, published and unpublished, trace the energy and the unfortunate brag: "I fucked three times [he writes on his fiftieth birthday], shot ten straight at pigeons (very fast ones) at the club, drank with five friends a case of Piper Heidsick Brut and looked the ocean for big fish all afternoon. There was nothing although the current was strong and the water very dark."

How does one account for his manic rage at the success of James Jones's war novel (published by Scribner's), *From Here to Eternity*? "I hope he kills himself as soon as it does not damage his or your sales," he writes his publisher. "If you give him a literary tea you might ask him to drain a bucket of snot and then suck the puss out of a dead nigger's ear." Only a man who thought Jones had done violence to his personal code, his faith in the valor of men in the army, could have roused himself to that kind of wrath. It would be a mistake to think it was an aberration, a momentary outburst. There are other insulting letters, probably not sent. To Cardinal Spellman, who had attacked Eleanor Roosevelt: "In every picture that I see of you there is more mealy mouthed arrogance, fatness and overconfidence. . . . You will never be Pope as long as I am alive." To Senator Joseph McCarthy: "You can come down here and fight for free, without any publicity, with an old character like me who is fifty years old and weighs 209 and thinks you are a shit, Senator, and would knock you on your ass the best day you ever lived." The thoughts, perhaps, of a man on his way down? Or is it simply rage from the bottle?

There are the other, generous, serious or joking letters that show him in a better light. When Bill Smith, having served as a speechwriter for Labor Department officials during the Truman administration, came under suspicion of disloyalty, Hemingway wrote Marion Smith, "If there is anything he wants me to do or anyone he wants me to write to I will gladly do so." It was ridiculous that Bill's loyalty to his government should be questioned:

> Am sure I am regarded as a premature anti-Nazi myself but believe showed my loyalty or at least willingness to work for and fight for

> during 1941, 42, 43, 44, 45 in a sufficiently drastic manner so that I may possibly still have a little credit to exhaust. I might just compromise Bill further. But might also be able to fight our way out of the average damp paper bag.

Writing from the Gritti Palace in Venice, he recommended that Bill seek the support of his old friend Buck Lanham, who was working for General Omar Bradley at the Pentagon. It paid to have friends in high places.

"Publicity, admiration, adulation, or simply being fashionable are all worthless and are extremely harmful if one is susceptible to them," he told Bernard Berenson, with whom he had started up a lengthy and revealing correspondence. Berenson, whom Mary had met in Florence in 1948, became another of the carefully selected, necessary older confidants of Hemingway's life after the unexpected death of Charlie Scribner. Whatever else he was, Hemingway was a strategist of the word, knowing the calculated weight and force of a sentence, a thought, its probable effect on the reader of his books, the recipient of his letters.

⁊⁊⁊

Whatever progress Hemingway made in resolving the tangle of structural problems on his Sea trilogy he attributed to Adriana's visit to Cuba in 1950. On the day after Christmas, he had written Charlie Scribner that, in a surge of work, he had completed the segment he called "The Sea When Absent." (Even more remarkably, in the new year, he was hard at work on "The Sea in Being," which became *The Old Man and the Sea.*) Otherwise, his Sea Book was never published during his lifetime. Edited by Mary, Charles Scribner, Jr., and Carlos Baker, it would be issued posthumously as *Islands in the Stream.* It would borrow heavily from the circumstances of Hemingway's life, his children, assorted memories of his childhood in Michigan, his life in Paris, his Cuban *finca,* his empire of cats, the submarine hunts on the *Pilar.* (In the novel, there would again be a hated third wife who was a war correspondent.) The hero, Thomas Hudson, a successful but merely good painter who forgoes his opportunities to become a better one, has lived in Bimini and Cuba, has three sons, two of whom, along with their unfortunate mother, die in an automobile accident. The third son is killed in the war. Hudson, too, in a sea chase for the maurauding sailors of a German submarine, would join the list of fatalities among Hemingway's final heroes.

Tactically, Hemingway's decision to publish *The Old Man and the Sea* as a short novel was one of the fortunate moves of his career. As he explained to Wallace Meyer when he sent the uncorrected manuscript of the book to Scribner's early in March 1952, "Publishing it now will get rid of the school of criticism that I am through as a writer. It will destroy the school of criticism that claims I can write about nothing except myself and my own experiences." He had already convinced himself that the story had a special, perhaps magical, quality. Having read portions of the manuscript to various friends (among them Aaron Hotchner and the film producer Leland Hayward), he informed Meyer, "It affected all of them in a stronger way than anything that I have ever written." He had originally intended it as an epilogue to his long book about the sea, but it might well serve, he suggested, "as an epilogue to all my writing and what I have learned or tried to learn, while writing and trying to live."

A writer's sense of timing, of readiness, is one of his great assets. The story that he had told, in brief, in one of his *Esquire* articles, sixteen years before, of the old fisherman, alone in a skiff far out to sea, who had caught a great marlin only to have it destroyed by sharks, now served as a more dramatic personal metaphor. About the meanings of fiction, Hemingway had once contended, to Mary at least, "If you have a message, call Western Union." Yet he was not above spelling out the moral of a story as he had with Harry Morgan's message that a man alone "ain't got no bloody fucking chance." The story of the old Cuban fisherman, Santiago, down on his luck, having gone eighty-four days without catching a big fish and considering himself unlucky, and the boy, Manolino, who still believes in him, although his family has forced him to fish with someone else, points to a later, more universal moral. After his grueling three-day ordeal at sea, after fighting off the sharks, Santiago symbolizes Hemingway's belief in the human spirit: "But man is not made for defeat. A man can be destroyed but not defeated."

Hemingway distrusted symbolism, felt that the thing itself, accurately described, was symbol enough. Readers and critics alike, however, saw his tale of an old man wresting a victory out of defeat as a Christian parable. It would have been impossible for any reader to overlook the deliberate, if understated, symbolism of Santiago's bleeding hands, or the low groan of his "Ay" when he sees a pair of sharks heading as deliberately as fate toward the marlin trussed to the side of his skiff. ("There is no translation for this word," Hemingway explains, "and perhaps it is just a noise such as a man might make, involuntarily, feeling the nail go through his hands and into the wood.") Nor is the three-day span of the ordeal without significance, nor Santiago's exhausting Calvary climb, when he stumbles and falls, carrying the mast on his shoulders up the hill to his cabin. After such symbolism, what denial?

Still, Hemingway tried to deny it. Having sent an advance copy of the book to his father figure, Bernard Berenson, and having received a letter of praise in return, Hemingway asked, apologetically, if Berenson might be willing to write two or three sentences about the book for Scribner's use. After cautionary references to Homer, to *Moby Dick,* and to the sea in general as "*la puta mar,*" Hemingway let Berenson in on a secret. There was, he told Berenson, no symbolism in his book: "The sea is the sea. The old man is an old man. The boy is a boy and the fish is a fish. The sharks are all sharks no better and no worse." Berenson, taking his cues from Hemingway, as Hemingway quite probably intended, neatly obliged with a perfect blurb: "Hemingway's *Old Man and the Sea* is an idyll of the sea as sea, as un-Byronic and un-Melvillian as Homer himself, and communicated in a prose as calm and compelling as Homer's verse. No real artist symbolizes or allegorizes — and Hemingway is a real artist — but every real work of art exhales symbols and allegories. So does this short but not small masterpiece." Hemingway couldn't have been happier if he had written it himself — as, perhaps, he had.

The sharks, however, would not go away. Critics read them and their actions as tropes for critics. In a letter to Edmund Wilson, Hemingway insisted on setting the record straight: "You know I was thinking about actual sharks when I wrote the book and had nothing to do with the theory that they represented critics. I don't know who thought that up." But Hemingway, with a new book in process and still smarting over the critical reception of *Across the River,* was promulgating his own metaphors of the artist at bay. In a letter to Harvey Breit, he spoke of the lobo wolf: "He is hunted by everyone. Everyone is against him and he is on his own as an artist is." There is no doubt that *The Old Man and the Sea* was a surrogate fable of Hemingway's own life as a writer who had dared to venture too far from the shore on the wide blue Gulf Stream, which had become Hemingway's major metaphor for the mysterious force of life. ("No," Santiago tells himself, "you violated your luck when you went too far outside.") Hemingway, too, was a former champion trying for a comeback, as Santiago was formerly El Campeón, not only a great fisherman but rather awkwardly — it is one of the sentimental flaws of the novel — the champion arm wrestler of the island. The too easy identification of Santiago with Hemingway himself unavoidably taints the narrative with a kind of self-pity.

Whatever its flaws, *The Old Man and the Sea* remains a moving and forceful story; it builds to its climax in the way that only a master knows how to pace and structure a work. It is the near masterpiece the public took to be the overwhelming masterpiece the media created. Santiago's boat pulled through the night by a mysterious force, fathoms deep, that the old fisherman, from his lifelong experience, can only guess at — this idea is conjured with the simplicity that only a major writer dares to attempt. An undercurrent of animism runs through the book, enlivening its descriptions of nature: the unexpected flight of wild ducks etched against the sky, the shadow of an airplane scaring the schools of flying fish, Santiago's ruminations on the sea. They are among the best prose moments Hemingway created in his career. And probably the most indicative example of Hemingway's essence as a writer is his account of Santiago's recurrent dream of the lions on the beach, a memory that harked back to the old fisherman's youth when he slept on deck off the coast of Africa. It demonstrates all that was best in Hemingway, the authority of genius. "He no longer dreamed of storms, nor of women, nor of great occurrences, nor of great fish, nor fights, nor contests of strength, nor of his wife. He only dreamed of places now and of the lions on the beach. They played like young cats in the dusk and he loved them as he loved the boy."

Hemingway had no reason to complain about the reception of *The Old Man and the Sea.* Its success was phenomenal. The Book-of-the-Month Club offered it as one of its dual main selections for September 1952, with a guarantee of $21,000. More important, *Life* paid him $40,000 to publish the text in its entirety in its September 1 issue, with a cover photo of Hemingway by Alfred Eisenstadt. In two days, the magazine sold some 5,300,000 copies. Advance sales of the Scribner's edition ran to 50,000, with weekly sales thereafter of 3000. For six months it remained on the best-seller lists. The later sale of the film rights (to Leland Hayward), including Hemingway's services as a technical adviser, would bring him $150,000.

The reviews of the book were a vindication of Hemingway's status as an American writer. Most reviewers proclaimed it a masterpiece. In *The New Republic,* Mark Schorer called Hemingway "unquestionably the greatest craftsman in the American novel in this century." Orville Prescott, in the *New York Times,* claimed, "Here is the master technician once more at the top of his form, doing superbly what he can do better than anyone else." Reviewers who had harshly criticized *Across the River and Into the Trees* were relieved. Cyril Connolly in the London *Sunday Times* wrote, "I believe this is the best story Hemingway has ever written. Get it at once, read it, wait a few days, read it again, and you will find (except for an occasional loose 'now' or 'until') that no page of this beautiful master-work could have been done better or differently."

Critics inevitably praised the book as a parable of the human spirit. The reviewer for *Time* saw deeper implications: "It is a poem of action, praising a brave man, a magnificent fish and the sea, with perhaps a new underlying reverence for the Creator of such wonders." Carlos Baker went public with his earlier praise for the manuscript version in the *Saturday Review of Literature*: "Hemingway has enhanced the native power of his tragic parable by engaging, though unobtrusively, the further power of Christian symbolism." The book, he said, was "destined to become a classic in its kind." But Philip Rahv, a sobering voice amid the runaway praise, in his *Commentary* review, tried to deflate the praise the book was receiving throughout the fall of 1952. If one were to judge by the reviews, Rahv said,

> the meaning of *The Old Man and the Sea* is to be sought in its profound symbolism. It may be that the symbolism is really there, though I for one have been unable to locate it. . . . Hemingway's big marlin is no Moby Dick, and his fisherman is not Captain Ahab nor was meant to be. It is enough praise to say that their existence is real, and that their encounter is described in a language at once relaxed and disciplined, which is a source of pleasure.

The review that might have irritated Hemingway most, though he made no direct reference to reading it, was William Faulkner's, written for the Fall 1952 issue of the little magazine *Shenandoah*. Faulkner claimed that the book was Hemingway's best: "Time may show it to be the best single piece of any of us. I mean his and my contemporaries." But Faulkner went on to state, "This time [Hemingway] discovered God, a Creator. . . . It's all right. Praise God that whatever made and loves and pities Hemingway and me kept him from touching it any further." Hemingway may have read the review after all — at least in his letters following publication, the themes of Faulkner, the Nobel Prize, and Faulkner's relationship with the Almighty induced attacks of spleen. "I cannot help out very much with the true dope on God," he wrote Lillian Ross, "as I have never played footy-footy with him . . . nor won the Nobel Prize. It would be best to get the true word on God from Mr. Faulkner."

Hemingway was aboard the *Pilar* on May 4, 1953, when he learned over the ship's radio that *The Old Man and the Sea* had been awarded the Pulitzer Prize. (Archibald MacLeish's *Collected Poems* won that year as well.) He didn't know what difference it would make to the book. "Can't hurt it, I guess," Hemingway dryly wrote Wallace Meyer at Scribner's. Actually he was pleased, he said, though he couldn't take it seriously, considering that *A Farewell to Arms* hadn't received it, also remembering that the year that *For Whom the Bell*

Tolls should have received it, the committee had given no award in literature. It was a good thing he was at sea and away from the phone, he told Meyer, or he might have told interviewers that he was sorry his favorite dog, Black Dog, hadn't received it.

Throughout that spring, Hemingway was more preoccupied with another of his sentimental journeys, a trip to Africa, this time accompanied by Mary. It would also provide him with an occasion to visit his son Patrick, who with his young wife, Henny, had bought a 2300-acre farm in the remote highlands of Tanganyika. Hemingway's plans, however, were delayed by visitors and business arrangements for the filming of *The Old Man and the Sea.* Early in April, Leland Hayward and his wife, Slim, arrived for conferences, accompanied by Spencer Tracy. Hemingway at first liked Tracy, who, though eager to play Santiago, would not be available for some time because of contract obligations. Hemingway was convinced they could make a terrific killing on the movie if they could make a great picture, but only, he wrote his agent, Alfred Rice, if "Tracy and I carry the ball most of the time. He knows it and I know it." Rice and Hayward had agreed upon a $25,000 advance on the use of the novel and the same amount for Hemingway's services in the filming of the sequences of the giant marlin, which involved exploring sites in the Caribbean. (Eventually these sequences were filmed off the coast of Peru.) Also in May, Hemingway entertained an editor from *Look,* William Lowe, and his wife. Lowe, eager for a story on the African safari, offered $15,000 toward the expenses of the trip, with another $10,000 for the world rights on a 3500-word article. The magazine would supply the photographer, Earl Theisen. It was an offer Hemingway could hardly refuse.

Despite the fact that Franco was in power, Hemingway also wanted to make another pilgrimage to the July *feria* at Pamplona, as well as a leisurely tour through Spain, before beginning the journey to Africa in August. On June 24, he and Mary boarded the SS *Flandre,* scheduled to arrive in Le Havre on June 30. In Le Havre, they were met by Adriana's brother, Gianfranco, who, having failed in his Cuban career, had returned to Europe in January, hoping for more success as the director of a steamship line. He had secured the services of a friend from Udine, a cheerful young funeral director who would chauffeur the Lancia they would use on their Spanish tour. In his younger days, Hemingway made his vacation trips in the company of a few friends; in his celebrity years, an entourage would become a fact of life. At Pamplona they met Tommy Shevlin and his wife and Peter Viertel. It was the occasion, too, for a reunion with Juanito Quintana, who accompanied them on the tour. Quintana had lost his hotel in the civil war, and Pamplona was so crowded that the Hemingway party had had to take rooms in the village of Lecumberri, twenty-five miles distant. The first corrida was a disappointment; Hemingway was furious because the picadors had overworked the fine bulls, the blood pumping from their shoulders; but the second day, he and his friends had been impressed by the young Antonio Ordóñez, slim and dark and unhurried in the arena, a genius with the cape, according to Hemingway. Ordóñez was the son of Niño de la Palma, the Pedro Romero of *The Sun Also Rises.*

In Madrid, they put up at the Hotel Florida, where Hemingway and Martha had stayed during the civil war. Mary was bothered by the arid climate of the plateau and even more by the noise of the streetcars that ran all night past the hotel. She enjoyed the paintings in the Prado, so Hemingway said, although it was he who had insisted on spending an hour in the museum each morning. He was particularly enthralled with Hieronymus Bosch's crowded, undecipherable dream-triptych, *The Garden of Earthly Delights.* "No discovery in Madrid pleased him more," Mary claimed. Hemingway wrote Berenson, "If it is of even comic interest, I prayed for you sincerely and straight in Chartres, Burgos, Segovia and two minor places. It is sort of cheerful for a non-believing 1/8 Northern Cheyenne to pray for a Jew but if they have it to sell I am a buyer."

But during the "miserable passage" from Marseilles to Mombassa aboard ship, some taint of sourness or dissatisfaction crept into the pilgrimage, or his "chicken-shit crusade," as Hemingway referred to it, writing to Berenson. (They had boarded with sixty-four pieces of luggage, including three guns, a typewriter, two book bags, and a Spanish wineskin.) Mary claimed that Ernest had enjoyed the voyage, made friends, done some reading. But out of the blue, apropos of Mary, Hemingway told Berenson, "Sometimes it is as hard to trust a woman who has never born a child, being of the age for it, as it is to trust a banker or a high priced surgeon." Whores, he thought, were probably nicer, more trustworthy emotionally and with regard to money. At Mombassa, it was raining when they disembarked on August 22. Philip Percival, twenty years older than when Hemingway had first met him, and now heavier, was awaiting them at the dock. Mario "Mayito" Menocal, one of Hemingway's Cuban friends, the son of a former Cuban president, and Earl Theisen were expected to join them at the temporary encampment on Percival's Kitanga Farm.

"This is a fine trip," Hemingway wrote Berenson in a better frame of mind from the Kajiado district, south of Nairobi. The irony of his writing to one of the world's sophisticates about roughing it in the African veldt seems not to have crossed his mind. It was, in fact, a corroboration of his sense of the equality of artists everywhere. In Kajiado, he struck up an immediate friendship with the young game warden of the district, Denis Zaphiro, and adopted him as a younger brother. Zaphiro returned the favor by deputizing Hemingway as an honorary ranger in the war against the cattle-killing lions that were marauding the herds of the Masai. For Berenson's benefit perhaps, Hemingway seemed bent on overturning a few of the myths, particularly those surrounding the Masai, considered one of the more aristocratic of the African tribes. He depicted them as local capitalists, telling Berenson, "The Masai are all very rich in cattle and there is no reason for the lions not to kill a few. But like most rich people they are very avare and we only kill one for every ten they want killed." Mary, he noted, was very well; they were in desert and oasis terrain, and she finally found a country that was as tough as she. "We get up at 5 a.m. and hunt in the early morning light. The birds are very beautiful and we usually see elephant and rhino every day."

But, unfortunately, Hemingway was drinking heavily and his marksmanship was not always up to that of Menocal, who was a crack shot. As the celebrity of the trip, he was expected to pose for suitable pictures for Theisen to illustrate his *Look* article. When he and Menocal took shots at a leopard, Hemingway took credit for the kill and posed for the photographs. In private, Mary scolded him until he promised, "I'll get a leopard to salve your conscience." And when, later in the safari, Hemingway took up with a young Wakamba woman whom he called Debba and spoke of as his "fiancée," Mary kept her cool, suggesting only that Debba ought to have a needed bath. While she was away on a trip to Nairobi to buy Christmas presents, Hemingway shot a leopard and, in the ensuing drunken celebrations, brought a carload of the local girls to a nearby village to buy them dresses, then back to his camp for a riotous party in his tent in which Mary's cot was broken. Writing to Harvey Breit about the episode, Hemingway described Debba as "sort of like Brenda Frazier in the old days only black and beautiful." He shaved his head, wounds, welts and all, to please his black fiancée. "Miss Mary," he stated with more than a modicum of male fatuousness, "just stays the hell away from it and is understanding and wonderful."

Hemingway's extracurricular partying apparently caused no rupture in his relationship with his wife. In fact, their sexual relationship seems to have freed Hemingway from any lingering Oak Park inhibitions, if one is to believe his and her reports. A few days before Christmas, Hemingway wrote a long, strange, how-do-I-love-thee-let-me-count-the-ways passage in Mary's diary, noting that he loved her hair, wanted her to be a platinum blonde again as she had been in Torcello years before, when the beech logs burned in the fireplace and they "made love at least every morning, noon and night and had the loveliest time Papa ever knew of." Mary, he wrote,

> has always wanted to be a boy and thinks as a boy without ever losing any femininity. If you should become confused on this you should retire. She loves me to be her girls, which I love to be, not being absolutely stupid . . . I loved feeling the embrace of Mary which came to me as something quite new and outside all tribal law. On the night of December 19 we worked out all these things and I have never been happier.

But Hemingway's second safari soon turned into a nightmare nearly as bizarre as anything Bosch might have imagined. As a Christmas gift to "Miss Mary," Hemingway chartered a sight-seeing flight to the Belgian Congo region in a Cessna 180. The flight began on January 21, the Cessna piloted by Roy Marsh, a spic-and-span young bush pilot who had already taken them on hedgehopping excursions over the nearby herds in Kenya. There was a mishap on the first day when the travelers put down in Mwanza because of generator problems, but they managed afterward to fly over Lake Victoria, stopping the first night at Bukavu, where there was a first-class hotel. On the second day, they made a flight northward past the sulphurous clouds of two active volcanoes and on to the Mountains of the Moon, which were obscured by heavy cloud cover. It was on their third flight, edging up along the western shore of Lake Albert and the Victoria Nile, sighting hippos and mixed herds of elephant and buffalo, that they reached Murchison Falls, the spectacular cataracts descending in various levels into the gorge. Marsh circled several times while Mary snapped photographs.

Breaking away to return to Entebbe, the plane encountered a large flock of birds. Diving sharply to avoid collision, Marsh struck an abandoned telegraph wire, damaging the plane's radio atenna and rudder. He managed to crash-land in some low trees and heavy brush. Fortunately the plane did not explode or catch fire, and the three passengers were able to escape. For a frightening moment, Hemingway could not get a pulse from the dazed Mary. Only later did she learn that she had broken two ribs. Hemingway had dislocated his right shoulder; Marsh was bruised but unharmed. The plane was definitely out of commission. More seriously, Marsh could not get any reply from his messages on the damaged radio. There was nothing to do but move higher up the riverbank away from the animal life — the banks were infested with crocodiles. They spent an uneasy, cold night, comforted by a bottle of Grand MacNish that had miraculously survived the crash.

The next morning, they sighted a launch, the *Murchison,* puffing up the river. It had been chartered by an English surgeon, Dr. McAdam, his family, and his in-laws, who were celebrating their fiftieth wedding anniversary. The McAdams were delighted to take them back to civilization at Butiaba. (The launch, they learned later, had been used in the filming of *The African Queen.*) At Butiaba, a Captain Reggie Cartwright was waiting to receive them. The news services had already spread the word that they had been killed in the crash, and Cartwright was eager to fly them in his De Havilland Rapide to meet the press gathered at Entebbe. Though it was growing dark and the runway at Butiaba was little more than a stretch of furrows, Cartwright assured them they could make it easily. That proved not to be the case. The biplane bumped and lifted, set down, and was suddenly airborne and then just as suddenly crashed with a sound of wrenching metal. Flames broke out. Mary and Roy Marsh managed to escape by kicking out one of the small windows; the pilot at the last moment exited from the front. Hemingway, trying to get out the port door, found it jam-closed by a piece of metal. With the flames leaping in the cabin, he used his head as well as his already dislocated shoulder as a battering ram on the door, forcing his way out onto the lower left wing. None too soon; the plane had become a bonfire. In his escape, he had given himself another damaging concussion. His scalp was bleeding, and cerebral fluid was seeping down behind his left ear.

With her dry acerbity, Mary, in her memoir, recounted the rest of the two-accident ordeal and the rigors of colonial life. At Masindi, where they had driven that night, the telegrapher refused to open the telegraph office because of Sunday regulations. The dining room at the Railway Hotel being closed by the time they arrived, they had no dinner, only a few sandwiches. The following morning, the local doctor did little more than bandage Hemingway's head and make a perfunctory cleaning of the gashes on his knees and legs, as well as a cut on Mary's knee.

Later that day, at Entebbe, they were met by the press, eager for interviews. After the premature death notices, Hemingway was now being billed as "Invulnerable Papa." His demise and resurrection in a three-day period made headline news in the major papers. In Nairobi, recuperating at the New Stanley Hotel, Hemingway rested and read his obituaries with some bemusement. "In all obituaries, or almost all, it was emphasized that I had sought death all my life. Can one imagine that if a man sought death all of his life he could not have found her before the age of 54?" Hemingway asked in the lengthy two-installment account of the experience, "The Christmas-Gift," he provided for the readers of *Look.* In time, he managed to answer some of the cables and letters from friends congratulating him on his narrow escape. Writing to Harvey Breit, he admitted that the second accident was "a little bit bad." He had had to take two deep breaths in the fire, he joked, "which is something that never really helped anybody except of course Joan of Arc, the reincarnation (admitted) of Gen. Charles de Gaulle." In a garbled dig and with his usual association of prizes and buggery, he added, "Harvey it was a little more rugged than Nobel Prize winners corncob by FAULKNER."

By late February, when Hemingway was able to make a planned fishing holiday with the Percivals, Zaphiro, and Patrick and his wife at Shimoni on the coast near Mombassa, it was clear to Mary that his recuperative powers were not what they once were. Though he managed to keep up his usual bantering and continuous conversations, telling his often repeated jokes, he was obviously in pain much of the time. ("Semi-unbearable suffering" was how he referred to it in Mary's diary.) He fished only a few times during his stay. There were bouts of irascibility, one of them in which he harangued Patrick so unmercifully for failing to prepare the bait for a fishing expedition that Henny broke down and cried. At the end of the ordeal, Patrick answered, "I'm leaving," and gave orders to have his things loaded onto his Land-Rover.

It was not until months later, at Venice, according to Mary, that they learned the full extent of Hemingway's injuries: "two disks of his spine cracked and impacted, his liver and one kidney both ruptured, a paralysis of the sphincter, his right arm and shoulder dislocated, his skull broken open." There were good reasons for believing that the man was indestructible.

⸙ ⸙ ⸙

For years, Hemingway had coveted the Nobel Prize but always denied wanting it. He made a point of ridiculing the prize itself and, generally, those who had received it. When Sinclair Lewis was awarded it in 1930, Hemingway thought Ezra Pound and James Joyce were far more deserving. When Faulkner received it in 1950, he sent a cable, "as good a cable of congratulations as I know how to write," and never received an acknowledgment. Around that slight, he concocted an odd rationalization for the benefit of Harvey Breit: "You see what happens with Bill Faulkner is that as long as I am alive he has to drink to feel good about having the Nobel Prize. He does not realize that I have no respect for that institution and was truly happy for him when he got it."

But there was clearly jubilation at the Finca Vigía when, early on the morning of October 28, 1954, the United Press phoned Hemingway to tell him he had been awarded the Nobel Prize in Literature. "My kitten, my kitten," he told Mary, waking her, "I've got that thing." His first call was to Buck Lanham, to whom he also blurted out that he had got "that thing." Through most of that day, crowds of newspapermen, photographers, and well-wishers gathered at the house. When they had finally left, Mary danced around the sitting room, singing a parody version of a Gershwin tune: "Somebody loves you, I wonder who — the Swede Academy." Although the award patently recognized the achievement of *The Old Man and the Sea,* there must have been a lingering suspicion in Hemingway's mind that his obituary notices had played a part in the academy's decision. When Harvey Breit interviewed him over the phone for the *New York Times,* he suggested with the sudden generosity and false modesty that characterized his public persona that he might have been happier if the prize had gone to Isak Dinesen or Bernard Berenson or Carl Sandburg. "You know I know more or less what category of writer I am but that's no reason to act swelled headed," he explained in a letter to Buck Lanham. Sandburg, he reasoned, was an old man who would appreciate it, and Dinesen was a damned sight better writer than any Swede they'd ever given it to. "Berenson I thought deserved it (no more than me) but I would have been happy to see him get it." He was, he told Lanham, "in a belle epoque" of writing if people would only leave him alone. What he had, in fact, begun was another of his uncompleted projects, a semifictitious account of his African safari with Mary which would eventually stretch to some 200,000 words. (Some 50,000 words of it would be published posthumously as "African Journal" in three installments in *Sports Illustrated* in the winter of 1971–1972.) "I've gotten back into the country and I live in it every day," he told Lanham, "and some of the stuff I think you'll like unless you have too strong views on mis-cegenation." He asked, "If you had to make a Nobel speech, what would you say? That's an easy one for you maybe. Looks impossible to me."

Hemingway was not eager to attend the ceremonies in Stockholm. He had a real distaste for the podium, and perhaps he was a little miffed that the committee, in commending his "powerful, style-making mastery of the art of modern narration," had also felt it necessary to characterize his early writings as "brutal, cynical and callous." Instead, he pleaded poor health and wrote out his address to be delivered by John Cabot, the American ambassador to Sweden. His message, though dignified and brief, began with a reminder of worthy writers who had not received the prize. But it was certainly one of Hemingway's best and most measured acknowledgments of his profession:

> Writing, at its best, is a lonely life. Organizations for writers palliate the writer's loneliness but I doubt if they improve his writing. He grows in public stature as he sheds his loneliness and often his work deteriorated. For he does his work alone and if he is a good enough writer he must face eternity, or the lack of it, each day.

Hemingway took the occasion to reinforce what Santiago had represented in *The Old Man and the Sea,* a man who had gone out too far: "For a true writer, each book should be a new beginning where he tries again for something that is beyond attainment. . . . It is because we have had such great writers in the past that a writer is driven far out past where he can go, out to where no one can help him." But even so, something still nagged at his pleasure in an award that should have meant the vindication of his career. In a later conversation with Janet Flanner, Hemingway said that he regretted that André Malraux, one of the rumored candidates that year, had not received the prize. He felt that it meant that Malraux would not likely be considered again. He was worried, he said, that Malraux might commit suicide. Flanner attributed the cause of Hemingway's unusual concern to a talk they had once had about the predisposition to suicide in families where a parent had already taken his or her life. Flanner's father had killed himself, as had Hemingway's and Malraux's, and she admitted to Hemingway that given the right circumstances — if facing a painful terminal illness, for instance — she would consider taking her own life. But Flanner's explanation would hardly account for Hemingway's fears about Malraux. Was it, in some way, an eerie confession of guilt — or of the magic of revenge, as if the price of his winning the prize had to be paid for by a rival's suicide? There is in every life, as Freud once observed of every dream, a point where it becomes unfathomable, a central point that is connected to the unknown.

Hemingway's good fortune did not escape the meaner attention of his peers; it was a condition of the literary life. Edmund Wilson and John Dos Passos, meeting for lunch in New York a few months after the award, talked about Hemingway and *The Old Man and the Sea.* Wilson remarked on how much pressure Hemingway, after the failure of *Across the River and Into the Trees,* had brought to bear on everybody to applaud the new book and make his "good enough little story appear a masterpiece." Dos Passos agreed; he was fascinated by the "operation" and Hemingway's timing of it so as to get the jackpot. "I was so fascinated by the 'operation,'" Dos Passos said, "that I could hardly judge the story: it was like a magician's stunt — when he makes the girl float through the hoop, you don't notice whether she's pretty."

III

"It is only when you can no longer believe in your exploits that you write your memoirs," Hemingway had written when he was in his prime. In 1957, it seems, he had arrived at that stage of disbelief. He had begun work on an article about Scott Fitzgerald, how he had first met Scott and what Scott was like then. It was intended for the centenary issue of *The Atlantic Monthly*. But then, perhaps remembering his objections to Mizener's biography, he put the article aside, sending the magazine instead a twin bill of stories, both about men who had gone blind as a result of accident or violence. They were published as "Two Tales of Darkness" in the November issue of *The Atlantic*. Hemingway, however, did not abandon the project he had from time to time teased his editors with — the writing of his own memoirs, specifically of his early years in Paris. Over the next year or more he began sketching out the brief chapters of what would become *A Moveable Feast*. He may, perhaps, have been inspired by the recovery of two suitcases that had been sitting in the basement of the Paris Ritz for twenty-eight years. They were a time capsule from the Paris years, containing manuscript notebooks, typescripts of early stories, newspaper clippings. So, at least, the discovery was reported in a Leonard Lyons column in the *New York Post*, on December 12, 1957. (At least one scholar, however, has questioned whether the "treasure trove" of found documents provided the material for *A Moveable Feast*, as Mary would later claim — even whether the suitcases existed.) Hemingway, quite probably, would have written his story of the Paris years even if the memorabilia had never been found.

But *A Moveable Feast* was not "the confessions of the real Ernest Hemingway" that Gertrude Stein had taunted him with in her autobiography. It was a superbly written, well-paced idyll in which Hemingway invented an unlikely persona for himself and created a romanticized version of his marriage with Hadley that bore little resemblance to their actual lives. When it came to his colleagues, Hemingway settled many old scores — finishing off Stein with a humiliating story of her lesbian submission to Alice Toklas, dredging up again his oft-told story about Fitzgerald's worries over the size of his penis. Hemingway more than paid back Dos Passos for his treatment of him in *Chosen Country*, picturing him as the sycophantic pilot fish who had led the real sharks toward Hemingway — the innocent, unoffending Gerald and Sara Murphy, who purportedly ruined his marriage to Hadley and, above all, destroyed his talent with their corrupting wealth.

Toward the end, the writing of the sketches did not go all that easily. The malice that must have originally sharpened the faultless prose suffered as Hemingway's memory no longer served his rising anger. Once he had to make a pathetic call to Hadley when he could not remember the names of his intended victims, the man and woman who had exploited the writers in Paris, Ernest Walsh and Ethel Moorhead, the editors of *This Quarter.* He was clearly worried about the problem of libel, an old worry that may have manifested itself with more force in his last troubled years. In discarded pages from the preface, in which, in the published version, he gave the reader leave to consider his book a work of fiction, he claimed that he did not want to hurt Hadley or Pauline, neither alive nor dead, or the children. In the discarded draft he announced outright, "This book is fiction. I have left out much and changed and eliminated and hope Hadley understands." His ambivalence toward Pauline was clear; a passage referring to Pauline's deceit in her relationship with Hadley, as well as his own guilt, was removed: "For the girl to deceive her friend was a terrible thing but it was my fault and blindness that it did not repel me." In his easier moments, he seemed prepared to give charity if not justice to Pauline. He admitted that after Hadley had married Paul Mowrer, his life with Pauline was better and he felt no remorse: "I never worked better nor was I happier and I loved the girl truly and she loved me truly and well. And we had as good a life together for many years as early Paris had been." A sentimental passage, lacking the ring of authenticity, and one that was deleted from the book, as well. The part about Pauline, he added, he was saving for the start of another book: "It could be a good book because it tells many things that no one knows or can ever know and it has love, remorse, contrition and unbelievable happiness and the story of truly good work and final sorrow." But Hemingway left his passing tribute to Pauline and that account of the reality of their marriage buried in the slag of his memoirs. It had become easier to keep up the needed public image he had created, rather than to negotiate with the hard truths of his feelings, his marital affairs.

"No one can write true facts in reminiscences," he claimed in a deleted passage that must have been a warning to himself. "Evan [Shipman] would back you up but he is dead. Scott would disagree. Miss Moorhead would sue you if you published anything against Walsh and she has many letters and much basis to sue on."

One can only speculate on what a memoir of the Paris years by the real Ernest Hemingway might have been, just as one might wish that Hemingway's coverage of World War II had been written by the major writer, the man of genius, the real artist — rather than the man eager for celebrity. He had been at the center of a cultural revolution unequaled in its wide-reaching effects on Western culture except by the Italian Renaissance; had been — in his early years — a leader among the extraordinary band of writers, artists, playwrights, composers, architects, publishers, publicists, scholars, and critics who had shaped the art of their time anew, in Paris, Berlin, Moscow, London, New York — veritable creators in a period of insidious violence and destruction.

When Hemingway had the right audience — not the hangers-on, the idlers, the fawners with whom he seemed content to spend much of his time in his later years; when he found the right confidant, as he did with the old-world, fatherly figure of Bernard Berenson, he could, occasionally, dispense with the burdensome celebrity he had saddled himself with and allow himself to be the sharply prejudiced, interesting observer he was.

Writing to Berenson in March 1953 (before the disastrous accidents in Africa), he acknowledged the circumstances under which he practiced his profession. "The violence is the violence of our time," he told Berenson. "It is my heritage, not yours. I feel terribly that you should have been exposed to its idiocy. You came from a good time." In his letters to Berenson, there are hints of the memoirs he might have written in the brief character sketches he culled from his Paris years for Berenson's benefit, though they are not without the occasional brag or the invigorating malice he reserved for his more threatening rivals:

> Claudel always seemed ridiculous. When I first started to be published in French he thought I was a wonderful writer and it made me very uneasy and I thought, "There must be something wrong with this stuff that I do not see. If Claudel likes it there has to be something wrong." Gide had that awful lascivious protestant coolness; like the pastor of the Fourth Presbyterian Church who is caught by the janitor interfering with little boys behind the church organ. . . . Valery was a nice man. We were quite good friends but just before he died he expressed a wish to meet me and Sylvia Beach and Adrienne Monnier wanted to make a party for the event. I suppose I should have gone. But I was hurt, I suppose, that he did not remember me when I was a very quiet boy whose name nobody knew.

Forgetting the modesty or the self-deception: When was he a very quiet boy? When was his name not known in the Paris crowd? What might his memoirs have been if he had trusted his genius for the word, for the concentrated scene? In an autobiography (had he begun it earlier without the erosion of his gifts or his personality), he might have traced out the network of relationships and circumstances that would have summed up his career, summed up his age better than any American writer of his generation. He was the man who had all the credentials, who witnessed the time — the people, the events, the wars, the names that were being elevated into history — from his first afternoon visits to the cluttered salon on the rue de Fleurus, when he began to make a mark with his good looks, his talents, his persevering ambition, to the summons from Stockholm that crowned his career, some thirty years later. Of those last years, one has to fight back the feeling that Hemingway had let himself down, badly.

⁊ ⁊ ⁊

Ever since Hemingway had captured the Nobel Prize, the Finca Vigía had been besieged by guests and visitors, some welcome, some unavoidable: George Plimpton, Charlie MacArthur and Helen Hayes, who had brought Anita Loos (all right if you liked gnomes, which he didn't, he once commented on the diminutive Loos). And there were the "film people": Hayward and his wife; Fred Zinneman, the initial director of *The Old Man and the Sea;* and assorted staff members, which meant conferences and more guests. The "Picture Business" interrupted his morning work with calls to the kitchen phone and someone at the end of the line canceling an appointment or changing a date. "Coops," he wrote a sympathetic Gary Cooper, "after the Old Man and the Sea is finished I will not ever have anything to do with pictures again so Help Me God. God is Capitalized." There were temperamental squabbles among the cast and crew; there was the problem of the great marlin that had to be lashed to Santiago's boat during the long vigil. (The solution was the huge model fish with the startled glassy eye used in some of the sequences.) There were difficulties with "the artist," as Hemingway referred to Spencer Tracy, who had come down with a bad case of self-doubt and resorted to the bottle. "But they say that is all straightened," he wrote Gianfranco Ivancich, "and we have a docile artist now, but to me in the stills I saw last night he still looked very fat for a fisherman and the boy looks very tiny. There is nothing that a rubber fish cannot fix." And there had always been the problem of tourists, who arrived at San Francisco de Paula in busloads, the more aggressive among them pushing open the iron gates, herding toward the patio in search of Hemingway unless Mary caught sight of them in time. She was now typing episodes from his memoirs, until he came to a stop and picked up once more on *The Garden of Eden*. But for Hemingway, now, writing was becoming a matter of false starts and unreachable endings.

With the ominous signs of revolution brewing in Cuba, life became more dangerous and untenable at the Finca Vigía. (Batista's soldiers had shot one of Hemingway's dogs.) Having seen revolution in Spain, Hemingway was wary. It seemed wise to go back to Idaho over the fall and winter, where there were old friends, Lloyd and Tillie Arnold and Taylor Williams, and the crowd that went hunting and fishing. "Cuba is really bad, now," he wrote Patrick from Ketchum in November 1958. "Knowing what sort of stuff and murder will go on when the new ones come in — seeing the abuses of those in now — I am fed on it." He was in Idaho on New Year's Day, in fact, when the news came that Fulgencio Batista had fled the country and that Castro had taken Havana. The wire services and the *New York Times* had phoned Hemingway, asking his opinion, and he had answered that he was "delighted." Mary cautioned him that it was too strong a word, not knowing what excesses might be committed in the name of the revolution, and Hemingway reluctantly called the *Times* city room and changed the word to "hopeful."

And then he received an invitation from a wealthy friend, Nathan "Bill" Davis, to come to Spain to witness the *mano a mano* between Antonio Ordóñez and his brother-in-law Luis Miguel Dominguín, scheduled for the following season. Hemingway agreed and persuaded Mary to go with him, despite the fact that they were just buying a house in Idaho. It stood on a hillside overlooking the Big Wood River in Ketchum, with a back bedroom that would make a perfect study for Hemingway and views of the mountains across a valley forested with aspens and cottonwoods.

The trip to Spain that summer — the summer of Hemingway's sixtieth birthday — went badly. Word of the trip had gotten round, and the Paris office of *Life* had contacted him to do an article on the new season of bullfighting. The visit had the makings of a triumphal return tour, and it was true that whenever he attended a bullfight he was a favored visitor, with the most difficult bulls dedicated to him. In the midst of an attentive crowd, he stood now to acknowledge the ovations — and at Madrid had even taught the *presidente* of the corrida a lesson for having failed to appreciate the artistry of a young bullfighter, Segura: Hemingway stood up (in one of those last gestures of an old man confronting authority) and faced the *presidente* down, forcing him to acknowledge the performance and award the bullfighter the two ears of the bull. But he was in a restless state of mind, working spasmodically (on his preface, "The Art of the

Short Story," for a collection of some of his stories), drinking heavily again, traveling from *feria* to *feria* in the embarrassing pink Ford that Davis had rented for him. In Madrid, the midnight dinners, the irregular hours, and the liquor took their toll. Hemingway developed kidney trouble and was treated by Dr. George Saviers, his Idaho physician, who was in Spain that summer with his wife, Pat — members of the growing Hemingway entourage that included Hotchner and Juanito Quintana, Gianfranco Ivancich and his wife, and a new fresh-complexioned nineteen-year-old Irish girl, Valerie Danby-Smith, an aspiring journalist (a stringer for a Belgian news agency), whom Hemingway took under his wing as a secretary and called "Daughter" in his usual fashion.

Buck Lanham had arrived in time to celebrate Hemingway's birthday. Hemingway was moved to tears when Buck presented him with an affectionately inscribed history of the Twenty-second Infantry Regiment, but two nights later, at a birthday dinner at the Hotel Miramar, they quarreled bitterly when Lanham, in a warm gesture, grasped Hemingway's shoulder and accidentally brushed against the back of his head. As Carlos Baker, who had gotten the story from Lanham, described it, Hemingway "winced as if he had been burned" and in a loud voice declared that no one was permitted to touch his head. (Hemingway's reaction suggests that he may have winced in pain, raising the possibility that the five concussions he had sustained in his lifetime might have had far more serious consequences in his mental deterioration than has been recognized.) Lanham left the room white with anger. Hemingway, full of remorse, followed after him to apologize, weeping, explaining that he had combed his hair forward to cover a growing baldness. It was not the only incident Lanham found hard to forget or forgive; he was put off by Hemingway's "unhealthy nostagia for his young manhood" and the increasing obscenity of his language.

The birthday party that Mary had organized for weeks at the Davises' spacious home, La Consula, in the hills above Málaga, had seemingly gone well, with guitar players, flamenco dancers, Japanese lanterns in the gardens, fireworks, a shooting gallery. (Hemingway, as a demonstration of his marksmanship, shot lighted cigarettes from Ordóñez's lips.) But afterward, Hemingway accused Mary of spending his money for the party, although she had paid for most of it with an article she had written for *Sports Illustrated.* His moods were becoming volatile. He would start a harangue over minor things — accusing her of not having bought him Listerine (which she had), berating her for drinking too much water. Sometimes arguments would continue on into the small hours of the morning.

They did not make the return trip home together. Because Hemingway had invited Antonio Ordóñez and his wife to visit them in Cuba and then in Idaho, Mary had left early to prepare for their visit. Hemingway had seen her off at Orly; she felt it had been only a dutiful farewell. From Cuba, she wrote him that since he seemed to have so little need of her in his life, she was prepared to find herself an apartment in New York, though she intended to make the Finca and the house in Ketchum ready for his guests like a responsible wife. Hemingway cabled his thanks for her work at the Finca and was sorry, but disagreed with her assessment of personal matters — though he respected her views. "STILL LOVE YOU," he added. It was not very convincing. Nor was she any more convinced when he arrived in Cuba, bearing a peace offering of a diamond pin. While the Ordóñezes basked in the sun (the bullfighter had no liking for fishing expeditions on the *Pilar*), Hemingway tried writing his *Life* article, on which he had written 5000 words in Spain, but which proved to be only a beginning.

Hemingway had been hoping to impress Ordóñez with the duck shooting in Idaho, but he was bitterly disappointed. Soon after their arrival there, Ordóñez received an unexpected call from his sister in Mexico announcing that she was separating from her husband. The couple had to leave Ketchum in a hurry. Then Mary, only slightly less accident-prone than her husband, while out duck shooting with Hemingway and George Saviers, fell and shattered her elbow. While she was groaning with pain on the way to the Sun Valley hospital, Hemingway scolded her, "You could keep it quiet. . . . Soldiers don't do that." Invalided for a long spell — the bones did not set properly and had to be reset — she endured Hemingway's complaints when he had to help her undress. He complained to Buck Lanham that Mary was a bad patient who required all his forbearance: "Some people are better handling pain than others. Anyway let's put it that pain hurts Mary bad and is hard on her nerves. Under those circumstances . . . whoever they know the best receives the smallest ration of their heroism."

One evening early in the new year, when there were at their friends the Arnolds' for dinner, Ernest, looking out the window, saw lights on in the windows of the local bank, and said, "They're checking our accounts." He was convinced that the FBI was trying to get something on him, although Mary and the Arnolds tried to persuade him that there were more plausible reasons for the lights — that the cleaning women were there or that the bank manager was working late. But even paranoids have real enemies: the FBI, in fact, had opened a file on Hemingway at the time of his Crook Factory operations in Cuba. J. Edgar Hoover had an agent in the American embassy in Havana, Raymond Leddy, with whom Hemingway had had some embarrassing run-ins. Leddy was reporting regularly to the chief on Hemingway's activities.

In mid-January, Hemingway and Mary returned to the Finca Vigía, where he hoped to finish his article for *Life*. His activities under the Castro government could only have aroused the further suspicion of the FBI. When he had returned from Spain in November 1959, he had been met by newsmen and expressed his support for the Castro regime, saying he hoped the Cubans would not regard him as a Yanqui, and unfortunately kissed the hem of the Cuban flag. Hemingway's support of Castro would in time cost him the friendship of some of his Cuban friends, like Mayito Menocal, who were later driven into exile. Even the welcome relief that spring of the marlin-fishing tournament, which Hemingway had organized and in which some forty boats took part, had its political implications. The Castro government had taken over many of the luxury boats left behind by wealthy Cubans, and Castro himself had appropriated one, entering it in the competition. Under the watchful eyes of the guests aboard the *Pilar,* who took turns studying him through a pair of U.S. Navy binoculars, Castro, hewing strictly to the rules of the competition, won the trophy, a silver cup, which Hemingway awarded him on the dock that evening.

Throughout that spring and early summer, the *Life* article was expanding beyond reason and control, and Hemingway could not bring it to an end. The original 10,000 words the magazine had asked for stood at 63,000 words when he wrote his publisher, Charles Scribner, Jr., on April 1, advising him that the Paris book would have to be scratched from the fall list. With Mary still incapacitated, he had no one to help him with the typing, and he sent for Valerie Danby-Smith, paying for her flight. And still the manuscript grew. In June, in answer to Hemingway's repeated and anxious phone calls, Aaron Hotchner arrived at the Finca to help him cut the manuscript, which was now at 120,000 words. Hemingway, often writing irrational and petulant notes to Hotchner's suggested cuts, was still unwilling to make concessions. "What I've written is Proustian in its cumulative effect," he explained to Hotchner, "and if we eliminate detail we destroy that effect." Early in July, so Hemingway wrote Charles Scribner, Jr., the article stood at 70,000 words. Hotchner took the manuscript to *Life,* where Ed Thompson, the managing editor, agreed to make further necessary cuts and pay $90,000 for the rights to publication in the magazine and another $10,000 for the Spanish language rights. Even so, Hemingway felt it would be necessary to make another trip to Spain before "The Dangerous Summer" could be finalized.

With the manuscript in the works, he made plans, reluctantly, for his return to Spain to check facts and collect photographs, as well as accompany Ordóñez on his 1960 tour. Mary was not planning to go with him, choosing to remain behind in New York in the apartment Hotchner and other friends had found for them on East Sixty-second Street. For the first time, in 1960, Hemingway decided he wanted no birthday celebration. Four days after July 21, he, Mary, and Valerie took the ferry to Key West. They had left everything behind, expecting to return in the fall or winter. Fortunately, Hemingway had lent his — or Hadley's — Miró, *The Farm,* to the Museum of Modern Art for an upcoming exhibition; but Hemingway's collection of works by Gris, Braque, Klee, and Masson had remained at the Finca, as well as his library of some four to six thousand books. Reams of Hemingway's unpublished manuscripts were deposited in Mary's bank in Havana. The timing was unfortunate; they would never return to San Francisco de Paula together. After the Bay of Pigs, the Castro government appropriated the Finca Vigía. At Key West, a minor incident assumed ominous proportions in Hemingway's suspicious imaginings. Valerie Danby-Smith's visa had not been properly renewed, and Hemingway, despite assurances from the customs officials, brooded over it, sure it would bring him trouble.

Hemingway's summer in Spain was to be a far more dangerous summer than the one he had chosen as the subject of his *Life* article. For Mary, it had begun on August 8, four days after Hemingway had flown on TWA to Madrid. Hotchner called her in New York to say that he had heard over the radio that Hemingway had collapsed in Málaga and might be dead. After agonizing phone calls to the wire services and anxious queries from friends, it turned out to be a false alarm. Hemingway cabled her from Granada that he was all right. But his letters after that were ominous, or ought to have been to Mary, who inexplicably ignored the warning signals. For months she had continued to tell herself that he was overtired, that everything would be all right when he finished the assignment. "Kitner, I don't know how I can stick this summer out," he wrote her. "Am so damned lonesome and the whole bullfight business is now so corrupt and seems so unimportant and I have so much good work to do. . . . If I lie down and try to rest somebody calls me dead." He wrote her in the same letter, "Only thing I am afraid of, no, not only thing, is complete physical and nervous crack-up from deadly overwork." In a later letter, he more than pleaded, "I wish you were here to look after me and help me out and keep [me] from cracking up." Perhaps she did not want to believe the message he was sending her. Mary did not go to Spain to be with him, but Valerie went, and later Hotchner. On September 2, Mary cabled Hemingway the good news that the first installment of the *Life* article, "The Dangerous Summer," was a big hit in New York. Scribner's windows were full of copies of his books and blowups from the article. He found that encouraging, but the cover portrait seems to have brought him face to face with the celebrity he had become. The magazine made him sick, he said, "the horrible face on the cover . . . the comparing journalism with 'The Old Man'. . . . Just feel ashamed and sick to have done such a job."

What his letters to Mary only hinted at was grim reality to those who were with him in Spain. At La Consula, the bewildered Davises bore the brunt of Hemingway's breakdown. He kept to his bed for days, was stone silent whenever they drove him anywhere. (He told Hotchner that Davis was trying to kill him in a car accident, not having succeeded the year before.) It was clear to Hotchner that Hemingway was suffering from delusions. Hemingway ranted that after all the time he had spent getting the right pictures, the photographs used in the second installment of his *Life* story were not fair to either Ordóñez or Dominguín; it made him look like "an all-time fool and a double-crosser." When they tried to arrange for his flight home, he was convinced the airline would not allow him on the plane with all his luggage. Nothing would change his mind until Hotchner got a signed statement from the airline officials. He was a man on his way down.

In New York, Mary met him at Idlewild. She thought he looked better than expected but after a few days found it impossible to get him out of the flat. "Somebody waiting out there," he said. Still, she could not bring herself to broach the subject of psychiatric help. Instead, she lost patience, told him to stop acting like a fugitive. Hemingway became silent and brooding. Finally, she did manage to get him on an afternoon train to Chicago, thinking that the return to Ketchum would be the best cure. But after the tiresome journey, when she and Hemingway were settled into George Saviers's car at the Shoshone station, Hemingway caught sight of two men in topcoats passing by and muttered, "They're tailing me out here already."

In Ketchum, he was besieged by dire suspicions about Valerie's visa problems, obsessed by the idea that he would be accused of conspiring in her illegal entry into the country. On the phone, he would refer to her secretively as the "guest." He was full of undue worries about his financial situation, as well. Mary tried to rid him of his fears by having the vice president of the Morgan Guaranty Trust in New York call with the balances of his various accounts. Though Hemingway listened in on the extension phone, he was unconvinced: "He's covering up something," he argued.

It was not until late November, and at the suggestion of Hotchner and Dr. Saviers, that Mary agreed to consider the possibility of psychiatric treatment. Saviers found Hemingway at least responsive. But concerned about publicity, he refused to go to the Menninger Clinic, the leading psychiatric center: "They'll say I'm losing my marbles." On November 30, he entered the Mayo Clinic in Rochester, Minnesota, registering at St. Mary's Hospital under the name of George Saviers, presumably there for treatment of high blood pressure. A few days later, Mary arrived, registering at a nearby hotel as Mrs. Saviers. The medical reports, according to Mary, indicated that Hemingway was suffering from a mild form of diabetes mellitus (though one of the doctors suspected Hemingway might be suffering from hemochromatosis, an inherited metabolic disorder involving heavy accumulations of iron in the system which irreversibly affect the liver, heart, and other organs). The doctors thought it best to take him off the reserpine he had been taking for his blood pressure, since one of its side effects was to induce depression. Their principal recommendation was electric shock therapy twice a week for a period of several weeks.

While in the hospital, Hemingway wrote a pathetic letter "To Whom it may concern," intended to exonerate Mary from any charges of illegal acts or misdeeds relating to his finances or for registering under an assumed name. When the news of Hemingway's hospitalization made the headlines in January, six weeks later, Mary told Patrick the official version that his father was being treated for high blood pressure, that the tests and laboratory reports were promising. Hemingway was heartened by the letters and cards from friends and well-wishers and by an invitation, by telegram, from the newly elected president, John F. Kennedy, to attend the inauguration in Washington. Hemingway declined for reasons of health. He and Mary watched the ceremony on television. It was not until January 22 that the doctors felt he was well enough to return to Ketchum.

For a time, it seemed that the therapy had helped. He and Mary took long winter walks along Route 93. He had begun work once again on his Paris book. "Try to only think from day to day and work the same," he wrote his editor at Scribner's, L. H. Brague, Jr., "but things have been rough and are rough all over. Cuba situation — lack of library to work from — etc." But he was beset by fears that he might be sued for libel. Sometimes he stood at his desk for hours, shuffling papers back and forth. Asked to contribute to a presentation volume for President Kennedy, he was tormented by writer's block, writing and rewriting a simple message for hours and then days. During the day, his silences were ominous. At night, he stood at the door to Mary's bedroom, haranguing her as she lay in the dark, complaining that she spent too much on groceries, upbraiding her for not being concerned enough about the dangers of living in Idaho. One day, he broke down in front of Dr. Saviers, crying that he couldn't write anymore, that the words just wouldn't come. He was sure the shock treatments had destroyed his capacity to write. Day by day, in slow motion, an avalanche of fears and worries was descending on him.

↑↑↑

One morning, when Mary came downstairs, she found him standing in the vestibule with the shotgun in his hands, the shells ready to be loaded. She talked to him slowly and patiently, trying to convince him that he had much to live for, that the writing would come as it always had, that he had to live for his sons. Fortunately, it was time for Dr. Saviers's visit, and they managed to take the gun from him. They took him to the Sun Valley hospital. It was plain he would have to be readmitted to the Mayo Clinic. After a stay of a few days at Sun Valley, Hemingway wheedled Dr. Saviers into allowing him to go home, accompanied by a husky friend, Don Anderson, and a nurse, to pick up things he would need at Rochester. No sooner had they stopped in front of the house than Hemingway stepped out of the car, and, like an alcoholic with the jingle of sudden money in his pocket heading for the nearest bar, he took off, blindsided, hurrying to the back door and down the basement stairs to the gun cabinet. There was a scuffle as they wrested the gun away from him. He stood there glum and silent. Anderson brought him back to the hospital. The next day Dr. Saviers and Anderson flew with him to Rochester. Even then, on the runway at the fueling stop at Rapid City, in the blaze of the bright sunlight, he walked steadily toward the propeller of another plane before the pilot cut his engine in time.

At St. Mary's, they assigned him to the closed ward, which had bars on the windows and no locks on the doors. Mary had been advised to remain in Ketchum while he underwent further shock treatments. When she visited him, weeks later, they were allowed a little dinner party alone, outside the locked ward. But he accused her of setting things up in Ketchum so that he would have to go to jail. "You think as long as you can keep me getting electric shocks, I'd be happy." A few weeks later, she received an urgent call from

St. Mary's; Ernest was feeling better, his sexual urges had revived, could she come to Rochester? Love on prescription. In his cell-like room, they lay together on his narrow bed. "Like Africa," she said to him, as shuffling inmates pushed through the door, "hollowed-eyed men looking for something we could not give them," so she described them in a bereft bit of poetry in her incriminating prose. Ernest, she noted, seemed to accept the situation as part of his incarceration. (Only a year and a half earlier, he had written, "Without pride I would not wish to continue to live nor to write.") Then, a day or two after their sad tryst, Mary was told that he was well enough to go home. Mary, amazed, knowing that he must have fooled the doctors, seeing him standing there in the doctor's office, in his dress suit, grinning like a Cheshire cat, was unable to protest. Time was against them.

Time was, when he was a man in control of his life, a man in charge, commanding approval, admiration . . .

Time was, when cruising outward on the waters of the great blue river, the bow of the *Pilar* slapping against the waves, he had heard the slithering, silk-tearing noise of flying fish leaping, watched the man-of-war hawk dipping toward the waves as they broke . . .

It was late June, and in the heady summer the trees were in full leaf along the Big Wood River. In Ketchum he seemed eager to greet the friends who came round on Saturday nights, but his interest soon waned and he sat in a corner saying nothing. On July 1, a Saturday night, when Ernest and Mary went to a restaurant with a friend, Hemingway spotted two men at a table across the room and asked who they were and was told they were salesmen. "They're F.B.I.," he muttered. That night as they were undressing for bed, Mary sang "*Tutti mi chiamano bionda,*" and he joined in on the refrain. That night, as he had been doing, he slept in his back bedroom instead of in the front bedroom with Mary.

It must have been then, as he lay waiting for sleep, waiting for morning, that the resolve became fixed in his mind like a remembrance of some brave moment in the past ("And is dying hard, daddy?" a small boy in an imagined scene had asked his father years before), and whatever a man might think on the way down, Hemingway must have thought that next morning as he padded down the stairs, early, stepping softly so as to make no sound. Reaching for the keys on the kitchen windowsill ("No one had a right to deny a man access to his possessions," Mary had reasoned), he went to the locked storage room in the basement, turned the key, and picked up the double-barreled shotgun that he had used so often it might have been a friend. With a deft hand he inserted the shells and then, moving stealthily, climbed the stairs and passed into the foyer. He bent toward the certainty of the hard steel and, setting his forehead against the muzzle, pulled the trigger (and Mary, stirring in her sleep, heard what sounded like a bureau drawer slamming shut), and Hemingway, whatever else he knew, knew for all time that the questions he had asked in a lifetime were answered, and those that remained were no longer of any consequence.

Acknowledgments

Every biographer of Hemingway stands indebted, in some way, to the late Carlos Baker, who did the solid groundwork with his 1969 biography and later provided the vital resource of the *Selected Letters.* Carlos was particularly generous in his encouragement and in providing documentary material and information when I began work on this biography some seven years ago and I am grateful for his help. I am grateful, too, for the continuing work of Michael Reynolds, whose painstakingly detailed study of Hemingway is proceeding volume by volume; it has provided a safeguard against unfortunate errors. Paul Smith's *A Reader's Guide to the Short Stories of Ernest Hemingway,* although it was published late in my research, is the essential sourcebook for anyone trying to work out the troublesome chronological sequence of the composition of Hemingway's short stories in conjunction with the details of his life. Other biographers and critics — whether or not one agrees with their interpretations of the life or of the work — inevitably play a part in the shaping of one's own biographical decisions, and their works are duly cited in the notes and bibliography. But from the beginning, this study of Hemingway was meant to be the final volume of a trilogy that examined what seemed to me then, and is even more so now, the miraculous outcropping of genius and achievement in literature, art, music, theater, publication, architecture, and design which created the long span of the modern movement. It was Hemingway's role and his achievement in that context — his relationships with other literary and artistic personalities like Stein and Pound, as well as to the events of his time — that particularly concerned me.

Every biographer is indebted to the curators, scholars, and staff members of the institutions and archives which house the documentary records of the past. The Hemingway Collection in the John F. Kennedy Library in Boston is the most valuable single resource on the work and life of Hemingway, and my feeling is that the related papers and manuscript drafts there constitute a resource that will, in time and with further study, afford us an even deeper understanding of Hemingway's character and a truer measure of the life of a great writer in its particular relationship to the work. My suspicion is that Hemingway deliberately salvaged his diaries, papers, letters, and the many drafts of his stories and novels, transporting them across oceans and from residence to residence, for the express purpose of making them available for scholarly study, though he had no high regard for the academic mind. (It was Mary Hemingway's recollection, in a 1973 interview, that, at one point, Hemingway himself had considered leaving his papers to the New York Public Library so that they would be available for such study.) In this narrative, my interpretation of the relationship of Hemingway's life to the work, his personal relationships with his contemporaries, his habit of using and referring to them in the early drafts of his novels and stories, has benefited from this resource. I want to thank Joan L. O'Connor, former Curator of the Hemingway Collection at the Kennedy Library, and Megan Desnoyers, the present Curator, for their assistance and encouragement. Lisa Middents, Associate Curator of the Hemingway Collection, and, more recently, Stephen Plotkin have with great patience and persistence answered queries and supplied information. Alan Goodrich of the Kennedy Library photographic archives has also answered questions and put me on to photographic materials.

During the twenty and more years that I have been engaged in this trilogy, Donald Gallup, former curator of the Yale Collection of American Literature at the Beinecke Library at Yale, has been unfailingly helpful and supportive. And I am grateful to David Schoonover, his successor, and to Patricia Willis, the new Curator, for their interest in and support for this project. I also owe thanks to the staff members at the Beinecke, but particularly so to Stephen Jones, who, for over fifteen years, has gone out of his way to track down uncatalogued or difficult-to-find material. At the Princeton University Libraries, Ann Van Arsdale was especially helpful during the research on *Invented Lives* and was equally obliging during research jaunts for the Hemingway volume. I want to thank, as well, Jean Preston, the former Curator of Manuscripts, and Don C. Skemer, the present Curator.

For responses to queries, for providing needed documentary material and photographs, or for suggestions on sources or dealing with the necessary rights and permissions, I thank Peter Antheil; Deonna M. Ard of the Kansas City Public Library; Mel Arden; Elizabeth B. Carter; the late Malcolm Cowley; Gary Cummings and Marcy Barstow of the Henry Carter Hull Library of Clinton, Connecticut; Gioia Diliberto; Mrs. John Dos Passos; Hugh Ford; Katharine Hepburn; Robert Hull of the Manuscripts Department of the Alderman Library, University of Virginia; John Idol, Jr.; Waring Jones; Robert W. Lewis; Debbie and Doug Miles, who salvaged a valuable but badly damaged computer disk; James Nagel; Kerry Prior; Carley Robison, archivist at Knox College, Archives and Manuscript Collections; Margaret F. Sax of the Watkinson Library, Trinity College, Hartford; Charles Scribner, Jr.; George Seldes; G. Thomas Tanselle; Henry Serrano Villard; Alex Walker; Lydia Zelaya.

Barbara Williams at Houghton Mifflin was patient and thorough in bringing some needed order and authority to the many vagaries of copyright permissions. And I especially thank John Hemingway, who, in the course of granting permission to quote from Hadley Hemingway Mowrer's published and unpublished letters, took time to talk about the "spookiness" of deep-sea fishing.

Biography, inevitably, leads a biographer into strange pastures. Paul Whitehead of the Peabody Museum in New Haven and Pat Brunauer of the Museum of Natural History in New York have provided information on the odd sexual nature of the spotted hyena. Both Ed Migdalski, former professor in the Department of Zoology at Yale, and Terry Frady of the New England Fisheries Center at Woods Hole, Massachusetts, provided information on the sexual odysseys of the jewelfish and groupers. And Eric Prince of the South East Fisheries Center in Miami, Florida, was the source of information that countered Hemingway's speculations about the sex lives of the marlin in the deeper waters of the Gulf Stream.

There are the personal debts. It was Nan Talese, my former editor at Houghton Mifflin, who broached the subject of a Hemingway biography and thereby provided me with the opportunity to complete this "Lost Generation" trilogy. I want to thank, too, Janet Silver, my editor at Houghton Mifflin, for her sensitive editing and commentary on the various drafts of the manuscript, and John Sterling, editor in chief, for his continuing support. Jayne Yaffe did the often tedious but altogether vital job of copy-editing a long manuscript with charm and good humor. John Blades helped me by dredging up copies of Hemingway's review of Gertrude Stein's *Geography and Plays* and the news clippings of the Wanda Stopa affair from the *Chicago Tribune* files. John Rewald provided information on the exhibition of Cézanne works that Hemingway saw at Bernheim-Jeunes in Paris in March 1924. Sue Davidson Lowe offered her files of the *Transatlantic Review* and *The Dial.* I also want to thank my literary agent, Georges Borchardt, for keeping the enterprise afloat, and Denise Shannon for looking after my best interests.

And at the end of this long project it seems appropriate, at last, to thank those to whom I need to express a long overdue gratitude:

Albert Capaccio, over the years, has done many favors and been the best of company. It was Mitchell Levitas who, twenty-four years ago, as an editor of the *New York Times Magazine,* by front-paging my first article for the magazine section (on Gertrude Stein and her artist friends), launched me into what became a career in biography. There are the high school teachers in Gloucester, Massachusetts — Hortense Harris and Frances McGrew of the English Department, Henry Rosen of the French Department — who began my interest in just about everything that I now write about. Hilton Kramer, in the course of a friendship that dates back to high school, has voluntarily furthered my career in several ways. I thank him for his generosity. My cousin June Mellow has been a distinct influence in my life from childhood through our high school years and beyond. It was in high school that we first began reading Freud and Joyce together and started wondering about the incalculable mysteries of human nature. But my debt to her is given in more eloquent terms on the dedication page. And there is a debt to the wide-ranging members of the Capaccio-Attanasia-Garmendi-Montalbano-Mangano-Quigley clan, an extended second family, who have provided steady interest in my work and the perennial hospitality of well-remembered family feasts at Christmas and Easter year after year.

Lastly, my debt to Augie Capaccio, who throughout this project has done dog work as transcriber, researcher, traveling companion, copyreader, part-time editor, and loyal supporter. He has, from time to time, even managed to get a semireclusive hedgehog to check out the fox's broader terrain.

In my family, friends, and career I have been a very lucky man.

Notes

Abbreviations

SA	Sherwood Anderson
CB	Carlos Baker
JDP	John Dos Passos
FSF	F. Scott Fitzgerald
CEH	Clarence Edmonds Hemingway
EH	Ernest Hemingway
GHH	Grace Hall Hemingway
HR, HRH, HRM	Hadley Richardson, Hadley Richardson Hemingway, Hadley Richardson Mowrer
MW, MWH	Mary Welsh, Mary Welsh Hemingway
AVK	Agnes von Kurowsky
RMcA	Robert McAlmon
MP	Maxwell Perkins
EP	Ezra Pound
WS	William Smith
GS	Gertrude Stein
ABT	Alice B. Toklas
EW	Edmund Wilson
AFTA	*A Farewell to Arms*
AMF	*A Moveable Feast*
ARIT	*Across the River and Into the Trees*
DIA	*Death in the Afternoon*
FWTBT	*For Whom the Bell Tolls*
GOE	*The Garden of Eden*
GHOA	*Green Hills of Africa*
NAS	*The Nick Adams Stories*
OMATS	*The Old Man and the Sea*
SAR	*The Sun Also Rises*
SL	*Ernest Hemingway: Selected Letters* (edited by Carlos Baker)
SSEH	*The Short Stories of Ernest Hemingway*
THAHN	*To Have and Have Not*
TOS	*The Torrents of Spring*
JFK	Hemingway Collection, John F. Kennedy Library
PUL	Princeton University Library, Department of Rare Books and Special Collections
YCAL	Yale Collection of American Literature, Beinecke Rare Book and Manuscript Library, Yale University

The Country Is Always True

PAGE

3 "For years it had obsessed him": *SSEH*, 152.
"He had seen the world change": Ibid, 164.

4 "After all . . . there is the career": Stein, *The Autobiography of Alice B. Toklas*, 266.
"I don't like to leave anything": *SSEH*, 156.
"Of the place where he had been a boy": *NAS*, 5.

6 "He is contented": GHH scrapbooks, JFK.
"He comes and slaps you": Baker, *Ernest Hemingway: A Life Story*, 4.
"'Fraid a nothing!": GHH scrapbooks, JFK; Meyers, *Hemingway*, 9.
"not in the regular discharge": Ibid., 579.

7 "You tend to your practicing": Sanford, *At the Hemingways*, 54.
"anytime you could wake Grant": EH to Robert Cantwell, August 25, 1950; *SL*, 710.

8 "But do you really see it?": Sanford, *At the Hemingways*, 20.
"Suddenly the flower": Ibid.

10 "But I have you children": Ibid., 58.
"dear boy" . . . "the blessed doctor": Ibid., 15.
"When he first thought about him": *NAS*, 257.

11 "played with small china tea sets": Sanford, *At the Hemingways*, 62.

12 "Chumpy dear, this boy": Ibid., 12.
"the frayed end of a rope": Ibid., 5.
"Your Daddy loves you and prays": CEH to EH, July 18, 1907, JFK.
"I am so pleased and proud": CEH to EH, July 20, 1915, JFK.

13 "with onion on her breath": Sanford, *At the Hemingways*, 34.

15 "My First Sea Vouge": Baker, *A Life Story*, 12.

16 "were going through a period of great religious fervour": MS. 194-1, JFK.
"the disgrace or extinction": Ibid.
"too terrible even to be warned against": Ibid.
"high, gallant, hooked purple nose": Ibid.
"It seemed strange that any thing": Ibid.

17 "haven of refuge": Max Westbrook, "Grace under Pressure" in Nagel, *Ernest Hemingway: The Writer in Context*, 84.
"The best thing we raise": Miller, *Ernie*, 23.

18 "My precious boy, a 'real boy'": GHH scrapbooks, JFK.
"All Four Children": Miller, *Ernie*, 20.

19 "and I remember": *NAS*, 147.
Indian artifacts: See Meyers, *Hemingway*, 21.
"I've been cleaning": *NAS*, 147.
"The best arrowheads": Ibid., 148.

20 "Dearest Muv": Reynolds, *The Young Hemingway*, 79.
In 1908, she funded: Sanford, *At the Hemingways*, 112.

21 "Do you want me to let": GHH to CEH, October 17, 1908; Max Westbrook, "Grace under Pressure" in Nagel, *The Writer in Context*, 88.
Hemingway's high school grades: Meyers, *Hemingway*, 581n.
"Your dad is having": CEH to EH, October 12, 1910; Baker, *A Life Story*, 11.
"Once I remember": Sanford, *At the Hemingways*, 134.
"bachelor friends": Baker, *A Life Story*, 19.

22 "The Old Brute": Ibid.

"the Great Physician": Sanford, *At the Hemingways,* 127.
"Leads to hell": Ibid., 143.
According to Grace's memory album: Miller, *Ernie,* 70.
"No particular prize": Mrs. Robert Craig Corlett to Charles Fenton, June 10, 1952, Charles Fenton papers, YCAL.
"All his bachelor friends": Baker, *A Life Story,* 19.

23 "There was one summer": Sanford, *At the Hemingways,* 99.
"from cover to cover": Ibid., 134.
"Emerson, Hawthorne, Whittier": *GHOA,* 21.
"They had minds, yes": Ibid.

24 "dignified, rather quiet, unexpressive man": Sanford, *At the Hemingways,* 137.
"was a very frank": Fenton, *The Apprenticeship of Ernest Hemingway,* 7.
"more interested": Ibid., 8.
"She has ripe eyes": Fannie Biggs to Charles Fenton, February 24, 1952, Charles Fenton papers, YCAL.

25 "I never saw any of the family": Ibid.
"was recognized": Arthur Bobbitt to Charles Fenton, May 13, 1952, Charles Fenton papers, YCAL.

26 "After a gasping, breathless": Montgomery, *Hemingway in Michigan,* 45.
"It is the judgment": Ibid.
"a pusson of color": Ibid., 48.

27 "It was really a very neat job": Ibid., 52.

The Two Good-byes

28 "He was a beautiful shot": *By-Line,* 188.
"Dad had keen, piercing eyes": Miller, *Ernie,* 97.
"Don't tell": CEH to EH, July 8, 1907, JFK.

29 "Sure" . . . "Cheyenne?": EH to Bernard Berenson, March 20–22, 1953; *SL,* 815.
"is not the redskin": Montgomery, *Hemingway in Michigan,* 51.

30 "She's a good kid": Ibid.
"I never saw any evidence": Miller, *Ernie,* 26.
"lay back, we want to talk private": Ibid.

31 "Nick . . . felt hollow and happy": *NAS,* 29.

32 "quite a time": Ibid., 31.
"I just heard them threshing around": Ibid., 32.
"In the morning": Ibid., 33.
"One little Injun": Paul Smith, "The Tenth Indian and the Thing Left Out" in Nagel, *The Writer in Context,* 69. I am indebted, obviously, to Smith's thorough examination of "Ten Indians," pp. 53–74, though the more general conclusions here are my own.

33 "Dear God, for Christ's sake": MS. 729, JFK.
"a certain vague loneliness": "The Art of the Short Story," *The Paris Review* (Spring 1981), 97.
"His father came back to him": *NAS,* 264–65.
"His father had summed up": Ibid., 259.
"I've seen him": Smith, *A Reader's Guide to the Short Stories of Ernest Hemingway,* 309.

34 "I no mind Billy": *NAS,* 261.
"Son a bitch": Ibid., 263.

"Make plenty baby what the hell": Ibid., 264.
"Could you say she did": Ibid., 266. In another unused fragment, Nick tells his son about Trudy: "She / had a baby / went away to be a hooker": MS. 382, JFK.

37 "Oh, Lord, give up Thy dead": Ludington, *John Dos Passos,* 266.
"Ernest was a husky, sharp-eyed kid": William Smith, "The Hunter's Eye," YCAL.
"It took an old pal": Ibid.

38 "change-work": Donald St. John, "Hemingway's Bill Gorton" in Sarason, *Ernest Hemingway and the Sun Set,* 172.
"to keep the feel of it": William Smith, "The Hunter's Eye," YCAL.
"penal servitude": Donald St. John, "Hemingway's Bill Gorton" in Sarason, *Sun Set,* 167.

39 "I may stay up here": EH to Anson Hemingway, August 6, 1917; *SL,* 1.
"is just as headstrong": CEH to GHH, August 12, 1917; Max Westbrook, "Grace under Pressure" in Nagel, *The Writer in Context,* 89.
"very glad to hear": CEH to EH, September 18, 1917, JFK.
"all crippled up": EH to CEH, September 19, 1917; *SL,* 1.
"I wanted to hire": Ibid., 2.

40 "He had told his father": *NAS,* 265.
"May the Lord watch": *FWTBT,* 405.

41 "His father had been": Ibid., 405–406.
"a stern disciplinarian": Fenton, *Apprenticeship,* 33.
"Use short sentences": *Star* copy style in Bruccoli, *Ernest Hemingway: Cub Reporter,* n.p.

42 "the best rules I ever learned": *Conversations with Ernest Hemingway,* 21.
"He liked action": Fenton, *Apprenticeship,* 34.
"You covered crime, usually small": Ibid., 35.
"the Union depot, hotel life": Thomson, *Virgil Thomson,* 3.
"Yankee territory, windy and dry": Ibid., 4.
"The surgeon opened": Bruccoli, *Cub Reporter,* 28.
"'It was just a friend of mine, boss'": Ibid., 30.

43 "Wops . . . I can tell": *SSEH,* 253.
"awful lust": Ibid., 492.
"He was a big, good-natured": Fenton, *Apprenticeship,* 36.
"Working under Pete": EH to Charles Fenton, July 29, 1952; *SL,* 775.
"Every newspaper man I knew": Fenton, *Apprenticeship,* 37.

44 "No stream of consciousness nonsense": Ibid., 41. Lionel Moise to George T. Bye, n.d. but ca. May 1952, per letter from Bye to Charles Fenton, May 23, 1952, Charles Fenton papers, YCAL.
Moise and Dorothy Day: See Miller, *Dorothy Day,* 124ff.
"the fastest man on a typewriter": MS. 553, JFK; also, "He drove": Baker, *A Life Story,* 35.
"I never, to my knowledge": EH to Charles Fenton, July 29, 1952, *SL,* 774.

45 "Like all real writers": Lionel Moise to George T. Bye, n.d. but ca. May 1952, per letter from Bye to Charles Fenton, May 23, 1952, Charles Fenton papers, YCAL.
"Don't let anyone": Fannie Biggs to Charles Fenton, February 24, 1952, Fenton papers, YCAL.
"When I get a little excited": Brumback, "With Hemingway Before *A Farewell to Arms*" in Bruccoli, *Cub Reporter,* 3.

“We all have that bad eye”: Sanford, *At the Hemingways,* 156–57.
Home Guard: See EH to Family, November 19, 1917, *SL,* 2.

46 “They are the regular army stuff”: EH to Dad and Mother, December 6, 1917; Villard and Nagel, *Hemingway in Love and War,* 202.
“very aggressive and opinionated”: Carl Edgar to Charles Fenton, April 13, 1952, Charles Fenton papers, YCAL.
“Sometimes I think”: Bruccoli, *Cub Reporter,* 5.
“Now dry those tears”: EH to GHH, January 16, 1918; *SL,* 3.

47 “Now Mother, I got awfully angry”: Ibid., 4.
“Dear Mither . . . a multitude of starving”: EH to GHH, March 2, 1918; Ibid., 4–5.

48 “He came back”: *Conversations,* 21.
“Your good letter rec’d”: CEH to EH, April 17, 1918, JFK.
“Dear Old Kid”: GHH to EH, April 17, 1918, JFK.
“I sure was glad”: EH to Dear Folks, April 19, 1918; *SL,* 5.

49 “If it comes to a death notice”: Fannie Biggs, “Memories of Ernest Hemingway,” YCAL.

50 “The heart of Greenwich Village”: EH to Family, May 14, 1918; *SL,* 6.
“from the Harlem River”: Ibid., 7.
“I do trust you will think twice”: GHH to EH, May 16, 1918, JFK.

51 “PLEASE CONSIDER MOST SERIOUSLY”: CEH to EH, May 16, 1918, JFK.
“You could do”: CEH to EH, May 18, 1918, JFK.
“It reminded me so of you, Ernest”: GHH to EH, May 18, 1918, JFK.
“Cheer up Ye old Pop”: EH to CEH, May 19, 1918, JFK. (Grace’s message, perhaps, had crossed in the mail; Hemingway did not mention it.)

52 “Your wire explaining the ‘joke’”: CEH to EH, May 19, 1918, JFK.
“but I have been out to see Mae”: EH to Dale Wilson, May 18 [misdated May 19], 1918; *SL,* 8.
“by virtue of his manly form”: Ibid.

53 “They did a good business”: MS. 340, JFK.
“I have to do that”: Ibid.
“I used to have a lot of fun”: MS. 341, “Crime and Punishment,” JFK.
“Thirty seven dollars”: MS. 340, JFK.

54 “so hot and brown to scald”: Ibid.
“Dear Boy no one knows”: GHH to EH, May 20, 1918, JFK.

And Wounds Don’t Matter

55 “Count Galinski and Count Horcinanowitz”: EH to Family [ca. May 27, 1918]; *SL,* 9.
“She had blonde hair”: *NAS,* 137.

56 “You’ll get better wine”: Ibid., 141.
“He’s not like us”: Ibid., 142.
“That isn’t what I mean”: Ibid.
“Sure. If she loved you”: Ibid.
“not as quaint and interesting as Bordeaux”: EH to Family, June 5, 1918; Griffin, *Along With Youth,* 64.

57 “A terrible scene greeted us”: Milford Baker diary, Friday, June 7, 1918, Carlos Baker papers.

"I must admit, frankly": *DIA,* 136.
"I recall one or two of us": Ibid.

58 "After the first shock": Milford Baker diary, Friday, June 7, 1918, Carlos Baker papers.
At Schio: See Milford Baker diary, Ibid.
"God they are a nasty crew": Dos Passos, *The Fourteenth Chronicle,* 183.

59 "joyful at the idea of going": Ibid., 186.
"a wonderful lot of souvenirs": EH to Dear Folks, July 21, 1918; Villard and Nagel, *In Love and War,* 172.

60 "You see I'm ranked a soto Tenente": EH to Ruth Morrison, ca. June 22, 1918; *SL,* 11.
"I crawled out over the top": Ibid.
"I died then": Malcolm Cowley, "A Portrait of Mr. Papa" in McCaffery, *Ernest Hemingway: The Man and His Work,* 47. As with many of the details of the various stories about the night of Hemingway's wounding, it is not clear whether there were two or three soldiers with him. See also "Now I Lay Me," *NAS,* 144; *Conversations,* 4; *AFTA,* 54.

61 "Gravely wounded": Lewis, "Hemingway in Italy," 224.
"I didn't carry anybody": *AFTA,* 63.
"They did a fine job": EH to Dear Folks, August 18, 1918; Villard and Nagel, *In Love and War,* 177.

62 "killed by a shell": Robert W. Lewis, "Hemingway in Italy," *Journal of Modern Literature* (May 1982), 215. See also Villard and Nagel, *In Love and War,* 22.
"How splendidly the Italians are fighting!": Reynolds, *Hemingway's First War,* 148.
"That trip to Milan": EH to James Gamble, December 12, 1923; *SL,* 108.
"Capt. Bates thought it was best": EH to Dear Folks, July 21, 1918; Villard and Nagel, *In Love and War,* 170.
"several wounded Italian soldiers": Hanneman, *A Comprehensive Bibliography,* H3.
"The concussion of the explosion": Theodore Brumback to the Hemingways, July 14, 1918, JFK, reprinted in Sanford, *At the Hemingways,* 162.
"I'm not near so much": Baker, *A Life Story,* 46.
"I do hope and pray": CEH to EH, July 17, 1918, JFK.

63 "Please believe that the Great Physician": CEH to EH, July 18, 1918, JFK.
"That is wise don't you think Dad?": EH to Dear Folks, July 21, 1918; Villard and Nagel, *In Love and War,* 170.
"coming on in rare shape": EH to GHH, July 19, 1918; Ibid., 172.
"The Italian I had with me": EH to Dear Folks, August 18, 1918; Ibid., 176.
"WOUNDED 227 TIMES": *Oak Leaves,* October 5, 1918; see Miller, *Ernie,* 84.
"I thank God for you": GHH to EH, September 15, 1918, JFK.
"hysterical with excitement": Sanford, *At the Hemingways,* 171.
"Anyway, don't worry about me": EH to CEH, September 11, 1918; Villard and Nagel, *In Love and War,* 183.

64 "And wounds don't matter": EH to Family, October 18, 1918; Ibid., 187.

"Killed Piave — July 8 — 1918": *Complete Poems,* 35; see the earlier version, MS. 534a, titled "Killed — San Dona di Piave; June 15, 1918," JFK.

65 "In Italy, when I was at the war there": "On Writing in the First Person," MS. 179a-1, JFK.

"Also Mom, I'm in love again": EH to GHH, August 29, 1918; Villard and Nagel, *In Love and War,* 181.

66 "I'm afraid I'm forgetting Daddy": AvK diary, June 19, 1918; Ibid., 52.

67 "simply full of personality": AvK diary, June 30, 1918; Ibid., 55.

"wonderful evening": AvK diary, July 2, 1918; Ibid., 56.

"Talk about Fate!": AvK diary, July 9, 1918; Ibid., 59.

"I'm glad my Amer. friends": AvK diary, July 11, 1918; Ibid., 59.

"It's so funny": AvK diary, July 13, 1918; Ibid., 60.

"The Capt. walked home": AvK diary, July 20, 1918; Ibid., 62.

68 "Sunday, July 21": AvK diary, July 21, 1918; Ibid., 62.

"This tempestuous Italian mode": AvK diary, July 22, 1918; Ibid.

"Another letter from Daddy": AvK diary, July 24, 1918; Ibid., 63.

"Cavie thrills over all the tidbits": Ibid.

"My Capt. grows even more ardent": AvK diary, July 26, 1918; Ibid., 63.

"Wednesday, July 31": AvK diary, July 31, 1918; Ibid., 65.

"a peach of a hospital": EH to Family, July 21, 1918; Ibid., 170.

69 "broken doll": Baker, *A Life Story,* 48.

"smarty": Reynolds, *First War,* 195.

"He always seemed to have": Ibid.

"ostensibly to call": AvK diary, August 2, 1918; Villard and Nagel, *In Love and War,* 65.

"Last night I had a lecture": AvK diary, August 4, 1918; Ibid., 66.

"is devoted to that man": AvK diary, August 8, 1918; Ibid., 67.

"a good-looking son-of-a-gun": Ibid., 8.

70 "younger sonning it in Italy": EH to GHH, August 29, 1918; Ibid., 179.

"got wet about wanting to see my wounds": Donaldson, *By Force of Will,* 188.

"You know how he was": Baker, *A Life Story,* 49.

"Oh, go out to dinner with the Captain": Reynolds, *First War,* 198.

"I thought this is some sort of place": Ibid.

"spent a ton": Ibid., 199.

71 "peach of a job": EH to Family, August 18, 1918; Villard and Nagel, *In Love and War,* 177.

"Saturday, August 10": AvK diary, August 10, 1918; Ibid., 68.

"but how the Kid worried": AvK diary, August 21, 1918; Ibid., 72.

72 "a whiff of beer": Ibid.

"Now Ernest Hemingway": AvK diary, August 25, 1918; Ibid.

"old affair": AvK diary, August 26, 1918; Ibid.

"that Ernie had been smitten": Villard and Nagel, *In Love and War,* 28.

"romance with Hem": Ibid.

"You had a great case on her": Baker, *A Life Story,* 50.

"mia ammalato": AvK diary, August 30, 1918; Villard and Nagel, *In Love and War,* 73.

"how little an act": AvK diary, September 11, 1918; Ibid., 78.

73 "gay" . . . "I didn't win a cent": AvK diary, September 12, 1918; Ibid.
"having a high old time": AvK diary, September 19, 1918; Ibid., 80.
"Lo'dy, Lo'dy, Goodness me": AvK diary, September 7, 1918; Ibid., 77.
"I would take out the pins": *AFTA*, 114.
"I think Hemingway and I": Reynolds, *First War*, 202.

74 "Maybe I am reforming him": AvK diary, September 13, 1918; Villard and Nagel, *In Love and War*, 78.
"at midnight as per order": AvK diary, September 25, 1918; Ibid., 82.
"Don't forget to come back to me": AvK to EH, September 25, 1918; Ibid., 93.
"This beats paradise": Brian, *The True Gen*, 24.
"one of the richest men in Italy": EH to Family, September 29, 1918; Villard and Nagel, *In Love and War*, 185.

75 "took charge of me": Ibid.
"to bring me up": EH to General Charles Lanham, September 11, 1950; *SL*, 715.
"My Kid came back tonight": AvK diary, September 30, 1918; Villard and Nagel, *In Love and War*, 84.
"Every time I try to tease him": AvK diary, October 7, 1918; Ibid., 86.
"And, Mister Kid, my dear": AvK to EH, [October 8, 1918]; Ibid., 96.
"He says he can't stand": AvK diary, October 13, 1918; Ibid., 88.

76 "an unprecedented performance": AvK diary, October 15, 1918; Ibid., 88.
"Perhaps that's why": AvK to EH, October 15, 1918; Ibid., 97.
"kept wishing I had you": AvK to EH, October 16, 1918; Ibid., 99.

77 "Dear old furnace man": AvK to EH, n.d.; Ibid., 94–95.
"Why Girls Leave Home": AvK to EH, October 17, 1918; Ibid., 100.
"Your Mrs. Kid": AvK to EH, October 21–22, 1918; Ibid., 108.
"Gosh — if you were only here": AvK to EH, October 17, 1918; Ibid., 101.
"Everything I see or read": AvK to EH, October 19, 1918; Ibid., 104.
"3 old pals": AvK to EH, October 16, 1918; Ibid., 99.
"the 3 original Campfire Girls": AvK to EH, October 8, 1918; Ibid., 97.
"But anyhow, you said": AvK to EH, October 16, 1918; Ibid., 99.
"Miss Jessup thinks": AvK to EH, October 21–22 [1918]; Ibid., 107.

78 "I like Miss Jessup, the day nurse": AvK diary, October 19, 1918; Ibid., 89–90.
"Don't let me gain you": AvK to EH, October 25, 1918; Ibid., 113.
"Give HER my best": GHH to EH, September 24, 1918, JFK.
"Last night I was wishing": AvK to EH, November 1, 1918; Villard and Nagel, *In Love and War*, 122.

79 "& I remember how you burst out": AvK to EH, November 5–6, 1918; Ibid., 127.
"Yours of the 4th": AvK to EH, November 7, 1918; Ibid., 128.
"Well it's all over!": EH to Dearest Family, November 11, 1918; Ibid., 189.
"The war to make the world safe": Ibid., 190.
"We trust you will be guided": CEH to EH, September 24, 1918, JFK.

80 "I am very happy indeed": AvK to EH, November 25, 1918; Villard and Nagel, *In Love and War*, 132.

"Please don't think I'm ashamed of you": AvK to EH, November 28, 1918; Ibid., 133.
"up at the front": EH to Dear Folks, November 28, 1918; Ibid., 193.

81 "Viva la Pace": MS. 604, JFK.
"We were in a garden at Mons": *SSEH,* 203.
"Dearie me": AvK to EH, December 1, 1918; Villard and Nagel, *In Love and War,* 135.

82 "My idea was": Kert, *The Hemingway Women,* 63–64.
"I sometimes wish": AvK to EH, December 1, 1918; Villard and Nagel, *In Love and War,* 135.
"and every now & then": AvK to EH, December 8, 1918; Ibid., 138.
Details of trip to Treviso: See EH to Dear Folks, December 11, 1918; Ibid., 194.
"I'd hoped to get back to Paris": AvK to EH, December 10, 1918; Ibid., 139.

83 "I wrote to my mother": AvK to EH, December 13, 1918; Ibid., 140.
"For a while I was going": EH to Dear Folks, December 11, 1918; Ibid., 195.
"So I'm going to hit the States": EH to WS, December 13, 1918; *SL,* 20.
"Every minute that I'm away": Ibid.
"Your news was somewhat startling": AvK to EH, December 16, 1918; Villard and Nagel, *In Love and War,* 143.
"It's strange how circumstances": AVK to EH, December 15, 1918; Ibid., 142.
"Be nice, now": AvK to EH, December 20, 1918; Ibid., 145.

84 "Your steady is here": AvK to EH, January 9, 1919; Ibid., 153.
"Now the only thing lacking": James Gamble to EH, December 11, 1918, JFK.
duke of Bronte: See EH to Charles T. Lanham, September 11, 1950; *SL,* 715.
"except a bedroom window": Reynolds, *First War,* 204–205.

85 "when drunk I boasted": *Complete Poems,* 75.
"If I'm doleful": AvK to EH, December 31, 1918; Villard and Nagel, *In Love and War,* 147. I am indebted to the private collector who owns this and several more of the subsequent letters (and who wishes to remain anonymous) for his cooperation in unraveling the mystery of Agnes's last meeting with Hemingway.
"superior officer": Ibid., 148.

86 "You know I wouldn't promise": AvK to EH, January 7, 1919; Ibid., 152.
"I'm beginning the New Year": AvK to EH, January 1, 1919; Ibid., 148.
"particularly dull and uninteresting": Ibid., 149.
"So now when you get blue": Ibid., 148.
"You were a dear last night": Ibid., 149.
"Capt. Moore was teasing me": AvK to EH, December 31, 1918; Ibid., 147.
"I forgot to tell you": AvK to EH, January 7, 1919; Ibid., 152.

87 "a spoiled child": AvK to EH, March 7, 1919; Ibid., 163.
"This was the first [spring] day": January 21 [1919]; Ibid., 158.
"to escape the R.C. censor": AvK to EH, January 6, 1919; Ibid., 151.
"Hence, we suffered": Ibid., 150.

The Art of the Short Story

88 "Has 227 Wounds": *Conversations,* 1–2.
"Worst Shot-up Man": Hanneman, *A Comprehensive Bibliography,* H8.
"Here boy!": Sanford, *At the Hemingways,* 177.

89 "It was pretty glorious": Leicester Hemingway, *My Brother, Ernest Hemingway,* 53.
"brain food": EH to James Gamble, March 3, 1919; *SL,* 22.
"Smoke that, kid": Miller, *Ernie,* 89.
"Don't be afraid to taste": Sanford, *At the Hemingways,* 184.

90 "so I would not be lonely": EH to Arthur Mizener, June 2, 1950; *SL,* 697.
"There was some laughter": Frank Platt, from a transcript of a panel discussion on Hemingway's Oak Park years, given at Triton College, River Grove, Illinois, September 24, 1974, Carlos Baker papers.
"Hemingway, we hail you": *Conversations,* 5.
"He had been shot in the chest": Ibid., 3.
"When the thing exploded": Ibid., 4.
"like a snowball, so hard": Ibid.
"was conferred personally": Ibid.

91 "You've let this sort of thing": Sanford, *At the Hemingways,* 187.
"They've tried to make a hero": EH to James Gamble, March, 3, 1919; *SL,* 21.
"Every minute of every day": Ibid.

92 "I've written some darn good things": Ibid., 22.
"the great amourist": MS. 834, JFK; Reynolds, *Young Hemingway,* 58.
"soul-searing": "Ash Heel's Tendon," Griffin, *Along With Youth,* 179.

93 "'Wop?' asked Graves": "The Mercenaries," Ibid., 106.
"blue-black hair": Ibid., 109.
"Carissima!": Ibid., 110.
"one of those little 7.65 mm.": Ibid., 111.

94 "a little tenente": AvK to EH, January 15–16, 1919; Carlos Baker papers.
"We all worked": AvK to EH, January 21, 1919; Villard and Nagel, *In Love and War,* 157.
"Sometimes I think": Ibid., 158.
"is giving me a desperate rush": AvK to EH, February 3, 1919; Ibid., 159.
"the wildest of them all": AvK to EH, February 15, 1919; Ibid., 161.

95 "I can't begin to keep up with you": AvK to EH, March 1, 1919, Ibid., 162.
"One arm is paralyzed": Ibid.
"Oh, I'm going to the dogs": Ibid.
"very *cattiva* tonight": Ibid., 163.
"because we always seemed": AvK to EH, March 7, 1919; Ibid., 163.
"Then — & believe me": Ibid.
"show what a man you really are": Ibid., 164.

96 "very gentle, a gentle, nice soul": Reynolds, *First War,* 209.
"Read it": Sanford, *At the Hemingways,* 188.
"I'll tell you the sad truth": Griffin, *Along With Youth,* 113.
"and Bill, I forgot all about religion": Ibid., 114.

"All entangling alliances": Ibid., 117.
"Poor Hemmy": James Gamble to EH, May 23, 1919, JFK.
"She has fallen out": EH to Howell Jenkins, June 16, 1919; *SL,* 25.
Carraciolo burned the letters: But see Reynolds, *First War,* 209. Agnes's statement there might be read as that Caracciolo demanded his own letters back and burned them. See also Agnes's statement in Brian, *The True Gen,* 29: "Caracciolo was very jealous; he threw away all the letters I had from Hemingway."

97 "very jolly": Reynolds, *First War,* 209.
Luz for Ag, etc.: See *SL,* 469; and Smith, *Reader's Guide,* 26. A manuscript version of the vignette, titled "Love" and begun in 1923, was cast as a first-person narrative, MS. 633, JFK. As an added precaution, Hemingway also wrote a disclaimer for the edition: "There are no real people in this volume; both the characters and their names are fictitious. If the name of any living person has been used, the use was purely accidental."

98 "They were all about": *SSEH,* 239.
"he should go home": Ibid., 240.
"It was understood he would not drink": Ibid.
"On the train from Padua to Milan": Ibid.
"I tried hard to make you": AvK to EH, March 7, 1919; Villard and Nagel, *In Love and War,* 163.
"and she had never known": *SSEH,* 240.
"The major did not marry her": Ibid.

99 "The major never married her": MS. 633, "Love," JFK.
"got a dose of the clap": See James Steinke in Reynolds, *Critical Essays on Ernest Hemingway's In Our Time,* 220.
"That's some of his writing": Brian, *The True Gen,* 28.
"I think I felt — more or less": Reynolds, *First War,* 204.

100 Agnes in Key West: Ibid., 182.
"he did not want to see his friends": *SSEH,* 240.
"and we foregather": EH to James Gamble, March 3, 1919; *SL,* 21.
"dope" . . . "I don't know": EH to Lawrence Barnett, April 30, 1919; Ibid., 24.

101 "was plagued with more sore throats": Leicester Hemingway, *My Brother,* 59.
"Fine country": EH to James Gamble, April [27?] 1919; Griffin, *Along With Youth,* 118.
"You birds better bring": EH to Howell Jenkins, July 16, 1919; *SL,* 27.
"priceless" . . . "Fever, I lost one": EH to Howell Jenkins, ca. September 15, 1919; Ibid., 29.
"coming home beat to the wide": "The Art of the Short Story," *The Paris Review* (Spring 1981), 88.

102 "the need for thinking": *SSEH,* 308.
"So the war": "The Art of the Short Story," *The Paris Review* (Spring 1981), 88.
"a little haven of refuge": Max Westbrook, "Grace under Pressure" in Nagel, *The Writer in Context,* 84.
"dear wife Grace Hall-Hemingway": Ibid., 85.
"the place became hateful": Ibid., 86.

103 "Some women cling to their husbands": Sanford, *At the Hemingways,* 197.
"Your father does not always": Ibid.
104 "so insane on the subject": Marcelline Hemingway to GHH, August 31, 1919; Reynolds, *Young Hemingway,* 81.
"No distance": Ruth Arnold to GHH, August 4, 1919; Ibid., 80.
"If your mental attitude": GHH to CEH, n.d.; Ibid., 80.
"androgynous": Ibid., 81.
105 "pot boilers": EH to Harvey Breit, July 3, 1956; *SL,* 861.
"The funny feature of the writing business": Baker, *A Life Story,* 68–69.
"Hope to God": Meyers, *Hemingway,* 50.
"ghastly dream": WS to EH, December 18, 1919, PUL.
"stuff" . . . "anent the Bayites": WS to EH, November 7, 1919; JFK.
106 "a whang — a pearl": WS to EH, November 13, 1919, JFK.
"But now most everyone": Griffin, *Along With Youth,* 125.
"the only regular fellow": Ibid., 124.
"After a while": Ibid.
107 "For Dutch Pailthorp": Reynolds, *First War,* 277.
108 "Fie on you": WS to EH, November 14, 1919, JFK.
"the gift of tongues": WS to EH, January 24, 1920, JFK.
"You know everything": *SSEH,* 208.
"I feel as though everything": Ibid.
"Did she go all right?": Ibid., 209.
"Bill didn't touch him, either": Ibid.
"without touching each other": Ibid.
109 "He lay there until he felt Bill's arm": Smith, *Reader's Guide,* 54.
"Once a man's married": *SSEH,* 220.
"I tell you, Wemedge": Ibid., 222.
"Nothing was finished": Ibid.
"None of it was important now": Ibid., 223.
110 "It was the kind of thing we read": Sarason, *Sun Set,* 164.
"I don't know. There's a difference": *SSEH,* 222.
"No. I don't honestly think": Sarason, *Sun Set,* 174.
111 "Liz liked Jim very much": *SSEH,* 179.
"The boards were hard": Ibid., 183.
"Oh, it isn't right": Ibid.
"Even Further Up in Michigan": Sarason, *Sun Set,* 175.
112 "more reasonable to die than to live": Baker, *A Life Story,* 66.
"engaged, or partly so": EH to Charles Fenton, October 9, 1952; *SL,* 786.
"the original Peruvian Doughnuts": EH to Howell Jenkins, December 20, 1919; Ibid., 30.
"So it doesn't look like": EH to Grace Quinlan, January 1, 1920; Ibid., 31.
113 "very young old soldiers": EH to Dorothy Connable, February 17, 1953; Ibid., 806.
"wonderful worthless servants": Ibid.
"one of the finest, loveliest": EH to Charles Fenton, October 9, 1952; Ibid., 786.
"exceptional child": Ibid.
"a great character builder": CEH to EH, February 4, 1920, JFK.

114 "I was very pleased": CEH to EH, April 13, 1920, JFK.
Cozy Curls: Griffin, *Along With Youth,* 131.
"introduced anger into art": *Dateline: Toronto,* 4.
"The Free shave etc. story": CEH to EH, March 20, 1920, JFK.
"You will be able to talk": *Dateline: Toronto,* 11.

115 "As long as I live": Fenton, *Apprenticeship,* 115.
"I did this for her": EH to Charles Fenton, October 9, 1952; *SL,* 787.
"Say, I renewed my youth": CEH to EH, May 9, 1920, JFK.
"You were awfully good to me": EH to Harriet Connable, June 1, 1920; *SL,* 34.
"Marcelline, my older sister": Ibid., 35.

A Life Without Consequences

116 "Do hope dear Ernest": CEH to EH, June 4, 1920, JFK.
"little Wop automatic": Ibid.

117 "Dear Ones at Windemere": CEH to Family, June 11, 1920; Leicester Hemingway, *My Brother,* 63.
"I will write to Ernest": CEH to GHH, June 13, 1920; Ibid.
"I heard three nominating speeches": CEH to EH, June 13, 1920, JFK.
"I had a letter from Ernest": CEH to GHH, June 16, 1920; Leicester Hemingway, *My Brother,* 63.
"92 Saturday, 94 Sunday": CEH to GHH, June 28, 1920; Ibid., 64.
"I advised him to go with Ted": CEH to GHH, July 18, 1920; Ibid., 64–65.

118 "took it for granted": CEH to GHH, July 21, 1920; Ibid., 65.
"In the last mail last night": CEH to GHH, July 25, 1920; Ibid.
"My dear Gracie" . . . "advising him he must move": CEH to GHH, July 26, 1920; Ibid.
"I so wish that Ernest": Ibid., 66.

119 "Your letter I handed to Ernest": GHH to CEH, July 28, 1920; Max Westbrook, "Grace under Pressure" in Nagel, *The Writer in Context,* 81–82.
"the air was *blue* with condemnations": Miller, *Ernie,* 67.
"Of course Ernest called me": GHH to CEH, July 27, 1920; Max Westbrook, "Grace under Pressure" in Nagel, *The Writer in Context,* 82.
"I called Ernest": Ibid., 81.

120 "Unless you, my son, Ernest": GHH to EH, July 27, 1920; Reynolds, *Young Hemingway,* 137–38. Grace also took the legalistic precaution of making a dated copy of the document: "Copy of a letter handed to Ernest Miller Hemingway, Tuesday July 27, 1920."
"Do not come back": Ibid., 138.
"He is a very unusual youth": CEH to GHH, July 28, 1920; Leicester Hemingway, *My Brother,* 66.
"the last act of his was his finish": CEH to GHH, July 30, 1920; Ibid., 67.

121 "Mother was glad of an excuse": EH to Grace Quinlan, August 8, 1920; *SL,* 37.
"Didn't we rate a great moon": Ibid., 36.
"In as much as there": CEH to EH, September 18, 1920, JFK.

122 "His lies were quite unimportant lies": *SSEH,* 244.

"In the war that I had known": Robert W. Lewis, "Hemingway in Italy," *Journal of Modern Literature* (May 1982), 236.
"A distaste for everything": *SSEH,* 243.

123 "Ernest is very much like me": Sanford, *At the Hemingways,* 198.
"all work is honorable": *SSEH,* 249.
"Interest in Mother's ideas": Reynolds, *Young Hemingway,* 137.

124 "Don't you love your mother": *SSEH,* 249–50.
"Krebs kissed her hair": Ibid., 250.
"There is a picture": Ibid., 243.

125 "complicated world of already defined": Ibid., 245.
"Krebs acquired the nausea": Ibid., 244.
"He did not want any consequences": Ibid., 245.
"Having been barred": EH to Howell Jenkins, September 16, 1920; *SL,* 38.

126 "At present the best rainbow trout": *By-Line,* 9.
"It being now decided": William Horne to EH, October 13, 1920; Griffin, *Along With Youth,* 138.

127 "propinquity": WS to CB, September 17, 1965, Carlos Baker papers.
"practice made *her*": Ibid.
"a good-looking young man": EH to Y. K. Smith, October 1, 1921; *SL,* 55.
"an intense feeling": Leicester Hemingway, *My Brother,* 71.

128 "hulky, bulky something masculine": Kert, *The Hemingway Women,* 86.
"would become a second rate": HR to EH, August 7, 1921, JFK.

129 "I sort of appealed to her": HR to EH, June 7, 1921, JFK.
"Hadley Richardson was here": EH to Grace Quinlan, November 16, 1920, YCAL.

130 "two rounds of Bronxes": EH to WS, November 25 [1920], PUL.
"What would have caused J. C. Odgar": Ibid.
"Came one Saturday night": EH to GHH, December 22, 1920; *SL,* 42.
"It's a very extra comfortable": Ibid.

131 "work like hell": EH to WS, ca. December 1920 [misdated 1918 or 1919], PUL.
"and gave us the cold dope": EH to GHH, January 10, 1921; *SL,* 44.
"I'd be much happier too": EH to HR, December 23, 1920, JFK. Hemingway's letters to Hadley during their courtship were presumably destroyed by Hadley after their divorce, an act she later regretted.
"a nawful good sport": HR to EH, December 20, 1918, JFK.
"Suppose when you tell me how nice Dick is": EH to HR, December 23, 1920, JFK.

132 "I was feeling so blue": HR to EH, January 1, 1921, JFK.
"corking little Irene": HR to EH January 8, 1921, JFK.
"Jim Gamble is great": EH to HR, December 23, 1920, JFK.
"Rome sounds so wonderful": HR to EH, January 1, 1921, JFK.
"Rather go to Rome": EH to James Gamble, ca. February 24, 1921; *SL,* 45.
"bold penniless dash to Wopland": HR to EH, January 12–13, 1921, JFK.
"I want to be your helper": HR to EH, January 12–13, 1921, JFK.
"I'm not at all the woman": HR to EH, February 8, 1921; Sokoloff, *Hadley,* 22.

133 "picked up and loved to death": Griffin, *Along With Youth,* 157.

"to be everything to you": HR to EH, April 27, 1921, JFK.
"Do you remember the morning": HR to EH, January 15, 1921, JFK.
"Ernest, *I* never have taken": HR to EH, November 25, 1920, JFK.
"It's about time": Griffin, *Along With Youth,* 160.
"thought out, not felt out": HR to EH, January 12–13, 1921, JFK.
Anderson would talk to a chair: See Anderson, *My Thirty Years' War,* 39.

134 Reading *Omar Khayyam:* See HR to EH, January 7, 1921, JFK.
"those two 'old fellows'": Griffin, *Along With Youth,* 165.
"bout the novel busting loose": HR to EH, April 20, 1921, JFK.
"My feeling for you": Ibid., JFK.
"I will give you a Corona": HR to EH, April 22, 1921, JFK.
"sheer gaiety": HR to EH, August 7, 1921, JFK.
"Kate says Nick is *mad* over you": HR to EH, July 14, 1921, JFK.
"Don['t] get too awfully lonesome ever": HR to EH, April 22, 1921, JFK.

135 "How many scarves of mine": HR to EH, May 1, 1921, JFK.
"Through the hot, pounding rhythm": *Complete Poems,* 33.
"the svelte jewess": Griffin, *Along With Youth,* 189.
"Very, very sorry": HR to EH, June 2, 1921, JFK. This portion of the letter is dated Thursday afternoon (June 2).
"It's amazing you happened": Griffin, *Along With Youth,* 190.

136 "At least she'll have lived": Sarason, *Sun Set,* 159.
"the wallop": EH to WS, April 28, 1921; *SL,* 48.
"She plays worse than ever": EH to WS, [ca. March 1921], PUL.
"Yen's words to me": Ibid., PUL.

137 "chorines" . . . "was the only person": HR to EH, April 3, 1921, JFK.
"stuttering with terror": Griffin, *Along With Youth,* 215.
"Ernest has written me": HR to GHH, June 12, 1921, JFK.
"We were not made to be friends": Kert, *The Hemingway Women,* 93.
"Suppose you want to hear": EH to Grace Quinlan, July 21, 1921; *SL,* 51.

138 "In your wide and diverse acquaintance": EH to Grace Quinlan, August 19, 1921; Ibid., 55.
"I think it is grand": Marjorie Bump to EH, July 12, 1921, PUL. The letter is signed "Red." Hemingway's letter to Grace Quinlan, August 1, 1920, says his sister Ursula was visiting Red. Clarence's letter to Grace Hemingway, July 30, 1920, says "I am glad that Ursula is having a few days at Marjorie Bump's. Hope she will not see Ernest." (Leicester Hemingway, *My Brother,* 67.) Red, then, is Marjorie Bump.
"Old dear — what's this?": HR to EH, July 7, 1921, JFK.
"dearest letter" . . . "all played unto you": HR to EH, July 13, 1921, JFK.
"so easily forthcoming": Ibid.
"warm weather pomes": HR to EH, July 14, 1921, JFK.
"It is cool at night": *Complete Poems,* 30.

139 "I'm awfully grateful": HR to EH, July 13, 1921, JFK.
"At night I lay with you": *Complete Poems,* 32.
"and talked and jibed": MS. 546, JFK.

141 "Many telegrams were received": Montgomery, *Hemingway in Michigan,* 195.

142 "probably well-thumbed correspondence": EH to Y. K. Smith, October 1, 1921; *SL,* 55.

"You can readily understand": Y. K. Smith to EH, ca. October 2, 1921; Ibid., 56.

The Mecca of Bluffers and Fakers

145 "Paris is cold and damp": EH to Howell Jenkins, December 26, 1921; *SL,* 60.
"What a town": EH to SA, ca. December 23, 1921; Ibid., 59.
"but you can find": EH to SA, March 9, 1920; Ibid., 62.
"about as long as little Traverse Bay": EH to WS, ca. December 20, 1921; Ibid., 58.

146 "Written a chunk": EH to Howell Jenkins, January 8, 1922; Ibid., 61.
"the deserted boomtowns of Nevada": *Dateline: Toronto,* 87.

147 "only local weather and not something": *AMF,* 7.
"All good books are alike": *By-Line,* 184.
"Will you and Mr. Hemingway": GS to HRH, n.d. [February] 1922, JFK.
"Sherwood has told us": HRH to GS [February 7, 1922], YCAL. Hadley wrote her acceptance on a Tuesday, for the following day. Since Hemingway's March 9 letter to Anderson says he had been seeing a lot of Stein, that would mean their first meeting would have taken place on Wednesday, February 8. The Wednesday prior to Hemingway's March 9 letter would have been March 8, only the day before, hardly allowing time enough for them to see a lot of each other. The earlier, February, date, therefore is the more creditable one, since Anderson, on March 13, wrote Stein, "I had a charming letter from Mr. Hemingway, stating how glad he is to know you." (SA to GS, March 13, 1922; *Sherwood Anderson/Gertrude Stein,* 19.) He could hardly be referring to Hemingway's March 9 letter: it would have taken much more than four days to receive a letter from France. Anderson's letter also indicates an earlier letter (not the March 9 one) from Hemingway to Anderson about his first meeting with Stein. Hemingway's passport indicates that he and Hadley had returned to Paris on February 2, 1922, in time for the February 8 meeting with Stein.

148 "It was like one of the best rooms": *AMF,* 14.
"beautiful eyes": Ibid.
"petrified": See HRH to EH, March 5, 1928, JFK.
"made one conversation": *AMF,* 14.

149 "Mr. Hemingway is an American writer": SA to GS, December 3, 1921; *Sherwood Anderson/Gertrude Stein,* 11.
"Gertrude Stein and me": EH to SA, March 9, 1922; *SL,* 62.
"We love Gertrude Stein": Ibid., 63.
"They are charming": GS to SA, [March? 1922]; *Sherwood Anderson/Gertrude Stein,* 18.
"rather foreign looking": Stein, *The Autobiography of Alice B. Toklas,* 261.

150 "A sentence is not emotional": Stein, *How to Write,* 23.
"He wanted to write like Cézanne painted": *NAS,* 239.
"one true sentence": *AMF,* 12.
"invaluable for analyzing anything": EH to EW, November 25, 1923; Wilson, *The Shores of Light,* 118.

151 "Soldiers like a fuss": Stein, *Geography and Plays,* 394.
"a rebuilding, an entire new recasting": Ibid. (Anderson preface), 8.

"It made a big hit with Gertrude": EH to SA, March 9, 1922; *SL*, 62.
"Madame, all our words": *DIA*, 71.
"wandering line" . . . "the manner for the matter": Stein, *The Autobiography of Alice B. Toklas*, 258.

152 "profoundly occupied": HRM to Charles Fenton, March 25, 1952, Charles Fenton papers, YCAL.
"direct, Kiplingesque": Stein, *The Autobiography of Alice B. Toklas*, 261.
"Begin over again and concentrate": Ibid., 262.
"*inaccrochable*": *AMF*, 15.
"She liked it about his mustache": MS. 799, JFK.
"She had . . . discovered many truths": *AMF*, 17.
"She's the best head I know": EH to WS, February 26, 1925, PUL.

153 "a fine old femme": EH to Howell Jenkins, March 20, 1922; *SL*, 65.
"I am hoping that you didn't": Mildred Aldrich to GS, March 21, 1922, YCAL.

154 "One has to keep going east": Colum, *Life and the Dream*, 263–64.
"enfeebled or adolescent Amurkn mind": EP to William Rose Benét, January 23, 1933; Pound, *Selected Letters*, 244.
"glared at one another": Edel, *Henry James, The Master*, 481.
"strange how all taint of art": Ibid.
"They will come no more": Carpenter, *A Serious Character*, 323.
"Mistrust any poet": Norman, *Ezra Pound*, 95.
"Vurry Amur'k'n": EP to Alice Henderson, [March 1913]; Pound, *Letters*, 14.

155 "the only hippopoetess": Norman, *Ezra Pound*, 155.
"the swirl of the prairie wind": EP to William Carlos Williams, November 10, 1917; Pound, *Letters*, 124.
"any new idea": Stock, *The Life of Ezra Pound*, 242.
"sort of great clot": Ibid.
"The literary life of Paris": *The Dial* (December 1920), 635.
"village explainer": Stein, *The Autobiography of Alice B. Toklas*, 246.

156 "the homely finish": Scofield Thayer to Alyse Gregory, July 30, 1921, *Dial* papers, YCAL.
"so awkward as unintentionally": Joost, *Ernest Hemingway and the Little Magazines*, 9.
"a splendidly built young man": Meyers, *Hemingway*, 84.
"pretty sporting of him": EH to SA, March 9, 1922; *SL*, 62.
"I believe some of the ideas": Kert, *The Hemingway Women*, 113.

157 "Ezra Pound sent": HRH to GHH [February 1922]; Sokoloff, *Hadley*, 50.
"the chap seems to have": EP to Scofield Thayer [February 1922], *Dial* papers, YCAL.
"enough young blood": Scofield Thayer to EP, March 5, 1922, *Dial* papers, YCAL.
"silly cantos": Scofield Thayer to Alyse Gregory, October 22, 1922, *Dial* papers, YCAL.
"poem including history": Kenner, *The Pound Era*, 360.
"Mankind lives in the few": Ibid., 330.

158 "The 'age demanded' chiefly": Pound, *The Selected Poems of Ezra Pound*, 62.
"The age demanded that we sing": *Complete Poems*, 53.
"which aims at filling the student's head": Stock, *Pound*, 236.

"two halves of what might have made": EP to William Carlos Williams, September 11, 1920; Pound, *Letters*, 160.

159 "sodomitical usurers": EP to EH, November 28, 1936; Ibid., 283.

"Celto-Kike": EH to EP, January 1, 1923; *SL*, 77.

"a 19 year old Bloomsbury kike intellectual": EH to EP, ca. May 15, 1924, YCAL.

Pound had seen only a half dozen: See Nagel, *The Writer in Context*, 181; based on EH to Charles Fenton, September 23, 1951, Charles Fenton papers, YCAL.

Together in Paris in fall: See EP to his father, October 30, 1922, YCAL, saying Hem back from Constantinople fed up even with Turks.

"distrust adjectives": *AMF*, 132.

"learned more about how to write": EH to EP, July 22, 1933, YCAL.

"There is also several stale jokes": EH to Arnold Gingrich, March 13, 1933; *SL*, 383.

"Erudition shouldn't show": EH to Malcolm Cowley, August 1952; James D. Brasch, "Invention from Knowledge: The Hemingway-Cowley Correspondence" in Nagel, *The Writer in Context*, 222–223.

160 "sold himself to the god dollar": Norman, *Ezra Pound*, 461.

"never knew one human being": Kenner, *The Pound Era*, 528.

"the 1922 Edition of E.M.H.": WS to EH, February 19, 1922; *SL*, 66n.

"the Madam" . . . "poisoning": EH to Howell Jenkins, March 20, 1922; Ibid., 64.

"Once he took a dislike": Milford, *Zelda*, 116.

"'Blood is thicker than water'": *Complete Poems*, 41.

161 "about eight hundred dollars worth": EH to Howell Jenkins, March 20, 1922; *SL*, 65.

"fonder of Stut than of Bill": Ibid.

"prehistoric": Y. K. Smith to Charles Fenton, May 17, 1952, Charles Fenton papers, YCAL.

"was that of being larger than the founder": Joost, *Little Magazines*, 42–43.

162 "almost instinctive": William Smith memoir, "The Hunter's Eye," Charles Fenton papers, YCAL.

"All the love went into fishing": *NAS*, 235.

163 J. C. Edgar on Bill Smith's breakdown: See undated [ca. March 1952] Edgar memoir, Charles Fenton papers, YCAL. Also Hemingway's coded reference to Smith as W.G., "recently recovered from manic depression which followed nervous breakdown," in *DIA*, 468.

"Bill forgave him": *NAS*, 234.

164 "heart-busted bunch": Sokoloff, *Hadley*, 32.

"The scum of Greenwich Village": *Dateline: Toronto*, 114.

"You can find anything": Ibid., 115.

"Paris is the Mecca": Ibid., 119.

"the canadian viewpoint": Stein, *The Autobiography of Alice B. Toklas*, 262.

"a super-Sodom and a grander Gomorrah": *Dateline: Toronto*, 117.

165 "It is from tourists who stop": Ibid., 89.

"Cook and Co. . . . a Famous London house": EH to Howell Jenkins, January 8, 1921; *SL*, 58.

"never having lived in New York": MS. 276A, JFK.

"I have seen the favourite crash": Baker, *A Life Story*, 90–91. See Reynolds, *Hemingway: The Paris Years,* 47–49, 95–97. The original version was apparently lost along with the "lost manuscripts" and rewritten in 1923. See also *Complete Poems,* xxii, xxiii.

166 "my sister born beyond the sea": Fitch, *Sylvia Beach and the Lost Generation,* 145.
"half convent and half farm": Monnier, *The Very Rich Hours of Adrienne Monnier,* 13.
"but it is always he": Ibid., 90.

167 "brown eyes that were as alive": *AMF,* 35.
"Even the dead writers": Ibid.

168 "No one that I ever knew": Ibid.
"ugly and repugnant": Ibid., 20.
"do nothing that they are disgusted by": Ibid.
"You have to find someone": Virgil Thomson conversation with James Mellow.

169 "Paris was where the twentieth century was": Stein, *Paris France,* 11.
It was in Paris: it was what the cultural historian and archaeologist George Kubler would call a "good entrance." See Kubler, *The Shape of Time,* 6.
"I don't know why it is": Dupin, *Miró,* 96.

170 "Sit down. You're just a best seller": McAlmon and Boyle, *Being Geniuses Together,* 34.
"a seismographic station": Ehrenburg, *People and Life,* 150.
"Like all the rest of the world": *Dateline: Toronto,* 98.
"ran with the idiot fringe": EH to Carlos Baker, November 22, 1951, Carlos Baker papers.

171 "Everyone just sits around": Field, *Djuna,* 116.
"a faintly sensitized, dried up old bitch": EH to Ernest Walsh, January 2, 1926; *SL,* 187.
"For we have thought the longer thoughts": *Complete Poems,* 34.
"her eager body's unimmortal flower": Kennedy, *Dreams in the Mirror,* 113.
"He, I may add": John Peale Bishop to EW, October 5, 1923, YCAL.

172 "E. E. Cummings married to": EH to EP, ca. May 2, 1924; *SL,* 114.
"Damn it all, midnight": Chisholm, *Nancy Cunard,* 86.
"What Broom and the Skyscraper Primitives": MS. 276a, JFK.
"the unlovely aftermath": Stearns, *The Confessions of a Harvard Man,* 203 (originally published as *The Street I Know*).
"self-conscious and self-assured": Ibid., 300.

173 "He has never let me down": Stearns, *The Confessions of a Harvard Man,* 367.
"It was a useless, silly life": Ibid., 277.
"the City of Dreadful Night": Crosby, *Shadows of the Sun,* 147.
"Dinners, soirees, poets": Crane, *Letters of Hart Crane,* 333.
"strange-acting and strange-looking breed": *Dateline: Toronto,* 114.

174 "enjoy life, without respecting it": Ibid., 118.
"with anything he could get his hands on": Sokoloff, *Hadley,* 56.
"sudden marvelous smile": Sarason, *Sun Set,* 149.
"This goddam newspaper stuff": EH to SA, March 9, 1922; *SL,* 62.
"'I did it,' said Cock Robin": Mary Hickok to Charles Fenton, May 7, 1954, Charles Fenton papers, YCAL.

175 "He tried to spit out the truth": *Complete Poems,* 39.

176 "I know monks masturbate": *Complete Poems,* 52.
"A letter from Ernest Hemingway": Joost, *Little Magazines,* 41.
"If George Antheil asks you": MS. 376a, JFK.
"Ernest would always give a helping hand": Bruccoli, *Scott and Ernest,* 166.

Chasing Yesterdays

177 "the casual and childish nature": *Dateline: Toronto,* 131.
178 "a masterpiece of tact and kindliness": Ibid., 155.
"coldly intellectual": Ibid., 156.
"had nothing to gain": Ibid., 155.
"the greatest compromiser": Ibid., 148.
"His charm, his fresh coloring": Ibid., 166.
"like the left hand one": Ibid., 166.
179 "Chicherin said to me": Ibid., 127.
"We are changing": Ibid.
"the dawn of a new era": Ibid., 167.
"I worked very hard": EH to CEH, May 2, 1922; *SL,* 66.
180 "the industrial dictator of Germany today": *Dateline: Toronto,* 155.
"black derby hat and his ready-tied neckties": Ibid., 156.
"the same sensation": Ibid.
"This is a *new* language": Seldes, *Witness to a Century,* 313. Seldes may be the source of this anecdote via Carlos Baker; the mistake may be that he was still there for the end of the conference when Steffens arrived, whereas Hemingway had left for Paris on April 27. It was at the later Lausanne conference that Hemingway and Steffens most probably met.
But Steffens, covering the conference: for dates, see Steffens, *The Letters of Lincoln Steffens,* vol. 2, 586ff. Hemingway's letter to his father from Paris is dated May 2, and he says he has been laid up for four days with a sore throat.
181 "has a very rich wife": *Dateline: Toronto,* 145.
"a big, jolly, middle-western college professor": Ibid.
"gentle and unassuming": Eastman, *Great Companions,* 43. For the history of the *Masses* and the *Liberator,* see O'Neill, *The Last Romantic.*
"all about how scared he had been": Max Eastman to Charles Fenton, February 3, 1952, Charles Fenton papers, YCAL.
"descriptions of scenes and incidents": Ibid.
182 "I have every word of it": Eastman, *Great Companions,* 45.
183 "Wasn't that an awful way": HRH to GS and ABT, May 13, 1922, YCAL.
"It is all fly fishing": EH to CEH, May 24, 1922; *SL,* 68.
"I believe I wanted Chink": Kert, *The Hemingway Women,* 119.
"alcoholic clairvoyance": EH to GS and ABT, June 11, 1922; *SL,* 69.
184 "has the quiet and peaceful look": *Dateline: Toronto,* 175.
"Mussolini was a great surprise": Ibid., 173.
"The crowd loves strong men": Denis Mack Smith, *Italy,* 397.
"The crowd is like a woman": Ibid.
185 "Severely wounded in the fighting": *Dateline: Toronto,* 173.
"a very good reason": Ibid. By 1938, Hemingway was more than ever convinced of Mussolini's fakery: "You have to know that he was not

hot stuff in the war . . . that he was never wounded in action but took advantage of slight wounds caused by the explosion of an Italian trench mortar to leave the front permanently early in the war." Stephens, *Hemingway's Nonfiction,* 192.
"the most beautiful moment in my life": Denis Mack Smith, *Mussolini,* 28.
"adventurer for all roads": Ibid., 33.

186 "And for Christ's sake": EH to William Horne, July 17–18, 1923; *SL,* 85.
"a brand new ugly town": Ibid., 86.
"We can't ever go back": Ibid., 85.
"the supreme, deadly, lonely dullness": *Dateline: Toronto,* 176.
"recreate something for my wife": Ibid., 180.

187 "They were good troops": Ibid., 178.
"A writer's job": Donaldson, *By Force of Will,* 248.
"If you make it up": *By-Line,* 216.

188 "bloomin' prairies": *Dateline: Toronto,* 181.
"I shall keep the series": EP to William Carlos Williams [August 1] 1922; Pound, *Letters,* 183.

189 "and we have all cheered up": EH to Harriet Monroe, November 16, 1922; *SL,* 72.
"Even though I kissed you Dorothy": EH to Dorothy Butler, n.d. [ca. 1924], JFK.
"We can't afford to leave this country": EH to GS, August 22, 1922, YCAL.
"Because the mark keeps dropping": EH to Family, August 25, 1922; *SL,* 71.

190 "It meant drowning": *Dateline: Toronto,* 214.
"All the symbolism that people say": EH to Bernard Berenson, September 13, 1952; *SL,* 780.
"In the cafes the Frenchmen": *Dateline: Toronto,* 94.
"The people are tired": Ibid., 95.

191 "as brown as an Ojibway": MS. 773b, JFK.
"as though the whole trip": Ibid.
"No . . . I will not go to Canada": Ibid.
"No . . . No. No. I have nothing to say": Ibid.
"It is nice here, eh?": Ibid.

192 "great Canadian paper": Stephens, *Hemingway's Nonfiction,* 51.
"to pass up your excellent color": John Bone to EH, September 25, 1922, JFK.
"I can only tell the truth": MS. 773b, JFK.
"Going to America": Ibid.

193 "I never had a quarrel with him": Bird chronology, Carlos Baker papers.
Discussion of homosexuality with Bill Bird: During a visit to Yale when he was on his way to being honored at Trinity College (his alma mater), Bird told this story to the scholar Norman Holmes Pearson, who told it to Donald Gallup, from whom I heard it, December 5, 1991.
"WONDERFUL ASSIGNMENT": EH to John Bone [ca. September 18, 1922], JFK.

194 "You ought to make it": EH to GS, [October 1922], YCAL.
"like a ripe blackberry in a bunch of daisies": *Dateline: Toronto,* 149.

“If you attempt to leave Bulgaria”: Ibid., 150.
“There are no internal problems”: Ibid.
195 “I will take up the question”: Ibid., 229.
“the sickening, cold, crawling fear-thrill”: Ibid., 230.
196 “The Mudania conference will determine”: Ibid., 219.
“Eliminating the Greeks”: Ibid.
“It may not go off”: Ibid., 234.
197 “newly arrived Constantine officers”: *SSEH,* 163.
“rose-petal, syrupy, smooth-bellied”: Ibid.
“Nice open country”: EH to CEH, November 7, 1923; *SL,* 100.
198 “It is better than sleeping”: *Dateline: Toronto,* 250.
“ghastly, shambling procession”: Ibid., 249.
“They’ve all had Karagatch”: Ibid., 251.
“It is not only the fault”: Ibid., 252.
“trying to make”: EH to Mrs. Paul Pfeiffer, October 16, 1933; *SL,* 397.
“Why don’t you come back”: EH to GS, November 3, 1922, YCAL.
199 “I have a necklace to show you”: HRH to Miss Stein and Miss Toklaz, November 25, 1922, YCAL.
“At any rate, I have had it out”: EH to John Bone, October 27, 1922, JFK.
“but that usually means two years”: EH to Harriet Monroe, November 16, 1922; *SL,* 72.
200 “representative of English letters”: Mizener, *The Saddest Story,* 324.
Hemingway meets Ford at Pound’s Notre Dame de Champs studio: See EH to EP, September 8, 1956, YCAL.
“Poor dear little Wicky Poo” . . . “sweet little feather kitty”: EH to HRH, November 28, 1922; *SL,* 73–74.
“we haven’t lost so much time”: Ibid., 74.
201 “I’m so sick of this”: Ibid., 73.
“Mason has kiked me so”: Ibid.
“registering Dictator”: *Dateline: Toronto,* 255.
202 “the biggest bluff in Europe”: Ibid.
“genius for clothing small ideas”: Ibid.
“big-whited African eyes”: Ibid., 256.
“smiled her way into many interviews”: Ibid.
“Power!”: Sheridan, *Nuda Veritas,* 312. Sheridan gives November 24 as the date for their arrival in Rome.
“Above all, keep your heart a desert!”: Ibid., 314.
203 “The adventurer must be unsocial”: Bolitho, *Twelve Against the Gods,* 3.
“but he would turn pale”: *Dateline: Toronto,* 258.
“The boy who was kept in dresses”: Ibid., 259.
“that were the beginning”: *By-Line,* 222.
“the malady of power”: Ibid., 227.
204 “cadging drinks”: Duranty, *I Write As I Please,* 95, 169.
“the beginning, really the beginning”: Stein, *The Autobiography of Alice B. Toklas,* 264.
“history of every kind of them”: Stein, *The Making of Americans,* 191.
“If you keep on doing newspaper work”: Stein, *The Autobiography of Alice B. Toklas,* 262.
“You must be prepared to work”: *By-Line,* 185.
“you told what happened”: *DIA,* 2.
“Remember what the noises were”: *By-Line,* 219.

205 "was the best advice she gave me": Fenton, *Apprenticeship,* 159.
"had it coming to him": *SSEH,* 303.
"I was seeing the scene": Steffens, *The Autobiography of Lincoln Steffens,* 834.

206 "He was gay, he was sentimental": Ibid., 835.
"a certain overbearing attitude": Charles F. Bertelli to Charles Fenton, August 19, 1952, Charles Fenton papers, YCAL.
G. Ward Price: Hemingway was familiar with the *Century,* but it is not certain that he had read Price's article in his researches on the campaign for *A Farewell to Arms.*
"The Monocled Prince of the Press": *By-Line,* 223.
"one of the best newspapermen": Ibid.
"good-looking dark young man": G. Ward Price to Charles Fenton, August 30, 1952, Charles Fenton papers, YCAL.

Memory Is the Best Critic

208 "I told her that no matter": *AMF,* 74.

209 "just back": GS to Etta Cone, February 6, 1923. A Christmas postcard, dated December 19, 1922, from Hadley to Stein and Toklas (YCAL), was forwarded to them at the Hôtel de Provence in St.-Rémy. They did not return to Paris until early February, according to the letter Stein wrote to Etta Cone from 27 rue de Fleurus, saying, "Here we are just back" per letter from Donald Gallup to James Mellow, September 2, 1987.
"No use, I think": Steffens to EH, December 9, 1922, JFK.
Bird's letter: See William Bird to EH, December 11, 1922, JFK.
"the kind of Christmas": *Dateline: Toronto,* 423.

210 "had made the job complete": EH to EP, January 23, 1923; *SL,* 77.
"act of Gawd": EP to EH, January 27, 1923, JFK.
"I thank you for your advice": EH to EP, January 29, 1923; *SL,* 79.
"What was going to be my first novel": EH to CB, April 1, 1951, Carlos Baker papers.
"a whole winter in Petoskey": Ibid.
The lost manuscripts: on those that survived, see Paul Smith, *Reader's Guide,* xxvi–xxvii; and also Reynolds, *Paris Years,* 95–96, on the Parisian sketches.

211 "I've traveled nearly 10,000 miles": EH to CEH, March 26, 1923; *SL,* 81.
Lincoln Steffens witnessing scene: Kert, *The Hemingway Women,* 127.
"truly wonderful chapters": HRM to Charles Fenton, March 25, 1951, Charles Fenton papers, YCAL.
"That painful subject again!": Kert, *The Hemingway Women,* 127.

212 "It was sacred to himself": Reynolds, *First War,* 277.
"He closed and locked the suitcase": *GOE,* 219.
"to forget it and put it out of my mind": EH to CB, April 1, 1951, Carlos Baker papers.
"It was a bad time": *AMF,* 74.

213 When the early checks failed: See EH to Alice Langelier, INS, December 5, 1922, JFK.
Hadley's possible involvement: See Mason wire to EH, October 1, 1922, ending, "Advised address wifeward regards Mason," JFK.
"puritan soul": Kert, *The Hemingway Women,* 124.

"Pay for it": cable transcripts, EH to Frank Mason or INS, November 27?, 1922, JFK. The first version was crossed out; later revision said, "Twenty-four-hour service costly."

"DONT UNDERSTAND WHETHER": Frank Mason to EH, November 28?, 1922, JFK.

The real break came in mid-December: See EH to Frank Mason, wire incorrectly dated September/October 1922, JFK; also Frank Mason to EH, December 14, 1922, JFK.

"SUGGEST YOU UPSTICK": EH to Frank Mason, [ca. December 14, 1922], JFK.

"I can only regard it": EH to Frank Mason, December 15, 1922, JFK.

"Mussolini told me at Lausanne": EH to EP, January 23, 1923; *SL,* 76.

214 "to eat bad food": Baker, *A Life Story,* 105.

Seldes's expulsion: See Seldes, *Witness to a Century,* 212ff.

"If Mussolini would have me taken out": *Dateline: Toronto,* 255.

Mussolini's two-day appearance at the Lausanne Conference: See Smith, *Mussolini,* 59–60.

215 "You mustn't tease Benito": EP to EH, January 27, 1923, JFK.

"new stuff": EH to EP, January 23, 1923; *SL,* 77.

"Drop this unbecoming delicacy": EH to EP, January 29, 1923; Ibid., 78.

"The Fascio is very quiet": EP to EH, January 27, 1923, JFK.

"COME NOW": MS. 298, JFK.

216 "I tried to explain": EH to CB, April 1, 1951, Carlos Baker papers.

"I've been working hard": EH to GS, ca. February 18, 1923; Ibid., 79.

"That guy who tried to stop us": EH to EP, March 10, 1923; Ibid., 80.

217 Stein's "A Saint in Seven," *What Are Masterpieces,* 45: Consider the following lines from the Stein poem written at St.-Rémy:

> Louise makes rugs and reasonably long
> Heloise makes the sea and she settles well away from it.
> Amelia does not necessarily please.

"Baron Hayashi gets in and out": *Complete Poems,* 63.

"Lord Curzon likes young boys": Ibid.

"Lincoln Steffens is with Child": Ibid., 64.

"He and his wife went away": Stein, *The Autobiography of Alice B. Toklas,* 262. It is perhaps possible that this visit to Stein, if made after her return from Provence in February, was also the visit after which he wrote "They All Made Peace."

218 "crabbing" to Stein: EH to EP, July 22, 1933, YCAL.

"There is no sure preventative": Steffens, *Autobiography,* 835.

"I've thought a lot": EH to GS, ca. February 18, 1923; *SL,* 79.

"I had a wonderful time with the book": Ibid, 80.

219 "In the photograph": Stein, *Geography and Plays,* 415.

"You can cut out any": EH to GS, ca. February 18, 1923; *SL,* 79.

"the unbelievably stupid": *Chicago Tribune,* Paris edition, Monday, March 5, 1923.

"Gertrude Stein is a sort of gauge": Ibid.

"Gertrude Stein is probably": Ibid.

220 "was mutilated": GS to EH, March 6, 1923 [misdated February 1, 1923], JFK.

"The place aint much": EH to GS, ca. February 18, 1923; *SL,* 79.
"corking portrait": EH to EP, March 10, 1923; Ibid., 81.
"hurt far more than I was": *AMF,* 74.

221 "Gee . . . don't you wish": *SSEH,* 284.
"George and Nick were happy": Ibid.
"There isn't any good in promising": Ibid., 286.

222 "I get so tired of it": Ibid., 267.
"And I want to eat at a table": Ibid., 268.
"thrilling rescue": AvK to Dear Kid, October 17, 1918; Villard and Nagel, *In Love and War,* 101.
"was 4 months pregnant": EH to FSF, ca. December 24, 1925; *SL,* 180–81.
"an almost literal transcription": Ibid.

223 "Of course you haven't got the guts": *SSEH,* 274.
"He felt uncomfortable and afraid": Ibid., 275.

224 "I'm sorry you feel so rotten, Tiny": Ibid., 273.
"What in hell makes him say marsala?": Ibid., 272.

225 "I hold Rome in the hollow of my hand": McAlmon and Boyle, *Being Geniuses Together,* 134.
"innocent young Canadian": RMcA to Norman Holmes Pearson, February 28, 1952, Charles Fenton papers, YCAL.
"deliberately hard-boiled": McAlmon and Boyle, *Being Geniuses Together,* 157.
"If the world's going to hell": Ibid., 203.
"in a boyish way": RMcA to Norman Holmes Pearson, February 28, 1952, Charles Fenton papers, YCAL.

226 "We've got to": *SSEH,* 286.
"If I can't have long hair": Ibid., 268.
"It's a rotten day": Ibid., 275.
"Sometimes when I wake up": RMcA to Norman Holmes Pearson, February 28, 1952, Charles Fenton papers, YCAL.
"disturb my bachelorhood": Meyers, *Hemingway,* 68.
"I never was more pleased": AvK to EH, December 22, 1922; Villard and Nagel, *In Love and War,* 164.

227 "It is so nice to feel": Ibid., 167.
"But his wife said": *SSEH,* 164.
"McAlmon came and stayed": EH to EP, March 10, 1923; *SL,* 80.
"Both men and women": Fitch, *Sylvia Beach,* 86.
"McAlmon has given us the dirt": EH to EP, March 10, 1923; *SL,* 80.
"Re: Robt. I dare say": EP to EH, March 26, 1923, JFK.
"You're it . . . Go to it": Ibid.

228 "who was much more courageous": Norman, *Ezra Pound,* 461.
"He had some stories": RMcA to Norman Holmes Pearson, February 28, 1952, Charles Fenton papers, YCAL.
"were fresh and without derivation": McAlmon and Boyle, *Being Geniuses Together,* 158.

229 "He has written a really fine": EH to Edward J. O'Brien, September 12, 1924; *SL,* 124.
"Village is absolutely first rate": EH to RMcA, [late January or early February 1925], YCAL.
"damn important — It is god damn important": EH to EP, [n.d., possibly 1924 but misdated 1929], JFK.

"I have never yet succeeded": EH to Ernest Walsh, January 2, 1926; *SL*, 186.
"His interests . . . are all those": EH to EP (fragment misfiled in 1954–59 letters, may be portion of an earlier letter), YCAL.
"Their experiences get to be": EH to Charles Poore, January 23, 1953; *SL*, 800.
Ideally a writer would know everything: See EH to Malcolm Cowley, August 1952; James D. Brasch, "Invention from Knowledge: The Hemingway-Cowley Correspondence" in Nagel, *The Writer in Context*, 222–23.

230 "Minarets stuck up in the rain": *SSEH*, 195.
"Everybody was drunk": Ibid., 187.
"We were in a garden at Mons": Ibid., 203.
"It was a frightfully hot day": Ibid., 211.
"The kid came out": Ibid., 257.
"They shot the six cabinet ministers": Ibid., 225. On the several newspaper accounts of the execution of the ministers, some false and some more accurate, see Reynolds, *Critical Essays*, 31–33; also *Paris Years*, 115–16.

231 "Excellent": John Bone to EH, March 7, 1923, JFK. In the letter, Bone repeated the wording of the wire he had sent Hemingway: "Your letter February Eighteenth received. Stop. Please make trip proposed therein," which suggests that Hemingway had initially proposed the trip.
"Your tiny": HRH to EH, "3:30 Thurs, Cortina" [March 1923?].
"a man of undisciplined genius": Secrest, *Between Me and Life*, 293.
"and such like beauty aids": EH to GS, [August 1924], YCAL.
"To write about Germany": *Dateline: Toronto*, 260.

232 "whose plot could not even be outlined": Ibid., 264.
"It is a very intimate politics": Ibid., 265.
"Military intrigue by the French": on verso of draft of Hemingway's letter to John McClure, the editor of *The Double-Dealer*, [November 1922], JFK.

233 "You have only to hear M. Viviani": *Dateline: Toronto*, 261.
"Lord knows I worked hard on them": EH to CEH, June 20, 1923, JFK.
"RUSSIA UNFEASIBLE": EH to John Bone, May 9, 1923, JFK.

234 "The articles you are sending": John Bone to EH, August 20, 1922, JFK.
"Can you let me know anything definite": John Bone to EH, November 2, 1922, JFK.
"Delighted to know": John Bone to EH, cable and letter, March 7, 1923, JFK.
"Oh Hem would like to go there too": RMcA to Norman Holmes Pearson, February 28, 1952, Charles Fenton papers, YCAL.
"need to love the art of bullfighting": McAlmon and Boyle, *Being Geniuses Together*, 161.

235 "A Mexican is to take his place": Stein, *Geography and Plays*, 70.
"I forget war and fear": Ibid., 74.

236 "I was trying to write then": *DIA*, 2.
"the feeling of life and death": Ibid., 3.
"*El sol es el mejor torero*": Ibid., 15.

237 "Hell, Mac, you write like a realist": McAlmon and Boyle, *Being Geniuses Together,* 160.
"great one": *Dateline: Toronto,* 342.
"Only thing that brings man": MS. 295, JFK.
"Oh, for Christ's sake, more flamingos": Bird memoir, Carlos Baker papers.
"You know I'll take anything": Baker, *A Life Story,* 111.
"a beauty of a dream scene": RMcA to Norman Holmes Pearson, February 28, 1952, Charles Fenton papers, YCAL.

238 "I am very anxious": EH to GS, June 20, 1923; *SL,* 83.
"Swell fights": EH to Isabel Simmons, June 24, 1923; Ibid.
"a stalwart pre-natal influence": Ibid, 84.
"made blood-red stripes across your heart": Sokoloff, *Hadley,* 62.
"embroidering in the presence": Ibid., 63.
"dark, spare and deadly looking": *Dateline: Toronto,* 352.
"*Era muy hombre*": *DIA,* 82.

239 "and God how it's played": EH to Greg Clark [July 12, 1923], JFK.
"It will make some very fine stories": EH to CEH, June 20, 1923, JFK.
"We're both crazy": EH to William Horne, July 17–18, 1923; *SL,* 88.
"You are the publisher": EH to RMcA, August 5, 1923; Ibid., 90.
"made it any amount stronger": Ibid., 91.
"Nobody will buy a book": Ibid., 90.
"Maera felt everything": *SSEH,* 305.

240 "When they are read altogether": EH to EP, ca. August 5, 1923; *SL,* 91.
"Like all Greeks": Ibid., 92.
"You just won't be the same": Sokoloff, *Hadley,* 64.
"Christ, I hate to leave Paris": EH to Isabel Simmons, June 24, 1923; *SL,* 84.

The Perpendicular Pronoun

241 "absurd assignments": HRM to Charles Fenton, March 25, 1952, Charles Fenton papers, YCAL.
"I have understood": EH to GS and ABT, October 11, 1923; *SL,* 94.
"I am now undertaking": EH to EP, October 13, 1923; Ibid., 95.
"Someday someone will live here": Ibid., 96.

242 "young Gallito": EH to GS and ABT, October 11, 1923; Ibid., 93.
"Felt dreadfully about Hadley": Ibid., 94.
"Compromised by telling him": EH to EP, October 13, 1923; Ibid., 96.
"The paper wants all day": EH to Sylvia Beach, November 6, 1923; Ibid., 97.
"#3 sturries and ten pums": Ibid., 98.
"in the morning a story starts": EH to Edward J. O'Brien, ca. November 20, 1923; Ibid., 104.
"You ruined me as a journalist": EH to GS and ABT, [misdated November 9, 1923; should be after November 27, following the publication of Stein's November 27 review of *Three Stories and Ten Poems*]; Ibid., 101.
"Do knock off something": EP to EH, [late September/early October 1923], JFK.
"Feel that I'm so full of hate": EH to EP, October 13, 1923; *SL,* 96.

243 "See here Ole Bungo": EP to EH, December 3, 1923, JFK.
"Above the hell-rot": Pound, *The Cantos of Ezra Pound,* 62.
"After Hell": EP to EH, October 24, 1923, JFK.
"And Ernie Hemingway went to it": Pound, *The Cantos of Ezra Pound,* 72.
"decoyed": EH to EP, October 13, 1923; *SL,* 96.
"Prince Charming, the Ambassador of Empire": EH to EP, ca. September 6, 1923; Ibid., 92.
"one of the few surviving idealists": *Dateline: Toronto,* 336.

244 "has written, with the exception": Ibid., 384.
"If Yeats hasn't written swell poems": EH to Ernest Walsh, January 2, 1926; *SL,* 187.
"The paper is full": EH to GS and ABT, November 9, 1923 [misdated; should be after November 27, following the publication of Stein's November 27 review of *Three Stories and Ten Poems*]; Ibid., 101.
"The great qualification to hold office": EH to EP, June 16, [1926], YCAL.

245 "[Bobby] Reade and [Greg] Clark sit around and talk": Baker, *A Life Story,* 120.
"I see . . . I just wanted to see": Callaghan, *That Summer in Paris,* 29.
"You don't know anything in Canada": EH to EW, November 11, 1923; *SL,* 102.
"As far as I can think": EH to EW, November 25, 1923; Ibid., 104.
"Sherwood has written about boys and horses": Ibid., 105.

246 "She is where Mencken and Mary Colum": Ibid.
"Three stories and ten poems": Ford, *The Left Bank Revisited,* 257.
"It seems very sound to me": EH to GS and ABT, [misdated November 9, 1923; should be after November 27, following the publication of Stein's review]; *SL,* 101.
"I can feel it in the papers etc.": Ibid.
"I have some good stories to write": Ibid., 102.

247 "Mr. Hindmarsh *says*": EH to John Bone, ca. December 26, 1923; Ibid., 109.
"local staff of the Star": EH to John Bone, ca. December 27, 1923; Ibid. Possibly the tentative dates of the two resignation letters are incorrect and relate to Hemingway's October quarrel with Hindmarsh over the Apponyi episode, in which case Hemingway, having threatened to resign, may have been tactfully transferred to the *Star Weekly.* A third possibility is that the earlier letter, in which he only raised the issue of his quitting the *Star,* should be dated October, while the later one represents the official letter of resignation which he tendered late in December.
"From now until Christmas": EH to CEH, November 11, 1923; Ibid., 99.
"She is a corker Jim": EH to James Gamble, December 12, 1923; Ibid., 106.
"All this is frightfully full": Ibid., 107.

248 "Don't show this to the family, Marce": Sanford, *At the Hemingways,* 215–16.
"a big world vision": GHH to EH, December 26, 1923, JFK.
"way out of season": HRH to GHH, January 2, 1924, JFK.

Hadley, in fact, felt so guilty: See Jack Hemingway, *Misadventures of a Fly Fisherman,* author's foreword.
"I feel like running away": CEH to EH, January 10, 1924, JFK.
"I have about 7 stories to write": EH to EP, February 10, 1924; *SL,* 110.
249 "haywired" . . . "an enormous number": Ibid., 110–11.
"Ernest has written two dandy stories": HRH to Family, February 20, 1924, JFK.
"experimenting": EH to EP, March 17, 1924; *SL,* 112.
Baptismal certificate dated March 16, 1924, JFK.
"he was a triple deformity": Chink Dorman-Smith to EH, December 9, 1923, JFK.
"the two giant women gargoyles": Jack Hemingway, *Misadventures,* 248.
250 "Good literature is produced": T. S. Eliot in *Transatlantic Review,* vol. 1, no. 1 (January 1924), 96.
"Ford alleges he is delighted": EH to GS, February 17, 1924; *SL,* 111.
"simple middle class monotonous tradition," Stein, *The Making of Americans,* 34.
"So for the first time": Stein, *The Autobiography of Alice B. Toklas,* 264. While writing the book, Stein kept notebooks observing and analyzing the character of people she knew and of her own personality, developing a number of theories: "Picasso has a maleness that belongs to genius. Moi aussi," a theory congenial to Hemingway and his other mentor, Pound. It is quite possible that Hemingway's habit of making analytical character notes of his friends derived from this practice.
"eternal hymn of repetition": Walker, *Gertrude Stein,* 43.
"I am all unhappy in this writing": Ibid., 348.
251 "I think it is wonderful stuff": EH to Edward J. O'Brien, September 12, 1924; *SL,* 124.
"Once an angry man": Stein, *The Making of Americans,* 1.
"As I was saying every one": Ibid., 225.
"It wasn't just love": *NAS,* 218.
"I feel sick about it": EH to GS, ca. May 15, 1924; *SL,* 118.
252 "one of the very greatest books": EH to SA, May 21, 1926, Ibid., 206.
"Fuck Literature": EH to EP, March 17, 1924; Ibid., 113.
"He projects moments when life": Marjorie Reid in *The Transatlantic Review,* vol. 1, no. 4 (April 1924), 247–48.
"sensitive feeling for the emotional possibilities": Kennon Jewett, Ibid., 246.
"Burton Rascoe said In Our Time": EH to EP, July 19, 1924; *SL,* 119.
"here and there a sentence": Rascoe, "A Bookman's Day Book," *New York Herald Tribune* (June 15, 1924), 20.
"remarkably successful in suggesting": Wilson, *The Shores of Light,* 120.
"the only American writer": Ibid., 119.
253 "a naiveté of language": Ibid., 119–20.
"You are the only man": EH to EW, October 18, 1924; *SL,* 129.
"I wish you would print": EW to Alyse Gregory, September 4, 1924; Wilson, *Letters on Literature and Politics,* 114.
"Seldes, his sphincter muscle": EH to EP, February 10, 1924; *SL,* 111.
Probably "Soldier's Home": See EH to Donald Ogden Stewart, November 3, 1924, YCAL: "Sending Soldier's Home to the Dial for instance as

they seem disposed favorably toward me if I can believe what it says in Bunny Wilson's review."

"which we do not find wholly suited": Alyse Gregory to EH, December 4, 1924, YCAL.

"The Undefeated": See Joost, *Little Magazines,* 140ff.

254 "Mencken and I cannot agree": Reynolds, *Critical Essays,* 9.

"I wonder what was the matter": EH to Family, May 7, 1924; Reynolds, *Paris Years,* 198.

"I'm going to start": EH to EP, March 17, 1924; *SL,* 113.

255 "Down with gentlemen": EH to EP, Ibid.

"running the whole damn thing": EH to EP, ca. May 2, 1924; Ibid., 116.

"in the contemplation of whose work": "Chroniques," *Transatlantic Review* (May–June 1924), 356.

"Two of his paintings": Ibid.

256 "They are three kids": EH to Edward J. O'Brien, September 12, 1924; *SL,* 124.

"It is discouraging": Ibid.

"the admirable American prose writer": Poli, *Ford Madox Ford and the Transatlantic Review,* 106.

"the man whose tastes march": Ford in *The Transatlantic Review* (August 1924), 94.

"to publish everything": Ford, *It Was the Nightingale,* 295.

"The only stories I've got": EH to EP, ca. May 2, 1924; *SL,* 116.

257 "Ef yew see Ford; feed him": Lindberg-Seyerstad, *Pound/Ford,* 78.

"how very much better": *The Transatlantic Review* (August 1924), 103.

"a swell book": EH to FSF, December 15, 1925; *SL,* 176.

258 "acid estimates": Dos Passos, *The Best Times,* 141.

"both great guys": EH to Howell Jenkins, November 9, 1924; *SL,* 130.

"people that mattered": Dos Passos, *The Best Times,* 145.

259 "entirely of Mr. Hemingway's getting together": Poli, *Ford Madox Ford,* 106.

"should any large body of readers": Ibid., 107.

"the godamdest wild time": EH to Howell Jenkins, November 9, 1924; *SL,* 131.

"I appeared in the bull ring": EH to EP, July 19, 1924; Ibid., 118.

"gored": EH to Edward O'Brien, September 12, 1924; Ibid., 124.

260 "BULL GORES 2 YANKS": Hanneman, *A Comprehensive Bibliography,* H21.

"Bull gores Toronto Writer": Ibid., H22.

"spoil the last frenzied night": Stewart, *By a Stroke of Luck,* 133.

"We butchered them this summer": EH to Howell Jenkins, November 9, 1924; *SL,* 130.

"He was so intent": McAlmon and Boyle, *Being Geniuses Together,* 246.

"I've tried and tried": EH to EP, July 19, 1924; *SL,* 119.

261 "I found myself": JDP to John Howard Lawson [August 1924]; Dos Passos, *The Fourteenth Chronicle,* 358.

"It was fun": Dos Passos, *The Best Times,* 155–56.

"suffered sincerely and deeply": *DIA,* 467.

"he knew the ropes": RMcA to Norman Holmes Pearson, February 28, 1952, Charles Fenton papers, YCAL.

"It was one of those secrets": Ibid.

262 "He was tragic about it": McAlmon and Boyle, *Being Geniuses Together,*

246–47. Michael Reynolds, in *Hemingway: The Paris Years* (218–19), believes that Hemingway was morose because Hadley had missed her period and suspected that she might be pregnant again; but after the departure of McAlmon and the others, they discovered that Hadley was merely late.
"a good fat book": EH to Edward J. O'Brien, May 2, 1924; *SL,* 117.
"The Transatlantic killed my chances": EH to EP, July 19, 1924; Ibid., 119.
"In the meantime": EH to Edward J. O'Brien, May 2, 1924; Ibid., 117.
"bitched financially": EH to EP, July 19, 1924; Ibid., 119.

263 "I take great and unintellectual pleasure": Ibid.
"In all the other arts": Ibid.

264 "go to hell on or about": EH to GS and ABT, October 10, 1924; Ibid., 127.
"only a supplementary reward": *The Transatlantic Review* (September 1924), 300.
"Practically all the people": Ibid., 301.
"If I knew that by grinding": Ibid., 341.
"We were besides convinced": Joost, *Little Magazines,* 116.

265 "dancers, expounders": Loeb, *The Way It Was,* 207.
"There was blood": Ibid., 208.
"Pay for your own drinks": Rascoe, *We Were Interrupted,* 185.
"There are a good many": EH to GS and ABT, October 10, 1924; *SL,* 127.
"Ezra goes to Italy": Ibid.
"E[rnest] had AWFUL dreams": HRH to GS and ABT, [September 19, 1924], YCAL.

266 "The town isn't much fun": EH to GS [late August/early September 1924], YCAL.
"I've worked like hell": EH to EW, October 18, 1924; *SL,* 128.
"Like looking with your eyes": Ibid.
"looks like a modern": Stein, *The Autobiography of Alice B. Toklas,* 266.

267 "Periplum, not as land looks": Canto LIX, in Makin, *Pound's Cantos,* 57.
"The advance was going like clockwork": MS. 633, "Love," JFK.

268 "Take your stuff and get out": *NAS,* 24.

269 "Remember, that he who ruleth his spirit": Ibid., 25.
"The doctor wiped his gun carefully": Ibid., 25–26.
"Dear, I don't think": Ibid., 26.

270 "I know your memory is very good for details": CEH to EH, March 8, 1925, JFK.
"I'm so glad you liked the Doctor story": EH to CEH, March 20, 1925; *SL,* 153.
"because you or Mother sent back": Ibid.

271 "trying to do the country like Cézanne": EH to GS and ABT, August 15, 1924; Ibid., 122.
"awfully to read it": GS to EH, August 12, 1924, JFK.
"There is, in none of them": Stein, *Lectures in America,* 184; see also James R. Mellow, "The Word Plays of Gertrude Stein" in Stein, *Operas and Plays.*
"burned-over country": *NAS,* 177.

272 "the need for thinking": Ibid., 179.
"Nick looked down": Ibid., 177.

"Ahead of him, as far": Ibid., 179.
"He wanted them long": Ibid., 183.

273 "I've got a right to eat": Ibid., 184.
"Nothing could touch him": Ibid.
"There was a heaviness": Ibid., 193.
"He did not want to rush": Ibid., 194.
"tragic" . . . "Nick did not want it": Ibid., 198.
"long gray-white strips of milt": Ibid., 199.
"There were plenty of days coming": Ibid.
an eleven-page rumination: See EH to Donald Ogden Stewart, November 3, 1924, YCAL.

274 "He went on up the trail": *NAS,* 241.
"holding an umbrella": Ibid., 236. The eleven-page deletion was eventually published as "On Writing" in *NAS,* 233–41.
"Everyplace they had been together": Ibid., 234.
"Helen thought it was because": Ibid., 235. In one of the earlier versions, she is identified as Hadley.
"the greatest man": Ibid., 237.

275 "Everything good he'd ever written": Ibid., 237.
"so he was terrible": Ibid., 238.
"They would all turn into clichés": Ibid., 239.
"one of the great books": Ibid.
"Nick in the stories": Ibid., 238.
"You had to do it": Ibid., 239.
"the soldiers undressing": Ibid., 240. John Rewald very kindly wrote me (March 18, 1988) that the Cézanne exhibition at Bernheim-Jeune's took place from March 3 to 24, 1924, and that the landscape of trees with a house beyond might "conceivably" be Venturi No. 156, though no catalogue was issued for the exhibition. There is no painting bearing the title "Soldiers Undressing to Swim," but Rewald adds, "Indeed, it has often been said that for lack of models Cézanne went to the Arc River which flows near Aix and watched bathing soldiers there. This may very well have been the case and Hemingway obviously heard the anecdote."

276 "He always worked best": Ibid., 238.
"I think you would like it": EH to EW, October 18, 1924; *SL,* 128–29.
"little story of meditations": Stein, *The Autobiography of Alice B. Toklas,* 270.
"She'd know it if he": *NAS,* 239.
"I have discovered": EH to Donald Ogden Stewart, November 3, 1924; YCAL.

277 "mental conversation": EH to RMcA, ca. November 15, 1924; *SL,* 133.

The Dangerous Friend

278 "BOHEMIA GIRL": *Chicago Tribune,* April 26, 1924.
"with suitable moral comments": EH to WS, December 6, 1924; *SL,* 138.
"Is it good this way?": *NAS,* 227.

279 "Is my arm long enuf": WS to EH, November 21, 1924, JFK.
"You could have KO'ed me": EH to WS, December 6, 1924; *SL,* 136.
"I know how damn good": Ibid., 136–37.

"And we've got them all": Ibid., 137.
"I'll stake you to second class": EH to WS, ca. early 1925, PUL.
"You got the intelligence": EH to WS, February 17, 1925, PUL.
280 "If she's married and wants it": Ibid.
"to have it happen to them": Ibid.
"Get Mr. and Mrs. Haddock Abroad": EH to WS, December 6, 1924; *SL,* 138.
"He's a guy you'd like": Ibid., 137.
"Loeb is really good": EH to WS, March 4, 1925, YCAL.
"Should rate a laugh": EH to WS, January 30, 1925, YCAL.
"The reason the maternal speaks": EH to WS, January 9, 1925, PUL.
"But now I know": EH to WS, January 8, 1925, YCAL.
"This gets complicated as hell": Ibid.
"I dreamt night before last": EH to RMcA, December 10, 1924; *SL,* 140.
281 "This is the best short story": Ibid., 139.
"You'd better too": RMcA to EH, [December 1924], JFK.
"Anyhow this story is as good": EH to RMcA, ca. December 15, 1924, YCAL. Ironically, the fact that McAlmon was familiar with Hemingway's stories, including "Soldier's Home," from an early date, and that Hemingway was familiar with McAlmon's novel *Village* in manuscript form might suggest that the dramatic mother-son confrontation vital to both stories involved a bit of borrowing on either hand. It is more likely a coincidence than a matter of plagiarism. There are very distinct differences of style and content between the two episodes. More than likely it is a case of the envy, admiration, and competitiveness of the literary life — and one more reason for Hemingway's high opinion of McAlmon's novel. See Mellow, "Talent and All the Right Connections," *New York Times Book Review* (July 22, 1990), 9.
"an enormous check": EH to Harold Loeb, January 5, 1925; *SL,* 142.
282 "Every body had read it": Ibid., 143.
"WANT TO PUBLISH": Horace Liveright to EH, March 4, 1925, JFK.
"Mr. and Mrs. Elliot tried very hard": *SSEH,* 259. It is probably no coincidence that in *Mr. Midshipman Easy,* one of Hemingway's favorite Captain Marryat novels, Mr. Nicodemus Easy, who had no children, "was anxious to have them, as most people covet what they cannot obtain. After ten years, Mr. Easy gave it up as a bad job."
"a busted down pug": EH to JDP, April 22, 1925; *SL,* 157.
"This protects you as much": EH to Horace Liveright, March 31, 1925; *SL,* 154.
"unpublishably obscene": Ibid., 155.
283 "fine book" . . . "was written in a style": Ibid.
"My book will be praised": Ibid.
"I was greatly impressed": MP to EH, February 21, 1925, PUL.
"This is a pity": Ibid.
"We would certainly read it": MP to EH, February 26, 1925; Reynolds, *Paris Years,* 271.
"very excited": EH to MP, April 15, 1925; *SL,* 156.
284 "an awfully artificial and worked out form": Ibid.
"reflect life or describe life": Gertrude Stein in *Ex Libris,* vol. 2 (March 1925), 177. Reprinted in *Sherwood Anderson/Gertrude Stein,* 45.
"far and away the best": GS to SA, [November 1924], 42.

"There are very beautiful places": *Ex Libris,* vol. 2 (March 1925), 176–77.
"He is a very great writer": Ibid.
"all of them": SA to GS, [Spring 1925]; Anderson and Stein, *Sherwood Anderson/Gertrude Stein,* 43.

285 "crackerjack" blurb: SA to GS, [May 1925]; Ibid., 46. Anderson, however, did not write a review of *In Our Time.*
"Mr. Hemingway is young, strong": Ibid., 43.
"I can't write letters": EH to SA, May 23, 1925; *SL,* 162.
"Sure, probably I was wrong": Ibid., 161–62.

286 "the absolute secret": EH to Ernest Walsh and Ethel Moorhead, ca. January 12, 1925; Ibid., 145.
"The Editors of This Quarter": EH to Ernest Walsh, March 9, 1925; Ibid., 152.
"great news spreaders": EH to Ernest Walsh, January 29, 1925, JFK.
"He does first rate criticism": Ibid.
"his creative work, his editorship": vol. 4, "American Writers in Paris: 1920–1939," *Dictionary of Literary Biography,* 400.

287 "I owe a great deal": *This Quarter,* vol. 1, 219.
"He keeps to his hill": Ibid., 229.
"There is only one living poet": Ibid., 222.
"He never takes chances with it": Ibid., 223.
"he tries to advance": Ibid.
"Don't worry, there's going to be": EH to Ernest Walsh, July 20, 1925, JFK.
"I'm glad as hell": EH to Ernest Walsh [March 28, 1925], JFK.

288 "Jo-esus Bird": EH to WS, March 4, 1925, Charles Fenton papers, YCAL.
"completely worthless characters": *AMF,* 147.

289 "No. That's the way it takes him": Ibid., 150.
"He had the shyness about it": Ibid., 152.

290 "Didn't miss one vintage": EH to EP, December 11, 1925; YCAL.

291 "horror pictures": MS. 486, JFK. "I have not seen them for a year." In this version Hadley was with Hemingway at the Dingo when he first met Fitzgerald but did not meet Fitzgerald herself, being with other friends.
"golden blowsiness": Ibid.
"I did not like her": Ibid.
"Dear Friends": EH to GS and ABT, [June?] 1925, YCAL. Hemingway's meeting with Zelda then would seem to have taken place before, not after, the trip to Lyon. Stein and Toklas, per a letter to Carl Van Vechten (*The Letters of Gertrude Stein and Carl Van Vechten,* 115), had left for Belley on May 18, 1925. The date of Hemingway's letter to Stein and Toklas, then, should be in mid-May.
"The title seemed": RMcA to Norman Holmes Pearson, March 31, 1951; Sarason, *Sun Set,* 227.
"damned good-looking": *SAR,* 22.
"power of invention": MS. 179a-1, JFK.
"built with curves": *SAR,* 22.

292 "At all times the perfect lady": Sarason, *Sun Set,* 243.
"As far as I know": EH to Harold Loeb, June 21, 1925; *SL,* 164.

"various habits": MS. 194-I-4, JFK.
"enormously attractive to look at": Sarason, *Sun Set,* 197.
"awful mess and tramp": RMcA to Norman Holmes Pearson, February 28, 1962, YCAL.
"The primary idea": RMcA to Norman Holmes Pearson, March 31, 1951; Sarason, *Sun Set,* 225.

293 "lovely, a very fine lady": Sarason, *Sun Set,* 127.
"His portrait was superficial": Ibid., 236.
"They were good paintings": Ibid., 238.
For biographical details on Pauline Pfeiffer and the Pfeiffer family, I am indebted to Bernice Kert's *The Hemingway Women.*

294 "There's a lot of that aspect": Sarason, *Sun Set,* 156.

295 "Dear Better Half": Donald Ogden Stewart to WS, June 17, 1971, PUL.
"Tell the lad hello for I": WS to EH, November 22 [1925], JFK.
"I was talking to someone": Kert, *The Hemingway Women,* 156.
"F. Scatt" . . . "quite a bit of stuff": WS to EH, November 22, 1925, JFK.
"had a wit which expressed itself": Loeb, *The Way It Was,* 247.
"He was then": Milford, *Zelda,* 117.

296 "in every way a man's man": Kitty Cannell to Carlos Baker, Carlos Baker papers.
"bogus" . . . "Ernest, nobody is as male": Donnelly and Billings, *Sara & Gerald,* 21.
"I notice that in the Hemingway family": Milford, *Zelda,* 116.
"too assured a male": Ibid., 117.
"Before I die": Donnelly and Billings, *Sara & Gerald,* 166.

297 "You are a stimulus": Ibid., 171.
"He was extremely sensitive": Ibid, 164–65.
"is never difficult": Ibid., 167.
"the line has been drawn": Ibid.
"Ernest will have given": Ibid., 174.

298 "I never met or heard": MacLeish letter of February 28, 1979; reproduced in vol. 4, "American Writers in Paris: 1920–1939," *Dictionary of Literary Biography,* 263.
"We have learned the answers": MacLeish, *The Collected Poems of Archibald MacLeish,* 245.
"A poem should not mean": Ibid., 50.
"Veteran out of the wars": Ibid., 145.

299 "Fish killed": EH to CEH, August 20, 1925; *SL,* 168.
"male festival": Bruccoli and Clark, *Fitzgerald/Hemingway Annual 1973,* 87.
"little Paris books": Sarason, *Sun Set,* 198–99.
"a dangerous friend to have": Ibid., 198.
"It seemed, in some obscure way": Loeb, *The Way It Was,* 289.

300 "He went off muttering": Ibid., 291.
"You know that I do *not*": Ibid., 295.
"I was terribly tight": EH to Harold Loeb, July 12, 1925; *SL,* 166.

301 "Her eyes crinkled up": *SAR,* 134.
"fine" . . . "very fine": EH to GS and ABT, July 15, 1925; *SL,* 167.
"did everything Belmonte did": Ibid.

302 "I work from lunch": EH to WS, July 27, 1925, YCAL.
"I've written six chapters": EH to Sylvia Beach, August 3, 1925, PUL.

"Have 8 chapters done": EH to WS, August 5, 1925, YCAL.

303 "I just got back yesterday": EH to GS and ABT, August 20, 1925, YCAL.

"I am working all the time": EH to Ernest Walsh, [August 1925], JFK.

"I'm not going to be": *SAR*, 243.

304 "You know it makes one feel rather good": Ibid., 245.

"Oh, Jake . . . we could have had": Ibid., 247.

Leopold and Loeb: See MS. 194-I-13, JFK. It may have been a subconscious slip of the pen, but in a joking letter to Fitzgerald about the plot of his novel, Hemingway again merged Loeb's name with the Leopold and Loeb crime: "the heroine is a girl named Sophie Irene Loeb who kills her mother . . . The Sun Also Rises comes from Sophie's statement as she is strapped into the chair as the current mounts."

305 "terrific case of hero worship": Kitty Cannell, memo to Carlos Baker, Carlos Baker papers.

"She never had any new clothes": Ibid.

"I've taken your advice": Ibid.

"Yes that's the way it's done": MS. 194-II-20, JFK.

"During this time": MS. 194-I-12, JFK.

306 "fundamentally unsound": EH to Louis and Mary Bromfield, ca. March 8, 1926; *SL*, 195.

"Glenway Weskit": EH to EP, [1926], YCAL.

"I do declare": *SAR*, 20.

Sir Cedric Morris and Arthur Lett-Haines: See Sarason, *Sun Set*, 45; Cecil in Loeb's *The Way It Was*, 283. Morris and Lett-Haines later ran a private painting school in Dedham Vale in England. Lucien Freud was one of their students: *New York Times Magazine* (December 4, 1988), 96.

"Georgette Mangeuse le Blanc": EH to EP, ca. May 2, 1924, *SL*, 115.

"All these personages": Flanner, *Paris Was Yesterday*, 12.

307 "Other people can get killed but not me": *NAS*, 142.

"E.H. will be read": Fitzgerald, *The Notebooks of F. Scott Fitzgerald*, no. 1979.

"pretentious fake": EH to GHH, December 14, 1925; *SL*, 174.

"What made 3 Soldiers": EH to FSF, December 15, 1925; Ibid., 176.

"In them there was always": MS. 194-VI-21, JFK.

"You may recall my prediction": EH to EP, April 17, 1926 (not 1925), YCAL.

308 "Joyce is swell": EH to Ernest Walsh, January 2, 1926; *SL*, 186.

"I wanted to stay well outside": Svoboda, *Hemingway & The Sun Also Rises*, 133–34.

"Gerald Cohn is the hero": MS. 194-II-7, JFK.

"Gertrude Stein once told me": MS. 194-I-9, JFK.

"You are all a lost generation": *SAR*, Epigraph.

"One generation passeth away": Ibid.

"the ones between twenty two": MS. 202c, JFK. Although Hemingway claimed, in the preface, that he did not hear the remark until after he had finished the book, the preface was written, along with the early draft of the story "Ten Indians," in a notebook dated September 27, 1925, Chartres. Since Stein was away from Paris from May until late October that year (see *The Letters of Gertrude Stein and Carl Van Vechten*), Hemingway must have heard the remark sometime after the summer of 1924, when Stein and Alice first discovered the Hôtel Pernollet (see GS to EH, August 13, 1924, JFK).

309 "Then he stepped out": EH to GS and ABT, July 15, 1925; *SL*, 167.
"I saw him for the first time": MS. 193-I-1, JFK.

310 "Nobody ever lives their life": MS. 194-I-22, JFK.
"It was like a course in bull fighting": MS. 194-VI-11, JFK.
"It was like a course in bull-fighting": *SAR*, 219–20.
"In bull-fighting they speak": *SAR*, 213–14.

311 "His jaw only went further out": Ibid., 214.
"no longer had his greatest moments": Ibid., 215.
"Romero smiled": Ibid., 217.
"I know it": Ibid., 185.

312 "Irony and Pity. When you're feeling": *SAR*, 114.
"You're an expatriate": Ibid., 115.
"Listen. You're a hell of a good guy": Ibid., 116.
"That was what the Civil War": Ibid.
"It is funny that a thing": MS. 194-III-15, JFK.
"I'm crazy": Ibid.

313 "I have a rotten habit": *SAR*, 13.
In the realization of this chapter, I am indebted to William Balassi's day-by-day breakdown of the writing sessions of the first manuscript version of *The Sun Also Rises*, published in the *Hemingway Review*, (Fall 1986), 65–78.

All Things Truly Wicked

314 "His language is": Hanneman, *A Comprehensive Bibliography*, H29.
"Make no mistake": Ibid., H34.
"may puzzle the reader": Reynolds, *Critical Essays*, 20.
"The characters are alive": Ibid., 17.
"says all of it": EH to FSF, December 31, 1925–January 1, 1926, *SL*, 182.

315 "The flat, even banal": Reynolds, *Critical Essays*, 15.
"belong with cubist painting": Ibid., 18.
"What a lot of Blah Blah": EH to GHH, December 14, 1925; *SL*, 175.
"Hemingway has always been ripe": Joost, *Little Magazines*, 147–48.
"I have to be restrained": EH to Ernest Walsh, January 2, 1926; *SL*, 187.

316 "But the hell of it is": Ibid.
"an augury": Fitzgerald, *In His Own Time*, 147–48.
"Many of us": Ibid., 149.
"Le Grand Gertrude Stein": EH to EP, November 8 (Rent Day), 1925, YCAL.
"You might, if you liked": Ibid.

317 "Naturally I regretted": EH to EP [November 1927; misdated, should be 1925], YCAL.
"Evidently they made up": EH to Harold Loeb, ca. November 25, 1925, JFK.
"a funny book": EH to EP, November 30, 1925, YCAL.

318 "I prefer 'Torrents of Spring'": EP to EH, November 18, 1926, JFK.
"My wife left me": *TOS*, 18.
"What was it all about?": Ibid., 41.

"Nurse . . . put out the candle": Ibid., 39.
"fairy tracings": Ibid., 3.
"Was he going to pieces": Ibid., 52.
"whom I consider": Ibid., 68.

319 "It was at this point": Ibid., 76.
"The Passing of a Great Race": Ibid., 71.
"Ah, there was a woman!": Ibid., 74.
"I loved it": FSF to MP, ca. December 30, 1925; Fitzgerald, *Dear Scott/ Dear Max,* 127.
"thoroughgoing wet blanket": Kert, *The Hemingway Women,* 170.
"damn good": Dos Passos, *The Best Times,* 158.
"Hem had a distracting way": Ibid.

320 "each one of which": EH to Horace Liveright, December 7, 1925; *SL,* 173.
"about the best comic book": FSF to Horace Liveright, before December 30, 1925; Fitzgerald, *Correspondence of F. Scott Fitzgerald,* 183.
"We shall try to do the young man": transcribed in EH to FSF, December 31, 1925–January 1, 1926; *SL,* 184.
"REJECTING TORRENTS OF SPRING": Ibid., 183.
"I have known all along": Ibid.

321 "It's up to you how I proceed": Ibid., 184.
"You, however, are an important cog": Ibid.
"Today is Thursday": Ibid.
"YOU CAN GET": FSF to MP, January 8, 1926; Fitzgerald, *Correspondence,* 187.
"PUBLISH NOVEL": Ibid. See note, 187.
"There can be no doubt": EH to Horace Liveright, January 19, 1926; *SL,* 191.
"You surely do not": Ibid.

322 "She was no better": *TOS,* 42.
"It has in it": Meyers, *Hemingway,* 166.
"Hem, you should have '*The Farm*'": Ibid.
"Will doubtless be referred to at death": EH to EP, November 30, 1925, YCAL.
"Pauline and I killed": EH to WS, December 3, 1925; Reynolds, *Paris Years,* 332.

323 "isn't his best stuff": EH to FSF, December 15, 1925; *SL,* 176.
"Turgenev to me": EH to Archibald MacLeish, December 20, 1925; *SL,* 177.
"I think MacLeishes": EH to FSF, ca. December 24, 1925; Ibid., 180.
"Oh my soul": Pauline Pfeiffer to EH and Hadley, January 16, 1926; Kert, *The Hemingway Women,* 173.
"If I am anything I am a Catholic": EH to Ernest Walsh, January? 1926, JFK.

324 "Although I am catolic": EH to Ernest Walsh, January 2, 1926; *SL,* 189.
"Then starting to think": MS. 194-III-30, JFK.
"I was a little ashamed": *SAR,* 97. In an equally interesting passage, which made it to the galley stage of the novel and was subsequently cut, Hemingway wrote, "So my name is Jake Barnes and I am writing the story, not as I believe is usual in these cases, from a desire for confession, because being a Roman Catholic I am spared that Protes-

tant urge to literary production." See Svoboda, *Hemingway & The Sun Also Rises,* 134–35.

325 "I feel he should be warned": Pauline Pfeiffer to HRH, January 17, 1926, JFK.
"I miss Hadley": EH to Ernest Walsh, February 1, 1926; *SL,* 192.
"wrote an awfully swell contract": EH to Louis Bromfield, ca. March 8, 1926; *SL,* 195.
"hells own amount of people": Ibid.
"Great love at first sight": EH to Isabel Godolphin, February 25, 1926; Ibid., 193.
"lecherous cat": EH to MP, January 10, 1929; Ibid., 293.
"playing the butcher's boy": Wilson, *The Bit Between My Teeth,* 522.
"Would have paid": EH to Louis Bromfield, ca. March 8, 1926; *SL,* 196.

326 Dawn Powell: See Gore Vidal, "Dawn Powell, the American Writer," *New York Review of Books* (November 5, 1987), 52–60.
"But the girl I was in love with": *AMF,* 208.
"and where we went and what we did": Baker, *A Life Story,* 165–66.
"I wished I had died": *AMF,* 208.
"All things truly wicked": Ibid.

327 "It is quite hard in texture": EH to MP, March 10, 1926; *SL,* 197.
"the last unalloyed good time": Dos Passos, *The Best Times,* 158.
"Ernest would stop": Donnelly and Billings, *Sara & Gerald,* 22.
"said that that he knew": Ibid. For a different account of Hemingway's use of the term "grace under pressure," see Mellow, *Invented Lives,* 265.
"pilot fish": *AMF,* 205.

328 "Those who attract people": Ibid., 206.
"Under the charm of these rich": Ibid., 207.
"If these bastards like it": Ibid.
"I want the Mss. back": EH to MP, April 24, 1926; *SL,* 201.
"'The Sun Also Rises' seems to me": MP to EH, May 18, 1926, PUL.
"The matter referred to": Ibid.

329 "Also the tragedy is real": Brownell report, PUL.
"Dear Charley, You wanted to know": MP to Charles Scribner, May 27, 1926, PUL.
"What he seemed to be saying to me": Kert, *The Hemingway Women,* 178–79.

330 Bumby, whooping cough: EH to FSF, ca. April 20, 1926; *SL,* 200.
"low as hell": EH to FSF, May 4, 1926; Ibid., 203.
"You'll be seeing Hadley": EH to FSF, ca. May 20, 1926; Ibid., 204.
"I was in love": "The Art of the Short Story," *The Paris Review* (Spring 1981), 97.
"You see I feel": EH to SA, May 21, 1926; *SL,* 205.

331 "and some gents": EH to CEH, May 23, 1926; Ibid., 207.
"I was very glad": EH to MP, June 5, 1926; *SL,* 208.
"sneers, superiorities": FSF to EH, [June 1926]; Fitzgerald, *Correspondence,* 193.
"I felt the lack": Ibid., 195.

332 "But remember this is a new departure": Ibid., 194.
"But you write like yourself": MP to EH, July 20, 1926, PUL.
"The bulls now without appendages": EH to MP, August 21, 1926; *SL,* 213.

"But in truth": MP to EH, July 20, 1926, PUL.

333 "Here it was": Kert, *The Hemingway Women,* 180–81.
"*Dansa Charleston*": Donnelly and Billings, *Sara & Gerald,* 25.
"I'm going to get a bicycle": Kert, *The Hemingway Women,* 182.

334 "that when life gets bumpy": Gerald Murphy to EH, Donnelly and Billings, *Sara & Gerald,* 25.
"collected people then": Baker, *A Life Story,* 593n.
"It is a truly gripping story": Hanneman, *A Comprehensive Bibliography,* H50.
"If there is better dialogue": Ibid., H49.
"writes as if he had": Ibid., H65.

335 "fascinating": Ibid., H56.
"the integrity achieved": Lynn, *Hemingway,* 331.
"It is not that Mr. Hemingway": Ibid.
"utterly degraded people": Hanneman, *A Comprehensive Bibliography,* H57.
"I took to my bed": Cannell memoir, Carlos Baker papers.
"No bullets whistled": EH to FSF, March 31, 1926; *SL,* 249.
"said the only thing": EH to FSF, ca. September 15, 1927; Ibid., 262.
"You certainly wrote out": WS to EH, [December 1926], JFK.

336 "You are all a lost generation": *SAR,* Epigraph.
"play off against the splendid bombast": EH to MP, November 19, 1926; *SL,* 229.
"one of the filthiest books": GHH to EH; Lynn, *Hemingway,* 357.
"You surely are now": CEH to EH, December 13, 1926, JFK.
"I mean that anywhere": John Dos Passos in *New Masses* (December 1926), 26.
"I've written a damn priggish": JDP to EH, November 10, 1926, JFK.

337 "I feel thoroughly sore": Ibid.
"I think it was fine": EH to MP, December 21, 1926; *SL,* 239.
"The fact that Mr. Hemingway": Ernest Walsh in *New Masses* (October 1926), 27.
"Except in the sense": EH to EP, [late 1926 or early 1927], YCAL.
"ALL FAIRIES": EH to EP [late 1926?], YCAL.
"I am sorry Mr. Walsh is dead": EP to EH, November 3, 1926, JFK.

338 "an awfully nice girl": JDP to EH, November 10, 1926, JFK.
"And how does she feel": Pauline Pfeiffer to EH, October 14, 1926; Kert, *The Hemingway Women,* 186.
"Ernest and Pfeiffer who tried": Pauline Pfeiffer to EH, October 29, 1926; Ibid., 188.
"a lousy terribly cheap self-pitying letter": EH to Pauline Pfeiffer, November 12, 1926; *SL,* 222.

339 "that you that are all": Ibid., 220.
"But now it is getting all out of control": Ibid., 222.
"The entire problem": HRH to EH, November 16, 1926, JFK.
"Please for the sake of peace": Ibid.
"I think your letter": EH to HRH, November 18, 1926; *SL,* 226.

340 "Will you please just take it": Ibid., 228.
"Haven't I yet made it": HRH to EH, November 19, 1926, JFK.
"You paid out 300 francs": Ibid.
"weeping down the street": Sokoloff, *Hadley,* 91.

"Anyway I'm now all through": EH to FSF, ca. November 24, 1926; *SL*, 232.

341 "La vie est beau avec papa": Ibid.

"The gossip is about": CEH to EH, December 13, 1926, JFK.

"I did not answer": EH to GHH, February 5, 1927; *SL*, 243.

342 "Our family has never": CEH to EH, August 8, 1927, JFK.

"I did not desert her": EH to CEH, September 14, 1927; *SL*, 257.

"I have seen, suffered": Ibid., 258.

"The reason I haven't made": Ibid., 259.

"if we can lay off": Ibid., 260.

The Master of Indirection

343 "You always do speak to me": SA to EH, [June? 1926], JFK. Anderson's letter precedes Hemingway's July 1, 1926, letter, which follows.

"the book will do you good": EG to SA, July 1, 1926; *SL*, 210.

"They're a swell lot": SA to EH, August 26, 1926, JFK.

344 "Well, here's how": Anderson, *Memoirs*, 465. For another version of their meeting, see Mellow, *Charmed Circle*, 280.

"He was not at all sore": EH to MP, January 20, 1927; *SL*, 241.

"Sherwood Anderson — A man's name": Townsend, *Sherwood Anderson*, 242.

"Hemingway had at one moment": Stein, *The Autobiography of Alice B. Toklas*, 265.

"Don't you come back": Ibid., 270.

345 "had attacked someone": *AMF*, 28.

"stupidly enough": Ibid., 117.

"Gertrude Stein was never crazy": MS. 423a, JFK.

"Miss Stein was always charming": MS. 593a, JFK.

"KEEP OUT. THIS MEANS YOU": Ibid. The same sign appears in *The Torrents of Spring*, 28, at the Petoskey pump factory.

"I would be glad": EH to EP, sometime after November 8, 1926, but before Pound's November 18 letter to Hemingway, which follows.

"Somewhat contented to see": EP to EH, November 18, 1926, JFK.

346 "Paulinose": Jack Hemingway, *Misadventures*, 5.

"I am going to look out for you": Pauline Pfeiffer to EH, November 29, 1926; Kert, *The Hemingway Women*, 198.

"Hickok and I": EH to EP, [1927], letter from Gstaad, YCAL.

"Italian tour for the promotion": Kert, *The Hemingway Women*, 200.

"sworn declaration of fact": See Meyers, *Hemingway*, 185 and 594, note 21.

"That's a young man": *SSEH*, 390.

347 "Forli last night": EH to EP, postcard from Rimini, dated Tuesday night and postmarked March 23, 1927, YCAL.

"Listen . . . let them go": *SSEH*, 393.

"very cheerful and clean": Ibid., 397.

Ada MacLeish luncheon: See Baker, *A Life Story*, 185.

348 "This is a fine place": EH to MP, May 27, 1927; *SL*, 252–53.

"I've been in love with her": EH to FSF, March 31, 1927; Ibid., 249.

"We sat at a table": Paul Smith, *Reader's Guide*, 204.

"They look like white elephants": *SSEH*, 371.

"Doesn't it mean anything to you": Ibid.
"Mss. for Pauline": Paul Smith, *Reader's Guide,* 206. Smith gives the most thorough examination of "Hills Like White Elephants" in his *Reader's Guide,* 204–13.
"*Look* at those god-dam": Ibid, 205.

349 "He had many problems": *GOE,* 13.
"delicate things on the fantastical side": "Philip Haines Was a Writer," *Hemingway Review* (Spring 1990), 2; see also 19, 32.
"In the daytime there was some sort": Junkins, "Hemingway's Paris Short Story," Ibid., 18. Hadley mentions the same sort of Persian figured cover, "a new Bagdad bed cover and student lamp," in a letter to "Stein and Toklaz," November 25, [1922], YCAL.

350 "He saw the upthrust curve": Ibid.
"a hollow feeling of unfaithfulness": Ibid.
"and she kissed him there on the sidewalk": "Philip Haines Was a Writer," Ibid., 2; see also Donald Junkins, "Hemingway's Paris Short Story," 34. Junkins seems to consider the Philip Haines story complete, but to me it is more like the opening chapter of a novel; the pistol that Haines buys has no function, but the ominous introduction of it into the story seems clearly intended for some later development.
"eggs and cold beer": Crosby, *Shadows of the Sun,* 151.

351 "And they both think Cocteau": Ibid., 131.
"It was very hard": EH to MP, August 31, 1927; *SL,* 257.
"new monumental work": EH to FSF, ca. September 15, 1927; Ibid., 260.

352 "and I think it's very important": EH to MP, December 6, 1926; Ibid., 237.
"malignancy of the machine": Ibid.
"Scribner's don't know it": EH to EP, [January 1927], YCAL.
"Now mong cher ami": EP to EH, January 30 [1926], JFK. Should be 1927. Sent to Hemingway in "GGGGG-staaaad Svizzz"; Hemingway was in Gstaad in January 1927.
"about the advance man": EH to MP, February 14, 1927; *SL,* 245–46.

353 "In all of these, almost": Ibid.
"*A basso gli ufficiali!*": *SSEH,* 366.
"a theory, like another": Ibid., 369.
"Thou hast committed": Eliot, "Portrait of a Lady," *The Complete Poems and Plays,* 8.

354 "I've been cleaning out the basement, dear": Paul Smith, *Reader's Guide,* 173.
"On those nights": *SSEH,* 462–63.
"You lie all night half funny": EH to Pauline Pfeiffer, December 3, 1926; *SL,* 235.
"A man ought to be married": *SSEH,* 468.

355 "I tell you, he was pretty good": Ibid., 456.
"The people he observes": Wilson, *The Shores of Light,* 339.
"In his hands": Ibid., 339–40.
"a truly magnificent work": Hanneman, *A Comprehensive Bibliography,* H81.
"but he so presents them": Ibid., H79.
"a collection of grim little stories": Ibid., H85.

356 "this rumor of modernity": *New York Herald Tribune Books* (October 9, 1927), 1, 8.
"They are the people": Ibid.
"Thus Mr. Lawrence, Mr. Douglas": Ibid., 8.
"At last we are inclined": Ibid.
357 "with his usual gentle": Wilson, *The Shores of Light,* 339.
"a sordid little catastrophe": Ibid., 340.
"a story about a man": Ibid., 341.
"a glimpse of one aspect": Ibid.
"his masterly relevance in indirection": Ibid., 341.
"Look at that bunch of camels": *SSEH,* 339.
"It would appear, then": Wilson, *The Shores of Light,* 341.
358 "The Virginia Woolf review": EH to MP, ca. November 1, 1927; *SL,* 264.
"friends" . . . "a pile of shit": EH to FSF, October 30, 1927, JFK.
"They probably belong": FSF to EH, [November 1927?]; Fitzgerald, *The Letters of F. Scott Fitzgerald,* 301.
"Did like White Elephants": EH to FSF, October 30, 1927, JFK.
359 "I thought the first paragraph": Archibald MacLeish to EH, [February 20, 1927]; MacLeish, *Letters of Archibald MacLeish,* 199.
"blind spell" . . . "It sounds like": EH to EP, [January? 1928] from Gstaad, YCAL.
"How the hellsufferin tomcats": EP to EH, March 11, 1928; Baker, *A Life Story,* 190.
"You poor dear old thing": HRH to EH, ca. March 11, 1928, JFK.
360 "But this next book": EH to MP, March 17, 1928; *SL,* 274.
"There is a *very very* good chance": Ibid., 273.
"I should have gone": Ibid., 274.
361 "interesting people to talk to": Dos Passos, *The Best Times,* 198.
"Nobody seemed ever to have heard": Ibid., 198.
362 "They picked her clean": *SSEH,* 476.
"At the moment": JDP to Robert Hillyer, [April 1928]; Dos Passos, *The Fourteenth Chronicle,* 385.
363 "You would best consider": CEH to EH, June 4, 1928, JFK.
"We are anxious to hear": CEH to EH, June 18, 1928, JFK.
"Pauline had a very bad time": EH to MP, July 23, 1928; *SL,* 280.
"They finally had to open Pauline": EH to Guy Hickok, ca. July 27, 1928; Ibid.
364 "1st day — worked": EH to Waldo Peirce, August 9, 1928; Ibid., 282.
"As it is have been": Ibid., 283.
"I think I will have to get": EH to MP, May 31, 1928; Ibid., 278.
"She is strong as a goat": EH to Waldo Peirce, ca. August 23, 1928; Ibid., 285.
"Were I thirty": *SL,* 255n (quoting letter from Owen Wister to Barklie McKee Henry).
"to let it lie": EH to MP, September 28, 1928; Ibid., 285.
"Have never felt": Ibid., 286.
365 "Where are you going to be": EH to FSF, ca. October 9, 1928; Ibid., 289.
"How does it feel": EH to FSF; Ibid., 287.
"It was agony for my mother": Sanford, *At the Hemingways,* 229.

366 "It was a beautiful mansion": Hotchner, *Papa Hemingway,* 121. For discussion of various versions, see Mellow, *Invented Lives,* 325–28.
"I am sorry I made": EH to FSF and Zelda, ca. November 18, 1928; *SL,* 290.
"Yale & Navy Games": Fitzgerald journal, November 1928, PUL.

367 "What Pauline did": Miller, *Ernie,* 55.
"But I don't see how": Sanford, *At the Hemingways,* 231.

368 "The bullet pierced the brain": Reynolds, "Hemingway's Home: Depression and Suicide" in Wagner, *Ernest Hemingway: Six Decades of Criticism,* 15.
"a hopeless case": Ibid.
"At the funeral": Leicester Hemingway, *My Brother,* 111.
"You were damned good": EH to FSF, ca. December 9, 1928; *SL,* 291.

Fathers and Sons

371 "My dear father died this morning": CEH to EH, October 7, 1926, JFK.
"Dear Dad, I am terribly sorry": EH to CEH, October 22, 1926, JFK.
Leicester's account of suicide: See *My Brother,* 109–10.
"As for my war trophies": Ibid.
"My father shot himself": EH to MP, December 16, 1928; *SL,* 291.
"I know how the death of your father": Archibald MacLeish to EH, December 14, [1928]; MacLeish, *Letters,* 220.

372 "My father shot himself in December": EH to Sylvia Beach, February 12, 1929, PUL.
"brave as a damned buffalo": Baker, *A Life Story,* 609n.
"outside of Patrick being born": EH to MP, January 5–6, 1932; *SL,* 351.
"Remember us writers": EH to FSF, April 12, 1931; Ibid., 340.
"I would have been glad": EH to EP, February 25, [1932 or 1933?], YCAL.

373 "Had never had": EH to Mrs. Paul Pfeiffer, January 26, 1936; *SL,* 436.
"Have you a father": *AFTA,* 154.
"But if you were born": Reynolds, *First War,* 41.
"There was a letter": *AFTA,* 135.

374 "Don't you care anything": Ibid., 304.
"Never worry": EH to GHH, March 11, 1929; *SL,* 295.
"How wonderful": GHH to EH, February 24, 1929, JFK.

375 "Any honors you could get": GHH to EH, March 7, 1929, JFK.
"Les wants you": GHH to EH, February 24, 1929, JFK.
"I will take care of it": GHH to EH, March 11, 1929, JFK.
"because Leicester says": GHH to EH, March 24, 1929, JFK.
"For Heaven's sake, Ernest": Baker, *A Life Story,* 200.

376 "Buried our fathers": *Complete Poems,* 95. See also MS. 816, "We are the generation whose fathers shot themselves," JFK.
"The Gulf Stream is alive": EH to MP, January 8, 1929; *SL,* 292.
"It makes too crazy dreams": Ibid., 293.
"For God's sake come down": EH to JDP, February 9, 1929; Ibid., 295.

377 "He built him up to me": Miller, *Ernie,* 113.
"I will have you back": MP to FSF, January 23, 1929; Fitzgerald, *Correspondence,* 223.
"AWFULLY PLEASED": See Reynolds, *First War,* 68.

"long tale of transalpine fornication": EH to Guy Hickok, January 9, 1929, YCAL.
"don't know what the hell": EH to Guy Hickok, February 26, 1929, YCAL.

378 "Abstract words such as glory": *AFTA,* 185.
"I watched them go down the road": Ibid., 206.
"In the late summer": Ibid., 3.
"At the start of the winter": Ibid., 4.

379 "It came very fast": Ibid., 6.
"in conscious imitation": Ross, *Reporting,* 218.
"Oh Jesus shoot me": *AFTA,* 55.
"medical wallahs" . . . "Lift him very carefully": Ibid., 58.

380 "blood brother and roommate": Ibid., 65.
"nights in bed, drunk": Ibid., 13.
"and we were still friends": Ibid., 14.
"He makes big preparations": Ibid. 65.
"Oh I love to tease you, baby": Ibid., 66.
"You do not love Him at all": Ibid., 72.

381 "It is another thing": Ibid.
"Very bitter": Ibid., 280.
"You're my religion": Ibid., 116.
"and Bill, I forgot all about": Griffin, *Along With Youth,* 114.
"But do you think": AvK to EH, [October 15, 1918]; Villard and Nagel, *In Love and War,* 98. I believe it is a St. Anthony that Hemingway had sent or given Agnes when she took the train to Florence, and that she refers to again in a later letter, November 1, 1918. See Villard and Nagel, 121.
"God please make her not die": *AFTA,* 330.

382 "You're my religion": Ibid., 116.
"and we'd be just alike": Ibid., 299.
"In a month": MS. 256, JFK.
"the bark of a young white birch tree": *GOE,* 81.

383 "and he helped with his hands": Ibid., 17. A recent bit of scholarship (see K. J. Peters, "The Thematic Integrity of The Garden of Eden," *Hemingway Review* [Spring 1991], 17–29) contends that the strange sexual performance is only the missionary position in reverse. It relates, apparently, to some mystical mumbo jumbo that Hemingway introduced into the novel and also to a Rodin sculpture, *The Metamorphosis of Ovid,* which figures prominently in the manuscript version but was cut before publication. Considering that some 130,000 words were cut from the 200,000-word manuscript, almost any argument might seem plausible but not altogether conclusive.
"brush away the Villa Rossa": Ibid., 168.
"Oh, yes. All my life": Ibid., 169.
"I am the snake": Ibid., 170.

384 "separate peace": Ibid., 243.
"You're like a snake": Ibid., 246.
"Don't you smile at him": Ibid., 247.
"Think how much we have": Ibid., 257.
"You don't know much, darling": Ibid.
"But I don't think about them much": Ibid., 298.
"I could tell": Reynolds, *First War,* 47. See also Robert W. Lewis, "Hem-

ingway in Italy," *Journal of Modern Literature* (May 1982), 209ff, for other details.

385 "Scott sailed last Saturday": MP to EH, March 8, 1929, JFK.
"Please don't under any circumstances?": EH to MP, [April 3, 1929?], PUL.
"Certain coldness": Fitzgerald journal, June 1929, PUL.

386 "In Cat in the Rain": Fitzgerald, *Correspondence,* 226.
"Our poor old friendship": Ibid.
"I mean — you're seeing him: Ibid., 227.
"Where's that desperate": Ibid.
"Kiss my ass": Ibid., 228.
"She's read all that silly": Callaghan, *That Summer in Paris,* 101.

387 "You would not believe it": EH to MP, August 28, 1929; *SL,* 302.
"So interested to see if I": Ibid.
"If you want to see me": Callaghan, *That Summer in Paris,* 214.
"the magic was in the way the words": Ibid., 107.

388 "Always remember this": Ibid., 108.
"Hey you old pornographer": JDP to EH, July 1, 1929, JFK.
"Certainly those letters": EH to MP, June 7, 1929; *SL,* 298.
"emasculation": EH to Archibald MacLeish, July 18, 1929; Ibid., 300.
"carried out on the shoulders": EH to Guy Hickok, July 30 [1929], YCAL.

389 "one of my most outspoken admirers": Franklin, *Bullfighter from Brooklyn,* 164.
"In depth, in range, in drama": Hanneman, *A Comprehensive Bibliography,* H117.
"a moving and beautiful book": Ibid., H118.

390 "Hemingway's farewell to a period": Ibid., H121.
"the most interesting novel of the year": Butcher, *Chicago Tribune,* September 28, 1929.
"Yay, Fannie": GHH inscription, Ibid.
"I'm sure I *personally*": GHH to EH, October 5, 1929, JFK.
"They must have all been by people": EH to Archibald MacLeish, November 22, 1930; *SL,* 331.
"That terrible mood": EH to FSF, September 13, 1929; Ibid., 306.
"Look what tripe": EH to FSF, ca. October 24 or 31, 1929; Ibid., *SL,* 310, but should be November 28 or December 5, 1929. See Mellow, *Invented Lives,* 351, and endnote on the misdating of the letters.

391 "hard, almost metallic": Hanneman, *A Comprehensive Bibliography,* H132.
"found in the war": Ibid., H133.
"The book has stirred up": EH to MP, December 15, 1929; *SL,* 316.
"I should need to be strong": John Peale Bishop to EH, October 15, 1929, JFK.
"Dear Hem, do you realize": JDP to EH, October 24, 1929, JFK.
"Looks like you'll be able": Ibid.
"Damned glad to hear": EH to JDP, September 4, 1929; *SL,* 303.

392 "I hope to Christ": EH to MP, October 31, 1929; Ibid., 311.
"the only obstacle": MP to FSF, October 30, 1929; Fitzgerald, *Dear Scott/ Dear Max,* 157.
"In reality, between ourselves": MP to FSF, November 20, 1929; Fitzgerald, *Correspondence,* 233.

"I only write when Scott": EH to MP, December 15, 1929; *SL,* 316.
"what does McAlmon do": MP to FSF, October 30, 1929; Fitzgerald, *Dear Scott/Dear Max,* 157–58.
"God knows he shows": FSF to MP, ca. November 15, 1929; Ibid., 159.
"scandalous story of something": Callaghan, *That Summer in Paris,* 84–85.

393 "I was impressed with McAlmon's 'Village'": MP to FSF, November 20, 1929; Fitzgerald, *Correspondence,* 233.
"was at his old dirty work": FSF to MP, January 21, 1930; Fitzgerald, *Dear Scott/Dear Max,* 161.
"claims you are the one": EH to FSF, ca. October 22 or 29, 1929; *SL,* 308, but should be ca. November 26 or December 3, 1929; see Fitzgerald's January 21, 1930, letter to Perkins in Fitzgerald, *Dear Scott/Dear Max,* on the dating of Hemingway's letters before and after the Stein party.
"Gertrude has taken me back": Tate, *Memoirs and Opinions,* 64.
Pauline Hemingway to GS, n.d. and February 27, 1928, YCAL.
Mildred Aldrich had died ca. February 19, 1928. See Mellow, *Charmed Circle,* 329.

394 "good hangover": EH to FSF, [November 28 or December 5, 1929]; *SL,* 309.
"She was praising her head off": Ibid.
"I like to have Gertrude": Ibid., 310.

395 "a legend very important": Callaghan, *That Summer in Paris,* 240.
"HAVE SEEN STORY IN HERALD TRIBUNE": Bruccoli, *Scott and Ernest,* 101.
"If you remember": EH to FSF, December 12, 1929; Ibid., 312.
"You'll remember though": Ibid., 313.

396 "one remarkable one": Crosby, *Shadows of the Sun,* 281.
"He told me about this girl": EH to FSF, December 12, 1929; Bruccoli, *Scott and Ernest,* 314.

A Thousand Intangibles

397 "A man can be": EH to Henry Strater, October 14, 1932; *SL,* 369.
"Nobody but Fairies": EH to FSF, September 4, 1929; Ibid., 305.
"To Scott from his old bedfellow": See Mellow, *Invented Lives,* for photograph, from the collection of Matthew Bruccoli.

398 "my other self": *Kansas City Star* (October 21, 1931), 17.
At Grace's door: Leicester Hemingway, *My Brother,* 135–36. See also EH to Guy Hickok, December 12, 1931, YCAL: "My damned imposter is out in Hollywood."
"ineradicable": EH to Arnold Gingrich, June 4, 1935; *SL,* 413.
"When you have a phony": EH to CB, February 17, 1951, Carlos Baker papers.

399 "Hemingway by K.O.": Hanneman, *A Comprehensive Bibliography,* H393.
"the 'tough guy'": Raeburn, *Fame Became of Him,* 105.
"I saw Ernest again": Meyers, *Hemingway,* 66.
"He has an accent I like": Baldwin, *Man Ray,* 150.
"an Era that is over": Klüver and Martin, *Kiki's Paris,* 9.
"never had a Room of Her Own": Ibid.

"perversion"..."There's no necessity": *SSEH,* 498.

400 "and I knew the story too too well": Smith, *Reader's Guide,* 224.

"the mechanics of it": EH to EW, November 8, 1952; *SL,* 795.

"is nothing but straight reporting": EH to MP, November 16, 1933; Ibid., 400.

"the necessity to put a thousand intangibles": *GHOA,* 28.

401 "The dead grow larger": *DIA,* 137.

"In this you drown in mucus": Ibid., 139.

"code" . . . "We didn't begin": Josephine Herbst, "The Hour of Counterfeit Bliss," 7, YCAL.

"Hem came up in a rush": Ibid., 9.

402 "grand venture to the Dry Tortugas": Ibid., 15.

"They were going to fish": Josephine Herbst to Katherine Anne Porter, April 1, 1930; Langer, *Josephine Herbst,* 109.

"the dreaminess of the place": Josephine Herbst, "The Hour of Counterfeit Bliss," 4, YCAL.

"Have been working hard": EH to MP, ca. April 11, 1930; *SL,* 321.

"Dos lost one": EH to Henry Strater, May 20, 1930; *SL,* 322.

"a hell of a good book": EH to MP, August 12, 1930; Ibid., 327.

"So far I've killed": EH to Henry Strater, ca. September 10, 1930; Ibid., 328.

"He had the leadership principle": Dos Passos, *The Best Times,* 205.

"The inside of the arm": EH to Guy Hickok, December 5, 1930, *SL,* 332.

"The most hair raising": Archibald MacLeish to CB, August 9, 1963; Ibid., 332n.

404 "can only write about 400": EH to FSF, April 12, 1931; Ibid., 339.

"She wouldn't have wanted": Ibid.

"It looks like a dull voyage": EH to Waldo Peirce; May 4, 1931; Ibid., 340.

405 "bravest and most honorable": *DIA,* 223.

"Chances for Marxian revolution nil": EH to JDP, June 26, 1931; *SL,* 342.

"If the people of Spain": *DIA,* 264.

406 "the moment of truth": Ibid., 174.

"Leave us get bulls straight": EH to EP, [1926], YCAL.

"He gives the feeling": *DIA,* 213.

"Now I've got it": Ibid., 253.

"I see death": Ibid., 264.

"All stories, if continued": Ibid., 122.

"the feeling of life and death": Ibid., 3.

407 "Courage comes such a short distance": Ibid., 222.

"We used to bring the makings": Franklin, *Bullfighter,* 196.

408 "I have never cared for any man": Mary Welsh Hemingway, *How It Was,* 426.

"the unsuccessful matadors": *DIA,* 271.

"Make all that come true again": Ibid., 272.

"a complete coward": Ibid., 227.

"has not the courage of a louse": Ibid., 251.

409 "Then you could walk across": Ibid., 277.

"cider in Bombilla": Ibid., 271.

410 "The little devil": *SSEH,* 428.

"[The damned kid]": MS. 341, "Crime and Punishment," JFK. An earlier version of the sketch also appears in MS. 340.

411 "I write some stories": EH to MP, November 16, 1933; *SL,* 400.
"Keep out of my business": *SSEH,* 514.
"What kind of blood is it": Ibid.
"the mincing gentry": *DIA,* 205.
"There's a queen for you": *SSEH,* 517.

412 José Ortiz: See Franklin, *Bullfighter,* 49; Hemingway told Arnold Gingrich (*SL,* 393) that "The Mother of a Queen" was a true story about the Mexican bullfighter Ortiz.
"sure he's a queen": *SSEH,* 513.
"Immediately after the accident": Franklin, *Bullfighter,* 185.
"ruined by sea water": *SSEH,* 515. Franklin, too, had had his luggage and bullfighting paraphernalia damaged in the hold of a freighter. See *Bullfighter,* 98.
"I won't bother you with any more letters": GHH to EH, April 5, 1932, JFK.
"The good parts of a book": EH to FSF, September 4, 1929; *SL,* 305.

413 "Now she is all about me": *SSEH,* 514.
"except the suicide": *DIA,* 122.

414 "My bloody book is finished": EH to Guy Hickok, December 12, 1931, YCAL.
"Very black hair. Solemn pan": Ibid.
"I imagine Hitler": EH to Guy Hickok, Ibid.
"an absolute model": JDP to EH, [February 1932]; Dos Passos, *The Fourteenth Chronicle,* 402.
"I'm only doubtful": Ibid.
"The volume is so hellishly good": Ibid., 403.

415 "4½ galleys of philosophy": EH to JDP, May 30, 1932; *SL,* 360.
"DID IT SEEM": Baker, *A Life Story,* 229.
"You know I am superstitious": EH to MP, June 28, 1932; *SL,* 361.
"a cook book and a telephone directory": Ibid., 362.
"an extraordinarily fine piece": Hanneman, *A Comprehensive Bibliography,* H197.
"excellent reading, full of the vigor": Ibid., H185.

416 "Fortunately the author": Ibid., H195.
"spiritual autobiography" . . . "tragic masterpiece": Kirstein, *By With To & From,* 284, 288.
"It also defines": Ibid., 284.
"stands head and shoulders": Ibid., 288.
"There are passages": Hanneman, *A Comprehensive Bibliography,* H191.
"There weren't any cracks": EH to Robert Coates, October 5, 1932; *SL,* 368. Hemingway's letter appeared in the November 5, 1932, issue of *The New Yorker.*
"you can't go wrong": *DIA,* 173.
"The Eliot thing": EH to Robert Coates, October 5, 1932; *SL,* 368.
"I would shoot my own mother": Ibid., 369.

417 "He is, of all critics": EH to MP, August 12, 1930; Ibid., 326.
"*wonderful* reporting": EH to JDP, May 30, 1932; Ibid., 369.
"is sometimes boring": EH to JDP, October 14, 1932; Ibid., 374.
"I suppose I am an anarchist": Ibid., 375.
"will sound honester in 20 years": Ibid.

"pretty maudlin": EW to FSF, November 7, 1932; Wilson, *Letters,* 229.
"basilisk stare": Wilson, *The Thirties,* 301.
"Hemingway was now a great man": Wilson, *The Bit Between My Teeth,* 522.

418 "not to overdo it": Wilson, *The Thirties,* 302.
"pretending to be unconscious": Wilson, *The Bit Between My Teeth,* 522.
"I have the impression": Wilson, *The Thirties,* 303.
"with the utmost seriousness": Wilson, *The Bit Between My Teeth,* 522.

419 "but he simply took off": Wilson, *The Thirties,* 302.
"No confidence, eh?": Ibid.
"a terrible bat": FSF to MP, January 19, 1933; Fitzgerald, *Dear Scott/Dear Max,* 177.
"You did call me up, by the way": MP to FSF, January 27, 1933; Ibid., 178. For another version of this incident, see Mellow, *Invented Lives,* 407.
"gorgeous pages": "Bull in the Afternoon" appeared in the June 7, 1933, issue of *The New Republic,* quoted, here, from Eastman, *Great Companions,* 53–54.
"that shallow cult": Ibid., 55.

420 "It is of course a commonplace": Ibid., 54.
"It was as though": *DIA,* 94. It is probable that Mejías was the second of the unnamed "fairies" Hemingway mentions in his glossary definition of *maricón,* "a sodomite, nance, queen, fairy, fag," in *DIA,* 417–18, among the matadors he knew about. (Ortiz was the other.) On Sánchez Mejías's bisexual tendencies, see Gibson, *Federico García Lorca,* 198.
"the birth records": Archibald MacLeish to the Editors of *The New Republic,* ca. June 8, 1922; MacLeish, *Letters,* 261.
"Mr. Max Eastman elaborate": two letter drafts, EH to the Editors of *The New Republic,* dated June 12, 1933, JFK.
"Is it a matter of numbers": EH to Bruce Bliven, June 19, 1933, JFK.
"Mr. Alexander Woollcott": EH to the Editors of *The New Republic,* June 12, 1933; Baker, *A Life Story,* 242.

421 "every bit as good as the novel": Hanneman, *A Comprehensive Bibliography,* H157; Young's review appeared in the October 8, 1930, issue of *The New Republic.*
"What a slimy lying shit he is": EH to Archibald MacLeish, June 21, 1933, JFK.
"I will get my own redress": EH to MP, June 13, 1933; *SL,* 394.

422 "meritorious" . . . "the Picasso part": Flanner, *Paris Was Yesterday,* 90.
"Gertrude S. I was very fond of": EH to Janet Flanner, April 8, 1933; *SL,* 387.
"Poor old Papa": Ibid.
"a little proud and a little ashamed": Stein, *The Autobiography of Alice B. Toklas,* 265.
"a rotten pupil": Ibid., 266.
"Ernest is very fragile": Ibid., 267–68.
"He looks like a modern": Ibid., 266.

423 "They admitted that Hemingway was yellow": Ibid., 265–66.
"a woman who isn't a woman": Stephens, *Hemingway's Nonfiction,* 126.
"Learned from her too": EH to EP, July 22, 1933, YCAL.
"Well gents": Ibid.

The Green Hills of Africa

424 "We have a fine house here": EH to Janet Flanner, April 8, 1933; *SL*, 387.
"Ernest loves Jane": Baker, *A Life Story*, 228.
"Too much was going on": Kert, *The Hemingway Women*, 249.

425 "Am having large nose": Ibid., 247.
"Don't worry Mrs. Mason": Meyers, *Hemingway*, 245.
"was at loose ends": Evans, *Evans at Work*, 62.

426 "I refused to do Hemingway": Mellow, "Walker Evans Captures the Unvarnished Truth," *New York Times* (December 1, 1974), 37–38.
"Leave for Europe Aug. 7": EH to EP, July 22, 1933, YCAL.
"I weigh 187 now": Ibid.
"No kick to gun": EH to Henry Strater, ca. June 20, 1930; *SL*, 324.
"I may have become a naturalist": EH to EP, July 22, 1933, YCAL.
"An if you are goin to be": EP to EH, August 13, 1933, JFK.

428 "While the peasants are as bad off": *By-Line*, 146.
"All I do is go out": Ibid., 155.
"As I write this valediction": Bald, *On the Left Bank*, 142. Bald's farewell appeared in the July 25, 1933, issue of the Paris *Herald Tribune*.
"I am tired of jiggling a corpse": Ibid., 143.
"People must be expected": *By-Line*, 157–58.

429 "He and I are good old friends": Fitch, *Sylvia Beach*, 341.
"A fool like [H. S.] Canby thinks": EH to MP, November 16, 1933; *SL*, 400.
"after a wonderful start": Ibid., 399.
Lucia Joyce: See Maddox, *Nora*, 291.
Dinner with the Joyces: See *GHOA*, 71, 195; Baker, *A Life Story*, 608.
"Ah Jim could do with a spot": EH to Bernard Berenson, October 14, 1952; *SL*, 789.
"promised us a living lion": Ellmann, *James Joyce*, 695.
"He's a good writer, Hemingway": Ibid.

430 "Hemingway, blasphemy's no sin": EH to Bernard Berenson, October 14, 1952; *SL*, 789.
"Go easy on the beer": EH to Patrick Hemingway, December 2, 1933; Ibid., 402.
"Nothing that I have ever read": *By-Line*, 160.
Philip Percival: *GHOA*, 281.

431 "Mama *piga Simba*": *GHOA*, 42. See also Kert, *The Hemingway Women*, 256, for details from Pauline's diary.
"Hey la Mama!": Ibid.
"Very splendid; wished I had": Kert, *The Hemingway Women*, 256.
"chosen as the one to bear": *By-Line*, 159.
"belonging to the weasel family": Kert, *The Hemingway Women*, 258.
"very gay and handsome": Ibid.

432 "very unpleasant" . . . "she could and would put pen": EH to MP, August 27, 1942; *SL*, 541.
"We had not treated him badly": *GHOA*, 86.
"I was, truly, very fond": Ibid.

433 "They were the color": Ibid., 276.
"the biggest, widest, darkest": Ibid., 291.

"We have very primitive emotions": Ibid., 293.
"in a stupor of silent worship": Wineapple, *Genêt*, 67–68; see also Baker, *A Life Story*, 238 and note.
"The Dumb Ox" appeared in the April 1934 issue of the English publication *Life and Letters* and was later reprinted in *Men Without Art*.
"One might even go so far": Lewis, *A Soldier of Humor and Selected Writings*, 282.

434 "an art of the surface": Ibid., 274.
"Poor Ernest . . . he is really": Fitch, *Sylvia Beach*, 343.
"The men rose": Kert, "This Week," *New York Herald Tribune* (February 13, 1955), 8.

435 "The hell of it": EH to MP, April 30, 1934, PUL.
"Did you like the book": FSF to EH, May 10, 1934; Fitzgerald, *Letters*, 307.
"If you take real people": EH to FSF, May 28, 1934; *SL*, 407.
"In the first place": Ibid.

436 "Of all people on earth": Ibid., 408.
"The old charming frankness": FSF to EH, June 1, 1934; Fitzgerald, *Letters*, 308.
"I think it is obvious": Ibid., 309.
"that I no longer listen": Ibid. 310.
"A strange thing is that": MP to FSF, April 8, 1935; Fitzgerald, *Dear Scott/Dear Max*, 219.
"But I still believe": FSF to MP, April 15, 1935; Ibid., 219.

437 "If I ever write anything": *GHOA*, 193.
"I loved the country so": Ibid., 72.
"how far prose can be carried": Ibid., 26–27.
"A country, finally, erodes": Ibid., 109.

438 "minds, yes. Nice, dry, clean minds": Ibid., 21.
"all modern American literature": Ibid., 22.
"At present, we have two good writers": Ibid., 23.
"When is your World Genius": EH to MP, December 26, 1931; *SL*, 347.
"At a certain age": *GHOA*, 24.
"Woman of letters. Salon woman": Baker, *A Life Story*, 267, 612n.

439 "quick-legged across the road": *GHOA*, 35–36.
"It was a cow rhino": Ibid., 99.
"hearing the rustle of night things": Ibid., 58.
"me scared of snakes": Ibid., 58.
"*Fisi*, the hyena": Ibid., 38.
"obscenely loping, full belly dragging": Ibid., 37.
"There was that comic slap": Ibid.

440 "Are not the white marlin": *By-Line*, 175. On the sexual changes of the jewelfish and the grouper, I am indebted to Ed Migdalski, former professor in the Zoology Department at Yale University, and Terry Frady of the New England Fisheries Center, Woods Hole, Massachusetts. For information on the two different genera of marlin Hemingway mistakenly thought of as hermaphroditic members of the same genus, I am grateful to Eric Prince of the South East Fisheries Center, Miami, Florida. Both Paul Whitehead of the Peabody Museum in New Haven and Pat Brunauer of the Museum of Natural History in New York City supplied information on the strange case of the hyena.

"It wasn't much of a roe": Ibid., 177–78.
"pretty evenly divided between big game": Hanneman, *A Comprehensive Bibliography,* H260.
"the best written story": Ibid., H264.
"A pretty small book": Ibid., H262.
"Would Hemingway write better books": Ibid., H269.
441 "He inveighs with much scorn": Wilson, *The Shores of Light,* 619.
"went all the way to Africa": Ibid., 619–20.
"rubbishy": Ibid., 621.
"But for reasons": Ibid.
"without question one of the finest": Ibid., 622.
442 "I think he read the criticisms": EH to Ivan Kashkin, January 12, 1936; *SL,* 430.
"One can imagine": Wilson, *The Shores of Light,* 621.
"The next thing he knew": *SSEH,* 119.
443 "She was always lovely": *GHOA,* 73.
"He had always had": *SSEH,* 121.
"All in all they were known": Ibid.
"They're not dangerous": Ibid., 108.
"What would happen": Ibid., 129.
444 "They are, he thought, the hardest": Ibid., 107.
"Macomber, as he fired": Ibid., 134.
"a sudden white-hot, blinding flash": Ibid., 135.
"Mrs. Macomber, in the car": Ibid.
445 "the bits of horn": "African Sketch," JFK.
"He said Karl's and my fire": Ibid.
446 "He quoted what I said": Meyers, *Hemingway,* 262.
"Gave White Hunter": "African Sketch," JFK.
"Not any more": *GHOA,* 65.
"complete with handles": "The Art of the Short Story," *The Paris Review* (Spring 1981), 93.
"a brave man": *SSEH,* 110.
447 "more than shame he felt": Ibid.
"He lay awake with that knowledge": Ibid., 121.
"Well, you're a coward": Ibid., 122.
448 "That was a pretty thing to do": Ibid., 135.
"Francis' wife hates him": Meyers, *Hemingway,* 273.
"No, I don't know": "The Art of the Short Story," *The Paris Review* (Spring 1981), 95.
"a really nice and really fine": Ibid.
"what would happen to a character": Ibid.
449 "a major story" . . . "fool proof": EH to MP, April 9, 1936; *SL,* 442, 444.
"put into one short story": "The Art of the Short Story," *The Paris Review* (Spring 1981), 96.
"Close to the western summit": *SSEH,* 150.
"because there is so much dialogue": EH to MP, April 9, 1936; *SL,* 443.
"The marvellous thing": *SSEH,* 150.
450 "What have we done": Ibid., 153.
"Very painful": Kert, *The Hemingway Women,* 258.
451 "It came with a rush": *SSEH,* 162.
"He lay still and death": Ibid., 169.
"It can be two bicycle policemen": Ibid., 172.

“A fourth planed down”: Ibid., 151.
“You can’t die”: Ibid.
“is it absolutely necessary”: Ibid., 155–56.
452 “Why don’t you use your nose?”: Ibid., 165.
“with her well-known, well-loved”: Ibid.
“a spy in their country”: Ibid., 157.
“the people he knew now”: Ibid.
“If you hadn’t left”: Ibid., 153.
“I love you now”: Ibid.
453 “You rich bitch”: Ibid., 156.
“He is part of the metaphysics”: “The Art of the Short Story,” *The Paris Review* (Spring 1981), 96.
“explainers, apologists, stoolies”: Ibid.
“Put it down to *omertà*”: Ibid.
“*No, he had never written about Paris*”: *SSEH,* 169.
“*He had never written any of that*”: *SSEH,* 164.
“*He had seen the world change*”: Ibid.
454 “as wide as all the world”: Ibid., 174.

Politics, Women, Drink, Money, Ambition

457 “make yourself responsible”: *GHOA,* 148.
“when you write truly and well”: Ibid., 148–49.
“and when on the sea”: Ibid., 42.
“as the load spreads”: Ibid., 149–50.
458 “and the palm fronds”: Ibid., 150.
“just one faded snap-shot more”: EH to Charles Fenton, July 29, 1952; *SL,* 777.
“Eyes went haywire in Spain”: EH to MP, January 5–6, 1932; Ibid., 351.
459 “14 stitches in face”: Ibid.
“A life of action”: EH to Ivan Kashkin, August 19, 1935; Ibid., 419.
“And the point of it is”: “The Art of the Short Story,” *The Paris Review* (Spring 1981), 92.
“Along before Christmas”: EH to Sara Murphy, February 11, 1936; Donnelly and Billings, *Sara & Gerald,* 171.
“felt simply awful”: EH to JDP, February 11, 1936, JFK.
“started going out in the stream”: Donnelly and Billings, *Sara & Gerald,* 171.
“calendar of slaughter”: FSF to MP, [before March 19, 1937], Fitzgerald, *Letters,* 272.
460 “who cannot write because”: *GHOA,* 23.
“very supercilious”: EH to JDP, December 17, 1935; *SL,* 427.
“That means, anyhow”: EH to FSF, December 16, 1935; Ibid., 424.
“Also you are like nobody”: Ibid., 425.
“since I have stopped giving”: EH to FSF, December 21, 1935; Ibid., 428.
“You put so damned much value”: Ibid.
461 “only a mediocre caretaker”: Fitzgerald, *The Crack-Up,* 71.
“never sank below the level”: Ibid., 77.
“like an old plate”: Ibid., 72.
“So there was not an ‘I’ any more”: Ibid., 79.
“the test of a first-rate intelligence”: Ibid., 69.

"a qualified unhappiness": Ibid., 84.
"he seems to almost take a pride": EH to MP, February 7, 1936; *SL,* 437–38.
"My god did you read": EH to JDP and Katy, January 13, 1936; Ibid., 433.
"These are the bad times": EH to Sara Murphy, ca. February 27, 1936; Ibid., 440.

463 "because the people are so much nicer": EH to Marjorie Kinnan Rawlings, August 16, 1936; Ibid., 450.
"If I hadn't been such a bloody fool practicing Catholic": Mary Welsh Hemingway, *How It Was,* 243.
"break your bloody heart": EH to Marjorie Kinnan Rawlings, August 16, 1936; *SL,* 449.
"Tell me first what are the things": *GHOA,* 28.
"the struggle between two fighting males": Meyers, *Hemingway,* 248. For a fuller discussion of Kubie's thesis, see Meyers, 247–49.

464 "Have won 350 bucks": EH to Arnold Gingrich, June 4, 1935; *SL,* 415.
"My Mr. Cooper": Kert, *The Hemingway Women,* 270.
"Goddam editor comes down to Bimini": Gingrich, "Scott, Ernest and Whoever," *Esquire* (October 1973), 374.
"a magnificent and mysterious phenomenon": JDP to Stewart Mitchell, [March 27, 1935]; Dos Passos, *The Fourteenth Chronicle,* 468–69.

465 "What they do out here": Katy Dos Passos to Pauline Hemingway, September 28, 1934, JFK.
"We called it the lit royale": Dos Passos, *The Best Times,* 219.
"You remember": Katy Dos Passos to Sara and Gerald Murphy, December 3, 1934; Dos Passos, *The Fourteenth Chronicle,* 421.
"a crazy mixture of luxury, indigence": Katy Dos Passos to Gerald Murphy, June 20, 1935; Ibid., 422.
"They came like express trains": Katy Dos Passos to Gerald Murphy; Ibid., 423.
"to see the bullets": Ibid.

466 "Gosh Hem — this novel business": JDP to EH, [February 7, 1936]; Ibid., 483.
"Don't let the goddamned novel": EH to JDP, February 11, 1936, JFK.
"Mrs. Mason" . . . "almost as apt": EH to JDP, April 12, 1936; *SL,* 445.
"Have something very funny": Ibid.
"By God I wish I had": EH to Sara Murphy, ca. February 27, 1936; Ibid., 439.

467 "so good": Ibid.
"As I say am always": EH to JDP, April, 12, 1936; Ibid., 447.
Stevens-Hemingway fight: See also Brazeau, *Parts of a World,* 97–99.
"Most people don't think": Wallace Stevens to Henry Church, July 2, 1942; Stevens, *Letters of Wallace Stevens,* 411–12.
"Gosh Hem, it was a tough proposition": JDP to EH, May 21, 1936, JFK.
"Will make a good trip soon": EH to JDP, July 16, 1936, Carr, *Dos Passos,* 348.
"You must have had hell": Ibid.

468 "In hunting you know": *By-Line,* 239.
"What size of a fish": Ibid.

"half crazy from his loss": Ibid., 240.

469 "The rich were dull": *SSEH,* 170.

"a most lovable, nervous and sensitive": Berg, *Max Perkins,* 378.

"He is so great an artist": Ibid., 379.

"They are the only people": Baker, *A Life Story,* 288.

470 "The Stewarts were ruined": EH to JDP, September 4, 1929; *SL,* 303.

"was ruined by Mrs. Bishop's income": Ibid.

"Always try not to be": EH to Charles Scribner, July 22, 1949; Ibid., 659.

"He remembered poor Scott Fitzgerald": See manuscript copy in Bruccoli, *Scott and Ernest,* 130.

"And there in the cafe": Lynn, *Hemingway,* 214.

471 "Dear Ernest" . . . "Please lay off me": FSF to EH, [August 1936]; Fitzgerald, *Letters,* 311.

"yellow dog": Gingrich, "Scott, Ernest and Whoever," *Esquire* (October 1973), 152.

"quite as nervously broken down": FSF to Beatrice Dance, September 15, 1936; Fitzgerald, *Letters,* 543.

472 "Somehow I love that man": FSF to MP, September 19, 1936; Fitzgerald, *Dear Scott/Dear Max,* 231.

"The only difference between the rich": MP to Elizabeth Lemmon, August 16, 1936; see Bruccoli, *Scott and Ernest,* 131.

"As for what Ernest did": MP to FSF, September 23, 1936; Fitzgerald, *Dear Scott/Dear Max,* 232.

"It was a damned rotten thing": FSF to MP, March 4, 1938; Ibid., 241–42.

"As to the Scott passage": MP to EH, August 23, 1938; Bruccoli, *Scott and Ernest,* 140.

473 "Poor Scott; and didn't he know": EH to Arthur Mizener, January 4, 1951; *SL,* 716.

"spoiled us for anything less good": James Rorty to EH, September 8, 1926, JFK.

"They just took the Walsh thing": EH to EP, [1926], YCAL.

"I find five numbers": Stock, *Ezra Pound,* 265.

474 "*The Revolution*": EH to EP, [1927], YCAL.

"said a very funny thing": EH to MP, January 20, 1927; *SL,* 241.

"Fuck the new masses": EH to EP, [1927], YCAL.

"interesting phenomena": Carpenter, *A Serious Character,* 458.

"but what makes you think": EH to EP, [1926], YCAL.

475 "had all his old political opponents": *By-Line,* 226.

"Waal, me deah Hombo": EP to EH, November 28, 1935; YCAL.

"to achieve ECONOMIC INDEPENDENCE": Carpenter, *A Serious Character,* 535.

"are in the air": *By-Line,* 235.

"have been beaten because": Ibid., 234.

"a confidential agreement": Ibid., 233.

476 Mussolini's "economic penetration" of Ethiopia: For details of the negotiations with France, see Denis Mack Smith, *Mussolini,* 191.

"in order that their return": *By-Line,* 229.

"boys from the little": Ibid., 235.

"Now watch one thing": EH to JDP, March 26, 1932; *SL,* 354.

477 "Leftward Swing": EH to Paul Romaine, July 6, 1932; Ibid., 363.

"Your idea that I stay": EH to Paul Romaine, August 9, 1932; Ibid., 365.
"Dos Passos doesn't swing": EH to Paul Romaine, July 6, 1932; Ibid., 363.
"middle-class liberal" . . . "'camp follower'": Dos Passos, *The Fourteenth Chronicle,* 382, 383.
"Anyway as I says": JDP to EH, January 15, 1927, JFK.
"If you keep away": JDP to EH, [November 1, 1928], JFK.
"Tell us . . . are you for us": Dos Passos, *The Best Times,* 196.
Kirov murder: See Kennan, *Russia and the West,* 302–303; also Kennan, *Memoirs,* 64–65.

478 "has completely destroyed": JDP to EW, December 23, 1934; Dos Passos, *The Fourteenth Chronicle,* 459.
"I regret that Stalin": EW to JDP, January 11, 1935; Wilson, *Letters,* 255.
"My enthusiastic feelings": JDP to EW, [January 1935]; Dos Passos, *The Fourteenth Chronicle,* 462.
"The great joker about the USSR": JDP to EH, December 24, 1928, JFK. For an account of Hemingway's publication in Russia, see Deming Brown, "Hemingway in Russia," in Baker, *Hemingway and His Critics,* 145–61.

479 "again and again he was writing": Kashkin, "A Tragedy of Craftsmanship" in McCaffery, *The Man and His Work,* 93.
"It is a pleasure": EH to Ivan Kashkin, August 19, 1935; *SL,* 417.
"Here criticism is a joke": Ibid., 417–18.
"Everyone tries to frighten you": Ibid., 418–19.
"P.P.S. Don't you drink?": Ibid., 420.

480 "what is, in fact, perhaps": Wilson, *The Shores of Light,* 620.
"rotten old capitalist world": Ibid., 625.
"that arch-bourgeois, arch snob": Ibid.
"who would never knowingly sit": EH to Ivan Kashkin, January 12, 1936; *SL,* 430.
"You write like a patriot": Ibid., 432.
"Well what the hell": Ibid.

481 "but writing isn't silly": Ibid.
"between 700 and 1000 dead": EH to MP, September 7, 1935; Ibid., 421.
"The veterans in those camps": Ibid.
"naked, tossed up into trees": Ibid., 422.
"those poor bonus march guys": Ibid.
"And what's the punishment": *New Masses,* vol. 16 (September 17, 1935), 4.

482 "You have all the luck": JDP to EH, September 20, 1935; Dos Passos, *The Fourteenth Chronicle,* 482.
"I don't think it's entirely": JDP to Malcolm Cowley, December 1, 1934; Ibid., 456.
"Marx the whimpering bourgeois": Baker, *A Life Story,* 612n.

The Politics of Desperation

483 "none of the female vices": Kert, *The Hemingway Women,* 288. For biographical information on Martha Gellhorn, I am indebted to Bernice Kert's volume and to Carl Rollyson's more recent *Nothing Ever Happens to the Brave.*

"Nothing ever happens to the brave": *AFTA*, 139.

484 "Who is this Martha Gellhorn?": Kert, *The Hemingway Women*, 289.
"a beautiful blonde in a black dress": Ibid., 282.
"very lovable and full of fire": Ibid., 291.
"My new system": Ibid., 292.

485 "It was by now visible": Carr, *Dos Passos*, 363.
"a peach, both good and intelligent": Shi, *Matthew Josephson*, 178.
"They [American Communists] have certainly": Ibid.
"received these observations": Ibid.
"We must now protest everywhere": Ibid., 179.
"I could stay on here forever": Meyers, *Hemingway*, 302.

486 "came from selling": *THAHN*, 240.
"collected writers": Ibid., 150.

487 "a silly ass": MS. 204, JFK.
"What can you do": *THAHN*, 245.
"And I said": Ibid., 259.
"I guess you find out": Ibid., 261.
"I've seen you bitter": Ibid., 186.
"Don't mind him": Ibid., 189.

488 "No matter how": Ibid., 225.
"What the hell do I care": Ibid., 168.
"The funny thing": Franklin, *Bullfighter*, 206.

489 "John, they goin' make": Ludington, *John Dos Passos*, 364.
"conspirators": Martha Gellhorn to EH, February 15, 1937; Kert, *The Hemingway Women*, 294.

490 "When finish this book": EH to MP, September 26, 1936; *SL*, 454.
"This is the dress rehearsal": EH to the Pfeiffer Family, February 9, 1937; Ibid., 458.
"leader of the Ingrates battalion": Ibid., 457.
"but they are the people": Ibid., 458.

491 "a young man high up": EH to JDP, April 12, 1936; Ibid., 447.
"the politics of desperation": EH to Harry Sylvester, February 5, 1937; Ibid., 456.
"exploited working people": Ibid.
"I think that's a dirty outfit": Ibid., 457.
"but you can't preserve": EH to the Pfeiffer Family, February 9, 1937; Ibid., 457.
"I would sort of worry": Ibid., 458.
"After the first two weeks": EH to Mrs. Paul Pfeiffer, August 2, 1937; Ibid., 461.

492 "a major victory": Watson, "Hemingway's Spanish Civil War Dispatches," *Hemingway Review*, vol. 7, no. 2 (Spring 1988), 19.
"the battle of Brihuega": Ibid., 22.

493 "They did not look like men": Ibid., 19.
Capa's falling soldier: See Whelan, *Robert Capa*, 95–100.
"a good general": EH to MP, December 15, 1936; *SL*, 455–56.
"must either encircle Madrid": Watson, "Hemingway's Spanish Civil War Dispatches," 20.

494 "This is a strange new kind": Ibid., 33.
"I am tired of explaining": Gellhorn, *The Face of War*, 17.
"a lovely tinkling musical sound": Ibid., 20.

"all kinds of liaisons": Baker, *A Life Story,* 308.

495 "who bought us all our food": Watson, "Hemingway's Spanish Civil War Dispatches," 44.

"NOTIFY HEMINGWAY": Ibid., 26.

"REQUEST HEMINGWAY": Ibid., 33.

"Well I was not in Guernica": EH to Mary Pfeiffer, February 6, 1939; *SL,* 476. For various accounts of the destruction of Guernica, see Beevor, Eby, Hugh Thomas, Gordon Thomas, and Max Witts.

"It was a feeling": Gellhorn, *The Face of War,* 15.

496 "a journalist friend": Ibid., 16.

"I think it was the only time": Kert, *The Hemingway Women,* 299.

"much that is brave and good": Raeburn, *Fame Became of Him,* 87.

497 "She was a legend": Hemingway's blurb was blazoned on the front of the dust jacket.

"a piece of fiction": Mora, *In Place of Splendor,* 290.

"Party pride": Matthews, *Half of Spain,* 94.

"Oh Lord, deliver us": Pétrement, *Simone Weil,* 272.

498 "I like Communists": Baker, *A Life Story,* 330.

"Of all the pigheaded kids": EH to Jack Wheeler, June 2, 1938; Watson, "Hemingway's Spanish Civil War Dispatches," 121.

"pricks and fakers": EH to MP, May 5, 1938; *SL,* 467.

"before it really started": Ibid.

"phony": EH to Charles Lanham, April 15, 1948; Ibid., 634.

"*Pense? Moi pense pas*": EH to Evan Shipman, August 25, 1942; Ibid., 538.

499 "Really good writers": *Conversations,* 193.

"all the foreign correspondents": Ludington, *John Dos Passos,* 376–77.

500 "enormously tall, very charming": EH to Mrs. Paul Pfeiffer, August 2, 1937; *SL,* 460.

"THE PICTURE WAS": FSF to EH, July 13, 1937; Fitzgerald, *Correspondence,* 475.

"whirlwind": FSF to MP, ca. July 15, 1937; Fitzgerald, *Dear Scott/Dear Max,* 238.

501 "What do you mean": Baker, *A Life Story,* 317.

"the Croton Mauler": Eastman, *Great Companions,* 68. Eastman gave a detailed account of the fight and the press coverage in his memoir.

"political gesture": Ibid.

"He jumped at me like a woman": Ibid., 66.

"He is living at the present": FSF to MP, September 3, 1937; Fitzgerald, *Letters,* 275.

"I had a plan for Hemingway": Ivens with Watson, "Joris Ivens and the Communists: Bringing Hemingway into the Spanish Civil War," *Hemingway Review,* (Fall 1990) 13.

Sources for information on the Russian staff officers, etc.: Hugh Thomas, *The Spanish Civil War;* Beevor, *The Spanish Civil War;* Eby, *Between the Bullet and the Lie.*

502 "thinking it was mined": EH to EW, November 8, 1952; *SL,* 794.

"I am *Général Soviétique*": *FWTBT,* 8.

"War's a dirty business": Ehrenburg, *Memoirs,* 385.

"petit bourgeois indecision": Beevor, *The Spanish Civil War,* 144.

503 "spoiled cry babies": Eby, *Between the Bullet and the Lie,* 27.

"a mentally sick man": Ehrenburg, *Memoirs*, 397.
"He knew I was not a communist": EH to Bernard Berenson, October 14, 1952; *SL*, 789.
"acted as Stalin's agent": Beevor, *The Spanish Civil War*, 122.
"I wondered how this man": Spender, *World Within World*, 209. See EW to Arthur Schlesinger, 1964; in Wilson, *Letters*, 197, who recounts the incident as told to him by Spender: "[Hemingway] was perfectly serious and natural when he talked about Stendhal and other literary matters, but switched into his bogus public character the moment there was publicity in the offing."

504 "Don't expect an analysis": Herbst, *The Starched Blue Sky of Spain*, 133.

505 The POUM was the Trotskyite Partido Obrero de Unification Marxista; the CNT, the Anarcho-Syndicalist Trades Union; the PSUC, the Partido Socialista Unificataluna, the Catalan Socialist-Communist Party.
"Ask Hem who is fighting": Langer, *Josephine Herbst*, 211.
"Hem good guy": Ibid., 214–15.
"If you don't stop talking": Ibid., 112.
"When I had finally": Ibid., 214.

506 "put iron into me": Ibid., 210.
"seemed to be naively embracing": Herbst, *The Starched Blue Sky of Spain*, 151.
"professed ignorance and chagrin": JDP to the Editors of *The New Republic*, [July 1939]; Dos Passos, *The Fourteenth Chronicle*, 526.

507 "romantic American Communist sympathizers": Ibid., 528.
"It was only too likely": Ibid.
"As always in such cases": Ibid.

508 "After all, this is a war": Herbst, *The Starched Blue Sky of Spain*, 150.
"Shall always remember": JDP to Josie Herbst, [Summer 1939]; Dos Passos, *The Fourteenth Chronicle*, 524.
"only one story among thousands": JDP to the Editors of *The New Republic*, [July 1939]; Ibid., 529.

509 "BABY, SEE YOU SOON": Hotchner, *Papa Hemingway*, 132.
"Of course, we were all": Ibid., 133.

510 "Perhaps he was still a little afraid": Ludington, *John Dos Passos*, 373.
"You do that": Dos Passos, *The Fourteenth Chronicle*, 496.
"Why Ernest": Ibid.
"between the Marxist concept": Ludington, *John Dos Passos*, 378.
"remaining alas in a state": Ibid., 376.
"Fascism is nothing": JDP to John Howard Lawson, [Fall 1937]; Dos Passos, *The Fourteenth Chronicle*, 514.

511 "A war is still": EH to JDP, ca. March 26, 1938; *SL*, 463.
"Then there is Nin": Ibid., 464.
"I would like to be able": Langer, *Josephine Herbst*, 227.
"When people start": EH to JDP, ca. March 26, 1938; *SL*, 463.

512 "a very good friend": *Ken*, June 30, 1938, 26.
"The Barbarism of Fascist": *Hemingway Review*, vol. 8, no. 2 (Spring 1988), 114. See also William B. Watson, "Discovering Hemingway's Pravda Article," *Washington Post*, November 28, 1982.

513 "During the last fifteen months": Ibid., 116.
"He was hungry": Ibid., 117.
"The crimes committed by Fascism": Ibid., 118.

"great 37–38 epoch": EH to Archibald MacLeish, April 4, 1943; *SL,* 544.
"Have you ever seen": EH to EW, November 8, 1952; Ibid., 793.

514 "I often wish our husbands": Katy Dos Passos to Pauline Hemingway, October 31, 1938, JFK.
"one of the most considerable": Wilson, "Hemingway and the Wars," Hanneman, *A Comprehensive Bibliography,* H384.
"You can go proudly": Thomas, *The Spanish Civil War,* 558.

515 "You were the first critic": EH to EW, December 10, 1938, JFK.
"the mess everything's in": EH to MP, October 28, 1938; *SL,* 474.

516 "The dead sleep cold": *New Masses,* February 14, 1938; Matthews, *Half of Spain,* 216.
"I have bad dreams": EH to MP, February 7, 1939; *SL,* 479.
"I would like to be able to write understandingly": EH to Ivan Kashkin, March 23, 1939; Ibid., 480.

517 "have never worked harder": EH to HM, ca. July 15, 1939; Ibid., 489.
"It is the most important thing": EH to Tommy Shevlin, April 4, 1939; Ibid., 484.
"But remember this": *FWTBT,* 432.

518 "He had put in it": Ibid., 248.

519 "That damned woman": Ibid., 135.
"because it seemed too luxurious": Ibid., 228.
"In a revolution": Ibid., 229.
"It is better to die on your feet": Ibid., 309.
"Dolores always made me vomit": Baker, *A Life Story,* 347n.
"We shot French": *FWBTW,* 419.
"some sort of secretary": Josephine Herbst, "The Hour of Counterfeit Bliss," 38, YCAL.

520 "ideology boys": EH to MP, December 8, 1939; *SL,* 498.
"Listen, *guapa*": *FWTBT,* 155.
"You please me, *Inglés*": Ibid., 156.

521 "I'll never forget how sick": Ibid., 338–39.
"I wonder what I would have been": Ibid., 339.
"This is the best book": Hanneman, *A Comprehensive Bibliography,* H430.
"I do not much care": Ibid., H436.

522 "Hemingway the artist": Ibid., H438.
"For here, we feel at once": Ibid., H454.
"finest achievement": Ibid., H442.

523 "the usual 'amicable' divorce": Gregory Hemingway, *Papa,* 23.
"enormously on the make": *SSEH,* 51.
"I want to make an absolutely colossal mistake": Ibid., 49.
"It will be odd to think of Ernest": FSF to MP, October 14, 1940; Fitzgerald, *Dear Scott/Dear Max,* 266–67.

524 "He was a genius, that uneasy word": Brian, *The True Gen,* 305.

A Very Lonely Trade

525 "the actual model": EH to MP, November 15, 1941; *SL,* 528.
"very nice with a good tough": Ibid., 529.
"as tight about money": Ibid.
"wants me to cover": EH to HRM, November 24, 1939; Ibid., 497.
"Not this August": *By-Line,* 205.

"Never again should this country": Ibid., 206.

526 "ideal for Japanese Intelligence": Gellhorn, *Travels with Myself and Others,* 22.

"Through our (American) laziness": EH to Charles Scribner, December 12, 1941; *SL,* 532.

527 "Ernest, you are certainly": Baker, *A Life Story,* 374.

"the most careless, shiftless": EH to MP, December 11, 1941; *SL,* 531.

"Chances are there aren't": EH to Charles Scribner, December 12, 1941; Ibid., 532.

528 "No lunch today": Gregory Hemingway, *Papa,* 95–96.

"What drove me crazy": Kert, *The Hemingway Women,* 364.

"Never laugh at a cat": Baker, *A Life Story,* 387.

"a wonder cat": EH to Patrick Hemingway, October 7, 1942; *SL,* 542.

"felt awful about it": Ibid.

"The place is so damned big": EH to HRM, November 25, 1943; Ibid., 555.

"Ernest could be the kindest": Kert, *The Hemingway Women,* 363.

529 "She is at present": EH to MP, August 27, 1942; *SL,* 541.

"I wish we could": Martha Gellhorn Hemingway to EH, June 26, 1943; Kert, *The Hemingway Women,* 379.

"I would like": Ibid., 380.

"What I wanted": EH to Carol Hemingway, [1945]; Fuentes, *Hemingway in Cuba,* 387–88.

"I'll show you": Gregory Hemingway, *Papa,* 91–92.

"ARE YOU A WAR CORRESPONDENT": Kert, *The Hemingway Women,* 391.

530 "I think no one": EH to Bernard Berenson, October 14, 1952; *SL,* 789.

"funny, unconceited, over-enthusiastic": EH to Carol Hemingway Gardner, [1945]; Fuentes, *Hemingway in Cuba,* 387.

"Introduce me to your friend": Mary Welsh Hemingway, *How It Was,* 106.

"I don't know you, Mary": Ibid., 108.

531 "This war may keep us": Ibid., 108–109.

"I hope and pray": GHH to EH, May 26, 1944, JFK.

"fully provided for": EH to Henry La Cossitt, November 16, 1944, JFK.

532 "On the beach": *By-Line,* 349.

533 "The enemy had waited": Boussel, *D-Day Beaches Revisited,* 114.

"I hit the beaches": EH to Henry La Cossitt, August 27, 1945, JFK. See also Fuentes, *Hemingway in Cuba,* 380, in which he repeats the same story in a letter to Martha which may not have been sent: "All I did for them was hit beaches on D Day when should have been in hospital and have had terrible headaches ever since."

"the day we took Fox Green beach": *By-Line,* 340.

Gellhorn's landing ashore: See Gellhorn, *The Face of War,* 109–20.

"Martha worked as nobody": EH to Henry La Cossitt, August 27, 1945, JFK.

534 Hemingway and the general: *By-Line,* 390ff.

"lie on same blanket": EH to MW, August 1 and 6, 1944; *SL,* 562.

"In war, my experience": *By-Line,* 374.

"*un bel accrochage*": Ibid., 377.

535 "what happens when two cars": Ibid., 378.

"It was much too beautiful": Ibid., 377.

"I took evasive action": Ibid., 378.
"because there now, below us": Ibid., 383.
"Small Friend": EH to MW, August 27, 1944; *SL,* 564.
536 "Have strong feeling my luck": Ibid., 564–65.
"Funny how it should take": EH to MP, October 15, 1944; Ibid., 574.
"lovely and touchable": EH to MW, August 27, 1944; Ibid., 565.
"Mary and I": EH to HRM, April 24, 1945; Ibid., 591.
537 "Picasso's face": Mary Welsh Hemingway, *How It Was,* 134–35.
"He came to see me": Huffington, *Picasso,* 306; see also EH to MW, August 1 and 6, 1944; *SL,* 563: "But have insignia cut from real officer (dead)."
"the Practical Nurse": Mary Welsh Hemingway, *How It Was,* 153.
538 "She would not do anything": EH to Patrick Hemingway, September 15, 1944; *SL,* 571.
"very fine girl": Ibid., 572.
"I hope you were quite serious": EH to MW, September 13, 1944; Ibid., 569.
"I walked down and back": EH to MW, November 15, 1944; Fuentes, *Hemingway in Cuba,* 348.
539 "Dearest Pickle my beloved": EH to MW, November 18, 1944; Ibid., 353.
"a fight such as has been": EH to MW, November 21, 1944; Ibid., 358.
"But then about yest.": EH to MW, November 23, 1944; Ibid., 361.
540 "I love Walton very much": EH to MW, August 27, 1944; *SL,* 564.
"especially gay, without internal conflicts": Kert, *The Hemingway Women,* 413.
"I'm cheerful as hell": EH to MW, November 13, 1944; Fuentes, *Hemingway in Cuba,* 347.
"drunks and slobs": Mary Welsh Hemingway, *How It Was,* 149.
"You poor coward": Ibid., 150.
"You're pretty": Ibid.
"There wasn't a hell of a lot": EH to W. G. Rogers, July 29, 1948; *SL,* 650.
541 "Now sleeps he": *Complete Poems,* 107.
"Many of the rules": Hayman, *Sartre,* 98.
"the greatest writer of our time": Ibid.
Influence on Camus: Ibid., 203.
"sort of a faintly wormy character": EH to Charles Poore, August 4, 1949, in notice of auction sale in Hemingway clipping file, YCAL.
542 "If Nelson is as tough": EH to Harvey Breit, July 3, 1956; *SL,* 863.
"I *can't* throw you away": EH to MW, November 25, 1944; Fuentes, *Hemingway in Cuba,* 365.
543 "as the hotshot warrior": Kert, *The Hemingway Women,* 416.
"We don't fight anymore": EH to Patrick Hemingway, November 19, 1944; *SL,* 576.
"Last night after I sent": EH to MW, Christmas night 1944; Fuentes, *Hemingway in Cuba,* 372.
544 Yet another account: Baker, *A Life Story,* 440–41.
"Remember this, Ernest": Ibid., 441.
"They made one break": EH to MG, n.d., probably not sent; Fuentes, *Hemingway in Cuba,* 377. See also Jack Hemingway, *Misadventures,* 194ff.
545 "We lost all the best mango trees": Ibid., 378.

"As filler for scenario": Ibid.
"Dearest Mook, if you want to marry": Ibid., 380.
"I spent a lot of time": EH to Charles Scribner, October 29, 1947; *SL*, 630–31.
"She is at her best": Ibid., 630.
"I never can think of her": Ibid., 631.
"to both parties": Kert, *The Hemingway Women*, 423. Though Hemingway paid for the storage of Martha's furniture for several years, he finally and reluctantly shipped some of her china and silver, some of it inherited, some years later.
"Apparently there are stories": Mary Welsh Hemingway, *How It Was*, 168.

546 "And now you are marrying again": GHH to EH, March 25, 1945; JFK.
"Don't know how it is with you": EH to MG, n.d., probably not sent; Fuentes, *Hemingway in Cuba*, 381.
"a rich and spoiled paralytic": *SL*, 674–75n.
"I hate things like Dongo": EH to Bernard Berenson, March 20–22, 1953; Ibid., 815.

547 "*Exercise utmost security*": Carpenter, *A Serious Character*, 653.
"A man on whom": "Canto 74," Pound, "The Pisan Cantos," *The Cantos*, 8.
"now ruled by Jews": Pound, *Ezra Pound Speaking*, 339.
"fetish value of metal": Ibid., 271.
"I think it might be": Ibid., 289.
In the Warsaw ghetto in July 1942: See Dawidowicz, *The War Against the Jews*, 301ff, 339.
"Will you please": EH to Archibald MacLeish, ca. May 5, 1943; *SL*, 544–45.
"One time I killed": EH to Charles Scribner, August 27, 1949; Ibid., 672.

548 "People dying this year": Baker, *A Life Story*, 366.
"all the realization": EH to MP, November 15, 1941; *SL*, 527.
"certainly the worst-invented": Wilson, *Eight Essays*, 102.
"Hemingway has been getting worse": EW to Florine Katz, March 7, 1941; Wilson, *Letters*, 387.

549 "Writers are certainly dying": EH to MP, April 29, 1941; *SL*, 523.
"It is just your book": Vita Sackville-West to Violet Trefusis, March 30, 1941; YCAL.
"terrible with his admirers": EH to Bernard Berenson, October 14, 1952; *SL*, 789.
"Writing is a very lonely trade": EH to Malcolm Cowley, September 3, 1945, JFK transcript; the letter is in the Maurice Neville collection, Santa Barbara, California.

550 "What is the answer?": Toklas, *What Is Remembered*, 173.
"Who *is* that?": Berg, *Max Perkins*, 566.
"great, great editor": EH to Charles Scribner, June 28, 1947; *SL*, 622.
"Did I tell you": EH to Charles Scribner, October 29, 1947; Ibid., 631.
"Please bury Max's ghost": EH to Charles Scribner, May 18–19, 1951; Ibid., 726.
"When Max died": EH to Wallace Meyer, February 21, 1952; Ibid., 750.

551 "Give Ezra good wishes": EH to Dorothy Pound, October 22, 1951; Ibid., 742.

"Can you enter the great acorn of light": Pound, "Canto 116"; Alexander, *The Poetic Achievement of Ezra Pound,* 195.

552 "Who is there now": Carpenter, *A Serious Character,* 888.
"As you know": EH to Charles Poore, January 23, 1953; *SL,* 800.
Land, Sea, and Air trilogy: See EH to MP, October 15, 1944, *SL,* 574, for first mention of the book.
"Let us cross": *ARIT,* 307.

553 "I have not the talent": Ibid., 135.
"pale almost olive-colored skin": Ibid., 80.
"Also that I love [Adriana]": EH to Charles Scribner, July 9–10, 1950; *SL,* 704.

554 Accident on the *Pilar:* Neil B. Houston and Ann Doyle, "Letters to Adriana Ivancich," *Hemingway Review* (Fall 1985), 19.
Adriana sketches: See Meyers, *Hemingway,* 445. According to a Scribner's advertising and promotion director, the drawings were "so bad we had to have them skillfully redrawn."
"I never thought of being in love": Kert, *The Hemingway Women,* 443.
"were busily launching a flirtation": Mary Welsh Hemingway, *How It Was,* 283.
"We were all happy": Ibid., 298.

555 "From his voice": Kert, *The Hemingway Women,* 450–51.
"Other people were fine": *ARIT,* 71.

556 "No matter what you say": Mary Welsh Hemingway, *How It Was,* 323.
"It is now one hour": Ibid., 286.

557 "It seemed to me his weariness": Ibid., 285.
"a character who needed": *ARIT,* 125.
"who possibly never told the truth": Ibid., 116.
"another jerk of the third": Ibid., 134; also a "high born jerk": 217.
"strictly the Epworth League": Ibid., 125.
"some politician in uniform": Ibid., 234.
"the career girl": Ibid., 251.
"Raincoats my ass": Ibid., 185.
"They teach them how": Ibid., 178.
"How do you feel about the Russians?": Ibid., 70.
"Don't we have fun with food?": Ibid., 127.
"putting years on it": Ibid., 130.
"because it combines sexology": Ibid., 87.

558 "He kissed her then": Ibid., 153.
"Let's do it again": Ibid., 155.
"Here's to you, Daughter": Ibid., 165.
"I was unhappy": Mary Welsh Hemingway, *How It Was,* 283.
"The girl is boring": Kert, *The Hemingway Women,* 456.
"with what seemed to me a formidable": Mary Welsh Hemingway, *How It Was,* 287.
"fifty plus one": *ARIT,* 75. See also 8.

559 "He smiled as only the truly shy": Ibid., 129.
"This is just warming up": EH to Charles Scribner, August 25–26, 1949; *SL,* 667.
"I am happy": EH to Arthur Mizener, April 22, 1950; Ibid., 691.
ARIT appeared in the February–June 1950 issues of *Cosmopolitan.*
"a little bit *pédéraste*": *ARIT,* 96.

560 "Reporter: Mr. Hemingway": Mary Welsh Hemingway, *How It Was,* 425.
"worst novel": Hanneman, *A Comprehensive Bibliography,* H640.
"This novel reads like a parody": Rahv, *Image and Idea,* 188.
"I shall wait": Hanneman, *A Comprehensive Bibliography,* H636.
"lamentable": Ibid., H633.
"Hemingway is bitter about nobody": *Conversations,* 58.
"Hemingway has no opinion": Ibid.

561 "Sure, they can say anything": Ibid., 61–62.
"with three-cushion shots": Ibid., 62.

The Undertaker Pleases

562 "fabricated geniuses": *By-Line,* 218.
"I tried for Mr. Turgenieff": EH to Charles Scribner, September 6–7, 1948; *SL,* 673.
He hated the idea of the "shit" that would be written: EH to Ivan Kashkin, January 12, 1936; Ibid., 432.
"It is my wish": Ibid., xxiii.

563 "He overcompensates": Malcolm Cowley to Kenneth Burke, August 16, 1948; Burke and Cowley, *The Selected Correspondence of Kenneth Burke and Malcolm Cowley,* 283.
"I know how good and friendly": EH to Malcolm Cowley, March 9, 1949; Nagel, *The Writer in Context,* 206.
"I truly think that we suffer": EH to Malcolm Cowley, June 10, 1949; Ibid., 207.
"That's why I don't want": EH to Malcolm Cowley, March 9, 1949; Ibid., 204–205.

564 "Cowley got a chance": EH to Marion Smith, May 31, 1948; *SL,* 634–35.
"So remember": EH to Charles Scribner, June 3, 1948; Ibid., 637.
"and now, since Cowley": EH to Charles T. Lanham, September 11, 1950; Ibid., 715.
"but think of poor old Cowley": EH to Charles Fenton, January 12, 1951; Ibid., 719.

565 "This is absolute": EH to Charles Scribner, August 27, 1949; Ibid., 670.
"that magazine bitch": EH to Charles Scribner, October 4, 1949; Ibid., 678.
"But I hate her guts": EH to Charles Scribner, August 27, 1949; Ibid., 670.
"diligence and your lovingness": EH to GHH, September 17, 1949; Ibid., 675.
"I do not care": Ibid.
"which I burned the midnight oil": GHH to EH, September 25, 1949, JFK.
"Am going to try": Bruccoli and Clark, *Fitzgerald/Hemingway Annual 1973*; galley proofs of *New Yorker* profile, 199.

566 "I really trust Hotchner": EH to Charles Scribner, October 4, 1949; *SL,* 680.
"inside gen" . . . "made a small poetic speech": Mary Welsh Hemingway, *How It Was,* 280.

567 "Honest, kid, we would both go crazy": EH to Harvey Breit, September 1, 1950; PUL transcript.

"lovely, golden, wasted talent": EH to Arthur Mizener, April 22, 1950; *SL,* 689.
"I get sick of Bunny Wilson writing": EH to Arthur Mizener, May 12, 1950; Ibid., 694.
"I'd done 42 galleys": EH to Arthur Mizener, June 1, 1950; Ibid., 696.

568 "It is a splendid piece of re-search": EH to Arthur Mizener, January 4, 1951; Ibid., 716.
"and you've buried him": Ibid., 717.
"good undertaking": Ibid.
"Mizener made money": EH to Wallace Meyer, February 21, 1952; Ibid., 751.
"Imagine what they can do": Ibid.
"has assembled in a spirit": EW to Christian Gauss, February 24, 1950; Wilson, *Letters,* 475.
"It is queer": Ibid., 477.

569 "I guess old Cranny": EH to Charles Fenton, January 12, 1951; *SL,* 719.
"cease and desist": EH to Charles Fenton, June 18, 1952; Ibid., 764. See also EH to Charles Fenton, October 9, 1952; Ibid., 786.
"a fairly complicated": EH to Carlos Baker, February 17, 1951, Carlos Baker papers.

570 "I am resolved to not aid": Ibid.
"directly and analytically": CB to EH, February 21, 1951, Carlos Baker papers.
"You are seen": Ibid.

571 "About the Mann": EH to CB, March 10, 1951, Carlos Baker papers.
"to be poised against fatality": CB to EH, March 6, 1951, Carlos Baker papers.
"I love to have": EH to CB, June 30, 1951, Carlos Baker papers.

572 "A writer has": EH to CB, February 17, 1951, Carlos Baker papers.
"has suddenly gotten afraid": EH to CB, November 22, 1951, Carlos Baker papers.
"It was really a great relief": EH to CB, June 30, 1951, Carlos Baker papers.
"protecting, or trying to protect": EH to CB, October 7, 1951; see also EH to CB, November 2, 1951, Carlos Baker papers.
"The wave of remembering": EH to Charles Scribner, October 2, 1951; *SL,* 737.

573 "some sort of sneak thing": EH to CB, October 7, 1951, Carlos Baker papers.
"Criticism is getting": EH to Wallace Meyer, February 21, 1952; *SL,* 751.
"with some horror": EH to Thomas Bledsoe, December 9, 1951; Ibid., 744.
"You are ruined": Bruccoli and Clark, *Fitzgerald/Hemingway Annual 1973,* 206–207.

574 "About our old piece": Ibid., 206.
"that the book is not biography": EH to Philip Young, March 6, 1952; *SL,* 760.
"No part of this is good": Ibid., 761.
"I average": EH to Charles Fenton, July 29, 1952; Ibid., 776.

575 "P. Young: It's all trauma": EH to Harvey Breit, July 23, 1956; Ibid., 866–67.

"Hope that won't set": EH to CB, January 16, 1961, Carlos Baker papers.
"We became great students": *AMF,* 202.
576 "A major art": *DIA,* 99.
577 "flashing that 'say cheese' smile": Gregory Hemingway, *Papa,* 107.
"I fucked three times": EH to Charles Scribner, July 22, 1949; *SL,* 658.
"I hope he kills himself": EH to Charles Scribner, March 5, 1951; Ibid., 721.
"In every picture": EH to Francis Cardinal Spellman, July 28, 1949; Ibid., 661.
"You can come down here": EH to Senator Joseph McCarthy, May 8, 1950; Ibid., 693.
"If there is anything he wants": EH to Marion Smith, ca. late 1948, PUL.
"Am sure I am regarded": Ibid.
578 "Publicity, admiration, adulation": EH to Bernard Berenson, September 24, 1954; *SL,* 837.
579 "publishing it now": EH to Wallace Meyer, March 4 and 7, 1952; Ibid., 758.
"It affected all of them": Ibid., 757.
"If you have a message": Mary Welsh Hemingway, *How It Was,* 513.
"ain't got no bloody fucking chance": *THAHN,* 225.
"But man is not made for defeat": *OMATS,* 114.
"There is no translation": Ibid., 118.
580 "The sea is the sea": EH to Bernard Berenson, September 13, 1952; *SL,* 780.
"Hemingway's *Old Man and the Sea*": Baker, *A Life Story,* 505.
"You know I was thinking": EH to EW, November 8, 1952; *SL,* 793.
"He is hunted by everyone": EH to Harvey Breit, June 29, 1952; Ibid., 771.
"No, you violated your luck": *OMATS,* 128.
581 "He no longer dreamed": Ibid., 27.
"unquestionably the greatest craftsman": Hanneman, *A Comprehensive Bibliography,* H764.
"Here is the master technician": Ibid., H727.
"I believe this is the best": Ibid., H740.
"It is a poem of action": Ibid., H742.
582 "Hemingway has enhanced": Ibid., H734.
"the meaning of *The Old Man and the Sea*": Rahv, *Image and Idea,* 194–95.
"Time may show it to be": Baker, *A Life Story,* 503–504.
"I cannot help out": EH to Lillian Ross, February 20, 1953; *SL,* 807.
"Can't hurt it, I guess": EH to Wallace Meyer, May 6, 1953; Ibid., 821.
583 "Tracy and I carry the ball": EH to Alfred Rice, April 26–27, 1953; Ibid., 817.
584 "No discovery in Madrid": Mary Welsh Hemingway, *How It Was,* 388.
"If it is of even comic": August 11, 1953; *SL,* 824.
"Sometimes it is as hard": Ibid., 823.
"This is a fine trip": EH to Bernard Berenson, September 15, 1953; Ibid., 825.
585 "I'll get a leopard": Mary Welsh Hemingway, *How It Was,* 412.

"sort of like Brenda Frazier": EH to Harvey Breit, January 3, 1954; *SL,* 826.

586 "made love at least every morning": Mary Welsh Hemingway, *How It Was,* 426.

"has always wanted to be a boy": Ibid.

587 "Invulnerable Papa": *New York Post* (January 25, 1954), 3.

"In all obituaries": *By-Line,* 460.

588 "a little bit bad": EH to Harvey Breit, February 4, 1954; *SL,* 829.

"Semi-unbearable suffering": Mary Welsh Hemingway, *How It Was,* 449.

"I'm leaving": Ibid., 450.

"two disks of his spine cracked": Ibid., 444.

"as good a cable": EH to Harvey Breit, June 27, 1952; *SL,* 769.

589 "My kitten, my kitten": Mary Welsh Hemingway, *How It Was,* 472.

"Somebody loves you": Ibid., 475.

"You know I know more or less": EH to Charles T. Lanham, November 10, 1954; *SL,* 839.

"I've gotten back into the country": Ibid.

"If you had to make a Nobel speech": Ibid., 841.

"powerful, style-making mastery": Baker, *A Life Story,* 528.

590 "Writing, at its best": *Conversations,* 196.

André Malraux and the Nobel Prize: Janet Flanner conversation with James Mellow, Paris, October 1969.

"good enough little story": Wilson, *The Fifties,* 302.

591 "It is only when you can no longer": "Pamplona Letter," *Transatlantic Review* (September 1924), 301.

"treasure trove": Baker, *A Life Story,* 536, 663n. See also Tavernier-Courbin, "The Manuscripts of *A Moveable Feast,*" *Hemingway Notes* (Spring 1981), 9–15. Also Tavernier-Courbin, "The Paris Notebooks," *Hemingway Notes* (Fall 1981), 23–26.

"the confessions of the real Ernest Hemingway": Stein, *The Autobiography of Alice B. Toklas,* 265–66.

592 "This book is fiction": Tavernier-Courbin, "The Manuscripts of *A Moveable Feast,*" *Hemingway Notes* (Fall 1981), 13.

"For the girl to deceive": Ibid.

"I never worked better": Kert, *The Hemingway Women,* 484–85.

"No one can write true facts": Tavernier-Courbin, "The Manuscripts of *A Moveable Feast,*" *Hemingway Notes* (Fall 1981), 13.

593 "The violence is the violence of our time": EH to Bernard Berenson, March 20–22, 1953; *SL,* 808.

"Claudel always seemed ridiculous": Ibid., 809.

594 "Coops, After the Old Man and the Sea": EH to Gary Cooper, March 9, 1956; Ibid., 855.

"the artist": EH to Gianfranco Ivancich, May 25, 1956; Ibid., 858.

595 "Cuba is really bad, now": EH to Patrick Hemingway, November 24, 1958; Ibid., 888.

"delighted" . . . "hopeful": Mary Welsh Hemingway, *How It Was,* 527, 528.

596 "winced as if he had been burned": Baker, *A Life Story,* 548.

"unhealthy nostalgia": Ibid.

597 "STILL LOVE YOU": Mary Welsh Hemingway, *How It Was,* 550.

"You could keep it quiet": Ibid., 552–53.
"Some people are better": EH to Charles T. Lanham, January 12, 1960; *SL*, 899.
"They're checking our accounts": Mary Welsh Hemingway, *How It Was*, 554.

598 "What I've written": Hotchner, *Papa Hemingway*, 242.

599 "Kitner, I don't know how": Mary Welsh Hemingway, *How It Was*, 563.
"Only thing I am afraid of": Ibid., 564.
"I wish you were here": Ibid., 565.

600 "the horrible face": Ibid.
"an all-time fool and a double-crosser": Hotchner, *Papa Hemingway*, 253.
"Somebody waiting out there": Mary Welsh Hemingway, *How It Was*, 566.
"They're tailing me": Ibid., 567.

601 "He's covering up something": Ibid., 568.
"They'll say I'm losing my marbles": Ibid.
"Try to only think": EH to L. H. Brague, February 6, 1961; *SL*, 917.

602 "You think as long": Mary Welsh Hemingway, *How It Was*, 575.

603 "Like Africa": Ibid., 576.
"Without pride I would not": "The Art of the Short Story," *The Paris Review* (Spring 1981), 100.
"They're F.B.I": Mary Welsh Hemingway, *How It Was*, 579.
"No one had a right": Ibid., 578.

Bibliography

Books

Alexander, Michael. *The Poetic Achievement of Ezra Pound.* Berkeley: University of California Press, 1979.
Anderson, Margaret. *My Thirty Years' War.* New York: Horizon Press, 1969.
Anderson, Sherwood. *Sherwood Anderson's Memoirs: A Critical Edition.* Edited by Ray Lewis White. Chapel Hill: University of North Carolina Press, 1969.
Anderson, Sherwood, and Gertrude Stein. *Sherwood Anderson/Gertrude Stein.* Edited by Ray Lewis White. Chapel Hill: University of North Carolina Press, 1972.
Antheil, George. *Bad Boy of Music.* Garden City, N.Y.: Doubleday, Doran, 1945.
Arnold, Lloyd. *Hemingway: High on the Wild.* New York: Grosset & Dunlap, 1968.
Baker, Carlos. *Ernest Hemingway: A Life Story.* New York: Charles Scribner's Sons, 1969.
———. *Hemingway: The Writer as Artist.* Princeton, N.J.: Princeton University Press, 1952.
———, editor. *Ernest Hemingway: Selected Letters.* New York: Charles Scribner's Sons, 1981.
———, editor. *Hemingway and His Critics.* New York: Hill & Wang, 1961.
Bakewell, Charles. *The Story of the American Red Cross in Italy.* New York: Macmillan, 1920.
Bald, Wambly. *On the Left Bank.* Edited by Benjamin Franklin V. Athens: Ohio University Press, 1987.
Baldwin, Neil. *Man Ray: American Artist.* New York: Clarkson N. Potter, 1988.
Beevor, Antony. *The Spanish Civil War.* New York: Peter Bedrick Books, 1983.
Benson, Jackson J., editor. *The Short Stories of Ernest Hemingway.* Durham, N.C.: Duke University Press, 1975.
Berg, A. Scott. *Max Perkins: Editor of Genius.* New York: Simon & Schuster, 1978.
Bolitho, William. *Twelve Against the Gods.* New York: Simon & Schuster, 1929.
Boussel, Patrice. *D-Day Beaches Revisited.* Garden City, N.Y.: Doubleday & Company, 1966.
Brazeau, Peter. *Parts of a World: Wallace Stevens Remembered.* New York: Random House, 1983.
Brian, Denis. *The True Gen.* New York: Grove Press, 1988.
Bruccoli, Matthew J. *Scott and Ernest.* Carbondale: Southern Illinois University Press, 1978.
———. *Some Sort of Epic Grandeur.* New York: Harcourt Brace Jovanovich, 1981.
———, editor. *Ernest Hemingway: Cub Reporter.* Pittsburgh: University of Pittsburgh Press, 1970.
Bruccoli, Matthew J., and C. E. Frazer Clark, Jr., editors. *Fitzgerald/Hemingway Annual 1973.* Washington, D.C.: Microcard Editions, 1974.

Buckley, Peter. *Ernest.* New York: Dial Press, 1978.
Burke, Kenneth, and Malcolm Cowley. *The Selected Correspondence of Kenneth Burke and Malcolm Cowley.* Edited by Paul Jay. New York: Viking Press, 1988.
Callaghan, Morley. *That Summer in Paris.* New York: Penguin Books, 1963.
Carpenter, Humphrey. *A Serious Character: The Life of Ezra Pound.* Boston: Houghton Mifflin Company, 1988.
Carr, E. H. *The Comintern & the Spanish Civil War.* New York: Pantheon Books, 1984.
Carr, Virginia Spencer. *Dos Passos: A Life.* Garden City, N.Y.: Doubleday & Company, 1984.
Chisholm, Anne. *Nancy Cunard.* New York: Alfred A. Knopf, 1979.
Colum, Mary. *Life and the Dream.* Dublin, Ireland: Doufour Editions, 1966.
Cowley, Malcolm. *Exile's Return.* New York: Viking Press, 1969.
———. *Think Back on Us.* Carbondale: Southern Illinois University Press, 1967.
Crane, Hart. *Letters of Hart Crane.* Edited by Brom Weber. New York: Hermitage House, 1952.
Crosby, Harry. *Shadows of the Sun: The Diaries of Harry Crosby.* Santa Barbara: Black Sparrow Press, 1977.
Dawidowicz, Lucy S. *The War Against the Jews: 1933–1945.* New York: Holt, Rinehart & Winston, 1975.
Donaldson, Scott. *By Force of Will: The Life and Art of Ernest Hemingway.* New York: New York Press, 1977.
Donnelly, Honoria Murphy, with Richard N. Billings. *Sara & Gerald.* New York: Times Books, 1982.
Dos Passos, John. *The Best Times.* New York: New American Library, 1966.
———. *Chosen Country.* Cambridge: Riverside Press, Houghton Mifflin Company, 1951.
———. *The Fourteenth Chronicle: Letters and Diaries of John Dos Passos.* Edited by Townsend Ludington. Boston: Gambit, 1973.
Douglas, George H. *Edmund Wilson's America.* Lexington: University Press of Kentucky, 1983.
Draper, Theodore. *American Communism and Soviet Russia.* New York: Vintage Books, 1960.
Dupin, Jacques. *Miró.* New York: Harry N. Abrams, 1962.
Duranty, Walter. *I Write As I Please.* New York, Simon & Schuster, 1935.
Eastman, Max. *Great Companions.* New York: Farrar, Straus & Cudahy, 1942.
Eby, Cecil. *Between the Bullet and the Lie.* New York: Holt, Rinehart & Winston, 1969.
Edel, Leon. *Henry James, The Master: 1901–1916.* Philadelphia: J. B. Lippincott, 1972.
Ehrenburg, Ilya. *Memoirs: 1921–1924.* Cleveland: World, 1955.
———. *People and Life.* New York: Alfred A. Knopf, 1962.
Eliot, T. S. *The Complete Poems and Plays.* New York: Harcourt, Brace & Company, 1959.
Ellmann, Richard. *James Joyce.* New York: Oxford University Press, 1982.
Fenton, Charles A. *The Apprenticeship of Ernest Hemingway: The Early Years.* New York: Viking Press, 1954.
Field, Andrew. *Djuna: The Life and Times of Djuna Barnes.* New York: G. P. Putnam's Sons, 1983.
Fitch, Noel Riley. *Sylvia Beach and the Lost Generation.* London: Souvenir Press, 1983.

Fitzgerald, F. Scott. *As Ever, Scott-Fitz 1919–1940.* Edited by Matthew J. Bruccoli. London: Woburn Press, 1973.
———. *Correspondence of F. Scott Fitzgerald.* Edited by Matthew J. Bruccoli and Margaret M. Duggan. New York: Random House, 1980.
———. *The Crack-Up.* New York: New Directions Books, 1956.
———. *Dear Scott / Dear Max: The Fitzgerald-Perkins Correspondence.* Edited by John Kuehl and Jackson R. Bryer. New York: Charles Scribner's Sons, 1971.
———. *In His Own Time.* Edited by Matthew J. Bruccoli and Jackson R. Bryer. New York: Popular Books, 1971.
———. *The Letters of F. Scott Fitzgerald.* Edited by Andrew Turnbull. New York: Charles Scribner's Sons, 1963.
———. *The Notebooks of F. Scott Fitzgerald.* Edited by Matthew J. Bruccoli. New York: Harcourt Brace Jovanovich, 1980.
Flanner, Janet. *Darlinghissima: Letters to a Friend.* Edited by Natalia Danesi Murray. New York: Random House, 1985.
———. *Paris Was Yesterday: 1925–1939.* New York: Viking Press, 1972.
Flora, Joseph M. *Hemingway's Nick Adams.* Baton Rouge: Louisiana State University Press, 1982.
Ford, Ford Madox. *It Was the Nightingale.* Philadelphia: J. B. Lippincott, 1933.
Ford, Hugh. *Four Lives in Paris.* San Francisco: North Point Press, 1987.
———. *Published in Paris.* New York: Macmillan, 1975.
———, editor. *The Left Bank Revisited: Selections from the Paris Tribune, 1917–1934.* University Park: Pennsylvania State University Press, 1972.
Franklin, Sidney. *Bullfighter from Brooklyn.* Englewood Cliffs, N.J.: Prentice-Hall, 1952.
Fraser, Ronald. *Blood of Spain.* New York: Pantheon Books, 1979.
Fuentes, Norberto. *Hemingway in Cuba.* Secaucus, N.J.: Lyle Stuart, 1984.
Gallup, Donald, editor. *The Flowers of Friendship: Letters Written to Gertrude Stein.* New York: Alfred A. Knopf, 1953.
Gellhorn, Martha. *The Face of War.* New York: Atlantic Monthly Press, 1936.
———. *Travels with Myself and Another.* London: Eland Books, 1983.
Gibson, Ian. *Federico García Lorca.* New York: Pantheon Books, 1989.
Grebstein, Sheldon N. *Hemingway's Craft.* Carbondale: Southern Illinois University Press, 1973.
Griffin, Peter. *Along With Youth.* New York: Oxford University Press, 1985.
Hanneman, Audre. *Ernest Hemingway: A Comprehensive Bibliography.* Princeton, N.J.: Princeton University Press, 1967.
———. *Supplement to Ernest Hemingway: A Comprehensive Bibliography.* Princeton, N.J.: Princeton University Press, 1975.
Hayman, Ronald. *Sartre: A Biography.* New York: Simon & Schuster, 1987.
Hemingway, Ernest. *Across the River and Into the Trees.* New York: Charles Scribner's Sons, 1950.
———. *By-Line: Ernest Hemingway.* New York: Charles Scribner's Sons, 1967.
———. *Complete Poems.* Lincoln: University of Nebraska Press, 1979.
———. *The Complete Short Stories of Ernest Hemingway.* New York: Charles Scribner's Sons, 1987.
———. *Conversations with Ernest Hemingway.* Edited by Matthew J. Bruccoli. Jackson: University Press of Mississippi, 1986.
———. *The Dangerous Summer.* New York: Charles Scribner's Sons, 1985.
———. *Dateline: Toronto.* New York: Charles Scribner's Sons, 1985.
———. *Death in the Afternoon.* New York: Charles Scribner's Sons, 1932.

———. *Ernest Hemingway on Writing.* Edited by Larry W. Phillips. New York: Charles Scribner's Sons, 1984.
———. *A Farewell to Arms.* New York: Charles Scribner's Sons, 1929.
———. *For Whom the Bell Tolls.* New York: Charles Scribner's Sons, 1940.
———. *The Garden of Eden.* New York: Charles Scribner's Sons, 1986.
———. *Green Hills of Africa.* New York: Charles Scribner's Sons, 1935.
———. *Islands in the Stream.* New York: Charles Scribner's Sons, 1970.
———. *A Moveable Feast.* New York: Charles Scribner's Sons, 1964.
———. *The Nick Adams Stories.* New York: Charles Scribner's Sons, 1972.
———. *The Old Man and the Sea.* New York: Charles Scribner's Sons, 1952.
———. *The Short Stories of Ernest Hemingway.* New York: Modern Library, 1938.
———. *The Sun Also Rises.* New York: Charles Scribner's Sons, 1926.
———. *To Have and Have Not.* New York: P. F. Collier & Son, 1937.
———. *The Torrents of Spring.* New York: Charles Scribner's Sons, 1972.
Hemingway, Gregory H., M.D. *Papa: A Personal Memoir.* Boston: Houghton Mifflin Company, 1976.
Hemingway, Jack. *Misadventures of a Fly Fisherman.* Dallas: Taylor Publishing Company, 1986.
Hemingway, Leicester. *My Brother, Ernest Hemingway.* Cleveland: World, 1962.
Hemingway, Mary Welsh. *How It Was.* New York: Alfred A. Knopf, 1951.
Herbst, Josephine. *The Starched Blue Sky of Spain.* New York: HarperCollins, 1991.
Hotchner, A. E. *Papa Hemingway.* New York: Random House, 1966.
Huffington, Arianna Stassinopoulos. *Picasso: Creator and Destroyer.* New York: Simon & Schuster, 1988.
Joost, Nicholas. *Ernest Hemingway and the Little Magazines: The Paris Years.* Barre, Mass.: Barre Publishers, 1968.
Kazin, Alfred, editor. *F. Scott Fitzgerald: The Man and His Work.* New York: Collier Books, 1951.
Kennan, George. *Memoirs: 1925–1950.* Boston: Little, Brown & Company, 1967.
———. *Russia and the West.* Boston: Little, Brown & Company, 1961.
Kennedy, Richard S. *Dreams in the Mirror: A Biography of E. E. Cummings.* New York: Liveright, 1980.
Kenner, Hugh. *The Pound Era.* Berkeley: University of California Press, 1971.
Kert, Bernice. *The Hemingway Women.* New York: W. W. Norton, 1983.
Kirstein, Lincoln. *By With To & From.* Edited by Nicholas Jenkins. New York: Liveright, 1991.
Klimo, Vernon (Jake), and Will Oursler. *Hemingway and Jake.* New York: Doubleday & Company, 1972.
Klüver, Billy, and Julie Martin. *Kiki's Paris.* New York: Harry N. Abrams, 1989.
Kubler, George. *The Shape of Time.* New Haven: Yale University Press, 1962.
Langer, Elinor. *Josephine Herbst: The Story She Could Never Tell.* Boston: Atlantic–Little, Brown, 1983.
Lewis, Wyndham. *A Soldier of Humor and Selected Writings.* New York: New American Library, 1966.
Lindberg-Seyerstad, Brita. *Pound/Ford: The Story of a Literary Friendship.* New York: New Directions, 1982.
Loeb, Harold. *The Way It Was.* New York: Criterion Books, 1959.
Lovell, Mary S. *Straight on Till Morning.* New York: St. Martin's Press, 1987.
Ludington, Townsend. *John Dos Passos: A Twentieth Century Odyssey.* New York: E. P. Dutton, 1980.
Lynn, Kenneth S. *Hemingway.* New York: Simon & Schuster, 1987.

MacLeish, Archibald. *The Collected Poems of Archibald MacLeish.* Boston: Houghton Mifflin Company, 1962.
———. *Letters of Archibald MacLeish, 1907–1982.* Edited by R. H. Winnick. Boston: Houghton Mifflin Company, 1983.
———. *Riders on the Earth.* Boston: Houghton Mifflin Company, 1978.
Maddox, Brenda. *Nora.* Boston: Houghton Mifflin Company, 1988.
Makin, Peter. *Pound's Cantos.* London: George Allen & Unwin, 1985.
Marryat, Captain. *Mr. Midshipman Easy.* New York: Grosset & Dunlap, 1928.
Matthews, Herbert L. *The Education of a Correspondent.* New York: Harcourt, Brace, 1946.
Matthews, Herbert L. *Half of Spain.* New York: Charles Scribner's Sons, 1973.
McAlmon, Robert. *A Hasty Bunch.* Carbondale: Southern Illinois University Press, 1990.
———. *Village.* Albuquerque: University of New Mexico Press, 1924.
McAlmon, Robert, and Kay Boyle. *Being Geniuses Together: 1920–1930.* San Francisco: North Point Press, 1984.
McCaffery, John K. M., editor. *Ernest Hemingway: The Man and His Work.* New York: Cooper Square Publishers, 1969.
McLendon, James. *Papa.* New York: Popular Books, 1972.
Mellow, James R. *Charmed Circle: Gertrude Stein & Company.* New York: Praeger Publishers, 1974.
———. *Invented Lives: F. Scott & Zelda Fitzgerald.* Boston: Houghton Mifflin Company, 1984.
Meyers, Jeffrey. *Hemingway: A Biography.* New York: Harper & Row, 1985.
Miller, Madelaine Hemingway. *Ernie: Hemingway's Sister Sunny Remembers.* New York: Crown Publishers, 1975.
Miller, William D. *Dorothy Day.* San Francisco: Harper & Row, 1982.
Milford, Nancy. *Zelda: A Biography.* New York: Harper & Row, 1970.
Mitgang, Herbert. *Dangerous Dossiers: Exposing the Secret War Against America's Greatest Authors.* New York: Ballantine Books, 1988.
Mizener, Arthur. *The Saddest Story: A Biography of Ford Madox Ford.* New York: World, 1971.
Monnier, Adrienne. *The Very Rich Hours of Adrienne Monnier.* Translated, with an Introduction and Commentaries, by Richard McDougall. New York: Charles Scribner's Sons, 1976.
Montgomery, Constance Cappel. *Hemingway in Michigan.* New York: Fleet, 1966.
Mora, Constancia de la. *In Place of Splendor.* New York: Harcourt Brace, 1939.
Munson, Gorham. *The Awakening Twenties.* Baton Rouge: Louisiana State University Press, 1985.
Nagel, James, editor. *Ernest Hemingway: The Writer in Context.* Madison: University of Wisconsin Press, 1984.
Norman, Charles. *Ezra Pound.* New York: Macmillan, 1960.
O'Neill, William L. *The Last Romantic: A Life of Max Eastman.* New York: Oxford University Press, 1978.
Orwell, George. *A Collection of Essays.* Garden City, N.Y.: Doubleday & Company, 1954.
Painter, George D. *Marcel Proust,* Vol. 1. New York: Random House, 1978.
———. *Marcel Proust,* Vol. 2. New York: Random House, 1959.
Pétrement, Simone. *Simone Weil.* New York: Schocken Books, 1976.
Poli, Bernard J. *Ford Madox Ford and the Transatlantic Review.* Syracuse, N.Y.: Syracuse University Press, 1967.

Pound, Ezra. *The Cantos of Ezra Pound.* New York: New Directions, 1948.
———. *Ezra Pound Speaking.* Edited by Leonard W. Doob. Westport, Conn.: Greenwood Press, 1978.
———. *Selected Letters, 1907–1941.* Edited by D. D. Paige. New York: New Directions, 1971.
———. *The Selected Poems of Ezra Pound.* New York: New Directions, 1956.
Powell, Dawn. *Angels on Toast.* New York: Vintage Books, 1990.
———. *The Golden Spur.* New York: Vintage Books, 1990.
———. *The Wicked Pavilion.* New York: Vintage Books, 1990.
Raeburn, John. *Fame Became of Him: Hemingway as Public Writer.* Bloomington: Indiana University Press, 1984.
Rahv, Philip. *Image and Idea.* New York: New Directions, 1957.
Rascoe, Burton. *We Were Interrupted.* Garden City, N.Y.: Doubleday & Company, 1947.
Reynolds, Michael S. *Hemingway's First War.* Princeton, N.J.: Princeton University Press, 1976.
———. *Hemingway's Reading, 1910–1940.* Princeton, N.J.: Princeton University Press, 1981.
———. *Hemingway: The Paris Years.* Cambridge, Mass.: Basil Blackwell, 1989.
———. *The Young Hemingway.* New York: Basil Blackwell, 1986.
———, editor. *Critical Essays on Ernest Hemingway's In Our Time.* Boston: G. K. Hall, 1983.
Rollyson, Carl. *Nothing Ever Happens to the Brave*: The Story of Martha Gellhorn. New York: St. Martin's Press, 1990.
Rood, Karen Lane, editor. *Vol. 4 of Dictionary of Literary Biography. American Writers in Paris, 1920–1939.* Detroit: Gale Research Company, 1980.
Root, Waverly. *The Paris Edition.* Edited and with an Introduction by Samuel Abt. San Francisco: North Point Press, 1987.
Ross, Lillian. *Reporting.* New York: Simon & Schuster, 1964.
Samuelson, Arnold. *With Hemingway.* New York: Random House, 1984.
Sanford, Marcelline Hemingway. *At the Hemingways: A Family Portrait.* Boston: Atlantic–Little, Brown, 1962.
Sarason, Bertram D. *Hemingway and the Sun Set.* Washington, D.C.: Microcard Editions, 1972.
Scribner, Charles, Jr. *In the Company of Writers.* New York: Charles Scribner's Sons, 1990.
Secrest, Meryle. *Between Me and Life: A Biography of Romaine Brooks.* Garden City, N.Y.: Doubleday & Company, 1974.
Seldes, George. *Witness to a Century.* New York: Ballantine Books, 1987.
Sheean, Vincent. *Not Peace But a Sword.* New York: Doubleday, Doran & Company, 1939.
———. *Personal History.* New York: Modern Library, 1934.
Sheridan, Clare. *Nuda Veritas.* London: Thornton Butterworth Limited, 1927.
Shi, David E. *Matthew Josephson, Bourgeois Bohemian.* New Haven: Yale University Press, 1981.
Slocombe, George. *The Tumult and the Shouting.* New York: Macmillan, 1936.
Smith, Denis Mack. *Italy: A Modern History.* Ann Arbor: University of Michigan Press, 1969.
———. *Mussolini.* New York: Alfred A. Knopf, 1982.
Smith, Paul. *A Reader's Guide to the Short Stories of Ernest Hemingway.* Boston: G. K. Hall, 1989.

Sokoloff, Alice Hunt. *Hadley: The First Mrs. Hemingway.* New York: Dodd, Mead, 1973.
Spender, Stephen. *World Within World.* New York: Harcourt, Brace & Company, 1948.
Stanton, Edward F. *Hemingway and Spain.* Seattle: University of Washington Press, 1989.
Stearns, Harold. *The Confessions of a Harvard Man.* Sutton West and Santa Barbara, Calif.: Paget Press, 1984.
Steffens, Lincoln. *The Autobiography of Lincoln Steffens.* New York: Harcourt Brace, 1931.
———. *The Letters of Lincoln Steffens.* Edited by Ella Winter and Granville Hicks. New York: Harcourt Brace, 1938.
Stein, Gertrude. *The Autobiography of Alice B. Toklas.* New York: Harcourt, Brace & Company, 1933.
———. *Geography and Plays.* Boston: Four Seas Company, 1922.
———. *How to Write.* Paris: Plain Edition, 1931.
———. *Lectures in America.* New York: Random House, 1935.
———. *The Letters of Gertrude Stein and Carl Van Vechten,* Vol. I, 1931–1935. Vol. II, 1935–1946. Edited by Edward Burns. New York: Columbia University Press, 1986.
———. *The Making of Americans.* New York: Something Else Press, 1966.
———. *Paris France.* London: Batsford, 1940.
———. *What Are Masterpieces.* Los Angeles: Conference Press, 1940.
Stephens, Robert O. *Hemingway's Nonfiction: The Public Voice.* Chapel Hill, N.C.: Chapel Hill Press, 1968.
Stevens, Wallace. *Letters of Wallace Stevens.* Edited by Holly Stevens. New York: Alfred A. Knopf, 1981.
———. *Transport to Summer.* New York: Alfred A. Knopf, 1951.
Stewart, Donald Ogden. *By a Stroke of Luck! An Autobiography.* London: Paddington Press, 1975.
Stock, Noel. *The Life of Ezra Pound.* San Francisco: North Point Press, 1982.
Svoboda, Frederic Joseph. *Hemingway & The Sun Also Rises.* Lawrence: University Press of Kansas, 1983.
Tate, Allen. *Memoirs and Opinions, 1926–1974.* Chicago: Swallow Press, 1975.
Thomas, Gordon, and Max Morgan Witts. *Guernica: The Crucible of World War II.* New York: Stein & Day, 1975.
Thomas, Hugh. *The Spanish Civil War.* New York: Harper & Brothers, 1961.
Thomson, Virgil. *Virgil Thomson.* New York: Alfred A. Knopf, 1966.
Toklas, Alice B. *What Is Remembered.* New York: Holt, Rinehart & Winston, 1963.
Townsend, Kim. *Sherwood Anderson.* Boston: Houghton Mifflin Company, 1987.
Villard, Henry Serrano, and James Nagel. *Hemingway in Love and War: The Lost Diary of Agnes von Kurowsky.* Boston: Northeastern University Press, 1989.
Wagner, Linda W. *Ernest Hemingway: Six Decades of Criticism.* East Lansing: Michigan State University Press, 1987.
Walker, Jayne L. *Gertrude Stein: The Making of a Modernist.* Amherst: University of Massachusetts Press, 1984.
Weeks, Robert P., editor. *Hemingway: A Collection of Critical Essays.* Englewood Cliffs, N.J.: Prentice-Hall, 1962.
Whelan, Richard. *Robert Capa.* New York: Alfred A. Knopf, 1985.
Williams, Wirt. *The Tragic Art of Ernest Hemingway.* Baton Rouge: Lousiana State University Press, 1981.

Wilson, Edmund. *The Bit Between My Teeth.* New York: Farrar, Straus & Giroux, 1939.
———. *Eight Essays.* Garden City, N.Y.: Doubleday & Company, 1954.
———. *The Fifties.* Edited by Leon Edel. New York: Farrar, Straus & Giroux, 1986.
———. *The Forties.* Edited by Leon Edel. New York: Farrar, Straus & Giroux, 1983.
———. *Letters on Literature and Politics 1912–1972.* New York: Farrar, Straus & Giroux, 1957.
———. *The Shores of Light.* New York: Farrar, Straus & Giroux, 1952.
———. *The Thirties.* Edited by Leon Edel. New York: Farrar, Straus & Giroux, 1980.
———. *The Twenties.* Edited by Leon Edel. New York: Farrar, Straus & Giroux, 1975.
———. *The Wound and the Bow.* Boston: Houghton Mifflin Company, 1941.
Wineapple, Brenda. *Genêt: A Biography of Janet Flanner.* New York: Ticknor & Fields, 1989.
Wolff, Geoffrey. *Black Sun: The Brief Transit and Violent Eclipse of Harry Crosby.* New York: Random House, 1976.
Young, Philip. *Ernest Hemingway: A Reconsideration.* University Park: Pennsylvania State University Press, 1966.

Selected Articles and Essays

Balassi, William. "The Writing of the Manuscript of *The Sun Also Rises,*" *Hemingway Review* (Fall 1986): 65–78.
Brasch, James D. "Invention from Knowledge: The Hemingway-Cowley Correspondence." In *Ernest Hemingway: The Writer in Context,* edited by James Nagel, 201–236. Madison: University of Wisconsin Press, 1984.
Donaldson, Scott. "Dos and Hem: A Literary Friendship." In *Ernest Hemingway: Six Decades of Criticism,* edited by Linda W. Wagner, 41–59. East Lansing: Michigan State University Press, 1987.
Gingrich, Arnold. "Scott, Ernest and Whoever": *Esquire* (October 1973): 151–54, 374–80.
Hemingway, Ernest. "The Art of the Short Story," *The Paris Review* (Spring 1981): 85–102.
———. "Philip Haines Was a Writer," *Hemingway Review* (Spring 1990): 2–8.
Houston, Neal B., and Ann Doyle. "Letters to Adriana Ivancich," *Hemingway Review* (Fall 1985): 14–29.
Junkins, Donald. "Hemingway's Paris Short Story: A Study in Revision," *Hemingway Review* (Spring 1990): 10–47.
Lewis, Robert W. "Hemingway in Italy: Making It Up," *Journal of Modern Literature* (May 1982): 209–36.
Mellow, James R. "Reading Hemingway with One Eye Closed," *New York Times* (April 24, 1988): 33, 38.
———. "Stein Salon Was the First Museum of Modern Art," *New York Times Magazine* (December 1, 1968): 48–51.
———. "Talent and All the Right Connections," *The New York Times Book Review* (July 22, 1991): 9.
———. "Walker Evans Captures the Unvarnished Truth," *New York Times* (December 1, 1974), 38D.

———. "The Word Plays of Gertrude Stein." In *Operas and Plays,* by Gertrude Stein. Barrytown, N.Y.: Station Hill Press, 1987.

Peters, K. J. "The Thematic Integrity of The Garden of Eden," *Hemingway Review* (Spring 1991): 17–29.

Solomon, Barbara Probst. "Where's Papa?" *The New Republic* (March 9, 1987): 30–34.

Tavernier-Courbin, Jacqueline. "Ernest Hemingway and Ezra Pound." In *Ernest Hemingway: The Writer in Context,* edited by James Nagel, 179–200. Madison: University of Wisconsin Press, 1984.

———. "Fact and Fiction in *A Moveable Feast,*" *Hemingway Review* (Fall 1984): 44–51.

———. "The Manuscripts of *A Moveable Feast,*" *Hemingway Notes* (Spring 1981): 9–15.

———. "The Paris Notebooks," *Hemingway Notes* (Fall 1981): 23–26.

Vidal, Gore. "Dawn Powell, the American Writer," *New York Review of Books* (November 5, 1987): 52–60.

Watson, William Braasch. "Hemingway's Spanish Civil War Dispatches" and subsidiary articles, *Hemingway Review* (Spring 1988): 4–122.

Westbrook, Max. "Grace under Pressure: Hemingway and the Summer of 1920." In *Ernest Hemingway: The Writer in Context,* edited by James Nagel, 77–106. Madison: University of Wisconsin Press, 1984.

Index

← BAr-Code INside